Audubon

AN INTIMATE LIFE OF
THE AMERICAN WOODSMAN

"A curious event, this life of mine."

JOHN JAMES AUDUBON
in his Journal March 15, 1827

By

STANLEY CLISBY ARTHUR

The Story of the Battle of New Orleans

The Fur Bearing Animals of Louisiana

The Birds of Louisiana

Old Families of Louisiana
[with George C. H. Kernion]

The Story of the West Florida Rebellion

Old New Orleans

JOHN JAMES AUDUBON by himself.

The earliest known and probably the best likeness of The American Woodsman. Painted in oils while looking in a mirror. Made at Beech Woods, Feliciana Parish, Louisiana, 1822, when he was 37 years old.

Audubon

AN INTIMATE LIFE OF

THE AMERICAN WOODSMAN

BY

STANLEY CLISBY ARTHUR

"My motto is: '*Les temps decouvrir la vérité.*' "
(Time will uncover the truth.)
JOHN JAMES AUDUBON, in his Journal.

A
FIREBIRD
PRESS
BOOK
Gretna 2000

Manufactured in the United States of America
Published by Pelican Publishing Company, Inc.
1000 Burmaster Street, Gretna, Louisiana 70053

To My Wife

John J Audubon

CONTENTS

List of Illustrations

Prologue

"THE AMERICAN WOODSMAN"

"I have a rival in every bird."
LUCY AUDUBON in a
letter to her sister Eliza.

". . . . *but I love indepenn and piece more than humbug and money.*"

JOHN JAMES AUDUBON, in a letter to his wife, dated Washington D. C. July 25, 1842

"THE. AMERICAN WOODSMAN"

JOHN JAMES AUDUBON gathered for himself a fame and recognition which stamps him as one of the greatest of bird artists and naturalists of all time. A bronze bust of him occupies a niche in America's Hall of Fame, and a full length figure, compelling in its beauty of poise, surmounts a granite block in a park bearing his name in New Orleans, where many times he walked the narrow streets penniless, where he knew of the gnaw of hunger and the pain of disrepute. A set of his bird drawings, frequently characterized as the greatest monument erected by art to nature, which he humbly hawked throughout the United States and the ancient cities of England, Scotland, and France a mere century ago, sells today for more than twelve times the original subscription price.

Audubon was a gifted artist, quasi-naturalist, sometime dandy, quondam merchant, unkempt wanderer, many-sided human being. As a man he is far more interesting than aught he accomplished. A halo of romance surrounds his entire career, and he was generally regarded as mad because of his strange self-absorption, his long hair, tattered garments, and persistence in chasing about the countryside after little birds.

Vagabond at heart, Audubon let no responsibility or family tie keep him from the woods and the sound of bird music. He was alternately a fastidious dandy of the cities and a ragged, penniless wanderer of the by-ways and forest trail. He had a way with the ladies. He could play the flute and flageolet, bow the violin, and dance the cotillion with delicate grace. He liked his pinch of snuff and glass of grog, was superstitious about numbers, favoring the odd ones. He was skillful at plaiting hair. He was, withal, spectacular in his good looks and powerful of bone and sinew. Always he presents a figure of splendid genius.

He died just before completing his sixty-sixth year, and perhaps no other conspicuous character of the past hundred years has had more written and less revealed of his actual individuality than the excitable and gifted delineator of the birds of America, whose name, in scarcely a third of a century after his death, became and remains the shibboleth of wild life conservation.

Through half a hundred years the real Audubon was obscured by a biographical screen consisting of a heterogeneous combination of fact, fancy, and misrepresentation. Some of the contributions to this shroud were penned by loving but misguided relatives who through domestic partiality when writing about him colored his life misleadingly. His own account of himself and his affairs, which was never completed and was generously edited before being given to the public, is manifestly not four-square with facts . . . for Audubon had a romantic imagination which defeats verification.

A granddaughter, presenting a record of her distinguished ancestor from his closely guarded journals, letters, and diaries, maintained she had "tried to put only Audubon *the man*" before her readers, "and in his own words so far as possible, that they may know what he was and not what others *thought* he was" . . . and then suppressed the very passages in those documents that would more clearly illumine his true character. Other journals and diaries were burned "so they would not fall into vandal hands," and the remaining data, when put into print, have been in many instances so edited, changed, deleted, and interpolated as to cloud the true portrait. Scarcely "his own words."

One outstanding biography, however, is by an earnest student and ardent admirer of the artist naturalist. Professor Francis Hobart Herrick, after painstaking research, reached into the tantalizing obscurity of Audubon's birth and, aided by age-worn documents, revealed with clear and unbiased words heretofore unsuspected details of this event. Details not subscribed to by The American Woodsman's descendants.

The present work is also by a student and admirer of the

celebrated bird artist who, after twenty years of research, after a diligent study of the naturalist's original works . . . pictorial, literary, and familiar, and after years spent in the same bird paradise, the state of Louisiana, from which Audubon gathered the bulk of his material, is constrained to write the portrait found in the pages to come.

The mystery of Audubon's birth and parentage has been made the subject of particular attention. No final decision is reached. What his descendants believe, what Audubon himself would have his wife believe, is offered for the first time for your consideration.

To whichever belief one gives credence in reading the man's life, John James Audubon presents a fascinating figure in American history, a high light in American romance, a model in American achievement.

Close study reveals him as sportsman rather than student, as hunter-naturalist rather than ornithologist, one who loved nature more than he loved science, yet whose tenderness and love of bird life were coupled with the lust to kill the objects of his admiration . . . the wonder subjects of his facile pencil. He who reflected the birds with crayon, brush, and water colors in the mirror of his magnificent genius, gained literary fame only through the ability of a ghost writer. Humility was his, he was at times the victim of an inferiority complex, yet he knew over-weening vanity and tenacity of purpose, his apparent laziness found contrast in his avidity for work.

A truly remarkable woman, a rosy-cheeked English girl had much to do with moulding this long-haired, gesticulating Frenchman into heroic proportions. A woman who worked when her husband seemed to dawdle, a wife who had perfect and beautiful faith in the eccentric genius she had married, and who never lost that faith. Had it not been for her devotion, her prodding tongue, her zeal, her self-sacrifice, the world would probably never have heard of Audubon. Therefore, for every plaudit we give the man for his accomplishment, a like acclaim must be reserved for Lucy Bakewell.

The story herein presented of Audubon's life and works has been carefully sifted and is set forth without intentional unkindness and with a faithful adherence to all obtainable truth and fact.

In recreating The American Woodsman, as Audubon so delighted to characterize himself, it is with the hope that I shall let him speak for himself, and set him wandering again in the printed pages as he did, a century and more ago, through the magnolia forests of his beloved Louisiana.

Book One

The Boy Audubon

"*The precise period of my birth is yet an enigma to me.*"
JOHN JAMES AUDUBON, in his
autobiography "*Myself.*"

CHAPTER 1

La Gerbetière on the Loire

THE DATE and place of John James Audubon's birth have been for years matters of dispute. He would have his wife and sons believe that an enigma shrouded the question of his parentage and throughout his diaries and journals he makes conflicting statements regarding the place of his nativity and his age. In a printed autobiography he refers to the "puzzling background" of his life. Certain passages in his many writings contain references to his "great secret," to his "noble birth," as well as an underscored declaration that he was an "aristocrat." Many of these illuminating entries have been repressed—some of them even changed when given to the world via the printed page.

Today, descendants, having absorbed such references throughout their lives, refer guardedly to a Bourbon resemblance and hint that Audubon may have been the subject of that strange and interesting problem of the Lost Dauphin of France, child of the martyred Louis *Seize* and Marie Antoinette, the little prince who by an ill turn of the wheel of fortune became the pathetic Prisoner of the Temple whose ultimate fate has proved to be the greatest riddle the world has yet been called upon to solve.

A granddaughter, having written a history of her distinguished grandfather and edited his journals before giving them to the world, sets at the bottom of a series of withheld extracts from his writings that it is her belief that John James Audubon was in fact "the Dauphin of France who mysteriously disappeared during the French Revolution!"

Such a possibility fires the imagination.

Yet—a bronze statue in New Orleans proclaims the bird artist a native son of Louisiana, and for years past the *Encyclopædia Britannica*, too evidently taking authority lightly, has published a record of "AUDUBON, JOHN JAMES, American naturalist said to have been born on the 5th of May, 1780, in Louisiana, his father having been a French naval officer and his mother a Spanish creole."

Subsequent to the publication in 1917 of newly-discovered documents by Francis Hobart Herrick, the *Britannica* altered the life sketch in later editions to read: "AUDUBON, JOHN JAMES (1785-1851) American naturalist born at Aux Cayes, Santo Domingo, now Haiti, April 26, 1785. By his father, Lieut. John Audubon, a French naval officer and planter, the boy was taken to the United States and then to France. Even in his petted boyhood he was fond of nature and began making collections . . . etc."

Neither Professor Herrick with his legally attested documents nor the latest edition of the *Encyclopædia Britannica* has prevailed generally. There are still those who persist in claiming that Audubon was born in Louisiana (somewhere "in the New World" was the vague phrasing in the *Introductory Address* to his *Ornithological Biography*). Some name the city of New Orleans as the actual spot, some the never definitely located Louisiana plantation of his father, some the plantation *Fontainebleau*, property of the exclusive Bernard de Mandeville de Marigny on the north shore of Lake Pontchartrain . . . there was even a claim that Audubon's mother was taken ill on a Mississippi flatboat when it was moored at Nine Mile Point, a short distance above New Orleans, and that the boy was born there!

All of which weaves an intricate tapestry background for Audubon's biography. The incredible suggestion of his noble birth is like a crimson thread glowing through it. Fact faces the reader, yet the breath of a mysterious whisper, emanating from the lips of the man himself, has obscured it.

The documents which Professor Herrick uncovered would establish as a fact that John James Audubon was born at Aux Cayes, on the island of San Domingo, on April 26, 1785, to a ship's captain named Jean Audubon and one Mlle. Rabin, styled, as was the custom at that time, a *créole de Saint-Domingue*. Captain Audubon's own wife, Anne Moynet Ricodel, a widow, whom he had married seven years previously, was then living in Nantes, France.

This left-handed boy of Captain Audubon's, the documents point out, was himself termed a *créole de Saint-Domingue*, and named Jean Rabin; that his mother died shortly after her son's birth; that the boy lived in Aux Cayes until he was a little more than four, and then was taken to the United States, with a half-sister named Muget Bouffard, a child also born to Captain Audubon in another and later island *affaire*. The ship's captain went on to France with his two natural children and when the three arrived at Nantes, Mme. Audubon received the trio with characteristic Gallic warmth and affection. When the boy, Jean Rabin, was eight, and his half-sister (her name changed to Rosa) was six, Captain Audubon and his wife legally adopted them and gave them the name of Audubon.

So much for divergent records of John James Audubon's origin. Detailed review of this event, extracts from various authorities, testimony of descendants on this clouded phase of his existence, conjectures, inferences, argumentations, conclusions, have been correlated in the pages of the appendix.

With the papers of adoption drawn before a notary, properly witnessed and filed in Nantes, the boy, in 1794, became Jean Jacques Fougère Audubon, and at that time we take up the thread of the story of this lad who became The American Woodsman, as he begins his eventful and colorful career—a legalized love child, presumably born in Santo Domingo, and reared in France when the thunders of the Revolution roared over that land.

2

Jean Jacques LaForêt Fougère Audubon, to give the lad the full complement of names borne at this period of his career, was given an education appropriate to Captain Audubon's purse, but this could not have been at all extensive, as young Audubon's original letters, journals, and diaries, either in French or English, disclose a marked inability to spell correctly. This is not strange for his school hardly deserved the name, so the boy tells us, and his private teachers were the means through which he "acquired the least benefit." Captain Audubon, who had long followed the sea and who, upon his return from Santo Domingo, joined the French navy, desired that the boy he had brought from Aux Cayes should follow in his steps on the quarterdeck. Finding that such a career failed to interest the lad to whom he had given his name, Jean Audubon expressed the wish that he would study to become an engineer.

An engineer? Ah, that was something different. Consequently, with such a career in mind, the boy studied drawing, geography, and mathematics, and also took up fencing and music for which he declared he had a natural talent. "I had a good fencing master, and a first-rate teacher of the violin; mathematics was hard, dull work, I thought; geography pleased me more," he wrote in one account of his youthful days. "For my other studies, as well as for dancing, I was quite enthusiastic; and well I recollect how anxious I was then to become the commander of a corps of dragoons."

Young Audubon confesses that, as his father was frequently away from home, his foster mother permitted him to do pretty much as he pleased. Instead of applying himself to the studies mapped out for him by his educators, he much preferred association with the boys of his own age and disposition in the village who were fond of seeking out birds' nests, birds' eggs, fishing, and shooting, and was not at all taken with the idea of conning spellers, doing sums in arithmetic and subjecting himself to other drudgeries of the schoolroom. Consequently, he became adept in playing hooky!

> Thus almost every day instead of going to school when I ought to have gone, I usually made for the fields, where I spent the day [he set down in his autobiography]; my little basket went with me, filled with good eatables, and when I returned home, during either winter or summer, it was replenished with what I would call curiosities, such as birds' nests, birds' eggs, curious lichens, flowers of all sorts, and even pebbles gathered along the shore of some rivulet.

Once when Captain Audubon returned to his country estate, *La Gerbetière*, on the outskirts of Couëron, a village situated on the banks of the Loire nine miles from Nantes, he showed an interest in the appearance of his adoptive son's room. "He was so pleased to see my various collections that he complimented me on my taste for such things," recalled the boy in later years. "But when he inquired what else I had done, and I, like a culprit, hung my head, he left me without saying another word. Dinner over, he asked my sister for some music and, on her playing for him, he was so pleased with her improvement he presented her with a beautiful book. I was next asked to play on my violin, but alas! for nearly a month I had not touched it; it was stringless: not one word was said on that subject.

" 'Had I any drawings to show?' Only a few, and those not so good. My good father looked at his wife, kissed my sister, and humming a tune left the room. The next morning at dawn of day my father and I were under way in a private carriage; my trunk, etc., were fastened to it, my violin case under my feet, the postilion was ordered to proceed, my father took a book from his pocket, and while he silently read I was left entirely to my own thoughts."

The journey ended at the military town of Rochefort. When the two had entered Captain Audubon's lodgings the elder seated young Audubon at his side and taking firm hold of his hands said: "My beloved boy, thou art now safe. I have brought thee here that I may be able to pay constant attention to thy studies; thou shalt have ample time for pleasures, but the remainder *must* be employed with industry and care."

The lad had an aversion to anything English and while at Rochefort voiced this feeling to Captain Audubon who replied: "Laforest, thy blood will cool in time, and thou wilt be surprised to see how gradually prejudices are obliterated and friendships acquired towards those at one time we held in contempt. Thou hast not been in England; I have, and it is a fine country." Years afterwards when the boy had become a man, when honors were being heaped upon him in England and Scotland, he remembered Jean Audubon's words.

When he was fourteen—this was in 1800—he was enrolled in the military school at Rochefort. However, neither a military nor an engineering career was the future's gift for this adoptive lad of Captain Audubon's—he cared more for the fields, the birds, the animals, the sunshine, and the trees than for tomes on the art of arms. He was no fighting man. From his own story we learn that after a short cruise as a midshipman he was back at Nantes and later at Couëron, where at the villa *La Gerbetière* he was once more in his element. "During all these years there existed within me a tendency to follow Nature in her walks," he wrote his sons in after years. "Perhaps not an hour of leisure was spent elsewhere than in the woods and fields, to examine either the eggs, nest, young, or parents of any species of birds constituted my greatest delight."

It was at this period of his career, when he was fifteen so he says, that he began the development of the ability that afterwards brought him fame. He made a series of drawings of the birds found in that part of France, which he continued until they numbered about two hundred. "They were all bad enough, yet they were representations of birds, and I felt pleased with them," he adds.

The boy's foster mother, in spite of the strange manner in which he came to her from over the seas, was devotedly attached to him. Far too much for his own good, he acknowledged, for she was desirous that he should be brought up to live and die "like a gentleman," and believed that fine clothes and filled pockets were the only requisites necessary to attain that end. "She, therefore, completely spoiled me," confessed the object of her adoration, "hid my faults, boasted to everyone of my youthful merits and, worst of all, said frequently in my presence that I was the handsomest boy in France."

The good Anne Moynet saw that all the boy's whims and idle notions were gratified the instant they were expressed, and she went so far as to give him *carte blanche* at confectionary shops. An earnest Catholic herself, she had the boy baptized in a church of that religion. To this he says, while he was surprised, he was indifferent. As he loved her as though she had been his own mother, the boy took to the catechism and studied it with other matters pertaining to the ceremony. It was not long before he learned the reason for this sudden religious flurry on the part of Mme. Audubon—she wanted him to become a priest.

When Captain Audubon learned of his wife's plans he flew into a rage. He refused to allow the boy to even think of embracing holy orders. He exacted from him a solem oath that he would never enter the Church. The captain's only explanation was—the boy must have heirs . . *legitimate heirs!*

Consequently Laforest Audubon did not become a priest nor did he even remain a Catholic. As a matter of fact, later in life he eschewed all religious beliefs and upon a number of occasions made most uncomplimentary references to the religion of his baptism. When in Kentucky he became a member of Free Masonry.

The boy's sixteenth and seventeenth years were spent at *La Gerbetière* and in the countryside that lay about Couëron. It is evident that at this period, 1802 and 1803, he was busy at what he termed his "bad enough representations of birds." Unfortunately none of these original drawings has been handed down to posterity so that we may pass judgment on them. It is quite likely that the captain realized the lad from San Domingo needed art instruction and to this end, or so Audubon claimed in later life, sent him to Paris to study drawing under Jacques Louis David, the popular artist of that period of the Revolution who, in spite of his pronounced enmity against the "last five despots of France," became the court painter for Napoleon. At David's *Louvre* studio young Audubon says he was set to drawing from manikins and began the study of the rudiments of the art by transferring to paper, by crayon and pencil, the designs of inanimate casts. The boy was disappointed. He had expected that he would be permitted to perfect himself in depicting animal life—something that would be alive and moving. To his disgust "eyes and noses belonging to giants, and heads of horses, represented in ancient sculpture," were his models.

As might be suspected, after a month or two at David's *atelier*, Laforest Audubon returned to Couëron and his doting foster mother, free again to roam fields and play with bird drawings. He drew the wingéd creatures of the meadows, river bank and roadside hedges because they intrigued him, because some stirring genius in him called for expression. There was something in his blood that claimed a kinship for the wild.

He has left us a pen picture of these early formative days:

When, as a little lad, I first began my attempts at representing birds on paper, I was far from possessing much knowledge of their nature, and, like hundreds of others, when I had laid the effort aside, I was under the impression that it was the finished picture of a bird because it possessed some sort of a head and tail, and two sticks in lieu of legs; I never troubled myself with the thought that abutments were requisite to prevent it from falling backward or forward; and, oh! what bills and claws I did draw, to say nothing of a straight line for a back, and a tail stuck in anyhow, like an unshipped rudder.

Many others in Couëron besides his foster mother and Captain Audubon inspected the boy's attempts to picture the feathered inhabitants of that section of France. Many there were who unstintingly praised these crude daubs, and Audubon in later years admitted that no boy was ever nearer being completely wrecked than he was by such flattery. Captain Audubon was not one of these praise spendthrifts. "He constantly impressed upon me that nothing in the world possessing life and animation was easy to imitate," remembered the boy throughout his life, "and that as I grew older he hoped I would become more and more alive to this."

Young Audubon tells us that his first bird drawings were all "represented *strictly ornithologically*, which means more or less in stiff, unmeaning profiles, such as are found in most works published to the present day. My next set were begun in America, and there, without my honoured mentor, I betook myself to the drawing of specimens hung by a string tied to one foot, having a desire to show every portion, as the wings lay loosely spread, as well as the tail."

In this manner, the embryo artist admits, he "made some pretty fair signs for poulterers."

We have it in his own words that this love for nature came to him early in life. In his justly celebrated *Ornithological Biography* Audubon devoted several prefatory pages to himself, in which he made only a single reference to his birth, but a great many to his infatuation for the birds and flowers.

"I received light and life in the New World," was his single contribution in his great work to the enigma of his birth. "When I had hardly yet learned to walk and to articulate those first words always so endearing to parents, the productions of Nature that lay spread all around were pointed out to me. They soon became my playmates; and before my ideas were sufficiently formed to enable me to estimate the difference between the azure of the sky, the emerald of the bright foliage, I felt that an intimacy with them, not consisting of friendship merely, but bordering on phrenzy, must accompany my steps through life."

As he developed into manhood his wishes grew with his form. "I was fervently desirous of becoming acquainted with Nature," he wrote, "but for many years was sadly disappointed," and adds: "forever it was my lot to have desires that could not be gratified. The moment a bird was dead, however beautiful it had been in life, the pleasure arising from possession of it became blunted, and although the greatest care was bestowed on endeavors to preserve the appearance of nature, I looked on its vesture as more than sullied, as requiring constant attention and repeated mendings, which, after all, it could not be said to be fresh from the hands of its Maker. I wished to possess all the productions of nature, but wished life with them. This was impossible. Then what was to be done?"

For an answer he turned to Captain Audubon and laid bare his problem, his disappointments, and anxiety. Captain Jean produced a book of *Illustrations;* just what they illustrated the budding artist did not state, but he did declare: "A new life ran in my veins. I turned over the leaves with avidity; and although what I saw was not what I longed for, it gave me a desire to copy nature. To nature I went, and tried to imitate her, as in the days of my childhood I have tried to raise myself from the ground and stand erect, before nature had imparted the vigour necessary for the success of such an undertaking."

For a number of years, he admits, his attempts to copy, to imitate nature were worse than the illustrations he had regarded as bad in the book Captain Audubon had given him. "My pencil gave birth to a family of cripples. So maimed were most of them, that they resembled mangled corpses on a field of battle, compared with the integrity of living men. These difficulties and disappointments irritated me but never for a moment destroyed the desire of obtaining perfect representatives of nature. The worse my drawings were, the more beautiful did I see the originals."

Consequently, he drew and drew. Hundreds of these crude and amateurish sketches of the birds that inhabited the woods along the Loire he says were produced day after day and then destroyed by his own hands. "They made bonfires on the anniversary of my birthday," he says . . . but withholds the date of his entry into this world!

3

In the summer of 1803, when the young man was eighteen, there came a momentous change in Laforest Audubon's life. Although it had long been believed by those inhabiting the pleasant little villa *La Gerbetière* on the Loire that it was Captain Audubon's unshaken intention that the boy, now nearing manhood, should be enrolled in Napoleon's army and like other sons of France should follow the First Consul's victorious eagles, the elder Audubon suddenly and strangely changed his mind and made hurried arrangements to send his adoptive son to far-off America.

He explained to Laforest that he had two objects in mind in wishing him to quit France—first, that the boy should begin to learn something about trade, and, secondly, the English language. The youth was provided with a letter to a rich Quaker of Philadelphia who had acted as Captain Audubon's agent for several years and intrusted with the supervision of a farm the captain had acquired in 1789. Being well supplied with funds when he left Santo Domingo, Jean Audubon, during his stay in Philadelphia before returning to France with the little boy and girl, had purchased a lovely stretch of country on the Perkioming Creek just above the spot where this gentle tree-lined stream empties into the historic Schuylkill River.

Here, at beautiful *Mill Grove* was the young *créole de Saint-Domingue*, so mysteriously hurried from France, to become intimately acquainted with the land he afterwards grew to love with a passion that knew no bounds.

CHAPTER 2

Mill Grove on the Perkioming

ALTHOUGH the exact time of John James Audubon's first voyage from France to the United States, the name of the vessel on which he sailed and such other details so dear to the heart of a biographer are not known, it can be set down in fact that the skipper of the ship that carried the young man across the Atlantic was named John Smith.

It was during the last days of August or the first ones in September of 1803 that the lad, to his "intense and indescribable pleasure," found himself in New York. His first American adventure came when he "caught the yellow fever by walking to a bank in Greenwich street to cash letters of credit." The illness that laid the young Frenchman low was not the dread "Yellow Jack" but a malignant fever of another type that was prevalent in New York in 1804. Whether from one fever or another, ill he became. So ill that Skipper John Smith took him to Morristown, New Jersey, and placed him in a boarding-house kept by two large-hearted Quaker ladies. Under their tender ministrations young Audubon was nursed back to health and from them learned his first words of the English language.

When Miers Fisher, Captain Audubon's agent in Philadelphia, heard of the eighteen-year-old boy's plight that gruff yet kindly Quaker hurried to Morristown in his carriage and removed the invalid to his own villa on the Trenton Road just outside the City of Brotherly Love . . . a city that was anything but that to Audubon in after years.

Miers Fisher had been Captain Audubon's trusted agent for a dozen years and the Quaker and the French naval officer entertained a common admiration for each other. So you may be sure good care was taken of the handsome youth who lay in one of the Fisher beds and that he became a personage of importance to the members of that Quaker family. "Indeed," Audubon set down a quarter of a century later in his oft-quoted *Myself*, "it would seem that Mr. Fisher was actually desirous that I should become a member of his family, and this was evinced in a few days by the manner in which the good Quaker presented me to a daughter of no mean appearance."

Laforest Audubon took an unconquerable dislike to the comely Quakeress, so he tells us, and, naturally, the match did not materialize. There were other objections . . . Miers Fisher opposed music of all kinds. He frowned on dancing. He could not endure the sight of the young man from Nantes carrying a fishing rod. He condemned in round terms most of the other things Audubon called amusements. Worst of all, he frowned upon the young man's constant habit of going out to the fields with a gun to shoot birds!

This last prohibition settled matters for Laforest Audubon who, in a mixture of broken English and excitable French, insisted on leaving the house of don'ts and being installed on Captain Audubon's estate. Early the next morning the austere Quaker had his carriage ready and young Audubon and his luggage stowed in it. The whip flicked over the horses' backs and at the end of the journey John James Audubon stepped for the first time on the soil of *Mill Grove*, a place destined to remain a milestone in his colorful remembrance of life.

The farm was in charge of a tenant, one William Thomas, another Quaker, who with his wife and sons cordially received the young man from far-off France. *Mill Grove* was a beautiful place and there was little to be desired when Audubon took possession of the farm except—yes, there *was* one fly in the ointment—he had become master of *Mill Grove* "under certain restrictions," he tells us, "which amounted to my not receiving more than enough money per quarter than was considered sufficient for the expenditure of a young gentleman."

Poof! What was money when there were hunting, fishing, drawing, music to occupy his every moment? To him *Mill Grove* became a blessed spot. In his early walks about the place he thought he detected traces of Captain Audubon's presence in the fences that surrounded the fields, the regular manner in which the trees had been planted in avenues, as well as the mathematical precision of the orchard trees. The mill on the rippling Perkioming was an ever-increasing joy. In a cave, where he discovered pewees building their nests and raising their young, he never failed to find soothing solitude and a delight in absorbing the secrets of nature. Here, in this cave, with the pewees as subjects, he carried on the first bird-banding experiments ever attempted in this country.

Of cares he had none "and cared nothing about cares," he boasted. He purchased excellent horses, visited such neighbors as he found congenial—they were few—and from the tenant Thomas and his wife learned a little English, which undoubtedly accounts for the many "thees" and "thous" and other Quaker idioms found in his mature writings. *Mill Grove* being near Philadelphia, Audubon thought nothing of walking to and from the town of Penn's Woods when no conveyance was at hand. As the distance is a matter of some twenty-five miles we might set this down to a piece of Audubon's characteristically enthusiastic writing but for the fact that other examples of long walks he records apparently prove him a most remarkable pedestrian.

Not far to the south of this Montgomery county farm was historic Valley Forge where Washington and his ragged and bloody-footed Continentals passed the winter of 1777-78. "It was at *Mill Grove*," Audubon wrote in his autobiography, "and only a few days before the memorable battle of Valley Forge, that General Washington presented my father with his portrait." This statement is far from being accurate, for there was no "battle" of Valley Forge, and during the winter that Washington and his ragged soldiers shivered in their rude huts, Captain Jean Audubon was on the high seas and far, far from Pennsylvania. Such slips are frequent in The American Woodsman's writings.

In the early summer the caretaker's wife informed the impetuous young Frenchman that a farm immediately across the Philadelphia road, called *Fatland Ford*, had been purchased by an Englishman who had moved into it with a large family, consisting largely of daughters. Mrs. Thomas coupled this information with the suggestion that Audubon observe the usual amenities and welcome the newcomers. The lad, just turned nineteen, shrugged his shoulders with an eloquent

Gallic gesture and replied that, as far as he was concerned, the English were merely English, and to him they "were nossing." He cared even less that the household boasted several handsome daughters . . . the beautiful pointer dogs, which he had perceived at a distance, would interest him more. "*Voila ce que c'est!*"

The Englishman, however, had no such aversions to young Frenchmen so he called on the young master of *Mill Grove* and, not finding him at home, the caller left his card, which bore the name of William Bakewell, and expressed to Mrs. Thomas his sincere regret at not finding Mr. Audubon in. The Englishman left a message—he would be honored if Mr. Audubon would join him on a shooting expedition. When the good Quakeress reported the call and delivered the message the boy was quick with his reply—he would not meet the new neighbors! They were English, and he, Audubon, had the greatest prejudices against all of that hated nationality! Return the call? Not he! All this in spite of the fact, inwardly, he recognized that his position was as absurd as it was ungentlemanly and impolite. He was determined to have "nossing" to do with the family Bakewell.

Summer waned. The woods glowed with their covering of autumnal gold and carmine. Broad maple leaves floated down from the tree tops in all their dying glory of scarlet and yellow. A sharp frost or two—then the first fine smattering of snow and a go after grouse called Audubon from the blazing fireplace of *Mill Grove.* As the youth with his ever-present gun was threading the thickets and the firs that lined the banks of the Perkioming, he came face to face with a ruddy-faced, white-haired man also intent on bringing down a brace of the birds. The elder spoke first and kindly, too, and the hot-blooded French boy, entering into conversation, was soon apologizing in broken English for his discourtesy in not returning the other's call. He admired the Englishman's dogs, noting in addition to their beauty of carriage, how well they had been trained. He later became impressed with the Englishman's expert marksmanship. So the oddly-assorted pair continued after the grouse, which were plentiful, and the banging of their muzzle-loaders resounded through the snow-clad woods.

"LA GERBETIERE"
Captain Jean Audubon's villa near Coueron on the River Loire, France. From a photograph made in 1910 by William Beer.

"MILL GROVE"
Captain Jean Audubon's Pennsylvania farm home outside Philadelphia on the banks of the Perkioming Creek. From a photograph made in 1931 by the author.

"FATLAND FORD"
The country home of the Bakewell family in Pennsylvania where Audubon courted his "beloved Lucy." From a photograph made in 1931 by the author.

THE PERKIOMING CREEK
Near "Mill Grove" where Audubon first became acquainted with American bird life and where he courted Lucy Bakewell.

The return call was made on a crisp morning. Whether or not it was the very next morning Audubon does not tell us, but knowing his impetuosity of that period we may be quite safe in surmising it occurred the day following the meeting in the woods. Thirty years later Audubon lived again the ecstasies of that momentous event when penning a short story of his life for the eyes of his two sons, Victor and John. The printed version that has been made public from this long-lost manuscript reads:

> Well do I recollect the morning, and may it please God I may never forget it, when for the first time I entered Mr. Bakewell's dwelling. It happened that he was absent from home, and I was shown into a parlor where only one young lady was seated at her work by the fire. She rose on my entrance, offered me a seat, and assured me of the gratification her father would feel on his return, which, she added, would be in a few moments, as she would dispatch a servant for him. Other ruddy cheeks and bright eyes made their transient appearance, but, like spirits gay, soon vanished from my sight; and there I sat, my gaze riveted, as it were, on the young girl before me, who, half working, half talking, essayed to make the time pleasant to me. Oh! may God bless her! it was she, my dear sons, who afterwards became my beloved wife and your dear mother.

The Englishman made his appearance in a short time and welcomed his young neighbor in hearty British fashion, introduced the members of his family to the caller who amused them by his quaint Gallic accent. Lucy, who was seventeen; Eliza, who was fourteen; Sarah, just twelve; Ann, nine; Thomas Woodhouse, then sixteen, and William Gifford, a tiny lad of five. Introductions over, Squire Bakewell, like a true Britisher, called for tea.

> "Lucy" was told to have luncheon produced. She now rose from her seat a second time, and her form, to which I had previously paid but partial attention, showed both grace and beauty; and my heart followed every one of her steps. Lucy, I was pleased to believe, looked upon me with some favor, and I turned more especially to her on leaving. I felt that certain "*je ne sais quoi*" which intimated that, at least, she was not indifferent to me.

So here we have in Audubon's romantic career, a typical case of boy meets girl, of love at first sight between a young Frenchman of nineteen, and a seventeen-year-old slip of a girl from England. This meeting between Lucy Green Bakewell and John James Audubon becomes one of the turning points in his well-rounded career, although not *the* pivotal point as far as his life's work was concerned . . . for that came seventeen years later and in a far distant place.

When the young man just emerging from his teens stalked into the home of one of the hated British and bowed low to the ruddy-cheeked English girl sewing by the open fireplace, his position in world of famous men became assured—for had it not been for Lucy Bakewell, you and I might never have heard of a man named Audubon.

2

Lucy Green Bakewell was born at Burton-on-Trent, England, January 18, 1787. Her father, William Bakewell, first came to America in 1798 and with his brother Benjamin started brewing English ale at New Haven, Connecticut. In that establishment the brothers Bakewell reproduced to perfection the famous Burton ales of Merrie England. A disastrous fire ended this business, and, after bringing his family to the infant United States in 1802, William Bakewell purchased *Fatland Ford* in 1804, and there, within a few months after arriving in her new home, his wife died.

Wherefore, we are first introduced to Lucy Bakewell, as was Audubon, soon after her father had been left a widower, and when the girl had been in America only two years. We do not know as much of her at that period as we do of the man she afterwards married and moulded into greatness, for Audubon, with rather bombastic frankness, told his sons a great deal about himself during these courting days and little of the object of his affections.

We learn that Audubon's first meeting with the family Bakewell was quickly followed by another at his home in *Mill Grove*. The Perkioming was congealed with ice and from all the neighborhood the young folk of the quiet Pennsylvania countryside were playing pranks on the glassy surface of the creek. Being a good skater, and anxious no doubt to display this accomplishment before the young lady who had so interested him, the young squire of *Mill Grove* sent a blanket invitation to the inhabitants of *Fatland Ford* to be his guests for dinner. Partridges and grouse, trapped by his tenant's sons, formed the main courses of the meal Audubon had set before his British guests.

Dinner over, all repaired to the ice of the creek "and there in comfortable sledges, each fair one was propelled by an ardent skater," Audubon recalled in after years. "Tales of love may be extremely stupid to the majority, so I will not expatiate on those days, but to me, dear sons, and under such circumstances as then, and thank God, now exist, every moment was to me one of delight."

Can there be any doubt that the sled propelled by Audubon over the mirror-like surface of the frozen Perkioming held the slight but comfortably furred figure of Lucy Bakewell?

The property owned by Captain Audubon and that purchased by William Bakewell were separated by a road linking Morristown with Pauling's Landing, a part of the main highway leading to Philadelphia; consequently, *Mill Grove* and *Fatland Ford* were less than a mile apart. The friendship deepened. Lucy Bakewell soon was teaching Laforest Audubon English and she received lessons in French and drawing in return. The two saw each other daily. That they had fallen in love astonished no one . . . not even the two most vitally concerned.

3

Audubon had purchased the best horses the country could afford. He rode well and was proud of his horsemanship. He possessed a large and varied assortment of firearms and fishing tackle, the most expensive that could be procured, in fact they were not wanted if they were not richly ornamented with silver. He spent a lot of time and money on his clothes. "Indeed, though in America," he admits, "I cut as many foolish pranks as a young dandy in Bond street or Piccadilly." Read his own pen-portrait:

> I was in plain terms what might be called extremely extravagant. I had no vices, it is true, neither had I any high aims. I was ever fond of shooting, fishing and riding on horseback; the raising of fowls of every sort was one of my hobbies, and to reach the maximum of my

desires in those different things filled every one of my thoughts. I was ridiculously fond of dress. To have seen me go shooting in black satin smallclothes, or breeches, with silk stockings, and the finest ruffled shirt Philadelphia could afford, was, as I now realize, an absurd spectacle, but it was one of my foibles, and I shall not conceal it.

This was the young man who made violent and tempestuous love to Lucy Bakewell. He was fond of music, dancing, and drawing. As he had been well instructed in each, he lost no opportunity to display these accomplishments. He had his share of love for amusements and never a ball, skating match, house party, or riding assemblage was given but that the young man with the excitable French manner of speaking, who gesticulated wildly, was very much in evidence, and became the life of every gathering. He declares he was not addicted to gambling, disliked cards, was "temperate to an *intemperate* degree," and that he never swallowed a glass of wine nor spirits until the day of his wedding. "The result has been my uncommon, indeed, iron constitution."

He was most finical, however, in his choice of foods and for this reason did not accept many dinner invitations because of his peculiarities in this regard occasioned comment. "Pies, puddings, eggs, milk or cream was all I cared for in the way of food," he declares, adding that on more than one occasion he robbed his tenant's wife of the cream she had setting for the Philadelphia market.

"All this time I was as fair and rosy as a girl, though strong, indeed stronger than most men, should I not have kept to that delicious mode of living? and why should not mankind in general be more abstemious than mankind is?"

This was the fop and dandy who preened his fine feathers before his neighbor's eldest girl. That he believed himself a fine bird is borne out in his characteristic sketch of himself at this period:

"I measured five feet, ten and one-half inches, was of fair mein, and quite a handsome figure; large, dark blue, and rather sunken eyes, light coloured eyebrows, aquiline nose and a fine set of teeth; hair, fine texture and luxuriant, divided and passing down behind each ear in luxuriant ringlets as far as my shoulders."

What wonder then that the eyes of Lucy Bakewell brightened, that her rosy cheeks became rosier still, that her heart beat faster and her breath quickened when such a romantic figure began paying her marked attentions.

Audubon and the father of the four Bakewell girls were always hunting and Audubon displayed time and again his proficiency with gold and silver encrusted guns. One morning while skating on the Perkioming with Tom Bakewell, he was challenged by Lucy's brother to hit his cap as it was tossed into the air, and while the shooter would be racing by at full speed. Audubon accepted the challenge—undoubtedly the fair Lucy was on the banks an interested spectator.

"I was to pass by at full speed, within about twenty-five feet of where he stood, and to shoot only when he gave the word," is Audubon's version. "Off I went like lightning, up and down, as if to boast of my prowess while on the glittering surface beneath my feet; coming, however, within the agreed distance the signal was given, the trigger pulled, off went the load, and down on the ice came the hat of my future brother-in-law, as completely perforated as if a sieve."

As a countryside sensation Audubon not only attracted the fair sex but men with whom he came in contact as well, as witness what David Pawling, a neighbor, wrote:

> Today I saw the swiftest skater I ever beheld; backwards and forewards he went like the wind, even leaping over large air-holes fifteen feet or more across, and continuing to skate without an instant's delay. I was told he was a young Frenchman, and this evening I met him at a ball, where I found his dancing exceeded his skating; all the ladies wished him as a partner; moreover, a more handsome man I never saw, his eyes alone command attention; his name, Audubon, is strange to me.

While John James Audubon was cutting capers on the ice of the Perkioming his business affairs were becoming entangled. Soon after his arrival at *Mill Grove*, the tenant Thomas called his attention to the presence of a lead-ore deposit on the farm. This information, likewise, had been communicated to Captain Audubon in France and he had sent a man named Francis Dacosta to develop the lead mine on a partnership basis. The man with the Portuguese name succeeded Miers Fisher as Captain Audubon's agent soon after his arrival, and exercised, or endeavored to exercise, a tutorship over the boy.

The young Frenchman took an instant and intense dislike to Dacosta. "A covetous wretch," he termed him. One reason for this feeling was due to the fact that Dacosta endeavored to persuade Audubon that his affection for the English girl was rash and inconsiderate. "He spoke triflingly of her and her parents, and one day said to me that for a man of my rank and expectations to marry Lucy Bakewell was out of the question," declares Audubon, who was certain his answers exasperated the new manager, for Dacosta immediately curtailed his allowances.

In spite of the antagonism between the two, Audubon relates how Dacosta influenced him in his efforts to portray birds on paper. The manager was always praising the youngster's ability in this direction and one morning while Audubon was endeavoring to properly portray a great blue heron, "he assured me that the time might come when I should be a great American naturalist. However curious it may seem to the scientific world that these sayings from the lips of such a man should affect me, I assure you they had great weight with me, and I felt a certain degree of pride in these words even then."

Dacosta, who was, according to Laforest Audubon, his "partner, tutor, and monitor," did more than curtail the boy's allowances. He secretly began making arrangements to ship Audubon off to India. When this information came to the Frenchman's ears he also heard the rumor that Dacosta had gone to Philadelphia to arrange his passage to Canton, China. India or China it was all the same to Audubon, who, wild with rage, followed his tutor to Philadelphia, denounced him for interfering with his affairs of the heart, and demanded enough money to enable him to sail at once for France and lay the whole matter before Captain Audubon.

The "cunning wretch," so states Audubon, gave him a letter of credit on a man named Kaufman in New York. The future naturalist returned to *Mill Grove* to bid adieu to his beloved Lucy and then, making hasty preparations for the journey, left for New York on foot. "It was winter, the country lay under a covering of snow, but withal I reached New York on the third day, late in the evening," so Audubon claims in his autobiography. The distance from the City of Quakers to New York is 93 miles, to which must be added the distance from Philadelphia to *Mill Grove*, a matter of 25 miles—which means he covered more than 39 miles a day over snow-covered roads!

In New York, when he had located Kaufman, who proved to be a banker, and presented his supposed letter of credit, he was told that the sealed missive Dacosta had given him merely advised the New Yorker to have Audubon arrested and shipped to Canton, China!

Laforest Audubon flew into a rage. He resolved to return to *Mill Grove* and kill Dacosta! He stormed and he threatened.

"The blood rose to my temples, it is well I had no weapon about me, for I feel even now quite assured that his heart would have received the result of my wrath," wrote the naturalist, describing his tumult of feelings at the time. However, he left the banker and, half bewildered, wholly mad, rushed back to his lodgings and sputtered out his story to his landlady, who was Benjamin Bakewell's sister-in-law. "I spoke to her of my purpose of returning to Philadelphia and there certainly murdering Dacosta. Women have great power over me at any time, and perhaps all circumstances. Mrs. Palmer quieted me, spoke religiously of the cruel sin I thought of committing, and, at last, persuaded me to relinquish the dreadful plan."

Happily, William Bakewell had provided his future son-in-law with a letter to his brother Benjamin, then a prosperous New York merchant. So from Benjamin Bakewell the young man borrowed $150, sufficient to pay his passage on the brig *Hope*, which was sailing direct to Nantes, and Laforest Audubon was off again on the broad reaches of the Atlantic. This time he was headed for La Belle France.

The *Hope* did not sail direct for the port at the mouth of the river Loire. The ship's captain, being newly married, wanted a week with his bride at New Bedford and Audubon declares the skipper bored holes in the hull below the waterline, which leaked enough to keep the men at the pumps until they made harbor. The week over, the ship's hull caulked, the *Hope* again set sail. Nineteen days later, after a stormy passage in which one of the crew was swept overboard, the American brig entered the Loire, and anchored off Paimbœuf, the lower harbor of Nantes.

4

The *Hope* had no sooner come to anchor than young Audubon made himself known to the customs officials when they boarded the ship in the morning, and was soon in a custom's barge on his way up the Loire river. Late that evening Laforest Audubon reached Couëron, the arms of Captain Jean Audubon, those of his half-sister Rosa, and the frantic embrace of his adored *chère maman.*

That Audubon's return to his home in France was not unwelcome is indicated by letters uncovered in the thorough research Professor Herrick made of the artist-naturalist's early life. Although the birdman frequently boasted of the wealth Captain Audubon possessed, we find the former planter of Aux Cayes confiding by letter to Francis Dacosta that he expected the boy to secure a position in the lead mine activities to be carried for the development of the deposit at *Mill Grove*, which would enable his adoptive son "to provide for himself, in order to spare me from the expenses that I can, with difficulty, support."

Captain Audubon's letters to Dacosta prove that the Portuguese was acting directly under the father's orders when he opposed the proposed marriage of Laforest to Lucy Bakewell. The lad had written to France of his infatuation, consequently the elder Audubon directed Dacosta to send him information concerning the parents of the girl and, "to oppose this marriage until I may give my consent to it. Tell these good people that my son is not at all rich, and that I can give him nothing if he marries in this condition."

In the same communication Captain Audubon gave a clear insight into the character of the lad he unhesitatingly calls "my son." Dacosta, it appears, had complained of Laforest's words and actions, especially his claim that *Mill Grove* was his sole property, and urged Captain Audubon to recall the lad to France. Admitting that he was annoyed, the father wrote: "One cannot be more vexed at the fact that you should have reason to complain about the conduct of my son, for the whole thing, when well considered, is due only to bad advice, and lack of experience; they have goaded his self-esteem, and perhaps he has been immature enough to boast in the house to which he goes, that this plantation should fall to him, to him alone."

Captain Audubon went on to advise Dacosta that he had every means at his command to destroy this presumption on Laforest's part. "It is known at Philadelphia," the letter continued, "that you have the same rights as I have, and that you are doing nothing but for our mutual advantage," and then added he was writing the boy on the subject to give him the rebuke his indiscretion deserved.

"To recall my son is not easier; the reasons which made me send him out there still remain," Captain Audubon penned —but did not explain what those reasons were. "Only an instant is needed to make him change from bad to good; his extreme youth and his petulance are his only faults . . . it is necessary that we endeavor, by gentleness, to reclaim him to his duty . . . This is my son, my heir, and I am old. When Mr. Miers Fisher shall have shown my letter to the would-be father-in-law, he will see that he is mistaken in his calculation upon the assumed marriage of his daughter, for if it should take place without my consent, all help on my part would cease from that instant . . . you may say to the would-be father-in-law that I do not wish my son to marry so young."

When this letter was written, in March of 1805, and dispatched to Philadelphia, the subject of the captain's solicitude was then on the *Hope* bound for France. Although he had left New York with murder in his heart for Dacosta he was not successful in ridding *Mill Grove* of this gentleman. Audubon claimed in his autobiography that he persuaded Captain Audubon to get rid of Dacosta; convinced him that "a greater scoundrel than Dacosta never probably existed," and obtained consent to his marriage to the rosy-cheeked Lucy. It may be that the boy convinced the parent that his partner and manager of *Mill Grove* was a scoundrel but Dacosta continued to keep his position and hold on the estate, as will be shown later.

Neither did the impetuous young lover fly back at once to his beloved Lucy. As a matter of fact he was exceedingly dilatory in making the return journey. He remained at Couëron for more than a year, and "in the very lap of comfort," spending the days quite happily. He went shooting, drawing every bird procured, and witnessed his sister married to Gabriel Loyen du Puigaudeau.

While roaming the countryside about *La Gerbetière*, the Audubon villa, he formed an intimate friendship with Dr. Charles Marie d'Orbigny, physician to Captain Audubon. Together they searched the woods, "procuring every bird we could, and I made drawings of everyone of them—very bad, to be sure, but still they were of assistance to me."

These nature forays in the woods, fields, and along the banks of the Loire with Doctor d'Orbigny probably proved to Audubon that there was much to be learned in communing with nature and in such fashion the physician became Audubon's godfather in natural history. At all events the two were inseparable. When a second son arrived at the d'Orbigny home, John James Audubon's name appears on the baptismal papers as tiny Gaston Edouard's *parrain*, and his half-sister Rosa's as the *marraine*. Before Audubon quitted France, a third son was added to the d'Orbigny family. Doctor d'Orbigny a score of years later was placed in charge of the museum of natural history at La Rochelle, and his eldest and youngest sons, Alcide Charles Victor, and Charles Jr., became distinguished naturalists. His influence on Audubon's future was considerable.

5

At the time of Laforest Audubon's return to France the Corsican despot who ruled the land had made himself emperor, and his empire was in a frenzy of activities preparatory to a conflict with Russia. To quote the lad's own words, France was in the throes of a great convulsion; the Republic had dwindled into a half monarchic, half democratic era—with the Little Corporal at the height of his success, overflowing the country as a mountain torrent floods the plains in its course to the sea. Levies, conscriptions by the wholesale, were the order of the day and, for some reason that does not today appear plain, Captain Jean Audubon felt uneasy over the

THE EUROPEAN MAGPIE
One of Audubon's early drawings, made in 1805 while at "La Gerbetière" villa near Coueron, France,, when he was twenty years old. Like all his later work the bird was drawn life-size and by a combination of crayon and water colors upon a thin inexpensive paper. On it he wrote: "La Pie, Buffon. Pye, Piot Magpye, Pianet, english. No. 44."

probability that this boy he had brought to France from far-off tropical San Domingo would be torn from the lap of comfort he had provided at Couëron, forced to shoulder a musket and take part in the strife then tearing Europe asunder. Captain Audubon insisted that Laforest return to America in spite of the fact he believed the whole Bakewell family was lying in wait to rush the boy to the altar.

Dacosta was writing Captain Audubon demanding additional funds so that he could push the lead mine activities. These demands Jean Audubon could not meet and he turned to a fellow-townsman, Claude François Rozier, a commercial judge in Nantes, and induced him to invest in the *Mill Grove* lead mine, which was to be consummated through a business partnership between Captain Audubon's adoptive son and Judge Rozier's son, Ferdinand. This partnership between Jean Jacques Laforest Fougère Audubon, then lacking a month and a few days of being twenty-one, and Ferdinand Rozier, who was a half year more than twenty-eight, was to endure for nine years, according to the written contract.

As Ferdinand Rozier played a prominent part in the early days of the bird artist, a brief resumé of his career up to the time he joined hands with Captain Audubon's adoptive son is not out of place here. He was the second son and fifth child of Judge Rozier and Renée Angelique Colas, and was born at Nantes November 9, 1777. The boy was given the benefits of good schooling and when he was twenty-five he entered the French navy during the time England and Bonaparte were struggling for the supremacy of the seas.

Young Rozier first served on *La Renommée*, commanded by a Captain Frichaud, which sailed for *Bonne Espérance* (Good Hope) and while at the island of France the man-of-war was captured by the British. In the year 1804 Ferdinand was a member of the crew manning the cutter *La Experiment* which visited a number of the Atlantic ports of the United States, including Philadelphia and Norfolk. From the last named harbor he sailed on *Le Président* for Nantes where he was discharged from service March 1, 1805. His visits to the coastal cities of the young United States had fired his imagination and made him desirous of making his fortune

EUROPEAN COOT

Another of Audubon's ambitious youthful attempts in depicting birds. Beneath his representation of the Old World "Mudhen" or "Poule d'eau," is written: "La foulque ou La Moselle—Buffon. Rivière Loire Josell—English the Coot."

in distant America. He prevailed upon his father to embrace Captain Audubon's offer and in a short while all arrangements had been completed, the papers of partnership signed, and all that was necessary in the month of March, 1806, was to secure passports which would permit two young Frenchmen to get out of France at a time conscription sergeants were combing the country for cannon fodder.

In spite of the fact that he had served in the French navy, Ferdinand Rozier's passport named him a Dutch subject—he could not speak a word of that language! No attempt was made to conceal young Audubon's name, but he had to be smuggled out by subterfuge. In consequence, Captain Audubon declared his adoptive son to have been born in New Orleans—therefore a citizen of the United States. When the inspection officer glanced over the young man's papers he congratulated him on being able to leave such an unhappy country and wished he could do the same.

Audubon described the brig *Polly*, on which he sailed from St. Nazaire on April 12, 1806, as being commanded by Captain S. Sammis, and said that the American flag was snapping in the breeze above the taffrail. "Our passengers were a medley crowd—two days out two monks appeared amongst us from the hold, where our captain had concealed them." The medley of humanity that crowded the brig was composed of many others besides Audubon and Rozier who were fleeing the iron rule of Napoleon. But they were a happy lot, we learn, and while the *Polly* danced over the waters on her six week's journey to distant America, those on board spent the time in amusements, which included gaming and dancing.

The *Polly* had not been out of St. Nazaire a fortnight, Audubon tells us, than a vessel gave chase to the fleet little brig. "We were running before the wind under full sail, but the unknown gained on us at a great rate, and after a while stood to the windward of our ship, about half a mile off. She fired a gun, the ball passed within a few yards of our bows; our captain heeded not, but kept on his course, with the United States flag displayed and floating in the breeze."

The commander of the pursuing craft sent ball after ball at the scuttling *Polly*, until the passengers, fearful of a broadside from the warship, prevailed on Captain Sammis to heave to. This he did after advising all to conceal valuables. Audubon, who was carrying the gold coins that constituted the fortune of the partnership, concealed them in the bow of the ship under the coiled cable ropes. Then a boat came alongside and two officers and a dozen sailors clambered to the decks, announcing they were from the *Rattlesnake*, an English privateer. The ship's papers were found to be in order, as were those of the passengers, but the brig was searched for treasure, robbed "of almost everything that was nice in the way of provisions, took our pigs and sheep, coffee and wines," writes Audubon "and carried off two of our best sailors despite all the remonstrances made by one of our members of Congress, I think from Virginia, who was accompanied by a charming young daughter.

Forty-four days after leaving the mouth of the Loire, the *Polly* sailed into New York harbor, dodging two British frigates lying in wait off Sandy Hook by sailing around Long Island, and the two partners set foot on American soil May 26, eager and ready for an adventure in business.

6

Laforest Audubon at once hurried to Philadelphia and then to *Fatland Ford* and his beloved Lucy. We learn from one of his journals that Captain Audubon had withdrawn his objections to a marriage with the English girl for we read: "I went to France not only to escape Dacosta, but even more to obtain my father's consent to my marriage with my Lucy, and this simply because I thought it my moral and religious duty to do so. But although my request was immediately granted, I remained in France nearly two years . . . Mr. Bakewell considered my Lucy too young (she was then but seventeen), and me too unbusiness-like to marry."

When the partners arrived at *Mill Grove* they found Francis Dacosta installed as half-owner and ready, and willing, to give them orders about the conduct of the lead mine operations. Audubon claimed in his autobiography: "Dacosta was at once dismissed from his charge . . . I was again my own master."

All of which did not take place. As a matter of fact, the two young Frenchmen, after trying for some months to form a company to exploit the lead mine, abandoned their share of the project, sold their half-interest in *Mill Grove* to Dacosta and others interested with him in the enterprise, and turned their attention to other pursuits. In such a manner did the *Mill Grove* property pass from the Audubon family forever.

Misstatements, similar to the ones he makes about Dacosta and *Mill Grove*, are characteristic of Audubon when he is writing about himself and they have proved puzzling to those who would weave a comprehensive story of his career from published works. He did secure Captain Audubon's consent to his marriage, for the Frenchman's first suspicions, planted in his mind by the crafty Portuguese, Senhor Dacosta, that the Bakewells were after the boy's supposed fortune, were dissipated when letters were exchanged between William Bakewell and Captain Audubon.

To marry the object of his affections, it was first necessary that Laforest Audubon sweep away Mr. Bakewell's objection that he was too unbusiness-like. What was there for him to do? He and Ferdinand, after selling *Mill Grove*, lived at *Fatland Ford* waiting for something to turn up. This delighted Lucy's three sisters, Eliza, Susan, and Ann, for they were greatly amused with the solemn-faced Ferdinand Rozier who, because of his inability to speak English, or even understand it, wanted to learn the strange tongue-tripping language from the laughing mischievous trio. When they would talk too fast for his rather slow comprehension, Rozier would cry, "*Dit donc—dit donc—dit donc!*" Whereupon, the three Bakewell girls promptly dubbed Ferdinand as "Didon" and for years referred to him by this nickname.

Audubon was content to remain at *Fatland Ford*. He was content to wander arm and arm with his beloved Lucy over the fields, along the banks of the purling Perkioming, content to sit for hours at the entrance of the grotto where he found the pewees building their nest and rearing their young—the very spot where he first confessed his love to Lucy and heard from her faltering lips the tender acknowledgment that he meant much to her.

THE INFERNAL MILL
Audubon's grist mill on the banks of the Ohio river at Henderson, Kentucky. Drawn from a photograph taken before it was destroyed by fire in 1913.

NATCHEZ ON THE HILL
Portion of a large oil painting made by Audubon showing the celebrated Mississippi river town as it was in 1822. The original hangs in "Melrose," a plantation home near Natchez.

THE MARQUIS AND MARQUISE DE SAINT-PIERRE

Black chalk portraits made by Audubon in 1819. The likeness of the marquis, "James Berthoud," was Audubon's first attempt at portraiture. The marquise, "Mme. Berthoud," according to family tradition, was at one time "dame d'honneur" to Marie Antoinette, queen of France and mother of the Lost Dauphin.

NICHOLAS BERTHOUD

Audubon's black chalk portrait of the son of the Marquis and Marquise de Saint-Pierre who married Eliza Bakewell, Lucy Audubon's sister. Reproduced from the originals owned by Nicholas Berthoud Ringeling, of Phillipsburg, Montana.

If Laforest Audubon wished to marry his daughter, said William Bakewell firmly, he must be in a position to support a wife. Could he do it? The lover admitted, at the present time, he could not, but had high hopes. The Britisher bluntly reminded the optimistic young Frenchman that one, much less two, could not live off hopes, and arranged to have him take a place in the counting house of his brother, Benjamin Bakewell, in New York, expressing the hope that his future son-in-law would become a business man. Ferdinand Rozier, because of his inability to learn and speak English, entered the employ of the French importing house of Laurence Huron, long established in Philadelphia.

In Benjamin Bakewell's commission house in New York, Audubon worked side by side with Tom Bakewell, Lucy's brother. Another Thomas Bakewell, son of the head of the firm, was also employed there, as was Thomas Pears, a nephew of Benjamin Bakewell's wife.

After he had been clerking for a year, Audubon wrote Captain Audubon a letter in English, doubtless to exploit a proficiency in his newly-acquired tongue, and in the course of the missive said ". . . about three weeks ago I went to Mill Grove for a/c of the latter and had the pleasure of seeing my Biloved Lucy who constantly loves me and makes me perfectly happy. I shall wait for thy Consent and the one of my good Mamma to Marry her. could thou but see her thou wouldst be pleased I am sure of the prudency of my choice . . . Good by, farwell good father believe me for life thy most sincere friend. be well be happy." For a postscript he added: "*J'espere que tu poura lire—adieu—adieu.*"

Beginning to acquire some mastery of the speech of his adopted land, we find him at this time expressing himself in the two languages. His writing then, as in future years, was a curious blend of both tongues. His English, with many "thees" and "thous" reflected the Quaker influence of the first friends he met after he landed in America. Undoubtedly, Audubon was one of the pioneer phonetic spellers, and not a few of his written words are quaint and most amusing. It must be remembered that quotations from his letters, diaries, and journals made public by relatives have in many instances been edited, the English polished, phrases rounded, and, indeed, in some instances, variously interpreted—even doctored!

All of which, in the absence of a check with the original documents, instigates a doubt of the authenticity of a number of statements relating to Audubon's strange life that have been handed down through the medium of the printed page. The correct language found in his *Ornithological Biography* was the work of his "ghost writer," William MacGillivray.

Although Audubon was ostensibly learning the art of business in Benjamin Bakewell's importing and exporting office, his thoughts were not on laces, gloves, linens, music boxes, indigo, coffee, and sugar, but on those delightful denizens of the woods and fields—the birds. Every moment of time he could steal from the mercantile establishment was spent shooting birds and drawing bird portraits in pencil, black chalks, pastels, and watercolors. The waterfowl fascinated him and he was constantly killing specimens and conveying them to his lodgings to crudely reproduce their likenesses on his tinted papers. He held some of his models so long that neighbors lodged complaints with the authorities because of the odors that issued from his room!

The paths of business did not suit Audubon. He was led through life more by the quest of adventure and novelty than business ambition. So we need not be surprised to find him complaining of the restraints of a business career in New York. Ferdinand Rozier was finding the Quaker City too slow and opportunities for making a fortune too limited and he wanted to go elsewhere. In the summer of 1807 Audubon and Rozier once more became partners. They decided to leave the eastern marts and branch out for themselves in the West.

CHAPTER 3

The Louisville Venture

THE WEST having been selected as a promising field for an initial independent venture, the particular spot in that frontier country was not as important as another problem. The two young men from Nantes required capital. Audubon borrowed $3,600 from Benjamin Bakewell on a promissory note, to fall due in eight months, and with this financial aid, together with what he had saved from his share of the sale of *Mill Grove* to Dacosta (Rozier had hoarded his share and it was intact) the two young Frenchmen laid in a considerable stock of goods which they freighted overland to Pittsburgh and then loaded on a flatboat which was to journey down the Ohio.

The West was investigated for business. The partners visited Maysville, Frankfort, Paris, Dansville, Lexington and, finally, in the early part of October, 1807, decided to open their store in Louisville. A young Kentuckian, Nathaniel Wells Pope, nineteen years old, at the time studying medicine under Doctor Dudley, was engaged as a part-time clerk. In such fashion did Audubon begin his mercantile career.

The following March Audubon left his partner and Nat Pope in charge of the store and returned on a brief but most momentous mission to *Fatland Ford*. The importance of the journey can be gauged by the fact that on the eighth of April, 1808, just before he reached his twenty-third birthday, he was married to his beloved Lucy by an Episcopal clergyman, and the next morning started with his bride for the Kentucky frontier home. Nor was this honeymoon journey without its hazards, for in crossing the Alleghany mountains their coach upset and Lucy was severely bruised.

The Louisville store, Audubon admits, "went on prosperously when I attended it; but birds were birds then as now, and my thoughts were ever and anon turning toward them as objects of my greatest delight. I shot, I drew, I looked on nature only; my days were happy beyond human conception, and beyond this I really cared not."

Louisville, in Audubon's day, was a trading post with a population of approximately one thousand, the surrounding country was settled by farmers, and agriculture supported the place. Rarely a day passed that he was not killing a bird, drawing its portrait, "or noting something respecting its habits," Audubon records, "Rozier meantime attending the counter. I could relate many curious anecdotes about him, but never mind them; he made out to grow rich, and what more could *he* wish for?"

On June 26, 1809, at John Gwathmay's hotel, the *Indian Queen*, a son was born to Lucy Bakewell and named Victor Gifford Audubon. At this time the two partners were feeling the pinch of poor business, additional funds were needed to keep the venture alive and Audubon turned, as he did many times in after life, to his wife for help. She proved equal to the demand (when did she ever fail him?) for she prevailed on her father to sell a portion of *Fatland Ford's* broad acres so that she might realize her interest in it. Against the wishes of his wife, for he had married again, William Bakewell disposed of 170 acres of the rich Pennsylvania farmland and deposited $7,838 to the account of the two struggling Louisville merchants. This loan was consummated in 1810 when Victor was not quite a year old.

At the age of twenty-five the future world figure was idling away his time. Business, whenever it interfered with the pleasure of wild life pursuit, was set aside and every invitation of gentlemen of the countryside for a shooting foray was accepted with alacrity—no matter how many customers might be hammering at the door of the store.

Shippingport, the village below the rapids, or "Falls of the Ohio," frequently saw Audubon on his bird quests. Here lived James Berthoud and his wife and son. The elder was a titled refugee from France and his real name was other than that by which he was known in America. Louisville, in that day, was a refuge for many émigrés who had fled from France to escape Doctor Guillotin's head remover. We are interested in old Mr. Berthoud's son, Nicholas, for he after-

Book Two

Audubon The Merchant

"Fortune if not blind certainly Must have his Lunatic Moments."

JOHN JAMES AUDUBON, in his journal.

wards married Lucy's younger sister Eliza. Other intimates of John and Lucy Audubon while they lived in that part of Kentucky were the Tarascon brothers, Major George Crogan, an old friend of Captain Audubon; Jonathan Clark, brother of General William Clark, companion of Meriwether Lewis on the famous expedition to the far West that bears their name; the Maupins, the Beals, the Booths, Dr. W. C. Gault, a botanist frequently consulted by Audubon on matters of natural history; John B. Gilly, who had a talent for drawing, and Charles Briggs, a frequent woods companion.

During the Louisville residence Audubon's collection of crude drawings of birds continued to grow in volume if his cash did not. These artistic endeavors, made without plan or scheme for future publication, were stiff and rather sketchy but they did exhibit a certain charm and a fidelity to nature, although they were decidedly inferior to the bird portraits he made ten years later during his residence in Louisiana. During these early Kentucky days he was courting nature for the love of seeking out the secrets of the birds that fell before his gun, and without the slightest conception that these creatures of his pencil and brush would ever bring him fame.

Only one of the drawings made at this period of his career became an original for his subsequently famous plates. It was the bird he afterwards named "Rathbone's Warbler." The original water color sketch bears the penciled notation: "Drawn from nature by John J. Audubon, Falls of Ohio, July 1, 1808," the floral decoration of bignonias was added fourteen years later when the artist was living in Natchez, Mississippi. These two little yellow warblers were the only ones Audubon ever saw, he writes, and, it might be added, they have never been seen by others since, save in his colored plates. According to Doctor Coues, they were probably "offsprings of imagination, stimulated by the artistic sense of their originator."

2

During his stay in Louisville, Audubon's attention was called by Major Crogan to a great hollow sycamore tree to which an incredible number of chimney swifts resorted regularly every night. Audubon visited the tree, found it to be about seventy feet high and eight feet in diameter at the basc. Just as the sun was setting behind the Silver Hills he saw great flocks of swifts pitching into the hole at the top of the towering stump. Placing his head against the tree he could hear a roaring noise on the inside as the birds settled for the night. He tells us:

> The next morning I rose early enough to reach the place before the appearance of daylight and placed my head against the tree. All was silent within. I remained in that posture probably twenty minutes, when suddenly I thought the great tree was giving way, and coming down on me. Instinctively I sprang from it, but when I looked up again, what was my astonishment to see it standing as firm as ever. The Swallows were now pouring out of it in a black continuing stream. I ran back to my post, and listened in amazement to the noise within, which I could compare to nothing else than the sound of a large wheel revolving under a powerful stream.

The swifts were a half hour vacating the immense tree trunk, Audubon affirmed, and he at once proceeded to examine the interior. He endeavored to enter it from the top by means of a long rope but this proving unsuccessful, the next day he cut a slice out of the trunk near the base and on the succeeding night entered the tree through this hole. With the aid of a lantern he saw the Swallows, as he termed swifts at that time, clinging to and even covering every inch of the inside surface of the giant sycamore.

> Satisfied with the sight, I closed the lantern. We then caught and killed with as much care as possible more than a hundred, stowing them away in our pockets and bosoms, and slid into the open air. Closing the entrance, we marched toward Louisville perfectly elated. On examining the birds we had procured, a hundred and fifteen in number, we found only six females. Eighty-seven were adult males; the remaining twenty-two the sex could not be ascertained, and I had no doubt they were the young of that year's brood.

The budding scientist roughly calculated the number of birds that clung to the interior of the sycamore stump. He figured the height and breadth of the hollow giant of the forest, concluded that 32 birds could cover a square foot, and then estimated that the tree contained at least 9,000 swifts. What he did with the one hundred and fifteen little dead birds he does not tell us.

3

Early in March, 1810, a wandering ornithologist visited Louisville. His name was Alexander Wilson, variously referred to as the "Paisley Weaver," the "Scotch peddler," the "Melancholy poet-naturalist," and the "Father of American Ornithology." The stranger carried under his arm two books, the first two volumes of the work that has since become famous as *Wilson's American Ornithology*. One of the first calls he made was at the store of "Audubon & Rozier, Merchants." He asked for Mr. Audubon.

In his *Myself*, Audubon records this historic meeting of rival ornithologists in only a few words: "In 1810, Alexander Wilson the naturalist—not the *American* naturalist—called on me." However, in his episode of *Louisville in Kentucky*, he gives a much fuller account of the meeting of the two men who afterwards became rivals for the title of foremost artist-naturalist of the early days of ornithology in the United States. He wrote:

> One fair morning I was surprised by the sudden entrance into our counting room of Mr. Alexander Wilson, the celebrated author of the "American Ornithology," of whose existence I had never until that moment been apprised . . . How well do I remember him, as he walked up to me! His long, rather hooked nose, the keeness of his eyes, and his prominent cheek bones, stamped his countenance with a peculiar character. His dress, too, was of a kind not usually seen in that part of the country,—a short gray coat, trousers, and a waistcoat of gray cloth. His stature was not above the middle size.

The stranger had two books under his arm, and as he approached the table at which Audubon was at work on a bird drawing, the Frenchman says he beheld something like astonishment on the stranger's face. Still eyeing Audubon's drawing the Scotsman proceeded to explain the object of his visit which was to procure subscriptions to his work on the birds of America. He opened his books, displayed the engravings in the last pages, which had been colored by hand, and read aloud a portion of the text. Then the little gray man solicited Audubon's patronage, stating that future numbers would be issued from time to time.

Naturally, John James Audubon was interested in the bird books. He turned over a few pages, examined a number of the plates, and took up a pen to set his name down as a subscriber at $120 for the set, which would comprise ten volumes when completed. The goose quill was poised and in another instant Audubon would have been the patron of the man nineteen years his senior, when Ferdinand Rozier interfered. "My dear Audubon," said the partner rather abruptly and in French, "what induces you to subscribe to this work? Your drawings are certainly much better and, again, you must know as much of the habits of American birds as this gentleman."

Audubon laid down the goose quill without signing.

Whether Wilson understood French, or sensed what had been said by Audubon's action in refusing to sign the subscription list is not known, but it was clearly to be seen the Scot was not pleased. "Vanity and the encomiums of my friend prevented me from subscribing," is Audubon's apology.

When Wilson asked him if he had done many drawings of birds Audubon quickly spread before the stranger the contents of his portfolio and "shewed him, as I would shew you, kind reader, or any other person fond of such subjects, the whole of the contents, with the same patience with which he had shewn me his own engravings." Wilson's surprise appeared great, and he admitted he had not the remotest idea that any other individual but himself had been engaged in forming such a collection. "He asked me if it was my intention to publish, and when I answered in the negative, his surprise seemed to increase . . . Mr. Wilson now examined my drawings with care, and asked if I should have any objection to lending him a few during his stay, to which I replied I had none."

Before Alexander Wilson left the counting room Audubon made arrangements with him to explore the woods in the vicinity of Louisville so that he could "procure for him some birds, of which I had drawings in my collection, but which he had never seen."

Wilson lodged at the *Indian Queen*, where Audubon lived with his wife and infant son, and there the young Frenchman endeavored to entertain the Scottish birdman. Said Audubon:

His retired habits exhibited either a strong feeling of discontent, or a decided melancholy. The Scotch airs which he played sweetly on his flute made me melancholy, too, and I felt for him . . . I exerted myself as much as was in my power, to procure for him the specimens he wanted. We hunted together and obtained birds which he had never before seen; but, reader, I did not subscribe to his work, for, even at that time, my collection was greater than his. Thinking he might be pleased to publish the result of my researches, I offered them to him, merely on the condition that what I had drawn, or might afterwards draw and send to him, should be mentioned in his work, as coming from my pencil.

Audubon declares he also suggested a correspondence, thinking an exchange of letters might prove beneficial to both, but he states Wilson made no reply to either proposal and a few days later left Louisville on his way to New Orleans.

Many years later, Audubon upon going through the ninth volume of *Ornithology* was chagrined to note the following printed extract from the Scot's diary:

March 23, 1810.—I bade adieu to Louisville, to which place I had four letters of recommendation, and was taught to expect much of everything there; but neither received one act of civility from those to whom I was recommended, one subscriber, nor one new bird; though I delivered my letters, ransacked the woods repeatedly, and visited all the characters likely to subscribe. Science or literature has not one friend in this place.

That entry from Wilson's diary was inserted in his book on birds by George Ord when he wrote a biographical sketch of the wandering Scot. As the "Father of American Ornithology" had passed away before this volume was printed, the entry was included for a purpose. Ord, at that time, was doing all he could to cast discredit on Audubon, whose first plates had made their initial appearance in Philadelphia and were creating a sensation. In publishing the excerpt from the diary Ord deliberately withheld other entries which bore out Audubon's version of the meeting of the two bird men. As an examination of the original diary shows, the Scot arrived at the *Indian Queen* tavern on March 17. Two days later he wrote he was "rambling around the town with his gun. Examined Mr. ————'s drawings in crayon—very good. Saw two new birds he had, both *Motacillae*." On the 21st Wilson wrote that he "went shooting this afternoon with Mr. A. Saw a number of Sandhill Cranes. Pigeons numerous."

All of which verifies Audubon's statement that the Scot

did note two warblers that were new to him in Audubon's collection of drawings; that Audubon hunted with him, and that they saw sandhill cranes while on the shooting expedition. In his *Ornithological Biography* Audubon maintained that Wilson copied his drawing of a "Small-headed Flycatcher" *Muscicapa minuta*, without acknowledgement. "He found in my already large collection of drawings, a figure of the present species, which being at that time unknown to him, he copied and afterwards published in his great work, but without acknowledging the privilege that had thus been granted to him."

Quite an ado about one small bird. The amusing part of it is that the "Small-headed Flycatcher" has become an ornithological phantom—a bird that has never been seen since!

In all probability it was an immature specimen of one of the warbler family. Doctor Coues believed it to be the young of the pine-creeping warbler, while Professor Spencer Fullerton Baird identified it (from Audubon's plate, of course,) as a female or young of the hooded warbler. Only one thing is certain, Audubon's plate and Wilson's engraving of this mythical bird have no resemblance in common, therefore, if Wilson copied Audubon's bird he did so from a drawing other than that serving as the original for the plate in Audubon's work.

In his biography of the whooping crane, Audubon states that he had the "gratification of taking Alexander Wilson to some ponds within a few miles of town, and shewing him many birds of this species, of which he had not previously seen other than stuffed specimens. I told him that the white birds were adults, and the grey ones the young. Wilson, in his article on the whooping crane has alluded to this, but, as on other occasions, he has not informed his readers whence this information came."

In this identification Audubon blundered, inasmuch as the white whooping crane and the grey sandhill crane are different species, and Wilson carried on the blunder, for he writes: "I . . . saw a flock at the ponds near Louisville, Kentucky, on the 20th of March . . . It is highly probable that the species described by naturalists as the Brown Crane (*Ardea Canadensis*) is nothing more than the young of the Hooping

Crane, their descriptions exactly corresponding with the latter."

One of the originals of Audubon's drawings of birds, now in the New York Historical Society's collection, bears the legend in ink: "*Chute de l'Ohio.* July 1, 1808. No. 31 J. A. *Que j'avais figure* 12 *pennes a la queue.*" The scientific designation, evidently added at a later date, is: "*sylvia Trochilus delicata; Sylvia delicata,* Aud." In lead pencil, in Audubon's hand, is the notation: "This bird was copied by Mr. Wilson at Louisville." As neither this drawing, nor the copy Wilson is alleged to have made of it, was published, the history of the "Dainty Warbler" ends here.

Audubon met Wilson once after the Louisville episode. His account of the second meeting reads:

> Sometime elapsed, during which I never heard of him, or of his work. At length, having occasion to go to Philadelphia, I, immediately after my arrival there, inquired for him and paid him a visit. He was then drawing a White-headed Eagle. He received me with civility, and took me to the Exhibition Rooms of Rembrandt Peale, the artist, who had then portrayed Napoleon crossing the Alps. Mr. Wilson spoke not of birds or drawings. Feeling as I was forced to do, that my company was not agreeable, I parted from him; after that I never saw him again.

It would appear that unfriendly feelings and charges and counter charges by ornithologists and naturalists have not altered much in the past hundred and twenty-five years. Audubon's accusations against Wilson were never proved. However, a much more serious charge of misappropriation came from Wilson's biographer, George Ord of Philadelphia, in which Audubon appears in a most unfavorable light. Ord stated flatly that the "female" Mississippi kite appearing in Audubon's plate of that species had been literally stolen from Wilson's engraving of the male Mississippi Kite, the original drawing of which the Scot had made in Louisiana in 1810, soon after his meeting with the French bird artist in Louisville. This charge of theft, as will be shown later, seems to have been well founded, and the full story of the "twin kites" most interesting.

4

At the time of the meeting of the two foremost pioneers in

early American ornithology, the firm of Audubon & Rozier was falling on evil times. Audubon claimed the business was suffering from over-competition. At any rate, whatever the cause, it was doomed to failure, in spite of Lucy Bakewell's sacrifice of her patrimony. The collapse was due as much to her husband's laziness and inattention to business as to any other factor. We have his own words for it:

> Louisville did not give us up, we gave up Louisville . . . Merchants crowded to Louisville from our Eastern cities. None of them were, as I was, intent on the study of birds, but all were deeply impressed with the value of dollars. I could not bear to give the attention required by my business, and which, indeed, every business calls for, and, therefore my business abandoned me.

Before the final step was taken, the artist conveyed his wife and infant son back to *Fatland Ford* where they remained a year with the Bakewells. The second Mrs. Bakewell did not like the mad artist her stepdaughter had married so Audubon, forced to cut his visit short, left Lucy and little Victor at the Pennsylvania farm. Back in Louisville, the three, Audubon, Rozier, and Nat Pope, endeavored to pull the business up by its own boot straps, but without success, and though the margin between original cost and selling prices was tremendous the sales were so few and irregular that it became a choice between closing up the shop or migrating. Audubon admits with disarming candor that he never thought of business beyond the engaging journeys which he was in the habit of making to Philadelphia and New York to purchase goods.

> These journeys I greatly enjoyed as they afforded me ample means to study birds and their habits as I traveled through the beautiful, the darling forests of Ohio, Kentucky, and Pennsylvania. Were I to tell you that once when traveling and driving several horses before me laden with goods and dollars, I lost sight of the pack-saddles, and the cash they bore, to watch the motions of a warbler, I should only repeat occurances that happened a hundred times and more in those days.

Before Mrs. Audubon's return from her old home in Pennsylvania, Rozier decided, so far as Louisville was concerned, he was done. Then, too, there was that old-time itch on the sole of Laforest Audubon's foot, a heritage, so it has been claimed, from Captain Jean Audubon.

In consequence the partners packed what they could salvage from the unprofitable Louisville venture, loaded the stock on a flatboat, floated down the Ohio river, and set up shop again at the village of Red Banks, or Henderson, as it later became known, situated one hundred and twenty-five miles below the Falls of the Ohio.

"When I for the time landed there my family was in accordance with the village quite small," wrote Audubon some years later. "The latter consisted of 6 or 8 houses, the former of 3 members—a child, a wife and the American Woodsman. The houses too were small, but fortunately for us we found an empty one, 'a Log *Cabin*'—not a 'Log *House*' Reader! Well there we were located—our neighbors were kind, the country around thickly populated, and all purchasable provisions rather scarce.

"We had brought flour, Bacon, Ham and other necessities of life. Our pleasures were those of young people, not long married and full of life and merriment. A single smile from our infant was by us far more valued, I assure you, than all the golden treasures of a Modern Crœsus would have been. The woods were amply stocked with Game, the river with fish and now and then the stores of busy bees were brought from some hollowed tree to our little fold. Our child's cradle was our richest piece of furniture, our guns and fishing lines our most serviceable implements, for although we began cultivating a garden, the rankness of the soil kept the seed we planted far beneath the tall weeds which overgrew the ground during the first year.

"I had then a 'Partner' a man of Business, besides whom a Kentucky youth who much preferred the sports of the forrest and the water than those of either Day Book or Ledger. He was naturally a good woodsman and marksman. He and I alone thought of the means to procure fish and fowl, and at it we went with all our energies."

The move to Henderson was made in the fall of 1810. While the future naturalist, his wife's brother, Will Bakewell, and Nat Pope, the clerk who preferred hunting to keeping the books of the small store, roamed the woods after game and sport, the patient partner Rozier "again stood behind the counter."

5

"Audubon & Rozier" tried out Henderson for six months. Then Rozier demanded a new field for he found the new location was even less profitable than Louisville. The West called to Rozier. He believed they would succeed better away from Kentucky and, as Audubon's wandering foot was developing its customary itch, he whole-heartedly agreed to the change, and the partners entered into a new compact to launch their mercantile venture in the infant and growing city of St. Louis.

Lucy Audubon disliked Rozier. Evidently dissatisfied with the manner in which Audubon had attended to his share of the partnership transactions, Ferdinand Rozier had been free with his criticism and insisted on greater cooperation. Audubon's wife possessed a sharp tongue, but no matter how much she could, and did, nag her husband, she would not tolerate his being hectored by others. So Rozier and the husband decided to leave Lucy and her child behind while they investigated greener fields in the distance. Audubon saw to it she would not have to rely on funds he might, or might not, send back for her maintenance—he secured for her a position as governess in the home of Dr. Adam Rankin, who owned and lived on a farm called *Meadow Brook* just outside of Henderson. As the husband and father expressed it: "I placed her and the children under the care of Dr. Rankin and his wife."

Their store of mixed goods was loaded on a keelboat which the partners planned to float down the Ohio to the point where it met the Mississippi, and then, with the aid of the stout crew of rivermen that had been engaged, to *cordell* the craft up the father of the waters to the city on its banks named in honor of Louis XIV. The cargo on the keelboat consisted of 300 barrels of Monongahela whiskey, sundry dry goods, and gunpowder. The departure was in December and the journey lasted nine weeks, although the actual length of the route by water was only 165 miles.

The current of the Ohio carried the keelboat along at the rate of five miles an hour. Audubon and Nat Pope were elated. Little work was needed on the part of the crew to keep the unwieldy craft in motion and there were high hopes of good hunting *en route.* "Thousands of wild waterfowl were flying to the river and settling themselves on the borders. We permitted our boat to drift past, and amused ourselves firing into flocks of birds," is one of Audubon's vivid written remembrances of the trip down the beautiful Ohio.

Three days after the start, the keelboat was propelled into the mouth of Cash Creek for harbor, for the merchants were warned that the Mississippi was covered with ice of a dangerous thickness. Two mornings later Audubon celebrated Christmas Day by joining an Indian hunting party going to a lake not far off where great flocks of wild swans were reported to be sporting in the water and feeding on the lily bulbs in the shallows. Audubon leaves a picturesque record of the hunt in the following:

> I seated myself on my haunches in the canoe, well provisioned with ammunition and a bottle of whiskey, and in a few minutes the paddles were at work, swiftly propelling us to the opposite shore. I was not much surprised to see the hunters stretch themselves out and go to sleep. On landing the squaws took charge of the canoe, secured it, and went in search of nuts, while we gentlemen hunters made the best of our way through the thick and thin to the lake.

The muddy shores of the waterbody were overgrown with a dense stand of cottonwoods and sycamores, favorite resorts of parakeets, which came at night to roost in their hollow trunks; slimy lagoons had to be hurdled or, when too wide, crossed by swimming. At last the lake was in view:

> And there were swans by the hundreds, and as white as rich cream, either dipping their black bills in the water, or stretching out one leg on the surface, or gently floating along. According to the Indian mode of hunting we had divided and approached the lake from different sides. The moment our *vedette* was seen it seemed as if thousands of large, fat, and heavy swans were startled, and as they made their way from him they drew towards the ambush of death; for the trees had hunters behind them, whose touch of the trigger would carry destruction among them.
>
> As the first party fired, the game rose and flew within easy distance of the party on the opposite side, when they again fired, and I saw the water covered with birds floating on their backs downwards, and their heads sunk in the water, and their legs kicking in the air.

When "the sport" was over, Audubon states he counted more than fifty of these beautiful birds, their skins destined for the decorations of the ladies of Europe, piled on the lake's shore. He adds:

> There were plenty of geese and ducks but no one condescended to give them a shot. A conch was sounded and after a while the squaws came dragging a canoe, collecting the dead game, which was taken to the river's edge, fastened to the canoe, and before dusk we were again at our camping ground. I had heard of sportsmen in England who walked a whole day, and after firing a pound of powder returned in great glee bringing one partridge; I could not help wondering what they would think of the spoil we were bearing from Swan Lake. The fires were soon lighted, and a soup of pecan nuts and bear fat made and eaten. The hunters stretched themselves with their feet close to the camp-fires, intended to burn all night. The squaws then began to skin the birds, and I retired, very well satisfied with my Christmas sport.

Perhaps it was well that the keelboat carried a goodly load of gunpowder or Audubon too would have found the time they were ice-bound in Cash Creek hanging heavily on his hands and have hated the delay as much as did his partner. "Mr. Rozier, whose only desire was to reach the destination and resume trade, was seized with melancholy at the prospect occasioned by the delay," chuckles Audubon. "He brooded in silence over a mishap which had given me a great occasion for rejoicing."

Finally the ice softened and the keelboat, dragged from its clutches, entered the Mississippi and turned upstream to breast the currents of the mighty Father of the Waters. Here was labor indeed for the crew, for the heavy boat with its load of whiskey must be moved northwards with setting poles, or laboriously *cordelled*—that is, pulled upstream by the crew trudging along the banks dragging the unwieldy craft, by the aid of long ropes, against the yellow, ice-encrusted flood of water.

"We made seven miles a day up the famous river," remembers Audubon, "but while I was tugging with my back at the *cordella*, I kept my eyes fixed on the forests or on the ground, looking for birds or curious shells." This warping against the current, both dangerous and exhausting, was not to continue without interruption, for when the wanderers reached the Tawapatee Bottoms at the great bend of the river, the ice again clutched the keelboat and prevented further advance upstream. It was found necessary to unship the cargo to protect the craft from being crushed by a great ice pack, and in winter quarters await the spring breaking up of the ice. So the party encamped on shore. There were about fifteen in all, some hunters, others trappers, and Osage and Shawnee Indians in encampments nearby came in numbers to the camp of the white men. Audubon studied the members of both tribes, and found the Osages far superior to the Shawnees. They delighted in watching him draw bird pictures, and when he made a "tolerable likeness of one of them in red chalks, they laughed excessively."

Here on the riverside, much to Audubon's elation, were new woods to be explored, new birds to be shot, new drawings to be made, new secrets of nature to be learned. "The sorrows of Rozier were too great to be described," gloated Audubon in after years when recalling the adventure. "Wrapped in a blanket, like a squirrel in winter quarters with his tail about his nose, he slept and dreamed his time away, not being seen except at meals."

The rest of the company made the best of the enforced stay in the snow-covered camp. Nat Pope played the violin, Audubon accompanied him on the flute, and trappers and hunters sang or danced to the lively tunes. Only Rozier gloomed.

While at this camp Audubon saw for the first time the bird he afterwards named for George Washington. It was the immature bald eagle in its wholly brownish-black plumage, but he believed that he added a new species to science in his "Washington Sea-eagle," or "Bird of Washington," as he usually termed it. He describes his first view of the eagle:

It was in the month of February 1814 [it was 1811, however], that I obtained the first sight of this noble bird, and shall never forget the delight it gave me . . . I lay stretched beside our patroon, a Canadian, who had been engaged many years in the fur trade. He was a man of much intelligence and, perceiving that the ducks had engaged my curiosity, seemed anxious to find some new object to divert me. An Eagle flew over us. "How fortunate!" he exclaimed; "this is what I could have wished. Look, sir! the Great Eagle, and the only one I have seen since I left the lakes." I was instantly on my feet, and having observed it attentively, concluded, as I lost it in the distance, that it was a species quite new to me. My patroon assured me that such birds were indeed rare.

Audubon saw no other specimen of this strange eagle until several years later and drew his celebrated pictures of the huge Bird of Washington only after eight years had gone by, and while he was engaged in a struggle for existence in New Orleans.

Things went on as Audubon desired at the winter camp for some days. Then the bread supply gave out. True, there was plenty of game to be secured but something besides meats were needed for the larder. For after using the breasts of wild turkeys for bread and bear's grease for butter, the stomachs of all revolted and it was decided certain members of the party should endeavor to find a way by land to the nearest settlement to obtain Indian meal and loaves of bread. Audubon, Nat Pope, and a woodsman who claimed he knew the way, volunteered for the overland expedition and the three started off on a short cut through the forest to escape a huge bend in the river.

On their way the trio sighted a herd of deer. Audubon killed one, and in trailing the others, lost his bearings. The three walked until nightfall but failed to reach the river's shore, and when Audubon came upon an Indian trail, the wanderers followed it for a while and—found themselves back in their own camp!

When Rozier realized they had lost their way, and had not returned with the expected wheaten loaves nor the bags of meal on their backs, he flew into a towering rage and called Audubon and his companions "*Niquads!* Boobies!" Then he wrapped himself in his blanket, took a place near the roaring camp fire, and glowered in silence until sleep time came.

The next morning, after a supper and breakfast of cold raccoon, the same three set forth again, "going directly across the bend, suffering neither the flocks of wild turkeys nor the droves of deer we saw to turn us aside until we had Cape Girardeau in full sight an hour before the setting of the sun," Audubon wrote. The next night the three came marching back into the camp with loaves of bread hanging on their gun barrels, and sacks of flour and corn meal sledded over the snow-incrusted ground.

When the weather moderated the party on the keelboat resumed the battle with the Mississippi's current, working their craft up the great river a few miles a day. The village of Cape Girardeau was passed, and Sainte Geneviève, a small settlement, twenty miles south of St. Louis, was reached. Audubon was not prepossessed with the place and characterized it as "not so large as dirty . . . with a population then composed of low French Canadians, uneducated and uncouth . . . but Rozier, on the contrary, liked it; he found plenty of French with whom to converse."

The three hundred barrels of Monongahela whiskey on the keelboat found a ready and enthusiastic welcome at Ste. Geneviève. The liquor had cost the partners twenty-five cents a gallon—but there was no difficulty in selling it at two dollars a gallon! The rest of the goods was disposed of at a like profit. The long journey from Henderson, with the constant bickerings, irritating delays, and daily flare-ups in temper between the two Frenchmen ended their partnership. Audubon proposed selling out to Rozier, who quickly agreed to the parting, and the bargain was struck, Rozier buying Audubon's share at so much cash and the remainder in notes. Nat Pope elected to stay in Ste. Geneviève, where he had found an uncle bearing the same name, so the bird artist bade his partner and clerk farewell, and set out for Henderson, April 6, 1811, after a six-weeks' stay at the Mississippi river settlement.

Whether John James Audubon walked back to Henderson from Ste. Geneviève will always remain a matter of conjecture for he has left us two divergent accounts of this return trip. In his usually-quoted *Myself* he claims he rode back to Henderson on "a beauty of a horse, for which I paid dearly enough." In his unedited journal of 1820 he says: "I parted with Mr. Rozier and walked to Henderson in four days 165 miles." Another remarkable example of pedestrianism!

At any rate, on the high-priced horse or on shank's mare, Audubon set out in high spirits, so he states in the opening paragraphs of his episode, "*The Prairie*," to rejoin his wife who was still working at Doctor Rankin's home. "The weather was fine, all about me was as fresh and blooming as if it had just issued from the bosom of nature. My knapsack, my gun, my dog, were all I had for baggage and company. But although well moccassined [he must have been afoot], I moved slowly along, attracted by the brilliancy of the flowers, and the gambols of the fawns around their dams, to all appearance as thoughtless of danger as I felt myself."

In his autobiography *Myself*, as printed, is found an entirely different version of what happened after he sold out to "*Dit Donc*" Rozier. After arranging affairs with his former partner, Audubon says: "I purchased a beauty of a horse, for which I paid dearly enough, and bade Rozier farewell. On my return trip to Henderson I was obliged to stop at a humble cabin, where I so nearly ran the chance of losing my life at the hands of a woman and her two desperate sons, that I have thought fit since to introduce this passage in a sketch called 'The Prairie,' which is to be found in the first volume of my '*Ornithological Biography*'."

This tale, which has frequently seen print in articles on Audubon, with its pronounced dime-novel flavor, its murderous-minded mother, her two blood-thirsty sons, the friendly one-eyed Indian, the dramatic entry, just in the nick of time, of passers-by, regulator justice, and the other wild and woolly dressing The American Woodsman gave to his tale, were probably as mythical as the high-priced horse. How Audubon must have enjoyed putting this piece of creative writing to paper!

Be that as it may, when the two Frenchmen dissolved partnership each set forth on paper his feeling regarding the other.

Audubon wrote: "Rozier cared only for money and liked Ste. Geneviève."

Rozier complained: "Audubon had no taste for commerce, and was constantly in the forest."

Ferdinand Rozier, who was then thirty-five and nine years the senior of Audubon, remained at the Missouri river settlement where he could talk French and pursue the business of merchant and trader to his heart's content. He married a girl of sixteen, Constance Roy by name, who could speak only French, and she, with somewhat regularity, presented Rozier with ten children. When Ferdinand Rozier was taken to the grave, in addition to his ten children, one hundred and ten grand and great grandchildren mourned his passing.

Rozier's business at Ste. Geneviève prospered and in the course of a few years after his parting with the bird artist he became recognized as one of the foremost merchants of Missouri and the upper Mississippi Valley.

Rozier studied trade and dollars.

Audubon ran after birds.

Rozier died rich and unknown to the world.

Audubon died in poverty—but his name will live forever.

Audubon's pen-and-ink sketch of a "fin-tail" (ruddy) duck on a page of his journal.

CHAPTER 4

HENDERSON AND THE INFERNAL MILL

BACK in the Kentucky settlement on the red banks of the Ohio Audubon found his wife busy with her job at Doctor Rankin's *Meadow Brook* farm. Here he remained while looking about for something to do to earn a living. What he did at first is not clear, but existing records show that shortly thereafter he launched upon one of the most prosperous and, then, one of the most disastrous periods of his life.

In the summer of 1811 he entered into partnership with his wife's eldest brother, Thomas Woodhouse Bakewell. Tom Bakewell had been previously sent to New Orleans by his uncle Benjamin Bakewell to attend to certain business details connected with his New York commission house. In the prosperous Creole City Tom became acquainted with a representative of Liverpool cotton milling interests, Alexander Gordon, son of Major William Gordon of Natchez. From what he learned of the cotton and other commission businesses from the Gordons, Tom Bakewell believed there was a splendid opening in the Louisiana city for a commission house handling pork, lard, and flour. He told his brother-in-law that he was confident that Audubon's French nationality would prove of marked advantage in such a business. He painted such a rosy picture that the firm of "Audubon & Bakewell" was thereupon formed and the new house, with Tom in charge, was opened June 12, 1812. Six months later President Madison declared war with Great Britain and the venture was doomed to failure before it had fairly opened its doors.

In the spring of 1812 Audubon was so pressed for funds that he undertook an overland journey to Ste. Geneviève to collect money he claimed was owed him by his former partner Rozier. He made the journey on foot in company a part of the way with a hunting party of Osage Indians, and returned in the same manner—no better off financially.

From some source, possibly through his wife's appeal to the Bakewell family, Audubon obtained sufficient funds to purchase a small stock of supplies at Louisville, half for cash and the remainder on a long time credit, and he opened a small store at Henderson. His second attempt at becoming a merchant seemed a successful venture from the first; indeed, so bright became the prospects and profits that Audubon purchased four one-acre lots with the intention of making Henderson his future home.

Flushed with success he journeyed to Pennsylvania to visit his father-in-law at *Fatland Ford*, and it was here that the plans for the New Orleans commission house were consummated. All was not business that intrigued him on this trip. He gave much of his attention to his first love—the birds—for while roaming over familiar ground alongside the purling Perkioming he collected the myrtle warbler, or "Yellow-rumped warbler" as he called the bird, following Wilson's designation, and drew its picture. The next day he killed and made his drawing of a hawk new to him which he termed *Falco temerarius* in Latin, and *Le Petit Caporal* in French, naming the bird after *Napoleon le Grand*, who then was in the zenith of his glory and preying, as a hawk, on all Europe. Audubon for some strange reason thought it most appropriate to call the *little* hawk after the Little Corporal. It is the same species the bird books of today call the pigeon hawk.

Three other drawings, all dated May 12, were also made at *Fatland Ford*—the bay-breasted warbler, the yellow-winged sparrow and the Blackburnian warbler. Five days later he made his portrait of the chestnut-sided warbler—these early drawings were reproduced in his celebrated work on the birds of America, although his best work was made later.

During the time Audubon remained at the Bakewell farm of many happy memories he also drew portraits of the male and female towee bunting, a pair of cardinals, and two purple grackles, these three early drawings being reproduced in this work direct from the originals now in the United States museum. On the eighth of June he collected and pictured one of his celebrated "mystery birds," the one he in later years named "Cuvier's wren" in honor of the Baron Cuvier, the distinguished French savant who pronounced Audubon's *Birds of America* the greatest monument ever erected by art to nature.

This little bird that Audubon shot out of a laurel tree was not a wren but, to judge by the portrait he made, was a kinglet. As drawn the tiny feathered prize had two black stripes on each side of the head and otherwise differed from known birds. It was the only one ever found or described. Writes Audubon in his *Ornithological Biography*:

> I killed this little bird supposing it to be one of its relatives, the Ruby-crowned Kinglet, whilst it was searching for insects and larvae amongst the leaves of the broad-leaved laurel, on a branch of which you see it represented, and was not aware of its being a different bird until I picked it up from the ground. I have not seen another since, nor have I been able to learn that this species has been observed by any other individual.

Cuvier's *Regulus*, as he afterwards baptized the bird, continues to be unknown to our present day, and it proves to be one more in the list of strange birds Audubon presented to the ornithological world—birds that no other bird student ever beheld.

2

Details connected with the starting of his New Orleans commission venture made it necessary for Audubon to transact some business in Philadelphia, and late in the fall he started back to Henderson on horseback. In December of that year he met Vincent Nolte, a prominent German merchant of New Orleans, who in his very readable *Fifty Years in Both Hemispheres*, has given us what must be recognized as an accurate pen picture of the bird artist at that time.

Audubon himself recalls the meeting in one of his episodes. As the two accounts are divergent and furnish interesting comparisons, both are given. Wrote Audubon:

> On my way homeward I met at the crossing of the Juniata River a gentleman from New Orleans, whose name is Vincent Nolte. He was mounted on a superb horse, for which he had paid three thousand dollars, and a servant on horseback led another for a change. I was

then an utter stranger to him, and as I approached and praised his horse, he not very courteously observed that he wished I had as good a one. Finding that he was going to Bedford to spend the night, I asked him at what hour he would get there. "Just soon enough to have some trout ready for our supper, provided you will join me when you get there." I almost imagine *Barro* [the name of Audubon's horse] understood our conversation; he pricked up his ears, and lengthened his pace, on which Mr. Nolte caracoled his horse, and then put him to a quick trot; but all in vain I reached the hotel nearly a quarter of an hour before him, ordered the trout, saw to putting away my good horse, and stood at the door ready to welcome my companion. From that day Vincent Nolte has been a friend to me . . . We rode together as far as Shippingport, where my worthy friend Nicholas Berthoud, Esq., resides, and on parting with me repeated what he had many times said before, that he had never seen so servicable a creature as *Barro.*

Audubon's praise of the virtues of his horse *Barro*, which is to be found in the episode "A Wild Horse," is evidently a true pen picture of the mount, but his tale of the meeting with Vincent Nolte differs from the account written by the other. The German merchant, who was accompanied by a young Livonian from Riga named Edward Hollander, after a voyage from Liverpool, was on his way from New York to the Crescent City. Nolte recounts that one morning he reached a small inn close by the falls of the Juniata river. The landlady showed him into a room and expressed the hope that he would not mind taking his meal with a "strange gentleman" who had already arrived.

This stranger, who struck Nolte as "an odd fish," was seated at a table before the fire. He had a madras handkerchief wound about his head exactly in the style of French mariners, or laborers, in a seaport town, observed Nolte.

I stepped up to him and accosted him politely with the words, "I hope I don't incommode you by coming to take my breakfast with you." "Oh, no, sir," he replied, with a strong French accent, that made it sound like "No, sare."

"Ah," I continued, "you are a Frenchman, sir." "No, sare, hi emm an Heenglishman." "Why," I asked in return, "how do you make that out? You look like a Frenchman, and you speak like one." "Hi emm an Heenglishman becas hi got a Heenglish wife," he answered.

Without investigating the matter further we made up our minds, at breakfast, to remain in company, and to ride together to Pittsburgh.

He showed himself to be an original throughout, but at last admitted that he was a Frenchman by birth, a native of Rochelle. However, he had come in his early youth to Louisiana, and had grown up in the sea service, and had gradually become a thorough American. "Now," I asked, "how does that accord with your quality of Englishman?"

Upon this he found it convenient to reply, in the French language, "When all is said and done, I am somewhat cosmopolitan; I belong to every country."

This man, who afterwards won for himself so great a name in natural history, particularly in ornithology, was Audubon, who, however, was by no means thinking at that time, of occupying himself with the study of natural history.

Nolte invited Audubon to travel with him on his flatboats, which Hollander, who had ridden on ahead, was to engage so they would be ready when the travelers reached Pittsburgh. Hollander, by birth a Livonian, was accompanying Nolte to New Orleans as a business helper, and afterwards became the German merchant's partner and later the Russian consul in that southern city. Ten years later Hollander befriended the naturalist when Audubon's fortunes were at low ebb. With their horses aboard the flats, which were loaded with barrels of flour, the journey was resumed early in January, when the Ohio was filled with ice.

In his account of the meeting, Nolte said he learned little of Audubon's traveling plans until the boats reached Limestone, now called Maysville, in Kentucky. Here they led their horses ashore and were dining at a tavern when Audubon suddenly jumped from his seat at the table and exclaimed in French, "Now I am going to lay the foundation of my establishment."

Waving his arms, Audubon strode to the doorway and, as the German gazed in surprise at his companion's strange actions, began searching his pockets. "With the words he took a card from his vest pocket and nailed it on the door," recounts Nolte. "The card read:

AUDUBON & BAKEWELL
Commission Merchants
Pork, Lard & Flour
New Orleans.

" 'Oh! Oh!' thought I, 'there you have a competition before you have got to the place yourself,' and as pork and lard were not articles in the way of trade, I consoled myself with the thought that competition of that sort would not amount to much."

Nolte rode with Audubon as far as Lexington where they parted company, the bird-man on his wild mustang *Barro* riding on to Henderson scattering his business cards wherever he put up for the night.

3

Mrs. Audubon was at the time still employed at Doctor Rankin's *Meadow Brook* farm, just outside of the village. During the husband's absence the Audubon family had been increased, for his second son, John Woodhouse Audubon, was born on November 30, 1812. This added responsibility no doubt superinduced Audubon's sudden spurt of energy and he attended diligently the small retail store he had started before his trip back to Pennsylvania, and for a time he gave up roaming the nearby woods for objects of natural history.

When customers were not in the store, Audubon whiled away the time dabbling with his paintings. One morning, while he was painting a picture of an otter held in a trap, his brother-in-law Tom Bakewell, whom he supposed was still in New Orleans, unexpectedly walked into the store. He carried wtih him the unwelcome news that owing to the outbreak of the war with Great Britain, the business experiment of "Audubon & Bakewell" had gone on the rocks. Bakewell remained at Doctor Rankin's a few days, talked much to Audubon and his sister about the misfortune that had come to their venture in trade, and then left for *Fatland Ford*.

In spite of this disastrous business failure, Audubon was cast down only for a few days. He shrugged his shoulders, tended the store and, when customers were few, picked up his gun and the seeking of birds and the painting of them went on merrily. Some of his drawings were good, but most of them were not, and these the budding storekeeper and merchant destroyed.

The unsuccessful pork, lard, and flour venture at New Orleans was not the last partnership into which Audubon entered with Tom Bakewell. To use his own words, he had done well with the little store and "in the space of a twelvemonth had again risen in the world." Mrs. Audubon quitted her work as governess at Doctor Rankin's when her husband erected a cabin, a story-and-a-half high, on a lot he purchased at what is now Second and Main streets in modern Henderson. The house boasted a wide porch, and in the little ground fronting it the naturalist dug a pond in which he kept wing-tipped wild geese and ducks and turtles for table use. *Soupe à la tortue* was one of his special delights and, like all *gourmets*, he never lost an opportunity to indulge his passion for unusual food. Therefore, he soon built up among the more plodding folk of Henderson the reputation of being a high liver.

With the proceeds from the sale of goods over the counter of the store he purchased a lot of ground and soon sold it at a profit. He purchased other pieces of real estate near his store and also turned them over to advantage. Court records show that he participated in a number of realty sales; that he bought no less than twenty-six separate acres of ground at a cost of $4,436.00 which were later sold for $27,620.84. Real estate transactions were not his only activities in buying and selling. He did a lucrative business in slaves—one deed on record shows that nine blacks cost him $10,550.00, and all his transactions in real and personal property while at Henderson reached a value of $49,606.84.

He was now a successful *négociant*, filling the same role in business Captain Audubon had filled before him in far-off San Domingo. "I was doing extremely well when Thomas Bakewell came once more on the tapis, and joined me in commerce," Audubon charges in his *Myself* when writing of the Henderson period. "We prospered at a sound rate for a while, but unfortunately for me, he persuaded me to erect a steam mill."

Again under the firm name of "Audubon & Bakewell," the brothers by marriage plunged into a hazardous business venture. They made application to the five town trustees of the village for a lease of the river front, covering a period of 99 years, for the purpose of erecting a steam grist mill, one that would also convert logs into lumber. After mature deliberation the town trustees, Daniel Comfort, William R. Bowen, W. .H. Ingram, Fayette Posey, and Bennett Marshall, consented and entered into the lease. The trustees were of the opinion the proposed mill would be of material benefit to the town, so the space of 200 by 220 feet at Water street and the bank of the river was leased to Audubon and his brother-in-law for $20 a year.

Soon the mill structure intruded its bulk against the beautiful view of the Ohio. The weather-boarding was of whip-sawed yellow poplar, the joists of unhewn logs, and the foundation was of stone. It was erected at enormous expense, "in a country then unfit for such a thing as would be now for me to attempt to settle in the moon," repented Audubon in later years. At first all went well. Steam hissed from the exhausts, smoke rolled from the tall chimney, the teeth of the blades bit into the logs sent to the mill to be converted into lumber, while the stones ground the corn into meal. In 1817, Thomas W. Pears, who had been a fellow-clerk with Audubon and Tom Bakewell in Benjamin Bakewell's New York commission offices, joined the others in the venture but, as it was then proving unsuccessful and Pear's wife cordially disliked Henderson, he soon quitted the place, selling his interest to the partners. The parting was not pleasant.

Audubon and Tom Bakewell struggled on alone with the load, and just when they were about to go under induced others to join them in the venture. One, a man named Apperson, was established at Shawnee Town; another was Benjamin Harrison, living at Vincennes in Indiana, and the third was Nathaniel Pope of Ste. Geneviève, an uncle of the young medical student who had clerked for Audubon and Rozier.

The infusion of new blood failed to revivify the mill's business and the naturalist's good fortune seems to have deserted him at this point. Every move he made had a disastrous ending. He purchased a tract of 1200 acres of government land and engaged a band of "hard-fisted Yankees" to fell and deliver the logs to the mill. These men were emigrants who had floated down the Ohio on a community ark and were in need of work, so they told Audubon. The strangers fulfilled their part of the contract for some weeks, but one day they failed to deliver the usual quota of timber. Audubon investigated and to his consternation found the entire party had vanished, taking with them on their craft all the plunder they could stow on board, including Audubon's draft oxen. Nothing was recovered, according to one report, and the bird man never saw them again.

In the face of impending business reverses and disaster Audubon did not give up his bird forays into the woods about Henderson. William G. Bakewell, Lucy's brother, now a sturdy lad of sixteen, usually was his companion on excursions to the Long Pond after ducks, or along the high banks of the shimmering Ohio to seek out possible strange birds, and he has left an interesting account of these happy hunting days:

> On these excursions we killed a great deal of game and often when without horses had such loads to carry that less enthusiastic hunters might have thought it more toil than pleasure, but to us with all the fatigue and hardships it was the grandest enjoyment the world could afford.
>
> One day Mr. Audubon and I went to a pigeon roost, about twelve miles from Henderson, and reached it about sundown and commenced firing at the clouds as they flew over us to see how many we could bring down at a shot than from any value we set on the birds—but soon gave it up, not considering them worth the ammunition. Next morning we filled four large bags, containing nine or ten bushels, with pigeons killed by upper branches of the trees (that were broken by the weight of the birds) falling on those roosting below. After the passenger pigeons left this neck of the woods the trees were so much broken and stripped of their limbs as to have the appearance produced in western and southern forests by the hurricanes they sometimes experience.

Will Bakewell was in his glory during such hunting forays with his brother-in-law. Audubon had first introduced him to the thrills of searching out nature's secrets at *Fatland Ford* just before he had married the small boy's sister, and had found him more useful, for the boy could shin up a tree like a squirrel. "I became an expert climber and went with Mr. Audubon nearly every day in quest of birds' nests, much to the annoyance of my father who feared I would fall and break my neck," Will Bakewell's memoir tells us.

> In order to remove my father's apprehension, Audubon made me jump from one of the highest trees in the orchard to show with what ease and certainty he could catch me if I should fall. Whenever I got up in one of the large trees in the forest, or on the side of the cliffs of the rivers in quest of eagles' or hawks' nests, it was plain to

see by his watchful eye and anxious countenance that he was not unmindful of how much might depend upon his strength and dexterity in catching me in case a branch or the bark (which latter was, after all, all I had to hold by) should give way.

It was on one of these excursions that I passed a silk handkerchief over a large hawk sitting on her nest at the top of a high tree in the woods near the Perkioming. Sometime previous to this, Audubon began to represent *all* his birds alive, in their natural attitudes. After he had painted the likeness of this hawk he opened the window and away it flew in a direct line towards the place where we had caught it.

Some months after, Audubon and my sister, whom he had married, went to Kentucky and lived several years at the Falls of the Ohio and, afterwards, in 1816, were settled at Red Banks, now called Henderson, where I visited them and remained two years doing little else but hunting, fishing, and exploring the country with Audubon in pursuit of new objects to add to his collection of paintings, already so numerous that it was very difficult to find any of the feathered tribe he had not painted.

At this time he had no idea of publishing his work and the World is indebted to an unfortunate mill, which is still to be seen on the bank of the Ohio river at Henderson, for the Birds of America.

Will Bakewell, in his narrative of the glamorous Kentucky days with his talented brother-in-law, recalled a number of instances whereby Audubon's fencing lessons taken in his youth stood him in good stead:

A person who had been in all the battles of Napoleon (according to his own account) came to the village of Henderson and was teaching the broad-sword exercise. He boasted that no man in the French army could touch him and he perfectly astonished the natives with the grand flourishes he made with his sword and the marvelous accounts he gave of his many adventures.

At length some of his pupils became disgusted with his boasting and wished to find someone who could test his skill as a swordsman, but it so happened there was no person except Mr. Audubon who pretended to know anything about fencing. Audubon was therefore applied to and requested to give the invincible gentleman a trial with the large wooden swords used by scholars. This Audubon declined to do as he said it would only create unpleasant feelings. Besides, it would be impossible for him to hit the gentleman, if he was a good fencer, without striking very quick and consequently with such force as to hurt and, in that case the gentleman, might become angry.

The "professor" declared there was no fear of his being touched, much less of his taking it amiss, no matter how hard it came and completely ridiculed the idea of his being struck. The young men of the village insisted that Mr. Audubon give him a trial, to which Mr. Audubon consented. The result was that in a very few passes Audubon gave the "professor" such a blow across the legs as to make him drop to the ground, as if he had been shot, and in the greatest agony. As soon as he recovered sufficiently, the broadsword expert left the village and was never heard from again.

Will Bakewell also related how his brother-in-law subdued a large and ferocious dog. A farmer had brought the animal into Henderson boasting that the dog could not only lick any dog in the place but that it could lick any man in the village.

Audubon listened quietly to the farmer's words of praise for his growling and snarling canine, secured a cudgel and advanced upon the dog. It immediately sprang at the man's throat but Audubon with unerring accuracy struck it so many times on the nose that the dog retreated to the safety of the wagon, and that night, under the vehicle, with its tail between its legs, slunk out of town.

4

While John James Laforest Audubon was battling adversity in the tiny Kentucky settlement on the banks of the beautiful Ohio, Captain Jean Audubon, in far-off France, at the age of seventy-four, passed away very suddenly. According to the Nantes registry of deaths the retired ship's master died away from his Couëron villa, at six in the morning of February 19, 1818, while "he was in the home of Mlle. Berthier, in the *Chaussée de la Madeleine*, No. 24, Fourth Canton." This fact being certified to in the presence of the town mayor by Gabriel Loyen du Puigaudeau, husband of Rosa Audubon, described "as a gentleman of leisure" in the official report, and the other witness, Francois Guillet, was designated a grocer of the *Quai de la Fosse*. His adoptive son did not learn of Jean Audubon's passing until a year later.

At the time of his death Captain Audubon was a pensioner of the state and he had nothing to leave his heirs save the villa *La Gerbetière*. His last will, dated at Couëron March 16, 1816, was to the effect that his wife, if she survived him, should enjoy the entire property during her lifetime, but upon her death it was to be equally divided between his two adoptive children. In this will he named the boy "Jean Rabin,

Créole de Saint-Domingue, husband of Lucy Backwell," and added a provision that in case his "dispositions in favor of Jean Rabain and Rose Bouffard, wife of Loyen du Puigaudeau, should be attacked and annulled," he bequeathed the entire estate, without exception, to his wife, Anne Moynet, for her sole use.

The will, as the old sea captain anticipated, was immediately attacked by four nieces through a suit based upon the French law which at that time debarred a natural child from inheriting property. The case was finally settled out of court by compromise but it only served to further impoverish the widow, who left the villa to live with Rosa and her husband at the du Puigaudeau home in Couëron, *Les Turtelles*.

Captain Audubon's estate had dwindled and the little that remained went to the widow and was eventually willed to her two adoptive children. Madame Audubon's last testament, made in the summer of 1821, just a month or two before her death, directed that the property should be equally divided between "Mr. Jean Audubon, called Jean Rabin, husband of Lucy Bakewell, and who I believe is at present in the United States of America, and to Rosa Bouffard, wife of M. Gabriel Loyen du Puigaudeau, my son-in-law, who is living at Couëron."

The estate was not valuable and the pleasant fiction of great wealth lost to John James Audubon, so feelingly referred to in many early biographies, was a tale founded on scant knowledge of the real state of affairs in France.

5

While Audubon was having sport afield with Will Bakewell, the grist mill was grinding on, and just as prospects were beginning to brighten for the harassed merchant, the newly-born Kentucky banks began crashing, and the mill venture was once more on the rocks.

Again Audubon and his brother-in-law searched for new partners. Nicholas Berthoud of Shippingport, joined the enterprise, but conditions went from bad to worse. The times were "bad," Audubon complains, but also admits: "I am persuaded that the great fault was ours, the building of that accursed steam-mill was, of all the follies of man, one of the greatest, and to your uncle and me the worst of all our pecuniary misfortunes," he wrote his sons.

"How I labored at that infernal mill!" he wailed. "From dawn to dark, nay at times all night." The business experiment ended, as had all of Audubon's other ventures, in flat failure. During the course of the dissolution Audubon became involved in a serious quarrel with a man named Samuel Bowen, whose name appears significantly in his printed journals as "S——— B———." The affair nearly cost Audubon his life and his adversary likewise came close to death in the sanguinary encounter.

According to the accounts at hand, Tom Bakewell had entered into a steamboat building partnership with David Prentice, a Scottish engineer, whose first work in this country had been the erection of a threshing mill at *Fatland Ford*, and who had erected the machinery in the Henderson steam mill. Prentice & Bakewell had for their first venture the construction of a small river steamboat, a pair of paddle wheels on a keelboat, which they named the *Pike*. Later they built another, the second to be constructed in Kentucky, which was named the *Henderson*. Prentice and Bakewell, on April 18, 1818, sold the boat to Samuel Adams Bowen, who formed a partnership with his brother William Russell Bowen, one of the town's trustees, and Robert Speed, Obadiah Smith, Bennett Marshall, and George Brent, for the transaction of boating business, and in payment gave Tom Bakewell and Prentice a promissory note for $4,250.00.

A year passed and the note had not been paid nor had Sam Bowen given back the craft. The note had been sold to Audubon when matters began to go awry with his milling venture and Tom Bakewell had quit the struggle in February of 1819. His wife, Elizabeth Rankin Page, had disliked the milling venture, she had disliked Henderson, and she disliked Audubon, consequently on the thirteenth of the month Tom assigned to his brother-in-law his portion of the mill site lease "for value received," as well as the Bowen note for the *Henderson*. Tom Bakewell returned to Cincinnati, his wife's home, and with his father-in-law went into the steamboat business and subsequently became wealthy, then poor.

After being left in the lurch by his wife's brother, the naturalist attempted to carry on his mill venture under the name of "J. J. Audubon & Co.," but only succeeded in getting himself entangled more and more and sunk deeper in debt. To add to his trials and tribulations the rumor came to him that Sam Bowen, and a rival Henderson merchant named Wilson, had taken the *Henderson* to New Orleans to be disposed of there and that Audubon would be left whistling for the payment of the note.

Realizing he had been outwitted, Audubon and his former partner held a conference and Bakewell suggested that Audubon hasten to New Orleans and endeavor to recover the craft. On May 8, so he sets forth in his account, he started in pursuit. "I travelled down to New Orleans in an open skiff accompanied by two negroes of mine."

There is something wrong with Audubon's dates or his method of traveling down the twisting Mississippi to the Crescent City. If he was rowed there in a skiff by two slaves, the negroes were wonders with the oars, indeed, for on May 12, four days after leaving Henderson!, Audubon was in the city that has since claimed him as its own, demanding his boat or the payment of his note from Sam Bowen, or threatening court action.

Bowen refused either to pay or deliver up the *Henderson* and the dusty archives of the civil district court show that on May 12, 1819, accompanied by a lawyer, James Workman, of the firm of Workman & DeArmas, John James Audubon appeared before James Pitot, judge of the New Orleans parish court, and represented that "Messrs. Wilson, Bowen & Co., merchants of Henderson, Kentucky, being indebted to Messrs. Prentice & Bakewell in the sum of $4,250.00 did on the 1st. day of April, 1818, make and did give their promissory note to Prentice & Bakewell for the above amount. And that the said John J. Audubon is the holder and lawful owner, etc., etc."

The petition further set forth that as Wilson and Bowen had refused to pay the face of the note, and as they had property within the jurisdiction of the New Orleans court, an attachment should be issued against the steamboat *Henderson.* Judge Pitot issued the attachment, but not before

Audubon posted a bond against wrongfully swearing to the facts in the case. Consequently his signature and that of a New Orleans merchant, Eben Fisk, were on the bond for the sum of $8,000.

When these legal formalities were out of the way, and J. H. Holland, the deputy sheriff, was seeking Bowen to serve him with the papers and plaster an attachment on the *Henderson*, the word came to Audubon that Bowen had outwitted him. On the day before Audubon landed in New Orleans, Bowen had surrendered the *Henderson* to "prior claimants" and no longer owned the craft. Still insisting on an attachment and alleging fraud, the court forced Audubon to post still another bond—and it raised the sum. Consequently, on May 15, Audubon and Romain Pamar, a crockery merchant, set their hands on an $8,500 bond. Later on in this chronicle of Audubon we shall see more of M. Pamar.

Four more days were needed to convince the bird artist that Bowen had completely out-maneuvered him. Frustrated in his efforts to recover the river boat, Audubon withdrew his suit, but he made known to many in New Orleans that he considered Sam Bowen a thief, and otherwise characterized his conduct in an excited but expressive mixture of English and Gallic. This satisfactorily accomplished, but still smarting under failure, Audubon engaged passage upstream on the river steamer *Paragon* and on the very last day of May, bade farewell to New Orleans which, according to records available, he had visited for the first time in his life.

Sam Bowen had already returned and when Audubon reached Henderson and word came to him that Bowen was making threats. Hardly had Audubon recited his experiences in New Orleans to his wife, her brother William G. Bakewell, and the émigré James Berthoud, when it became most evident that Sam Bowen was preparing to settle matters. "Old Mr. Berthoud told me Bowen had threatened to kill me," writes Audubon. "My affrighted Lucy forced me to wear a dagger."

The anticipated encounter took place. As Audubon recounts it, Bowen attacked him from behind as he was walking to the steam mill. Audubon had his right hand in a sling, he had injured it in the mill the day before, but he was prepared for eventualities, for Bowen had been pacing back and forth in front of the Audubon cabin carrying a club. That a conflict was inevitable was accepted by everyone at Henderson, for Bowen was noted for his violent and ungoverned temper. On the morning in question Bowen, flourishing his club, approached Audubon threateningly. "I stood still," wrote the naturalist, "and he soon reached me. He complained of my conduct to him at New Orleans and, suddenly raising his bludgeon, laid it about me. Though white with wrath, I spoke not nor moved not until he had given me twelve severe blows, then, drawing my dagger with my left hand, I stabbed him, and he instantly fell."

Audubon stumbled home, bruised and bleeding from the clubbing he had taken before he drove his knife into Bowen's body. While he was being ministered to by his frantic wife, old Mr. Berthoud, assisted by Will Bakewell and others, carried the bleeding Bowen to his home on a plank. His wound was severe and for a time it was feared he would die. The news spread and the townspeople were incensed—fighting with fists, with kicks, by wrestling, and gouging, or even with clubs was recognized, but knife stabbing was taboo—too damned Frenchy for the Kentuckians of that day.

As a result, Audubon's cabin was soon surrounded by a crowd of Bowen sympathizers intent on giving the long-haired Frenchman "regulator justice." The bird artist was in bed, only half conscious, suffering great pain from the clubbing Bowen had given him. Those gathered outside were clamoring for the horse-whipping they were determined to administer, so runs the account of the affair handed down by letters in the Bakewell family. James Berthoud, feeling that armed resistance of himself, Will Bakewell, and the carpenter from the mill, who had loaded Audubon's "long Tom" hunting gun, would be useless in the face of mob violence, stepped out on the porch and calmed the angry assemblage by his words.

"Will Bakewell used to tell how grand Old Mr. Berthoud looked with his white hair floating in the wind as he harangued the crowd who had come to whip Mr. Audubon who was lying wounded in the house," so one letter reads. "Will Bakewell always claimed that James Berthoud's appearance and his appeal had such an electric effect on those roughs that they cooled down and looked at the grand old man as a spirit from another world."

The clubbing and stabbing affray was later settled by Judge Broadnax and not by Judge Lynch, for Sam Bowen's wounds did not prove fatal, and Audubon soon recovered from the beating his adversary had so thoroughly administered. When both were able, the two participants in the brawl appeared in court, for Audubon had been charged with assault with a deadly weapon.

Evidence adduced, however, showed he had merely defended himself when attacked and the court found him not guilty. After the hearing had ended, and the Frenchman was being congratulated upon his acquittal by a small group outside the court building, Judge Henry Broadnax approached the man he had just freed and in a very gruff voice said:

"Mr. Audubon, you committed a serious offense, an exceedingly serious offense, sir—in failing to kill the damned rascal!"

6

James Berthoud died soon after he saved Audubon from the hands of the Bowen sympathizers and was buried at Henderson. We are interested in this émigré Frenchman and his wife because they were involved in what Audubon was prone to call the enigma of his birth. Their son, Nicholas Berthoud, had married Eliza Bakewell, first meeting Lucy Audubon's sister when she was on a visit to Henderson. As a consequence, the Berthouds and the Audubons were bound by closer ties than those of mere friendship.

"Old Mr. Berthoud," as Audubon frequently characterized him in his journals, was a well-liked, white-haired, aristocratic member of a colony of French émigrés who had settled in the Louisville section of Kentucky after escaping the terrors of the revolution that was drenching their native land in blood. Although he called himself "James Berthoud," it was not his name. In reality he was Bon Hervé de Belisle, with a right to the title of Marquis de Saint-Pierre. He was descended from a distinguished Norman family that had a chateau near

Valognes in that part of old Normandy now included in the department of Manche. His title and coat-of-arms came to him through his grand uncle, Bon Hervé Castel, Marquis de Saint-Pierre, who died in 1766 without issue, in consequence his *signeurie* and chateau passed on to his sister, Marie Louise Castel, who had married Jean Erard, seignor de Belisle.

Not a great deal is known of this Bon Hervé de Belisle, Marquis de Saint-Pierre, who mysteriously preferred to be known as "James Berthoud" in his American retreat. He was a grandson of the last named couple; a great grand uncle was no one less than the celebrated Abbé Saint-Pierre, author of a project for perpetual peace among the nations, in whose honor a statue has been erected at Saint-Pierre-l'Eglise. Another early writer in the same family was Jacques Henri Bernardin de Saint-Pierre, author of *Paul et Virginie* and other writings.

According to Berthoud family tradition, the wife of Bon Hervé de Belisle, who called himself in America "James Berthoud," was at one time a *dame d'honneur* to Queen Marie Antoinette, royal Austrian spouse of Louis XVI, and mother of Louis Charles Capet, the celebrated Lost Dauphin, the famous little Prisoner of the Temple, "The Boy" of the French Revolution whose ultimate fate has been so shrouded in mystery.

When the revolution flared forth in all its fury, Bon Hervé de Belisle, Marquis de Saint-Pierre, was living in Paris with his wife, a little daughter, and an infant son. They survived the first mad outbreaks of the *sans-culottes*, notwithstanding their intimacy with the royal family; saw the king and queen dragged from the Tuileries, witnessed the insanity of the days given over to the *Terror*, and the more diabolical machinations of the *Commune*. Early in 1795, when there was a fresh outbreak against the nobility, Bon Hervé de Belisle decided that flight was all that could save him from the guillotine. All over Paris the wild cry "Death to the aristocrats!" was welling from a thousand throats. The king had been beheaded, and Marie Antoinette had been ridden in a *tumbrel* to guillotine, but rumors were rife in Paris that the Royalists had effected the escape of the Dauphin from the Temple.

When he made his preparations for fleeing the land of his

birth the Marquis de Saint-Pierre found only one servant remained true to him—the family coachman, a Swiss named Jacques Berthoud. Although he wore a cockade on his chapeau and was ostensibly a rampant revolutionist, Jacques Berthoud planned the escape of his royalist master and his family. It was decided that the daughter should remain in her Paris convent while the father, mother, and eight-year-old son Nicholas, should make for a seaport and there take vessel for America. Faithful Jacques Berthoud secured the necessary passports, but in his own name. He was on the coachman's box and guided the horses that drew the carriage through the streets when they left Paris.

At the barrier the carriage was stopped by representatives of the *Commune.* Little Nicholas was secreted under a seat, for the members of the Committee of Vigilance had loudly announced, before examining the baggage, that they were searching for The Dauphin as rumor had it the young king had been removed from the Temple, and absconding Royalists were endeavoring to spirit the son of Louis XVI out of Paris. They searched the luggage but little Nicholas cowering under the seat escaped detection.

For days Jacques drove the carriage southwards. It passed through Orleans, Tours, Poitiers, Angouleme before the four-hundred-mile journey ended at Bordeaux. The journey was not without its thrills, for the story that the Dauphin had actually escaped the Temple and Paris, and was being smuggled out of France, had spread. As a consequence, the parents were kept in a constant state of anxiety fearing their little son might be mistaken for "The Boy."

At Bordeaux passage was engaged on a vessel sailing for distant America. To get on board the Marquis de Saint-Pierre was compelled to use his servant's name, and consequently he appeared on the ship's papers as "Jacques Berthoud." Upon his arrival in America, and subsequent settlement at Louisville, Bon Hervé de Belisle, Marquis de Saint-Pierre, not only dropped his title but even his own name, and continued to use that of Berthoud. He was buried under the name of the faithful coachman, and the name is still borne by descendants.

The son, Nicholas, grew to manhood in Kentucky, engaged

with his father in the flatboat, and later the steamboat, building trade; met Lucy Audubon's sister Eliza, married her, and took his bride to the Berthoud home, *The White House*, a large dwelling located in Shippingport, then a small village just outside of Louisville at the Falls of the Ohio.

The ci-devant Marquis de Saint-Pierre was strangely fond of the eccentric bird artist. So was his wife, the former *dame d'honneur* to Marie Antoinette, who was known to her intimates and others in Louisville only as "Madame Berthoud." These two titled émigrés, it is recorded in family documents, made frequent references to the Bourbon cast of Audubon's countenance, and Old Mr. Berthoud found a great deal of pleasure in being in the young Frenchman's company.

One day Audubon made a portrait of his elderly friend in black chalk—it was his first attempt at fashioning a human likeness, he tells us, and the result was so highly praised that he made one of Madame Berthoud, and later one of Nicholas. It was then Audubon discovered he possessed a talent for portrait making . . . a discovery that stood him in good stead in years to come.

When the Audubons left Louisville for Henderson, Old Mr. Berthoud made frequent journeys down the Ohio to spend days, even weeks, at the Audubon cabin. It was while on one of these visits that James Berthoud, the Marquis de Saint-Pierre, cowed the mob of Bowen sympathizers by his words and patrician appearance while his protege lay inside the cabin moaning from the pain of Sam Bowen's clubbing.

7

After the steamboat contretemps, the "bad establishment," as Audubon termed his infernal mill, worked worse and worse each day. He struggled on alone, worsted in everything he undertook in a commercial way. At this time he became involved in an affair which shows him at a disadvantage.

Early in 1819 he entered into a business transaction with a young Britisher named George Keats, a brother of John Keats, the English poet. George Keats had come to America to make his fortune and with his wife lived with the Audubons at Henderson. As an investment, Keats purchased from

Audubon a boat said to be loaded with merchandise which could be sold at a profit down river. True, the cargo was on board the boat, as Audubon had claimed, but, as Keats later learned, the boat, at the time of the sale, was at the bottom of the Ohio river!

George Keats incensed at what he termed a "Yankee trick," threatened to sue for a return of his purchase price, but found that Audubon had nothing which he could seize. In a letter to his poet brother, George complained of what had happened. John Keats' reply was direct and to the point. "I cannot help thinking Mr. Audubon is a dishonest man," he wrote. "Why did he make you believe he was a man of property? In truth, I do not believe you fit to deal with the world, or at least the American world. But, good God! who can avoid these chances? You have done your best. Take matters coolly as you can, and confidently expecting help from England, act as if no help was nigh."

Charging that Audubon had cheated him out of the small fortune he had brought to America, George Keats in the fall of 1819 found it necessary to return to England to obtain what remained to him of his father's estate. His poet brother John, although himself in financial straits, assisted him out of his own scanty purse. Upon George Keats' return to Louisville, he was befriended by Tom Bakewell and later, when he became a successful businessman, he was able to repay his friend in kind. However, at Keats' death the executors of his estate found he had endorsed Bakewell's paper to such an extent that the accumulations of an enterprising and thrifty lifetime had been swept away in making good these endorsements.

Audubon's brother-in-law, after deserting him at Henderson, became a wealthy builder of boats at Pittsburgh and Cincinnati, but his business crashed during the panic of 1837 and he never regained his financial standing. It is believed that Audubon's treatment of George Keats was one of the reasons for the break of pleasant relations between Tom Bakewell and his sister's husband.

8

Audubon continued to battle adversity at Henderson. His

steamboat troubles were not ended by his encounter with Sam Bowen for he was sued by Bowen and his associates for ten thousand dollars, the claim being that the bird artist had maliciously taken out an attachment on the steamboat *Henderson* at New Orleans, where it had been detained. Before being served with the writ, Audubon took steps to save what he could from the impending wreck of his fortunes. On July 13, 1819, he made over his interest in the mill to his brother-in-law Nicholas Berthoud for fourteen thousand dollars, and in another indenture, signed also by his wife, Audubon sold Berthoud his home and all his household effects for seven thousand dollars.

The Bowen brothers and their associates in filing their suit against the naturalist, represented to Judge Broadnax that Audubon was about to leave Kentucky and the jurisdiction of the court. Consequently they were successful in having a warrant issued and the sheriff took Audubon in custody. He would have stayed in jail had not Fayette Posey, one of the town trustees, posted a ten thousand dollar bail bond for Audubon's appearance at the trial. The case was never tried. Audubon declared at the preliminary hearing that a trial at Henderson would be unfair to him, so the court allowed a change of venue. The case was transferred to the neighboring court of Owensboro but, when called, Sam Bowen and the others asked for a continuation and, when the complainants failed to appear at the next term of court, the action was dismissed.

To top Audubon's misfortunes the bank at Henderson, together with two score like institutions scattered throughout Kentucky, failed. He could not meet the many bills that fell due. Creditors were clamoring for money. His wife was in a delicate condition. The mill was closed down and Audubon finally acknowledged himself bested by adversity. He recalled in later years:

> My pecuniary difficulties increased; I had heavy bills to pay which I could not meet or take up. The moment this became known to the world about me, that moment I was assailed with thousands of invectives; the once wealthy man was nothing. I parted with every particle of property I held to my creditors, keeping only the clothes I wore, my original drawings, and my gun.

Leaving his wife in Henderson, Audubon went to Louisville, but creditors pursued him and he was arrested, charged with debt, and incarcerated in the jail there. He took advantage, however, of the insolvency act before Judge Fortunatus Crosby and was released from prison.

While the husband and father was having his troubles in Louisville, his family was in sad straits in Henderson. Victor was ten, John Woodhouse was seven, and Mrs. Audubon carried a child, destined to join in memoryland a girl baby named Lucy who had lived only a short time and was sleeping in a tiny grave at *Spring Garden*, the old plantation home of General Samuel Hopkins outside of Henderson. Audubon admitted his wife "felt the pangs of our misfortune perhaps even more heavily than I, but never for an hour lost her courage; her brave and cheerful spirit accepted all, and no reproaches from her beloved lips ever wounded my heart. With her was I not always rich?"

Freed from jail, he tramped the few miles to Shippingport to the house of his brother-in-law, Nicholas Berthoud. What was he to do? He was without friends, without funds, and without prospects. He did not find a welcome at the *White House* for his wife's sister, Eliza Berthoud, was frankly displeased with him and indignant over his failure at Henderson. Humbly he asked his former partner, Tom Bakewell, to aid him in securing a position as a clerk on any of the steamboats then plying the Ohio river. Tom refused so the down-hearted artist turned to his other brother-in-law for assistance in securing a job, no matter how lowly, on the steamboats. Audubon wanted to get away—to flee the accursed Kentucky country! Nicholas Berthoud also turned thumbs down, curtly advising Audubon to find his own work.

While he was wandering about Louisville, wondering what he could do next, he received word that his wife was about to join him. She planned sailing on the next boat bound upstream, but her condition became such that it was deemed expedient she should leave at once and Isham Talbot's carriage and horses carried her and the two boys to her sister Eliza's home. Here, at the Berthoud's, the Audubons second daughter was born. The child, named Rosa, for the father's half-sister in France, lived only seven months.

9

In the exodus from Henderson, Audubon had retained his drawings of birds, his guns, his dog, and his black chalks and drawing papers. He had an idea of going to France to see his foster mother and sister, but while idling away his time, waiting for something to turn up, he inspected the portrait sketch he had made of the late Berthoud *père*, which hung on a wall in the great white house alongside a sketch he had made of Mme Berthoud. It was life-like—a striking likeness! An idea! Audubon was seized with a new ambition! He would put a heretofore unsuspected talent to work—to practical use! He resolved to enter upon the career of a portrait artist.

So at Louisville he began his portraiture experiment. "Nothing was left to me but my humble talents. Were those talents to remain dormant under such exigencies? Was I to see my beloved Lucy and children suffer, and want bread, in the abundant land of Kentucky? Was I to repine because I had acted like an honest man? Was I inclined to cut my throat in foolish despair? No!! I *had* talents, and to them I instantly resorted," he said in his autobiography many years later.

His charges for making portraits of the human "head divine," as he expressed it, at first were small but as he gained in reputation he raised his scale of prices until he was receiving five dollars, sometimes more, for each likeness made. In the course of a few weeks he had as much work as he could do, and was able to rent a house in a retired part of Louisville. Several summoned the artist into the surrounding country to make likenesses of those on their deathbeds. On one occasion a clergyman even had his dead child disinterred so a portrait could be made.

"My drawings of birds were not neglected meantime; in this particular there seemed to hover round me almost a mania, and I would even give up doing a head, the profits of which would have supplied our wants for a week or more, to represent a little citizen of the feathered tribe . . . I thought that I now drew birds far better than I had ever done before, misfortune intensified, or at least developed my abilities," he declared.

The saturation point was soon reached, the portraiture business fell off and he was once more destitute. The curse, or blessing, of the "wandering foot" was again troubling him, and he was shrouded in the black despair that always enveloped him when things were going wrong. His autobiography tells us:

One morning when all of us were sadly disponding, I took you both, Victor and John, from Shippingport to Louisville. I had purchased a loaf of bread and some apples; before you reached Louisville you were hungry, and we sat down by the river side and ate our scanty meal. On that day the world was blank, my heart was sorely heavy, for scarcely had I enough to keep my dear ones alive; yet through those dark days, I was being led to the development of the talents I loved, and which have brought so much enjoyment to us all.

Late in 1819, through the intervention of the Tarascon brothers, Audubon was offered a position at $125 a month, in a museum attached to the Cincinnati College, in the Ohio city of the same name, and there he was given an opportunity of exercising his talent for "stuffing fishes."

With an Englishman named Robert Best, who also had considerable talent in taxidermy, Audubon labored for a few months, while Mrs. Audubon remained in Louisville. This Kentucky town was quite gay at that period, if we may believe the contents of a letter from John Keats to his brother's wife. Wrote the poet:

I was surprised to hear of the state of society at Louisville; it seems you are just as ridiculous there as we are here—threepenny parties, halfpenny dances. The best thing I have heard of is your shooting; for it seems you follow the gun. Give my compliments to Mrs. Audubon, and tell her I cannot think her either good-looking or honest. Tell Mr. Audubon he's a fool, and Briggs that 'tis well I was not Mr. A——."

The Cincinnati engagement was not altogether a financial success. While the salary promised was ample it was not paid regularly. So the artist opened a school for drawing, and when his wife joined him she opened a school of her own. It was Lucy, so it appears, who really earned the family bread.

The stuffing of fishes at the museum did not interfere with his bird studies or drawings. He believed that he now drew birds better than he had ever done before. That this is an accurate estimate is proved by a number of drawings made at the time he was living in Cincinnati. These efforts, at least those that were afterwards reproduced by the engravers of his famous work, include the cliff swallow, drawn in May of 1820; the Henslow sparrow, painted a month earlier; the cedar waxwing, also drawn in April; the least bittern, sharp-shinned hawk, and several smaller birds.

Faced with the absolute necessity of earning a living for himself and his family, the bird man sought a position as drawing teacher in a school for young ladies. In an April issue of the *Western Spy*, an early Cincinnati newspaper, is printed:

MISS DEEDS

Respectfully informs the Ladies of Cincinnati, that her school is open for the reception of females of all ages, where they will be instructed in the various branches of education, at $5 per quarters. French $10.

DRAWING & PAINTING by
MR. AUDUBON

In the same publication, of the dates May 4 and 11, is to be found practically the same advertisement for a school conducted by a Miss Jacobs. She did not say that French was included in her curriculum but advised that instruction would be given in "Ornamental Needlework," and that Mr. Audubon would give lessons in drawing and painting—all for the modest fee of $5 a quarter.

Audubon did not stay long at either of these select schools for young ladies. His temperament and those of the school mistresses clashed. In consequence the former merchant and steam mill operator of Henderson opened his own private art academy. Among the score of pupils who studied under him was a boy just thirteen years old named Joseph Robert Mason, who exhibited such talent in depicting flowers and so pronounced a bent for botany that Audubon singled him out for special instruction. Not that he taught the boy to draw flowers, for that was a special gift which stamped the lad a budding genius. The teacher was quick to take advantage of the boy's talent and in a short time Joseph was supplying the floral decorations amongst which Audubon's birds were perched.

Audubon and the Mason boy became constant companions of the woods. When pupils were not clamoring for instruction, which was usually the case, the boy flower-artist and the bird artist were exploring the forests about Cincinnati, and across the river on the Kentucky side, in search of objects of natural history. The man, of course, was seeking feathered creatures while the boy was as intent in searching out fragrant, gala-hued blooms that grew in every field and copse of woods.

Joseph Robert Mason, who played a conspicuous part in the life of John James Audubon, as will be shown in the pages to come, was born in Cincinnati, July 24, 1807, and lived to the age of seventy-six. He was the son of James Wilson Mason and Mary Fletcher. He had two brothers, Jack and Henry, neither of whom married, and two sisters, Fannie, who married Henry Washburn, and Mary, who became the wife of William H. Shively. Joseph Mason early in life evinced a love of nature, particularly for flowers, and delighted to portray them, which he did with a fidelity and artistic treatment quite remarkable in one so young.

10

It was while Audubon and young Mason were combining their talents in the bird and flower infested countryside adjacent to Cincinnati, that the *Great Idea* seized Audubon! —he would draw from nature a comprehensive and complete collection of *all* the birds of the United States, depicting them in natural size, and in congenial and appropriate surroundings. He determined to acquire by his own observation a knowledge of the habits and homes of the birds.

What he would do with such a collection of bird pictures after he had made it, he did not know—that was a trifling issue which could be faced and solved later!

In the meanwhile pupils at the drawing school fell away—the teacher was more likely to be absent in the woods than in the school room when they called for instruction. In fact, so serious a problem as that of getting something to eat had to be met by patient Lucy, who secured a position as an instructor in one of the local academies for young ladies, and there she taught while Laforest Audubon lay on his back in the tangled wild wood listening to and memorizing a bird's song.

There can be no doubt that the companionship with Joseph Mason, young as he was, had much to do with the resolution to picture all the birds of America, for in the boy, just entering his teens, Audubon found one who not only could aid him greatly in identifying the flora of the country, but one sufficiently gifted to paint a glorious floral accompaniment to his bird figures. As he had determined to paint *all* the birds of America and, as *all* the birds were not to be found in the vicinity of Cincinnati, Audubon resolved to seek them out in their favorite haunts.

Wherefore, in October of the year 1820, the "wandering foot" was again dominating the man's mature judgment as he prepared for a nature pilgrimage to the South. He resolved to close an unprofitable school of art; he resolved to leave wife and children behind; he resolved (resolutions grew in his mind like weeds) to follow the feathered migrants then deserting the cold North for the salubrious swamps and marshlands bordering the Gulf of Mexico.

Audubon found a man named Shaw about to set down the Ohio and Mississippi rivers with two flatboats loaded with provisions for the trade of New Orleans and other river towns. He arranged that Mason and himself should make the trip without paying fare. Audubon would act as hunter and guaranteed to secure game for the members of the crew, while Joe Mason would serve as handy boy on board the arks. Audubon, with a wealth of glowing adjectives, prevailed on Mason's father to allow his son to join the pilgrimage, promising to make a great artist of the lad—all that Joseph needed was a little rubbing elbows with the world—roughing it a bit! Reluctantly, the father gave his son his blessing, and five dollars, and the oddly assorted two were off.

A crew of hardy rivermen was in charge of the cumbersome crafts. Joseph Aumack was in command of the flat on which Audubon and Mason lived, while the second broadhorn was under the direction of a man named Lovelace. Besides the crew of four on Aumack's flat, a sea captain and engineer named Samuel Cummings, who had formerly been in government service, took working passage for the long and arduous trip and almost before the journey was begun a curious and enduring friendship was struck up between the indigent engineer and the penniless bird artist.

This journey down the Ohio and Mississippi rivers to the distant city of New Orleans proved to be the most momentous one in Audubon's vivid and varied career. Before he again saw his wife and sons he had starved, encountered bitter and galling disappointments, and finally reached the pivotal point in his unique history when he turned from the dismal prospect of failure to the bright face of success and world acclaim.

He started on this important journey literally without a cent in the pockets of his well-worn gray breeches. However he had his gun—when was he ever without it? Other possessions included a violin, a flute, the first seven parts of Alexander Wilson's "*American Ornithology,*" and a worn, well-thumbed copy of Dr. William Turton's *Linné*, an English translation of the distinguished Swede's general system of nature, the volume that dealt with birds.

Audubon also carried his two portfolios of bird drawings, a quantity of black chalks, his watercolors, and a tin box, a long, rather bulky pipe-like contrivance in which he kept his rolls of drawing paper, and a large unruled blank book, measuring 8 x 13 inches. We must be interested in this book for in it he set down a daily record of this memorable trip and a great deal about what happened to him in New Orleans and Louisiana after the trip on the Father of the Waters was completed.

To his wife Audubon left the duty and task of caring for their two sons. Lucy, happily, had a satisfactory if not well-paying position as a teacher in a Cincinnati academy, and her husband's absence merely meant one mouth less to feed.

His destination was New Orleans, where he knew he would be in a world of wintering waterfowl when the flatboats would finally be tied up at the river front levees of the historic French city founded by Bienville on a crescent bend of the mighty Mississippi.

In such a fashion began the most important journey in the career of John James Laforest Audubon.

Book Three

Audubon The Wanderer

"Hopes are Shy Birds flying at a great distance seldom reached by the best of Guns."

JOHN JAMES AUDUBON, in his journal, December 8, 1820.

CHAPTER 5

ON A FLATBOAT DOWN THE MISSISSIPPI RIVER

IT was late in the afternoon of October 12, 1820, when the two flatboats left Cincinnati and they had not gone very far down *La Belle Rivière*, as Audubon and other Frenchmen delighted to call the Ohio, when he opened a new journal he had purchased for the purposes of the journey and on the first page set down this initial entry:

I left Cincinnati this afternoon at half past 4 o'clock, on Board Mr. Jacob Aumack's flat boat—bound for New Orleans—the feelings of a husband and a Father, were My Lot when I kissed My Beloved Wife & Children with a expectation of being absent for Seven Months—

I took with me Joseph Mason a young man of 18 years of age [1] of good family and naturally an amiable Youth, he is intended to be a Companion & a Friend; and if God will grant us a safe return to our famillies our Wishes will be congenial to our present feelings Leaving home with a Determined Mind to fulfill our Object—

Without any Money My Talents are to be My support and my Enthusiasm my Guide in My Dificulties, the whole of which I am ready to exert to keep, and to surmount.

The Watter is low, although a Little froth, sailed the river a few days since, about 4 1/8 feet. We only floated 14 miles by the break of Octobre the Day was fine. I prayed for the health of my family —prepared Our Guns and went on shore in Kentucky.

This excerpt is printed as nearly as type will do it *verbatim literatim et punct.*, after the original handwriting. It will be noted in this, and in extracts which will follow, that Audubon had his own way of spelling certain words, which have been greatly edited in the quotations which have appeared in previous printed versions released by descendants. This daily record of his activities, in which he faithfully wrote, for more than a year, all of his adventures gives us an intimate insight into his character as well as his acts.

[1]He misstates Mason's age by five years; the lad was just 13.

Captain Cummings accompanied Audubon and Joe Mason on the shooting expedition, and the three bagged "thirty Partridges—1 Wood Cock—27 Grey Squirrels—a Barn Owl—a Young Turkey Buzzard." A myrtle warbler was also shot during the foray and Audubon took occasion to bring Alexander Wilson to task for misnaming the bird. According to Audubon the bird he had killed was "an Autumnal Warbler, as Mr. A. Willson is pleased to denominate the Young of the Yellow-Rump Warbler—this was a Young Male in beautiful plumage for the season and I drew it—as I feel perfectly convinced that Mr. Willson has made an Error in presenting this bird as a New Specie I shall only recommend You to Examine attentively My Drawing of Each and His Description—its Stomach was filled with the remains of Small Winged Insects and 3 Seeds of Some Berries, the names of which I could not determine."

During the days that followed the flats drifted past many of the small settlements that lined the banks of the Ohio. One afternoon Audubon records: "I walked to *Bellevue* the former residence of a *Far Famed* Lady of our acquaintance, Mrs. Bruce; saw Thomas Newell and Capt Green—if my eyes did not err I saw my suspicions of her conduct the Evening Justified."

The discerning blue eyes of the long-haired voyager detected other things that day for on his way back from the far famed lady's place, Audubon noted about thirty grebes sporting on the surface of a small pond. He signaled to Joseph. Quickly triggers were cocked and pans primed. Audubon tells us they secured four out of the thirty:

> We approached them with ease to about 40 yards, they were chassing each other and Quite Merry when the Destructive fire through the Whole in consternation. The Many Wounded escaped by Diving the rest flew off—this is the second time I have seen this Kind, and they must be rare in this part of America.

Cold, disagreeable weather and the tendency of the lashed-together flats to run on rocks and sandbars, made the next few days uneventful for Audubon and little Joe Mason. There were no unusual natural history episodes in spite of the fact that Audubon and his gun were constantly ashore killing turkey cocks, partridges, robins, hawks, crows, grouse—anything that wore feathers and came within range of his long-barreled muzzle-loader. A week out from Cincinnati he records that he felt "poorly" all day, and supposed that drawing in the cabin of a flatboat, where he could not stand erect, was responsible for his violent headaches.

In the days that followed Joe Mason was initiated into the art of hunting and the use of firearms. He proved an apt pupil and Audubon was greatly elated when his portégé bagged three wild turkeys. "Shot *at once* by *Joseph* who was not a little proud when he heard 3 Chears given him from the Boats. This was his first essay on Turkeys." Audubon killed "a young Carolina Cuckow," and when back on the flatboat made an examination of its food. He listed his finding as: "2 entire Grass Hopers one Large Kid didid and the remainder of remains of Diferents colopterous Insects."

As the boats moved slowly down the Ohio towards Louisville a near-fatality almost cost Audubon the loss of his pupil-assistant. The flatboats had put to shore so that new sweeps could be made for steering the boats, when a flock of wild turkeys suddenly settled among the men ashore felling trees. Captain Aumack's pistols were immediately brought into play and, as Audubon expressed it, "one was bustted and the other wounded Joseph's Scull pretty severely."

When the first of November was marked off the calendar the flatboats had reached Evansville, and late in the afternoon Captain Cummings and Joseph put off in a skiff to cross the river to Henderson. Their mission was to secure Audubon's hunting dog *Dash*, which he had left in charge of a former neighbor, Charley Briggs. Audubon had refused to go for the dog himself—he did not want to set his foot in the village where he had experienced so much happiness and success . . . so much misery and woe. He was probably not on friendly terms with Mr. Briggs, anyway.

As the flatboats made their way down the river, Audubon's attention was attracted by three birds alighting on a red maple. He told the captain he believed them to be "brown pelicans," and prevailed on Aumack to make a landing. The naturalist and the boss of the flats, both in high excitement, went after the three strange birds. Aumack fired at two that had alighted on the same limb, but missed them —much to Audubon's chagrin, for he had counted on seeing them both fall. These strange "pelicans" puzzled him, and his failure to secure specimens so dampened his spirits that when he returned to the ark to record the incident in his journal, he added: "Extremely tired of my Indolent Way of Living not having procured a thing to draw since Louisville."

It was long after midnight when Captain Cummings and Joe Mason, successful in their quest for Audubon's hunting dog, returned to the flatboat. By daylight the boats were drifting on their way. A violent gale was blowing as the flats passed the village of Henderson, peaceful scene of Audubon's varying fortunes. He stood atop the cabin and glared at the collection of houses and the mill that bulked huge against the leaden sky. He endeavored to picture the place with pencil and paper but, as he afterwards confessed to his diary, he could only make a rough drawing because of the windstorm.

"I can scarcely conceive that I staid there 8 Years and passed them Comfortably for it is undoubtedly one of the poorest Spots in the Western Country according to my present opinion," he penned, with a splutter of the quill.

He meditated with further loathing upon the place as he gazed on the "infernal mill" from across the expanse of rough river water. "I looked upon the Mill perhaps for the Last Time, and with thoughts that made my Blood almost Cold, bid it an eternal farewell."

Luke, a shoemaker from Cincinnati, who had been acting as cook, and whom Audubon characterized as a poor sickly devil, did not share the artist's unflattering conception of Henderson, for Luke left the flatboat in a skiff, and the disagreeable task of cooking fell to Joseph's lot.

The voyage proceeded. There was very little to break the monotony of the drift down the Ohio. "My *Slut Dash* apparently good for nothing for want of employment," recorded Audubon one night, and he, like his dog, longed for an opportunity to go ashore. For a number of days he observed "many dears merely Gamboling on sand Barrs," which greatly excited the members of the crew but the captains only urged greater exertions on the part of the hired help that toiled at the sweeps, for the Mississippi must be reached before ice blocked traffic in the Ohio.

The flatboats were continually being passed by faster craft bound downstream, and Audubon consoled himself with the thought that the hunting would be poor even if he could get on shore with his gun on his shoulder and *Dash* at his heels.

2

A crew of hard-boiled gentry manned the flatboats. Audubon in his journal made word pictures of them for his sons and bemoaned the fact that his pen could not emulate his black chalks in furnishing a true likeness of each. His quaint pen picturization is worth repeating:

as I promised You a Picture of the Caracters We have on Board of Both Boats I will attempt to Copy them, could my Pen Act as a Black Chalk by the help of my fingers you might rely on the Exhibition of the figures—Yet I undertake it with pleasure, knowing how sweet this May be to you & Myself some Years hence, while sitting together by the fireside Looking at Your Dear Mother reading to us.

being on Board of Boats Much in the situation of Passengers, I am of Course Bound to give the preference to those who are termed Captains and Mr. Aumack is the First that I will bring to your attention—

You have seen him and of Course I have not much to say. the acquaintance of Man When unconnected by Interest is *plain* easily *understood* & Seldom Deviates . . .

he is a good Strong, Young Man, Generously Inclined rather Timorous on the River, yet Brave and accustomed to hardships—he Commands the Boat where I am—

Mr. Lovelace is a good Natured, rough fellow brought up to Work without pride, rather anxious to Make Money—playful & fond of Jokes and Women—

Mr. Shaw, the owner of Most of the Cargo, puts me in mind of some Jews, who are all Intent on their Interest & Wellfare; of a keen Visage & Manners; a Bostonian—Weak of Constitution but strong of Stomack—Would Live Well if at any one else' Expense—

The Crew is Composed as follows:

Ned Kelly a wag of 21. Stout Well Made, handsome if Clean, possessed of Much Low Wit, produces Mirth to the Whole even in his Braggardism—Sings, dances and feels always happy—he is a Baltimorian.

2 Men from Pennsylvania although not brothers, are possessed of a great sameness of Caracters—these are *Anthony P. Bodley* & *Henry* Sesler. They Work Well, talk but litle and are Carpenters by Trade.

The Last is Much Like the Last of every thing, the Worst Part—

Joseph Seeg, Lazy, fond of Grog, says nothing because it cannot help himself, sleeps Sound, for he burns all his Cloths, while in the ashes.

Cap^e Cummings Joseph & Myself for the Rear at Times and at Times the Van—you have seen the Life and there Likeness could not give you a better Impression than you have formed—We agree Well, and are Likely to agree Still—

The sixth of November found the cargo boats near the mouth of the Wabash river and Audubon, once more on shore, walked nine miles on an unsuccessful hunt for something to shoot. The wind proving favorable, the boats reached the Illinois shore "and 5 Guns went hunting, I shot 6 dear!" The next day, landing at Shawnee Town where the boats remained six hours, the members of the crew evidently patronizing the local doggeries, for from the pages of the journal we learn:

"This Evening Ned Kelly & his companion Joe Seeg, having drank rather freely of Grog, they had a little Scrape at the Expense of Mr. Seeg's Eyes & Nose."

The following morning, while Kelly and Seeg were sobering up by laboring at the sweeps, Audubon drew and colored a "Rusty Grakle *Gracula Ferruginea*, and made a handsome piece of it." The bird, a high plumaged male, had been killed the day before by Aumack. On Sunday the commander shot a duck out of a flock of five which, on examination, Audubon declared to be a "nondiscript." How this small member of the waterfowl family puzzled him! He first identified it correctly as a "ruddy duck," but later drew his pen through the words. Subsequently he set down: "I had the pleasure of Seeing Two of the same Ducks Swimming Deep, with their Tail *erect*, and diving for food—having never seen these Birds before, it was highly satisfactorily to Me." This was the artist's introduction to the agile ruddy duck and he made a sketch of it on a page of the journal.

Several days later he recorded that "Joseph made a *Faux Pas* this day—the Whole of our Folks not in the best Humour." What was the slip that set the burly boatmen on edge? Possibly something went wrong with Joseph's method of cooking or of serving the meals—we will probably never know, for the diary doesn't explain. Three days later, when the boats were tied up at a place called America, Audubon and Joseph went for a walk. It was late when they returned to the flatboats. What then occurred is best told by Audubon's entry in his well-scribbled journal:

At our Return at Night found Mr. Aumack in Bad humor, and after We had retired to our Cabin for the Night, received a *Humorous Lesson* that I shall Never forget.

My Dear Children if Ever you read these trifling remarks pay your attention to what follows—

Never be under what is Called obligations to Men not Aware of the Value of the Meaness of their *Conduct*

Never take a passage in any Stage or Vessell without a well understood agreement between you & the owners or Clerks & of all things. Never go for Nothing if you Wish to save Mental Troubles & Body Viscisitude.

Well aware that I shall never forget this Night as long as I Live, I close.

The moral is clear, but just what the "humorous lesson" was will perhaps never be known. One can only speculate on the sort of pranks likely to be indulged in on a flatboat and by men of the character manning it. Entries in his journal prove that Audubon's dignity and inflammable Gallic temper were easily ruffled, even by little things.

3

The day following, when the flatboats neared the junction of the two great rivers of the Mississippi valley, Audubon leaped into a skiff and rowed around the point where the Ohio empties into the Mississippi. That night he recorded his impressions:

Eleven Years ago on the 2 of January I ascended that Stream to St. Genevieve, Ferdinand Rozier of *Nantes* my partner in a large Keel Boat loaded with Sundries to a Large Amount *our* property

The 10th of May 1819 I passed this place in an open Skiff Bound to New Orleans with two of My Slaves.

Now I enter it *poor*, in fact, *Destitute* of all things and reliing only on that providential Hope, the Comforter of Wearied Mind—in a flat Boat a passenger.

The meeting of the Two Streams reminds me a little of the Gentle Youth who Comes in the World, spotless he presents himself, he is gradually drawn in to thousands of Dificulties that Makes him wish to keep, apart, but at Last he is over done and mixed, and lost in the Vortex.

The naturalist was intensely interested with the manner in which the currents of the two streams met, and he set down his observations in the well scribbled pages of his journal:

> The Beautiful & Transparent Watter of the Ohio when first entering the Mississippi is taken in small Drafts and Looks the more aquable to the Eye as it goes down surrounded by the Muddy Current, it keeps off as much as possible by running down the Kentucky side for several miles but reduced to a narrow strip & is lost . . . . here the Traveller enters a New World, the current of the stream is about 4 miles per hour, puts the steersman on the alert and wakes him to troubles and difficulties unknown on the Ohio, the Passenger feels a different atmosphere, a very different prospect—the Curling stream and its hue are the first objects—the caving in of the banks and the Thick Set Growth of the Young Cotton Wood is the next—the Watter's dencity reduced the thermoter from 62 to 20 degrees . . . I bid farewell to the Ohio at 2 o'clock P.M. and felt a fear gathering involuntarily, every moment draws me from all that is Dear to Me, My Beloved Wife & Children.

4

The Audubon who went ashore with Captain Cummings that afternoon was not the sprightly young popinjay of *Mill Grove* who played such havoc with Lucy Bakewell's heart, There was little of the dandy in the man who recorded in his diary: "When we left Cincinnati, we agreed to shave & Clean completely every Sunday—and often have been anxious to see the day come for certainly a shirt worn one week, hunting every day and sleeping in Buffalo robes at night soon become soiled and Desagreable."

He was more the "American Woodsman" at this period than at any other time of his career. The flatboats had separated upon entering the Mississippi, it being safer to navigate them singly, and the strong current carrying the laden craft southwards would not permit of forays on shore, except when the clumsy flats were forced to the banks by contrary winds. This was not much of a deprivation, as Audubon found "the Game not so plenty as on the Ohio and Much Shier."

It was on such a foray ashore that Captain Cummings captured alive an opossum and carried it back to the flatboat for the naturalist's inspection. Audubon has left us two records of the incident. One in an *Episode*, with the language smoothed by MacGillivray, and thereby robbed somewhat of its brutality; the other in his unexpurgated day by day record of his journey down the great river on Aumack's flatboat. In his episode on "The Opposum" it is printed:

Once, while descending the Mississippi, in a sluggish flat-bottomed boat, expressly for the purpose of studying those objects of nature more nearly connected with favorite pursuits, I chanced to meet with two well-grown Opossums, and brought them alive to the "ark." The poor things were placed on the roof or deck, and were immediately assailed by the crew, when, following their natural instinct, they lay as if dead. An experiment was suggested, and both were thrown overboard. On striking the water, and for a few moments after, neither evinced the least disposition to move; but finding their situation desperate, they began to swim towards our uncouth rudder, which was formed of a long slender tree, extending from the middle of the boat thirty feet beyond its stern. They both got upon it, were taken up, and afterwards let loose in their native woods.

The entry in the journal gives an entirely different version of the opossum episode. In the naturalist's uncensored words this is what happened:

Cap[e] C. Brought an Oppossum, *Dash* after having broke I thought all of its bones left—it was thrown over Board as if dead, yet the moment he toucht the Watter he swam for the Boats—so tenacious of Life are these animals that it took a heavy blow of the Axe to finish him—

Audubon worked on his drawing of a waterbird he called the Imber Diver, the loon of our present-day bird books. In addition to his full-sized drawing, he made a pen-and-ink sketch of the loon and the little ruddy duck on the pages of the journal, together with notes on the condition and plumage of the two birds. When the weather was disagreeable he kept to the interior of the flatboat's cabin, busy with his drawings. As he drew his bird pictures the current of the mighty Mississippi floated him nearer his destination.

5

When the flats tied up at New Madrid, Audubon found some old friends at the settlement. He wrote: "A Mrs. Maddis, formerly the lawful wife of Mr. Reignier of St. Geneviève, resides and keeps a small store in company with a French Gentleman. We are told that the Partnership was rendered agreable to both by a mutual wish of Nature. Went to this Lady's house who knew me first and exhibited much of the french Manners."

But he felt depressed that evening, he confided to his journal, for "every object that brings *forward* the *Background* of My Life's Picture shews too often with poignancy the difference of situation." This is one of the artist-naturalist's very few references to his "background" that has been put into print unedited. His day-by-day record of his life shows that he was treading high in air one moment, and wallowing in the depths the next.

"Every Sunday," he writes, "I look at my Drawings and particularly that of My Beloved Wife—& like to spend about one hour in thoughts devoted to my family." Let the boat drift to the shore and be held there by the winds, and Audubon is routed from his dour reveries and, gun in hand, with *Dash* leaping before him, he is off seeking what he can shoot.

The heavily laden flats did not move down the river as fast as the cargo owner or crew desired. "The winds on this River are Contrary to our Wishes as that of an Ole Rich *Maid* to the wishes of a Lover of Wealth," the hunter of the expedition wrote. "We are anxious to Make progress on account of our Situation—but it is disposed of Diferently by a *Superior Power.*" Therefore, the naturalist was compelled to do his shooting from the deck of the ark. On one occasion he says he "killed a *Red Tailed Awk* a great distance with a ball," as well as a barn owl and a goose, but also records he missed a "black hawk" that passed within a few yards of him because he had a rifle in his hands at the time and could not hit the bird on the wing with a ball.

Otherwise life on board the ark, slowly drifting with the current along the winding course of the Father of the Waters, was without excitement. The daily breakfast was bacon and grease-soaked biscuits. The members of the crew manned the sweeps to keep the awkward craft in the middle of the stream and off sand bars, and when night came the boats were tied up to a convenient shore. After a supper of this rough fare had been served all hands played cards until bedtime, which by common agreement was nine o'clock.

6

It was late in November, when the boats were floating past Little Prairie, a point a few miles south of New Madrid, that Audubon took Joseph with him for a shooting expedition on shore. "As soon as we had eat our *Common Breakfast* fried Bacon and Soaked Biscuits—Joseph went to his station and I to Mine, i.e., he rowed the skiff and I steering it—Went to the *Little, Prairie* shot at a Brown Eagle probably 250 yards and yet cut one of its legs." The two were surrounded on all sides by a considerable collection of birds, "mostly Red-breasted Thrushes," as Audubon then named robins, "the sungs of Which revived our spirits and Imparted within us the Sweet sensation that Spring brings to Minds of *our* kind."

Suddenly a great white-headed eagle swooped through the air and settled on a tree top. Its form bulked in silhouette against the morning sun as Audubon took careful aim with his rifle. In spite of the fact that the eagle was 150 yards off, the ball sped true to its mark, and the imperious bird of freedom, surveying its domain from the high cypress, reeled at the impact of lead, clutched impotently with talons at the perch and hurtled to the ground, its lifeless form bounding from limb to limb as it fell.

It proved to be a handsome male and Audubon, struck with the majestic and high plumaged appearance of the emblematic bird of his adopted country, decided to make it live again on paper. Joseph rowed the artist back to the ark without loss of time and Audubon set to work with pencil, crayon, watercolor, and pastel fashioning the likeness that appears in one of his most celebrated plates, which portrays the White-headed Eagle devouring a catfish.

As he fixed the dead eagle with wires and arranged its pose the better to transfer its image to paper, he examined his specimen in hand minutely and set down in his journal: "Since I killed the one before me I am convinced that the *Bald Eagle* and the *Brown Eagle* are two different species."

He labored on his life-sized drawing of the Bald Eagle four consecutive days. As Joseph had killed a particularly fine Canada goose, Audubon used it in the composition, setting the eagle tearing at the bird's breast. Many years later, Audubon when in London, redrew this picture, faithfully copying the eagle but substituting a catfish for the goose, and thus it appears in the famous engraving.

White-headed eagles were very numerous during this part of the journey, affording Audubon many opportunities for observing their habits. His interest in them was always acute as he was positive the brown eagle, his Bird of Washington, was a valid species and was constantly on the lookout for one suitable for a drawing. He had first seen one of these brown eagles ten years before when he and his partner Rozier were laboring with a keelboat and its load of whiskey up the Mississippi on their way to Ste. Geneviève. The tremendous size of the brown bird, the absence of white head and white tail feathers, convinced the embryo-naturalist that the two were separate and distinct species, whereas today we know that the wholly brown birds were only the immaturely plumaged bald eagles, which do not acquire the characteristic white head and tails until their third or fourth year.

From the deck of the flatboat Audubon kept sharp lookout for eagles, using his long brass telescope to better observe the birds. He noted that the eagles were:

> Becoming very Numerous, hunt in pairs, and roost on the Tall trees above their Nests—One this morning took up the head of a Wild Goose thrown overboard, with as much ease as a man could with the hand—they chase Ducks and if they force one from the Flock he is undoubtedly taken, carried on a Sand Bank and eat by Both Eagles —they are more shy in the afternoon than in the morning—they seldom sail high at this season, Watch from the tops of trees and Dash at any thing that comes near them—to secure a Goose, the Male & Femelle, Dive alternately after it and give it little time to breath that the poor fellow is forced in a few Minutes.

Audubon's drawing of his eagle was finished on Monday, November 27, and on the same day all on board were made ill by eating too freely of a buck deer that had been killed two days before. Audubon, sick in mind as well, brought out his drawing of Lucy. "While looking at My Beloved Wife's Likeness this day I thought it altered and Looked sorrowful, it produced an Immediate sensation of Dread or her being in Want—yet I cannot hear from her for Weeks to Come—but Hope she and our Children are well."

CHAPTER 6

His Own Story of His Early Life

THERE WAS LITTLE in the weather the next morning to cheer his gloomy meditation, for the blue devils were pounding him the day the flatboats moved downstream in a drenching downpour of rain. Unable to hunt, cooped up in a tiny stuffy cabin, dejected, and still ill from the attack of indigestion brought on by over-eating fresh venison, Audubon took up his journal and penned what is undoubtedly the first account of his early life and parentage he ever set to paper.

Those who have studied this strange yet gifted man's life have heretofore been forced to accept versions of his writings only as they were copied from his original documents by descendants. In many instances these versions did not actually print what he wrote. In the account which follows, transcribed *verbatim et literatim* from the pages of Audubon's journal of 1820-21, we have the opportunity of not only knowing exactly what he penned but of comparing portions of this unexpurgated "life" to the autobiography *Myself* he is said to have written fifteen years later.

This valuable journal of his trip down the Mississippi river on a flatboat, in some way not now known, escaped the fire to which other Audubon manuscripts were consigned by a granddaughter so that certain facts in them would never be known, and it comes to us intact save for the mutilation of two lines on one page where Audubon describes his own mother, and the absence of eight whole pages which detailed his adventure in New Orleans with a ravishingly beautiful widow when he drew her portrait in the nude. Fortunately these eight pages have been preserved, and that amusing episode can be told, with its wealth of detail, in its proper place.

The entry which had to do with his early existence, like other incidents, inscribed in the journal, was addressed to his two sons so they might know something of his life and antecedents. After dating the top of the page Tuesday, November 28, 1820, Audubon wrote:

"As it is a rainy morning, I cannot hunt, and will take this opportunity to retailing to you such incidents relative to my Life as I think you may at some future period be glad to know—

"my Father John Audubon, was born at Sables D'Olonne in France; the son of a man who had a very Large family, being 20 males & one femelle. his Father started him at a very early age *Cabin Boy* on Board a Whaleing Ship—of course by education he was nothing; but he naturally was quick, industrious and soberly Inclined, his voyage was a hard one but he often assured me that he never regretted it—it rendered him Robust, active and fit to go through the World's rugged paths. He soon became able to command a Fishing Smack, to purchase it, and so rapidly did he proceed on the road to Fortune, that when of Age, he commanded a small Vessel belonging to him, trading to St. Domingo.

"A Man of Such Natural Talents and enterprise could not be confined to the common drudgery of the Money Making Annimal, and entered an officer in the French Navy's Service under Louis the 16th was fortunate and Employed as Agent at St. Domingo to Carry the trade—every movement was a Happy hit, he became Wealthy—the American Revolution brought him to this Country Commander of a Frigate under the Count Rochambeau, he had the honor of being presented to the Great Washington, and Major Crogan of Kentucky who has told me often that he then Looked Much Like me was particularly well acquainted with him. My Father was in several Engagements in the American service and at the taking of Lord Cornwallis.

"Before his Return to Europe he purchased a Beautiful Farm on the *Schuillkill* and *Perkioming* Creek in Pennslyvania; the Civil Wars of France and St. Domingo, brought such heavy sweeps of Fortune on his head, that it was with the utmost Dificulty that his Life was Spared.

"he along with thousands more saw his Wealth Torn from him, and had Little More left than was Necessary to Live

Tuesday November 28th 1820.

as it is a rainy Morning, I Cannot hunt, and will take this opportunity of relating to you such Incidents relative to my Life as I think you May at some future period be glad to Know. ——

My Father John Audubon, Was born at Sables D'Olonne in France; the son of a Man who had a very Large familly, being 20 Males & one famille; his Father placed him at a very Early age Cabin Boy on Board a Whaleing Ship — of Course ~~his youth~~ his education ~~was as Was then~~ ~~what we call here a~~ Nothing; but he Naturally Was, quick Industrious and Soberly Inclined; his Voyages was a hard one but he often assured Me he never regretted it — it rendered him Robust, active and fit to go through the World's rugged Paths. he soon became able to Command a Fishing Smack, to purchase it, and so rapidly did he proceed on the road of Fortune, that when of Age, he commanded a Small Vessel belonging to him, trading to St Domingo — a Man of Such Natural Talents and Enterprise Could not be confined to the common drudgery of this... Making animal, and entered an Officer in the French Navy's Service under Louis the 16th was fortunate and Employed as Agent a St Domingo to Carry the trade — Every Movement was a Happy hit, he became Wealthy —— the american Revolution brought him to this Country Commander of a Frigate under the Count Rochambeau, he had the honor of being presented to the Great Washington, and Major Croghan of Kentucky who has told me often that he then looked Much like me was particularly well acquainted with him; My Father was in several Engagements with american service and at the taking of Lord Cornwallis.

before his Return to Europe he purchased a Beautifull Farm on the Schuilkill and Perkioming Creek in Pensylvania; the Civil Wars of France and St Domingo, brought such heavy reverses of Fortune on his head, that it Was with the utmost Dificulty that his Life Was Spared—

he along with thousands more saw his Wealth, Gone from him, and had little More left than was Necessary to Rear and Educate Two Children Left out of five having 3 Older Brothers Killed in the Wars—

he remained in France residing in the Service under the Bonaparte; but the French Navy prospered not and he retired to a Small ~~but~~ beautifull Country Seat, three Leagues from Nantes in Sight of the Loire and ended his Life happy— Most Men have faults; he had One that never left him untill followed by a Long Life Common to Many Individual, but this was Counter balanced by Many qualities— his Generosity was often too great— as a Father I never complained of him and the Many Durable Friends he had prove him to have been a good Man—

[redacted]

My Mother, who I have been told was an Extraordinary beautifull Woman, died Shortly after My Birth and My Father having Remarried in France I was removed thereto when only Two Years Old and received by that Best of Women, raised and Cherished ~~by her~~ to the Extremity of her Means— My Father gave me and My Sister Rosa Good education appropriate to his purse I studied Mathematicks at an early Age, and had Many Teaching of agreable Talents, I perhaps would have Much fitted up, if The Continual Wars in Which France Was engaged had Not forced Me away when only Fourteen Years Old— I entered in the Navy and Was Rec'd a Midshipman at Rochefort Much against my Inclinations— the Short Peace of 1802 between Engl. & France ended My Military Career, ~~by [illegible]~~ the Conscription determined My Father on sending me to and Educate Two Children Left out of five—having 3 younger[1] Brothers Killed in the Wars.

"he remained in France reentered the Service under Bonaparte; but the French Navy prospered not and he retired to a Small but beautifull Country Seat, Three Leagues from *Nantes* in sight of the Loire and ended his Life happy—Most Men have faults, he had One that never Left him untill sobered by a Long Life common to many Individual, but this Counter balanced by Many qualities—his Generosity was often too great—as a Father I never complained of him and the Many Durable Friends he had prove him to have been a *good* Man—

[The next two lines in the journal have been heavily marked with black ink, different from that used by Audubon in writing his entries. It is evident that the obliterated entry has to do with the identity of his mother and his birth, as the succeeding lines indicate.]

My Mother, who I have been told was an Extraordinary beautiful Woman, died shortly after My Birth and my father having married[2] in France I was removed thereto when only Two years old and received by that Best of Women, raised and cherished by her to the utmost of her Means—My Father gave me and My Sister *Rosa* such education appropriate to his purse I studied Mathematics at an early Age, and had many Teachers of Agreable Talents, I perhaps would have much stored up, if the Continental Wars in Which France Was engaged had not forced me away when only Fourteen Years old— I entered the Navy and was Recd a midshipman at Rochefort much against my Inclinations—the Short Peace of 1802 between England & France ended my military Carreer, by law, but the Conscription determined My Father on sending me to *America* and Live on the *Mill Grove* Farm I have mentioned above—he sent me to the care of Miers Fisher, Esqr a rich and honest Quaker of Philadelphia who

[1]The word "younger" is written over in a different ink, evidently at a later period, and in a different hand, to make the word read "older." See reproduction of page of original journal on the opposite page.

[2]The word "married" in the original has been changed, by a different hand and in different ink, evidently at a later date, by the addition of "re"—to make it "remarried." (Note reproduction.) This was undoubtedly an attempt on the part of one who successfully obliterated the lines, for the ink is the same, to change the meaning in an effort to prove that Lieutenant Audubon "remarried" in France, whereas Audubon truthfully stated that the man he called father was already married when he was born.

had been his agent for many years, and who received me so Politelly that I was sure he Esteemed My Name.

"A Young Man of *Seventeen*[1] sent to America to *Make Money* (for such was My Father's Wish) brought up in France in easy Circumstance who had never thought on the Want of an article I had had at Discretion but was ill fitted for it.

"I spent much Money and One Year of My Life as Happy as the Young Bird that having Left the Parents sight carolls Merily, While Hawks of All Species are Watching him for an easy prey.

"I had a Partner with whom I did not agreed, he [several words blotted out in different ink evidently at a later period] waited his opportunity [several words inked out] We parted forever.

"Here it is well I should Mentioned, that I Landed in *New York*, took the Yellow Fever and did not reach Philadelphia for Three Months.

"Shortly after My Arrival on My Farm, Your Mother *Lucy Bakewell* came with her Father's Familly to a Farm Called *Fatland Ford* and divided from mine only by the Philadelphia Road.

"We soon became acquainted and *I* attached to her. I went to France to Obtain My Father's Consent to Marry her, and returned with a Partner, Ferdinand Rozier of Nantes entered in Business for the thoughts of Marriage brought Ideas so new to me that I began with pleasure in the Business War to secure my Future Wife and Familly the Comforts We had both been used to. I travelled through the Western Country and Made Louisville my Choice for a residence. On my return and being of age I married your Beloved Mother on the *5th* of April 1808 and removed to Kentucky. Louisville did not suit our Plans and we left that place with a View to Visit St Louis on the Mississippi but it is so seldom that our wishes are favored that we did not reach that Place, for My Partner not being on good Terms with My Wife, I left her and you *Victor* at Henderson, you were then a babe, having reached St. Genevieve through Many Difficulties, Ice,

---

[1]If Audubon was seventeen in 1802, this would make his birth year 1785.

&c I parted from Mr Rozier and Walked to Henderson in Four Days 165 Miles.

"Your present Uncle T. W. Bakewell Joined me in opening a House at New Orleans that the War with England Made us Remove to Henderson. This Place saw My best days, My Happiest, My Wife having blessed me with Your Brother Woodhouse and a sweet Daughter I Calculated, to Live and died in Comfort, Our Business Was good of course We agreed. but I was intended to meet Many Events of a disagreeable Nature; A Third Partner Was taken in and the Building of a Large Steam Mill. the Purchasing of Too Many goods sold on credit of course Lost. reduced us—Divided us.

"Your Uncle who had married a Short time previous removed to Louisville. Men with whom I had Long been connected offered me a Partnership. I accepted and a small ray of Light reappeared in My Business but a *Revolution* occasioned by a Numberless quantities of Failures, put all to an end; the Loss of My Darling Daughter affected Me Much; My Wife apparently had Lost her spirits. I felt no wish to try the Mercantile Business. I paid all I could and Left Henderson, Poor & Miserable of thoughts.

"My Intention to go to France to see My Mother and Sister was frustrated and at Last I resorted to My Poor Talents to Maintain You and Your Dear Mother, who fortunately became easy at her Change of Condition, and gave me a Spirit such as I really Needed, to Meet the surly Looks and Cold receptions of those Who so shortly before were pleased to Call me Their Friend.

"in Attempting the Likeness of James Berthoud, Esqr a Particularly good Man and I believe the Only *Sincere* Friend of Myself and Wife We ever had—to please his Son & Lady, I discovered such Talents that I was engaged to proceed and succeeded in a Few Weeks beyond my Expectations.

"Your Mother who had remained at Henderson to come by watter, was at Last obliged to come in a Carriage, and for the second time You had a sweet sister born. How I have dwelt on her Lovely features, when sucking the nutritious food from her Dear Mother. Yet she was torn away from us when only 7 months old. Having taken all the likeness Louisville could afford I removed to Cincinnati, leaving you all behind untill satisfied of some Means of Making something for a Maintanance. Through Talents in stuffing Fishes I entered in the service of the Western Museum at One Hundred and Twenty five Dollars per Month, and raised a Drawing School of 25 pupils, Made some Likeness, and had You around Me Once More, but small towns do not afford a support for any time.

"Ever since a Boy I have had an astonishing desire to see Much of the World & particularly to Acquire a true Knowledge of the Birds of North America, consequently, I hunted when Ever I had an Opportunity, and Drew every New Specimen as I could, or dared *steel time* from my Business and having a tolerably Large Number of Drawings that have been generally admired, I Concluded that perhaps I Could Not do better than to Travel, and finish My Collection or so nearly that it would be a Valuable Acquisition. My Wife Hoped it might do Well, and I Left her Once More with an intention of returning in Seven or Eight Months; I wrote to Henry Clay Esqr with Whom I Was acquainted and he Enclosed Me in a Very Polite & Friendly Letter One of General Introduction. I received Many from Others, General Harrison &c

"from the day I left Cincinnati untill the present My Journal gives you a rough Idea of My Way of Spending the tedious Passage in a Flat Boat to New Orleans."

Audubon's sketch in his journal of the "Imber diver," as he then termed the loon.

CHAPTER 7

Birds, Broadhorns and Keelboats

TIME hung heavily on the hands of the travelers moving down the Mississippi. Audubon's journal tells us the "rain lowered the smoake so *Much* that it was impossible to see beyond 20 or 30 yeards; played a great deal on the flutes. looked at my Drawings, read as much as I could and yet found the day very long and heavy Although I am Naturally of light spirits and have often tried to Keep these good, when off from my Home, I have often dull Moments of Anguish."

The Chickasaw Bluffs, now the site of Memphis, Tennessee, were passed in a rain so deluging that the naturalist could not draw a picture of these uplands, and he was confined to the low cabin of the flatboat, a prey to his homesick thoughts. The boat he was on ran a race with the flat commanded by Lovelace through a certain course in the river known to rivermen as the *Devil's Raceground*. "But the whole of the Mississippi being so much of the same nature," Audubon complained to his diary, "it feels quite immatereal to follow the Devil's tracks any where along its Muddy Course. Many places on this River are render More terrible in Idea by their Extraordinary Names than real difficulties."

The race of the broadhorns ended in an acrimonious dissension, which prompted the naturalist to observe: "it reminded me of Gamblers that although playing for Nothing are allways grieved by Lossing."

The first day of November dawned clear but the weather was intensely cold. Great flocks of mergansers flew over the boats in long V formations; hundreds of gulls were gathered on a sandbar, and many purple grackles winged by the arks. Audubon observed four white-headed eagles feasting off the carcass of a deer, and was elated when Mr. Shaw killed five

Canada geese, four falling before one discharge of the cargo-owner's double-barreled shotgun.

Always on the alert for something pertaining to eagles, Audubon recorded their mating antics in his diary.

I saw this afternoon Two Eagles Coatiting—the femelle was on a Very high Limb of a Tree and squated at the approach of the Male, who came Like a Torrent, alighted on her and quakled shrill untill he sailed off the femelle following him and ziz zaging herself through the air—this is scarce proof I have the pleasure of witnessing of these and all the *Falco Genus* breeding much Earlier than any Other Land Birds.

His method of hunting during the early days of December, while the cumbersome flats slowly floated southwards, was to take the skiff and, with Joseph Mason providing the propelling power, keep well in advance of the heavily laden arks. Should game be sighted the two hunters would lie flat in the small boat and float within range. He wrote:

Shot at a Large W. H. Eagle and a *Black Hawk*. Missed Both. This Latter in going off *flapped* his Wings Like a Pigeon, they are more Swifter than any bird in their Common flight. I could Not Well account My Missing these birds, they were not more than 100 yds. off. I shot 3 Turkeys at 2 shots—their Crops completely filled with *winter Grapes* Gizzards of the seeds of the same and large gravel. They were extremely gentle. I floated immediately to them and Came within 25 yds. Cold days force the geese away from shore—the woods literly filled with Parokeets. great Many Squirls—and many *Snow Birds*. begun raining about one—Now & then a Wood Cutter's Hut is seen in a Small Parcel of cleard Land between Two Thick Cane Brakes.

The following Sunday Audubon described seeing in "the setting sun hundreds of Malards travelling *South* and the *Finest* rainbow I ever beheld, the Clouds were also beautifull apposite it. Looked at My Beloved Wife's Likeness. Shaved and Cleaned, One of the few enjoyments Flat Boats Can Afford. The Goose we eat at Dinner extremely fishy. Joseph who is now obliged to officiate as Cook does not appear to relish the thing. The more I see of Cape C. the more I like him. Wish that we could say the same thing of all the World."

The next few days were very disagreeable. The wind was high and kept the boats knocking against sandbars. Few birds were seen, and although some white-headed eagles were noted through his spy glass, Audubon failed to observe any "brown eagles." The bald eagles were courting and the males "busy chasing off the Batchelors." One morning, while skinning a large catfish Audubon's attention was diverted from his chore by seeing "several hundred of those Black Birds yet unknown to me that I dominate *Black Pelicans*, flying South forming a very obtuse Angle, without uttering any Noise—have some hopes therefore to see some of them on the Watters of the Red River or Washita."

Long lines of birds, all bound for the hospitable Louisiana marshlands, flew over the boats. Sandhill cranes, geese, trumpeter swans, green-winged teal were among the species observed by Audubon from the deck of the flatboat. The high V's of geese interested the naturalist as much as did the flocks of mysterious birds he called "black pelicans." He noted the methods of sky travel the honkers followed, setting down: "While Geese are in a Travelling order the Young or Smallest are about the center of the *Lines* and the larger Gander Lead the Van, the Oldest Goose Drives the Rear."

The weather was beautiful but cold, and Audubon opined that "the frogs that Wistled so merily Yesterday," were well buried in the mud. The boat he was on made an awkward landing and lodged in the mud for half an hour consequently "our Commander had a good opportunity for Exercising his Powers at Swearing, more particularly when Anthony broke his Sweep Oar." However, the arks made thirty miles that day, and when they were finally tied to shore at night, the naturalist credits Captain Cummings with the cryptic observation: "Fine Weather but no Fish."

The next morning dawned clear, save for a few clouds in the sky, and as the commanders of the flats were anxious to overtake a flotilla of other broadhorns that had passed them the day before, so as not to be the last of the provision boats to reach the New Orleans' market, a start was made at daybreak. When the mouth of the St. Francis river was passed, Audubon took the skiff, with Joseph at the oars, and landed at Big Prairie where he saw "a Monstrous Turkey Cock, I think the largest I ever saw; it appears considerably Larger than the one I weighed that was over 31 lb." His anxiety to secure the bird, he confessed, affected his aim and the great bird flew off.

While at the Big Prairie Audubon recalled the fact that it was here he had first seen Mississippi kites flying over the forests. This was eighteen months before, in the month of June, when he was ascending the river on the steamboat *Paragon* following his unsuccessful trip to New Orleans to recover his steamer from Sam Bowen, and he remembered that the kites "were busily Employed in Catching small Lizards off the Bark of dead Cypress Trees, this effected by Sliding beautifully by the Trees and suddenly Turning on their side and Graple the prey. Having at that time no Crayons or Paper, did not Draw one, and determined Never to Draw from a Stuffed Specimen."

This resolve, made from the deck of a Mississippi river steamboat, was not rigidly observed in after years. Audubon's drawings have been criticised for the postures in which he placed many of his bird subjects, attitudes which have been declared too violent of action. Some critics say his paintings were too flat, and in many instances exhibit defective drawing. Other critics complain there is too much detail in the feathers. Others grumble that he paid too much attention to backgrounds and plant accessories. Then there are those who aver he did not pay enough attention to backgrounds.

He had his own original method of transferring the bird subject from life, or death, to the surface of his large sheets of paper. In addition to his pencils, chalks, watercolors and pastels, the artist carried rolls of wire. When he killed a specimen he wished to draw he decided in advance the posture it was to assume in his drawing by forming a picture of the whole in his mind's eye. He then fixed the bird to a background, which was marked off in squares, and with the aid of wires secured the legs, head, tail, and wings of the dead bird in the attitude he desired. As he made all of his drawings exactly life size, he marked off the paper in squares corresponding in proportion to the squares on the background that held his wired subject. In this manner he could make sure of exact proportions, and could examine thoroughly the bill, nostrils, eyes, legs, and claws, as well as the structure of the wings and tail, and colors of the feathers. Being ambidextrous, he could use his left hand as well as his right in fashioning his picture, sometimes he even drew with *both* hands.

Whenever it became necessary to secure proportions where the cross lines on the background were concealed by the bird's body, a frame with wires, set the same distance apart and corresponding with the lines on his paper, was laid over the bird's body so he could more correctly obtain his outlines. Parts, such as wing-lengths, size of bill, legs, toes, and even talons, were measured with a pair of compasses. The general proportions and outline finished to his satisfaction on the first sheet, Audubon then transferred the first rough drawing to a second sheet of drawing paper by pouncing or tracing, so the original painting would not be marred with his first sketching strokes.

A few ornithological critics have complained that Audubon was guilty of exaggeration in endeavoring to give his birds life and action—like his own French manner, he gesticulated too much! Compared with Alexander Wilson's drawings of the same species of birds, Professor Herrick notes that the birds drawn by the Paisley weaver were more cautious or sedate, as became a canny Scot.

However closely Audubon's work, that is, his mature or better bird drawings, which developed during his flatboat journey down the Mississippi river, approached the mechanical, they were never too unnatural. It must be remembered, also, that he was confronted with a mighty problem in delineating his birds. His resolve, from which he never deviated, was to show them in life size, whether it was the tiny hummingbird or the long-legged whooping crane. True, he was forced to place the tall waders in attitudes that permitted them "to fit," so to speak, the largest piece of drawing paper he could then secure—a sheet thirty by forty inches in size.

In these large subjects, such as his splendid white-headed eagle, the original drawing shows every feather, with *every barb* of every feather, precisely in place. The yellow feet of the eagle, ending in the powerful and sharp talons, reveal every scale. Whenever he placed a bird subject on a limb or branch of a tree or shrub, every leaf and flower were in exact detail. In drawing the accessories he had a proficient assistant in Joseph Mason who, according to penciled legends on many of the originals, drew the flowers and leaves.

Indeed, comes the evidence to this from a staunch champion of the boy, one John Neal, editorial writer on *The New England Galaxy* of Boston, who in 1835 gave Audubon a triple toasting in the columns of that newspaper. Neal claimed that this thirteen-year-old lad "did all the botanical drawings, and used to paint the feet, legs, eyes, and beaks of all the birds in water colors—the rest being done by Audubon, who rubbed the colors on dry."

The hunting of birds, the killing of them, and the making of bird and flower drawings went on whenever weather permitted. Audubon brushed up on botany, with the boy's help and artistic pencil, and in return the man taught the boy much about birds and expounded his ideas as to how they should be represented on paper. The oddly-assorted comrades exchanged many confidences. It is related that Audubon even told the boy that he had been born in San Domingo and that he remembered distinctly the escape of his father, sister, and himself, when the negroes revolted . . . that a faithful negro slave, who afterwards became a general in the French army, spirited the three on board a ship, by blackening their faces, loading coffee in bulk, and hiding Captain Audubon's fortune in the coffee cargo.

So passed the days as the flatboats drifted ever southwards with the placid current of the great river. All on board were anxious for the completion of the tedious journey, for prevailing winds from the south prevented the clumsy craft from traveling as rapidly as the current. Other flats, also loaded with produce, had passed them; so one evening Aumack and Lovelace held a conference with the cargo owner as to the best method of overtaking competing arks which lay moored to the banks some four miles below. It was decided that a start should be made an hour before daybreak and "run down the Dd Rascals." Next morning the headwinds still prevailed and prevented the maneuver.

While waiting for the wind to lull, Aumack winged an eagle and "brought it alive on board, the Noble Fellow Looked at his Ennemies with a Contemtable Eye. I tied a string to one of its Legs this Made him Jump over Board. My Surprise at Seeing it Swim well Was very great, it used its Wings with great Effect and Would have Made the Shore distant there about 200 *yds* Dragging a Pole Weighing at Least 15 *lbs*—Joseph went after it with a Skiff, the Eagle defended itself. This specimen rather less than the one I draw—the femelle hovered over us and shrieked for some time exhibiting the *true sorrow* of the *Constant Mate* . . . Our Eagle Eat of Fish freely about one hour after we had him, by fixing a piece on a stick and putting it to its Mouth. However, while I was friendly Indian toward it, it Launched one of its feet and caught hold of my right thum, making it feel sore."

Nursing his sore thumb, Audubon prepared a bed for his dog *Dash*, "expecting her to be delivered from her Burthen every Day," and as he walked about the deck the tortured eagle hissed at him. Audubon was eagerly watching for the opening that led to the Arkansas Post, then the seat of government of the new territory of that name. He began a letter to his wife, which he intended mailing back from that stopping place, which the boat's commander hoped to reach on the morrow, "but Hopes are Shy Birds flying at a great distance seldom reached by the best of Guns," he sighed.

Audubon had a reason for wishing to reach the fort other than that of mailing a letter. He had subsisted that day on raw sweet potatoes and was not to be blamed for scribbling in his journal: "how Surly the Looks of Ill fortune are to the poor." He had become greatly dissatisfied with the behaviour of those in charge of the flats and confided to Mason his determination to leave the boats. "I hope," he set down in his diary, "to Leave the boat I am now in if there is What the Kentuckians Term a '*half Chance*.' Our Commander's Looks and acting are so strange that I have become quite Sickened."

The Arkansas Post was not located on the banks of the Mississippi but several miles up the course of the Arkansas river, which emptied into the larger stream in two places. The flatboats floated to the Caledonian Point, or Petite Landing, about four miles above the actual mouth of White River, and Jacob Aumack hopped to shore, to make an overland journey to the Post. After making inquiries concerning the road, Audubon decided to go by water to the mouth of what natives called the Cut-off, and then tramp the rest of the way to the settlement. Joseph Mason and Anthony Bodley joined him on the excursion, and the skiff, double-oared, began the trip. "We left at ten o'clock with Light hearts, Small Bottle of Whiskey, a few Biscuits, and the determination of Reaching the Post that Night," Audubon records.

The three had an adventurous journey and did not attain their objective until nine that night. Audubon describes their arrival: "We entered the Only Tavern in the Country—Wearied, Muddy, Wet & hungry—the Supper was soon calld for, and soon served, and to see 4 Wolfs taring an Carcass would not give you a bad Idea of our Manners while helping *Ourselves*. The *Bright Staring Eyes* of the Land Ladies Notwithstanding . . . however, I found Mrs. Montgomery a handsome Woman of good Manners and rather superior to those in her rank of Life—to Bed and sleep sound was the next Wish for 32 Miles in such a Country May be Calculated as a full dose for any *Pedestrian per day*—Led into a Large Building that formerly perhaps saw the great *Concils of Spanish Dons* we saw 3 beds containing 5 men. Yet all was arranged in a few moments and as the Breaches were Coming off our Legs, Mr. Aumack & Anthony slided into one and Joseph & myself into Another, to force Acquaintance with the strangers being of course necessary, a conversation ensued that Lulled Me a Sleep, and Nothing but the Want of *Blankets* Kept Me from Resting Well, for I soon found a Place between the *Tugs* that Supported about 10 lbs of Wild Turkey Feathers to save (?) My roundest Parts from the Sharp Edges of An Homespun Bedstead."

In spite of sleeping discomforts morning arrived at last and with the light of the new day came the songs of a multitude of birds, for notwithstanding the fact that it was the eleventh of December, Audubon records that there was "Mirth *all about us*, the *Cardinals*, the Iowa Buntings, the Meadow Larks and Many Species of Sparrows, chearing the approach of a Benevolent sun Shining day." He was quickly dressed, up and about, met several old acquaintances, and made inquiries regarding the place, especially the upper country drained by the Arkansas river. He learned with regret that General James Miller, the territorial governor, was absent from the post, having gone to a place then called *Petite Rocke*, today known as Little Rock, about 150 miles distant, where the "new seat of government would probably be situated." Consequently, the letter of introduction he carried to the executive was left with a friend to be delivered to the governor upon his return, and Audubon turned to a survey of the place and an inventory of its bird life. He wrote:

> The Post of Arkansas is Now a poor, Nearly deserted Village, it flourished in the time that the Spaniards & French kept it, and One 100 years passed it could have been called and agreable Small Town—at present, the decripid Visages of the Worn out Indian Traders and a few American Famillies are all that gives it Life, the Natural situation is a handsome One, on a high Bank formerly the Edge of a *Prairie* —but rendered extremely sickly by the Back Neighborhood of Many Overflowing Lakes & Swamps . . . the Town now Prospering at *Point Rock* is highly healthy and in the Center of a Rich tract of Wood & Prairie Lands —and probably may flourish.

A French gentleman, one who evidently was endowed with an acute taste for joking, told Audubon that he had recently killed a hawk, all white save for its bright red tail. This so excited the naturalist that he began a frantic search for its remains, but not even a red tail feather was located. Nor was this the only thing to excite him at the old *Poste*, for he "Saw there a *Velocipede*. Judge how fast the Arts & Sciences Improved in this Southwestern Country," he wrote his wife.

Failing to meet Governor Miller and thus conclude an arrangement to explore the Arkansas to its headwaters, Audubon reluctantly abandoned his secret plan to desert the flatboats. After a breakfast at the old *Poste*, the four manned the skiff and by evening had returned to the moored arks. Several days were spent tied up to the banks however before they were again off down the Mississippi.

A day or two later, while engaged in drawing a marsh hawk, the naturalist's attention to his task was diverted by a flock of his mysterious "black pelicans" settling on a sandbar but the ball he sent into their midst failed to touch a single feather. Not only that, the next night Aumack, "who was *rather Merry*," tried to shoot one of these birds "to Cool himself," so the artist informs us, but the flatboat captain was equally unsuccessful in the attempt to pot a pelican. The mysterious black birds proved most elusive and by this time the whole crew shared with Audubon his desire to obtain a specimen.

The next morning there was excitement aboard the flatboat—*Dash* had augmented the passenger list with ten whimpering little pups. The next natural history event was the shooting of a number of green and yellow paroquets. Before starting on a drawing of one of the wild parrots, Audubon consulted his copy of Wilson's ornithology, turning to the chapter which dealt with these birds and read to the curious crew the Scot's assertion that a general opinion prevailed throughout the backwoods of America that "the brains and intestines of the Carolina Paroquet are a sure and fatal poison to cats." Audubon read aloud this passage, which recounted a number of experiments that had been brought to Wilson's attention which seemed to prove that cats immediately expired after feasting on the parrots. This caused an immediate and heated argument for many of the boatmen scoffed at the assertion that the seeds of cockleburs, on which paroquets fed, were deleterious to cats—or any other animal, for that matter.

According to Wilson's printed account the Scot had never tried the experiment himself because he had "never met with a suitable *patient* on whom, like other professional gentlemen, I might conveniently make a fair experiment," and was in doubt as to what might happen to Mistress Puss. This determined Audubon to test the alleged poisoning action of the birds on mammals. Not having a cat on board he decided to try it on the dog. He was spurred on by the assertion of one of the crew that he had been told that the heart of the "parakeet" contained a poison, and that it was a known fact that seven cats had died after eating the hook-billed birds. His journal tells us:

"We boiled 10 Parokeets to night for Dash who has had 10 Welps—purposely to try the Poisoning effect of their hearts on animals."

He did not record, however, the result of the experiment but, as all references to *Dash* and her puppies here abruptly cease in the pages of the journal, it may be surmised that the worst happened.

3

Two days before Christmas the flats passed the mouth of the Yazoo river when Audubon seeing "a Large flock of My unknown *Blackbirds* that I supposed Brown Pelicans," sprang into action, and was rowed by Joseph in the skiff to a sandbar. Landing below the birds, Audubon says that "after crawling on My belly for about 300 yards I arrived within about 45 yeards. I fired at 3 that were perched Close together on a dead Stick 7 feet above the Watter, at my shot they all fell as so many stones. I expected them to be all dead but to My surprise, those and about 20 swimming took Wing after running on the Watter about 50 Yds at the exception of the one I had taken aim on—it would not raise, the Skiff was brought up. We rowed after it, diving below, up the Yazoo one Mile. Yet I could not give it up, it became Warier, & remained Less under Watter the Nearer We approached when at Last Joseph shot at its *head* & Neck (the only part in view Looking much Like a Snake) and Keeled it over. I took it up with great pleasure and Anxiety—but I could not ascertain it Genus—for I could not make it an *Albatros*, the only bird I can discover any relation to."

Back on the flat, Audubon began his drawing of the "black pelican" which had a small gular pouch. He puzzled over its identity for some hours, thumbing over Wilson and Turton but found nothing like it in either of the bird books. He was finally told that the common name along the river for the bird was "Irish Goose," probably a *mot* coined by Ned Kelly or another of the jesting crew. A few days later, however, his journal records that he saw "*Millions* of *Irish Geese* or Comorants," flying southwards—the mystery was solved, for his "pelicans" were in fact double-crested cormorants on migration.

4

Christmas Day found the arks tied up to the Louisiana shore fifteen miles above the town of Natchez, and Aumack, who appears to have been expert with the shotgun, when sober, killed a fine specimen of duck hawk which Audubon, who at that time slavishly followed Wilson's nomenclature, called the Great Footed Hawk. He set down in his journal:

Great Footed Hawk, the *Bird* Alexander Willson heard so many wonderful Tales of—these Birds are plenty on this River at this season every Year according to all the accounts I have collected but allways extremely Shy, and I believe few Men Can Boast of Having killed Many of them, for 15 years, that I have hunted and seen probably one hundred I Never had the satisfaction of bringing one to the Ground—I often have seen them after hearing the Cannon Ball Like wissling Noise through the Air seize their Prey on the wing . . . We have seen about 50 since a few Weeks—they fly fast, with quick motions of their Wings, seldom Sailing except when about alighting; the Specimen before me is a very Old Bird and a beautiful one, when on the wing they appear Black and are often mistaken for the *Falco Niger*.

When Audubon began his drawing of the male duck hawk, it was predicted that the flatboats would reach Natchez the next day so he closed his entry with the "hope that My Familly wishes me as good a Christmas as I do them—Could I have spent it with My Beloved Wife & Children, the exchange of situation would have been most Agreable."

As soon as there was sufficient daylight the next morning he was again at work on his ambitious and spirited drawing of the duck hawks and was still laying in color and fashioning feathers when the flats floated to the landing place at Natchez Under the Hill.

It was just past the noon hour when he hurried ashore and at the post office of the lower town found two letters from his wife. In one was enclosed a letter from Gabriel Loyen du Puigaudeau, husband of his half-sister Rosa. It read:

Two years have passed without our having any news of you. What a long lapse of time, and in what anxiety are we plunged! In God's name give us some news about yourself, if it be but a word to set us at rest in regard to your situation. I should not know how to persuade myself that you were not on friendly terms with me, since I have given you no cause; if it is so, be generous enough to relieve me from this anxiety. The business matters of Mr. Audubon are at last concluded, and I await only the return of the papers from Aux Cayes to set them in order with justice . . . Madame Audubon is coming to live with us; she found herself isolated at *La Gerbetière*, and was very dull there; I wish that she may be contented here. She does not cease to speak of you, and is as much astonished as I am that we receive no news of you.

Audubon returned to the flatboat, wrote a letter to his wife, and resumed his work on the drawing of the great footed hawks, destined to become one of the more noteworthy of the large plates in his *Birds of America.* The next morning he cleaned up and went up the hill to Natchez proper. There, to his surprise, he came face to face with his brother-in-law Nicholas Berthoud, "who accosted Me Kindly." He invited Audubon to leave the flats and accompany him to New Orleans in his keelboat, for Berthoud was making a fast down-river trip with a party of French gentlemen. The invitation was accepted with alacrity.

5

Not having one cent when he landed, Audubon looked about for "something to do in the likeness Way for our Support (unfortunately Naturalists are Obliged to eat and have some sort of Garb) I entered the room of a Portrait Painter Naming himself *Cook* but I assure you he was scarcely fit for a Scullion, Yet the *Gentleman* had some politeness and procured me the drawing of two Sketches for 5$ each, this was fine sauce for our empty stomacks."

Audubon did not earn ten whole dollars by his portrait sketching commissions, for as he wrote his sons while "one was immediately paid for, the other, a very excellent resemblance of Mr. *Mathewson*, probably never will be, for that Gentleman absented the same Evening and never Left orders for any body to pay—I merely put this down to give you the Best advice a Father Can present you with, Never to Sell or Buy without immediately paying for the same—a constant adhereance to this Maxim will Keep your Mind and person all times free & Happy."

The artist Cook expressed himself greatly pleased with Audubon's ability to catch a likeness and the rapidity with which he made his sketches, and suggested he and Audubon could carry on a successful and profitable portraiture business. What sort of an agreement would Mr. Audubon consider? The naturalist replied that he would accept a compensation of two dollars a day, monthly in advance, providing Mr. Cook furnished one-third of the whole expenses, and provide the necessary materials. Cook considered the proposition and promised to join the bird artist in New Orleans in a week or two, but nothing ever came of the proposed partnership.

With a few dollars jingling in the pockets of his worn grey breeches Audubon, taking Joseph Mason with him, repaired to the Natchez House for dinner. The two found it "a good House built on the Spanish plan, i.e. with Large Piazas and Many Doors and Windows—well kept by Mr. John Garnier and is the rendezvous of all Gentile Travellers and Boarders."

Life on the flatboat had changed the young dandy of the Perkioming. His hair, which he had always worn long, was now straggly and unkempt, his clothes were little better than rags, and his manners, too, had become frayed. Thus he describes himself at this time:

> The awkwardness I felt when I sat to Dinner at the Hotel was really justified to me; having not used a fork and Scarcely even a Plate since I left Louisville, I involuntarily took Meet and Vegetables with My fingers several times; on Board the flat Boats We seldom eat together and very often the hungry Cooked, this I performed when in need by Plucking & Cleaning a Duck, or a Partridge and throwing it on the Hot embers; few Men have eat a Teal with better appetite than I have dressed in this manner.
>
> Others prefering Bacon would Cut a Slice from the *Side* that hung by the Chimney and Chew that raw with a hard Biscuit—Such Life is well intended to drill men Gradually to hardships to go to Sleep with Wet Muddy Clothing on a Buffalo skin stretch on a board—to hunt through woods filled with fallen trees, entengled with Vines, Briars, Canes, high Rushes and at the same time giving under foot; produces heavy sweats.
>
> strong Appetite, Keeps the Imagination free from Worldly thoughts. I would advise *Many Citizens*, particularly our Eastern *Dandys* to try the experiment—leaving their high heeled Boots, but not their Corsets, for, this would no doubt be Servicable whenever food giving way, they might wish to depress their Stomacks for the occasion.

The meal at an end, the two artists strolled about the river town until they met Nicholas Berthoud, who asked how they had enjoyed the voyage. Audubon needed no prompting to give his brother-in-law a vivid description of the hardships that had been their lot aboard the broadhorns, whereupon Berthoud invited Laforest to share his lodging in the Natchez hotel. There was no polite remonstrance and an hour later, with Mason's help, he moved his guns and drawing paraphernalia off the flatboat and stored them in Berthoud's room.

The transfer accomplished Audubon inquired of the innkeeper, John Garnier, a French gentleman of agreeable manners, who among the residents of Natchez were subscribers to Alexander Wilson's *Ornithology*. M. Garnier named James Wilkins as one interested in birds and Audubon promptly hunted him out. The artist relied on the Scottish ornithologist for practically all his bird science at this period of his career and while he had the earlier volumes he had not seen the eighth number of Wilson's birds. Mr. Wilkins, fortunately, had received his number and Audubon conned it from cover to cover, comparing, of course, the engraved plates of Wilson's to the drawing he had made of the same species. Audubon found, so he tells his journal, his own drawings much, *much* superior to Wilson's efforts!

The next day, having drawn two crayon portraits, for which he was paid five dollars each, Audubon ransacked the town in a search of Wilson's ninth number, which had been issued, but neither Mr. Wilkins nor any of the other Natchez subscribers had received his copy. Thereupon, Audubon spent the entire day copying from the eighth volume "writting the Name and Such Description of the Watter Birds in Willson as would enable me to Judge whenever a New Specimen falls my Praise." He meant "prize," of course.

The flatboats left Natchez on a Saturday, Captain Cummings remaining on board Jacob Aumack's ark for the remainder of the journey to New Orleans. Audubon was delighted to leave the rough crew of the flats but expressed his regret at parting with the engineer, whom he found a "really agreeable *Compagnion*." Berthoud had consented to find a place for Joe Mason on the keelboat, which was scheduled to start down the river Sunday morning, so their luggage was placed on board but it was not until after the noon hour on the last day of the year 1820 that the trip was under way. Arrangements had been made for the steamboat *Columbus* to tow the keelboat down stream, thus making faster time than would be accomplished by the eight negro slaves who usually labored at the oars.

The keelboat was made fast to the *Columbus* by two ropes, and a gay and festive party was aboard the boat hauled along in the wake of the steamer. Nicholas Berthoud had given his friends a sumptuous midday meal at the Natchez House. It was called a breakfast and the diners had done full justice to everything the genial M. Garnier had set before them, both solids and liquids, in consequence there was much of what Audubon termed "French gaiety" at the table, and also when Nicholas Berthoud, his French gentlemen guests, and Audubon staggered down the hill to the boat landing. The French gaiety continued unabated as the boat in tow of the *Columbus* sped down stream. Late in the afternoon Audubon threw the party into a different sort of an uproar.

For the first time since leaving Natchez he took stock of his scanty belongings and, to his consternation, found that his smaller portfolio, containing fifteen bird drawings, his crayon likeness of his "dearest friend," and some preservative papers, was missing. With Mason's help he had carried all his luggage from the upper town to the keelboat, placed the various pieces on the wharf, and ordered Simon, Berthoud's body servant, to stow the assortment on board. He had then returned to the hotel to partake of the lively breakfast.

The lost portfolio was not his larger one, which contained the major portion of his best and most important work, but among the bird pictures in the missing container were those of three birds Audubon termed "Non Descripts," one of these being the curious and rare duck he called a *Fintail*, which we have already learned was the ruddy duck. He had made a rough pen-and-ink sketch of it in the pages of the journal but he bemoaned the loss of his finished drawing, declaring that failure to recover this particular drawing "may retard My return home very Considerable," and wound up his account of the loss:

> I unfortunately Went off to Natchez again to breakfast the servant forgot my Folio on the Shore and now I am Without any Silver paper, to preserve my Drawings, have lost some very Valuable Drawings, and my Beloved Wife's Likeness—the greatest Exertions I now Must Make to try to find it again, but so dull do I feel about it that I am nearly Made Sick. I wrote to Mr. John Garnier, requesting him to advertise and procure someone to try and find my Port Folio but no Hopes can I have of ever seeing it when Lost amongst 150 or 160

flat Boats and Houses filled with the Lowest of Caracters —No doubt my drawings will serve to ornement their Parlours or will be Nailed to some of the Steering Oars.

Audubon's Natchez experiences clear up some incidents that have been given to the reading world through Buchanan's and Mrs. Audubon's versions of the Mississippi river trip, and as printed in two of the naturalist's Episodes—*Natchez in 1820* and *The Lost Portfolio*. One of the oft-repeated tales is that Audubon and a companion, being "down at the heels" in more ways than one, needed new shoes. Neither having money to purchase the footgear, the bird artist hunted up a shoemaker and volunteered to make portraits of the cobbler and his wife in exchange for two pairs of boots. The offer was instantly accepted, and Audubon set to work with his black chalks, finishing the likenesses in two hours. Then he and his unnamed companion, having thrust their feet into the new boots, went their way rejoicing.

Audubon's original diary, in detailing the Natchez visit, makes no mention of this shoeing incident, nor is it mentioned in the Episodes printed in the *Ornithological Biography*. Interesting and unique as the experience sounds, it probably was a bit of fiction on someone's part and was so passed on to Buchanan, for we find the first mention of the two pairs of shoes in that biographer's work.

6

New Year's Day, 1821, found Berthoud's keelboat gliding down the tawny waters of the Mississippi river far in the wake of the puffing, wood-burning *Columbus*. Audubon, denied the opportunity to hunt, having no birds to draw, and with the loss of his portfolio uppermost in his mind, eased his depressed feelings by an entry in his much-scribbled-in journal:

This day 21 Years since I was at *Rochefort* in France. I spent most of that day at Copying Letters of My Father to the Minister of the Navy.

What I have seen, and felt, since would fill a Large Volume —the whole of Which Would end *this Day January 1st* 1821. I am *on Board a Keel Boat going down to New Orleans the poorest Man on it*—& What I have seen and felt has brought some very dearly purchased Experience, and Yet Yesterday I forgot that No servant could do for Me What I might do Myself; had I acted accordingly; My Port Folio Would now have been safe in my possession.

Not Willing to dwell on Ideal futurity, I do not at this moment attempt to forsee where My Poor Body may be this day 12 Months.

At noon, that first bright day of the new year, the *Columbus* arrived at Bayou Sarah, the most important river town between Natchez and New Orleans during early days of boating on the big river, and a place ever to be associated with Audubon's career, although he little dreamed it at the time. The steamboat tied up at the small settlement at the mouth of the bayou that gave the place its name for a supply of wood for the boilers, at the same moment another river steamer, bound down stream, put off. This boat was the *Alabama* and as Captain D'Hart of the *Columbus* was apprehensive the rival craft would reach Baton Rouge in advance of his own boat and secure a load of cotton bales and other freight awaiting transportation, he ordered Berthoud's keelboat to cast loose so as not to curtail the *Columbus*' speed as she attempted to catch up to and pass the *Alabama*. Consequently, when the keelboat left Bayou Sarah and headed for New Orleans it was sent downstream by the back-bending efforts of the eight black slaves who manned the oars and the slight current of muddy waters.

Row as lustily as they would the blacks did not put the keelboat opposite Baton Rouge until after six o'clock and, although Captain D'Hart had agreed to wait three hours for them there, the *Columbus* had gone on. Only the smoke from its single stack was visible to the party on the more slowly moving craft.

Audubon was now in lower Louisiana, a part of the state he eventually grew to love with an undying affection. He described in some detail in his journal his impressions on beholding the plantations on either side of the river, and noted that the shores of the Mississippi had much the appearance of the lands adjoining some of the large rivers in France. He was greatly interested in the fact that when viewed from the surface of the river only the roofs of houses and tops of trees could be seen above the levees.

The craft progressed downstream all night and by next morning was fifty miles below Baton Rouge. The day broke cloudy and raw. A head wind developed which considerably impeded speed. Intent on bird life Audubon wrote in his diary that he saw more common crows after leaving Natchez than he had ever seen in his whole life, and that he looked in vain for fish crows. He was enjoying this phase of his trip down the Mississippi. He was overjoyed to be away from Jacob Aumack and his tough crew of flatboatmen. "Our Situation in this Boat is quite Comfortable," he recorded. "We have a good Servant to wait on us, are served with regular Meals, clean and in Plates—Move much faster than with Messrs Aumack & Lovelace, having here 8 Roaers who dare not contradict orders."

Finally rain and a hard blow on the river, coupled with the cold, caused the commander of the craft to put to shore about a mile below the mouth of Bayou Lafourche, near the settlement of Donaldsonville. Audubon and Mason took to land without loss of time and tramped to a swamp that lay to the rear of a plantation. A new bird note, so Audubon supposed, struck his ear and for some moments he searched for the mysterious feathered songster; then—"I found the deceiving Mocking Bird close by me and Exulting with the Towee Bunting's *cheep*."

Joseph Mason killed two warblers, one a red poll, of which there were a dozen, more or less, flying about, but the other Audubon was at first unable to identify. The bird was a male in high plumage and the artist returned to the keelboat to preserve its likeness. Daylight failing he completed the drawings of the birds in outline only, to conserve time for completing them in color the next day. Before rolling up in his buffalo robe that night he penned in his journal:

> how Sweet for me to find Myself the 1st. of January in a Country where the woods are filled with Warblers, Thrushes, and at the same time see the Rivers and Lakes covered with all kinds of Watter Birds . . . the Pewees are quite gaily, I have see this day 3 Cat Birds—if this is not the winter retreat of all our Summer Birds it is at all Events that of very many—how happy would I feel to see some future January surrounded by the diferent species of Swallows Skeeping about, like the Whippoorwill & Night Hawk.

Early the next morning he was at work on his two birds. The first was posed on a plant in full bloom that he plucked near the levee where the keelboat was moored, and on his original drawing of his plate of the tiny warbler he wrote in lead pencil: "Yellow Red-poll Warbler, Male *Sylvia Petcopia,* drawn from Nature by John J. Audubon, Bayou La Fourche, January 1, 1820." His mistake in the year is a natural one . . . practiced today by many folk during the first days of a new year.

His other bird was not a warbler. It puzzled the naturalist and he searched his copy of Wilson for a clue as to its identity and finally concluded it to be a Solitary Flycatcher, or Greenlet, following the Scot's nomenclature of that time. He posed the male and another he had secured on bits of common cane growing along the banks of Bayou Lafourche and made the drawing that was later reproduced as the twenty-eighth plate of his monumental work. Later he learned its true identity and the little pair were listed in the printed works as Solitary Vireos, although his lead pencil notes on the margins of the original painting designate the species as *Musciapa solitaria.*

While the Frenchman was hard at work on his bird drawings, plantation folk of the neighborhood gathered about the keelboat. They interested the artist and he noted: "We were visited by several *french Creoles,* this is a breed of animals that Neither speak French, English nor Spanish correctly and Complimented Me very Highly. On asking them the names of about a dozen different Birds then lying on the Table they Made at once and without hesitating a Solid Mass of *Yellow Birds* of the Whole. One of them, a young man, told Me that he could procure 3 or 4 dozen of them every Night by hunting the Orange trees with a Lantern—'I can,' said he 'see the Rascalls White belies and Knok them down with a Stick very Handy.' Few of these good Natured Souls could answer any valuable account of the country."

At sunset the wind, which had been blowing furiously all day, suddenly lulled, whereupon Dickinson, commander of the craft, pressed the oarsmen to work and again a start was made for New Orleans, the keelboat's captain promising the city could be reached by morning. The slaves were given a good supper, and the long pull began. By four in the morning the wind was so violent, the surface of the broad river so rough, and the cold so intense, that the boat was rowed to land and moored to the levee opposite the brick Catholic church at *Bonnet Carré*.

At daylight Audubon, gun in hand, walked over the cultivated land to the swamp that lay not far from the levee. His attention was caught by the movements and songs of great flocks of large black birds. Their notes were strange to his ears and he decided they were "non described *Cuckoos*," when detailing his walk in his journal that night. He saw many warblers, robins, bluebirds, cardinals, grackles, sparrows, goldfinches, flickers, wrens, sparrow hawks, and one red-headed woodpecker, but the long-tailed blackbirds caught his fancy and he endeavored to get in proper gun range so as to have a specimen in hand. His excursion ashore was cut short for Captain Dickinson ordered the keelboat to make another start as the winds were lulling. The boat had proceeded down stream but a little ways when the blow gathered in intensity and they were once more moored to the levee about a mile below the *Bonnet Carré* church.

Audubon returned to shore and walked back to the church to pay his respects to the pastor and make inquiries respecting Major George Crogan, a former Louisville friend; a man named Lecorgne, and to gather information concerning the surrounding country. "But," he wrote after questioning the priest, "I found only a tall thin dirty Creole who could not say much besides the prayer for the prosperity of the Brick Church now erecting—from this pennsionary of Bigots I went to a School House."

Sighting more of the "black cuckoos" on the levee, Audubon killed three, a male and two females, and watched another beautifully plumaged male bird busily engaged in carrying stems of straw to the limbs of a mammoth live oak, draped with long gray festoons of Spanish moss. He was frankly puzzled over the bird's actions, for it was too early in the year for it to be nest building. He had Joseph bring him his gun and secured the glossy male, while the boy knocked down a female specimen. Back on the keelboat both birds were triced up on wires, set against the checkered position board and the drawing was begun.

Puzzled as to the identity of the birds, Audubon turned to the French-speaking natives for enlightenment. Some replied that they were called *etourneaux* or "starlings," while others said that they were named "Chocks," in imitation of the peculiar note uttered by the birds." Audubon commented drily in his journal that the natives' rejoinder to nearly all questions was "a constant 'Oh *Oui!*' " He studied the live birds noting: "on the ground their walk is Elegant and Stately carrying their Long concave tails rather high—feed Closer to each than Swamp Black Birds." He thumbed Turton's *Linné* and noted Wilson's engravings closely but found no such bird described by either or illustrated by Wilson. Was he discovering a new species? He listened to the *chuck*-like note, quite unlike that of the purple grackle; studied the keel-like shape of the tail feathers—then the solution flashed upon him. He had collected the "Great Crow Blackbird, or Boat-tailed Grackle!"

While still laboring at his drawing, the wind lulled just long enough to encourage a new start. But the rain came down in torrents and the rough water soon drove the keelboat inshore again, and Audubon finished his painting in the stuffy cabin.

The next morning "the french Gentlemen wrapd up in their Cloaks Kept their Handkerchiefs to their Noses—What would become of them on the Rockey Mountains at this Season?" he inquired of his journal. A light snow fell and the wind blew violently, so Audubon kept at his drawing of the grackles which became in after years the only bird picture of his to be reproduced in Bonaparte's *American Ornithology*. Later his attention was distracted by a number of white-winged birds flying over the water, their evolutions made more beautiful and graceful by the boisterous wind then churning the river's surface into froth. He writes:

> I saw some Terns Winowing in the Eddy just below us. Killed Two of them on the Wing. On the Falling of the first, the second approached as if to see What was the Matter. I shot it dead, when the remaining Two that were coming fast, wheeled and flew out of our Sight immediately. These Birds flew Lightly with their Bills perpendicular over the Watter on which they appeared to Keep a close attention, Now & then falling to it and taking up Small fragments of Buiscuits thrown from our boat.

PURPLE GRACKLES

An early example of Audubon's attempts to picture American birds. Of interest because he later used it as the basis for his magnificent drawing made in Feliciana and engraved by Havell in London, as Plate VII.

KENTUCKY CARDINALS

An early drawing by Audubon on which he wrote: "Cardinal Grosbeck. A. Wilson. Loxia Cardinalis. Cardinal de Buffon—Nos. 194 & 195. Henderson, 17th May, 1811. J. A."

That day Audubon drew the outlines of one of the terns he had shot. It was a species of sea bird new to him and again he ransacked Turton's *Linné* and the descriptions he had copied from Wilson's latest edition, but failed to find one that would describe the prize. It was undoubtedly a tern, he could tell that by the shape of the bill. Had he collected a new species of "watter" bird? He was perplexed and set down: "Yet I do not Consider this a New Speci untill I see Willson's 9th. Volume."

Eventually he decided that he had added another bird to America's avian fauna, for on the original drawing he wrote: "New Orleans in the winter of 20-21 when thousands of the same species were gambolling over the River—I then drew it but have no skins of it; and through fear of confounding myself I dare not publish it—I have notwithstanding named it 'Black-billed Tern' *L. Sterna Ludoviciana.* J. J. A."

Years later when this drawing of the "Louisiana Tern" was engraved it was combined on the plate with another species of tern, one named by Audubon for Dr. James Trudeau, of Louisiana, who had secured the sea bird at Great Egg Harbor, New Jersey. When plate 140 was published the white-winged bird collected on the Mississippi just above New Orleans, was not designated by Audubon as either a "Black-billed Tern," or even a "Louisiana Tern," as the Latin term might indicate such was his intention. He named it Havell's Tern, scientifically *Sterna Havelli*, in honor of Robert Havell, the talented engraver of his famous bird plates.

Havell's tern however, proves to be the white sea bird we now know as the Forster tern. At the time Audubon took his specimens these terns were in their winter plumage, when the black cap, so characteristic a mark in summer, gives way to two black bars on the sides of the head, and the reddish bill coloration of the breeding season becomes blackish. This particular tern was first described in print fourteen years later by Nuttall who in 1834 named the bird after John Reinhold Forster from specimens taken on the Saskatchewan river in Canada. Audubon did not publish his description of Havell's tern until 1838. Therefore, although he was first to note a species new to science, he fails to receive the credit because of the stringent law of priority that governs the science of ornithological nomenclature. On the other hand, Trudeau's tern, a bird he named, described and pictured from a stuffed specimen, is credited to him.

While awaiting favorable weather to complete the final run of the keelboat to New Orleans, Audubon solved one thing about the boat-tailed grackles which had so puzzled him the day before—the rice straws the "Gracule" carried to the tops of the oak trees were not borne aloft for nest building purposes; they were gathered on the ground and taken to the trees so that the bird could pick out the grains contained in the heads. Audubon was learning much of bird habits on this momentous voyage down the Mississippi river.

The wind lulled at sunset of January sixth. The moon rose, flooding the broad expanse of the Mississippi with mellow enchantment, assuring the impatient voyagers a calm and tranquil night. All were ordered on board and "we left our station to drop within a few miles of the City," Audubon wrote in his journal. "Tomorrow perhaps May take us there, yet so uncertain is This World that I should not be Surprised if I never Was to reach it—the Stronger my anxiety to see My familly again presses on My Mind—but Nothing but the astonishing desire I have of Compleating my work Keeps My Spirits at par."

Havell's Tern redrawn from Audubon's plate.

Book Four

In Old New Orleans

"*how Surly the Looks of Ill fortune are to the poor.*

JOHN JAMES AUDUBON, in his journal,
December 8, 1820.

CHAPTER 8

The Portrait Sketcher

WHEN John James Laforest Audubon entered the city which afterwards claimed him as a native son and raised a bronze monument to his memory, he was without a dollar in the pockets of his well-worn gray pantaloons.

It was a Sunday morning when the keelboat tied up to the levee near the French market, where hundreds of fish crows dashed and rose and dashed again to the surface of the river water like gulls after food. Audubon was quickly ashore and inquired the way to the office of Gordon, Grant & Co., he was in search of Alexander Gordon, a cotton commission factor, who three years later became his brother-in-law by marrying Ann, the youngest of the four attractive Bakewell girls.

The ragged wanderer's first inquiry was for news of his wife. Was she well? Gordon reassured him and said that a letter from her was then lying in the post office but, as Monday would be a holiday, to be given over to celebration of the sixth anniversary of the Battle of New Orleans, Audubon would be compelled to wait until Tuesday to secure his Lucy's letter.

In consequence, Sunday promised to be a dull day for the bird artist. Although Alexander Gordon invited him to dine, Audubon did not look forward with any real pleasure to a meal in the stylish Gordon home. He called on Felix Arnaud, an old friend of James Berthoud, who lived in the *rue de la Lévee*. He was so cordially pressed to remain and be a member of a party Arnaud was giving that afternoon that Audubon cut the dinner with the Gordons for the more Bohemian attraction promised by the hospitable M. Arnaud.

We had a really good dinner and a great deal of Mirth that I call *french Gayety* that really sickened me. I thought Myself in Bedlam, and every body talk[d] at once and the topics dry Jokes—Yet every one appeared good, well disposed Gentleman, were very polite to us—A Monkey amused the Company a good deal by Gambols and pranks—formerly I would have been able as well as anxious to go to the Theatre but now I only partake of the Last; . . . I retired to the Keel Boat; with a bad head Hake occasioned by drinking some Wine.

In the morning, though still annoyed by his "head Hake," Audubon and Mason visited the market, having been informed that many birds would be found there on sale. Indeed, they found displayed an amazing assortment of mallards, teals, widgeons, Canada and snow geese, mergansers, robins, bluebirds, red-winged blackbirds, godwits, and other shorebirds. All were high in price, ducks selling for $1.25 a pair, while the geese brought $1.50 each. Audubon was surprised and amused to find barred owls dressed and offered for sale at twenty-five cents each. In spite of the varied and abundant supply of slaughtered birds he could not find a single specimen fit for picturing.

Sauntering along *rue Chartres* Audubon met a number of his former Louisville friends, including Major George Crogan, but as he was not over enthusiastically received by any he fell into one of his peculiar fits of melancholia and returned to the keelboat. There Joseph found him, his head buried in his arms. The boy, who had been out viewing the town, declared that he was not at all prepossessed in its favor, either. This declaration did not raise Audubon's feelings an inch.

Yet old New Orleans was in a festive mood that day. The sixth anniversary of the Battle of New Orleans was being celebrated with great pomp. The Louisiana Legion took arms early in the morning and with the local veterans of General Jackson's army which had defeated the flower of England's troops, staged a parade. Roused from his melancholia, Audubon attended the review and had occasion to remember the Eighth of January with more than historical significance. His pockets were picked! He lost no money—for he had none to lose—but his pocketbook in which he had placed letters of introduction to Governor Robinson, Henry Clay's brother, and a number of other notables, had been deftly lifted from his coat pocket.

Discovering his loss he hastened to Nicholas Berthoud, who was having coffee in Maspero's Exchange with a number of French-speaking worthies, and in great agitation, accompanied with a flourish of his arms, told of what had befallen him.

Berthoud laughed loud and long, and finally said, "Oh, Laforest, you must be a greenhorn!"

Audubon drew himself erect. "I do not know ze color of *my* horns," he replied with withering scorn, "bud well I know *zose* of some neighbors of mine!" Turning indignantly on his heel he stalked off followed by a burst of laughter from Berthoud and his companions of the coffee shop. In a black and towering rage, Audubon returned to the keelboat heaping colorful French imprecations on the head of the man who had married his wife's sister.

Later, when he had regained his temper and composure and turned, as usual, to his journal, he chronicled the episode, winding up the account of the loss of his pocketbook with the philosophic observation:

> Not blaming fortune as is generally the Case I peaceably pack the Whole to Myself and will try and grow Wiser if possible—I think the Knave who took it is now a good deal disappointed and probably wishes I had it—the Parade was only tolerable.

Tuesday morning Audubon got his wife's letter from the post office and after reading it admitted his "Spirits very low," and earnestly wished he had remained in Natchez. He called on John W. Jarvis, the portrait painter, in his Custom House street studio, and later on the street ran into an old Shippingport friend, John B. Gilly, now a New Orleans merchant, who invited the artist to breakfast with him. The remainder of the day was spent in endeavoring to find work—and to forget the contents of his wife's letter. Unsuccessful in both endeavors he "remained on board the Keel Boat, opposite the Market, the dirtiest place in all the Cities of the United States," and penned a letter to John Garnier, again asking the Natchez hotel keeper to redouble his efforts to recover the lost portfolio.

For days Audubon fairly combed the city for work, and kept Joseph busy inquiring for the lost drawings of every boat that landed from Natchez. The weather contributed its share to further depress his spirits for there was "much rain and absolutely no work for a man of his talents and inclinations." The rain came down in torrents on the tenth of January; so he confined himself to the keelboat's cabin and wrote letters to his brother-in-law du Puigaudeau and his foster-mother in France. While engaged in this task, which he acknowledged was a long-neglected duty, the flatboats commanded by Aumack and Lovelace drifted into the collection of broadhorns tied up opposite the market and Captain Cummings sought out Audubon, who welcomed the engineer warmly, invited him to dine and live with them. Captain Cummings, so Audubon wrote, was down on his luck and "his appearance much Worst."

When the cold drizzle at length stopped, and the sun peered through high black clouds, Audubon took up his search for work. He met Fogliardi, an Italian scene painter at the St. Philip Theatre, due to be opened in a week or two, who evinced an interest in drawings, so Audubon took Fogliardi to Nicholas Berthoud's rooms at an inn and showed the scenic artist his finished drawing of the white-headed eagle. The Italian was fulsome in his praise and hurried the bird artist to the theatre where he introduced him to its proprietor and manager, who "very roughly offered me 100$ per Month to paint with Mons L'Italian." What! Audubon a scene painter? He curtly refused the post and stalked away affronted, to complain later to his journal: "I believe really now that my talents must be poor or the Country." According to a story coming from young Mason, Audubon demanded a wage of eight dollars a day for himself and five dollars a day for "his boy."

That night he pocketed his pride, washed, shaved, combed out his long hair, and dined with the Gordons, where he discussed birds and drawings, and exhibited his work again and again as guests filtered in and out of the smart Gordon home in St. Philip street.

The next day he called on Romain Pamar, the crockery merchant who had gone on his bond eighteen months before when he was endeavoring to gain possession of his steamboat from Sam Bowen. He had been informed Pamar wished portraits made of members of his family and Audubon asked for the commission. Later he wrote of the unsuccessful interview with the merchant: "but Audubon was poor today and Pamar knew it when I made my bow."

Saturday Audubon rose early "tormented by many disagreeable thoughts, nearly again without a cent, in a Busling City where no one cares a fig for a man in my situation. I walked to *Jarvis* the painter and shewed him some of my Drawings—he overlooked them, then Leaned down and examined them minutely but never said they were good or bad. Merely that when he drew an Eagle for Instance, he made it resemble a Lyon, and covered it with Yellow hair not feathers. Some fools entered the room, were so pleased at seeing my Eagle that they prised it, Jarvis wistled. I called him aside, while Joseph rolled up our Papers, and asked him if he needed assistance to finish his portraits i.e. the Clothing and Grounds—he stared. I repeated my question and told him I would not turn my Back to any one for Such employment and that I had received good Lessons from Good Masters. He then asked me to come the following day and Would think about it."

Audubon and Mason wandered out into Custom House street and upon meeting Nicholas Berthoud, Joseph was sent back to the keelboat with the bird drawings while Berthoud led his brother-in-law to Pamar's Magazine street warehouse where, much to his surprise, Pamar asked the naturalist what he would charge for a drawing of each of his three children. Audubon replied that his usual fee was $25 a head. Pamar deliberated a moment then said: "I have three children—what will you charge for putting the likeness of the three on one sheet of paper?" Audubon replied: "In that case I must have $100 for such a drawing."

As Pamar was turning the matter over in his mind, Berthoud suggested that Audubon make a sketch of the merchant's little girl who was in the shop at the time. Audubon called for a piece of blank paper, sharpened a pencil, sat on a crate, using another for a table, and set to work. In a short time he presented the paper to the father with a magnificent flourish. "The Likeness was striking," writes the artist. "The Father Smiled, the Clerks stared me emased and the servant was dispatched to shew My Success (as it Was Called) to

Mistress—Monsieur Pamar *Civilly* told me that I must do my Best for him and Left it to Myself as to the Price. I would have liked to earn half of the Money that day, but the Eldest Daughter could not be ready perhaps for several Days. Yet here is found Hopes. How I calculated on 100 Dollars; What relief to My Dear Wife and Children for, Said I, if I get this, I may send it to her and no doubt I will soon procure some more Work."

Sunday, exactly a week after his arrival, Audubon dressed as neatly as he could in the only clothes he possessed and again called on John Jarvis. The portrait painter led the naturalist to his painting room and put many questions to him, so many, indeed, that Audubon thought Jarvis *feared* his assistance. The portrait painter ended the interview abruptly, stating he did not believe Audubon could be of the slightest help to him. Audubon rose, bowed low, and walked out of the studio without a word. "No doubt he Looked on Me, as I did on Him, as an Original and a Craked Man."

John Wesley Jarvis, nephew of the renowned John Wesley, originator of Methodism, was English by birth but had lived in the United States from the time he was five years old. He was a singular character, talented as an artist, but vastly affected as to dress and manner. His *mots* were the talk of the town as were his mode of life and his conviviality. One of the earliest American painters to give serious attention to the study of anatomy, he also painted many portraits of prominent people of his day. In New Orleans, at the time of the war with England which culminated in the historic conflict on Chalmette's field, Jarvis became a boon companion of Jean Laffite, the noted pirate of the Gulf, and spent many a hectic week at the freebooter's Barataria stronghold, *The Temple*, drinking with Jean and Pierre Laffite, Dominique You, Ronaldo Beluche, Gambino, and others of the notorious smuggler gang. As a painter he was a leader, for even Thomas Sully and Henry Inman had been among his assistants in portraiture. Jarvis was certainly an "original," but whether or not he was a "Craked Man," as Audubon would have us believe, we only have the bird artist's word for it.

Rue de la Levée was crowded as Audubon left Jarvis' studio and joined the promenade. He found, strolling by the river's edge, persons of varied kinds and colors. The church bells were ringing, from the many cafés came the sound of knocking billiard balls, and the sound of guns were heard all around. "What a display this is for a Steady Quaker of Philadelphia or Cincinnati," he wrote in his diary. "The day was beautiful and the crowd Increased considerably—I saw, however, no Handsome Women and the Citron hue of allmost all is very disgusting to him who likes the rosy Yankee or English cheeks."

So Audubon returned to the keelboat for his gun, rowed out to the middle of the river, and killed a fish crow. "When the one I killed fell, hundreds flew to him and appeared as if about to Carry him off, but they soon found it to their Interest to let me have him." Taking the crow on board the keelboat he began at once on its portrait, working unceasingly until darkness put a stop to his task. He walked to the Gordon home, paid a call on J. F. Laville, a meat inspector, at 33 Custom House street, where he saw "some *White Ladies* and Good Looking ones." Later, passing along Condé street, on his way back to his bunk on the keelboat, "the Quadroon Ball attracted My View but as it cost 1$ Entrance I merely Listened a Short time to the Noise and came Home—as we are pleased to call it."

The next several days were spent exclusively in looking for work. He was bitterly disappointed upon calling on Romain Pamar at the crockery store to be told that the merchant had taken up with his wife the matter of having their childrens' portraits drawn but, Mistress Pamar had decided against black chalk sketches and wished the likenesses in oil. Audubon had never worked in this medium and bemoaned the fact that there was no one in New Orleans who could give him lessons.

His intention of showing New Orleans his ability as a portraitist was frustrated until a few days later when he made a pencil drawing of his Kentucky friend John B. Gilly "for the purpose of exposing it to the public. It is considered by every one who knows him to be perfect." Although nothing more than a hurried sketch, Gilly's portrait accomplished what Audubon expected of it, for soon he had a number of orders and was highly elated. There was one cloud to his otherwise sunny day. Always subject to extremes of emotion, he bemoaned in his journal the receipt of "a letter from My Beloved Wife who ruffed My Spirits Sadly."

The next ten days were busy ones for the aspiring portraitist. He drew a likeness of John Davidson, the British consul; made black chalk portraits of Lucien Forstall, his wife and son; another of Etienne Carraby and, much to his surprise, was finally commissioned to make chalk likenesses of Mrs. Pamar and each of her three children. As he received twenty-five dollars a drawing, by Saturday he was well supplied with funds. Sunday he turned from men, women, and children to birds and put in the entire day and a good part of the night drawing a young brown pelican. Before retiring he triumphantly penned in his journal that he was "fatigued, Weary of Body but in good Spirits having plenty to do at good Prices, and my Work much admired—only sorry the Sun sets."

The next morning he purchased a crate of Queensware crockery from Pamar's store for his beloved Lucy, the thirty-six-piece dinner set setting him back $36.33. He also sent her $270.00 by letter. Fortune was now smiling instead of frowning upon him, although the necessity of earning money prevented him from making as many bird portraits as he wished and, worst of all, put a stop to gunning expeditions in surrounding swamps. When not making likenesses, Audubon was either canvassing the town for new patrons, inquiring for the ninth volume of Wilson's *Ornithology*, or searching the array of birds on sale at the market for specimens suitable for drawing. He was impressed by the number of robins brought into the *Halles*, as the market was usually called. Every stall was covered with them yet the price of 6¼ cents apiece seemed exorbitant to Audubon.

On the fifteenth of February, Nicholas Berthoud left New Orleans by steamboat for his return to Kentucky. Audubon prevailed upon him to carry back to his wife a collection of his new bird drawings. In the collection were eight birds "Not described by Willson"—the Common Gallinule, Common Gull, Boat-tailed Grackles, Snipe, Bath Ground-Warbler, Brown Pelican, Turkey hen, and Cormorant. The others were his drawings of the Marsh Hawk, Common Crow, Fish Crow, Sora, Marsh Tern, Hermit Thrush, Yellow Red-poll

Warbler, Savannah Finch, Great-footed Hawks, Carrion Crow or Black Vulture, Imber Diver, and White-headed Eagle. Some of these originals were afterwards reproduced in his plates and they show conclusively the man's improvement in delineating birds at this period of his career. He was sending the drawings to his wife so that she could see for herself how he had progressed in his ambitious scheme to picture the birds of America.

2

The warmth of the spring-like February days had their effect upon the birds as well as upon the man who had consecrated his life to picturing them and the swamps that bounded New Orleans were fairly alive with many species preparing to travel the air routes to their northern breeding regions. So Audubon and young Joe Mason with their guns were afield many times when they should have been seeking work. The swallow tribe interested Audubon in more ways than that of picturing their airy flight with his facile pencil and paint-charged brushes. Popular tradition of that day had it that swallows hibernated during the winter months in the muddy bottoms of ponds, marshes, and other waterways. In his copy of Wilson's *Ornithology* he had studied the Scot's apostrophe to the Barn Swallow "Yet this little winged seraph, in a few days, and at will, can pass from the borders of the arctic regions to the torrid zone, is forced, when winter approaches, to descend to the bottoms of lakes, rivers, and mill-ponds, to bury itself in the mud with eels and snapping turtles; or to creep ingloriously into a cavern, a rat-hole, or a hollow tree, there to doze, with snakes, toads, and other reptiles, until the return of spring!"

That the swallow, on whom Heaven alone had conferred superior powers of wing, must sink into torpidity at the bottom of rivers, Wilson went on to state, was something he did not believe. Audubon, likewise, refused to put credence in the widely-believed tale that swallows passed the colder season of the year in mud, therefore any flight of these birds was sure to catch his keen blue eyes. He tells us that on this nineteenth day of February he "saw Three Immense flocks of *Bank*

Swallows that passed over Me with the Rapidity of a Storm, going Northeast, their Cry was heard distinctly, and I knew them first by the Noise they made in the air coming from behind Me; the falling of their Dung resembled a heavy but thinly falling Snow; No appearance of any feeding while in our Sight—which Lasted but a few Minutes—I was much pleased to see these arbingers of Spring but Where could they be moving so rapidly at this early season I am quite at a Loss to think &c., yet their Passage here was long after the Purple Martins that went by on the 9th. Instance."

Two days later Audubon "Saw Many Green Baked White Belied Swallows and four Purple Martins All of them very Lively and not exhibiting much of the Muddy Appearance that immersion in the Swamps about this City would undoubtedly give them, had they remained buried in it since Last December at Which time late in that Month they were plenty . . . and the Millions of Musquitoes that raise from the Swamps Would Sufice to feed the Swallows of the World."

Audubon resolved to study the entire swallow tribe, especially during the winter months so, when the proper time came, he would present irrefutable evidence to the world that swallows did not hibernate in the mud. As a matter of fact, a few years later, his first contribution to ornithological literature was a paper upon swallows in wintertime.

Matters were running smoothly for the embryo naturalist . . . he was in funds, his work was being admired and, in some quarters, extravagantly praised. He was content with his lot—for were not he and Joseph Mason, and Captain Cummings, who was still down on his luck, eating regularly? The trio was happy though still quartered on Berthoud's keelboat moored to the levee near the old market.

CHAPTER 9

Mme. André and the Souvenir Gun

IT was during those February days that Laforest Audubon, as he preferred to call himself, had an unique and colorful adventure with a woman whom he dubbed "his Fair Incognito." The *affaire* was unfolded in its most intimate details in his journal but, years later, these eight pages were cut from the book and suppressed by horrified feminine descendants.

Early one afternoon, as he trudged along the narrow *banquette* of *rue Royale*, bulky portfolio balanced on his shoulder, he was accosted by a heavily veiled woman just as he reached the intersection with St. Louis street, a junction he afterwards called "the corner of events." Although the veil hid her features Audubon allowed his eyes to play over her garb, noted she was richly dressed, of a fine form, and evidently quite young.

"Pray, sir, are you the one sent by the French Academy to draw the birds of America?" she asked in French.

"No, madame, I draw them for my pleasure," was his reply.

"Thou art he that draws likenesses in black chalks so remarkably strong?" continued the voice behind the black veil.

Audubon admitted he was earning his living in New Orleans by making portraits in that medium and awaited the next question from the woman who had so strangely accosted him.

"Then call in thirty minutes at 26 *rue Amour*, near the corner of *rue Histoire*, open the door, which you will find unlatched, and walk upstairs." The instructions were given in a low voice, almost a whisper. "I will await you there," she added as she moved off. "Do not follow me," she called over her shoulder in evident alarm as he took a step or two after her. He obeyed but followed her retreating form with puzzled eyes. Jotting down the street and number in his note book, he walked to a nearby book shop.

"There I waited some time," runs the record in his journal, "agitated by a feeling of astonishment undescribable. Recollecting, however, how far I had to walk, I started for her home, being satisfied if she reached the address before me she had employed a carriage."

Audubon found the house without difficulty. He tried the door. It opened to his touch. He entered, mounted the steps, and at the top of the flight of stairs was received by the same woman who had invited him to her home. Her features were still hidden by the heavy veil.

"I am glad you have come," she said in a low voice. "Walk in quickly," was her command as she threw open a door that led to a room just off the hallway.

Audubon recalled, when setting down the details of the adventure in his journal that his "feelings became so agitated that I trembled like a leaf. This she perceived and shut the door with a double-lock. Then throwing back her veil, shewed me one of the most beautiful faces I ever saw." He admits he stood tongue-tied as the young woman smiled.

"Have you been or are you married?" she asked after a long silence.

"*Oui, mademoiselle.*"

"Long?"

"Twelve years, mademoiselle."

"Is you wife in this city?"

"*Non, mademoiselle.*"

"Your name is Audubon?"

"*Oui, mademoiselle.*"

"Very well, monsieur," she laughed lightly. "Sit you down and be easy." She smiled at him again (with the "smile of an angel" the man wrote in his account). "I will not hurt you," she added softly.

The last words were his undoing. His self possession left him. "I felt such a blush and breathlessness through me that I could not answer, and when she handed me a glass of cordial, so strange was all this to me, that I drank it—for I needed it! but awkwardly gave her the emptied glass to take back."

On this early drawing of a pair of Towhee Buntings Audubon wrote: "Emberiza Erythropthalma. hogon de la Caroline de Brisson. Towe Bunting femelle. A. W. May 6, 1812. Pennsa. drawn by J. J. Audubon." This as well as the drawings of the Grackles and Cardinals are now owned by the United States Museum, Washington, D. C.

GENERAL JEAN BAPTISTE BOSSIER

An example of Audubon's black chalk portraiture. Drawn in New Orleans April 28, 1821, for which General Bossier, of Sainte Geneviève, paid $25. The original is owned by Mr. Barat A. Guignon, Kansas City, Mo.

The beauty sank into a chair opposite that occupied by the confused Audubon and looked at him steadfastly before she again spoke.

"Do you think you can draw my face with your black chalks, monsieur?" Her face was wreathed in a dazzling smile as she questioned.

"Indeed, I fear not," was the embarrassed man's admission.

She laughed again. "But I am sure you can—if you will." The last words came softly, caressingly. "But, before I can say more . . . what is your price?"

"Generally twenty-five dollars," stammered Audubon.

She smiled again, most sweetly. "Will you keep my name, if you discover it, and my residence a secret?"

Audubon bowed his head. "If you require it mademoiselle."

"I do require it," was her instant reply. "You must promise that to me. Keep my name forever sacred although I do not care about any thing else."

The bewildered artist promised. "I will keep your name and your place of residence to myself." There was a long pause before she again spoke.

"Have you ever drawn a full figure?" she asked finally.

"*Oui, mademoiselle.*"

"Naked?"

Audubon wrote: "Had I been shot with a 48-pounder through the heart my articulating powers could not have been more suddenly stopped." He could not trust himself to speak.

"Well, why do you not answer?" the composed beauty demanded.

Audubon finally managed to stammer a mumbled "*Oui.*" The woman left her chair and paced the floor of the small room a few times before she again took her seat and then, in a most matter-of-fact voice, said:

"I want you to draw my likeness and the whole of my form naked. But as I think you cannot work now, leave your portfolio and return in one hour. Be silent!" she warned.

Audubon sprang to his feet and bowed. "She had judged my feelings precisely. I took my hat, she opened the door, and I felt like a bird that makes his escape from a strong cage filled with sweet meats. Had I met a stranger on the stairs no doubt I would have been suspected for a thief. I walked away fast, looking behind me. My thoughts rolled on her conduct. She looked as if a perfect Mistress of herself and yet looked, *as I then thought*, too young, not supposing her more than sixteen (a mistake, however) and apparently not at all afraid to disclose to my eyes her sacred beauties. I tried to prepare myself for the occasion. The time passed and I arrived at the foot of the stairs."

As before the woman motioned him to enter quickly. She shut and bolted the door. She then moved close, very close to Audubon, whose heart was again beating madly at his ribs, and in a voice just above a whisper she said:

"Well, how do you feel now? Still trembling a little?—what a man you are! Come, I am so anxious to see the outline you will make. take your time and be sure do not embellish any part with your brilliant imagination. Have your paper sufficiently large. I have some beautiful and good chalks. The drawing will be completed in this room." She moved to an *armoire* and drew out a large sheet of elephant-size drawing paper. "And you will please do it on this."

Audubon bowed and took the paper to arrange it on his portfolio. "The die was cast. I felt at once Easy, ready and pleased," is his version. "I told her I was waiting for her convenience. She repeated the urgency of Secrecy, which I again promised."

At one end of the room Audubon noted a superbly decorated couch. Above it was draped a pair of parted portiere. With a smile to him she walked to the couch and dropped the curtains which hid her from his view. As he sat anxious for the next scene in his amazing adventure, he could distinctly hear sounds from behind the heavy drapes that told him the girl was disrobing. He cleared his throat and shuffled his feet. Then the sound from behind the portiere ceased. All he could hear was the beating of his own heart. Then came the unmistakable sounds which informed him she was arranging herself on the divan.

Suddenly, into the stillness of the room, came her voice. "I must be nearly in the position you will see me . . . unless your taste should think proper to alter it by speaking."

"Very well," was his answer, although he admitted he felt

very strange and would never forget the moment. He had to wait a short time, however, then—

"Draw the curtains and arrange the light to suit yourself," came her voice and Audubon instantly sprang to his feet, his hand reaching for the portiere that concealed the woman's form from his eyes.

The man set down in his diary, days afterwards: "When drawing hirelings in company with twenty or more, I never cared but for a good outline, but shut up with a beautiful young woman, as much a stranger to me as I was to her, I could not well reconcile all the feelings that were necessary to draw well, without mingling with them some of a very different nature. Yet I drew the curtains and saw this Beauty!"

She lay coiled on the couch in a very graceful attitude, one calculated to do full justice to all her physical charms. "Will I do—so?" she asked when his eyes at last found hers.

His eyes again played over her figure . . . he let drop his black lead pencil from trembling fingers.

"I am so glad you are so timid," she whispered, "but, tell me, will I do—so?"

Writes Audubon. "Perceiving at once that the position, the light and all had been carefully studied before, I told her I feared she looked only *too* well for *my* talents. She smiled —I began."

For fifty-five minutes by his watch the bird artist drew with the black chalks. Under his deft manipulation the unclothed figure of the reclining beauty on the divan began to take form on the large sheet of paper. When the hour was nearly up, she spoke. "Please close the curtains." In an instant she had regarbed herself and was standing back of Audubon's chair, closely inspecting his drawing.

"Is it like me? Will it be like me? I hope it will be a likeness," she breathed. "I am a little chill—can you work any more without me today?"

When he found his voice Audubon said he could make some corrections on the rough outlines without having her resume the pose, but he would have to see her in the same position again before the portrait could be finished.

"Very well, be contented and work as much as you can.

I wish it were done—it is a folly, but all our sex are more or less so," she added as she pulled at a bell cord. A few moments later a woman servant entered bearing a waiter holding glasses of wine and cakes. The fair model ordered the artist to rest a while, insisted he join her in a glass of wine. "She made me drink, asked me a thousand questions about my family, residence, Birds, way of traveling, of living &c &c and certainly is a well informed femelle, using the best expressions and in all her actions possessing the manners necessary to Insure Respect & Wonder."

He worked two hours longer before he completed his work of blocking in or correcting some of the lines of her curved figure. The woman again inspected the work and announced herself very much pleased with the progress that had been made at the first sitting. "She remarked, very properly, an error and made me correct it," says Audubon who, from this and other suggestions and criticisms she made, decided she had herself received lessons in drawing. He questioned her in this regard and begged for her name.

"Not today," she replied, "and if you are not careful and silent you will never see me again."

He assured her he would be discreet—dumb.

"*Bien*, I have thought well of you from hearsay and hope not to be mistaken." Her face was rather serious as she spoke.

Audubon assured her the trust was not misplaced. "I felt now different thoughts from those I had while she was undressing in her curtains and asked when I must return again."

"Every day at the same hour until the portrait is done," was the reply. "But never again with your portfolio."

He bowed, took up the heavy collection of bird drawings and left the house in the *rue Amour*. "For ten days, at the exception of One Sunday that she went out of the city, I had the pleasure of this beautiful woman's company about one hour naked, and two talking on different subjects. She admired my work more every day—at least was pleased to say so,—and at the fifth sitting she worked on it in a style much superior to mine."

At the second posing, the *Fair Incognito*, as Audubon termed her, asked the artist what he was going to ask of her for the making of the portrait.

"I will be satisfied, mademoiselle, with whatever you will please give me," was the gallant's answer.

"*Bien*, I will take you at your word—It will be *un souvenir!* One who hunts so much needs a good gun or two. This afternoon see if there is one in the city and give this on account"—she slipped a five dollar bank note in his hand—"if you wish to please me to the last, I must see the gun, and if I do not like it, you are not to have it."

Audubon mumbled his thanks and warned that in all probability the firearm would prove a high-priced piece.

"That will probably be necessary to insure one of good quality,—do as I bid," she added imperiously. Audubon bowed again, placed the bank note in the pocket of his well-worn grey breeches and, with a "*Bon jour, mademoiselle*," took his departure.

Once in the street and on his way to the center of town, Audubon declares he was undetermined whether to seek out a gun or not, but ended by searching through the stores until he found a good shotgun. He left his name and the five dollar bill as down payment, telling the shopman he did not know when he would call for the gun and make final payment. The next day he told the *Fair Incognito* of the result of his shopping and that the gun he had selected would cost one hundred and twenty dollars.

"No more?" she laughed. "Well, we will say nothing more about it until I see how pleased I am with your part of the compact."

Whereupon down he sat to work once more on the drawing and the fair one resumed her *tout nu* pose on the divan. Audubon recounts he worked from one day to another "drawing a 25 dollar Likeness every day, to be sure a little at the expense of my eyes at night, but how could I complain? how many artists would have been delighted of such lessons. I finished my drawing, or rather she did, for when I returned every day I allways found the work much advanced. She touched it, she said, not because she was fatigued of my company daily but because she felt happy in mingling her talents with mine in a piece she had in contemplation to have done, even before she left the country she came from. I suppose from Italy or France but never could ascertain."

Audubon also tells that his beautiful model often took his pencil, so she "could compose a device to have engraved on the gun barrels." She had asked the artist to suggest a maxim of his own. This, however, Audubon says he refused to do, declaring that any lettering to be engraved on the Souvenir Gun should be left to her own taste and will. At last she decided on an inscription, wrote it out, and ordered him to have it engraved on the firearm.

There was one rift in the pleasant relationship between the artist and the model. As Audubon set it down in his journal: "Met this morning with one of those discouraging Incidents connected with the life of artists; I had a likeness Spoken of in rude terms by the fair Lady it was made for, and perhaps will Loose my time and the reward expected for my Labour, —Mrs. André, I here mention the Name as I May Speak More of the likeness as occasion Will require."

But the next day all was well again when Audubon went to the rendezvous in the *rue Amour*. The widow was quite satisfied with the rendition of her physical charms for she had it appropriately displayed in the little upstairs room. "She had a beautiful frame on the portrait the last morning I went to her home, on which she asked my opinion. This, of course, I gave her as I thought her desires inclined. She put her name at the foot of the Drawing as if *her own* and mine in a dark shadded part of the Drapery; when I close it and put it in a true light she gazed at it for some moments and assured me that her wish was at last Gratified, and taking me by the hand gave me a delightful Kiss.

" 'Had you acted otherwise than you have,' she said, 'you would have received a very different recompence. Go, take this,' she pressed $125 in bills in my fingers. 'Be happy, think of me sometimes as you rest on your gun. Keep forever my name a secret.' "

Audubon says he begged to kiss her hand and "she held it out freely—we parted probably forever. The Lady was kind, the Gun is good, and here is the inscription on it—'*Ne refuse pas ce don d'une amie qui t'est reconnaissante puisse t'il tégaler bonté.*' "[1]

Under the barrel, concealed by the ramming rod, he later

[1] "Refuse not this gift of a grateful friend; may it equal you in goodness."

had engraved, "Property of Laforest Audubon, February 22d 1821." Then, so the "lost" pages of the journal tell us, "Her name *I* engraved on it where I do not believe it will ever be found."

Audubon made no secret of this *affaire*; he informed his wife of his meeting with the "Fair Incognito" in a lengthy letter, in fact, he copied the entire extract from the pages of his journal for her perusal. "She never asked to see me when we parted," the artist lamented. "I have tried several times in vain, the servants allways saying 'Madame is absent,' I have felt a great desire to see the drawing since to judge of it as I all ways can do best after some time."

A few days later, so we learn from the age-yellowed pages of his New Orleans journal, Audubon tested the weapon Mme. André had given him.

"Walked out this Morning with Joseph to try my Souvenir Gun and found it an excellent One. Shot many Green Backed Swallows on the Wing."

Green-backed Swallows redrawn from Audubon's plate.

CHAPTER 10

CHEESE AND SNUBS

ASIDE from receiving his Souvenir Gun from the fascinating Mme. André, Washington's Birthday proved otherwise eventful, for on the twenty-second of February Audubon and young Mason, accompanied by Captain Cummings, left the keelboat that had so long been their home to move into a house at 34 Barracks street, near the corner of Royal. This, the bird artist's first New Orleans studio was situated between two grocery shops, one kept by Joseph Canales, the other by Isidor Pitie, and a few days after setting up his scanty effects Audubon records that in the room where they ate, slept, and drew he heard "at once all the New Matter that Issues from the thunderous mouths of all these groupes," that gathered to tell what was going on in town—and there was plenty to gossip about in old New Orleans in those days.

The landlady, Madame Louise Ménard, had not been overly prepossessed with the appearance of the shabby individual who bargained with her for the *chambre à louer* for she bluntly demanded the rent, ten dollars, be paid before he moved in. "The *Honest Woman* spoke much of honesty in strangers and required one Month paid in Advance, this however, I would not do and satisfied her with one half." The landlady offered a receipt but the artist waved the written slip aside with a haughty Gallic motion of his hand. When Madame Louise became urgent he accepted it and a warring passage of words was averted.

Settled in the new abode, Audubon again walked about the city "in search of work & Willson's Ornithology but was not favored with any success . . . am very much fatigued with New Orleans—where I cannot Shoot Two Birds with one Stone."

Audubon's first studio was located in the oldest part of the city, in the *carré* or parallelogram founded by Bienville and laid out by Adrien du Pauger, the assistant King's engineer. Many of the streets named by the surveyor still bear the original baptisms, but Barracks street had been first christened *rue des Quartier* because it fronted the old quarters or barracks of the troops, and about the time Audubon arrived the name was being Anglicized by the inhabitants. Up and down the narrow *banquette*, or sidewalk, trooped fiery Louisiana Créoles who, instead of wearing rapiers ready for instant response to real or fancied insult to their zealously guarded honor, carried the *canne à épée*, the so-called "American Stick," or sword-cane, which was just then coming into popular favor.

Life in the studio in *rue des Quartier* was alternately dull and eventful. Although the necessity for working at portraits kept him out of the cypress swamps which hedged in New Orleans, in the evenings Audubon had frequent opportunities to gather notes on birds, as many of the feathered tribe were flying about the city. He makes frequent mention of these bird observations in his journal but none is more charming than that describing the singing of a mockingbird:

> Near our House a Mocking bird regularly resorts to the South Angle of a Chimney top and salutes us with the Sweetest Notes from the arising of the Moon untill about Midnight, and every Morning from about 8 o'clock untill 11, when it flys to the Convent Garden to feed. I have remarked that Bird allways in the Same Spot and Same Position, and have been particularly pleased at hearing him Imitate the Watchman's Cry of *All's Well* that Issues from the fort about 3 Squares Distant, and so well has he sometimes performed that I would have been mistaken if he had not repeated too often in the Space of a 10 minutes.

Mealtime at the artists' makeshift studio was a hit and miss affair. When sitters were frequent Audubon, Mason, and Captain Cummings (for the engineer was still down on his luck and still with Audubon—waiting for something to turn up), lived high, patronizing the French market and its gamebird supply. At other times, when there was a scarcity of sitters, meals were meager affairs.

Cheese formed a conspicuous part of the daily diet, in fact

it was the *pièce de résistance* of a certain meal minutely recorded in the journal:

While at Dinner We were all surprised at the astounding Leaps that some *Maggots* took about our Table, they Issued out of a Very good piece of Cheese to perform this. I remarked them drawing up their heads toward the Tail untill Nearly runing both half of the Body Parell and Then Suddenly striking one of the ends, Could not see Which, they through themselves about 50 or 60 Times their Length, some time One Way sometimes another apparently in Search of the Cheese.

Audubon did not always receive money for his black crayon portrait sketches. A certain sitter was so pleased with his own likeness, he asked the bird artist to make one of his wife but, complaining that he could not afford to pay for it in cash, proposed that Audubon accept his wife's riding saddle in payment.

"So I made a likeness to day for a Lady's Sadle, a thing I had not the Leass use for, but the Man Wanted his Wife's so much and Could not Spare Money and Not to disappoint him I Sufered Myself to be Sadled." A few weeks later Audubon shipped it to Louisville so his Lucy could make use of it.

Audubon's neighbors in the Barracks street studio were a Spanish family named Puich. The head of the household was constantly calling on a seemingly inexhaustable fund of "amusing Jokes," while his nieces sang creditably and played a number of musical instruments. Consequently, many of the nights in *rue des Quartier* were enlivened by music and laughter, in which Audubon's flute and fiddle played their part—but not on those nights when his spirits were cast down because of a dearth of sitters or a sharp letter from his wife.

Friday, March 16, 1821, was a day of bright and joyful portent in Audubon's life, for he received a letter from Tony Bodley, one of the men who had manned the sweeps on Aumack's flatboat. On his way back to his Pennsylvania home, Tony had stopped off at Natchez and in a waterfront doggery found Audubon's lost portfolio of bird drawings. Bodley immediately deposited the collection in the office of the *Mississippi Republican*, a Natchez newspaper, where, so he wrote, it awaited Audubon's forwarding orders. Wondering how the portfolio could have escaped Host Garnier's search, the artist hastened to Alexander Gordon's offices and implored the cotton merchant to communicate with some trustworthy Natchez friend who could be relied on to send the drawings on by the first river boat bound for New Orleans.

The recovery of the portfolio was a matter of such moment that in holiday mood Audubon seized Mme. Andre's Souvenir Gun and hurried along Bayou St. John to participate in what proved to be an unbelievable wholesale slaughter of shorebirds. The entry in his journal, which was the basis for the account found in his *Ornithological Biography* dealing with the life history of the golden plover, gives the story of the bird carnage in his own words and presents a more vivid pen picture than the printed recital which was polished for the purposes of publication by his amanuensis MacGillivray.

In reviewing this bird killing episode it must be borne in mind that the golden plover is famous in ornithological literature which acknowledges it to be the most remarkable of bird migrants, as it makes the longest non-stop flight of any land bird over water. Golden plovers breed in the Arctic circle and, after its young are hatched and reared to the flight stage, move southeast from the breeding grounds, feeding on the curlew berry and accumulating thick layers of fat, until they reach Nova Scotia. Here the plovers take off, flying over the Atlantic Ocean for approximately 2,500 miles before they reach the northern shores of South America. On this steady flight the birds are a-wing day and night for forty-eight hours. Upon reaching South America the hardy migrants proceed in easy stages overland until the pampas of the Argentine are reached. Here they winter. The return journey to their breeding homes in the far north in the spring is by a different route. In this spring flight the plovers fly overland to Colombia, over the Isthmus of Panama, Central America, Mexico and the Yucatan peninsula, then hurdle the Gulf of Mexico by a mere 700-mile flight, which is made in a single night, landing on the shores of Louisiana and thence up the great Mississippi Valley flyway to take up their nesting duties.

Follows the uncensored account, in Audubon's own words, of the slaughter which took place March 16, 1821, the usual spring migration date for the golden plover in Louisiana:

I took a Walk with my Gun this afternoon to see the Passage of Millions of *Golden Plovers* Coming from North Est and going Nearly South—the distruction of these innocent fugitives from a Winter Storm above us was really astonishing—the Sportsmen are here more numerous and at the same more expert at shooting on the wing than any where in the U. States on the first sight of these birds Early this Morning assembled in Parties of from 20 to 100 at Diferent places where they Knew by experience they told me the birds pass and arrange themselves at equal distances squatted on their hams as a flock Came Near every man Called in a Masterly astonishing Manner, the Birds Imediately Lowered and Wheeled and coming about 40 or 50 yards, run the Gantlet every Gun goes off in Rotation, and so well aimed that I saw several times a flock of 100 or More Plovers destroyed at the exception of 5 or 6—the Dogs after each Voleys While the Shooters charged their Pieces brought the Same to each Individuals—this continued all day. When I Left One of these Lines of Sharp Shooters then the Sun Setting, they appeared as Intent on Killing More as when I arrived at the spot at 4 o'clock. A Man near where I was seated had Killed 63 dozens—from the firing before & behind us I would suppose that 400 Gunners were out. Supposing each Man to have killed 30 Dozen that day, 144,000 must have been destroyed. On Enquiring if these Passages were frequent I was told that Six Years ago there was about such an Instance, immediately after 2 or 3 days of Very Warm Weather a blow from the Northeast brought them, Which Was Nearly the same to day—some Few Were fat but the Greatest Number Lean, and all that I opened showed no food—

On the following day Audubon noted "The Market was pleantifully suplied with Golden Plover and *Grives*," *grive* being the name given by the French-speaking population of Louisiana to the robin.

2

It was not all work and no play for the Audubon who lived in New Orleans in the year 1821. In spite of the uncertain battle he was waging with Dame Fortune, he had his moments of pleasure and recorded a number of them in his journal. One Sunday afternoon affair, when he participated in a mock Masonic initiation, made him forget momentarily his heavy cares and light purse. He was on his way to the Pamar residence, when he met, Augustin Liautaud on the levee. The Creole insisted that Audubon join him in an elaborate breakfast being given in the offices of Liautaud Brothers and Delhonde, 36 *rue de la Levée*. The mercantile establishment was appropriately set for the entertainment, and gathered about the tables was a considerable party of debonair gentlemen of the town.

"They were well engaged around an Old Gentleman and Pleasing him by the most extravigant round of praises," says Audubon. "I understood the Character was rather Moony, and very gay When Well managed, productive of Much Mirth to his hearers." During the breakfast, which Audubon declares was a very bountiful one, "on which one *Prince Guest* touched heavily," the company was regaled with volleys of verses that were composed for the occasion. Everyone enjoyed himself, particularly the versemakers. Each was roundly applauded—"sometimes, to be sure, to put an end to his Loquacity."

Breakfast ended, Audubon arose to leave but was detained by the host, who whispered that the best part was yet to come, for the guest who was being bantered was about to be received a Mason. "My being a Brother entitled me at once to a seat," he writes in explaining why he witnessed the mock ceremony. "This was conducted in a most Ludicrous Manner as any one can concieve, and I really pitied the Newly Initiated. When all Ceremonies Were over the Man Was Burned in several parts, baptized in a Large Bucket of Watter, Tossed in a Blanket, and Made to Crawl Over about 50 Casks of Wine on his belly and Knees, and when at Last given up for want of Invention, the Poor Devil Who had been praying for Mercy during all this was Left in the Necessary.

"To this Man Might be done perhaps again, but few could bear such treatment and I expected several times that his Cries or a Change of sensation from Cowardice to Courage would shew a very diferent scene but all however was Ended as Intended and the poor fellow took it for Granted that he really was a Mason."

The mock ceremony ended, Audubon made a likeness of Louis Louaillier, and another crayon portrait of Philip Guesnore, a clerk in the Bank of Orleans, and on his way back to the Barracks street studio stopped at the market and purchased a great blue heron, the choice of five offered for sale. This "Blue Crane," a male in splendid plumage, became the subject of his spectacular plate in *The Birds of America* which shows the heron in the act of spearing a fish.

The buffeting he was receiving at the hands of fortune caused Audubon to become very wearied of New Orleans. If the truth must be known his wandering foot was itching again. This time the West was calling him. He made earnest endeavors to secure a position as draftsman with a proposed expedition which was to run a division line in the western part of Louisiana to mark the boundary between Spain and the United States. He hoped, if he secured the position, to leave in a short time for Natchitoches. The possibility of such a journey fired his blood and he says that the mere thought of it caused him to "walk out in the afternoon seeing Nothing but New Birds, in Imagination and supposed Myself often on the Journey." His descent from these roseate clouds was abrupt when he was informed that the governor of Louisiana had said that nothing would be done about running the boundary for many months and then—only surveyors would be needed. Audubon describes himself "going through the Street Not unlike I dare say a Wild Man thinking too much to think at all," when he met his old-time Louisville friend Major George Crogan, who advised the artist to write directly to the president. Audubon hurried towards his lodgings "Walking fast and Looking Wild," and "sat to the Paper & Wrote in Great a Hurry." The missive finished Audubon ran with it to David Prentice who declared it all-sufficient. "Feeling a great Weight off My Shoulders I returned to My Room, took Gun, Ammunition & Joseph & to the Woods Went in Search of New Species."

Even during the afternoon's foray in the cypress swamps the man could not erase from his mind the prospect of the western expedition. His fixation at the time was that, in some way or another, he would be successful in making the journey. At night he confided to his journal: "My Life has been strewed with Many thorns but I could see Myself & the fruits of my Labour safe, with My Beloved familly *all Well* on a return from Such an expedition, how grateful Would I feel to My Country and full of the Greatness of My Author."

As portraiture fell off during the latter part of March Audubon found more time for his bird drawings and constantly sought out new specimens. In the market one morning he saw "Three of what Willson *Calls Bartram's* Snipes, they Were very fat—are called here *Papacots*."[1] Purchasing one he made his drawing from it. The next day a hunter brought him a splendid specimen of the American egret. The big white plumed wading bird was in perfect order and, setting it in position with his wires, Audubon set to work. He kept diligently at his task the whole day and when he laid down his pencil and watercolors that night he admitted it had been the most difficult bird he had yet tried to transfer to paper. Two days later he was still working on his heron and when he was finally through with his model confessed it "smelt so dreadfully that When I opened it I Could only take time to see how plainly it proved to be a Male." This drawing, though not reproduced in his plates, is among the collection of original drawings preserved in the archives of the New York Historical Society. An examination of the drawing bears out Audubon's plaint that the egret was "difficult to imitate."

For the next several days he tells us "I spent my time . . . More at thinking than anything else—and often indeed have I thought My Head very Heavy." He was forced to the unpleasant realization that the saturation point in crayon portraiture had been reached in spite of the fact that other artists, who painted in oils, were reaping a golden harvest in old New Orleans, particularly John Vanderlyn, who was exhibiting his canvasses in a studio at Royal and St. Louis streets, Audubon's "corner of events" where he had been accosted by the beautifully formed fascinating Mme. André.

Audubon determined to call upon Vanderlyn—he should have paid his respects long ago but the naturalist had decided *he* would not run after any successful artist—so on the last day of March he selected a number of his black chalk sketches and a few of his bird studies and went hopefully to Vanderlyn's stylish studio. The account of this meeting, as first published by Buchanan, Mrs. Audubon, and all others who copied what was set down by the first biographer, gave the story of this amusing encounter between two famous

[1] Papabotte is the name prevalent even today in Louisiana for the Upland Plover or Bartramian Sandpiper.

American artists in not only an abbreviated, but in a much-edited form. The unexpurgated extract from the journal, which follows, is just as Audubon set it to paper.

I called on Mr. Vanderlyn the Historical Painter with my Port Folio—to shew him some of my Birds with a View to Ask him for a few lines of recommendation—he examined them attentively and *Called* them *handsomely* done, but being *far* from possessing any Knowledge of Ornithology or Natural History, I was quite satisfied *he* Was No Judge but of their being or Worst *Shaded* Yet he spoke of the beautifull Coloring and Good Positions and told Me that he would With pleasure give me a Certificate of his having *Inspected* them—Are all Men of Talents fools and Rude purposely or Naturally? I cannot assert, but have often thought that they were one or the other.

When I arrived at Mr V's Room, he spoke to me as if I had been an abject slave, and told Me in Walking Away to Lay my Drawings down *there*, *the Dirty* ——— —— — ————— [Audubon scratched out the epithet, or someone else did it for him in later years and with different ink] and that he would return presently and Look them over. I felt so vexed that My first Intention Was to *Pack* off, but the Expedition Was in View, I thought how Long Kempbell the Actor Waitted Once at the theatre in England, and stood patiently *although* not Laying My Drawing *Down there*

About 30 Minutes Elapsed, he returned with an officer and with an air More becoming a Man Who *Once Was Much* in My situation ask me in his private room. Yet I could plainly see in his Eye that selfish Confidence that allways destroy in some degree the Greatest Man's Worth.

the Swet ran down My face as I hastily opend My Drawings and Laid them on the floor; I lookd up to him. he Was looking at them, the officer's *By God* that's handsome, struck my eyars Vanderlyn took up a Bird Lookd at it closely put it down and said they Were *handsomely done.*

I breathed, Not because I thought him a Man of the Most Superior Talents, for to come to such a pitch one Must have no faults, and I With My Eyes *half* Closed (as you know pretended Juges of our Day Look at Painting) saw a great Deffect in One of his figures of Women (the deffect that had being Corrected by the Lady I drew Lately.) but because this Gentleman had *some Talents*, that he Was Lookd on as a Very Excellent Judge and that I had been Told that a few Words from him Might be serviceable—of My Likeness he spoke very diferently, the one I had Was fair, hard, and Without Effect, although he Acknowledged it Must have been a Strong one.

he sat, he Wrote, and I thinking More of Journeying to the Pacific Ocean, than of Likenesses, Cared Not a *Pecayon* about these Later Observations.

Audubon gathered his drawings, placed the letter Vanderlyn had written in his pocket, and after another glance at the canvases Vanderlyn was painting, left the studio, murmuring his thanks and bowing low first to the painter then to the naval officer.

"As I was Walking away from his house corner of St. Louis and Royal Streets—the *Corner of Events* the officer who had followed me, askd me, the price of My *Black Chalk* Likeness and where I resided—all answered; I thought how Strange it was that a poor Devil Like me Could Steal the Custom of the Great Vanderlein—but fortune if not *blind* certainly Must have his Lunatic Moments—the officer said he would Call on Me Liking My Style Very Much."

Audubon returned to his lodgings "with a compound of Ideas Not Easily to be described," and brooded over what he considered his mistreatment by John Vanderlyn. Before copying it in his journal he re-read the letter.

> Mr. John J. Audubon had shewed me several Specimens of his Drawings in Natural History—such as Birds, with their Natural Colors, & other Drawings in plain Black & White Which Appear to be done With great truth & Accuracy of representation as much as I have seen in any Country—the Above Gentleman wishes Me to give this as My Opinion in Writing believing it may Serve as a recommendation to his being employed as a Draftsman in an Expedition to the interiors of our Country.
>
> J. Vanderlyn
>
> NEW ORLEANS 20th March 1821

In spite of the friendliness of the letter, Audubon wrote above the transcription: "The Politeness of Mr Vanderlyn Will be remembered—a long time by me; and When ever I Look over these Scrawls it will do me good to have a Litle of the same feelings."

3

It was the fifth of April before Audubon's lost portfolio was in his hands again. "Mr. Garnier sent it to me a fortnight ago to the Care of his son, the trouble this gave me I will mention hereafter. I have to thank Mr. Garnier but More *he* that found it on the River Bank and took Such remarkable good

Care of it—for on opening it I found the Contents in as good order as the day it Was Lost and *Only* One Plate Missing."

Five days later the Barracks street studio lost one of its occupants when Captain Samuel Cummings left for Philadelphia. Audubon noting "the Poor Man had not *One Cent* with him." For a week Audubon and Mason made short trips out of the city hunting birds "Wading often to our Midles through the Swamps then Walking through the Thickest Woods I believe I had ever yet seen." The quest for human subjects was sporadic and pursued only when money was absolutely needed. Audubon trapped some painted buntings and endeavored to keep them in cages so as to study the male bird's song. He noted a large number of young mockingbirds for sale in the market place and was told by the Creoles that if the parent birds were allowed to get to the caged young they are "often Poisonned by them, this *unatural* conduct demands *Self* Confirmation," he added, properly suspicious of local bird lore.

Returning from one of his bird forays in the swamps Audubon found that a Dr. Louis Heermann and his wife had called at the Barracks street studio. Early the next morning he hurried to the doctor's residence in the smart *rue de la Levée* and was informed by the physician that it was Mrs. Heermann's desire to be instructed in drawing. Could Mr. Audubon accept the post? Mr. Audubon could and when asked how soon he could begin the lessons, replied: "Tomorrow morning, *mon docteur*."

Whereupon began a romantic friendship between the young, beautiful, and flirtatious pupil and the eccentric, talented, and long-haired art instructor.

Several days later, after leaving the Heermann residence where he had been instructing the doctor's vivacious wife in the rudiments of art, Audubon called upon an artist who had lately arrived in the city to exhibit an ambitious life-sized portrait of General Andrew Jackson. He was Ralph E. W. Earle, a portrait painter who had married Jane Caffery, niece of Rachel Jackson, and was therefore considered one of the Jackson family. The portrait pretended to show "Old Hickory" astride his horse at the Battle of New Orleans. Earle was in New Orleans for the avowed purpose of selling the huge canvas to the city for $1,000. Therefore a great deal of interest was being displayed in the portrait because General Jackson, who was also in New Orleans, had told Mayor Joseph Roffignac he considered Earle's the best likeness that had been made of him. Taking the broad hint the city council voted the appropriation, and today it hangs in the mayor's parlor of the City Hall.

Audubon was, to say the least, not at all impressed with Earle's effort. After leaving the exhibition hall he noted: "Called on a New Phenomena in Painting, Mr. Earl . . . saw Mr. Earl's *Jackson*—Great God forgive Me if My Judgement is Erroneous—I never Saw a Worst painted sign *in the streets of Paris!*"

Years later, through the kindness of Ralph Earle, Audubon and his wife were honor guests of President Jackson at dinner in the White House. Although we have no record of the conversation nor the repartee that probably sparkled at the table, one may be quite certain that nothing was then said about Paris street signs!

Although Audubon had managed to obtain other pupils, and his lessons given Mrs. Heermann were continued regularly, he managed to do a few bird drawings. He completed a likeness of the little snowy heron, the result of his labors pleasing him immensely; Joe Mason killed two beautiful specimens of the parula warbler, then called the "Blue Yellow-back Warbler," and Audubon posed them perched on a stem of the "Louisiana Flag," as he called the coppery iris. The drawings of the little birds finished, Audubon had Joseph draw and color the floral decoration and in such a fashion the original of the fifteenth plate of the *Birds of America*, one prized by collectors, was drawn.

In the market he found a gallinule, distinguished from the ordinary purple gallinule, by its red legs, and a fine specimen of the blue grosbeak—both birds had their likenesses transferred to paper and were later immortalized in his famous plates. He devoted considerable time to drawing a black-poll warbler, and when finished to his satisfaction, he compared the fruits of his skill to the plate of the same bird found in Wilson's *Ornithology*—then declared himself better pleased with his own work.

I am forced here to Complain of the bad figure that My friend Willson has given the Warbler I drew yesterday, in the Bill only the length exceed that of Nature 1/8 of an Inch—an enormous diference—and he has runned a broad White line over the Eye that does not exist.

Unfortunately for the cause of art and ornithology, starvation diet was the regime of the moment in Barracks street. Pay for the lessons Audubon was giving the charming Mrs. Heermann were being put on the doctor's cuff, no cash payments being forthcoming. Week after week the artist charged up the lessons, too abashed to render a bill to the physician or the fascinating pupil. Returning one morning from a lesson at Heermann's, and while walking along the levee on his way back to Barracks street he was surprised to meet John Gwathmay, the former keeper of the *Indian Queen* inn of Louisville, where Victor had been born, and now host at the Merchants' Exchange in Conti street. "He was *à la guetté* on the Levée," Audubon wrote his wife. "The appearance of My Clothes did Not please him. We talked but Little together." Audubon was clearly at outs with himself and former friends. Trifles plunged him into a surly ill-humor and one night, when setting his thoughts to the pages of his journal, he touched on the similarity of his own and Captain Audubon's dispositions. "In temper we much resemble each other, being warm, irascible and at times violent, but it is like the blast of a hurricane—dreadful for a time, when calm almost instantly returns."

Happily for Audubon's purse, the steamboat *Columbus* arrived at the river front having on board several of his old time Kentucky friends as passengers, and he made crayon sketches of some of them. He was so successful in picturing David Hall, a sea captain who lived in the *Champs Elysees*, that Mrs. Hall commissioned him to make a black chalk likeness of John D'Hart, commander of the *Columbus*, the same river smoke-belcher that had towed the Berthoud keelboat from Natchez to Bayou Sarah. Upon delivering the finished likeness of Captain D'Hart to Mrs. Hall, Audubon records he "spent a few hours with her extremely agreeably."

The next morning, learning of the arrival of Jean Baptiste Bossier, of Ste. Geneviève, a friend of his former partner

Rozier, Audubon went aboard the steamboat *Hecla* and received his customary fee twenty-five dollars for Bossier's portrait. He "made it good," he states in his journal. Fortunately this example of Audubon's portrait-making of that period is still in existence—for only a very few of these early sketches appear to have escaped destruction. General Bossier's portrait gives us an excellent idea of Audubon's style and manner of handling black chalk at this period of his career.

Swallowing his pride and breaking the resolution he had made following his first call, Audubon climbed the steps leading to John Vanderlyn's studio one April morning so that he could exhibit some new bird drawings as well as one or two black chalk portraits he had made of well-known Orleanians. "Paid a visit to the Amiable Vanderlyn," is the way he records the call in his journal. "This Gentleman like all substantial Men gained on Acquaintance. He complimented me on My Drawings, I thought too much to be true," he added suspiciously. While Vanderlyn was inspecting the other's work, Audubon glanced about the painting room and held a critical eye on the portrait painter's big canvas of "My Fair Pupil Mrs. H—— the Likeness good but roughly painted," was his comment. There was undoubtedly a tinge of green in his unvoiced appraisal . . . Vanderlyn was a successful painter —Audubon was not.

When the bird artist reached the narrow *banquettes* of *rue Royale* he found them crowded. Saint Louis, Conti, and Chartres streets were likewise thronged. He asked the reason for the outpouring and was informed by an excited passer-by. The city's entire population—so it appeared when judged by the jostling men, women, and children, black, white, and red —was out to bid farewell to General Andrew Jackson who was that day bringing to a close his first visit to the city he had six years before saved from an invading army.

At noon Audubon found himself rubbing elbows with many in the narrow streets so that he might see the grim-faced warrior ride to the boat landing. He was interested in "Old Hickory's" features and took them in with an artist's eye as he ran from one street to another like an urchin to behold the hero.

"I saw him *thrice*. Found Vanderlyn's Likeness the Only

good One I have seen, *Sully's* Plate *Miserable*," was his appraisal.

As he raised his voice to cheer, John James Laforest Audubon, penniless and half-starved bird artist, garbed in ragged gray breeches and torn shirt, who ran over the cobbled streets of old New Orleans in poorly shod feet, certainly never imagined for one fleeting instant that, three short years later, he would be standing in Andy Jackson's boots!

4

May came and was partly gone when Audubon wrote his wife a lengthy letter giving her a word picture of his life in the Crescent City:

We now and then of Moon Shining evenings ramble to what is called the Museum Coffee Shop; then (when it costs nothing) we hear a few indifferent Musicians and amuze our taste for critics on the poor collection of Paintings &c that fill the Gallery—and often walk up to the Roulette table to infuse a strong sketch of Intentness on our minds, it is there that one may well Judge of Tempers.

Mosquitoes are at this season so troublesome that we seldom can set in our room, after dark we fix ourselves about the middle of the street until bedtime, piping the flageolet, or blowing the flute—We sometimes have a Painter for company and then we talk of the Arts.

I have so far gone on toward giving you a Idea of our daily expenditure of time that I will I believe enter upon our actual way of Living.

We cannot be Epicures—our Purse is not that that suits best strong appetites; We generally have a ham on the Nail, and convenience makes us cook it by slices when hungry.

During the cooler Weather we had cheese but the heat that disperses and sends one part of the Inhabitants of this Place brings on Miryads of others called Maggots with which we are not englishmen enough to desire very close acquaintance—salt Makerell are good, for they are very cheap, we suffer the want of pure Cool Watter, this cannot well be purchased by us—the Vegetable Market is as good as in any part of America, and very early in the season—fresh Meat we never taste it we see it hanging in the Market House and that satisfy us completely. Our rent, washing, *cooks wages* amount about at One Dollar and 50 *cts* per day.

Audubon had been importuning his wife by every letter to relinquish her position in Louisville and join him in New Orleans. In spite of his strongly worded persuasions, Mrs. Audubon hesitated to leave the city by the falls of the Ohio, where she could remain at a brother's or sister's home, where a few pupils were providing her with a means of livelihood for herself and her two boys. "And who, recalling her early married life, can wonder that she hesitated before leaving this home for the vicissitudes of an unknown city?" asks a granddaughter.

One night, after receiving a letter from his wife announcing her determination not to leave Louisville, the husband wrote:

Thou art not, it seems, as daring as I am about Leaving one place to go to another, without the Means. I am sorry for that, I will never fear *Want* as long as I am Well, and God will grant me that as I have received from Nature my little talents—I would dare go to England without *one* Cent, one single Letter of Introduction to anyone, and on Landing would make Shillings or *Pence* if I could not make more but no doubt I would make *enough.*

Prejudice and habits carry many *I think* too far but I am thinking that I can rise the means; I intend to try.

After many pertinent references to items of Louisville gossip that his wife had written him, Audubon took up the matter of his young charge, Joseph Mason.

Now sweet Girl to the next question of thy Letter "What will I do with Joseph Mason"—as Long at Least as I travel I shall keep him with me, I have a great pleasure in affording that good Young Man the means of becoming able to do well. his talent for painting if I am a Judge is fine—his expenses very moderate and his Company quite indispensable. We have heard of his Father's death and on that a/c I am more attached to him—he now *draws Flowers* better than any man probably in America. thou Knowest I do not flatter young artists much, I never said this to him, but I think so—to show his performance will bring me as many pupils as I can attend to, any where.

One morning, when Audubon called to give Mrs. Heermann her drawing lesson, he found her "more amiable if Possible than usual," and that afternoon, on the strength of her stimulating pleasantness, purchased fifteen yards of yellow nankeen for a new suit of summer clothes. While the tailor was taking his measurements Audubon exacted a promise of speedy delivery of the finished garments.

Audubon's shabby and unkempt appearance, ragged clothes, lack of tonsorial attention, and his general slip-shod manner during these weeks did much to militate against his receiving proper attention or respect from those whom he sought as patrons. Edward Hollander, the Livonian who had accompanied the German merchant Vincent Nolte on his trip from New York to New Orleans in 1811 when Audubon and Nolte had their odd meeting at the inn near the Juniata river was now not only a well-to-do partner of Nolte's, but the Russian consul in New Orleans, and in charge of all of the German merchant's affairs in Louisiana. Hollander had not forgotten Audubon, nor the ride down the river from Pittsburgh, and consequently made friendly overtures to the bird artist. Because Hollander was now rich and Audubon poor, the proud, though thread-bare Frenchman, had studiously avoided the Livonian for weeks. One day, when the two came face to face in the street and there was no chance of dodging, Hollander accosted Audubon. "He, I believe, saw that I had no wish to disgrace the Handsome Rich furniture of the Wealthy with my Intrusions when reduced to my Grey Breeches, and taking Me by both Hands One day as I was about to Make Way from him, he said 'My dear Mr. Audubon, Come and see me. I promise you I shall Not have any one at table and I will try and Raise your Spirits. I have some fine Paintings, and please bring your Birds that I am anxious to see.' "

Audubon, demurring at first, accepted the invitation and later made note of his reactions to Hollander's kindness. "You see that although I lived extremely retired and generally showd those that I thought I Would Incommodate, I now & then stumbled on an Less Indifferent Member of this Life toward his fellows Who like Me have been rich and poor alternately."

The suit of yellow nankeen he had ordered would restore him, he felt, to a higher level, just as the jingle of a few dimes in one's pocket makes the world seem a more livable place. Portrait making had picked up a little. The money thus earned, coupled with the returns he expected from the drawing lessons he was giving Mrs. Heermann, made prospects seem brighter, but his revived spirits were again plunged to the depths when he received a letter from his wife which he admitted was "not very agreeable to my feelings." As he walked along the *rue de la Levée* he accosted Philip Guesnor, the bank clerk with whom he had been on most friendly terms since making his portrait in chalks, but the young banker made it plain he had been affronted by some action on Audubon's part and refused to speak to him.

Audubon was disturbed, for duels over women were quite prevalent in old New Orleans in those days, and that evening he wrote: "Thought to day that a Certain Gentleman to whom I go daily felt *uncomfortable* While I was present, seldom before My coming to New Orleans did I think I was Looked on so favorably by the *fair* sex as I have Discovered Lately." Then he dropped around to the tailor's shop to see how his new suit of nankeen was coming on. The smart, new outfit was ready.

With the old gray breeches thrown in the discard, his long hair carefully combed, and a shave every day, Audubon was fast resuming the position once held by the gay young popinjay of the Perkioming, who played havoc with maiden hearts by his dazzling convolutions on the ice-covered creek at *Mill Grove*. If his newly furbished appearance was a hit with the ladies, it did little to attract sitters, and drawing pupils were few and far between. However, with the coming of summer, planters with their wives and children flocked into the city from the countryside, all looking for culture.

One of those who called upon Audubon in regard to drawing lessons was Mrs. James Pirrie, wife of a prosperous cotton planter of the Feliciana country, and owner of a pretentious plantation home a few miles from the twin-towns of Bayou Sarah and St. Francisville. Her daughter Eliza, a girl of fifteen, was eager to be instructed in drawing and the girl became Audubon's pupil at two dollars a lesson.

This meeting with Mrs. Pirrie marked a turning point in Audubon's career. During the ten days that elapsed from the day he found himself looked upon as a "ladies' man," his journal "suffered from the same cause that affects me—attention," and very few events were penned. However, in one of his letters to his wife, Audubon described the planter's daughter:

"She is the daughter of a rich Widow lady, her name Eliza Perry, and resides near Bayou Sarah during the Summer heat—Yesterday I begged to hear her Sing and play on the Piano. I played with her on a flute and made the mother stare. She was much surprised to hear me sing the notes—This Lady askd me if I would go with them and teach her daughter (about 16, an interesting age) until Next Winter—I am to think of the terms and give an answer. This I have already formed in my mind—she must pay me 100$ per month in advance, furnish *us* with our room, our board and washing and I will devote *one half* of each day for her Daughter—it is very high but I will not go unless I get it. If she acceeds I will have an excellent opportunity of forwarding my collection, being able to draw birds every day."

These arrangements were not concluded immediately for Mrs. Pirrie was the wife of a Scotsman (and not a widow), therefore she did not choose to close a bargain at its first offering.

While the bird artist was rushing about, endeavoring to make up his mind, or rather, have others make up their minds, the *Columbus* came into port from up river and it carried a letter from Lucy Bakewell to her husband. In it she frankly explained her situation in Louisville—she was in want—she insisted that her husband send her some money. If he could not—he need not return to her!

Audubon, on the last day of May, answered the plea and the ultimatum:

Wert thou not to give me *hints* about money I should be sorry, as I know it is as necessary for the support of *thy Life* as thy affection is to the comfort of *Mine*—I admire the Family B's maxim extremely—I am not afraid of the Climate. but already feel very powerfully the effect of the Intense Heat on my faculties—I can scarcely draw for the Perspiration.

I am very sorry that *thou* are so intent on my *not* returning to thee—if that Country we Live in cannot feed us *Why* not fly from it? . . . Your great desire that I should stay away is I must acknowledge very unexpected—if you can bear to have me go a Voyage of at least three years without wishing to see me before—I cannot help thinking that Lucy probably would be better pleased should I *never* return—and so it may be.

The next morning he repented the words he had written the night before, so he added a postscript:

My Dearest Girl. I am sorry for the last part I wrote yesterday, but then I felt miserable. I hope thou wilt look on it as a momentary Incident. I love thee so dearly, I feel it so powerfully that I cannot bear anything from thee that has the appearance of Coolness . . . God Bless thee. Thine for ever

for Life Yours really devoted

Audubon.

5

The bird artist was in a blue funk. He had failed to establish a paying school. He had failed to draw, during the winter that had just gone, the many birds that migrated to Louisiana to pass the colder months. He had failed to win the fame he desired as a portrait artist. He had failed in everything he had attempted in New Orleans. He had been cutting a fine figure in his new clothes but the letter from his wife had come to him when his spirits were at their lowest.

Then, too, he had broken with Mrs. Heermann. The abrupt termination of that episode rankled and hurt. The doctor's wife had led him on in the *affaire*, Audubon believed, although when the break came he unbundled his wrath and sarcasm on the woman's husband as well when he wrote in his diary:

"a personnage who had some week ago boasted of his Interest towards me, and who on one occasion carried his attention quite too far and awkwardly must first take my attention—and here I will give you a Lesson, should you ever be Employed as a Teacher to any ostantatious oppolent person—*flatter*, Keep flattering and end in flattery or else expect no pay.

"My misfortunes often occur through a want of attention to that Maxim in similar Cases. after having with assiduity attended on a Gentleman's Lady (Whose Name I will not at present Mention) for forty Days, I received the rudest of dismisal and My pride would not admit me to the House—even to ask any compensation—how agreable the first Lessons were I shall allways remember. *She Thought* herself endowed with superior talents, and her Looking glass pleasing her Vanity I dare say made her believe She was a Star dropped from the heavens to ornament this Hearth—but dificulties augmented and of Course drawing seased to please. I could not well find time to finish every piece that I began for her, and Constancy the lady said was never to be found the Companion of Genius. Toward the last she Would be unwell when I walked in, Yawnd and posponed to the morrow—I believe the Husband saw her Weakness, but the good Man Like *one* or *Two* More of My Acquaintances Was Weaker still.

"I Knew well that My conduct had been correct and I felt a great pleasure in Leaving them, and, the One hundred Dollars I had hearned, *with Them.*"

6

The meeting with Mrs. Pirrie and her daughter Eliza, at this juncture was a meeting fraught with considerable and fortunate significance to the naturalist. Indeed, it marked a pivotal point of his career. Audubon was bereft at that time of not only funds but incentive. Having made an ignominious failure of a quest to the South which was to enrich his portfolios of bird drawings, he now made another resolution—he would banish from his mind forever the tenacious idea of completing or even of continuing that ambitious project! Birds? He was through with them—*fini!*

The wife of a Feliciana cotton planter came upon him when he was sunk deep in a slough of despond. He was a failure, this he admitted for the first time, and for the first time, too, he was deserted by the optimism that had thus far carried him along his bird-picturing career. He yearned to leave New Orleans—he had grown to hate the place. Each step he took along the crude *banquettes* of the *Vieux Carré* seemed to resound to the maddening reiteration of "failure, failure, *failure, failure!*" The dandified capers he had cut before Mrs. Heermann and the affair with the fascinating Widow André were bitter memories.

To quit New Orleans and return to his wife, as she was now insisting, required passage money on one of the many steamboats making the long Mississippi river trip, else a tedious journey a-foot over traces and trails to the North. Of course, there was Alexander Gordon from whom he could borrow—but the Bakewells would learn of it. Give them that satisfaction? Never! Beaten though he was his pride was still with him, and nothing would drive him to that ultimate humiliation.

Then into the enthralling drama of his life came the mother of Eliza Pirrie. As he tells it:

"I had attended a Miss Pirrie to Enhance her Natural tallen for drawing for some days When her Mother, Whom I intend Noticing in due time, asked Me to Think about My Spending the summer and fall at their farm near Bayou Sarah; I was glad of such an overture, but would have greatly prefered her Living in the Floridas—We concluded the Bargain promissing me 60 Dollars per Month for One half My time to teach Miss Eliza all I could in Drawing Music Dancing &c &c for Joseph & Myself—so that after the One hundred Diferent Plans I had form^d^ as Opposite as Could be to this, I found Myself bound for several Months on a Farm in Louisiana."

7

That is how Audubon came to know the lovely Feliciana country of Louisiana. Why he ever after referred to the beautiful magnolia woods of "*my* Louisiana." Why he designated in later writings that state as his "favorite portion of the Union."

His meeting with Mrs. Pirrie and his subsequent bargain to teach her daughter made it possible for him to study the bird life of a region without an equal in such opportunity. Made it possible for him to give full bent to his desire to seek out new birds and transfer their likenesses to paper. Proof of this is that more than one-fourth of the bird pictures that won for him his imperishable fame, were drawn in this section of the state he grew to love so passionately.

One smiling June morning he and Joseph made ready to depart. As much as Audubon regretted the loss of money due him for Mrs. Heermann's lessons, and his parting with that delightful "star of the heavens," he was truly saddened at leaving the Pamar family. On his last evening with them he recalled the many happy times he had spent at the crockery merchant's home. A frequent guest at dinner time, especially on Sundays, he was beloved by the Pamar children, for he would frolic with them and tell them amusing nature stories in his quaint Gallic idiom. He admitted he felt as though he was parting with his own sons when he said good-bye to the little folk in Magazine street.

Hurriedly he and Mason packed their scanty belongings, carted them to the river front, and placed portfolios, pencils, paints, black chalks, as well as guns, violins, flutes and flageolets on board the steamboat *Columbus*, the same river craft that had towed him downstream six months before. This time it was to transport him back to the very place where it had cast off the two lines of Nicholas Berthoud's keelboat.

Leave was taken of the jolly neighbor, Juan Puich, and his gifted nieces, and the señor was assured his jokes would be missed.

"We left our abode in Quartier street and Old Miss Louise without the least regret," wrote Audubon, "the filthiness of her Manners did not agree with our feelings; and by this time We had discovered that a Clean Sweet Housekeeper is quite Necessary to a Naturalist."

French Market, New Orleans from a sketch by Charles A. LeSueur.

Book Five

Audubon's Happyland

"The State of Louisiana has always been my favorite portion of the Union, although Kentucky and some other states have divided my affections."

JOHN JAMES AUDUBON in his *Ornithological Biography.*

CHAPTER 11

FELICIANA

IN Louisiana there are two places forever to be associated with the name of John James Audubon—New Orleans, where he starved; West Feliciana parish, where he feasted on beauty. There he roamed the most beautiful of all Louisiana's beautiful woods, studied the birds that abound in them, drew their portraits, and learned many of nature's innermost secrets. In Feliciana it was that his wife earned sufficient money by her years of teachings to send her husband to Europe, to fame, to immortality.

One woman was inseparably linked with Audubon's career and his final achievement—Lucy Bakewell, his wife, who through hardships, penury, and woe believed in him and his ultimate triumph. Other women, however, were responsible for many other opportunities that came to him during his slow and difficult climb up the ladder of fame. Lucy Alston Pirrie, who came upon him when his enthusiasm for his great work was at its lowest ebb, when he was about to give up his cherished dream of greatness, was one of these—she furnished him with an opportunity given few men. Eliza, her fifteen-year-old daughter, whose need of culture and art instruction paved the way, must also be included in this list of helpful women.

Had it not been for the Pirries, Audubon might never have known the bird-infested Feliciana country, the region that proved to be his ornithological mecca. True, he was induced to go there against his will, when his wandering feet were turning to Florida, itching to be off to the headwaters of the Arkansas, or to the far, far West. Distance, to Audubon, always had its enchantment.

It was a hot sultry day, June 18, 1821, when the *Columbus* put into the landing at Bayou Sarah just long enough to allow the passengers bound for that busy little river village to debark. Those landing—those we are interested in—included Mrs. Pirrie, her daughter, Joseph Mason, and the long-haired drawing teacher, encumbered with his portfolios, violin and flute cases, his guns, and other luggage. From the landing place he waved a farewell to Alexander Gordon, who was bound upstream on a business trip to the East, then climbed the hill that led to the settlement of Saint Francisville on the top of the bluffs. The whole party proceeded to *Wyoming*, the home of Judge Robert Semple, just outside the village where a meal was spread for the travelers.

"Dinner was set, but Not My Heart for it," writes Audubon. "I wished Myself on Board the *Columbus*, I wished for My Beloved Lucy, My Dear Boys—I felt that I would be Awkward at table and a good opportunity having offered to go to Mr Pirrie's place, We Walked slowly on, guided by some of their servants dispatchd with the news of our coming and some Light Baggage."

As the negro slaves led the way along the dusty road that wound its way to *Oakley*, Audubon and Mason followed slowly, observing the country they were being introduced to for the first time. Audubon has recorded his impressions of that walk:

> the Aspect of the Country entirely New to us distracted My Mind from those objects that are the occupation of My Life—the Rich Magnolia covered with its Odoriferous Blossoms, the Holy, the Beech, the Tall Yellow Poplar, the Hilly ground, even the Red Clay I Looked at with amazement. such entire change in so Short a time appears often supernatural, and surrounded once More by thousands of Warblers & Thrushes, I enjoyed Nature.
>
> My Eyes soon Met hovering over us the Long Wished for Mississippi Kite and Swallow Tailed Hawk, but our guns were packd and We could only then anticipate the pleasure of procuring them shortly.

The five miles appeared all too short and when the two arrived at *Oakley* they were met by Squire Pirrie, who received them kindly. "Anxious to Know him," says Audubon, "I Inspected his features by Lavater's directions."

James Pirrie was a Scotsman, born in Fifeshire, who had settled in that part of Louisiana when it was under the domination of Great Britain and known as West Florida, to differentiate it from East Florida, now the present state of Florida. Later, this narrow strip of territory along the Gulf from the Perdido to the Mississippi river, fell under the domination of Spain. In 1810 West Florida was summarily annexed to the United States by President Madison, and apportioned to Louisiana, Mississippi, and Alabama. That part allotted Louisiana, from the Pearl to the Mississippi river, was at the time Audubon first knew it, and is to this day for that matter, called the "Florida Parishes."[1]

Under the rule of the Dons, Squire Pirrie had been an *alcalde*, or judge, and, like other Scots, Britishers, and Irishmen who had settled this fertile land when the Union Jack waved over it, was forced to take an oath of allegiance to Spain, which he and the others were required to renew annually by the suspicious Spaniards. In 1810 the West Floridians, led by the planters of the Bayou Sarah region, revolted, ousted the Spanish rule by attacking the fort at Baton Rouge and shooting down its defenders. Spanish officials were jailed or expelled, the planter patriots of Feliciana set up an independent government, under a lone-star flag, which lasted only seventy-four days. For, after the people won their independence at the point of the bayonet, the United States stepped in, after seven years of futile diplomatic fencing with Madrid, and President Jimmy Madison blandly announced that West Florida belonged to the United States under the terms of the Louisiana Purchase, ignored the Tom Thumb republic, and ran up the stars and stripes.

James Pirrie had played only an inconspicuous part in this spectacular revolt, in which a Southern people rebelled to *become* a part of the American Union. A few years before the revolt he married the widow of Ruffin Gray, a prosperous planter of Homochitto in the Mississippi Territory and of *Oakley* in Feliciana. She was Lucretia, or Lucy Alston, daughter of Captain John Alston, a Carolinian, prominent in the affairs of the province when the British controlled West Florida. Upon his marriage to the Widow Gray Squire Pirrie not only adopted the children of his wife's first marriage, Ruffin and Mary Ann Gray, but *Oakley* plantation as well and here, on October 6, 1805, his daughter Eliza was born.

[1]The various political subdivisions of Louisiana are called parishes and not counties.

Eliza Pirrie grew into a girl of striking beauty, with artistic ambitions. When prosperity came to her parents, she was given all the attainments a doting and wealthy cotton planter of the old regime could lavish on an only child. There were no schools in the rich Feliciana country in those early days, all education being supplied by private tutors. Culture was in demand and those who could supply it were, naturally, highly regarded. It was while Mrs. Pirrie was in New Orleans, seeking a teacher who could add something to the native accomplishments of her daughter, that she met the eccentric but talented artist with a pronounced Gallic accent and mirth-provoking mannerisms, who could play the violin and flute, do simple sums, and, though faulty in spelling, was fairly proficient in writing and speaking English, French, and Spanish.

It was this same tall, angular-faced Frenchman, so variously endowed, with long, flowing locks, and arrayed in flapping nankeen clothes, who presented an unforgettable figure when he arrived at the gates of *Oakley*. He at once waxed enthusiastic over the prospect of completing his work on birds. During the five-mile walk he had shaken off his depression. His mercurial spirits had risen to fever point by the warmth of a glad bird chorus. Before he entered the plantation house yard "his great work" was again engrossing his thoughts to the exclusion of all else! His fingers itched for the feel of a pencil. He had reached his Mecca—an ornithological treasure house—this Feliciana—this well-christened Happyland!

The deep magnolia woods of the smiling country into which he had just come sheltered birds by the thousands, and of many, many species, all now busy with their nesting duties. No time was to be lost. With gun, and paper, and pencil, and colors, he went to work. As a consequence Audubon's collection of bird drawings grew daily. Enthused as never before he threw himself with a fanatical energy into a work that, in New Orleans only a week or two before, he had abandoned forever!

The countryside surrounding the Pirrie plantation became his bird heaven. Inspiration was here and he let it flood his soul and flow from his deft fingertips.

The influence of the Feliciana region on Audubon's paintings is most apparent to anyone who studies his collection of original drawings. Those made while he was at *Oakley* testify to a sudden, an amazing improvement in delineating the objects of his affection. Many of the new species he contributed to American ornithology were first seen and pictured in this happyland where he had the opportunity to spend unlimited time in the woods observing the birds and their habits without the harassment of earning his daily bread. Here he could shoot and study his birds at the same time. In New Orleans he had been forced, in a great measure, to rely upon birds picked up at the market or brought in to him by hunters while he earned his bread and cheese by delineating in black chalks that which he was so fond of terming "the human phiz."

His June introduction to the Feliciana woods was responsible for his oft-repeated statement of later years, when he had achieved fame and recognition as the foremost bird naturalist of his time, that Louisiana was his favorite section of the America he loved so passionately. In this Feliciana wonder-spot he found many birds, some he had met before, others he had only heard of, or read of in Alexander Wilson's printed works, others he believed to be "non-descripts," species not yet described. These latter he named for the first time in ornithological literature.

Among the birds he was to find in the Feliciana country and to propose as new species were: Louisiana water thrush, Bonaparte's flycatcher, Bewick's wren, Selby's flycatcher, Stanley's hawk, Louisiana warbler, Harlan's hawk, Roscoe's warbler, American crow, king rail, Harris's buzzard, Carolina chickadee, Children's warbler, Rathbone warbler, and the rough-winged swallow. He was in error in assuming as new species some of the birds he first designated as "Non-descripts," for many of them have since been proved to be young of known species in their immature plumage. No fault must be found with the budding, self-taught naturalist for it must be remembered that bird books were rare then and Audubon had to rely wholly upon the descriptions published by Wilson, or those contained in his copy of Turton's Linné.

The region about Saint Francisville gave him exceptional opportunities to find and handle many birds of which he had only heard of, to draw their portraits, and to study the intimate things about their lives he afterwards set forth in such a wealth of detail in his voluminous *Ornithological Biography*. To realize that it was in the Felicianas that the splendid genius of the man for bird portraiture burst into full and imperishable bloom, one need but examine his drawings of birds made first in France, then those drawn at *Mill Grove*, in 1808; at Henderson, from 1812 to 1819; at Cincinnati in the early part of 1820, and compare those formative efforts with such splendid Feliciana drawings as the wild turkey cock, yellow-throated vireo, American redstart, summer tanager, mocking-birds defending their young from a rattlesnake, the swallow-tailed kite, Tennessee warbler, yellow-throated warbler, the mourning doves, the assemblage of Louisiana paroquets, the ivory-billed woodpeckers, cerulean warbler, wood stork, roseate spoonbill, or the Baltimore orioles and their hang-nest to appreciate just what the Feliciana country of Louisiana meant to him and his art.

He remained the foremost American bird delineator until Louis Agassiz Fuertes appeared on the ornithological horizon in 1900, to be followed by such gifted bird artists as Robert Bruce Horsfall, Major Allen Brooks, Francis L. Jaques, and George Miksch Sutton. Thus, for the eighty years intervening between 1820 and 1900, Audubon's birds were not surpassed by any other American artist's brush.

2

On June 18, 1921, one hundred years to the day that Audubon walked from Bayou Sarah to the hospitable plantation home of the Pirrie family, the writer of this biography traversed the same road afoot to commemorate the centennial of the day The American Woodsman was introduced to a region that ever after remained fresh and green in his memory.

Making the identical pilgrimage, I could picture the artist's delight in the woodland scenes that lay on every side of the long twisting road that led to *Oakley*. The magnolia trees were in bloom, the holly and the beech trees were covered with verdant leaves, the slim yellow poplars reached high into the blue and cloud-flecked sky above the hilly ground and red clay. I, too, like Audubon, was surrounded on every side by warblers and thrushes making the soft summer air glad with their chorus.

Treading the same route, at the same time of the year, I could easily comprehend Audubon's instant infatuation with this truly beautiful region. From every shrub and every bush and every tree the birds sang their nuptial lays, as their gaudily colored forms flitted from branch to branch and tree to tree. A bird paradise, one indeed beyond compare.

They were all here, the king and principal soloist of the vast avian tribe, the beloved mockingbird, imitating the love notes of others and improvising runs and trills of his own to ease his impassioned heart; the flaming red Louisiana cardinal, whistling like a happy boy; the pert Carolina wren, praying to God on high as it sang; the clownish blue jay, screaming like an inebriate; the deep-throated brown thrasher, voicing his intoxication of love from the tip-top of a wide-spreading pecan; the twittering kingbird, distracted from his family duties for the moment to drive a black-headed vulture from his domain; timid wood pewees, uttering their sad, sweet calls from the depths of the magnolia woods; the ever-singing yellowthroat, calling *wichity, wichity, wichity, wichity* with force and energy from the thickets.

The chestnut-and-black orchard oriole, joining in Nature's hymn with musical efforts that so suggest the finished performance of a trained vocalist; its cousin, the yellow-and-black Baltimore oriole, singing and whistling loudly as his mate busied herself with the construction of the swaying and pendulous hang-nest that was to cradle the babies; a blood-red but black-winged scarlet tanager flashed through the deep green of the woods, illuminating the prospect with its color, cheering with its rhythmical carol as he traveled northwards to his nesting zone; the beloved bluebird, with its violet of song; the sociable meadowlark, fluttering over the fields, leaving behind a stream of mellow, bubbling flute-like notes; a summer tanager, soft-voiced in the tumult of other bird notes, carried its sweet song to the edge of the copse; the gaudy painted bunting, always shy and retiring, sang feebly yet concisely from its hiding place; a modest indigo bunting, making its way from a lower branch to the top of a tree on rungs of song, gave a flash of its purplish-blue robes; an acrobatic yellow-breasted chat performed aërial somersaults as he whistled his eccentric marital lay, and the towhee bunting sang, as it scratched among the leaves, the *chewink towhee* that has earned it its own version of its name.

The spotted wood thrush, from the distant depths of the forest, uttered its calm, restful song so truly like a hymn of praise pouring pure and clear from a thankful heart; twittering purple martins, dashing to and from homes in empty yellow gourds; a company of chimney swifts, performing intricate aërial evolutions in the azure of the sky over a cluster of negro cabins; while warblers, too many to be named, filled the heavily-wooded glades with a tumult of sweetness. In a tapestry of green leaves I glimpsed the cerulean, the parula, and the flashing golden prothonotary. A red-eyed vireo was declaiming his incessant song; mingled with it the tinkle of a Louisiana water thrush, while from the grasslands and the thickets of the blooming Chickasaw rose came an oft-repeated —*BOB, Bob White!*

Verily a place to delight the heart of a bird lover! Scarcely is there a spot in this broad land to compare with Feliciana, and what an ecstasy it must have been to Audubon!

A century later, it must be confessed, one looked in vain for the flocks of chattering parokeets. No longer was to be heard the hammerings of the ivory-billed woodpeckers on the decaying trunks of the forest's trees. One can scan the cloud-flecked heavens of the Felicianas for years and not see the floating flight of swallow-tailed kites. For some of the birds that Audubon knew there have passed on.

The yellow-billed cuckoo, however, still croaks its doleful *cow-cow* from the pawpaws, the belted kingfisher still rattles its note over the water-courses, the pileated woodpecker is to be discerned on the barkless trunk of a dead tree, uttering its *witchew* between its probings for grubs, the mourning dove still voices its sad, sweet *coo-o-o, ah-coo-o-o--coo-o-o* while hidden in the lush green foliage; the red-tailed hawk still sends its squealing whistle through the magnolia groves, and the snowy heron still flaunts its pure white delicate *aigrettes* in the green fastnesses of the Feliciana swamps.

Then *Oakley* itself! Could any place be more enchanting than this great two-storied house a century and more old? It is still surrounded by its moss-hung oaks, white blossoming magnolias, and towering poplars. Its spacious gallery is still shuttered against the heat of the day. Mockingbirds and cardinals still sing as sweetly in its gardens, and diminutive ruby-throated hummingbirds still sip nectar from the flowers that border its walks. *Oakley* stands as firm and as solid as it did when John James Audubon arrived at its portals on the eighteenth of June, eighteen hundred and twenty-one.

3

When Audubon and his pupil-assistant Joseph Mason joined the company at *Oakley*, the Pirrie household contained Squire Pirrie, fifty-two years of age, kind of manner, florid of face, fond of the good things of life, accomplished in the growing of cotton and the judging of good liquor; Mrs. Pirrie, austere but hospitable, in her forty-ninth year, kind to those she liked and who liked her; Eliza, daughter of Squire Pirrie, a beautiful, spirited girl, just approaching her sixteenth birthday; her half-sister Mary Ann, who with her husband Jedediah Smith, spent part of her time at the Pirrie home and part at her own home, *Locust Grove*, not far from *Oakley;* a Mrs. Harwood of England, with her two-year-old daughter; and Miss Eliza Throgmorton of New Orleans, visiting the Pirries for the summer, completed the group.

For four months Audubon gave daily lessons to the fair Eliza in drawing, music, dancing, mathematics, French, and such lesser accomplishments as plaiting, weaving, and working hair. Only part of the day was devoted to lessons, the remaining hours were left to the naturalist, free to roam the near-by swamps and woods to study birds, draw their portraits, and add to his collection of bird forms through the agency of his ever-present Souvenir Gun.

In short, he made the most of the rich opportunities offered by the bird-populated country of Feliciana. Accompanied by Joe Mason he explored the swamps edging the Mississippi river, hunted the wood stork on the border of Ball's lake and traversed the winding courses of Alexander's and Thompson's Creeks. Birds he knew only by hearsay fell before his ubiquitous gun, and in the intervals of teaching he painted bird portraits, while his pretty pupil looked on and applauded.

Soon after his arrival at *Oakley*, a Choctaw Indian, a hunter for Squire Pirrie, brought Audubon a female specimen of the Chuck-Will's-Widow. It was a welcome addition to his collection for he had heard the cries of the male birds monotonously repeating their name during the evening hours, but had not succeeded in securing a specimen for a drawing. The workers about the plantation regaled him with tales of the bird and its habits, and he was anxious to see these strange habits with his own eyes.

"Many of the Planters think that this bird has the Power and Judgment of removing its eggs when discovered, sometimes several yards—these are usually laid on the bare earth under a small bush or by the side of a Log," he set down in his journal, which proves that this observation which appeared in his *Ornithological Biography* was not founded upon personal observation, but upon hearsay. The declaration Audubon made that the bird picks up its own egg with its bill and in this manner removes it a considerable distance away, has been thoughtlessly repeated and quoted by many writers.

Day in and day out he combed the woods for birds. Many of the feathered inhabitants fell before his gun. "To kill a bird for science was to him a tragedy, and he shrank from it," wrote Hezekiah Butterworth in his *In The Days of Audubon*, a remarkable volume of misinformation regarding the life of the naturalist which is found on the shelves of juvenile sections of most libraries. "He sometimes destroyed life for scientific purposes, but always with regret . . . Only a mean mind and a low nature can be cruel."

To properly evaluate The American Woodsman it is necessary we follow him on a bird foray. One July day, soon after arriving in the Feliciana country, Audubon explored a lake situated in a swamp near the Mississippi river where he collected a female Mississippi kite and her fledgling under particularly touching circumstances. As he described the adventure in detail in his journal we will let him tell the tale:

In going there [the lake in the swamp] I was much pleased to observe the *sound* that We heard on Sunday and had taken for the Plaintive Note of the *Wood Pewee* was in fact that of a Young Mississippi Kite while waiting for the return of the Parents with food.

This Young it seems had Actually remained on the same tree Where we had heard it before but could not then discover it. This Morning perceiving that a long Vine reached near the Top of the Tree and hearing the Noise without knowing it nor where it actually issued from, I Walked toward it still looking up to the Topmost branches when I perceived something like a dead stick Lodged Cross ways on a limb—I eyed it particularly and saw it Moved. I Shot at it and the Noise stop[d] but the Young M. Kite Closed her wings and destroyed the Dead Stik like appearance it had before my fire—I waited for it to fall, it cried again shortly and then I saw the Old Bird bringing food and alight Close to the young with one of those Large Grass hopers that abound in the Mississippy flats—but the young was too far gone to relish food. The Mother exhibited much distress and after several trials to Make the young Bird take it, it dropt it and taking hold of her offspring by the feathers of the back, carried it off with ease for about 25 yeards to another tree where I follow[d] and Killed both at One Shot. The Young instead of having the head of a Light blue ash color, like its Mother, had it of a handsome buff and remaineder of the body Was Nearly black.

I intended drawing Both and I purposely hided them under a Log, but on my return some quadrupedes had discovered them and eat them both—I regret much the Loss, the young Bird was nearly fully grown.

Audubon had good cause to regret losing the female Mississippi kite and the young so wantonly shot. He had already drawn a portrait of the adult male bird but, to make his depiction of the species complete, a likeness of the female and a young in immature plumage was needed. The probabilities are that he never succeeded in securing either, for when his engraved plate of the Mississippi kite was published the male bird he had drawn at *Oakley* appears as the upper figure, while the lower bird, designated in the inscription on the plate as the female, got Audubon into exceedingly hot water a few years later.

George Ord, a Philadelphia ornithologist and Alexander Wilson's biographer, when Audubon's plate No. 117 reached Philadelphia from London, openly charged The American Woodsman with "stealing" the female bird from an engraving in Wilson's work. The Scot's kite portrait depicts a male bird he had secured and drawn when at Sir William Dunbar's *Wildwoods* plantation near Natchez in 1810, shortly after the historic meeting at Louisville of the rival ornithologists, when Audubon had refused to subscribe to the other's work. According to Ord's charges, Audubon had taken Wilson's *male* bird, reversed its position from left to right, and palmed it off as his own drawing—of a *female* kite!

Among the original Audubon drawings in the New York Historical Society's collection is the painting of the male Mississippi kite only. It is the same bird that was placed on the upper part of the engraved plate and in ink, in Audubon's hand, is written: "Mississippi Kite, *Falco Mifsifsipiensis.* Length, 14, inches; breadth, 3 feet ½ inches; weight, 10¾ Ouces; tail feathers, 12. Drawn from Nature by John J. Audubon, Louisiana, parish of Feliciana, James Pirrie's Esqr. Plantation, June 28, 1821."

On Audubon's *published* plate the lower bird, termed a female, is an identical twin of the Wilson bird—indeed, a tracing of the Scot's male reversed fits exactly over Audubon's female! They are identical with one exception—Wilson's bird exhibits four toes clasping the branch, while the one engraved by Havell for Audubon's plate shows only three toes!

When George Ord, with all the spleen he possessed, made this charge of theft, Audubon's reply was a dignified silence.

Therefore it would seem that the heartless killing of the innocent baby kite and its distressed mother had an embarrassing aftermath.

4

Audubon's own story of his discovery and naming of the rough-winged swallow again illustrates his insatiable desire to kill many of the creatures that inspired his art. He collected these birds, which he later discovered to be of a species new to ornithological science, while hunting in the Feliciana woods. The story told in his own words, the phrasing polished and corrected by his Scottish ghost writer, is:

> I was walking along the shores of a forest-margined lake, a few miles from Bayou Sarah, in pursuit of some Ibises when I observed a flock of small Swallows bearing so great a resemblance to our common Sand Martin, that I at first paid little attention to them. The Ibises proving too wild to be approached, I relinquished the pursuit, and being fatigued by a long day's exertion, I leaned against a tree, and gazed on the Swallows, wishing that I could travel with as much ease and rapidity, and thus return to my family as rapidly as they could to their winter quarters.

> How it happened I cannot now recollect, but I thought of shooting some of them, perhaps to see how expert I might prove on other occasions. Off went a shot, and down came one of the birds, which my dog brought to me in his lips. Another, a third, a fourth, and at last a fifth was procured. The ever continuing desire of comparing one bird with another led me to take them up. I thought them rather large, and therefore placed them in my bag, and proceeded slowly toward the plantation.

Audubon relates he examined the birds cursorily and perhaps might never have discovered the difference existing between the bank swallow and the birds he had killed merely to see how expert he was at wing shooting, had he not been spurred on by the writings of Vieillot on the swallow tribe. He found the birds he had collected were readily distinguishable from the bank swallow, which was at that time termed the sand martin, by drawing his finger along the edge of an outer wing feather, for "the stiff projecting tips of the filaments were felt like the edge of a fine saw."

Thus, in a moment of idle slaughter, did Audubon discover the rough-winged swallow, to which he gave the scientific designation of *Hirundo serripennis* in recognition of its "*saw wing*."

Nor was this strange desire to kill confined to the formative days of his career as a field naturalist. Ten years later, when Audubon was returning to the land of his adoption from London on the trans-Atlantic ship *Columbia*, after his first volume had been published and he was being recognized as a personage of importance in the realm of science, he killed many birds from the vessel's deck. He wrote Joseph B. Kidd, an Edinburgh artist, "I shot sixteen birds on the passage, which I got through the kind attention of our commander. I killed fifty more, when the *Columbia* was going too fast to stop for the purpose of picking them up."

A few months later, when he was in Florida seeking to extend his knowledge of bird life, Audubon wrote G. W. Featherstonhaugh, editor of the *Monthly American Journal of Geology and Natural Science*, that he was in the midst of an abundance of bird life and had "killed a bagfull of warblers." He detailed a hunt that began at sunrise: "The fact is that I was anxious to kill some 25 Brown Pelicans . . . to enable me to make a new drawing of an adult male bird . . .

I waded to the shore under the cover of the rushes along it, saw the pelicans fast asleep, examined their countenances and deportment well and leisurely, and after all, levelled my piece, and dropped two of the finest specimens I ever saw. I really believe I would have shot one hundred of these reverend sirs, had not a mistake taken place in the reloading of my gun. A mistake, however, did take place [he rammed in the balls first and the powder on top of them], and to my utmost disappointment, I saw each pelican, old and young, leave his perch, and take to wing, soaring off, well pleased, I dare say, at making so good an escape from so dangerous a foe."

Audubon, then in his forty-sixth year, complained of the scarcity of birds in Florida: "The birds, generally speaking, appeared wild and few—and you must be aware that I call birds few, when I shoot less than one hundred per day."

Birds *few* when he *shoots less than one hundred a day!* A true bird lover hesitates to consider what Audubon must have counted a *good* day's shooting.

Was Doctor Coues far from the mark when he suggested that Audubon's interest in a bird ceased from the moment he had transferred its likeness to paper?

All the evidence we have is Audubon's own words.

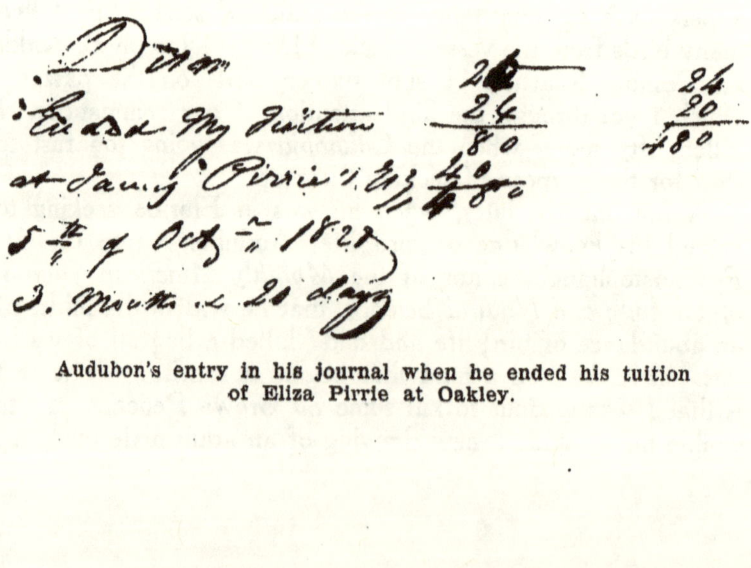

Audubon's entry in his journal when he ended his tuition of Eliza Pirrie at Oakley.

CHAPTER 12

His Bird Heaven

JOHN JAMES AUDUBON had not been long at *Oakley* before he appreciated that he was bound to a veritable bird paradise by a tie that could never be severed, and he proceeded to take full advantage of the opportunities offered on every side. In consequence his bird drawings grew in number and excellence. Many of the specimens he collected he compared to Alexander Wilson's printed descriptions and found what he considered errors on the Scotsman's part. "Willson's drawings" suffered when Audubon compared them to Audubon's drawings of the same species.

The Frenchman saw many new things in this bird heaven. Some of his observations were unique, one or two were—well, remarkable. The inclusion of the scarlet ibis in the bird fauna of the United States rests wholly on Audubon's record as published in his *Ornithological Biography*, which reads: "These birds occured at Bayou Sarah, in Louisiana on the 3rd of July, 1821. They were traveling in a line, in the manner of the White Ibis, above the tops of the trees. Although I only had a glimpse of them, I saw them sufficiently well to be assured of their belonging to the present species, and therefore, I have thought it proper to introduce it into our Fauna." His drawings of the adult and immature birds appearing in his plates, he admitted, were done from mounted specimens. (This in spite of his resolve never to draw from a stuffed bird.) Let us examine his journal, under date of July 4, 1821, and we find this brief entry: "Saw 3 Red Ibisses pass over the plantation Yesterday." A remarkable observation—but hardly sufficient for including so wholly tropical a bird as the scarlet ibis in our ornithological fauna.

While Audubon kept himself busy making portraits of the feathered tribe in the Feliciana woods, his talent for sketching "the human phiz," as he liked to express it, was not neglected. He began a portrait study of his vivacious pupil in pastels and worked at the likeness in odd times. He also guided Eliza's hand in making a portrait of her mother in the same medium. This was before he learned to paint in oils.

One night he was awakened, he tells us, by a servant who informed him he should dress and accompany Mrs. Pirrie to a neighbor's house, where a planter, who frequently visited *Oakley*, had suddenly fallen ill. "We went but arrived rather late for Mr. James O'Connor was Dead. I had the displeasure of Keeping his body's Company the remainder of the Night. On such Occasions time flys very slow indeed, so much so that it looked as if it had Stood Still like the Hawk that Poises in the air over its prey. The Poor Man had drink himself Literally to an everlasting sleep; peace to his Soul. I made a good Sketch of his head and Left the House and the Ladies engaged at preparing the ceremonial Dinner."

Shortly after his arrival at *Oakley* the artist found a sparrow hawk's nest with several young, and from the nestlings he chose one to raise. The bird grew rapidly and became a pet about the plantation home. As it developed to adult size it grew unmanageable and evidently quite cruel—probably living up to its baptismal name of *Nero*. Audubon recorded: "*Nero* has become extremely Temeraire, would fall on a Grown duck as if thinking all Must answer his Wishes when hungry."

During the first days of August, *Nero*, motivated by his insatiable hunger urge, fixed a baleful eye on one of a brood of baby chicks and proceeded to claim it for his own. The mother hen had very different ideas on the subject and no sooner had *Nero* sunk his talons about the chick than Biddy, with ruffled feathers, was atop the hawk, and how the feathers flew! A short but vicious battle ensued and *Nero* finally lay dead on the ground in the rear of the cook house.

Audubon bemoaned the passing of his pet, having become very much attached to the bird which he used as a model for several of the figures found in the plate of this species. "He flew at liberty about the Place, caught Grasshoppers with great ease and Would Catch in the Air any of the unfortunate Small birds Killed in our dayly walks when thrown toward

LUCY ALSTON PIRRIE

JAMES PIRRIE, ESQ.

James Pirrie, Esq., the master of "Oakley," his wife, and their daughter Eliza, from portraits of their period. Mrs. Pirrie's portrait, from the brush of Jacques G. L. Amans, and her husband's, by an unknown artist, hang on the walls of "Oakley." While family tradition has it Eliza's portrait, at "Rosedown," was by Audubon, it does not resemble his work in oil.

ELIZA PIRRIE

"Oakley," the Pirrie plantation home near Saint Francisville, West Feliciana parish, Louisiana, where Audubon first became acquainted with the birds of his "happyland."

Along the Little Bayou Sarah, Audubon's happy hunting grounds in West Feliciana parish, where he sought out the secrets of the Louisiana birds.

him for food—he regularly refused all putrid flesh. Never would touch Woodpeckers, but dearly received Bats & Mice. He had grown handsome from an apparent parcel of Moving Cotton—sailed with the Wild Birds of his Species, returning every Night to the Inner upper part of a Sash in Mr. P's Room—he seldome made use of the Note of the Old Birds but allmost constantly uttered his *Cree, Cree, Cree.*"

2

The Feliciana country is noted today, as it was in Audubon's time, as a warbler country. At first the naturalist was bewildered by the number and kinds of these forest-haunting birds that he found in the nearby woods. Bewilderment gave way to curiosity, and curiosity was succeeded by a desire to find birds new to science, and he became a confirmed new-species-seeker. One afternoon, while exploring the depths of a magnolia woods, he bagged a warbler he decided was new to ornithology. He had been unsuccessful in securing a similar bird the previous day, and after examining the bird minutely he was confirmed in his belief that he held a "Non-descript":

> It flew briskly from tree to tree or small bush to another, Not as if afraid of me, but as if anxious for food, hanging its Wing much like the Hooded fly Catcher and constantly Keeping its tail spread like the American Red Start. The Only Note it repeated every time it left a place for another was a simple soft single *Tweet*, all its Movements extremely quick gave Me much trouble to Shot it—this Bird I Have Never Met before, and of Course I consider it as a Very Scarce One, its Note attracted me as that of all New species do; More of its habit I would Like to Know.

As was his custom, he immediately made a drawing of his find and the bird (it proved to be a male) was the only one he encountered on his rambles until about three weeks later when he saw "a Male & femelle that I approached and Examined very attentively for some Minutes. They were in a Low damp & Shady part of the wood. I killed the femelle & have joined it to my drawing of a Male—I was anxious to procure her Mate but the discharge of my Gun so alarmed it that it flew off and I could not see it more—those Birds resemble the young of the Blue-eyed Warbler of Willson in much of their plumage but not in Manners and are a scarce species."

Satisfied he had discovered a valid species he named the birds for the state in which he found them. Although his original drawing bears the penciled legend: "Louisiana Warbler, male & female, *Sylvia Ludovicianna*, Drawn from nature by John J. Audubon, James Pirrie Esq's plantation, August 4, 1821." By a legend in ink, and obviously written many years later, the original Latin names were struck out and *Sylvia Childreni* substituted, thereby naming the warblers for John George Children of the British Museum and secretary of the Royal Society of London. These strange birds proved not to be a new species, as Audubon later acknowledged, but the young of the little yellow warbler, or "wild canary" of our day, in immature plumage.

Nor was this the only "new" warbler the budding naturalist erred in identifying in these days of combing the Feliciana swamps. One of his early and very beautiful plates in the magnificent collection of hand-colored engravings is one that bears the name of the Blue-green Warbler, so named by Alexander Wilson. Audubon at this time closely followed the Scot's second and third volume in his descriptions of birds, and had Wilson's bird in mind when he visited a certain swamp not far from *Oakley*. His excursion to this happy hunting ground was made one August Sunday in company with his constant companion Joseph Mason and is best told in his own words:

We left this morning after an early breakfast to go and explore a Famous lake about 5½ miles from this where we were to find (as told) great many Very fine Birds—the walk to it was pleasant being mostly through rich Magnolia Woods. We killed Two Wood Ducks in a Small pond that we had to leave on a/c of the depth of the Hole, but that were exceedingly wellcome to Two *Red Shouldered Hawks* that Carried them off in our Sight—these Last were the only Birds of this Kind that I have seen at this season in this part of Louisiana

We saw a singularly rich gold Spider that finding a Horse fly just entangled in her Net move it out in a stream and at the same time rolling the fly untill the whole Likened the appearance of a Small oblong ball of White Silk, the Spider then returned to the center of its Net—No doubt this is the Way of preserving the flies when the Spider is Not hungry.

When we left the ridges We at Once saw a diferent Country in aspect, the Tall White & Red Cypress being the Principal Trees in Sight with their thousand Knees raising Like so Many Loafs of Sugar —Our eagerness to see the Lake engaged us to force Our Way through Deep still Mud & Watter—We came to it and saw several Large Alligators Sluggishly Moving on the Surface, Not in the Least disturbd by our Approach.

Saw a White Ibis on a Log where it sat a Long time arranging its feathers using its scythe Shaped bill very dexterously; Could have Killed it but having No boat and afraid of Sending a Dog into the Lake Left it setting peaceably.

I was fortunate in Shooting a Male of the *Green blue Warbler*— One Week ago I had shot one but Never could fine it, there was at this time five in Company, and Within only a few feet of Me. Mr. Willson shot a femelle on the Cumberland River, and Never any more; about two Months since I Discovered One in a small Swamp Nearer Mr. Pirrie—these birds sing sweetly, and no doubt breed here. Look much like the *blue Yellow Back* Warbler and hang downwards by the feet like these and the Titmouse. Saw only the One I shot to day and having as much as I knew I could Well draw before they would be Spoiled by the heat of the Weather returned to the House.

Back at *Oakley*, Audubon closely examined his rare bird and after taking its measurements decided he had indeed secured a male of the Blue-green Warbler. He compared his with the description given by Wilson, noting: "All the Colors brighter & stronger than Willson's femelle, every Tail feather having White on their inner vane except the Two Midle Ones." He then triced it up on wires and began his drawing. He indicated its position on the branch of a small plant known to the country people as the Spanish Mulberry, and later Joseph Mason drew in the stalk and its dense whorl of globular purple berries. This bird, which appeared on his forty-ninth plate, was named, following Wilson's terminology, the Blue-green Warbler, *Sylvia rara.*

For many years Wilson's and Audubon's Blue-green Warbler was another mystery bird, finally other ornithologists decided that the little bluish-green bird was nothing more nor less than the young of the cerulean warbler in immature plumage.

This cypress swamp, which yielded so many ornithological treasures to Audubon, was near the Mississippi river and surrounded a body of water called Alligator Lake. It proved a veritable rendezvous for warblers of all kinds and the following Sunday Audubon and Mason were again there and busy collecting, and another "new" warbler was secured. When its likeness was published it bore the distinguished name of Bonaparte. The bird depicted came near bearing a more distinguished name . . . that of Audubon's wife. He tells of securing it:

> Arrived at the Swamp and there saw a great Number of Small Birds. Shot a beautiful *new* Species of Fly Catcher *Musciapa*, which I will give you Tomorrow when my Drawing of it Will be finished. I had the pleasure of seeing Two that appeared Much alike, they were quarelling when I shot at them but fell only One—cannot say More of this truly handsome birds having never seen any thing of them before to Day.
>
> My Litle fly Catcher had only one wing touch^{d} When I presented myself to pick it up, it spread its Tail & open its Wings and Snap its bill about 20 times in the Manner that Many of this Genus do when they seize a fly, particularly those that are Nearest the Standard of the Genus. I seldom have seen a bird of Such Small size With so Large & Beautiful an Eye. I took it home to James Pirrie's Esqr and had the pleasure of drawing it While a live and full of Spirit, it often Made off from My fingers by starting Suddenly and unexpectedly, and then would hop around the room as quick as a Carolina or Winter Wren would have done, uttering its *tweet tweet tweet* all the while, and Snapping every time I took it up. I put it in a Cage for a few Moments but it obstinatly forced the fore part of its head through the Lower part of the Wires and I relieved it by Confining it in my hat for the Night anxious to see more of its movements . . . My drawing an excellent one—finding this Bird very Weak in the Morning Killed it and put it in Whiskey.

It was Audubon's intention to first call this little bird the "Cypress Swamp Fly Catcher." Then he considered naming it for his wife, but later, when in Liverpool, proposed calling it after the Rathbones, a family of gentlefolk who befriended him when he first went to England to have his *Birds of America* published. Finally he named it for Charles Lucien Bonaparte, prince of Canino and Musigano, a nephew of the great Napoleon, the same Prince Bonaparte who continued Wilson's *American Ornithology* after the Scotsman's death. The titled name was not destined to live on a warbler in our ornithological literature . . . for the little bird Audubon secured in the Feliciana cypress swamp proved to be the young of the Canada warbler in immature plumage and not a new species.

In the published plate the bird is represented perched on a branch of the magnolia together with a cone of its ripe red fruit. This part of the drawing was executed by Joseph Mason, as a lead pencil notation sets forth on the original painting. In after years Mason complained of the effort it cost him to faithfully portray the carmine-colored seeds, a labor of four days, and the fact that Audubon had not given him on the engraved plate the promised credit for drawing the plant.

However, Audubon's errors in identification had their counterbalance in the new species he did add to American ornithology during his initial stay in the Feliciana country. One afternoon, it was the second of October, Audubon and Mason were returning to *Oakley* after a bird foray in adjoining woods when their attention was attracted to a small bird hopping along the trunk of a prostrate ironwood tree that lay close to a fence surrounding one of Squire Pirrie's cotton fields. The bird had a long tail and Audubon, ever on the alert for a "non-descript," shot it, so he asserts. He found the bird had the shape, color, and movements of the Carolina wren and something of the nervousness of the smaller house wren, but lacked the quickness of motion and sprightliness of these birds, and had proportionately a much longer tail with white spots on the outer feathers.

Upon his return to *Oakley* the new bird was triced up on wires and a drawing begun, the naturalist using as perch a piece of bark of the ironwood tree and some of its leaves. That the identity of the bird puzzled him is indicated by his pen notes on the original drawing. He first believed it belonged to the creeper family, and named it accordingly: "Long-tailed creeper, Male, *Certhia*. Length, 5 inches; breadth, 6½ inches; tongue, slender, jagged; mouth, yellow; rump feathers white beneath with central spots; tail feathers 10 inches. Drawn from Nature by John J. Audubon, Bayou Sarah, Octr 2." Added, but in different ink, and evidently at a much later date, are the words "Bewick's long-tailed wren," and the figures "19" are written over the "2" of the date, which indicates that Audubon later discovered his error in confusing this bird with the brown creeper and recognized it as a true wren. When he was in England he renamed it *Troglodytes Bewickii*, giving the ornithological world the well-known Bewick's wren, so christened in honor of Thomas Bewick, the celebrated wood engraver, whose *British Birds* is a standard work. Audubon ungrudgingly admired the aged English artist and, when he visited him in his Newcastle-upon-Tyne home, designated Bewick "the first woodcutter in the world."

There is another story, however, regarding the discovery and naming of this little bird—probably the correct one. It comes from Joseph Mason who complained that it was he who collected the bird, that Audubon had then pronounced it a *non-descript*, and had promised to name it for him by calling it "Mason's hive-creeper."

3

Three of Audubon's better known and more admired plates of American birds show snakes worked into the composition. One portrays brown thrashers battling a blacksnake intent on reaching an egg-filled nest; another shows a pair of chuck-will's-widows with a coral snake, while the third is his famous plate of mockingbirds defending their nest from a coiled open-mouthed rattlesnake.

The mockingbird picture was drawn in the Feliciana country. The artist selected for his floral composition a low bush covered with the flowers of the yellow jasmine, the very setting where he had found a mockingbird's nest. Audubon made a very spirited drawing of a scene he had witnessed. The parent birds, reinforced by a second pair, were shown battling a huge rattlesnake which had writhed its way into the low yellow-spangled jasmine bush with sinister designs on the blue-white eggs in the woven-grass cradle. This dramatic treatment later got Audubon into hot water—water almost as hot as that cooked up when George Ord accused him of stealing Wilson's Mississippi kite. It was the inclusion of the rattlesnake in Audubon's mockingbird picture, and an article on rattlesnakes written by him while in Edinburgh, that gave the editor of a Philadelphia magazine an opportunity to brand Audubon with the equivalent of the epithet used so freely during the strenuous Theodore Rooseveltian days . . . nature fakir!

While in the Scottish capital in 1827, seeking a publisher for his collection of bird drawings, Audubon wrote a paper on the habits of the rattlesnake, a reptile of great interest to the scientists abroad. His paper was read before the members of the Wernerian Society, and the mockingbird drawing which showed the snake with wide opened mouth and exposed fangs, was exhibited at the same time. Later Audubon's paper was published in an Edinburgh scientific journal and when a copy of the Scottish publication reached Philadelphia, Dr. Thomas P. Jones, editor of the *Franklin Journal and American Mechanic's Magazine*, picked up the article which was entitled "Notes on the Rattlesnake, by John James Audubon, F. R. S. E., M. W. S., &c," and ran it in his publication for the benefit of readers in America. Enemies of Audubon, among them George Ord, you may be sure, thereupon became conspicuously active and vigorously attacked a number of the statements made by Audubon.

In consequence, Editor Jones, in the following number of his periodical, denounced the very article he had "lifted" from the Edinburgh publication as a "tissue of the grossest falsehoods ever attempted to be palmed off on the credulity of mankind," and added that the "romances of Audubon rival those of Munchausen, Mandeville, or even Mendez de Pinto, in total want of truth, however short they may fall of them in the amusement they afford." It certainly wouldn't do for the Philadelphians to allow this French "trader-naturalist" to oust Alex. Wilson as America's Number One bird-man!

One mark upon which the critics focused their shafts was the statement which Audubon made with a wealth of detail, that he had seen a large rattlesnake climb a tree, pursue, capture, and kill by constriction, a gray squirrel, then devour it. The critics denied that a rattlesnake would, or could, climb a tree! Nor was criticism confined to the American side of the Atlantic. An English naturalist named Charles Waterton declared that not only was Audubon's drawing of a rattlesnake in his mockingbird plate a monstrosity, but he ridiculed the artist's representation of the shape of the reptile's fangs. Audubon had shown them *re*curved at the tips. According to Waterton, the fangs of poisonous snakes were always curved like a scythe, with their points bent inwards.

Audubon's journal sheds some light on the rattlesnake controversy. At *Oakley*, under date of August 25, he wrote he finished drawing a very fine specimen of a rattlesnake that measured five feet, seven inches in length, weighed six and a quarter pounds, and had ten rattles.

> Anxious to give it such a Position as I thought would render it most interesting to Naturalists, I put it in that position which that Reptile generally takes when on point to Inflict a Most severe wound—I have examined the Fangs of Many before and their position along the Superior Jaw Bones, but had never seen one Shewing the Whole exposed at the same time having before this thought that the probability was that those Laying Inclosed below the Upper one in Most Specimen Were to Replace these upper one Which I thought might drop periodically as the Animal Changes its Skin and Rattles—however on Dissection of these from the Ligament by Which they are fixed to the Jaw bones I found them Strongly and I think permanently attached & as follows—Two Superior Next the upper Like (I speak of one side of the Jaw only) connected Well together at the bases & running parrallel their Whole Length. They had appartures on the upper & Lower side of their bases to receive the Venom connectivly and the discharging one a short distance from the Sharp points on the inner part of the fangs—the Two next Fangs about one quarter of an Inch below connected and running on the Lower Side of each and the one at the point that issues the venom to the Wound—the 5th rather smaller is also about a quarter of an Inch below, Lonely appertures as in the Secondarius the scales of the Belly to Under part of the Mouth where they finished Numbered 170 and 22 from the vent to the tail—My Drawing I Hope Will give you a good Idea of a Rattle Snake although the Heat of the weather Would not permit me to Spend More than 16 hours at it.

This entry proves the thoroughness of Audubon's study at this period of nature's ways and her creatures and is all the more remarkable when it is considered that this man, so conversant with the habit of snakes, could have made the error he did in his written article on the rattlesnake where he confused the habits of the blacksnake, or blue racer, with those of the rattlesnake.

Audubon's statement that rattlesnakes climbed trees resulted in an acrimonious controversy a century ago. Ord and Waterton maintained that rattlesnakes never climbed trees! Others championed Audubon and affirmed that rattlesnakes did just that! A century later, in 1929, at *Waverly*, a plantation not five miles from *Oakley*, George M. Lester, while gathering figs from a tree in his yard, discovered a large rattlesnake on a limb of the fig tree twenty feet from the ground, and within arm's length of where he was gathering the fruit. It would be difficult indeed to convince Mr. Lester that the snake he killed could not climb a tree!

Waterton's vehement assertion that a rattlesnake does not have recurved fangs has been adequately refuted by Professor Herrick, who exhibited a six-foot Florida specimen which had the same recurvature of the fangs shown in Audubon's painting of a Louisiana rattlesnake. One champion who hastened to the defense of Audubon when he was being heckled by Waterton for his snake story, was the Reverend John Bachman of Charleston, who in later years joined with the American Woodsman in producing *The Viviparous Quadrupeds of America.* Doctor Bachman wrote in his "Defense of Audubon":

> Audubon has been rudely assailed about a 'snake story,' but Waterton has given us several stories that fairly fill us with wonder and dismay. Instead of a contemptible rattlesnake, as thick as a man's arm, he tells us of a great "Boa" which he encountered in his den. Dashing headlong on the Boa, he pierced him with his lance and tying up his mouth carried him as a trophy to the British Museum. The snake was so large that it took three men to carry it, and so heavy that they had to rest ten times.
>
> He gives another snake story—a snake ten feet long. Waterton was alone. He seized him by the tail, the snake turned around and came after him with open mouth, seeming to say "What business have you to meddle with my tail!" In this emergency, he put his fist in his hat, and rammed it down the snake's throat. Suffering the snake to wind itself around his body, he walked home in triumph . . . I am somewhat indifferent with regard to Mr. Waterton and his marvelous book; but it is well for the public to knew who this champion of truth is, that comes to accuse the American Ornithologist of exaggeration.

Little did Audubon suspect on that peaceful August day when he spent sixteen hours making a truthful drawing of the rattlesnake and its oddly-pointed fangs what a commotion its likeness would create a dozen years later. "My amiable Pupil Miss Eliza Pirrie also drew the same Snake," adds Audubon to his detailed account of the rattler's dental arsenal. "It is With Much pleasure that I now Mention her

Name expecting to remember often her sweet disposition and the Happy Days spent near her."

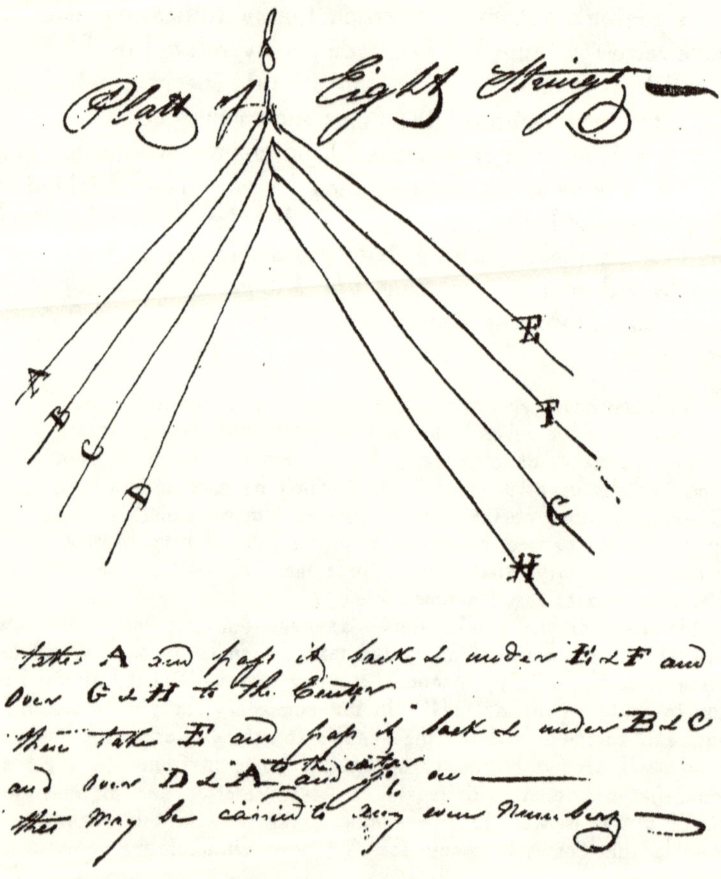

When at Oakley plantation Audubon taught Eliza Pirrie, among other things, how to plait hair. He drew a diagram in his journal, illustrating the necessary passes to make when making a braid of eight strands of hair, and his directions read:

"Take A and pass it back and under E & F and over G & H to the center.

"Then take E and pass it back and under B & C and over D & A to the center and so on—

"This may be carried to any even number."

CHAPTER 13

Shadows On Oakley

SUMMER days at *Oakley* passed swiftly and joyously. But as summer waned Audubon's pleasure at mentioning his fair pupil's name, sweet disposition, and the delightful hours spent in her company underwent a marked change during the last of the four months he and Joseph Mason lived at the beautiful Feliciana plantation home. The sunlight of cheer and light-heartedness that bathed *Oakley* was obscured by a cloud which shadowed friendship and put an abrupt end to lessons in music, dancing, and drawing.

Eliza Pirrie fell ill with a fever and a neighboring physician was called in attendance. Enamoured of the young lady's charms, Dr. Ira Smith looked with suspicion and envy on the undeniably attractive artist; so his first professional edict was an absolute ban on all drawing lessons for several months. He permitted the patient to eat any and everything pleasing her fancy, with the result, according to Audubon, Miss Eliza suffered several relapses of fever. The physician's mandates were strictly observed, however, as far as lessons were concerned. The tutor was not permitted to see his pupil during the convalescent period except at appointed times and hours. Doctor Smith was likewise successful in keeping John P. Colt, a young lawyer from Saint Francisville, also in love with the fair Eliza, away from the plantation home. The fact that his morning hours were not employed with lessons did not incommode the teacher in the least. To him it simply meant free and uninterrupted days in the magnolia woods and cypress swamps.

On the tenth of October, and for the first time since leaving New Orleans, Audubon sent his wife some money. She had written him several sharp letters on the subject, outlining her destitute circumstances, so he applied to Mrs. Pirrie for one hundred dollars of the amount due him for lessons he had given Eliza. This financial demand was the immediate cause of strained relations between the mistress of *Oakley* and the artist, for Audubon insisted on being paid for the first ten days of the illness of his pupil, although she could not attend lessons.

Mrs. Pirrie declined to honor the bill and there was an instant clash of temperaments—Gallic vs. Scot—for the mother insisted that the artist should not look for payment for work not performed. Audubon angrily persisted in his demand, whereupon Mrs. Pirrie summarily dismissed him.

Audubon was unwilling to leave *Oakley* at that time and pleaded that he and Mason be allowed to remain a week or ten days longer in the rôle of guests. Mrs. Pirrie, although feeling that Audubon had been unfair and unappreciative in his demands, agreed to his proposal, and the artist began collecting his scattered notes on birds, checking up on his drawings, and comparing what he had learned of the birds in the field with the printed matter found in Alexander Wilson's work. He recorded in his journal his "astonishment at the great many errors" found in the Scotsman's account of the life history of the various species he had the opportunity of studying while in the Feliciana parish.

The time for departure was set for Sunday, October 20, when the river steamer *Ramapo* would leave Bayou Sarah for its regular run down the river to New Orleans. Audubon worked at his notes late into the night but during the day he roamed the nearby woods for additional species of birds.

Upon leaving the fair Feliciana country, consumed with passionate regret, and while the paddle-wheels of the *Ramapo* were churning the brown waters of the Mississippi, Audubon took up his neglected journal and wrote in it his version of what had happened at *Oakley*.

As his own words are an index to his complex character, they are best passed on exactly as he wrote them:

"This morning about 8 o'clock We Left Mr. Pirrie's Plantation for New Orleans, which Place we Reached on Monday the 21st. at 2 o'clock but before I alight in this city, I must Poise Myself and give you a Short a/c of the Most

Remarkable Incident that have taken Place With us during our Stay at *Oakley* the Name of James P. Plantation.

"Three Months out of the 4 we lived there Were Spent in peaceful tranquility; giving regular Daily Lessons to Miss P. of Drawing, Music, Dancing, Arithmetick, and Some trifling acquirement such as Working Hair &c Hunting and Drawing My Cherished Birds of America; Seldom troublesome of Disposition, and not Caring for or Scarcely ever partaking or Mixing with the constant Trancient Visitors at the House. *We* were called *good Men*, and now & then received a Chearing Look from the Mistress of the House and *sometimes* also one Glance of Approbation of the More Circumspect Miss Eliza.

"Governor Robertson Visited us and then I formed a Still Stronger Opinion of that Man agreableness and Strength of Mind than I had before & Consider him as a really true Philosopher of the Age. Amongst our other Visitors the Brother of Henry *Clay*, Mr. John Clay of this City, I found a good agreable Man to all appearance. A Rather Singular Caracter Rich Wam Brand also spent some days at the House and Married in the Neighborhood—All Kindly Polite to us.

"Miss P. had no Particular admirers of her beauties but several very anxious for her fortune among Which a Certain Mr. Colt a Young Lawer Who appeared quite Pressing although Very uncivilly Received at First.

"Mr. P. a Man of Strong Mind but extremely Weak of Habit and degenerating sometimes into a State of Intoxication, remarkable in its Kind, Never associating With any body on such occasions and Exhibiting all the Madman's Actions Whilst under its Paroxism. When Sober; truly a good Man a *Free Mason*, generous and Entertaining—his wife Raised to opulence by Dint of Industry, an Extraordinary Woman—Generous I believe but giving Way for Want of understanding at times to the Whole force of her Violent Passions—fond of quizing her husband and Idolatring her Daughter Eliza.

"This Daughter Eliza of age 15 Years of a good form of *body*, not Handsome of face, proud of her Wealth and of herself cannot well be too Much fed on Praise—and God

Knows how hard I tryed to Please her in Vain—and God Knows also that I have vowed Never to try as much again for any Pupil of Mine—as usual *I* had to do 2/3 of all *her* Work. of Course her progresses Were Rapid to the Eyes of every body and truly astonishing to the eyes of some good observers.

"A Sister Mrs Smith I cannot say that I Knew or rather I never did Wish to Know; of Temper Much like her Mother, of Heart Not so good Yet God forgive her the Injuries She did me.

"her Husband a good, Honest Man and Citizen Viewed all the faults of her he Wedded With Patient Kindness and felt his reward through his own Correctness of Conduct—I admired him Much.

"About a Month before We Left Miss P. was taken seriously Ill, and as she was the only remaining Child unmarried and the 2nd. of 7, 5 of which had died in the Course of a very few years, Much fears were entertained of the Survival of this One, and No doubt Much too Much Care Was taken of her; Kept in bed Long after She was convalescent and Not permitted to leave her room for a Long time She became, Low of flesh and Crabed of Speech, every thing Must have gone on the Smoothest way to hurt her feelings. Her Phisician the *Man she Loved* Would not permit her reassuming her Avavocations near Me and told the Mother that it would be highly Improper Miss Eliza Should Draw, Write &c untill some Months; but that She Might Eat any thing Pleasing to her fancy—this fancy Was not Confined into small bounds. She Eat so plentifully of everything that could be procured that she had several Relapses of fevers. I saw her during this Illness at appointed hours as if I was an Extraordinary ambassador to some Distant Court—had to Keep the utmost Decorum of Manners and I believe Never Laughed Once With her the Whole 4 Months I was there.

"We perceived however during all this While that a remarkable Coolness had taken place from the Ladies toward us, seldom seeing any of them except at table and then With Looks far from Chearing My Spirits that Were during the Whole of My Stay there unfortunately very Low. Mrs Smith took an utter dislike to Me and one day While I was engaged in finish a Portrait of Mrs P. begun by her Daughter Eliza, Mrs S. addressed the Work and Me in the grossest Words of Insult, and afterwards Never Looked Directly at Me.

"She Busted at another time in a ridiculous Laugh at table. When her good Husband Interfered and told her She ought to Make Me some Amends for her Conduct—I Left the table unwilling to hear any More of this. Saturday Came and a Settlement of Money Matter Was Necessary. I charged for 10 days of Miss E. Ill time. My Bill was 204$ and Mrs P. in a perfect Rage fit told me that I Cheated her out of 20$. My Coolness sufered all her Vociferations to flow, I simply told her our formal mutual Engagements on that score —I figured the Bill and sent it to Mr P. Who Was then Labouring under one of his unfortunate fits of antoxication.

"He came to see Me, apologized in the Kindest Manner for his Lady's Conduct; Ordered his Son in Law Mr Smith to pay Me, and shewed Me all the Politeness he is possessed of. Mr Smith Congratulated My Firmness of Acting—and All Went on pretty well that Day.

"The Ladies early that Morning Left for St. Francisville Without bidding us any adieu, and expected that on their Return at Night We would be gone; this however was a disappointment for Mr *Pirrie* requested We should Stay, representing how easily We could reach the Steam Boat the Next Morning before her time of departure in the Course of this Afternoon. Mrs P. sent for Joseph and presented him with a full suit of fine clothes of her Deceased son—to the acceptation of Which I positively refused to acquiese, Knowing too Well how far some gifts are talked of—and Not Willing that My Companion should diminish the Self Respect I think Necessary for every Man to Keep towards himself however poor, when able by *Talents*, Health and Industry to Procure his own Necessities.

"Unfortunately there was Much Company in the evening. Sometimes after supper We Left our Room where Mr Pirrie and Mr Smith had Joined us on leaving the Table to go and bid our farewell to the female Part of the familly. My Entry before the Circle posessed none of that Life and Spirit I formerly Enjoyed on Such Occasion. I would gladly wished to be excused from the fatiguing Ceremonies, yet I walkd in followed by Joseph and approaching to Mrs. P. bid her good bye as simply as ever any Honest Quaker Did, touchd Slightly Mrs Smith's Hand as I boughed to her. My Pupil Raised from the Sopha and Expected a Kiss from Me—but None Were to be disposed off, I pressed her Hand and With a general Salute to the Whole Made My Retreat, No doubt Much to the great Suprise of Every one Present Who had heard those very Women Speak Constantly before of Me in Highest Terms of Respects, scarcely Deigning to Look at me Now. As Joseph Was following me he received a Voley of farewells from the 3 Ladies of the House put after him Ridiculously to Affect Me. but the Effect Was lost and it Raised a Smile on My Lips. We Joined again the Two good Husbands in our Lodging Chamber—they remained with us untill bed time; Cordially parted With us, retired to repose without Joining the Company.

"Day Light of Sunday Saw us Loading our Trunks and Drawing Table. Vaulted our Sadles and left this abode of unfortunate Opulence without a single Sigh of regret.

"Not so with the sweet Woods around us, to leave them was painfull, for in them We allways enjoyed Peace and the sweetest pleasures of admiring the greatest of the Creator in all his Unrivalled Works. I often felt as if anxious to retain the fill of My lungs with the purer air that Circulate through them Looked With pleasure and sorrow on the few Virgin blooming Magnolias—the 3 Colored Vines and as We desended the Hills of St Francisville bid that farewell to the Country, that under diferent Circumstances We Would have Willingly divided With the Ladies of *Oakley*."

Audubon's first New Orleans studio in Barracks street near Royal, where he and Joseph Mason lived before going to Feliciana.

"The Little House in Dauphine Street," New Orleans, where Audubon, Lucy, and the boys lived and where some of the drawings for the "Birds" were made. Old 55, now 505, Dauphine street.

LEVIN WAILES

MRS. WAILES

Audubon's black chalk portraits of four members of the family of Levin Wailes. The drawings were made in Natchez, Mississippi, in 1822, when the two sons accompanied him on bird forays.

EDMUND HOWARD WAILES

B. L. C. WAILES

Book Six

The Itch of A Wandering Foot

"Very much fatigued with New Orleans—where I cannot shoot two birds with one stone."

JOHN JAMES AUDUBON, in his journal,
February 23, 1821.

CHAPTER 14

The Little House in Dauphine Street

RAIN was falling and it was quite cool for that time of the year when the *Ramapo* discharged its passengers at the riverfront near the French Market. It was late of this October Monday afternoon when Audubon, with his long hair flying in the breeze, strode along the streets of New Orleans to the crockery store of his friend Pamar. On board the boat that carried him and Mason back to the Crescent City, Audubon had noticed with amused chuckles the amazement with which fellow passengers had looked upon his odd, unkempt appearance, particularly his unbuckled brown hair. As he walked along the narrow *banquettes* that carried him in the direction of Pamar's Magazine street home he noted that the effect of his free flowing hair was even more startling in the city.

"My Large Loose Dress of whitened Yellow Nankeen and the unfortunate *Cut* of My features made me Decide to be dressed as soon as Possible Like other folks," he set down in his journal that night, "and I had my *Chevelure*[1] parted from my head."

The family Pamar gave the naturalist a warm welcome and this raised his spirits considerably, for he was still smarting under what he considered indignities heaped upon him that last night at *Oakley*. After dinner was over he made a contract with a relative of Mrs. Pamar, one Lewis Adam, a well-known hunter, and arranged that the fowler would secure bird specimens for him. Audubon knew that he must remain in town seeking pupils and believed that between lessons he would draw the birds Adam would supply.

In the *rue Ste. Anne, No.* 29, he rented *une chambre garnie*, and soon he and Mason had their belongings removed

[1]Horse's mane.

from the *Ramapo* and installed temporarily in a furnished room whose windows looked out upon the *Place d'Armes*, as Jackson Square was then called. There they lived for three days while Audubon looked about town for a suitable studio and home for himself and family, for, elated over the ornithological success of his summer in the Feliciana country, he had resolved to reside in New Orleans permanently and in the Crescent City complete his growing work on the birds of America. He had notified his wife of this intention by letter, again urged her to relinquish her position in Louisville and join him in the city near the mouths of the Mississippi.

His search for a suitable studio was thorough. Little cardboard signs dangled from hundreds of *galeries* in the old part of town proclaiming "*Pension*," "*Pension Privée*," "*Chambres Garnies*," or simply "*Chambres à Louer*." The finding of suitable quarters was not a simple process for he had developed, with a few dollars in his pocket, a most finical taste for the right sort of a habitation. Up and down the narrow streets of old New Orleans he strode. He examined rooms in the street named in honor of the Duc du Maine, left-handed son of Louis XIV, then called *rue du Maine*, but today the preposition has become merged with the noun, and new New Orleans has a "Dumaine" instead of a Main street. His search was pursued in *rue de Ursulines*, *rue Royale*, *rue de Hôpital*, Chartres, Saint Philip, and Burgundy streets, and he entered all places in the *Vieux Carré* carrying the dangling rent signs of that period. The house-hunting journey even took him to the *rue Amour* of hectic memory. He gave wide berth only to Barracks street and Madame Louise's none too clean abode. Then he wandered the length of Dauphine street and there, at number 55, between Saint Louis and Toulouse, he found a suitable small house which he rented for seventeen dollars a month. Three days after his return from the Feliciana country he was established in "the little house in Dauphine street."

Aware of the general shabbiness of his appearance, he visited a tailor and was measured for a new suit. That much accomplished he impatiently awaited the completion of the outfit which was to render him presentable when drumming up pupils. The shearing of the "horse's mane" was not a complete mowing of his hirsute adornment—it was more in the nature of a trimming, for the chestnut locks still curled on his shoulders. Audubon had no intention of ever appearing like a shorn lamb.

He found Euphrosine Pamar much improved in music and manners and recounts that he enthusiastically complimented her upon the newly acquired talents. He made no other calls on erstwhile friends—his new suit was still in the process of making and he felt chagrined when men with whom he had been on friendly terms during his former stay in New Orleans deliberately cut him as he strolled along the levee, where the *ton* gathered daily. They "passed *Me* with out uttering a word to Me and *I as Willing* to shun those Rascalls," he recorded indignantly in his journal when he returned to Dauphine street.

For several days Audubon and Mason found time lying heavily on their hands. Each morning the market was unsuccessfully combed for game in the hope that some bird fit for drawing would be found, consequently Audubon expressed himself more than once as being greatly fatigued with his idleness and vowed that a month of such inaction "would render him sick of life."

In the Dauphine street studio he carefully went over his now heavy collection of bird drawings, listed and then appraised them.

> Since I left Cincinnati . . . I have finished 62 drawings of *Birds* & *Plants*, 3 quadrupeds, 2 snakes, 50 portraits of all kinds, and My Father *Don Antonio*. Have made *out to Live in humble Comfort* with Only My Talents and Industry, without *One Cent* to begin on at My Departure.
>
> I have Now 42 Dollars, health, and as much anxiety to pursue My Plans of Accomplishing My Collection as Ever I had and Hope God Will Grant Me the same Powers to Proceed.
>
> My Present Prospects to Procure Birds this Winter are More Ample than ever, being now Well Known by the Principal hunters on Lake Borgne, Barataria, Pontchartrain, and the Country of Terre a Boeuf.

Audubon's reference to his portrait of "my father *Don Antonio*" had to do with a large watercolor portrait he had begun just before leaving for the Feliciana country. It was the likeness of a Spanish monk, known to the pious French Créoles of New Orleans as Père Antoine, the same priest, Father Antonio de Sedella, who first came to the city in 1789, when Louisiana was dominated by Spain. He came and left under peculiarly inauspicious and unpleasant circumstances for the priest claimed he had been sent to New Orleans direct from Madrid as an emissary of the Holy Inquisition. Under his supervision began and ended the only attempt to introduce the Inquisition into the province.

Years later Père Antoine returned to New Orleans, but with the intention, he announced, of purifying the Orleanians with holy water instead of holy fire. He became an independent priest, was not particularly liked by the Jesuits and members of other orders of the Roman Catholic Church, and lived like an anchorite in a rude hut built of planks at the base of a tall, swaying date palm that rose from a lot he owned in Orleans Street.

Audubon was evidently deeply interested in this remarkable holy character of New Orleans, even though he professed hatred of the Catholic Church and its emissaries, and he watched Père Antoine closely whenever the priest appeared in the streets dispensing alms from a purse that dangled from his girdle. The little ones of the French Quarter followed him as children in the legend traipsed after the Pied Piper of Hamelin. These small folk would kneel in the mud of the unpaved streets to receive the monk's blessing and would never fail to tease for *lagniappe* in the shape of *picayunes* or *quartees*, small coins the good monk carried and which he never refused.

Needless to point out, so beloved a personage was a worthy subject for a popular portrait and, shortly after he was installed in the little house in Dauphine street, Audubon set to work on the likeness. This water color was apparently never finished to his satisfaction, for a year later we will find Audubon in Natchez reproducing the same picture in oils and sending the painting to Cuba so it could be hung in the Havana Cathedral.

When Père Antoine died in 1829 and was interred in the Saint Louis Cathedral, a great outpouring followed his remains to the last resting place. Among those in the long procession were the members of New Orleans Free Masonry, probably marking for the first time that Masons officially mourned the death of a Catholic priest. As word was whispered at the time that Father Antoine was himself a Free Mason and, as Audubon was a member of the craft, this may explain his peculiar interest in making the monk's portrait.

2

During his gunning expeditions about the city, Audubon watched with as much interest as he did in the spring the fall migration of members of the swallow tribe. He was still intent upon refuting the ridiculous theory that these birds hibernated in the mud at the bottom of waterbodies or in the muck of swamps and ooze of marshlands. He always carried a thermometer with him and when recording that October 30 was warm, he also set down: "Swallows Plenty and quite as gay as their flight in June—to find here those birds in abundance 3 months after they have left the Midle States, and to Know that they Winter Within 40 Miles in Multitudes is one of the Gratifications the Most Exquisite I ever Wishd to feel in Ornithological Subjects and that puts an complete *Dash* over *all* the Nonsense Wrote about their Torpidity during Cold Weather; No Man could ever have enjoyed the Study of Nature in her all Femine Bosomy Wild and errd so Wide."

3

When not out watching the swallows, Audubon was either working on the portrait of Père Antoine, canvassing the *Vieux Carré* for pupils, or worrying over the cut of his new clothes, while in far-off France his half-sister Rosa was plunged in grief. At *Les Tourterelles*, the du Puigaudeau home in Couëron, Anne Moynet Audubon, the *chere maman* of Jean Rabin's youth, suddenly died. She had left the villa *La Gerbetière* the year before to reside with her foster-daughter and she fell into her last sleep October 18, 1821. The once-pampered foster-son, however, knew nothing of this as he scurried about New Orleans intent upon birds.

Five years later we will find Audubon in England and

France—and then under the impression that his foster-mother is still alive! It seems incredible that Audubon should have remained so long in ignorance of her death, especially when we find him setting down in his journals and letters his impatience to be off to Nantes and Couëron just to hold her in his arms. At any mention of her in his diaries he always underscored the words which declared his nonceasing love for his doting *chere maman.*

Yet these are the facts and the Audubon private correspondence fails to throw any light upon this particular and peculiar phase of what The American Woodsman always termed the "enigma" of his life.

4

On a particularly bright and sunlit Sunday morning, a re-habilimented Audubon stepped forth from the door of the little house in Dauphine street and strolled along the Levee. So pleased was he with his appearance that he minutely described the figure he cut that Sabbath day:

Dressed all new, Hair Cut, my appearance altered beyond My expectations, fully as much as a handsome Bird is when robbed of all its feathering, the Poor thing Looks Bashfull dejected and is either entirely Neglected or Look[d] upon With Contempt; such was my situation Last Week—but When the Bird is Well fed, taken care of, sufered to Enjoy Life and dress himself, he is cherished again— Nai, admired! Such my situation this day—Good God, that 40 Dollars should thus be *enough* to Make a Gentleman! Ah, My Beloved Country When will thy Sons value more Intrinsectly each Brother's Worth? Never!!

That afternoon, following dinner at the Pamar home, he displayed his Feliciana drawings to the members of that family, and later called on John Clay and exhibited them to Mrs. Clay and a company of young ladies. The belles of the city were amused at the artist's words, expressions, gestures, manners, long hair, and particularly his accent, so he records with some glee that "he passed for a *German*" up to the time he took his leave. The company as a whole admired his bird pictures but he failed to secure the drawing pupils he had hoped to enroll as a result of his visit to the Clays.

The following morning he took stock of himself. This finished he determined on an exhibition of his drawings at a public place, "for I well recollect the effect of Lafontaine's Fable that says that a '*a l'oeuvre on connit L'Artizan.*' Unknown by most people here, I am like Many others who appear as advanturors, lookd on with Care, and Suspicion—but so Moves the World, and no doubt it is *Wright* it should be so."

Recalling the visit to *Oakley* of the wealthy builder William Brand, his marriage to Miss Anne Browder, a young lady of the Feliciana parish, and Brand's interest in his work on birds, Audubon called at Brand's home in quest of a pupil. He recorded: "Visited Rich Mrs. *Brand* was there very Politely received, 'Must Call again.' Mrs. Brand married a Large fortune, the Honey Moon is not yet *Set* and she looks well even on her Decline, promising full fullness bye & Bye."

The next day William Jr., a lad in his teens, and son of the builder by a former marriage, was enrolled as a pupil. Audubon was also promised that the young wife would also take up lessons in French and painting, for the second Mrs. Brand required culture. She had been reared on a Feliciana plantation and, beautiful though she was, her need of education was great. From the Brand home Audubon went to a college for young women but that visit was barren of result for, while his drawings were greatly admired, he found that another teacher in painting, one Torain, had arrived while he was in the Feliciana country and had enrolled many of the pupils Audubon had hoped to secure. It served to throw him into a sour mood, and he moped about the Dauphine street house for days without doing a thing. Each day at dawn he and Joseph would visit the market to look over the game displayed for sale, but the search was usually fruitless as far as finding new species was concerned.

One morning, while he was hurrying along the streets he met John Gwathmay, the former Louisville hotel keeper, who told Audubon he had sad news to impart, and announced the death of Mrs. Bakewell, Lucy's stepmother. The naturalist sped back to the little house in Dauphine street to record in his journal the passing of his step-mother-in-law, with whom he had never been on good terms . . . "My *Constant* Enemy . . . God forgive her faults."

Drawing lessons at the Brand, Dimitry, and Pamar homes, the addition of details to Father Antoine's portrait, and long walks in the outskirts of the city, to shoot specimens for his "Birds" and to watch migrating swallows, occupied his time for the recurring weeks. Financial returns from drawing lessons were slim, so Audubon renewed efforts to secure pupils at Mlle. Clothile Bornet's academy for young women at 173 Levee street. The exhibition of his work proved a failure, for the young ladies expressed themselves as being entirely prepossessed with the abilities of the rival artist Torain.

When finances had been reduced to copper cents—to picayunes—a young attorney named Joseph Hawkins called with an engraving, a copy of Vanderlyn's head of *Ariadne.* Would Mr. Audubon make a copy of it in colors? Mr. Audubon would indeed! A price of fifty dollars was agreed upon and in a few moments Audubon was making his pastels and water colors fly..

While Audubon was engaged on the copy of *Ariadne*, M. Basterop, painter for John Davis' celebrated Orleans street theatre, called and urged the naturalist to join him in painting a panorama of New Orleans. Even if money might be earned the proposition was declined and with many flourishes he penned: "My Birds, My Beloved Birds of America fill all my time, and nearly all my thoughts. I do not wish to see any other *Perspective* than the Last Specimen of them Drawed."

The first of the migrating waterfowl were filtering down to spend the winter in the hospitable Louisiana marshes when Audubon's hunter Gilbert sent him a gadwall duck to picture, but at the time the bird artist was racked by three worries: the non-arrival of his wife and two boys, for Lucy had finally agreed to abandon Louisville to try life with her husband in the far Southern city, although she had serious misgivings as to the success of the venture; second, a dearth of paying pupils who desired to be instructed in the rudiments of art, and third, a lack of specimens of waterfowl, for it had been Audubon's intention to devote most of his winter's work in depicting the various ducks, geese and shorebirds that wintered in Louisiana for his projected *Birds of America.* For this last purpose New Orleans was ideally situated, as migratory gamebirds from all sections of the continent sought the marshes adjacent to the city to escape the rigors of their northern nesting grounds.

A few of the birds he desired were brought to his studio, one being the white-fronted goose or speckle-belly, the first he had seen in the South, and as it had not been represented by Wilson in his work, Audubon lost no time in reproducing the bird in its natural colors. By the middle of November the migration of waterfowl from the snow and ice of the northlands was on in full force and many birds were sent to the little house in Dauphine street by the fowlers.

At this time Audubon drew a bird that has puzzled ornithologists for almost a hundred years. In his *Ornithological Biography* he states that he killed a Smew Merganser, or "White Nun," as the bird was termed by Wilson. Audubon thus established a southerly record for this Old World species, a bird that to this day has only been taken once or twice on the North American continent, one record being of a smew killed in Greenland, and the other reported from the Hudson Bay region. In his printed work Audubon wrote: "The only specimen secured by me was shot by myself on Lake Barataria, not far from New Orleans, in the winter of 1819. It was an adult female in fine plumage. How it had wandered so far south is an enigma to me; but having found it, I made a drawing of it on the spot."

Audubon's journal, under date of Wednesday, November 14, 1821, gives an entirely different account. It reveals he was not in the Barataria region that day, proving that he himself did not kill the mysterious bird, and that he could not have made the drawing "on the spot." The entry reads: "Gave my Lecons at Mrs. Brand's and Miss Delfosse's Work constantly the whole day—Drew a female of the *White Nun* or *Smew Merganser*—Weather Rainy & Raw."

In all probability the fowler Gilbert killed the bird, for it was he who hunted in the Barataria region, and Lake Barataria was better than a day's journey from the cobbled streets of old New Orleans. That night Audubon worked on his drawing of the alleged smew in the Dauphine street studio, finishing it by candlelight, and the result appears as the lower figure in his published plate, the one swimming on the surface of the water. But was it really a smew? Modern ornithologists think not, declaring the naturalist erred in his identification and confused this bird with the female of one of the other three species of mergansers common to North America.

He was distressed in mind the night he was at work on his bird, for he had received a letter from his wife that day, "the purport of Which Lower my Spirits very Considerably—alas, where does Comfort Keep herself now; retired certainly on a Desolate Rock unwilling to Cast even a Look on our Wretched Species . . . but My determination is bent and I Shall Philosophise Now on all things . . . Little Expectations of seeing My familly before the Latter Part of Winter."

Then he supped on bread and cheese and went to bed.

Next morning found him still downcast, but he worked throughout the day and finished three bird drawings after sunset by candlelight, worked at Vanderlyn's head of *Ariadne* and then turned to his journal admitting he was "Very Low of Spirits, Wished Myself off this Miserable Stage," and so to bed.

His principal worry was a lack of money, and he became so hard pressed that he swallowed his pride and sent Joseph to Doctor Heermann with a bill for one hundred dollars due him for the drawing lessons he had given the physician's wife in the spring. It will be remembered Audubon had cut quite a figure before the doctor's wife until the lady had given her drawing teacher what he described as a "rude dismissal." The physician accepted the bill and promised Mason he would pay it during the coming week. Four days later we find Audubon writing indignantly that he was "Shabbily used by Dr. Heermann—Who refused Paying My Well earned Bill."

His displeasure was dissipated that evening when hunter Gilbert appeared at the studio with a fine specimen of the whooping crane hanging over his shoulders. Audubon's delight knew no bounds and, although suffering from violent headaches and sore eyes, the next morning he was at his drawing board. He set the big white bird, which he first called a "Great Sand Hill Crane," in a position to allow the making of a life size reproduction. Three days later he had finished what is admitted to be one of the more noteworthy drawings of his amazing collection. It was the largest figure he pictured, and the whooping crane's peculiar attitude while spearing baby alligators with its long pointed bill, was made necessary by the limitations of the drawing paper.

During the days spent picturing the crane he found but little time to give Mrs. Brand her lesson, and even less to the instruction of Miss Fanchonette Delafosse in her home at 32 Maine street, so intent was he on his big bird drawing. Although he advised his journal, "My Spirits yet very Low," things were picking up for him in a monetary way. Attorney Hawkins paid him forty dollars on account for his copy of the head of *Ariadne*, and was profuse in his praise for the way Audubon had reproduced it in colors. An unexpected windfall was a hundred dollars he had sent his wife by Alexander Gordon, who had failed to deliver it, so Gordon returned it to him. Flush again, he paid out eight dollars for a portfolio which he purchased from Vigny, a New Orleans storekeeper. When he called on the fascinating Fanchonette Delafosse to give her a drawing lesson he found her as usual "beautiful and extremely agreable." Then he made arrangements for a check on a Philadelphia bank which he mailed to his wife at Louisville and urged her to make haste with her plans for moving down the river to New Orleans.

Giving lessons to regular pupils and working on bird portraits from specimens supplied by his hunters took up his time in the days that followed. They were without incident although he petulantly fretted over the non-arrival of his wife and sons, rushing down to the river front to inspect passengers filing off the gangplanks of every steamer that arrived from up-river ports.

5

While he was impatiently awaiting the arrival of his wife and boys he took to wandering about the city visiting others engaged in the profession of painting. One night, smarting under the treatment accorded him by some fellow-artists, he relieved his feelings by a lengthy entry in his journal:

I have but little time to spare at present to write of the Many Incidents connected with the Life I am forced to follow for My Maintainance and of Course hundreds of them are passed and forgotten although I am well assured that a Rearsal would at future period amuse My thoughts. *One* however so curious appeared Me this day that I Cannot let it escape—May you My Dear Sons reap some benefit from the details.

I am a Teacher of Drawing and have some Pupils My Style of giving Lessons and the high rate I charge for My Tuition have proved Me the Ill will of Every other artist in the City who Knows or had heard of My Maxims—I called on a *Bastard* of *Appollon* this day to see his *Labours.* I was unknown, tolerably well received and had the pleasure of seing the *Animal* in Action. I also heard his *Barkings* and saw his eyes gladening at the sight produced on the canvass before them. A Third unfortunate Dauber came in who it appeared Was an old acquaintance that Criticised at once on ease all that Was around us—as Every day arrivals by Sea and Land bring New hands to the bellows, the Names of Many Were Called forth and Mine amongst them—I Kept Myself and Waited & the following Picture was given Me Without any Varnishing, I assure You—"That Man Came No one knows from Whence—he goes thru the streets Like the Devil. I am told that he has as Many Pupils as he Wishes for and Makes a Wonderful quanity of What he Calls Portraits and Assures the good folks who employ him that in a few Months by his Method any One May become able Painter—and yet from What I am told the Man Never Drew but bought a set of handsome Drawings of Beasts Birds Flowers &c Which he Shews and Says are his own—all this a Lye and take in, While I Who Was Naturally Intended to Paint Teach &c an Without a Pupil or Portrait."

here I Took My Hat told the Gentleman where I resided and that I Would be happy to See him giving the Initials of My Name only for a Guide. From this Eloquent Member of the *Sans Culottes of the Trade,* I Moved pretty briskly . . . Not Well setled about the a/c of Myself I had so lately heard but thinking how strangely the good Man Will feel when *he* Calls on Me—if ever he does.

That was not the only humiliation to be suffered by Audubon that day. His sensitive nature received a further rebuff when walking along the street he came face to face with Eliza Pirrie. She did not deign to notice her former teacher, and Audubon hurried to the little house in Dauphine street to set his tumultuous thoughts to paper, and his journal entry for that day ends:

My Lovely Miss Pirrie of Oakley Passed by Me this Morning, but did not remember how beautifull I had rendered her face by Painting it at her Request with Pastelles; She Knew not the Man Who with the utmost patience and in fact attention *Waitted* on her Notions to please her—but thanks to My humble talents I can run the gantlet thru this World without her help.

His mind was still in its upset condition the next day and he endeavored to explain his feelings by a journal entry: "So Anxious Am I during the Whole of My present days to see My familly that My head is scarce at right With My Movements and yet I Must feel My sad Disapointments and retire to rest without the comfort of her so much Wanted Company." Before he laid the journal aside he added: "I saw to day a Work on Natural History with Colored Plates rather better than usual."

Audubon had not heard from his wife for a month—his record shows that it had been twenty-six days since he had received a letter—and three of the regular river steamboats had reached New Orleans from Louisville during that period. It was, therefore, a great relief to learn his beloved Lucy and the two boys were at last on their way South on the river boat *Rocket*, and that they were due to arrive within the next four or five days.

It was with a light heart that he called at the Brand home to give his lessons to the lady of the house. To his surprise he found Eliza Pirrie a caller. There was no snubbing of the former tutor by the lovely Miss Pirrie of *Oakley*. She was graciousness itself and, as Audubon expressed it, "the interview was Short, more friendly than I expected and We parted as if We Might see each other again With some Pleasure at some future Period."

Two days later Gilbert Broyart, his fowler from the Barataria region, sent Audubon a young trumpeter swan in its gray plumage. His delight over this acquisition knew no bounds and, although he worked at its drawing every spare moment, it was still unfinished on December 18, when his wife, with Victor and Johnny, debarked from the *Rocket*. The happy husband and father immediately took his family to the home of the hospitable Pamars for dinner, and later Mrs. Audubon and the boys moved into the little house in Dauphine street. The Audubons were reunited after a separation of fourteen months.

Lucy brought with her all her husband's early drawings,

including those he had made on the momentous flatboat journey down the Mississippi river the year before. Audubon reviewed his earlier efforts, those of the *Mill Grove* and Henderson days, with an appraising eye and "found them not so good as I expected them to be when compared with those drawn since last winter."

Audubon was correct in his own appraisement of his work. His summer in Feliciana had highly developed his ability as a delineator of bird life. Examination of his early work and that of after years makes unanimous the verdict that his best paintings were made during his Louisiana residence, particularly during the period spent in Feliciana, his happyland.

He was so elated over prospects of finishing his projected work in New Orleans that he painted for his wife their future in glowing and colorful words. Lucy wanted to believe the picture was not exaggerated so she withheld comment.

The day before Christmas Audubon's former partner Ferdinand Rozier arrived in New Orleans from Ste. Geneviève. He was invited to the studio home and for the first time in eleven years the two Frenchmen and Lucy Bakewell were again together. On Christmas day snow fell from daylight to noon and then froze hard. That night firecrackers were exploding in the streets but in spite of the cold there was cheer and warmth behind the doors and quaint shutters of the little house in Dauphine street.

The Whooping Crane redrawn from Audubon's plate.

CHAPTER 15

Failure in New Orleans

LUCY AUDUBON had been in New Orleans only a few days when she realized that her intuitions had been correct—the Crescent City would never prove to be the place for her talented, eccentric husband to make a permanent home or earn sufficient income to support her and their sons. But she remained quiet and hoped for the best. Victor and Johnny were sent to Professor Branard's academy, situated at Canal and Dauphine streets, where today a great dry goods emporium rears its lofty stories. There the two Audubon boys "received notions of geography, arithmetic, grammar, and writing, for six dollars per month each."

Audubon was kept busy searching out a sufficient number of drawing pupils to pay the house rent, tuition for the two boys, and provender for the family of five, for Joseph Mason was still one of the group. A sixth was added when Audubon encountered an old Kentucky acquaintance, one Matabon, "the famous flute player," wandering about the French market with his flute, but with no money with which to purchase a meal. Audubon, who had been in the same fix many times before, took the flutist home, gave him a bed and a share in the scanty meals. In consequence, night times in the little house in Dauphine street were musical intervals, for Lucy liked music as well as did her husband, sang and played creditably on the pianoforte, while the artist handled the flute and flageolet as competently as he did the violin. When Matabon left it was noted in the journal: "Mr. Matabon's departure is regretted by us all, and we shall sorely miss his beautiful music on the flute."

On Sunday, the last day but one in the year 1821, Audubon formed his New Year's resolution. He called into the studio Gilbert Broyart, the Créole fowler who regularly supplied the New Orleans market with game secured in the Barataria territory, and another market hunter named Robert, and made a solemn contract with them. Audubon had just completed a drawing of a brown thrasher, or as he then called it, a Ferruginous Thrush, and as he held the portrait up for inspection, told his wife and his two boys that he was resolved to draw ninety-nine other birds in the next ninety-nine days. He then completed his bargain with the hunters by agreeing to pay him one dollar per bird for each different bird the fowler would bring or send him. There was a proviso to the verbal contract . . . should the man with the gun not fulfill his part of the agreement, supply a different bird each day for the next hundred days, the gunman would receive only fifty cents each for the birds secured. Gilbert Broyart and Robert agreed, so Audubon set to work, drew the outlines of a cedar waxwing, and expressed the hope that the business of earning a living for himself, his wife, and children would not interfere too much with his work on the birds of America.

2

So ended the journal of 1820-21, whose pages have given us such a vivid and truthful self pen picture of the strange man whose name is reverenced today whenever birds are mentioned.

The succeeding journal, the one that detailed what occurred in 1822, while long in the possession of the Audubon family, was burned by a granddaughter. A number of censored extracts from it were published by Buchanan, copied from notes written by Mrs. Audubon, and many of these extracts have been republished by later biographers, who could not go to original sources. Late investigation proves many of these first published extracts underwent drastic doctoring.

According to Miss Maria Audubon's writings, the first entry in the 1822 diary reads: "Two months and five days have elapsed before I could venture to dispose of one hundred and twenty-five cents to pay for this book, that probably, like all other things in the world, is ashamed to find me so poor." According to what Lucy Audubon wrote Buchanan, this diary was made of thin, poor paper, and the entries were in keeping with his financial difficulties.

It has also been suggested that the naturalist probably set down some matters in this journal pertaining to his life, "even his puzzling background," which the Audubon family resolved, and successfully, to keep secret from the rest of the world.

In 1904 a number of Audubon enthusiasts, wishing more intimate details of his residence in New Orleans, particularly the exact location of the "little house in Dauphine street," endeavored to ascertain such matters from a granddaughter. Miss Maria Audubon's reply was that *all* the journals of the Louisiana period had been destroyed, and by her hands. Ruthven Deane wrote her that information had come to him to the effect that some of these writings had escaped the flames, to which Miss Audubon replied:

> The rather doubtful tone of the letter as to the destruction of the New Orleans journals is quite justified, most of the matter relating to that time *was* lost or destroyed years long gone, but the *one* I had and from which I quoted in "The Journals," had no number given to the house, I question whether "the little house in Dauphine street" had a number, and if it had whether the house has not long since been torn down. In the extreme poverty in which the family then were, it must have been truly a *little* and a *cheap* residence. I was quite truthful as to the destruction of the journals by fire so far as this one goes for *I burned it myself* in 1895. I had copied from it all I ever meant to give to the public, and if you will go back to that bitter year, *you* will perfectly understand why my mother, the other members of the family, and Dr. Coues who read it *all*, thought that in view of the existing circumstances, fire was our only surety that many family details should be put beyond the reach of vandal hands.

As we have seen, the journal of the 1820-21 period was not burned. It was written in a large unruled book, measuring eight by thirteen inches, and contained two hundred and one pages. This day by day account of his life was sold to Joseph M. Wade by the Audubon family when the descendants of the naturalist were in financial difficulties. Later it formed a part of the collection of Audubon and Wilson manuscripts owned by Colonel John E. Thayer and presented by him to Harvard University. Although excerpts from this journal have appeared in print from time to time, comparison of the original with extracts heretofore published shows that many of the quotations originally given out were not exact copies of what the naturalist wrote. Many incidents were suppressed. Others were drastically edited. Eight pages were cut from the journal—those that contained Audubon's story of his meeting with his *Fair Incognito*, Mme. André, and the gift of the Souvenir Gun.

Happily, other avenues of evidence have been found to guide the present biographer in recreating Audubon's days in New Orleans, where he never was successful; in Natchez, Mississippi, where he likewise was a failure; in the Louisiana countryside of Feliciana parish, where he mounted the first rungs of the ladder that carried him to fame.

3

Audubon was correct in his surmise that residence in the Creole City would afford him the choice of an infinite variety of game bird specimens, principally waterfowl which were brought into the market by the professional fowlers. During the month of February perfect specimens of pintail ducks, green-winged teal, scaups, mallards, gadwalls, and blue-winged teal were set up on wires in the Dauphine street studio and made to live again in his drawings.

One specimen sent in by the hunter Gilbert, who was evidently intent on collecting his dollar per day per bird, was a duck killed while keeping company with a flock of canvas-backs in Lake Barataria. Audubon immediately pronounced it a "non-discript." He searched through Wilson's accounts and the well-thumbed copy of Turton's *Linné*. He asked every hunter and sportsman in his circle if they had ever before seen such a duck? None had.

The duck, a young male, was posed, its image transferred to paper and designated a "Bemaculated Duck" by the puzzled naturalist forced to name the oddity. In the christening he took into consideration the many darkish spots on the breast feathers. When, several years later, the time came for Havell to engrave the painting, Audubon named it for Thomas M. Brewer, a young man living in Boston who had been most helpful to the artist. Brewer afterwards became a prominent physician and distinguished ornithologist. "Brewer's Duck," however, proved to be a hybrid, a cross between the green-headed mallard and the gadwall, and so again Audubon failed to add a new species to the extensive duck tribe.

With his wife by his side, Audubon found it imperative to confine himself closely to the duty of earning a living for his family. Lucy Audubon well knew how necessary it was to drive the accomplished but eccentric man she had married to the business of earning their daily bread. Apart from him she strove to accomplish this feat by correspondence, which caused the husband frequently to confide to his diary the depths of gloom to which he descended—driven there by his Lucy's severe pen-lashings. In his actual presence the English girl did not spare her tongue, and those who knew the family intimately have declared that the "wandering foot" of Audubon was frequently set to itching by the unleashing of certain poignant remarks from the lips of the woman he loved and who, there can be no doubt, devotedly loved him.

Drawing lessons were so few and far between that the man with the mighty ambition to picture all the birds of his adopted land in their natural sizes and true colors had time to draw many species on a gigantic scale. One of these was his famous "Bird of Washington," the wholly brown-plumaged young of the bald eagle he named after the first President of the United States.

The Bird of Washington, like some other "discoveries" of Audubon's, proved to be, not a new species, but the immaturely plumaged young of the bald eagle. In spite of the opinions of others, Audubon, to the day of his death, stubbornly maintained his *Haliaetus Washingtoni* was separate and distinct from the emblematic bird of his adopted land. His original drawing of the Bird of Washington, made in the Dauphine street house in New Orleans, however, bears the scientific designation "*Falco offsifragus*," the Latin name Alexander Wilson applied to the white-headed eagle, which would indicate he then believed it what it really was, the bald eagle in juvenal plumage.

The month of February was devoted to drawing. He tells us: "Every moment I had to spare I drew birds for my ornithology, in which my Lucy and myself alone have faith."

At this time he was seized with apprehensions regarding the appearance of the birds he had already painted. They were not good enough. They must be improved upon. But how? Other tasks were neglected to work out a solution, which resulted in the next few weeks being employed in "polishing up"—if the expression may be employed—all his bird pictures. He tells us:

> I thought I had improved them much by applying coats of watercolor under the pastels, thereby preventing the appearance of the paper, that in some instances marred my best productions. I discovered also many imperfections in my earlier drawings and formed the resolution to redraw the whole of them; consequently I hired two French hunters, who swept off every dollars that I could raise for specimens. I have few acquaintances; my wife and sons are more congenial to me than all others in the world, and we have no desire to force ourselves into a society where every day I receive fewer bows.

If he received fewer bows he received fewer pupils as well. Cheese began to make its appearance more frequently on the table in the little house in Dauphine street. Something must be done and, as had happened many times before, the wife stepped into the breach and announced her intention of securing employment. The husband spared his helpmeet the humiliation of seeking a job . . . he attended to that important matter in person.

The wife of the rich William Brand was expecting a child, and this put a stop to her drawing lessons, so Audubon approached the builder, explained his situation, and a few days later Mrs. Audubon was installed as governess to young William and companion to the builder's young wife, who was also in dire need of education. This masterstroke accomplished, Audubon went back to his drawing of birds with renewed vigor.

He drew the hermit thrush, eventually reproduced in his plates; the osprey, or sea eagle, rising from the water with a weakfish clutched in its talons; the rice bird, as he then termed the bobolink, was pictured singing atop a blade of grass, and the "Black-bellied Darter," his name for the anhinga, shown perched on a cypress stump with its mate. His snow goose drawing was also finished at this period, and with the adult white bird he pictured a blue goose, which he stated was the young of the snow goose in immature plumage—a mistake made by wiser and far better educated ornithologists fifty years later.

4

March crowded February off the calendar as springtime came tiptoeing in from the Gulf. An old restlessness seized Audubon, and as usual when this unrest fretted the naturalist he made a new resolution. This time the resolution, as was invariably the case, favored his "wandering foot," which had again started itching furiously. What about that expedition to the headwaters of the Arkansas river?

The month was exactly a week old when he inscribed in his diary: "Spring is advancing, with many pleasant associations, but my bodily health suffers from depression. I have resolved to leave for Natchez, but grieve to leave my family. My money is scarce and I find great difficulty in collecting what is owing me."

So the little house in Dauphine street was deserted. Mrs. Audubon and her sons were installed in the Brand home. Audubon visited the commander of the river steamer *Eclat*, and drew his portrait and that of his wife in payment of fares for himself and Joseph Mason to Natchez. On the sixteenth of March he was off again on a questing jaunt and, as many times before, without a cent in his pockets. He had with him however his old companions . . . drawing papers, crayons, watercolors, pastels, and, of course, his gun.

Flatboat at Natchez under the hill, sketched by Charles A. LeSueur

CHAPTER 16

NATCHEZ ON THE HILL

THE *Eclat* made many stops on its upstream trip on the yellow waters of the Mississippi and it was the twenty-fourth of March before it discharged passengers at Natchez Under The Hill. During the passage one of the passengers, during a general conversation on birds and the science of ornithology, accused Alexander Wilson of intemperate habits. "I had the satisfaction of defending his character from aspersion," Audubon righteously added, after setting down the calumniation in his journal. A few passengers aboard the steamboat had consented to have the bird artist dash off their portraits in black chalk so, when the *Eclat* tied up and Audubon debarked, he had a few dollars jingling in his pockets of his shabby nankeen trousers.

On the top of hill, where the streets of Natchez proper fanned out in several directions, Audubon called upon a friend and met with a cordial reception. What was there to do in this Mississippi river town? Prospects were bright, it seemed, as a certain Spanish merchant named Joseph Quegles, a native of the island of Majorca, desired a teacher of drawing, music, and French for his daughter Melanie. Audubon repaired to the Quegles' home where he was very graciously received by the merchant's wife. She had been Melanie Adam of New Orleans and welcomed anyone who might carry news from her native city. The matter of teaching was discussed with the little girl and her mother until Quegles arrived. His appearance "was by no means prepossessing," Audubon wrote his wife, "his small grey eyes, and corrugated brows, did not afford me an opportunity of passing a favorable judgment." In spite of this appraisal the artist was selected to instruct the daughter of the house in the attainments her parents wished her to cultivate and Joseph Quegles proved to be a kindly man who befriended Audubon many times.

Natchez holds the distinction of being the oldest settlement on the Father of the Waters and one of the interesting towns of the Mississippi Valley. It came into existence in 1716, when Jean Baptiste Le Moyne, Sieur de Bienville, built a fort on its present site. The written history of the place begins, however, in 1662 when the doughty and knightly La Salle, with his faithful Tonti of the Iron Hand, held pow wow with the Choctaw Indians inhabiting the high piece of ground. When Bienville built a fortification on the bluff he named it Fort Rosalie in honor of the beautiful wife of Louis de Phelypeaux, chancellor of France.

Natchez "On the Hill" and Natchez "Under the Hill" became famous in the colorful early history of the Mississippi Valley. Natchez "Under the Hill" was the name given then, as now, to that picturesque part of the settlement situated close to the river's edge and under the giant bluffs upon which the town proper perches. During the French, Spanish, and British regimes this river-front settlement was a wild, rough place, rendezvous for river boatmen, those stalwart sons of stalwart men who propelled the flatboats, arks, broadhorns, and keelboats up and down the broad river. Renegade whites, freed slaves, half-breeds, Indians, gamblers, outlaws, formed a cosmopolitan riff-raff that made this part of the Natchez settlement a law unto itself, a place the citizens on top of the hill left severely alone.

Audubon has left us two pictures of the place, one from his pen, the other from his brush. In his word picture he says:

> From the River opposite Natchez that place presents a Most Romantick scenery, the Shore is lined by Steam vessels, Barges and flat Boats, seconded by the lower Town, consisting of Ware Houses, Grogg Shops, Decayed Boats proper for the use of Washer Women, and the sidling Road raising along the Caving Hills on an oblique of a quarter of a Mile and about 200 feet High covered with Goats feeding peaceally on its declivities, while hundreds of Carts Horses and foot travellers are constantly meeting and Crossing each Other reduced to Minature by the distance renders the whole really picturesque; on the Top of this the Traveller comes in sight of the town as he enters the regularly Trees Leading to the diferent Streets running at right Angles towards the River; on the left the *Theatre* a poor framed Building and a New and Elegant Mansion the property of Mr.

Postlewait attract the anxious eye—on the right the rollings of the hearth thinly diversified by poor habitations soon close the prospect—advancing he is led into Main street; this as well as the generality of the place is too Narrow to be Handsome, is rendered less Interesting by the poorness & Iregularity of the Houses, few of which are Bricks, and at this season very much incumbered by Bales of Cotton—the Jail, Court House are New and tolerable in their form, the Lower part of the former a Boarding House of some Note. There are two Miserable Looking Churches; I dare not say unattended but think so.

Opposite the Natchez bluffs was the low-lying shore of Louisiana. In the front lands lay rich plantations which yielded splendid crops, save during those periods of the annual spring rise of the Mississippi. This Louisiana countryside proved another bird heaven for the naturalist, and he and Joseph Mason were frequently in the cypress swamps back of what is now the town of Vidalia seeking birds.

At Natchez Audubon made the acquaintance of Edmund Howard Wailes and his brother, B. L. C. Wailes, two young men of education as interested as Audubon himself in objects of natural history, and he soon became a habitue of their plantation home, located on the Louisiana side of the river. When Audubon went on his bird quests the Wailes brothers frequently accompanied him, and it was at the Wailes plantation that Audubon made his drawing of the Tyrant Flycatcher, as he then called the kingbird, and found the specimen of the orchard oriole which are reproduced in his splendid plates of these species, B. L. C. Wailes securing the orioles nest from a honey locust tree in the plantation yard. The following day the brothers watched Audubon wire a pair of towhee buntings on blackberry briars, and were greatly impressed with the deft manner in which he transferred their likenesses to drawing paper.

Audubon, in spite of his success in securing many bird subjects at Natchez and the Wailes plantation, still longed for the expedition to the head waters of the Arkansas. He had heard no word from the letters he had left at the Post of Arkansas the year before for the governor of that territory. During mid-April he seized upon an opportunity to go to the Post by steamboat hoping against hope that a personal interview with Governor Miller would result in his joining an expedition. He arrived at the old settlement, which he found unchanged from its former crude aspect, only to again suffer disappointment. No territorial expedition for a survey of the western limits of the United States was being planned.

The journey was not without result, as far as Audubon's cherished *Birds of America* was concerned, for while there he collected a new species of flycatcher. Observing a small bird flitting about the branches of a sweet gum tree, uttering a *wheet wheet* as it busily searched the leaves for insects, the naturalist watched it closely. He first thought it a wood pewee, then decided it was the small green-crested flycatcher, noting that it clearly articulated its *wheet wheet* while on the wing. The bird took a long flight from the highest branches of a low tree, skimming in zigzag lines close to the tops of tall grasses and, seizing different species of winged insects, returned to the same gum tree to alight. Its notes, Audubon observed, were uttered when on the point of leaving the branch. He watched a pair of the birds chasing insects and assumed they were mates with a nest in the immediate neighborhood. So he began the search and continued looking for the nest until he remembered it was only the middle of April . . . that was too early for the female to lay. Up went the ever-present gun and down came the birds. Upon dissecting the bodies he found five eggs, about the size of green peas, in the ovary of the female. "I could not perceive any difference in the coloring of the plumage between the sexes," says Audubon, and his drawing indicated the male in the inclined and rather crouching attitude which he observed the bird always assumed when it alighted on a branch.

He first named the bird *Muscicapa palustris* and also gave it a *vulgo* or common name, which has been obliterated on the original, and the words "Traill's Flycatcher, *Muscicapa trailli*" substituted. Audubon also made a pen and ink drawing of the bird's bill and the hairs growing about the gape, a very delicate and exact piece of work. The bird's locale was given as "Fort of Arkansas, April 17, 1822." In such a manner was Traill's flycatcher introduced to the avifauna of North America. Six years later, when this drawing was being engraved by Havell, Audubon named it "after his learned friend, Dr. Thomas Stewart Traill." Doctor Traill was a Scottish naturalist and one of the editors of the *Encyclopædia*

Britannica whom the American Woodsman had met at Liverpool when he was a'questing for fame.

Balked in his desire to travel to the headwaters of the Arkansas, Audubon returned to Natchez, and three days after securing his new swamp flycatcher he was at the Wailes plantation opposite Natchez collecting spring migrants. He secured several Black-throated Buntings (as he called the birds now best known as dicksissels) out of a flock of bobolinks leisurely making their way northwards, and here he also made his drawing of the wood thrush, next to the mockingbird his favorite among the sweet singers of the bird world.

It now became urgently necessary that Audubon find remunerative work of some sort, for the giving of drawing lessons and the making of pencil portraits were not sufficient to support him and Joe Mason. Happily, through the influence of Levin Wailes, a government surveyor who had been stationed for some years at Opelousas, in the Louisiana country, father of the two Wailes brothers so helpful to the bird enthusiast, Audubon secured a position at the Elizabeth Academy, the first college in this country to grant degrees to women. His duty was to give drawing lessons to the young ladies attending the academy which was located at Washington, a small village and the first capital of Mississippi, just a few miles from Natchez. This institution was headed by the Reverend B. M. Drake whose daughter later married Edmund H. Wailes.[1]

No sooner had Audubon assumed his duties at Dr. Drake's than he wrote to Lucy at New Orleans suggesting that his sons join him and share his new life at Natchez. A few days after receiving this welcome news Victor and Johnny left their mother in the Brand home and were on their way to join their father who placed them in Brevost's Academy in Natchez. For six weeks Audubon pursued his pedagogic role at the Elizabeth Academy with avidity, then his enthusiasm waned. He wanted to keep up his bird portraiture but having no opportunity to seek out the birds, and seeing only those inhabiting the woods that bordered the seven miles of dusty road connecting Washington with Natchez, which he tra-

[1]It has been believed for years that Audubon taught at Jefferson College at Washington. This proves to be an error. The institution was the female Elizabeth Academy.

versed afoot morning and evening, he yearned for the deep forests until it became an obsession.

He had finished one noteworthy and very beautiful drawing before joining the academy staff. It was his painstaking delineation of the chuck-will's-widow, which he says was known in the Natchez country as the "Spanish Whipper Will." He pictured a bird of each sex on the limb of a tree and his masterly treatment of the birds' soft plumage was as ably reproduced by Havell on copper. The lower figure, the female, was pictured with her wide mouth, bordered by stiff bristles, gaped wide open, while the upper bird was shown worrying a red-, black-, and yellow-ringed serpent which Audubon termed a Harlequin snake, and believed it "quite harmless." It is well that Audubon was not fanged when he took the reptile into his studio—for so well and correctly did he reproduce it in his drawing that a herpetologist will instantly recognize it as the very poisonous, even deadly, coral snake.

By the end of June Audubon could no longer endure the slight tasks assigned him at the academy. He was constantly depressed in spirits because "his work interferred with his ornithological pursuits." We also learn from the same journal that "constant exposure in the tropical climate, and the fatigue of my journeys to and from Washington, brought on fever." This his apology for quitting the post and the salary that meant, at least, a bare living for himself and boys.

The fever that stopped all work, ornithological or otherwise, brought the bird artist once more under the attention of a physician of Natchez, a deeply understanding man who not only treated Audubon for his ailment but "actually insisted on my taking his purse to pay for the expenses connected with the education of my sons." For the naturalist was again in his chronic condition—without employment and without funds.

The physician was Dr. William Provan who, besides proving a good Samaritan in this instance, rendered Audubon aid in other ways, and was instrumental in reintroducing the naturalist to Feliciana—that section of Louisiana he grew to love with a passion that never died.

Shortly after Audubon's recovery from his attack of fever, he secured temporary employment with Professor Brevost, who was then enlarging his academy of learning in Natchez. The slender salary earned by teaching drawing to those attending this seminary, together with the money secured from the few pupils who came to his Union street studio, brought him a glimmer of hope so he wrote his wife, urging her to forsake New Orleans and join him. His close application to earning money again irritatingly interfered with his work on the birds and fewer ornithological portraits came off his easel —fewer habits of the feathered denizens of the woods were studied.

"While work flowed upon me," he complained, "the hope of completing my book on the Birds of America became less clear; and full of dispair, I feared my hopes of becoming known to Europe as a naturalist were destined to become blasted."

2

In the last week in July, Audubon lost the faithful assistant who had stood by him for a year and nine months. Joseph Mason decided it was time to forsake his precarious and wandering existence with the bird artist. His father having died while he and Audubon were starving in New Orleans the spring before, the lad realized his place was at his mother's side. He planned to work his way back to Cincinnati on the steamboats, drawing pictures of passengers as a means of earning his fare.

"We experienced great pain at parting," says Audubon. "I gave him paper and chalks to work his way with, and the double-barreled gun I had killed most of my birds with, and which I purchased in Philadelphia in 1805."

Joseph Mason's contribution to Audubon's fame as an artist and delineator of birds in their habitat was considerable. Although several of the original drawings bear the penciled legends: "Plant by Jos. Mason," it must be admitted that Audubon was chary either in his printed works or on his engraved plates in giving a proper recognition to the very valuable assistance given him by the thirteen-year-old boy whose watercolors of flowers and leaves were gems of exactitude, grace, color, and composition. This can be determined for oneself by examining the plates of the blue yellow-back warbler, Bonaparte's flycatcher, American redstart, summer red bird, yellow-throated vireo, pine-creeping warbler, Kentucky flycatching warbler, yellow throated wood warbler, bay-breasted warbler, blue-winged yellow swamp warbler, white-throated finch, swamp sparrow, blue-eyed yellow warbler, and many others conspicuous for the beauty of the floral decorations.

3

Shortly after Mason's departure Audubon made a copy in colors of an engraving from John Trumbull's painting of the death of General Richard Montgomery before Quebec. Audubon's colored copy was admired by many who so praised his ability that he placed a valuation of three hundred dollars on the effort—but there were no purchasers. Doctor Provan, ever ready to assist the struggling artist, thereupon suggested it be raffled and personally disposed of the tickets. At ten dollars each all pasteboards were sold save one. "I'll set *your* name down for that ticket," the physician told Audubon, "and I hope it will prove the winning number." Following the drawing Doctor Provan returned with the picture and placing it in Audubon's hands said: "Your number has drawn it and the subscribers all agree that no one is more deserving of it than yourself."

On the first of September Lucy wrote her husband of the death of the Brand infant she had been nursing and, as she had wearied of living in New Orleans separated from her two boys, warned the father that she would join him within the next few days. Audubon, who had been idling away his time, bestirred himself and by the time Lucy arrived at Natchez had secured for her a position as governess in the family of a clergyman named Davis.

November came and with it the first hint of winter. Mrs. Audubon relinquished her position—she had found it difficult to obtain her salary from Parson Davis. So once more the Audubon family was in dire straits in the frame house which stood until late years at 118 South Union Street. Put to his utmost to earn a living for his wife and boys, Audubon more than once had to rely on the ever-proffered generosity of Doctor Provan to insure food being placed on the table, clothes for Victor and Johnny, and drawing materials for his illusory Birds of America.

Having found some sale for landscapes, Audubon was out one November day making a painting of the town of Natchez when he was accosted by a stranger who proved to be a traveling English naturalist named Leacock. The Englishman complimented the artist on the sketch and so Audubon invited him to his home to see his collection of bird drawings. Leacock was lavish in his praise.

"He advised me to visit England and take them with me," records Audubon. "But when he said I should probably have to spend several years to perfect them, and to make myself known, I closed the portfolio of drawings and turned my mind from the thought."

With the coming of December a wandering portrait painter visited Natchez. His name was John Steen and he hailed from Washington, Pennsylvania. He and Audubon drifted together attracted by the mysterious bond that exists between artists, who either like one another profoundly or are extremely antagonistic and become bitter enemies. Steen had a marked influence on Audubon's art, for it was he who taught the bird artist the use of oils.

"He gave me the first lesson in painting in oils I ever took in my life," Audubon tells us. "It was a copy of an otter from one of my water colors." It was not the only time Audubon made an oil reproduction of his favorite animal painting. This picture, showing the animal held fast in a trap, a few years later was destined to save *the Birds of America* from failure, for when the famous work was in the hands of Havell's engravers and money was required to pay the colorists, engravers, and paper makers, Audubon copied and recopied in oils the same trapped fur animal, selling the canvasses to London art shops and applying the proceeds to the costs attendant on the publication of his life's work.

Lucy Audubon, too, was desirous that her husband should master the use of oils and she enthusiastically seconded every move that would tend to make the man she loved and for whom she toiled more proficient in the delineation of his birds.

She agreed with the Englishman that Laforest should go to England and there find a publisher for his extensive collection, but she did not agree with Leacock that it would take her husband several years to perfect them. They were perfect as they were. Despite many things that might have shaken her faith, a staunch champion of the man she married was Lucy Bakewell.

The first sitters for Audubon, now trying his hand at portraiture in oils, were Victor and Johnny, and these two canvasses, treasured relics of Audubon's debut as a portrait *painter*, hang today in the home of Miss Florence Audubon, daughter of John Woodhouse Audubon, in Salem, New York.

When Audubon became used to the feel of a palette on his bare arm, the drag of the fitch hairs of the paint-charged brushes on the rough texture of stretched canvas, and began to find out something regarding the mixing of colors, he got out his water color of Père Antoine and, assisted by Steen, repainted the full-length portrait of the priest in oils. While Mrs. Audubon recorded that it was later sent to Havana, Cuba, to be hung in the cathedral, the portrait has apparently vanished.

A few pupils for instruction in painting were secured by Audubon and Steen. Among them was pretty Isabelle Munce, afterwards Mrs. Cyrus Marsh, who proved an apt pupil. The old Marsh home in Natchez has several of her paintings hanging on the walls, side by side with those Audubon painted of her parents, Thomas Munce and his wife, the former Margaret Campbell. These two treasured souvenirs of Audubon's initial essay in oil hang in places of honor in a quaint darkened parlor redolent with antiquity.

CHAPTER 17

The Perambulating Portrait Painter

THE first day of February 1823 brought a momentous change in affairs and conditions of the Audubon family. Mrs. Audubon was offered a position as teacher on a pretentious plantation in the Feliciana country, which she promptly accepted. This matter was arranged through the offices of Doctor Provan. The physician was frequently called in the course of his practice to the Louisiana plantation home of Mrs. Jane Percy, widow of Lieutenant Robert Percy, R. N., a former British naval officer. More than professional duties sent the doctor to *Beech Woods*, as the Percy plantation was named, for Sarah, one of the many Percy girls, afterwards became his wife.

Lieutenant Percy had been preceded to the West Florida section of America by his father, Charles Percy, a one-time British army officer, who emigrated to the New World when the southern section was under the domination of the English. After his death (he had thrown himself in a creek) his son visited the country to settle his father's estate, became enamoured with the country, and later brought his family to *Nuevo Feliciana*. He had married in London a Scottish lady named Jane Middlemist, and when Lieutenant Percy arrived in Louisiana he also brought from over the seas his two eldest daughters, Jane and Margaret. Settling in the prosperous cotton-raising section near Bayou Sarah in 1802, when it was under the domination of Spain, Robert Percy became a resident of importance and influence, was made an *alcalde*, and here were born his other children, Robert Dow Percy, Sarah, Christine, Thomas, and Charles. Lieutenant Percy was one of the leaders of the revolt of the Felicianians against the rule of Spain in 1810, and was designated one of the three members of the high court of the independent republic of West Florida, which had a life of seventy-four days.

The former British naval officer had been dead three years when the Audubons were introduced to *Beech Woods*. The main house had been builded in a grove of noble beech trees, thus giving the plantation its name, and it was here that Lucy Audubon taught the Percy children and daughters of neighboring planters.

The fact that their ancestors were instructed by the wife of the man who afterwards became so famous is reverently remembered by many descendants of the young ladies who received their early schooling at Mrs. Audubon's hands. Among these pupils were: Margaret Percy, who became Mrs. George Washington Sargent; Sarah Percy, who married Dr. William Provan; Christine Percy, later Mrs. Addison Dashiell; Augusta Randolph, who became Mrs. W. C. S. Ventress; Ann Eliza Ratcliff, later the wife of General Robert L. Brandon; Sarah Ann Yates Randolph, who married Colonel Tignal Jones Stewart; a Miss Marshall of Mississippi, and Ann Mathews, daughter of Judge George Mathews.

The young ladies of the Percy establishment and the daughters of neighbors needed instruction in reading, writing, and arithmetic, as well as social culture and music. Doctor Provan had convinced the Widow Percy that no one was better qualified to supply these requirements than the English wife of the eccentric French artist.

In such a fashion was Lucy Green Bakewell Audubon introduced to the pleasant Louisiana country which became to her, also, a happy land. With her two sons she moved to *Beech Woods* and opened her school. For seven years Lucy Audubon taught the young ladies of Feliciana and left a memory in that beautiful hill country of Louisiana as fragrant and enduring as the sweet scent of the magnolias that bloom there every summer.

2

Audubon and Steen remained in Natchez, busy with oils, making likenesses of those in town who desired to leave to posterity their features. As good paying sitters did not come to them the portraitists decided to go to their sitters, so in the late spring they decided on a perambulating portrait painting tour, so as to put to canvass likenesses of the wealthy planters and members of their families.

By March they were ready for the venture, and set out in *un chariot à la dearborn* via the historic tree-shaded Natchez Trace. The Homochitto and sandy Buffalo Bayou were forded; then over the hills into Woodville and into the Feliciana country creaked the wheels of the dearborn. At *Beech Woods* Victor joined the expedition, which headed in the direction of Baton Rouge. Steen was seeking sitters among the well-to-do planters of the broad, prosperous cotton fields, but Audubon, though ostensibly on the lookout for the same, had his eyes and ears alert for the flutter of a strange bird's wing or its note from every wayside bush.

"I had finally determined to break through all bonds and pursue my ornithological pursuit," Audubon stated. "My best friends solemnly regard me as a madman, and my wife and family alone gave me encouragement. My wife determined that my genius should prevail and that my final success should be triumphant."

The portrait painting expedition headed south and remained a few days at Jackson, then a thriving village on Thompson's Creek, and the seat of government of Feliciana parish. The artists were not prepossessed with Jackson, Audubon complaining he "found it a mean place, a rendezvous for gamblers and vagabonds." The old Rhea place, then one of the more pretentious mansions on Thompson's creek, was visited as were a number of other plantation homes in search of paying subjects. While in Jackson the two did a wholesale portrait job for David Fluker, keeper of the tavern, painting not only the host and his wife, but making likenesses of their two sons, David and John.

The firm of Audubon and Steen did not prosper. The partners did not agree on many things. There were bickerings and even quarrels, and the portrait painting venture went on the rocks. There was too much a-birding to suit Steen and, naturally Audubon did not agree with him that there could be too much attention paid birds. As a result of this difference of opinion the naturalist and his son returned to Jackson, but quickly quitted it "disgusted with the place and its people," while John Steen, poor fellow, went upon his birdless fameless way.

When the father and son appeared at *Beech Woods* they received a hearty welcome from Mrs. Percy, and Audubon was urged to remain at the plantation home and assist his wife in teaching the young ladies of the school what he could in music, drawing, and dancing.

3

Descendants of these pupils have many anecdotes handed down to them relating to Audubon and his wife. She was beloved by all who came in range of her lovable personality. Remembrance of the naturalist is tinged with a slight contempt, as it was recalled "he spent most of his time roaming the woods after birds." Audubon gave his wife's pupils lessons in dancing and French, but most vividly of all was it remembered that he taught the girls to swim in a large springhouse attached to *Beech Woods*, where the depth of the water could be regulated by the use of spills.

Beech Woods meant as much to the bird man as did *Oakley*. He wandered through the woodlands adjacent to Little Bayou Sarah, the Sleepy Hollow woods, and the swamps bordering the Mississippi, seeking out the secrets of the birds and making new acquaintances among the numerous planter families. At *Greenwood* he called upon his lovely Eliza Pirrie, a widow, bereft of her husband a few weeks after a romantic elopement.

The vivacious Eliza did not become the bride of the physician who had placed a taboo on Audubon's drawing lessons two years before. Although Dr. Ira Smith had been Mrs. Pirrie's choice, Eliza felt otherwise about it. A young and dashing gallant of the Feliciana countryside, Robert H. Barrow, a cousin of the girl he adored, won her affections. Robert pressed his suit with such ardor and persistence that Mrs. Pirrie forbade him the hospitality of *Oakley*—even refused to allow the two to correspond, but the young couple contrived a means of communication, Robert's missives of undying affection were placed in a hollow tree on the Pirrie estate by a trusted slave. Eliza had to resort to stratagem to secure them and send her answering letters of fidelity. In this the girl was aided by Mrs. Swazie, then living at *Oakley* as her companion, who exchanged the letters in the secret post box.

One rainy June morning Eliza was missing. By the time Squire Pirrie and his irate wife started in pursuit, Robert Barrow and his beloved were well on their way to Natchez, bumping and swaying over the roads in a carriage drawn by galloping horses. Past Woodville the runaway pair made their way and over Buffalo bayou, but when the Homochitto was reached this stream was running bank full, the result of a sudden summer downpour. Young Barrow held his lady fair high in his arms as he waded through the rushing waters. Then his team was led through the flood. The elopers were already married when the pursuing parents reached Natchez.

As a result of the wetting he had received in wading the Homochitto the young bridegroom contracted pneumonia. Six weeks after her elopement Eliza Pirrie was a widow. The fact that Eliza did not marry Doctor Smith proved no bar to the physician becoming a member of the Pirrie family for, several years later, when Mary Anny Gray, Eliza's half-sister lost her husband, Jedediah Smith, she retained her last name in a second marriage by becoming the wife of the persistent Doctor Ira Smith. Whenever Audubon's wanderings about the Feliciana countryside brought him in the vicinity of *Greenwood* he called on his former pupil, who received him graciously and, as in the days when he first knew her, displayed an interest in his bird pictures.

At *Beech Woods* Audubon worked daily in oil paints, striving to master this new medium of expression. As a matter of course, portraiture came in for a great deal of experimentation, for he was remarkably adept at catching a likeness and had a strong bent for truthfulness of color. He made oil portraits of Victor and Johnny and, seated before a mirror, painted his own picture and it is today probably the best likeness we have of the American Woodsman.

His predilection for truth in drawing and color led to an open rupture between Audubon and Mrs. Percy. As he describes it: "I continued to exercise myself in painting with oils and generally improved myself. I undertook to paint the portraits of my wife's pupils but found their complexions difficult to transfer to canvass." It was the yellowish tinge of their cheeks that Audubon persisted in imitating that led to the strained relations. Mrs. Percy admitted that the likenesses of her daughters were good, indeed, lifelike! But, she complained, the facial tones were too vivid . . . it made her girls look jaundiced!

This criticism ruffled Audubon, who could never tolerate anything but praise for his art, consequently he gathered his canvasses, his other painting material, picked up his gun, whistled to his dog and stamped out of *Beech Woods* in high dungeon, muttering imprecations upon the Widow Percy's head in the expressive tongue of his boyhood, and went to the village of Bayou Sarah.

Two or three days later the rage that had so completely engulfed him passed, and late one evening he was back at *Beech Woods.* When word was brought to Mrs. Percy by a servant that Audubon had returned, was then in his wife's room and in her bed! Mrs. Percy acted immediately. She not only ordered him out of bed but out of the house and away from the plantation as well! In a black tornado of rage and hate, Audubon was forced to trudge back across the long dusty road, to wade the Bayou Sarah ford and with only the stars to light his way he reached the village.

Four years later, in England, Audubon recalled this galling event when writing his wife his joy in learning Lucy had left Mrs. Percy's and was teaching at another plantation. He expressed the hope that the new family and situation were agreeable to her and added, "if I wanted to go to bed to thee there, I would not be sent back 15 miles on foot to Bayou Sarah instead!!!"

Mrs. Percy's action in turning him out as though he was a common vagabond of the highway threw the temperamental bird-artist into a fury. From the village he sent word for his elder son Victor to join him and bring all his effects from *Beech Woods.* This accomplished, father and son boarded a river boat and went to Natchez.

Back in the Bluff City, Audubon wandered about the town not knowing what next to do. The stormy scenes at the Percy plantation remained fresh in his thoughts, and Mrs. Percy's harsh words, as she ordered him from his bedroom, rankled.

To be driven from his wife's bed! It was degrading! He heaped Gallic imprecations on the head of the mistress of *Beech Woods.* Could Mrs. Percy tell *him* about Art? . . . not he! He confided to his diary that he knew not what course next to pursue. He was away from *Beech Woods,* but that was all. "I thought of going to Philadelphia, and again of going to Louisville," he set down in his journal, "and once more entering upon mercantile pursuits—but had no money to move anywhere!"

4

Mrs. Audubon had not sympathized with her husband in the stand he took regarding the portraits of the Percy children, and this time there was no monetary assistance forthcoming from his beloved Lucy. In consequence, he and Victor idled about Natchez, the father doing odd jobs, making a few portraits, and many, many vain resolutions.

He sought commissions from everyone and was overjoyed when a Mrs. Griffith, a wealthy woman to whom he had shown the hasty water color sketch of Natchez he had made the year before, commissioned him to make a large oil painting of the same. A price of three hundred dollars was agreed upon, and in high glee Audubon set to work on a pretentious eight-by-four-foot painting.

When it was finally finished he had portrayed Natchez as it was in 1823. On the left the bluffs which led down to the Mississippi river were shown with the ruins of old Fort Rosalie and the white-pillared Rumble residence. In the foreground appeared the old kilns which produced the bricks from which a number of the buildings standing in Natchez today were constructed. Surveying the scene was a group of men and women dressed in the quaint style of the period. High overhead a flock of black vultures was wheeling in wide circles, while other buzzards were at rest on the walls of the kiln and limbs of trees. Off to the right, among the other buildings, Audubon showed the dome of the old Episcopal Church, at that time a square building surmounted with a high dome. The old Catholic church, with its lofty spire topped with a cross, was also visible. Garnier's hotel, destroyed by a tornado in 1840, stood out in bold relief. The town's courthouse and jail were shown, and Profilet's store was among the group of buildings constituting the main section of town. In the lower right-hand corner of the picture Mrs. Elijah Smith, coming out of the deep-cut Natchez Trace driving a bob-tailed white horse harnessed to a high-wheeled gig, was made part of the composition.

Before Audubon put the finishing touches to his ambitious painting, Mrs. Griffith suddenly died and her heirs declined either to accept or pay for the picture. Audubon offered it for sale, but even at reduced prices there were no purchasers. He finally left it in the store of Emile Profilet to be sold. The huge painting hung on the walls of the store for many years until Profilet sent it overseas so that his relatives in France might see what manner of store he had erected in the American wilderness. In 1855, when Profilet visited his old home in France, he found the painting of Natchez hanging on its walls. The merchant had completely forgotten its existence. He boxed and shipped it on another sailing vessel, and some months later Audubon's panorama was back in Profilet's store. There it remained until purchased by Dr. Stephen Kelly, who removed it to his handsome ante bellum plantation home, *Melrose*, where it is now one of the cherished art treasures owned by a son, George M. D. Kelly.

With the disappointment attendant on his failure to collect what was due him, Audubon was again plunged into the depths of despair. He was indeed in desperate financial straits when he chanced to meet George Towers Duncan, owner of *The Towers*, an extensive plantation located several miles from Natchez in a locality known as "Second Creek." The plantation owner was an ardent sportsman and fisherman, with a pronounced leaning for any and everything connected with natural history. He invited Audubon and Victor to be his guests. The two men fished, hunted, and communed with nature to their hearts' content, nor was little Victor left out of this joyous slice of life in one of the prettiest spots in Mississippi.

It was August when the father, then the son, fell sick. Doctor Provan pronounced the malady yellow fever. Both were desperately ill and as they lay in the Duncan home the artist's only thought was for his wife . . . he called for her constantly. Advised of the plight of husband and son, Lucy Bakewell rushed over the high hills of the Woodville road to *The Towers* as fast as horse and gig could carry her, and was soon nursing her beloved ones back to health. During the first week of September word came from Mrs. Percy bidding Audubon forget past differences and return to *Beech Grove* to recuperate.

5

In the pleasant Feliciana country, where the birds sang as nowhere else, Audubon came back from the edge of existence to wander again through the magnolia woods he had learned to love. Strength regained, Mrs. Audubon proposed that her husband fulfill a long suppressed desire to go to Philadelphia and exhibit his bird drawings, in the hope that there he would find someone who would have them engraved and published. Lucy furnished the money for the journey.

It was decided, too, that Victor, then fourteen, was old enough to start out for himself and, as Nicholas Berthoud had agreed to find a place for the lad in his office at Shippingport, the mother agreed to part with her elder son. Audubon's collection of drawings was shipped on ahead and the father and son journeyed down the river to New Orleans where, during the first days of October, they took passage on the steamboat *Magnet* for the long trip up the Mississippi and Ohio.

Low water prevented the *Magnet* from entering the Ohio, Captain McKnight decided, so Audubon and Victor debarked and, in company with two other passengers, finished the journey to Louisville on foot. This long tramp was later detailed in two of his *Episodes*: "A Tough Walk for a Youth," and "The Hospitality of the Woods."

It was the twenty-fifth of October when father and son entered Louisville, the place where Audubon had been a struggling merchant, in whose jail he had once been a penniless and unwilling guest . . . now he had only thirteen dollars in his pocket.

Audubon found his wife's relatives and former friends very

cool, and confessed he realized his "position very insecure." After seeing his son installed in Berthoud's office, Audubon engaged rooms for himself and Victor at Shippingport and settled down for the winter, undertaking anything that came to hand, from making portraits in black chalk and oils and decorating interiors of steamboats then being rapidly built for the river trade, to the making of lettered and decorated signs for shops.

Why he put off his proposed visit to Philadelphia is not known but it may be surmised that he did not care to encounter the rigors of winter-time in the City of Brotherly Love . . . it was always cold enough to him in summer.

He was down-hearted at times and at others showed a surprising change of spirit—he resolved to do bigger and better things. One cold November day he confided to his diary: "Busy at work, when the weather permits, and resolve to paint one hundred views of American scenery—I shall not be surprised to find myself seated at the foot of Niagara."

6

One morning, late in January of 1824, Audubon was aroused from a sound sleep by the clatter of galloping hoof beats on the frozen road. The rider was making all speed possible in the direction of the Berthoud mansion. Audubon peered out of his window and by "the transparent light which is the effect of the moon before dawn, saw Doctor Middleton passing at full gallop towards the White House." Audubon dressed hurriedly and arrived at Berthoud's to find that his old and sincere friend, Madame Berthoud, had gone on to join her noble husband in the somber mystery of death.

"What a void in the world for me!" Audubon lamented in writing his wife of Madame Berthoud's death. "I was silent; many tears fell from my eyes accustomed to sorrow. It was impossible for me to work; my heart, restless, moved from point to point all around the compass of my life. Ah, Lucy! what have I felt today! how can I bear the loss of our truest friend? This has been a sad day, most truly; I have spent it thinking, thinking, learning, weighing my thoughts, and quite sick of life. I wished I had been as quiet as my venerable friend, as she lay for the last time in her room."

None mourned more sincerely than the tall, angular-faced Frenchman when the widow of the Marquis de Saint-Pierre was reverently lowered to her resting place. What were the thoughts that milled in Audubon's vortex of emotions as he stood by the side of the grave, a silent figure in the sorrowful ceremonies?

His heart, he had said, had moved from point to point around the compass of his life the night the former noblewoman had died. What was he thinking as the shovelsful of earth were being dropped on the casket that held all that was mortal of one who had been *dame d'honneur* to Marie Antoinette, the queen whose small son became the tiny prisoner of the Temple, the Shadow King of France—the celebrated, mysterious Lost Dauphin?

Seal and coat-of-arms of the Marquis de Saint-Pierre.

CHAPTER 18

SEEKING A PUBLISHER

IT was April, in the year eighteen hundred and twenty-four, before John James Audubon made his bow as a naturalist in the Quaker City, his portfolio of bird drawings in one hand, his hat in the other. He lacked one year of forty and should have known better, but he had journeyed to Philadelphia on a definite mission from the outposts of Louisiana and Kentucky, a desperate venture to obtain help in completing his ambitious ornithological enterprise.

Philadelphia was then the center of learning and science, and among the many luminaries living there and practicing their pursuits were Thomas Sully, the portraitist; the three Peale brothers, Robert, Titian, and Rembrandt; Doctor Richard Harlan, Thomas Say, Charles Alexandre LeSueur, talented French zoologist and artist, and George Ord, friend and biographer of Alexander Wilson. Others of distinction included Charles Lucien Jules Laurent Bonaparte, then just of age and intensely interested in the bird life of America, who was also the prince of Canino and Musigano, eldest son of a brother of Napoleon Bonaparte. There, too, were Alexander Lawson, engraver of the plates in Wilson's work on birds, and—although not quite so well known as the others—Edward Harris, a quiet, unassuming young gentleman-farmer from Moorestown, New Jersey, who was then just becoming interested in birds and other branches of natural history.

Audubon purchased a new suit of clothes and, "dressing with neatness," called upon an old-time friend, Dr. William Mease, and made known the reason for his being in Philadelphia. Doctor Mease introduced Audubon to Sully, whom he described as "a man after my own heart, who showed me great kindness." It was also through Mease that Audubon met young Bonaparte, George Ord, and a number of artists then making Philadelphia their headquarters. Ord was a naturalist of no mean ability, who had edited the eighth volume of Wilson's *Ornithology*, written the ninth and concluding volume, and done a biography of the Scotsman. Ord was financially interested in the success of Wilson's work, and had in mind, at the time of Audubon's appearance in Quaker Town, the publication of a new edition of the *American Ornithology*.

Audubon eagerly untied the strings of his portfolio and spread his portraits of life-sized birds on the floor for Ord's inspection. Wilson's champion was critical . . . hypercritical. He objected to Audubon's method of combining bird figures with plants, flowers, tree trunks, moths, butterflies, spiders, and scenic backgrounds. Ord pointed out the superiority of the engravings in Wilson's work, which showed the figure of the bird on a perch with no extraneous matter to detract the attention of the beholder. Ord had a jaundiced eye as far as Audubon was concerned.

The Prince Bonaparte, on the other hand, according to Audubon: "examined my birds and was complimentary in his praises. He was at the time engaged on a volume of American birds, which did not prevent him from admiring another man's work." The upshot of this meeting was Bonaparte's suggestion that Audubon contribute some bird pictures to the titled ornithologist's *Ornithology*, then in process of compilation, for which Titian R. Peale was doing the drawings and Alexander Lawson engraving the plates. When the nephew of Napoleon introduced Audubon with his armful of drawings to Peale and Lawson, it is not surprising to learn that there was small evidence of appreciation displayed for one another's work.

Titian Peale's method of drawing birds, stiff and in profile on the conventional perch, was abhorrent to Audubon, and with reason, for they were uncompromisingly artificial and stereotyped. Peale looked contemptuously on the "trader naturalist" and saw nothing in the Frenchman's bird drawings. The attitude of Lawson the engraver has been made clear by his biographer, William Dunlap: "Lawson told me that he spoke freely of Audubon's pictures and said they were ill-drawn, not true to nature, and anatomically incorrect."

Said Audubon of Lawson: "This gentleman's figure nearly reached the roof, his face was sympathetically long, and his tongue was so long that we obtained no opportunity of speaking in his company. Lawson said my drawings were too soft, too much like oil paintings, and objected to engraving them."

In another Philadelphia engraver named Fairman, the bird artist found a man better able to appreciate his work. Fairman, however, doubted the possibility of publication in the United States and advised Audubon to go to England to have his birds engraved in a superior manner.

Charles Bonaparte did not accept the valuation set by Lawson on Audubon's set of bird drawings, declared he would buy them all, and that Lawson would have to engrave them. "Weel, you may buy thim," replied the Scotsman, "but I weel na engrave thim—ornithology requires truth in th' forms, and correctness in th' lines. Here are neither." Other meetings followed but all ended the same way. Eventually Audubon set down in his diary that "those interested in Wilson's book on American birds advise me not to publish, and not only cold water but *ice* was poured on my undertaking." His rivals were jealous of his abilities.

Audubon reverenced the great. He had a habit of fawning on those who had achieved fame in their presence . . . he usually put them in a less flattering light when he discussed them in his journal at night! He too was jealous of his rivals, but this trait appeared in greater intensity in later years. In spite of the fact that George Ord had made it plain from their first meeting that he had no desire for the Frenchman's friendship, Audubon did his best to conciliate him; he wanted to force Wilson's biographer to a friendship which Audubon felt might prove of advantage to him in the publication of his work. He so expressed himself to Doctor Harlan and asked the physician to endeavor to bring about such a result. Harlan, who proved a real friend to Audubon, advised him to abandon any attempt to cultivate Ord, "since Ord has no heart for friendship—having been denied that blessing by nature itself."

Bonaparte was still insistent that he would use Audubon's drawings in his work; but Titian Peale remained stiff-necked about Audubon's work and Lawson, with characteristic Scottish prejudice and obstinancy, refused to engrave them. Audubon, meanwhile buoyed with hopes of having his precious work published, danced about from one to the other attempting to palliate and soothe the prejudiced ones. On the first day of May he writes: "shewed all my drawings to Titian Peale who in return refused to let me see a new bird in his possession. This little incident fills me with grief at the narrow spirit of humanity and makes me wish for the solitude of the woods."

Charles LeSueur, a vagabond Frenchman like Audubon, a first rate naturalist, and certainly a most talented artist, was delighted with the bird portraits, questioned Audubon minutely about the Mississippi river country and Louisiana, and gave him many valuable hints about the use of oil colors.

Audubon's hopes were dashed when Bonaparte visited the artist's rooms at Fifth and Minor streets, and suggested that negotiations be ended. The titled Frenchman advised Audubon to take his bird drawings to France so that they could be reproduced in all the glory and size of the pretentious originals. Whereat Audubon suggested that the prince give him financial aid so that he could cross the Atlantic and in Paris search out a publisher. Bonaparte, however "replied coldly and in the negative."

Before he took his departure the prince glanced through the collection and suggested an arrangement whereby he could reproduce the drawing of the boat-tailed grackles, the same picture Audubon had made at *Bonnet Carré* when on his way to New Orleans on Berthoud's keelboat. So, in spite of his declarations to the contrary, Lawson did engrave one of Audubon's bird drawings, but the grackles are the only birds of The American Woodsman that appeared in Bonaparte's work on the avifauna of America. Fortunately for Audubon's ultimate fame, the Scot, by his obstinacy, was an unwitting friend to the long-haired rival of Alexander Wilson.

Although mightily discouraged with conditions in Philadelphia, Audubon exhibited his drawings in a small hall. The bird show did not attract attention, and only a week was needed to prove it a financial and artistic failure. Next he endeavored to find drawing pupils but met with slight success in this effort. There were a few in Philadelphia who admired his work and under the spur of their enthusiasm Audubon wrote his wife, "I am now determined to go to Europe with my 'treasures' since I am assured nothing so fine in the way of ornithological representations exist."

Although Sully and LeSueur were barely making a living with their brushes, Audubon threw himself into oil painting with fanatical energy and, while he had one or two pupils offered him at thirty dollars a month, made little headway as a teacher.

He was wading knee-deep in a morass of melancholia.

2

Just when days were darkest, Audubon received visits from two old-time friends. The first was Ferdinand Rozier, then in Philadelphia obtaining supplies for his fast-growing and very successful mercantile venture at Ste. Geneviève. After Rozier had left, Audubon opened his journal and penned sarcastically that his former partner "was still thirsting for money."

His second caller was none other than Joseph Mason. The boy was now seventeen and he had grown physically and mentally. His contacts in Philadelphia had given him a poise, a maturity that completely changed the lad who had followed Audubon about so obediently three years before. He had also attained artistic fame and was employed at Barton's Botanical Gardens making drawings of trees, shrubs, leaves, and flowers—for which he was paid a salary of sixty dollars a month.

Audubon was overjoyed to again meet his former pupil. Mason told of his own success, while Audubon detailed what had transpired since the two had parted in Natchez, of his hopes of having his birds published abroad, and with pardonable pride displayed a number of the bird portraits he had made since his assistant had left him.

As Mason glanced over the collection, Audubon suggested that the boy again join forces with him, paint the floral decorations for the new pictures, go with him to New York, and from there to England, to France. Audubon held out the promise of glittering reward . . . five hundred dollars and expenses!

The young man did not receive the airy proffers of fame and fortune with enthusiasm. He turned over the bird drawings in silence, minutely inspecting one after another. Those he was most interested in were the pictures he and Audubon had made during the two years they were together in the South. Mason noted that on each drawing, in India ink, was written in a flowing hand, "Drawn from Nature by John J. Audubon," while "Plant by Jos. R. Mason," was still written in lead pencil. On some of the drawings on which he had spent hours, days, in depicting the flowers that made up the composition, the penciled words that he had drawn the plant had been erased. The boy remembered Audubon had promised his name would be engraved on the plates should they ever be published. So Mason closed the portfolio, bade his former drawing master good-bye and returned to the botanical garden.

Days passed, and as Mason did not revisit the studio, Audubon sought him out at the gardens. Inducements were renewed, but Joseph Mason declined to again join in a quest for fame, even though his former patron promised to be a father to him! Joseph had starved with him before and remembered the pangs of hunger. He did not relish another pilgrimage of uncertainty. The sixty dollars he was earning at the gardens were real, and they were paid him every thirty days.

On this occasion a man at the gardens who had seen Audubon's display of bird pictures not only complimented him on his ability to portray birds and flowers so perfectly, but expressed amazement at his industry in painting so many pictures in so short a period. Where had he found time to do all these things? Audubon pointed to Mason and said that "yon rascal did all the botany." But this oral acknowledgement did not satisfy the youth. He was now old enough to have the feelings and resentments of a man, and evidently sensed that the credit Audubon had promised him would never be forthcoming. He definitely told Audubon he would not go with him but would remain at Barton's gardens.

Later, Joseph Mason loosed his tongue and let it be known

among the naturalists in Philadelphia that it was he and not Audubon who had drawn the floral decorations on the majority of the more spectacular and beautiful pictures exhibited by the bird artist. The whispered story quickly went the rounds. George Ord and Titian Peale, and others of the clique that did not like Audubon, rolled the choice morsel of gossip on their lips.

Audubon, laboring assiduously at oil painting under the tuition of his new-found friend, Thomas Sully—who was giving the bird man lessons in oils without recompense of any kind—had been making excellent progress. "Sully gave me all the possible encouragement which his affectionate heart could dictate," acknowledged Audubon, who added that he preferred the style of Sully to that of Rembrandt Peale, who likewise admired the naturalist's work and offered him the encouragement his brother Titian had refused.

Three men in Philadelphia proved staunch to the disappointed, down-hearted bird artist: Dr. Richard Harlan, who stood by him faithfully and long; Thomas Sully, who gave him lessons in oil and much needed encouragement in his painting, and Edward Harris, who following a chance meeting became his patron, close friend, companion on adventures and expeditions in after years, and who extended needed financial relief to Lucy Audubon during her distress after the death of her husband.

Audubon had been commissioned by Fairman the engraver to draw a grouse so that he might engrave it on a banknote about to be issued by the state of New Jersey. In calling at Audubon's studio, the engraver brought with him Edward Harris, a wealthy young gentleman of leisure with a country estate at Moorestown, New Jersey. Harris at once expressed his admiration for Audubon's drawings of birds and told the artist some of his observations on bird life.

A week later Harris again called and inspected some of the drawings Audubon had placed on sale in an endeavor to raise sufficient money to pay his debts in Philadelphia and allow him to move on to New York. "Young Harris, God bless him, looked at the drawings and said he would take them *all*, at *my* prices," records Audubon. "I would have kissed him, but that is not the custom in this icy city."

As Harris was leaving with his purchases under his arm, Audubon offered him his painting of *The Falls of the Ohio*, a landscape he was very proud of, at what he considered a sacrifice price. Harris declined to purchase it, but as the two shook hands in parting he pressed a hundred dollar bill in the artist's hands, saying: "Mr. Audubon, accept this from me; men like you ought not to want for money."

The naturalist never forgot Edward Harris nor failed in after years to appreciate his whole-hearted generosity. "I could only express my gratitude by insisting on his receiving the drawings of all my French birds, which he did and I was relieved," penned Audubon. "This is the second instance of disinterested generosity I have met with in my life, the good Doctor Provan of Natchez, being the other.

"Now I have in hand one hundred and thirty dollars to begin my journey of three thousand miles. Before this I have always thought I could work my way through the world by industry; but I see I shall not have to leave here, as Willson often did, without a cent in my pocket."

The whispering campaign to the effect that the long-haired Frenchman had not done all the work on the magnificent set of bird pictures he had been displaying, reached his ears and got under his sensitive skin, and he was making ready to leave Philadelphia, on foot if needs be, at the time of his financial windfall from Harris. He resolved to follow the advice of Doctor Harlan, LeSueur, Sully, Fairman, Bonaparte, and others, to look elsewhere, preferably Europe, for a publisher.

Before he bade farewell to the City of Brotherly Love, Audubon paid a hurried visit to *Mill Grove* and *Fatland Ford* and allowed his thoughts to dwell tenderly on the times he had been known as the gay young popinjay of the Pennsylvania countryside and had won Lucy Bakewell, "a matchless woman," for his wife. Everyone was kind to him on the visit to his old haunts on the banks of the Perkioming and he returned to cold Philadelphia glowing with delight. Carrying with him a letter from Sully to Gilbert Stuart, Audubon left the Quaker City "in good health, free from debt, and free from the anxiety for the future," and was in New York on the first day of August.

3

Upon his arrival a cart took the luggage to his lodgings, "and about one hundred passengers perched about us, as I have seen chimney-swallows perched on a roof before their morning flight," was his description of the ride through the cobbled streets. He ran slap into disappointment the first day. Most of the notables to whom he carried letters of introduction and who might help him on to Europe, were out of the city and not expected back for weeks. Consequently he began to regret his hurried leave of Philadelphia.

He visited the museum but was not impressed with what he saw on display. He complained, "the specimens of stuffed birds were set up in unnatural and constrained attitudes. This appears to be the universal practice, and the world owes *to me* the adoption of the plan of drawing from animated nature. Willson is the only one who has in any tolerable degree adopted my plan." Whereupon he closed the journal and went to bed, doubtless to dream of greatness achieved.

The next morning he was up and about early. He called on John Vanderlyn, with whom he had had an unforgettable experience in New Orleans three years before. He looked over the portraits the painter was then working on, was shown the medal Vanderlyn had received from Napoleon, but "was not impressed with the idea he was a great painter."

Later he called on Dr. Samuel L. Mitchell, frequently described as the nestor of American science of that period, and presented letters of introduction. He requested permission to show his drawings to members of the Lyceum of Natural History and, if it could be arranged, to become a member of the institution. Doctor Mitchell, founder and president of the lyceum, gave the wandering artist a letter of introduction to a Doctor Barnes in which he stated he was "delighted and instructed by a display of the contents of a portfolio containing drawings done from life of North American birds which illustrated the connection of ornithology with botany." Doctor Mitchell added that in his judgment Audubon had superior attainments and skill in natural sciences. He recommended the Frenchman to Doctor Barnes' good offices in arranging a meeting with the society's membership, so that the bird drawings could be exhibited and Audubon made a member.

"I visited the Lyceum, my portfolio was examined by the members of the institution, among whom I felt awkward and uncomfortable," wrote Audubon of the meeting. "After being among such people I feel clouded and depressed—remember that I have done nothing—and fear that *I may die unknown!* I feel that I am *strange* to all but the Birds of America! In a few days I shall be in the woods and *quite forgotten!*"

However, the visit Audubon made to the Lyceum in company with Doctor DeKay was not productive of dire results. It turned out to be quite a successful affair. The bird drawings were praised and Audubon unanimously elected to membership. To justify his enrollment among these New York men of science he prepared two papers: *On the Hirundo fulva of Vieillot*, and *Facts and Observations connected with the permanent residence of Swallows in the United States.* These two papers, his maiden efforts in bird literature, were afterwards printed in the Lyceum's Annals for 1824, and marked Audubon's début as a writer on natural history subjects.

They were prompted by a paper written for the Lyceum by De Witt Clinton, governor of New York, who reviewed certain observations made by M. Vieillot in his *Historic Naturelle de Oiseaux d'Amerique Septentrionale*, who stated he had seen the cliff swallow "once in Santo Domingo."

Audubon's observations on this species followed Governor Clinton's paper. Audubon called the bird "the Republican Swallow in allusion to their mode of association for the purpose of building and rearing their young," said he had first seen them at Henderson in the spring of 1815, and in 1819 had found them again at Newport, Kentucky, when he had made his drawing of the birds and their mud nests.

The committee on publication of the Lyceum's Annals gave a flattering note to Mr. Audubon's work, stating: "This gentleman, with an enthusiasm only equalled by that of our lamented Wilson has devoted nearly twenty years to the study of American Ornithology. He has followed the birds into their most secret haunts, and traversed the United States in almost every direction. To the learnings of a naturalist, he unites the skill of an artist, and his magnificent collection of drawings, representing four hundred species, excels anything of the kind in this country, and has probably never been surpassed in Europe."

At a meeting on August 11, Audubon read to the members his first scientific paper on his observations and facts connected with the permanent residence of swallows in the United States. It will be remembered that there was a superstitious belief that the disappearance of certain birds, particularly the swallows, was due to hibernation, in which they passed into a torpid state and remained during the winter months hidden in caves, hollow trees, or even embedded in the mud at the bottom of streams, ponds, marshes, etc.—tales had even been printed that the birds had been seen flying directly into the water of the Gulf of Mexico, from which they did not reappear until spring . . . when they flew from the sea and thence northwards to their breeding grounds!

In one part of his paper Audubon said:

"Being extremely desirous of settling the long agitated question respecting the emigration or supposed torpidity of the swallow, I embraced every opportunity of examining their habits, of carefully noting their arrival and disappearance, and of recording every fact connected with their history.

"After some years of reflection and constant observation, I remarked that amongst all the species of migratory birds, those that remove farthest from us, depart sooner than those which retire only to the confines of the United States; and by a parity of reasoning, those that remain later, return earlier in the spring."

He included extracts of his notes and records of temperature while observing these birds in the vicinity of New Orleans, and proved they were most active during the coldest days and that he had seen no signs of torpidity among any of the swallow tribe.

4

In spite of this flattering reception of his birds and his exposé of the alleged torpidity of swallows in winter-time, he records in his journal that his spirits were low, that he longed for the woods again, and that the prospect of becoming better known alone prompted him to delay a proposed journey to Boston. He had been making exhaustive inquiries in New York concerning the possibilities of publication, but "found there is little prospect of the undertaking being favorably received," he confessed, and adds he had "reason to suspect that unfriendly communications from parties interested in Willson's volumes" had much to do with the refusal of New Yorkers to even consider his work on birds. The Philadelphians, it appeared, were still determined Audubon should not be allowed his place in the sun; that he should not be given an opportunity of filling Wilson's shoes as the American authority on birds.

The charge that Joseph Mason, and not he, had drawn the floral decorations and backgrounds of his bird pictures was now being openly bruited, which caused Audubon to set down in his journal that "the Philadelphians have represented that my drawings have not been wholly done by myself. Full of dispair I look to Europe as my only hope."

Joseph Mason's accusation proved the final blow. From that time on Audubon never mentioned the boy who had been of such service to him in the preparation of his magnificent series of bird pictures. An examination of these original drawings discloses that Joseph Mason did draw many of the floral designs, as has already been pointed out, but when the plates were engraved and issued there was no mention of the talented boy's part in making many of these bird plates real pictures.

Mason remained at Barton's botanical gardens in Philadelphia for several years and then returned to his home in Cincinnati, where he took up an art career. In 1830 he became engaged to Minnie Barleer, daughter of James Barleer, but in May of 1832, just a month before the ceremony was to take place, his pretty bride-to-be died of a fever. Joseph Robert Mason, true to his only sweetheart, never married. He died in Brown county, Ohio, September 24, 1883, at the age of seventy-four. According to a nephew, William Shiveley of New Richmond, Ohio, Mason never forgave Audubon for what he termed the bird man's selfishness in refusing him appropriate credit for his part in making so many of *The Birds of America* the beautiful examples of floral art they are today acknowledged to be.

5

Still downcast and morose over the action of the New York publishers in refusing to even look at, much less consider, his birds, Audubon again called at John Vanderlyn's studio where he found the portrait painter busy on a picture of General Andrew Jackson, a commission from the city of New York.

Vanderlyn had sketched in the composition, which showed "Old Hickory" in the field, sword in hand, as he appeared during the Battle of New Orleans. The warrior's face had been painted from the chiseled features of the old general himself, but that was as long as the hero of Chalmette would pose. Vanderlyn hailed Audubon's arrival with delight. The bird man must pose for the completion of the picture "since my figure considerably resembled that of the General more than any he had ever seen." Needing the money, Audubon donned the general's blue uniform, thrust his feet into the high boots, grasped the hilt of the unsheathed sword, slung the cloak over his left arm, grasped the hat just so, and struck the necessary pose, while the artist he had once so roundly cursed (in the privacy of his journal, however), mixed his colors and brushed on the paint.

Thus Vanderlyn's striking portrait of the hero of January Eighth, now hanging in the city hall, New York city, is "Old Hickory" from the shoulders up, but John James Audubon from the shoulders down. It is quite certain that ragged bird artist who stood in narrow Chartres street of old New Orleans, April 27, 1821, jostled by a cheering throng, who strained his eyes to catch a fleeting glimpse of the grim-faced warrior, had not the slightest suspicion then that one day he would be standing in Andy Jackson's boots!

"What a curious, interesting book, a biographer, well acquainted with my life, could write," Audubon afterwards predicted when writing to his wife from Edinburgh.

Five days later, the Jackson portrait finished, Audubon

left New York, but he did not go to Boston, as he had first intended. He decided on a boat trip up the Hudson to Albany in the hope of interesting De Witt Clinton in the publication of his *Birds*. He was doomed to another disappointment for he found Governor Clinton absent from the state capital. Deciding not to miss an opportunity of viewing Niagara Falls, Audubon journeyed on, thanks to the money Edward Harris had given him, and when he registered at a Buffalo inn, under his flourishing "John J. Audubon" he wrote: "who, like Willson, will ramble, but never like that great man, die under the lash of a book-seller!" The reference was to a story then going the rounds that the Scot's death had been hastened by the dishonesty of his publishers.

Audubon was all of a tremble, he says, when he reached the Falls of Niagara, "and, oh, what a scene! my blood shudders still, although I am not a coward, at the grandure of the Creator's power; and I gazed motionless at this new display of the irresistible force of His elements." The man did not paint the mighty torrent pouring over the rocks. He was satisfied, he declared, that Niagara had never been, and would never be, adequately painted.

" 'What!' thought I, 'have I come here to mimic nature in her grandest enterprise, and add *my* caricature to one of the wonders of the world to those that I here see?' No; I give up the vain attempt. I shall look upon these mighty cataracts and imprint them, where alone they may be represented—on my mind!"

He had a "good dinner" for twelve cents and went to bed "thinking of Franklin eating his roll in the streets of Philadelphia, of Goldsmith traveling by the aid of his musical powers, and of other great men who had worked their way through hardships and difficulties to fame, and fell asleep, hoping by persevering industry, to make a name for myself among my countrymen."

From Buffalo he went to Erie and, unable to afford a cabin berth, took deck passage on a boat at a fare of one dollar and fifty cents. "I was to furnish my own bed and provisions; my buffalo robe and blanket served for the former The captain invited me to sleep in the cabin; but I declined, as I never encroach where I have no right. The sky was serene, and I threw myself on the deck contemplating the unfathomable immensity above me, and contrasting the comforts which ten days before I was enjoying, with my present condition. Even the sailors, *ignorant of my name*, look upon me as a poor devil not able to pay for a cabin passage."

The next day the craft that carried him over the waters of Lake Erie ran into a gale, went upon a bar at the entrance of the harbor and the passengers had to be put ashore in a navy gig. Audubon was frantic with fear for a time that his portfolio of bird drawings would become watersoaked or lost, but his journal tells us that his "drawings were safely landed, and for anything else I care very little at the moment."

When he arrived in Erie, Audubon had exactly seven dollars and a half in his pocket. In spite of this scanty store of money, he started a-foot for Pittsburgh, which lay due south. He had picked up a companion for the tramp, a man who was also adept in the use of the pencil. Their heavy luggage was placed on a cart going to Meadville, which cost Audubon five dollars, and with blithe hearts the wanderers set off on shanks's mares. The night was spent at the home of the carter, and on a smiling Monday morning they entered Meadville and put up at the inn of "The Traveler's Rest," with a dollar and a half between them.

Audubon had relied on his black chalks in many a tight pinch before, so with a small portfolio under his arm he strolled about the village looking for heads. The search for the "human phiz" was successful and for that day and the next Audubon's black chalks were kept busy transfering to paper the physiognomies of many of the village aristocracy. His companion was fortunate in receiving payment for two sketches, so with pockets replenished the two set out on foot for Pittsburgh, sending the luggage in advance on a wagon.

6

Audubon arrived in Pittsburgh the first week in September and, according to his journal, was "more politely received than on former occasions . . . which I found was due to the reception I had met with in Philadelphia, some rumors of which had reached the West."

During his six weeks' stay in the growing town at the confluence of the Allegheny and Monongahela rivers Audubon was forced to rely upon his portrait sketching ability to keep himself supplied with food at meal times and a bed at night. Black chalks were kept busy, and he was fortunate in securing one pupil willing to pay for art lessons. She was Harriet Basham, who evidenced a pronounced talent for drawing flowers, and Audubon was frequently at the hospitable Basham home.

The Bashams were well-educated folk who delighted in gathering about them those of the artistic and scientific world. Charles Basham was an Englishman who had been in America more than a score of years. His wife, Elizabeth Beatty, came from County Cavan and she possessed all the wit Ireland usually bestows upon a favorite daughter. Among those Audubon met at the Basham home was a mysterious Frenchman, Doctor de la Motte by name, who had been forced to flee the land of his birth during the reign of Charles X, and he and the bird artist struck up an immediate friendship. M. de la Motte, suspected of bearing a title, had letters of introduction from the Marquis de LaFayette, and claimed that he was a physician planning to go to Mexico so he could find a cure for "a disease called goitre."

Another acquaintance made during the Pittsburgh stay was a Swiss landscape artist named George Lehman, and he, so we will find, again entered Audubon's life a few years later.

Giving lessons to Harriet Basham and making portrait sketches filled Audubon's time for several weeks. At first work flowed upon him and then, as in the past, the saturation point for delineations of the human phiz was reached and silver coins failed to rattle in the pockets of his well-worn pantaloons. Few bird drawings were made because the country about Pittsburgh yielded only the commoner species, and these Audubon had already pictured to his satisfaction.

One day he was called upon by a prominent, well-to-do merchant who told the bird artist he desired his portrait made in crayons. "But don't ask too much for it, Mr. Audubon," Henry Baldwin added.

Audubon did not answer immediately. He knew the prospective sitter's standing in the community but he did not like the last part of the merchant's request.

"At present, sar, I am engage with my bird," Audubon finally said. "Beside," here he slapped his trousers' pockets, "I 'ave so mooch in my pockets zat I mus' decline ze honor of making your picture." Then he stood up and bowed.

Baldwin was nonplussed. For a few moments he stammered for words, for the artist's curt action quite ruffled his temper. At last he found his voice.

"Will no inducement, sir, make you change your mind?"

"None, sar!" This time Audubon bowed his visitor to the door.

One Sunday he attended the Episcopal church presided over by the Reverend John Henry Hopkins, who later became the first Episcopal bishop of Vermont. Audubon was not a churchgoer. He opposed formal religion with a fervor that was matched only by his passion for drawing birds and listening to their music. "In my mind church attendance has been confounded with such rascally conduct otherwise that I cannot think of it without sadness," he set down in his journal.

Back in his lodgings, with the words of the Reverend Hopkins' sermon still ringing in his ears, he admitted to his journal that he had been brought to think, "more than I usually did, of religious matters; but I confess I never think of churches without feeling sick at the sham and show of their professors. To repay evils with kindness is the religion I was taught to practice, and this forever will be my rule."

Audubon's religion was that of the great out-of-doors. He communed with the trees and the birds. To him the clear and penetrating call of the mating bird had an infinitely deeper appeal to the Master Architect of the Universe than words in sermons, the swelling notes of a mighty organ, or the anthems from choir lofts in structures builded by man.

He loved, he worshipped nature . . . usually to the exclusion of all else, even family ties.

7

The last of October came and with it the first chilling

warning of approaching winter. Audubon was still in Pittsburgh and low in funds. This condition, and the biting cold, directed his thoughts longingly to the more salubrious climate of the Southland and especially to the magnolia forests and birds of Feliciana. How was he to get there? For days he meditated on the problem—should he purchase a skiff and row down the Ohio and Mississippi rivers to the land of his heart's desire?

After a period of indecision and changing resolutions, he purchased a small boat, filled it with provisions, and said goodbye to the Bashams and the few other new friends he had made in Pittsburgh. But he was not to journey alone. The Swiss artist Lehman and Doctor de la Motte decided to join Audubon on his river trip, their destination being New Orleans. Just before the start an Irishman was added to the party—the Celt was to labor at the oars in payment for his passage and keep.

In high spirits the quartette pushed off October 24, 1824. At nights the little boat was tied to the shore, Audubon using the skiff as sleeping quarters while the others found more or less comfortable places on the high bank. Five days after leaving Pittsburgh they reached Wheeling, but only after a very disagreeable experience—for it had rained almost continuously day and night. The oddly-assorted four were wetted to the skin and all suffered from the cold and exposure. There was a shortage of food, of money, and of temper.

The brawny Irishman was the first to abandon the journey. The Swiss Lehman was the next. Doctor de la Motte the next day announced his intention of remaining in Wheeling until he could go to Mexico in a more civilized manner. Audubon, left to himself, tried to add to his scanty store of small coins by hawking lithographs of General LaFayette. When he was finally convinced that likenesses of the French hero of the Revolution were not in demand, he decided to follow the example of his former companions and abandon ship. Fortunately he was able to sell the skiff for just enough to enable him to take passage on a keelboat carrying a number of army officers and other passengers to Cincinnati. Clutching his gun, journal, and portfolios of bird drawings, he climbed aboard, tightened his belt, and arrived in the Ohio city from which he had departed on his momentous flatboat journey four years before, and exactly as he left it—"without money or the means of making it."

Being broke was not his only embarrassment as he soon found out, for he had no sooner set foot in Cincinnati than he was "beset by claims for the payment of articles which years before I had ordered for the Museum, but from which I got no benefit." Money he must have, not for the insistent creditors of the museum where he had stuffed birds and fishes, but for himself if he was to continue on to Louisiana. He scurried about the town seeking someone who would trust him for a few dollars. "I applied to Messers Keating and Bell for the loan of fifteen dollars," he recalled in later years, "but had not the courage to do so until I had walked past their house several times, unable to make up my mind how to ask the favor."

Much to his surprise he got the loan cheerfully and with it he was able to purchase deck passage on a steamboat then leaving for Louisville. Although a deck passenger he was allowed to take his meals in the cabin, but at night was forced to sleep among some shavings he had managed to scrape together on the steamboat's open deck.

Audubon was ragged and unkempt; he had allowed his beard to grow, and his hair was even longer than usual. He had formed the habit of letting his personal appearance go by the board. His ablutions had been slighted for days. His spirits, habitually either at a very high pitch or sunk to the deepest depths of woe, were not seemingly affected that night by the depressed condition of his finances as he snuggled among the shavings. What if he was shivering? He had his portfolio, his gun, and his *confidente*—that well-known and much scribbled journal, in which he had just written:

"The spirit of contentment which I now feel is strange—it borders on the sublime; and, enthusiast or lunatic—as some of my relatives will have me—I am glad I have such a spirit."

He was Louisiana bound.

8

Audubon remained at Louisville long enough to discover

that his friends and his wife's relatives were impressed only with his ragged apparel, and to learn that those upon whom he had once conferred acts of kindness were inclined to remind him of his errors.

He held his son Victor in his arms, learned from him of the state of his wife's health, and that the boy was contented with his position in the Berthoud establishment. He secured another loan, and started down the Ohio on a steamboat headed for New Orleans. "I decided to go down the Mississippi to my old home of Bayou Sarah and there open a school, with the profits of which to complete my ornithological studies," was his resolution as he paid over eight dollars for passage.

Audubon arrived at Bayou Sarah "with rent and wasted clothes and uncut hair, and altogether looking like the Wandering Jew," he tells us. Yellow fever was raging at St. Francisville when the steamer arrived off the Bayou Sarah landing and the captain, fearing the scourge, would not tie up at the wharf, so his long-haired passenger and his bulky portfolios were put ashore in a small boat. The man's adventurous return to the Louisiana country he loved so well is best told in his own words:

"I was put ashore about midnight, and left to grope my way on a dark, rainy and sultry night to the village, about one mile distant. The awful scourge of yellow fever prevailed and was taking off the citizens with greater rapidity than had ever before been known. When I arrived the desolation was so great that the one large hotel was deserted, and I walked in, finding the doors all open, and the furniture in the house, but not a living person. The inmates had all gone to the pine woods.

"I walked to the post office, roused the postmaster, and learned to my joy that my wife and son were well at Mrs. Percy's. He had no accomodation for me but recommended me to a tavern where I might find a bed. The atmosphere calm, heavy, and suffocating, and it seemed to me that I was breathing death while hunting this tavern; finding it, the landlord told me he had no spare bed, but mentioned a German at the end of the village who might take me in; off there I walked, and was kindly received. The German, Maxmilian

Nübling, was a man of cultivation and taste, a lover of natural science, and had collected a variety of interesting objects. He gave me some refreshment, and offered me a horse to ride to Mrs. Percy's. The horse was soon at the door and with many thanks I bade him adieu.

"My anxiety to reach my beloved wife and child were so great that I resolved to make a short course through the woods, which I thought I knew thoroughly, and hardly caring where I should cross the bayou. In less than two hours I reached its shores, but the horse refused to enter the water, and snorting suddenly, turned and made off through the woods, as if desirous of crossing at some other place, and when he reached the shore again walked in and crossed me to the other side.

"The sky was overcast and the mosquitoes plentiful; but I thought I recognized the spot where I had watched the habits of a wild cat, or a deer, as the clouds broke away, and the stars now and then peeped through to help me make my way through the gloomy forests. But in this I was mistaken, for when day dawned I found myself in woods which were unknown to me.

"I was in the woods, the woods of Louisiana . . . my heart was beating with joy!

"However, I chanced to meet a black man, who told me where I was and that I had passed Mrs. Percy's plantation two miles. Turning my horse's head and putting spurs to him, a brisk gallop soon brought me to the house.

"It was early, but I found my beloved wife up, engaged in giving a lesson to her pupils and, holding and kissing her, I was once more happy, and all my toils and trials were forgotten."

Audubon arrived back in Louisiana penniless and in debt, but he was alive; so were his wife and son, and he was again in his adored Feliciana, his "Happyland"—so, what else mattered?

CHAPTER 19

Back in Happyland

EAGERLY and with characteristic enthusiasm the artist unfolded to his wife his ambitious plans for the future, as he exhibited additions to his portfolio of bird portraits. Europe—Success—Fame awaited him, could he but get there! But how? An entry in his journal the first day of December tells us:

> After a few day's rest I began to think of the future and to look about to see what I could do to hasten the publication of my drawings. My wife was receiving a large income—nearly three thousand dollars a year[1]—from her industry and talents, which she generously offered me to help forward their publication; and I resolved on a new effort to increase the amount by my own energy and effort.

Mrs. Percy, kind and helpful as always, agreed to forget the man's eccentricities for the sake of his lovable, kindly wife, for everyone who came under the spell of Lucy Audubon's charm became her devoted admirer.

For a year and a half Audubon lived at *Beech Woods*, and through every season of the year he roamed the fragrant magnolia woods for the warblers, the thrushes, and the vireos; the fields for the buntings, sparrows, and larks; the Tunica swamp for herons, ibises, spoonbills, bitterns, and rails; the broad Bayou Sarah for ducks, and geese, and shorebirds, moving north or to the south on their migrations. He haunted the woods bordering Little Bayou Sarah and sandy Thompson's creek for specimens of avian life. Gradually his portfolio swelled with added portraits and his knowledge of the birds grew. Many pictures made in previous years did not please him, for they failed to measure up to his new ability in delineation, so he re-drew some of them.

Upon his return to the Bayou Sarah region Audubon

[1]Mrs. Audubon's salary was only one thousand dollars per annum.

was overjoyed to find Nat Pope, his old-time clerk of the Louisville and Henderson days, settled in St. Francisville, married, rearing a family, and practicing medicine.

Audubon made another acquaintance at this time who proved invaluable to him in his chosen work. At *Bush Hill* plantation lived Augustin Bourgeat, of French descent—he would probably be called a Cajun today—who had married the daughter of Benjamin Collins. Bourgeat loved hunting as Audubon did and he too would neglect work at any time it interfered with the pleasure of a day in the woods with a gun. Small wonder, then, that these two drifted together, linked by a common passion for birds, chattering French, killing ducks, wood storks, parokeets, warblers, ibises, alligators, hawks, and owls. Augustin knew the resorts of all the birds; he was an accomplished alligator hunter, and many a happy excursion the two had together.

When Audubon called at *Greenwood* plantation he found Eliza Pirrie Barrow the mother of a little son, named for his father. Motherhood had only heightened the loveliness of his former pupil who, in spite of many opportunities to remarry, clung to her widowhood in order to devote herself more fully to the care of Robert Barrow's posthumous son. Squire Pirrie had died the previous March, and although her mother remained at *Oakley*, Eliza chose to stay on the Barrow plantation located not far from *Beech Woods*.

It was at this time that Audubon made his resolution regarding the manner in which his great work would be offered to the public. He said:

> Chance, and chance alone, had divided my drawings into three different classes, depending on the magnitude of the objects to be represented; and, although I did not at the time possess all the specimens necessary, I arranged them as well as I could into parcels of five plates—I improved the whole as much as was in my power; I daily retired farther and farther from the haunts of man, determined to leave nothing undone, which my labor, my time, or my purse could accomplish.

Audubon was constantly afield, whether Bourgeat or Doctor Pope could accompany him or not, and the sight of this able-bodied man roaming the woods of the Felicianas, killing little wrens and *ti-tits* and drawing their pictures in colors, while his wife earned the family living, was hardly a picture calculated to inspire respect among the men of Feliciana. Nor did the housewives of the countryside find many virtues to admire about him. Nevertheless, in the face of thinly disguised dislike and contempt, Audubon undauntedly pursued his way, saw much, learned much, and lived life fully in his own fashion.

There were two periods when he did pursue more remunerative occupations—teaching art to some of the young ladies at *Beech Woods* and giving French and violin lessons to others. He was equally proficient in each of these accomplishments. The sons of Judge Peter Randolph—John Hamden, Sidney, and Peter, by name—wished to become adept in fencing. Consequently Audubon, who could handle the foils as gracefully as he did the bow, made weekly journeys to the Randolph plantation near Woodville, Mississippi, and trained the young men in the intricacies of the *code duello*.

It was upon the occasions of Saturday night soirees that former pupils best remembered the artist, for when the cotton gin-house was not in use at *Beech Woods* its floor was swept clean and Audubon gave the beaux and belles dancing lessons. These affairs grew in favor and it was no unusual sight to see the gin-house filled to capacity, candles sputtering in brackets on the walls, and the long-haired Frenchman prancing up and down the floor, playing his violin as he danced, and showing the men the correct steps for the cotillion. When the men pupils were clumsy he would fly into a rage, calling them dolts, clods, idiots!

With the young ladies he was more patient, more gallant, and invariably addressed them in endearing terms. Isabel Kendrick told her daughter years later: "When I would make a misstep he would throw up his hands and 'De udder foot, my darling!' was his affectionate admonition."

The success of the dancing classes held at *Beech Woods* gained him a flattering reputation and prestige throughout the Feliciana country and it was not long before he had paying pupils at *Waverley*, a plantation home where he taught Emily McDermott, afterwards the wife of Dr. Henry Bains, and the mistress of the house, to trip the light fantastic toe—but in the decorous style of that period. Then his fame as a dancing master spread above the Mississippi state line and eventually a class of sixty pupils was gathered at Woodville for lessons every Friday and Saturday night during a three-month's term. Audubon has left us a word picture of inauguration of that first Mississippi dancing class:

> I marched to the hall with my violin under my arm, bowed to the company assembled, tuned my violin; played a cotillon, and began my lesson.
>
> I placed all the gentlemen in a line reaching across the hall, thinking to give the young ladies time to compose themselves and get ready when called. How I toiled before I could get one graceful step or motion! I broke my bow and nearly my violin in my excitement and impatience! The gentlemen were soon fatigued. The ladies were next placed in the same order and made to walk the steps; then came the trial for both parties to proceed at the same time while I pushed one here and another there, and all the while singing to myself to assist their movements. Many of the parents were delighted.
>
> After this first lesson was over I was requested to *dance to my own music*, which I did until the whole room came down in thunders of applause in clapping hands and shouting. Lessons in fencing followed to the young gentlemen and I went to bed extremely fatigued.

Woodville, which was a small town set in the very center of a prosperous cotton-growing community, gladly welcomed the artist who knew not only a great deal about birds but who also knew every step and prance of the dances of that period. Not only did the members of Judge Peter Randolph's family join his classes but many men of staid mein and ponderous dignity, as well as flesh, desired to "know their steps." Harry Cage, for instance, was a sportsman who loved a gun leveled at birds and a dash over the countryside after a gray fox; Major Feltus was a retired army officer who had served in the expedition against Canada in the War of 1812; William Ventress and Levin K. Marshall were fathers whose daughters had been sent to the Percy plantation in Feliciana so they could be educated by Lucy Audubon, a gentlewoman. Elderly all, but then the dancing school at Woodville had not been organized wholly for the benefit of the young, hot-blooded folk of the countryside. The middle-aged, especially the married men, attended these soirees devoted to Terpsichore in company with their children—as well as their parents. Shouts greeted their appearance on the floor. The juveniles would go into convulsions of mirth, tears of laughter streamed down their cheeks as they watched the solemn antics of fathers and grandfathers taking their first steps from that funny Mons. Audubon.

Those were the palmy, cotton-rich days of Woodville! when men in the twilight of their existence or those passing through middle years were not ashamed to unbend occasionally.

Audubon's dancing school became a sort of safety valve where a gathering of the grave, the gay, the old and the young could let off steam. As a result, some of Monsieur Audubon's elder pupils nearly ran him insane. Before the night's dancing lessons were ended he usually demonstrated that he had run out of temper.

When it came to teaching the doughty, and pouchy, Major Feltus his steps, the dancing master had a task cut out for him. The major's knee-joints, so it appeared from his cavortings on the floor, had acquired a rigidity to be matched only by an iron poker. The owner of the stiff knee-joints claimed this was due to military training and weary watchings on post at Fort Harrison during the late war with Great Britain. The excitable tutor either could not, or would not, believe that Feltus could not fling his legs about like wet dish rags. "Oh-h-h! Major Feltus, *mon ami*, why you do not bend those knee? *Avoir la danse libre!* Oh, *non*, *non*, eef you nod bend those knee you cannot geeve the extension necessarie! *Sacre bleu!* my frien', you geeve me no credit as *maitre à danser!*"

When Audubon took Harry Cage in hand it was evident there was nothing rusty about Mr. Cage's knee action. Indeed, the tutor complained that his pupil danced like a jockey riding in a steeple chase or like a gentleman a-horse after a fleeing fox. "*Mon cher ami*," the instructor would say, after he had stopped bowing the violin and endeavored to speak calmly so not to betray how near he was to letting slip his usually uncontrolled temper, "*Mon bon et digne ami*, w'y do you h'allow yourself so mooch motion? *Pourquoi*, you throw yourself ar-r-round too grand! You mus' gently, gently, saire, w'en you dance—you mus' nod run h'away wid these cotillon, saire!" This last injunction being coupled with a tremendous and withering glare from the blue eyes of the *maitre à danse*.

Audubon had no rival in this pleasant Southern country

in ornithology, certainly no peers or equals—unless it was Augustin Bourgeat, or Doctor Pope; he had no rival in the art of handling rapiers, single-sticks, or broadswords; as a shot with either shotgun, rifle, or pistol he was in a class by himself—even such an ardent and expert a sportsman as Harry Cage yielded the palm to Audubon when it came to bagging birds. In spite of his acknowledged superiority in these varied proclivities he did finally have a rival to his claim of being the best dancing master in the South, for one day a Monsieur Muscarilla daintily traipsed into Woodville from Natchez and introduced himself to town folk as *un professeur de danse* from Paris.

M. Muscarilla lifted a pudgy nose high above a wisp of a moustache while a spectator at one of Audubon's dancing classes and afterwards quoted a Spanish proverb, which was to the effect that to some men God hath given wisdom and understanding—to others He had given the art of playing the violin. As the newcomer from Paris carried with him such an instrument, he proceeded to demonstrate that the last part of the proverb fitted him like a glove. He expressed contempt of Audubon's fiddling and for the bird artist's dancing, too. He issued an invitation—let any *gentilhomme* accompany him to his salon and, in less than five minutes, he would prove that Audubon was "*ni musicien, ni maitre à danser! Violà!* H'i h'am suprise," continued the nimble-legged new-comer, "H'i h'am astonish thad theese man Audubon should 'ave took you h'in! He can no *danse*—He can no play *violon!*"

He was almost moved to tears when he was told the ladies of Woodville preferred Audubon, and in a characteristic Gallic outburst cried: "So, they prefaire these bird stouffer, *hein?* Oh, la, la, my *sacrée tete*! 'E does not comprehend *de poesie de motion*, him. 'E h'occupy his time stouffing *des oiseaux, et courant autour les bois et les champs!* 'E ees whad you call *vulgaire*, monsieurs. 'E, zis Audubon, 'ave so mooch de smell *des oiseaux* aboud 'im 'e is no fit to *approacher les Demoiselles*, mouch less to guide them through *les figures chassez rechassez, dos-à-dos, et la grand promenade, d'un cotillon parisien, et des autres fashionables.*"

That a war, one that would be fought with weapons other than words, even French words, was seen as inevitable. Audubon in rebuttal dubbed Muscarilla an interfering interloper —a *puante pravenu*, a stinking upstart—in the dancing profession. The lads about the village, scenting a rare time and some blood spilled, urged Monsieur Muscarilla to offer Audubon the opportunity of avenging these insulting words through the medium of the *duello*. He was about to send such a challenge when Harry Cage, the sportsman who rode a mean horse and handled a wicked shotgun when after birds, told the new dancing master that Audubon was the only man he ever met who could outshoot him.

"Why, M. Muscarilla," continued Cage in a confidential whisper, "this Audubon fellow told me, when out shooting partridges the other day, that he killed—at *one shot!*—one *more* bird than the whole covey numbered!"

Muscarilla never sent the challenge and a few days later left the dancing field to the bird artist.

Audubon's financial returns from his dancing lessons fell far short of the thousand dollars a year Lucy Audubon had earned from her teachings, and the little he received was spent for supplies for his beloved bird drawings.

2

Throughout the year things went on happily at *Beech Woods*. The young ladies of the school were amused at Audubon's odd ways and strange pronunciations in his high, French-accented voice. One of the Randolph girls, an uncommonly sedate member of the class, asked Ann Mathews to teach her a polite French phrase to address to Mr. Audubon in his native tongue. Ann, who knew her French, said "Go up to him very courteously and say, '*Bon soir, chat.*' "

Miss Randolph did as told, repeating the phrase as she made a graceful curtsey. To her consternation, Audubon flew into a violent rage and it became necessary for his wife to quiet him. Only then did the bewildered girl learn she had said "Good night, cat," to the artist who was long of hair but short of temper.

The young ladies of the school greatly admired the long brown curls that hung over his shoulders and, knowing Audubon's pride in his hirsute adornment, would beg for a tress so they might wear it, as was the fashion at that time, as an embellishing side curl in their own hair. Audubon would protest at first, pretending horror at the thought of parting from a single hair, but finally would throw up his hands with a typical Gallic gesture and cry: "Well, zen, bring ze scissor eef you mus' 'ave my 'air!" and beaming with good nature would bend his head while each girl snipped off a coveted trophy.

3

Much controversy has developed in late years as to when and where Audubon's famous bird plate, the lordly wild turkey cock, was painted. Henderson, Kentucky, and approximately a dozen places in Louisiana have bid for this fame. The celebrated picture was a result of one of his Feliciana quests and was drawn while Audubon was at *Beech Woods* in 1825. Arrived in England this was his favorite among his many bird pictures. He exhibited it on every occasion that presented itself to spread his collection of paintings before the scientific and the cultured. He selected it as the first subject to be engraved, and it led off the procession of birds in his ambitious work. In none of his earlier journals or diaries does he refer to this wild turkey gobbler, and it is quite certain had it been in existence, he would not have failed to mention what he considered the masterpiece of his collection. From 1826 on, his journals, letters and diaries have much to say of this prized bird.

The Sleepy Hollow Woods a few miles north of the Percy plantation was a favorite turkey hunting country, and Audubon and his constant woods companions, Augustin Bourgeat and Doctor Pope, haunted these tree-covered acres. Three of Mrs. Audubon's pupils recalled in after years watching the artist at work on his famous drawing. Miss Sarah Turnbull Stirling of Wakefield, who not only knew and talked with numerous former pupils of Mrs. Audubon's, but preserved in writing the many interesting tales about the Audubons that came to her ears, learned from those who saw the huge portrait in the making at *Beech Woods* that Audubon not only drew his original turkey picture there but even took it about to exhibit it to admiring friends.

We learn a great deal about the making of the wild turkey cock painting from the wife of Doctor Pope, who left behind her delightful manuscript reminiscences of the Audubons in West Feliciana. Before her marriage to Audubon's old-time clerk and woods companion of the hectic Kentucky days, Mrs. Pope was a passenger on board the *New Orleans*, the first steam-propelled vessel to ply the Mississippi, and while in the Crescent City met Mrs. Audubon when she was at the Brand home nursing the baby and instructing Mrs. Brand. According to Mrs. Pope, the builder's wife had been given only a slight education and Mrs. Audubon had been employed to rectify the deficiency.

"Mrs. Audubon was not handsome," recalled Mrs. Pope. "Her face was spoiled by her nose, which was short and turned up. She had fine dark gray eyes shaded by long dark lashes. Expression was her chief attraction. She was very gentle and intelligent. Her whole appearance impressed me with respect and admiration.

"Audubon was one of the handsomest men I ever saw. In person he was tall and slender, his blue eyes were an eagle's in brightness, his teeth were white and even, his hair a beautiful chestnut brown, very glossy and curly. His bearing was courteous and refined, simple, and unassuming. Added to these personal advantages he was a natural sportsman and natural artist.

"He kept his drawings in a watertight tin box, which remained in my parlour for months. His reputation was spread far and wide, and often our home was filled with visitors who came to see his drawings and paintings, which he would spread out on the floor for inspection, and he never seemed weary of unpacking and explaining them. He was very sociable and communicative, being the center of attraction in every circle in which he mingled."

Mrs. Pope, who left these delightful reminiscences of Audubon's stay in West Feliciana parish, was Martha Johnson, youngest daughter of an Englishman who settled in the West Florida section in 1776, when that part of Louisiana was under the domination of Great Britain. His name was Isaac Johnson and his father was a Liverpool divine. The pretty Martha Johnson married Nathaniel Wells Pope in 1823, when that young medico settled in St. Francisville to establish a practice. When Audubon returned from his wanderings he was enthusiastically welcomed by the physician.

"When Audubon came to St. Francisville on his way to or from the plantation where Mrs. Audubon was teaching, my husband invited him to make our house his home," so runs Mrs. Pope's narrative. "He often described to me the cottage in which he was born. It was on the banks of the Mississippi river, in lower Louisiana, and was surrounded by orange trees. When quite young his father sent him to France to be educated. He returned to the United States after completing his education, and married a young English girl, who was accomplished and dignified. They were married in Philadelphia from whence they migrated to Louisville, Kentucky. Here he opened a large store. Being hospitable and generous, his table was furnished with the choicest viands. Unfortunately he failed in business and was treated with much neglect by those who had shared his fortune, he told us.

"Stung to the quick by this treatment, he resolved to make a fortune and show these false friends that he could earn money as well as spend it. He would say: 'I mean to get me a coach-and-six and ride through the streets of Louisville yet!'"

Doctor Pope, "good friend Bourgeat," and Audubon were inseparable companions of the woods. Hunting and fishing and seeking birds, the three would absent themselves from their homes whole days at a time, starting at daybreak and not returning to the fireside until long after dark. Frequently their excursions into the swamps were matters of several days. As a rule the trio would come tramping back to Doctor Pope's home with the fruits of the chase. Here too Audubon usually brought his new bird drawings for comment, criticism, and praise, receiving all three from the friendly physician and his charming wife.

The day Audubon finished his ambitious drawing of the wild turkey cock he carried the water color to Doctor Pope's home, where it was hailed as a masterpiece, much to the artist's satisfaction. In his voluble way, illustrating with a wealth of gesticulation, he described the twenty-three hours of toil he had put into the drawing. He pointed out the correctness of each feather, the truthful coloring of the head and wattles, the bird's breast-beard, the stride it assumed in walking through the cane brake of the Sleepy Hollow woods where he and young Robert Dow Percy had spied it as they coaxed the suspicious gobbler within gun range by imitating the *cluck* of the female, using the second joint of a wing bone for a *yelper.*

Audubon also described the backward glance the handsome bird had given as it strode off when the cock discovered the kind of hen that had called him into the opening of the glade and how he had raised the Souvenir Gun and pulled the trigger. Dramatically he described the final thrashings of the big turkey cock that was destined to become his most famous model.

Back at *Beech Woods* the gigantic bird was triced up on wires and the drawing begun.

"The day Audubon showed us the painting of the wild turkey," wrote Mrs. Pope, "he compared it with the bird shown in Bonaparte's work, which he had lately procured. Audubon maintained that the superiority of his painting consisted in the shading of the legs, which Bonaparte had painted all one color, while those of his were shaded in different hues. Though no artist myself, I could see the difference after the explanation."

Robert Dow Percy in after years also told of the killing of the big gobbler. "It weighed twenty-eight pounds. Audubon pinned it up beside the wall to sketch and he spent several days lazily sketching it. The damned fellow kept it pinned up there till it rotted and stunk—I hated to lose so much good eating."

All of which indubitably ends a discussion of years and establishes the time and the place of the making of the wild turkey cock painting.

4

We will allow Mrs. Pope to tell us more of The American Woodsman at this period of his career:

"Mr. Audubon had always been fond of hunting and drawing, he told me, so when misfortune overwhelmed him he turned to these apparently frivolous pastimes as the means whereby his fortune could be made. His first sketch was of a wild duck sitting on her nest among the reeds of a marsh. Mrs. Audubon advertised for a situation as a teacher, and he started out on his career as a naturalist. In West Feliciana Mrs. Audubon taught at the plantation home of the Percys and in the family of my uncle, William Garret Johnson. Her schools were very popular and patronized by the elite far and near, for schools were not as accessible then as now.

"Mr. and Mrs. Audubon were always happy at our house, and discussed their plans for the future in our presence. He would relate to her the incidents in connection with his occupation and she would write them out for him for publication. His whole time was occupied in learning the habits of the birds on which he kept notes.

"On my return from church one Sunday—I think I had been to hear Lorenzo Dow preach—I found that Audubon had been to our home in my absence and hung in my parlour four of his oil paintings. One was of Hare Powell, the great boxer. It was a very fine picture. The handsome smiling face, with dark hair and eyes, the open shirt collar, showing the splendidly formed neck, made one of the finest specimens of athletic manhood I have ever seen. The other portrait was that of Mrs. Brown, and was his first attempt in this line of art. She had red hair, fair complexion, and was dressed in a low-necked dress, white with a crimson scarf thrown about her shoulders. The other two were vegetables and fruit. They were beautiful and Audubon hung them in my parlour as a present to me.

"Where are they now? They were destroyed during the Civil War. Audubon was anxious to paint my portrait but I would never consent to sit for one and would laughingly tell him I was too ugly to paint. I since have regretted that I did not comply with his request. I did not at the time reflect that he might have thought in this way to cancel somewhat the debt of obligation he was under to us, though he was always a cherished guest.

"Once when describing to us some of the scenes and incidents of his travels, he said: 'If I were to tell you one-half of what I see in those lonely ravines and swamps it would make your hair stand up on your head! I do not like to relate my adventures to everyone—for I might not be believed, madame. Yet everything I would say would be the truth!"

"Audubon was abstemious in his diet and did not drink tea nor coffee, nor did he use tobacco. He always drank a glass of weak whiskey and water, which he called grog, for his breakfast. After I had prepared my husband's coffee, I mixed his grog. Audubon was the most expert carver I ever saw and he cut the *bauxh hall* slice with the greatest dexterity. I never knew him to have a severe sickness, and do not think he drank any liquor except at meals, which the life he led necessitated. After spending a short time with his family he would start out again on his lonely journey in the woods, with his knapsack on his back, alone and on foot, often remaining in the open until his clothes were tatters, and his hair in long curls on his shoulders. His hair was beautiful!

"While he was wandering in the forests his noble wife was working in order to assist him in having his pictures engraved. It grieved him exceedingly to have it so. Every time he returned home he found her fading and drooping and he could not help but compare her to 'a beautiful tobacco plant cut off at the stem and hung up to wither with head hanging down,' as he put it in his quaint way of using similes."

5

There were other things in the Feliciana swamps that intrigued Audubon in addition to the innumerable birds. The great saurian of the wet places, the ungainly alligator, came in for special study and the bird man and Bourgeat, whom Audubon described as the most experienced alligator hunter in the Feliciana country, holding only sticks in their hands to ward off the big reptiles, waded waist-deep in the swamp waters with hundreds of 'gators swimming about them. Audubon learned that to go towards the head of the alligator courted no danger, and that he could safely hit its head with a four-foot club, until the monster would be driven away. It was necessary, however, to keep a close watch on the reptile's tail, as at each blow it received the tail would be thrashed violently from side to side.

Mrs. Pope related an alligator episode that illustrates Audubon's thirst for knowledge. During one of his trips to Pointe Coupée, just across the Mississippi river from Bayou Sarah, where he frequently visited the Labatout family in their fine old home situated near one of the largest live oak trees in the state, he and Augustin Bourgeat captured a lot of baby alligators. On their return Audubon placed a number of the small saurians in a tub of water in the room where he spent the night. When he removed his captives from the tub the next morning, preparatory to going on to the Percy home, one of the baby alligators was missing. The room was carefully searched but the truant was not to be found. Six months later the lady of the house discovered it in an old boot that lay under the bed in which Audubon had slept! It was alive and well! Word of the recovery was sent to Audubon, who returned to his friend's home posthaste, volubly expressing his amazement and joy. He thereupon compared its size with the others, which he had placed in more congenial surroundings at *Beech Woods*. The little alligator that had lived in a shoe was the same size!

"In Audubon's delight at making a scientific discovery, he did not reflect that the boot being found in the same place it had rested six months before was an evidence of a careless housewife," continued Mrs. Pope, "until the lady of the house laughingly reminded Audubon of that fact. He made her an ample apology."

Audubon's own story about the finding of the baby alligator differs slightly. He wrote that he and his friend Bourgeat, anxious to send some young alligators to a friend in New York, secured a bagful and brought them to Bourgeat's home at *Bush Hill*. "They were put on the floor," says Audubon, "to shew the young ladies, how beautiful they were when young. One accidently made its way out into a servant's room, and lodged itself snug from notice in an old shoe. The alligator was not missed but, upwards of twelve months after this, it was discovered about the house, full of life and, apparently, scarcely grown bigger; one of his brothers, that had been kept in a tub of water and fed plentifully, had grown only a few inches during the same period."

6

During these happy Feliciana days the collection of bird pictures was constantly growing. Many old efforts were touched up, floral decorations added to others, and some of the more complicated drawings completed, such as purple martins clinging to a nesting gourd; the screaming egg-robbing blue jays, the roseate spoonbill, the magnificent collection of ivory-billed woodpeckers, and the scythe-billed wood stork. His highly dramatic composition, which showed a hawk with outstretched wings and sharp, cruel talons extended, dashing on a covey of affrighted Bob White, was also made during this period of his career.

Audubon, Augustin Bourgeat, and Doctor Pope had long and frequently heated arguments relative to the precise function of the olfactory nerve in birds. It was acknowledged that with mammals it was the instrument of smell. The question arose regarding what sense attracted vultures to their prey—the sight or the smell of their carrion food.

Doctor Pope had an open mind on the subject. Bourgeat was inclined to the belief that the black vulture and the turkey buzzard smelled decaying carcasses from a great distance. Audubon denied this. He maintained that his observations had proved to him that vultures were not led to their prey by smell—that they were not even sensible of the nearness of carrion except when actually beheld with the eyes.

Bourgeat flatly denied that this was so. The consequence of the debate was a series of experiments in the Feliciana woods to prove or disprove Audubon's revolutionary contention. The result of the test furnished him with material for an article which he read before the learned Wernerian society of Edinburgh, and when this was published it established his fame as a naturalist, though it also brought down on his head a concentrated fusilade of abuse and ridicule from certain scientists who were prone to belittle everything the talented Frenchman did or said.

From the days of his youth Audubon had accepted the commonly believed theory that the vulture located its dead and usually decaying food through its sense of smell. While wandering the Louisiana fields and woods in pursuit of birds he observed that upon approaching the vultures unseen by them, they indicated no awareness of his presence nor did they take wing. Let them actually sight him, off they would fly, startled and affrighted. This action on the part of the birds led him to the conjecture that acuteness of sight and not the sense of smell guided the birds to their carrion prey.

To prove or disprove this conviction it was decided to make an experiment. Audubon and Bourgeat killed and skinned a deer, removed the skin from the carcass and stuffed it with dried grasses to give the appearance of swollen putrefaction. When the skin became dry and hard as leather, the dummy was conveyed to an open field, placed on its back, with the legs up and apart, giving the appearance of a dead and putrified deer. Audubon and his companions concealed themselves in bushes lining the field and awaited results. He wrote of the experiment:

> In the lapse of a few minutes a vulture, coursing round the field, tolerably high, espied the skin, sailed directly towards it, and alighted within a few yards of it. I ran immediately, covered by a large tree, until within about forty yards, and from that place could spy the bird with ease. He approached the skin, looked at it without apparent suspicion, jumped on it, raised his tail, and voided itself freely (as you well know, all birds of prey in a wild state generally do before feeding), then approached the eyes, that were here solid globes of hard dried and painted clay, attacked first one and then the other with, however, no further advantage than that of disarranging them.
>
> This part was abandoned; the bird walked to the other extremity of the pretended animal, and there, with much exertion, tore the stitches apart, until much fodder and hay was pulled out, but no flesh could the bird find, or smell; he was intent on discovering some where none existed, and, after reiterated efforts, all useless, he took flight, coursed about the field, when suddenly rounding and falling, I saw him kill a small *garter snake*, and swallow it in an instant. The vulture rose again, sailed about, and passed several times quite low over my stuffed deer skin, as if loath to abandon so good-looking a prey.
>
> Judge my feelings when I plainly saw that the vulture, which could not discover, through its *extraordinary sense of smell*, that no flesh either fresh or putrid, existed about that skin, could, at a glance see a snake scarcely as large as a man's finger, alive and destitute of odor, hundreds of yards distant. I concluded that, at all events, his ocular powers were much better than his sense of smell.

The contention remained unsettled in spite of the success of Audubon's initial experiment. Bourgeat was yet to be convinced. So a large dead hog was hauled into a field some distance from *Beech Woods*, and rolled into a narrow and winding ravine, about twenty feet deeper than the surrounding surface, and this depression was filled with briars, Chickasaw rose bushes and high cane. The negro slaves handling the carcass concealed the body of the hog by weaving cane stalks over it. As this experiment was undertaken in the month of July, barely two days elapsed before the concealed body began to make its presence known by an overpowering odor.

"I saw, from time to time, many vultures in search of food sail over the field in all directions, but none discovered the carcase, although during this time several dogs visited it and fed plentifully on it," recorded Audubon. "I tried to go near it, but the smell was so unsufferable when within thirty yards, that I abandoned it, and the remnants were entirely destroyed at last through natural decay."

This odoriferous experiment did not settle the matter, to Bourgeat's satisfaction, so Audubon next secured a young pig, plunged a knife through its neck and let the blood flow on the earth and grass at the same spot, then covered the body with leaves and made off to a place of concealment to watch the results. "The vultures saw the fresh blood, alighted about it, followed it down into the ravine, discovered the body of the pig, and devoured it when yet quite fresh," wrote Audubon.

This was sufficient proof for Bourgeat, but Audubon, still not satisfied in his own mind, made further researches. He found a nest of vultures containing two young about the size of pullets. Taking them to *Beech Woods* he put them in a coop and gave the youngsters his personal attention at feeding time. "I gave them a great many red-headed woodpeckers and parokeets, birds then easy to procure," he records. "So accustomed to my going towards them were they in a few days that when I approached the cage with hands filled with game for them, they immediately began hissing and gesticulating."

Later, when the young vultures had developed to the stage where the first black wing feathers began to appear, Audubon tried another experiment. He closed three sides of the coop with planks, leaving only the front open, and cleaned the cage of all decayed flesh. Then, barefooted, to insure noiselessness, and carrying dead rabbits or squirrels, Audubon would approach the cage from the closed side, so that the birds could not see him. The young vultures remained silent, giving no evidence of recognizing Audubon's presence until he revealed himself, then they would hiss violently and hurl themselves against the bars in an endeavor to secure the food.

"Satisfied within myself, I dropped these trials, but fed them until full grown, and then turned them out into the yard of the kitchen," he says, "for the purpose of letting them pick up whatever substances might be thrown them. Their voracity, however, soon caused their death. Young pigs were not safe if within their reach; and young ducks, turkeys, or chickens, were such a constant temptation, that the cook, unable to watch them, killed them both to put an end to their depredations."

Audubon wound up his experiments with the following conclusions: "I could enumerate many more instances indicating that the power of smelling in these birds has been grossly exaggerated and that, if they can smell objects at any distance, they can see the same objects much farther. I would ask any observer of the habits of birds—Why, if vultures could smell at a great distance their prey, they should spend the greater portion of their time hunting for it, when they are naturally so lazy that, if fed in one place, they will never leave it, and merely make such a change as is absolutely necessary to enable them to reach it?"

7

Many other experiments with birds, mammals, and alligators were carried on by the three boon companions in the Feliciana woods. Audubon continued his endless study of bird habits and stored in his mind all he learned. If he did not set all his observations on paper they were engraved on his retentive memory and when the time came to preserve them in words he was able, in far-off Edinburgh, to write, write, write, from early morning until late at night, the many things he learned in Nature's storehouse, the beloved woods of Louisiana's fairest spot—West Feliciana.

Audubon alternated his days in Feliciana between hunting and observing the birds in their habitats and making some of those he killed live again on paper. Meticulously each feather was made to lie just so; the length of wing and the breadth of bill were carefully measured. Every bit of plumage was colored with painstaking accuracy. He would spend hours in painting bird parts to which other artists might devote minutes. He was no laggard where his great work was concerned.

So, when the early spring days of 1826 starred the Feliciana hills with wild flowers, and when anon the dogwood and grancy graybeard and wild prune had ceased blooming; and beech, and holly, and tall yellow poplar had come into full leaf, Audubon's portfolios were filled to bursting with his bird pictures. In the first days of the long Louisiana summer he took stock of his possessions and his prospects.

He determined to go to Europe to seek a publisher and fame.

His meager financial returns from fencing and dancing lessons had accumulated, "and with this capital and my wife's savings I was able to see a successful issue to my great ornithological work."

The Wood Stork redrawn from Audubon's plate.

Book Seven

Europe and Fame

"*No work of mine shall be other than true metal—*
if copper, COPPER*; if gold,* GOLD*—but*
not COPPER GILDED!"

JOHN JAMES AUDUBON, in his journal,
September 29, 1826.

CHAPTER 20

AN ODD-FISH IN LIVERPOOL

JOHN JAMES AUDUBON started for Europe with two hundred and forty bird drawings, and $1,700.00 his wife had saved from her earnings, confident that he would find on the other side of the Atlantic a publisher who would reproduce the birds of his brush and pencil exactly as he had drawn them.

He left *Beech Woods* for New Orleans on the twenty-sixth of April. It was the anniversary of the birth of Jean Rabin, *créole de Saint-Domingue*, in tropical Aux Cayes exactly forty-one years before, and one wonders if Audubon was aware of the significance of the day. When he sailed down the winding Mississippi from Bayou Sarah to engage passage in New Orleans on an England-bound boat his wandering foot was itching as furiously for adventure as it had done twenty years before.

His portfolios were heavy and his purse was light, but his heart was singing within him—for he had resolved to seek fame, if not fortune, on this journey to the Old World.

The start of this eventful trip is set down in detail in his journal.

26 April 1826—I left My Beloved Wife Lucy Audubon and My son John Woodhouse on Tuesday afternoon the 26th April, bound for England. remained at Doct^{r} Pope at St Francisville untill Wednesday 4 o'clock P. M.: in the Steam Boat *Red River* Cap^{e} Kimble— having for Compagnons Messrs D. Höll & John Haliday—reached New Orleans Thursday 27th at 12—Visited Many Vessels for My Passage and concluded to go in the Ship *Delos* of Kennebunk Cap^{e} Joseph Hatch bound to Liverpool. Loaded with Cotton entirely—

The *Red River* Steam Boat left on her return on Sunday and I Wrote by her to Thee My Dearest Friend and forward^{d} Thee 2 small Boxes of Flowering Plants.

saw, spoke to & walked with Charles Briggs, much altered young man—

Lived at New Orleans at G. L. Sapinot in company with Costé.

During my stay at New Orleans, I saw my old and friendly acquaintances the familly Pamar; but the whole time spent in that city was heavy & dull—a few Gentlemen Calld to see My Drawings—I Generally Walked from Morning untill Dusk My hands behind me, paying but partial attention to all I saw—New Orleans to a Man who does not trade in Dollars or any Such Stuffs is a miserable spot—

fatigued and discovering that the Ship would not be ready for Sea for several days, I ascended the Mississippy again in the *Red River* and once more found Myself with my Wife and Child. I arrived at Mrs Percy at 3 o'clock in the morning, having had a Dark ride through the Magnolia Woods but the Moments spent afterwards full repaid me—I remained 2 days and 3 nights, was a wedding—of Miss Virginia Chisholm with Mr. D. Höll &c. I left in Company with Lucy Mrs Percy house at Sun rise and went to breakfast at My good frien's, Augustin Bourgeat.

It was the May Day when Audubon left the Feliciana country for the second time on his fame-questing journey to the Old World, but when he again landed in New Orleans he was faced with another delay. Captain Joseph Hatch Jr., a young down-East Yankee from the State of Maine who commanded the *Delos* of Kennebunk, informed the impatient Frenchman that the cotton ship would not sail for at least two weeks so Audubon again sought out friend Sapinot and Napoleon Costé for lodgings and then busied himself about town seeking letters of introduction to those in England who might prove of help in locating a publisher. Governor Johnson gave him a document, with the great seal of the state upon it, which saved Audubon the trouble of securing a passport, and Vincent Nolte insisted that he take a letter to Richard Rathbone, a prominent and wealthy cotton man of Liverpool. This letter, so we shall see, proved to be a most valuable piece of paper. Indeed, it turned out to be the *open sesame* to Audubon's after-fame in England. Consequently we may read a few of its lines: Nolte declared Audubon a gentleman of highly respectable scientific acquirements, a native of the United States, that he had spent more than a score of years in all parts of America devoted to the study of ornithology. "He carries with him a collection of over four hundred drawings, which far surpass anything of the kind I have ever seen, and afford the best evidence of his skill, and the perfection to which he has carried his researches. His object is to find a purchaser or a publisher for them, and if you can aid him in this, and introduce him either in person or by letter to men of distinction in arts and sciences, you will confer much of a favor on me." The letter closed with the prophecy that Audubon's drawings would convey a far better idea of American bird life than "all the stuffed birds of all the museums put together."

Impatient to be off, Audubon heaved great sighs of satisfaction when his luggage was stowed aboard the *Delos* on the seventeenth of May. At seven that evening the steamboat *Hercules* came alongside, made fast, and ten hours later put the ship loaded with 924 cotton bales through the South Pass and into the Gulf. Up went the sails and the long journey across the boisterous Atlantic began.

For the first day or two the artist suffered from seasickness, but when he was able to go on deck he began to take note of the birds that filled the air and the fish life in the water. "The first objects which diverted my thoughts from the dear ones left behind me, were the beautiful Dolphins that glided by the vessel like burnished gold by day and bright meteors by night," he wrote.

Audubon, Captain Hatch and some of the crew amused themselves luring these sea mammals (the naturalist set down in his journal that they were *fish!*) close to the side of the ship with baited hooks, then piercing them with a *grain*, as the five-pointed harpoon was called. Audubon examined the creatures' duck-bill-like snout, tail, and blowing apertures on the head, counted the teeth, carefully studied the intestines, and made sketches of several of the specimens hauled on board.

When birds came close to the vessel Audubon gave up his study of creatures of the deep for the creatures of the air. Of all things in nature on land, sea, or air he loved the birds and their ways the best.

2

Interesting things were to be seen and done when the sails of the *Delos* were spread to the breezes of the Gulf of Mexico. When the ship was in the doldrums so was Audubon.

When the wind failed and he had nothing to do he would be seized in the crushing grip of despondency, and frequently set down in his diary intimate matters pertaining to his early existence. It was at such times he would allude to "his noble birth." This is particularly true of an entry in his journal made on June fourth. This passage and others in his journals dealing with his journey to Europe and his adventures there have been withheld from public print by those who have had possession of the original diaries, and they form a part of the evidence upon which some of his descendants pitch their belief that Audubon was none other than the Lost Dauphin.

These references to *high birth* and his declaration to his journal that he was *an aristocrat* read:

"June 4, 1826. At sea.—We are a few miles south of the Line for the second time in my life—*What ideas* it conveys to me of my *birth*, and the expectations of my younger days. "*My high birth*, although *unknown to the world*, was always on my lips & I felt a pride unbecoming my *situation*, but I seemed unable to control it.

"I am an *aristocrat;* I Cannot divest my self of this knowledge—The feeling it brings remains with me; how can I help this?"

Did the reference to being "south of the Line for the second time in his life" apply to the tropic of Cancer? All we know is that the *Delos* on her way to Liverpool did pass south of that parallel and that San Domingo also lies south of it.

3

During such morose spells Audubon proved a poor sailing companion for the other two passengers, one being the son of Benjamin Swift of Saint Francisville on his way to visit relatives in Ireland. Let some new bird come sailing by the becalmed ship and Audubon was himself again! He would study the bird's wing beats with the unaided eye or through his long brass telescope.

The *Delos* was becalmed for many days in the Gulf of Mexico and Audubon admitted that he would have been dull indeed had it not been for the fishes and birds, his pen and pencil. After drifting along the Florida coast a stiff breeze rose and filled the sails. Audubon was elated; it was the last day of June and he looked for a more rapid voyage over the sea to England. Let us read an entry in his journal:

> The land birds have left us, and I—I leave my beloved America, my wife, my children, my friends. The purpose of this voyage is to visit not only England, but the continent of Europe, with the intention of publishing my work on the "Birds of America." If not sadly disappointed my return to these shores, these happy shores, will be the brightest day I have ever enjoyed. Oh! wife, children, friends, America, farewell! farewell! !

To keep his mind engaged while on the long slow sea trip, Audubon paced the deck of the *Delos* pencil in hand, making sketches of the sailors in their attitudes while engaged at their many tasks, and he tells us that he raised many a laugh by his rough sketches of Captain Joe Hatch, the mates, S. L. Bragdon and William Hobart, as well as his caricatures of the two other passengers. In spite of this diversion his thoughts continually milled about his mission to Europe, his mind was in a torment as to whether it would prove a successful venture or a dismal failure. One night he confided to his journal:

> My leaving America had for some time the feeling of a dream; I could scarcely make up my mind fixedly on the subject. I thought continually I still saw my beloved friends, and my dear wife and children. I still felt every morning when I awoke that the land of America was beneath me, and that I would in a short time throw myself on the ground in her shady woods, and watch for, and listen to the many lovely warblers. But now I have positively been at sea since *fifty-one* days, tossing to and fro, without the sight or the touch of those dear to me, I feel fully convinced, and look forward with an anxiety such as I never felt before, when I calculate that not less than four months, the third of a year, must elapse before my wife and children can receive any tidings of my arrival on the distant shores to which I am bound. When I think that many more months must run from Life's sand-glass allotted to my existence before I can think of returning, and that my re-union with my friends and country is yet an unfolded and unknown event, I am filled with sudden apprehentions which I cannot describe nor dispel.

4

Sixty-five days after leaving New Orleans, July 21, 1826, the *Delos* dropped anchor in the Mersey. Audubon was quickly ashore, took lodgings at the Commercial Hotel, and in Liverpool at last faced the second episode of his harebrained adventure of journeying to Europe to find fame and a publisher. His first visit was to the office of his brother-in-law, Alexander Gordon, who had recently established his cotton commission firm of Gordon & Forstall in the English mill city, and there was faced with his first disappointment—several of those to whom he carried letters of introduction, particularly Richard Rathbone, were out of the city for a few days. Dejectedly, he returned to his hotel.

The next morning, when he awoke from his first sleep in England, the sweet voice of a lark in a cage called him from his troubled dreams. He visited the customs where, to his consternation, he found he would have to pay tup'ns for each of his water color paintings and four pence a pound for each of his American-printed books. He drew on his purse, removed his books and precious bird drawings to his lodgings in the inn, and then went out to view the city.

As he trudged the streets of Liverpool "the noise of pattens on the sidewalk startled me very frequently; as if the sound was behind me. I often turned my head expecting to see a horse but instead I observed a neat, plump-looking maid, tripping as briskly as a killdeer."

As the days were marked off the calendar he met many of those to whom he carried letters of introduction, and had been in the famous cotton mill town but a short time when he had shaken hands with many leaders in the scientific and social life of the place, such as Edward Roscoe, after whom he named a bird; Dr. Thomas S. Traill, for whom he named the little flycatcher secured at the Arkansas Post; Jean Sismondi, the Swiss historian; Lord Stanley, fourteenth Earl of Derby, celebrated as a sportsman, patron of literature, art and the sciences, for whom the English horse-racing classic is named, and Audubon later honored him by baptising his unnamed hawk of the Feliciana woods—Stanley's Hawk.

When Audubon left Louisiana for his conquest of Europe he had in cash exactly three hundred and forty pounds sterling, a tidy sum his Lucy had accumulated during the period of her teaching in the Feliciana country. In spite of this scant store of cash, his first purchases in Liverpool were two watches, with necessary chains and seals. One was for his own use, the other for his "Beloved Friend," as he usually named Lucy in his letters. He laid out one hundred and twenty pounds for the time pieces, so with little more than two hundred pounds of the money his wife had given him left in his pocket-book, he faced the future.

He had not succeeded in meeting Richard Rathbone and time hung heavily on his hands for the first few days he spent in the mill town. "Being Sunday," he set down in his journal under date of July twenty-third, "I must expect a long and lonely day; I awoke at dawn and lay for a few moments only, listening to the sweet-voiced Lark; the day was beautiful; thermometer in the sun 65°, and in the shade 41°; I might say 40°, but I love odd numbers—it is a foolish superstition with me."

The queer-looking man from Louisiana, one week after debarking from the *Delos*, found a note had been left at his lodgings which informed him: "Mr. Martin, of the Royal Institution of Liverpool, would do himself the pleasure to wait on Mr. *Ambro* tomorrow at eleven o'clock."

Duly pleased to be the recipient of a gesture from this scientific body, Audubon could not conceal his annoyance at the misspelling of his name. "Why do people make such errors with my simple name?" he demanded of his journal. The next morning he prepared to receive the secretary and his description of his own appearance is, appropriately, bird-like. "A *full grown man* with a scarlet vest and breeches, black stockings and shoes for the coloring of his front, and a long blue coat, reminds me somewhat of our summer red bird (*Tanagra rubra*).[1] Both man and bird attract the eye, but the scientific appellation of the *man* is unknown to me."

Audubon does not tell us how his colorful *tout ensemble* impressed the secretary but we do know that before that gentleman left the Dale street lodgings he had arranged that Audubon's drawings of the birds inhabiting America would be exhibited in the rooms of the Liverpool Royal Institution. Therefore, ten days after the *Delos* had come to anchor in the Mersey, the doors of the institution were thrown open to

[1]While Audubon is quoted as writing he resembled the summer tanager, it is more probable he had in mind his resemblance to the male bluebird, Sylvia Sialis, as he would have then termed it scientifically. Such little slips were common with this colorful personage.

members and their friends so Liverpool could view a collection of painted birds. Audubon put up "two hundred twenty-five of my drawings; the *coup d'oeil* was not bad, and the room crowded . . . I was wearied with bowing to the many to whom I was introduced. Someone was found copying one of the drawings, but the doorkeeper, an alert Scotchman, saw his attempt, turned him out, and tore his sketch."

More than four hundred persons inspected the bird display on the second day and Audubon, as well as his pictures, became the talk of the town. When the first two weeks of the free show ended, the directors urged Audubon to continue the unique and undeniably popular exhibition with an admission charge. It netted him an even hundred pounds.

All this displaying of pictures and bowing and scraping to the elite, was not finding a publisher . . . anyway the rôle of showman did not please him. Arising very early in the morning he would tramp the streets of Liverpool tirelessly, eventually the watchmen ceased to look upon him with suspicion, "and think, perhaps, I am a harmless lunatic."

He was restless and distrait. He missed the live birds and the fragrant Feliciana woods separated from him by the width of the turbulent Atlantic. Invited to William Roscoe's home the stranger penned in his journal, "Charming as England is there is nothing in England more charming than the Roscoe family." However, when he surveyed a pond near the Roscoe country place he chafed to see no living thing in or near it, not even a frog. "No moccasin nor copper-headed snake is near its margin; no Snowy Heron, no Rose-coloured Ibis is ever seen there, wild and charming; no spritely trout, no waiting gar-fish, while above hovers no vulture watching for the spoils of the hunt, nor Eagle perched on dreary cypress in gloomy silence. No! I am in England, and I cannot but long with unutterable longing for America."

If Audubon's bird pictures created a sensation in Liverpool likewise did the man who made them. His clothes were unsightly, his hair as long as ever, and he stalked along the pavements of the city, a huge portfolio balanced on his left shoulder and his "American Stick," as he termed his sword-cane, grasped in his right hand, preoccupied with his own ambitious concerns and not caring a hang for appearances.

His sister-in-law, Anne Bakewell, now the wife of Alexander Gordon and living in Liverpool, harried him incessantly to cut his hair or, at least, to buy some fashionable clothes. At first he paid no attention to her almost frantic requests but finally yielded to her importunities to the extent of purchasing a new coat, and some other clothing necessities, but steadfastly refused to be shorn of his chestnut locks.

He became an "odd-fish" to the fashionable and unconsciously performed for many of them. He tells with charming naïveté how he amused Lady Douglass, a sister of Lord Selkirk, the former governor-general of Canada, "by eating some tomatoes raw; neither she, nor any of the company, had ever seen them on the table without being cooked."

On the first of September he wrote his son Victor that he had been in England upwards of a month and had been received so kindly that "I am in miniature in Liverpool what Lafayette was with us on our great Scale plan and habit of doing everything. My drawings are exhibited at the Liverpool Royal Institution and will continue so all this week—the proceeds are far beyond my expectations and it seems I am considered unrivaled in the art of Drawing even by the most learned of this country. The newspapers have given so many flattering accounts of my productions and of my being a superior ornithologist that I dare no longer look into any *of them*—

"You would be surprised to see the marked attentions paid me where ever I go by the first people of Liverpool—My exhibition attracts the *beau monde* altogether and the Lords of England look at them with wonder, more so I assure thee than at my flowing curling locks that again loosely are about my shoulders—the Ladies of England are Ladies indeed—Beauty, suavity of manners and the most improved education render them desirable objects of admiration." The letter closed with a request that Victor remember him to all in Louisville "who are not ashamed of my being a Relation or acquaintance."

If the stylish Gordons were not over-gracious to the man who was creating such a furore, others prominent in the life of the cotton port were, and his days and nights were busy ones, so many and varied were his invitations. He complained in a letter to Lucy about sister Anne's husband, "He has not been near me for two weeks although I have sent him word I wished much to see him and I cant think of troubling him any more."

5

Audubon had not been long in Liverpool before he was busy with drawing paper and water colors making pictures of the birds he found there. He also dabbled in oils, reproducing in this medium many of his favorite portraits of birds and mammals. Some of the pictures were for new-found friends in payment for kindnesses, some for sale as a means of support, and others as gifts in recognition of courtesies received from scientific societies.

The Rathbone family was most gracious to the long-haired artist and made him a welcome visitor to *Green Banks*, a country estate three miles from Liverpool. On one visit he was asked by his hostess, Mrs. William Rathbone, Sr., to make a very small sketch of his big wild turkey cock painting.

"I sat opposite my twenty-three hours' picture and made the diminutive sketch in less than twenty-three minutes," he wrote his wife. A few weeks later the gracious mistress of *Green Banks* presented him with a handsome gold-mounted seal—it was a replica of the famous Louisiana wild turkey, hardly an inch high, and lettered over the bird: "America, My Country." This seal has been used by members of the Audubon family ever since.

It was while in Liverpool that Audubon decided upon his sobriquet "The American Woodsman," for at this time we first find such a reference to himself in many of the entries he penned in his journal. He grew to like the many remarks about his personal appearance which caught his ear as he strode along the streets. Particularly pleasing were those directed at his flowing tresses. "My locks blew freely from under my hat in the breeze, and nearly every lady I met looked at them with curiosity," he recorded proudly.

While a visitor at *Green Banks* he discussed with the Rathbones and some of their friends his long premeditated plan for the publication of his *Birds of America*. As every subject had been drawn in its natural size he declared the work must be reproduced in the same life size. His listeners protested —such a thing was unheard-of. Nothing like it had ever been attempted—he was too ambitious!

The well-meaning Rathbones endeavored to dissuade him and pointed out the enormous expense involved in preparing such plates, the coloring of them, and the bulkiness of the finished product. They urged him to give up that part of his ambitious plan and be content with a reproduction of his birds on a smaller scale. Audubon would not bring himself to yield his cherished idea to more practical arrangements—not an inch!

A visiting bookseller from London named H. G. Bohn, one familiar with the publication business, agreed with the friendly Rathbones that such a gigantic work was impracticable and advised a smaller book suitable for what he termed the English market. Bohn urged Audubon to have the work reduced to "double Wilson," printed and finished in Paris, then have it brought to England to the number of two hundred and fifty copies, to be bound with a title page printed in Britain, and in this format issued to the people of England as an English publication.

Audubon flatly refused to even consider the suggestion. "*This I will not do,*" he declared with heat. "No work of mine shall be other than true metal—if copper, *copper;* if gold, *gold*—but *not copper gilded!*"

6

Brushing aside all advice, not deviating an iota in his determination to publish his beloved drawings as he had drawn them—life-size, Audubon went about securing subscriptions for his projected work before he had found either an engraver or a publisher. The Rathbones were the first to set their names on his list, then he found others in Liverpool who wanted the work, and so the conquest of Britain began. His quest for subscribers took him first to Manchester, but his visit there did not prove successful, neither from public interest nor from the standpoint of subscriptions. He had arranged to display his original drawings in a hall and when the pictures were at last hung to his critical satisfaction, he was asked if he desired a band of music. Turning with a glare on the man making the suggestion the artist said with withering scorn he "did not consider music necessary—in company with so many songsters that decorate the walls!"

The American consul at Manchester invited him to dinner so he could meet a party of influential Englishmen. "Judge to my surprise when, during the third course, I saw on the table a dish of Indian corn, purposely for me," writes the honor guest. "To see me eat it buttered and salted, held as if I intended gagging myself, was a matter of much wonder to the English gentlemen, who did not like the vegetable."

The Manchester exhibition ended, late in October Audubon began making ready for a visit to Edinburgh. Friends had guaranteed he would assuredly find a publisher in the Scottish city. The artist was assisted in packing his collection of drawings by Robert Bentley, the publisher, whom Audubon described as a "brother Mason who has been most kind to me."

When he boarded a coach bound for "fair Edina" he was animated with high hopes.

"Audubon at Green Bank. Almost Happy!!—Sep. 2, 1826."
From a pencil sketch drawn by himself for Mrs. William Rathbone.

CHAPTER 21

In Fair Edina

AFTER three days spent with coach and postillions, John James Audubon arrived at Edinburgh, October 26, 1826. He secured lodgings with a Mrs. Dickie in George Street, and then walked about the city, admiring all he saw, particularly the great breadth of the streets, the excellent pavements and footways, the beautiful buildings in their natural gray coloring, and the spotless cleanliness of everything. "Perhaps all was more powerfully felt," he adds to his account of his first impressions of the Scottish city, "coming direct from dirty Manchester, but the picturesqueness of the *tout ensemble* is wonderful."

The man who had looked forward with such enthusiasm and expectation to the visit to Edinburgh almost immediately after his arrival there was assailed with dire forebodings and doubts as to the success of his mission. He thereupon fell into one of his peculiar and periodic fits of depression. While it lasted Audubon alternately walked the streets or locked himself in his lodgings, giving way to a contemplation of his existence, his early life, and the secret of his birth. Turning to his journal he wrote:

> I unpacked my birds and looked at them with pleasure, and yet with a considerable degree of fear that they would never be published. I felt very much alone, and many dark thoughts came across my mind; I felt one of those terrible attacks of depression to which I so often fall a prey overtaking me, and I forced myself to go out and destroy the painful gloom that I dread at all times, and of which I am sometimes absolutely afraid.
>
> After a good walk I returned more at ease, and looked at a pair of stuffed pheasants on a large buffet in my present sitting room, at the sweetly scented geraniums opposite to them, the black hair-cloth sofa and chairs, the little cherubs on the mantlepiece, the painted landscape on my right hand, and the mirror on my left, in which I saw not only my own face, but such a strong resemblance to that of

my venerated father that I almost imagined it was he that I saw; the thoughts of my mother came to me, my sister, my young days,—all was at hand, yet how far away. Ah! how far is even the last moment, that is never to return again.

This reference was not the first the naturalist made to the likeness between himself and Captain Jean Audubon, and this entry in his Edinburgh journal would seem to refute the assertions harbored by the Audubon family for years that the bird artist was not the son, natural or otherwise, of Jean Audubon of Nantes, Aux Cayes and Coüeron. As will be shown later, John James Audubon made other references to his resemblance to "his father" . . . or, as he set it down in his journal, "not my adopted father, but my *own* father."

Depressed spirits, like summer thunder clouds, finally give way to sunshine, and Audubon's black moments were no exceptions to this rule. Meeting and hobnobbing with the great brought about a change in his volatile spirits. In turn The American Woodsman met Professor Robert Jameson, of the Edinburgh University; Dr. John Knox, a distinguished anatomist; Patrick Neill horticulturist and printer, and an engraver, then at work on the reproductions for Selby's *British Birds*, whose name was William Home Lizars. After meeting the picturesque stranger from over seas, the engraver accompanied Audubon to his lodgings to view his birds.

"I slowly unbuckled my portfolio," so Audubon records this private showing of his pictures, "and placed a chair for him, and with my heart like a stone held up a drawing. Mr. Lizars rose from his seat, exclaiming: 'My God! I never saw anything like this before!' He continued to be delighted and astonished, and said Sir William Jardine must see them, and that he would write to him—that Mr. Selby must see them."

Three days later Lizars again called upon Audubon; with him were his wife and a few friends so they too could view the eccentric American's collection. At the first meeting with the engraver, Audubon had shown only a few of his smaller drawings, but on this occasion he laid out some of his larger works made in the Feliciana country and in New Orleans.

These included the mockingbirds defending their nest from the rattlesnake; the two turkey representations—the lordly cock, and the hen and her little poults; the hawk, with outstretched wings and talons, pouncing on the seventeen affrighted partridges; the great white whooping crane devouring little alligators just hatched—dramatic pictures all, for Audubon knew when and how to dramatize.

Lizars pronounced them remarkable productions and enthusiastically announced his intention of engraving the lively group of Bob White fleeing the murderous hawk poised above them. But when Audubon spread out on the floor his drawing of the great-footed hawks, with bloody rags at their beaks' end, and cruel delight in their eyes, the Scotsman was mute with astonishment. Finally Lizars cried, "*That* I will engrave and publish!" When taking leave that night the engraver warmly pressed the hand of the man from over the seas and declared, "Mr. Audubon, the people here don't know who you are at all, but depend on it, they *shall* know."

The upshot of the impromptu exhibition at Mrs. Dickie's in George street was Lizars' agreement to join Audubon in his undertaking and engrave and bring out the first numbers. The giant Feliciana wild turkey cock was selected as the initial plate to be engraved, and work on it was begun November 20, 1826. A few weeks later when Audubon dropped into Lizars' shop he watched the engravers at work on the big copper plates. "I was delighted to see how faithfully copied they were, and scarcely able to conceive the great *adroit* required to form the lines exactly contrary to the model before them."

The yellow-billed cuckoo, pursuing a tiger swallowtail butterfly, was the second plate; the yellow prothonotary warblers, third; the purple finch, fourth, and Bonaparte's flycatcher was the final plate in the initial number. The turkey hen and her little poults, the purple grackle, white-throated sparrow, the tiny flycatcher he named on the impulse for Prideaux John Selby, and the brown lark were scheduled for the second number. Before New Year's Day, 1827, the five engravings for the first number had been pulled from the coppers and colorists had brushed on the various colors and tints, faithfully copying them from Audubon's original drawings set up in front of their easels.

The Great Work, after bitter and galling disappointments, was actually under way!

2

While the plates of the second number were being graved and bitten into the copper at Lizars' establishment the original drawings were being displayed on the walls of the Royal Institution of Edinburgh. Their reception by the public was immediate and most flattering . . . on one Saturday £15 were collected at the door. The long-haired American Woodsman had captured the town. He had given a thrill and topic of conversation to the dilettanti, the literati, and the men of science. Sir Walter Scott refused to attend the exhibition, but after Audubon had called upon him the bard set down in his diary: "I wish I had gone to see his drawings; but I had heard so much about them that I resolved not to see them—'a crazy way of mine, your honor.'"

Scientific, literary, and arts bodies of the Scottish capital raced each other to elect a bewildered Audubon to membership. His head was examined by phrenologists and molded in plaster. A prominent artist painted his portrait in shining new oils. Banquets were not complete without his presence, where he was the blushing subject of flowery toasts. The press gave his picture exhibition flattering notices. He was invited everywhere—he became the lion of the hour, declined no invitation, and roared appropriately.

"My situation in Edinburgh borders on the miraculous," he wrote jubilantly to Lucy, "without education and scarce one of those qualities necessary to render a man able to pass through the throng of the learned here I am positively looked on by all Professors & many of the principal persons here as a very extraordinary Man. I go to dine out at 6, 7, or 8 o'clock in the evening, and it is one or two in the morning when the party breaks up, then painting all day, with my Correspondence, that increases daily, my Head is like a hornet's nest and my body wearied beyond calculation—yet it has to be done. I cannot refuse a single invitation."

Audubon bore up well under the strain but often confided to his journal his longings for his family, the magnolia woods of far-off Feliciana, and his preference for hunting the wood stork and roseate spoonbill in the Tunica swamps, to being constantly dragged about Edinburgh from one friend's house to another's and fed to repletion. Many a night, after returning to his lodgings, satiated beyond expression, he recalled other meals in Barracks street and the little house in Dauphine street when a scanty fare of bread and cheese formed the meal, or when the fattest fletch from off a side of bacon composed the banquet.

The sumptuous dinners of Edinburgh overwhelmed him. "They are so long, so long, that I recall briefer meals I have had, with much more enjoyment than I eat the bountiful fare before me," he wrote in his journal. "This is not a goûter with friend Bourgeat on the Flat Lake, roasting the flesh of the orange-fleshed Ibis, and a few sun-perch; neither is it on the heated banks of Thompson's creek, on the Fourth of July, swallowing the eggs of a large soft-shelled Turtle; neither was I at Henderson, at good Doctor Rankin's, listening to the howling of the Wolves, while sitting in security, eating well-roasted and jellied vension—no, alas! it was far from all those dear spots, in Great King Street, No. 62, at Doctor Graham's, a distinguished professor of botany, with a dinner of so many rich dishes that I cannot remember them."

He had been in the Scottish capital nearly two months when, on December 21, 1826, he wrote his "Dearest Friend" details of the progress of the Great Work. "It is now a month since my work has been begun by Mr. W. H. Lizars of this city—it is to come out in the same size of my largest drawings that is called double eliphant—they will be brought up & finished in such superb style as to eclipse all of the kind in existence . . . Two of the plates finished last week . . . and are truly beautiful . . . I shall send thee the very first and I think it will please thee—it consists of the Turkey Male—the Cuckoos in the Pawpaws and three small drawings that I doubt thou dost remember but when you seeth them I am quite sure thou wilt—the little drawings in the center of those beautiful large sheets have a fine effect and an air of richness and wealth that cannot help but insure success in this country—I cannot yet say that I will ultimately succeed but at present all bears a better prospect than I ever expected to see. I think this under the eyes of the most discerning People in the World—I mean Edinburgh—if it takes here it cannot fail anywhere. It is not the naturalists that I wish to please altogether, I assure thee, it is the wealthy part of the community —the first can only speak well or ill of me but the latter will fill my pockets."

He took his beloved Lucy to task for not writing him. "After postponing day after day for the last two weeks writing to thee full of hopes that each new day would bring some tidings of thee or of some one connected with me in America, I am forced to sit and write filled with fear and sorrow. Many of the vessels I have wrote by have returned from America with full cargoes but nothing from thee." He dilated on his prospects of success and suggested that his wife give serious consideration to leaving Louisiana and joining him in Europe.

I am now better aware of the advantages of a family in unison than ever, and I am quite satisfied that by acting conjointly and by my advice we can realize a handsome fortune for each of us—it needs but industry & perseverance—going to America is a mere song and I now find that most valuable voyages could be made by procuring such articles as are wanted here and most plentiful there. It is now about time to know from thee what thy future intentions are. I wish thee to act according to thy dictates but wish to know what those Dictates are—think that we are far divided and that either sickness or need may throw one into a most shocking situation without either friend or help for thou sayest thyself "the World is not indulgent." Cannot we move together and feel and enjoy the natural need of each other—Lucy my friend think of all this very seriously—not a portion of the earth exists but will support us amply and we may feel Happiness anywhere if careful — When you receive this sit and consider well — Consult N. Berthoud, thy son Victor, or such person as Judge Mathews — then consult thyself and in a long plain explanatory letter give me thy own Heart entire.

Complaining of the fatigue that it entailed, Audubon penned his wife a colorful outline of his social obligations, rounds of company and dinners, and his daily task of painting, which consisted for the most part of copies of his more notable water colors done in oils. "My success in oil painting is truly wonderful—I am called an astounding artist &c What different times I see here courted as I am, from those I spent at *Beech Woods* where certain people scarcely thought fit to look upon me."

He confessed, "I have come to fine Dressing again—silk stockings and pumps, shave every morning and sometimes twice a day—My hairs are now beautifully long and curley as ever, and I assure thee do as much for me as my Talent for Painting."

3

It was when he began to receive invitations for breakfast in the homes of his new acquaintances that The American Woodsman grew concerned about the large proportion of working hours he was forced to surrender to social activities. He longed for the quiet of the Feliciana woods, "the only place in which I truly *live!*"

One Edinburgh admirer insisted upon Audubon having tea with him at four in the afternoon. Upon his arrival the naturalist discovered with consternation that he had left his lodgings in bedroom slippers! He worked so diligently on his drawings that he got no more than four hours sleep a night.

"Never before did I so long for a glance of our rich magnolia woods; I never before felt the want of a glance of our forests as I do now; could I be there but a moment, near the mellow Mock-bird, or the Wood Thrush, to me always so pleasing, how happy should I be; but alas! I am far from those scenes. I seem, in a measure, to have gone back to my early days of society and fine dressing, silk stockings and pumps, and all the finery with which I made a popinjay of myself in my youth."

Late in November, under the urging of Lizars, he consented to have his portrait done by John Syme. He records he went "to *stand up* for my picture, and sick enough I was of it by two; at the request of Mr. Lizars I wear my wolfskin coat, and if the head is not a strong likeness, perhaps the coat may be—but this is discourteous of me, even to my journal." The next day he again "stood" for his portrait and entertained hope that it might prove a good resemblance to "my poor self," and on the following day wailed that sitting for his portrait "has become quite an ardous piece of business. I was positively in 'durance vile' for two and a half hours."

On the last day of November John Syme's portrait of The American Woodsman was pronounced finished. After his visit to the artist's studio and a critical inspection of the work in oils, Audubon returned to his lodgings and set down his impressions of the likeness in his journal. "I cannot say that I think it a very good resemblance, but it is a fine picture, and the public must judge the rest."

Originally it was Lizars' intention to have the Syme portrait engraved and issued as a part of the prospectus on *The Birds of America,* but as the Lizars-Audubon partnership did not last, as will be detailed later, the engraving was not made. Previous biographies have had it that neither the Symes portrait nor an engraving of it has been found. As a matter of fact, a young Scottish artist named Joseph B. Kidd was instrumental in 1833 in having the portrait engraved by Charles Wands and published as a frontispiece in *The Miscellany of Natural History,* written by Sir Thomas Dick Lauder and Captain Thomas Brown, and this became the first *published* likeness of Audubon. Later, other engravings from the Syme portrait appeared in an English edition of Baron Couvier's *Animal World* and then in some American publications.

Audubon did not like Syme's portrait nor the engravings made from it, for we find him writing Dr. John Bachman: "I have seen my Portrait engraved—the Devil himself could not wish better fun than to catch me in such trim as this fellow has represented me in—Like me? God bless you not a bit of it!"

One afternoon a woman called on Audubon in his George street lodgings and introduced herself as a cousin of Samuel Gregg. She said she desired to meet him, look him over, and view his pictures.

"Just as I was finishing my dinner," wrote the mystified Audubon that night, "Mrs. F————, the cousin of Mr. Gregg, called; the ladies having the right to command, I went immediately, and found a woman whose features had more force and character than women generally show in their lineaments. Her eyes were very penetrating, and I was struck with the strength of all she said, though nothing seemed studied. She showed the effects of a long, well learned round of general information. She, of course, praised my work, but I scarce thought her candid. Her eyes seemed to reach my very soul; I knew that at a glance she had discovered my inferiority . . . I must say, the more I realized her intelligence the more stupid did I become."

The steady stream of visitors to Mrs. Dickie's house flowed on unabated and the artist records happily, "My room is a perfect levee; it is Mr. Audubon here, and Mr. Audubon there:—I only hope they will not make a conceited fool of Mr. Audubon at last!"

Sir William Jardine and Prideaux John Selby, both authors of works on British birds, were at the George street rooms day in and day out, taking lessons in depicting birds after the style of the suddenly famous man from the woods of America.

One cold morning, four days before Christmas, Audubon had a cock pheasant triced up on wires and placed in a strutting attitude on his position board. He outlined it on his coarse gray paper in order to pounce the outline on canvas. But his mind was not on his work—the weather was clear, with a sharp frost. "What a number of wild ducks could I shoot on a morning like this, with a little powder and plenty of shot—but I have other fish to fry!" he sighed.

He was tired. Physically undone. Invitations poured in on him. Invitations to dine, to attend musicals, science meetings, social soirees—so that the Scots and their ladies could hear a heavily-maned lion from the wilds of America roar. If Audubon enjoyed all these attentions, and we must believe they were not altogether distasteful, he did not admit it to his journal, for he wrote:

"My time is so taken up, and daylight is so short, that though four hours is all I allow for sleep, I am behind-hand, and have engaged an amanuensis. I go out so much that I frequently dress *three times a day!*—the greatest bore in the world to me; why I cannot dine in my blue coat as well as a black one, I cannot say, but so it seems."

He had determined on a large canvas, "Pheasants Attacked by a Fox," nine-by-six feet, the most ambitious piece of work he had yet attempted and in a medium that was as yet strange to him—oils. The morning of this twenty-first day of December passed but the stretched piece of canvas he had ordered did not arrive. Jardine and Selby had paid their call and taken their lesson. Audubon fretted. His fingers itched for the palette and brushes. The pricked outline of the pheasant cock was ready for pouncing. The wired bird, in all the glory of its red and gold feathers, was on the position board when Mrs. Dickie announced callers—Mrs. Lizars and the sickly-looking Dr. Charles Fox in company with some friends of Selby. They chattered, his birds were admired, but Audubon did not want to talk—he wanted to paint.

"I looked at the beautiful Pheasant with longing eyes, but when the canvas came and my guests had gone, daylight went with them. So I lost a precious day—that is a vast deal in a man's life-glass."

4

In spite of the fact that he was called from his work as many as twenty-five times a day to greet visitors and show them his bird drawings, Audubon found time to slave on his big canvas of the pheasants. Winter daylight in Edinburgh was of short duration, it was usually nine-thirty before it was light enough to begin on the ambitious work and by three in the afternoon he was forced to drop his brushes and take up the crow quill and by gaslight paint in words something of the birds of his America.

One of his essays on natural history had to do with his experiments in the Feliciana country with the vultures and their alleged power to find their carrion food by the sense of smell. He had told many of the learned in Edinburgh how he had definitely discovered that vultures had no sense in this direction but were guided to their food by keen eyesight alone. This so upset traditional belief he was asked to set down his discovery on paper so that it might be spread before the scientific world through the medium of the printed page. His account finished, Audubon called on Dr. David Brewster, an eminent scientist and philosopher, to read the results of his labor with the pen. He admitted that his nervousness affected his respiration.

"I paused a moment, and he was kind enough to say it was highly interesting," recounts the author. "I resumed, and went on to the end much to my relief. He who has been brought up an auctioneer, or on the boards of some theatre, with all the knowledge of the proper usage of the voice, and all the *aplomb* such a life would give, knows nothing of the bashfulness which agitated me, a man who never looked into an English grammar and who has forgotten most of what he learned in French and Spanish ones—a man who has always felt awkward and shy in the presence of a stranger—a man habituated to ramble alone, with his thoughts usually bent on the beauties of Nature herself—this man, *me*, to be seated opposite Doctor Brewster in Edinburgh, reading one of my puny efforts at describing the habits of birds that none but an Almighty Creator can ever know, was ridiculously absurd in my estimation, during all the time; besides, I also felt the penetrating looks and keen observation of the learned man before me, so the cold sweat started from me."

Audubon left the manuscript with Doctor Brewster, who promised to go over it and make some corrections, and have it in readiness so that it could be read before the next meeting of the Royal Academy.

It was his ability as a painter of birds that caught the fancy of the learned in Edinburgh. He was prevailed upon to give a demonstration of his work and many brought birds to his rooms to have drawn. "I showed these gentlemen how I set up my specimens, squared my paper, and soon had them at work drawing a squirrel," he writes. "They called this a lesson. To me it like a dream, that I, merely a Woodsman, should teach men so much my superiors."

While Audubon was basking in the warmth of praise for what he could do in depicting birds with his chalks and brush, he received a letter from his Liverpool friends the Rathbones. They were frank in telling him it was their opinion his work would not succeed on account of the unusual large size, and Mrs. Rathbone refused to allow Audubon the pleasure of naming a bird after her, on account of the publicity she feared would follow. "Yet I longed to do so," wrote the artist, "for what greater compliment could I pay any lady than to give her name to one of the most exquisite creations of the Almighty? The whole made me most dismal, but yet not in the least discouraged or disheartened about my work. If Napoleon by perseverance and energy rose from the ranks to be an emperor, why should not Audubon with perseverance and energy be able to leave the woods of America for a time and publish and sell a book?—always supposing that Audubon had *some* knowledge of his work, as Napoleon had *great* knowledge of his. No, no, I shall not cease to work for this end till old age incapacitates me."

So the year drew to a close. On New Year's Day he acquired a new journal to record his varied activities in the British Athens, and on the first page he penned:

"A Happy New Year to you, my book. Bless me! how fair you look this very cold day. Which way, pray, are you travelling? Travelling wherever chance and circumstance may lead you? Well, I will take you for my companion, and we will talk together on all kinds of subjects, and you will help me remember, for my memory is bad, very bad. I can never recollect the name of an enemy, for instance; it is only my friends whom I can remember, and to write down somewhat of their kind treatment of me is a delight I love to enjoy."

5

A changed and sartorially improved Audubon penned those lines January 1, 1827, for The American Woodsman had developed into a recognized dandy. He had learned to take a fashionable pinch of snuff, and had purchased an ornate and stylish box to hold the scented tobacco. He was dressed in the height of fashion when he called on Lord Morton, where, he recounts, "a man in livery opened the door, and I walked in, giving him my hat and gloves and my American Stick (that, by the bye, never leaves me unless I leave it)." His free and easy manners of the open still clung to him, for when it was time to dress for dinner at the earl's palatial estate, *Dalmachoy*, eight miles from Edinburgh, he set down in his diary: "My evening toilet is never a very lengthy matter—for in my opinion it is a vile loss of time to spend as many minutes in arranging a cravat as a hangman does in tying a knot—I was ready long before seven."

A changed man, indeed, from the unkempt, tousle-haired individual who journeyed down the Mississippi river on a flatboat a short six years previously, "forking" vegetables and venison with his fingers and gnawing wolfishly at the carcass of a teal duck hot off the embers, was the gentleman who now offered his arm with studied grace to the Countess of Morton and conducted her in measured steps to the great beamed dining room of the castle to be served by lackeys in powdered wigs and crimson liveries.

In "fair Edina" he was a continued success with the scientists. In rapid succession he became a Fellow of the Royal Society of Antiquarians, Member of the Wernerian Society of Natural History, Member of the Society of Arts in Scotland, in addition to his membership in the Philosophical and Literary Society and the Royal Institution in Liverpool. With many flourishes he added "F.R.S." to the signature on his original drawings of birds, for he placed a high valuation upon his election to the select Scottish society.

Audubon's paper relating to the power of sight and smell in the black vulture and turkey buzzard, which he had left with Doctor Brewster so that learned savant could couch it in better English, was sent back to him ready for presentation before the Wernerian Society. Eagerly the author opened the package when the revised sheets were delivered at his lodgings. His heart sank lower and lower as he rapidly scanned page after page. Before he left for the meeting place where his literary and scientific effort was to be read, he turned, as he frequently did when sunk in the depths of despair, to his journal and wrote: "Doctor Brewster had altered it so much that I am quited shocked it, it made me quite sick. He has, beyond question, greatly improved the style (for I have none), but he has destroyed the matter."

This piece of natural history writing, which recounted Audubon's experiments in the Feliciana woods when he demonstrated to the satisfaction of Augustin Bourgeat and Doctor Pope that vultures found their carrion food by sight and not by smell, was presented at the regular Saturday night meeting of the Wernerians when Patrick Neill, the printer of Old Fishmarket, read it, "not very well, as my writing was not easy reading for him," Audubon noted in his journal and added that it was his "maiden speech."

Well do I remember the uneasy feelings which I experienced. The audience was large and composed of many of the most distinguished men of that enlightened country. My paper was a long one, and it contradicted all former opinions on the subject under discussion; yet the cheering appearance of kindness which everywhere met my eye, as I occasionally glanced around, gradually dispelling my uneasiness, and brought me to a state of confidence. The reading of the paper being at length accomplished, I was congratulated by the president, as well as by every member present. Many questions were put to me; all of which I answered as well as I could. My esteemed and learned friend, Professor Jameson, requested permission to publish my paper in his valuable journal, which I most readily granted.

Strolling homeward I felt proud that I had at last broken the chain by which men had so long been held in ignorance respecting the natural history of our vultures, assured that the breach which I had made upon a general and deeply rooted opinion, must gradually dissolve it as well as many other absurdities which have for ages infested science, like a vile grub beneath the bark of the noblest forest tree, retarding its growth, until happily removed by the constant hammerings of the industrious woodpecker.

About the time Audubon was setting the naturalists of Edinburgh on their ears by his revolutionary ideas on the "nose smelling" of the vultures, he met a young landscape artist named Joseph Bartholomew Kidd. The Scot was only nineteen but he had already won a reputation for his work in oils. Kidd breakfasted with the bird artist and Audubon declared himself charmed with the youngster's talents and "thought what a difference it would have made in my life if I had begun painting in oil at his age and with his ability. It is a sad reflection that I have been compelled to hammer and stammer as if I were working in opposition to God's will, and so now am nothing but poor Audubon."

Audubon invited Kidd to visit him daily so they might discuss painting. He took down his portfolios and showed Kidd some of his work in bird portraiture. The young man was astonished and said: "How hopeless must be the task of my giving any instruction to one who can draw like that."

The elder says he pointed out to the younger that "nature is the great study for the artist, and assured him that the reason my works pleased him was because they are all exact copies of the works of God, who is the Great Architect and Perfect Artist; and impressed on his mind this

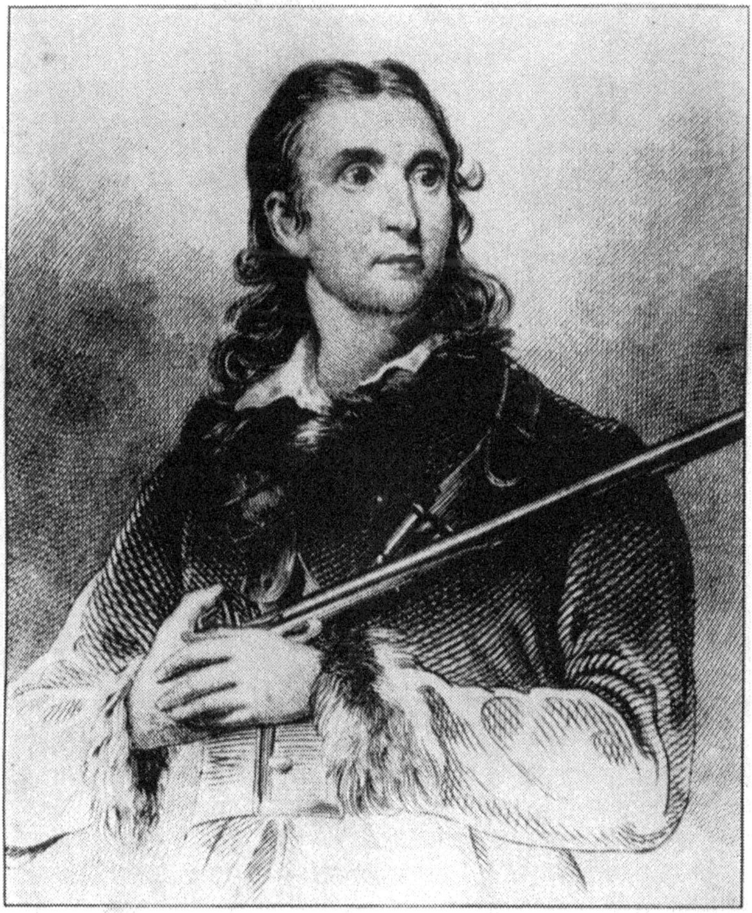

AUDUBON AT 41
The first published portrait of The American Woodsman. It is from an engraving by Charles Wands after the oil portrait by John Syme, Esq., S. A. Painted in Edinburgh, Scotland, November 1826, for William Home Lizars.

AUDUBON AT 46

Audubon's favorite likeness, a miniature by Frederick Cruikshank, painted in 1831. From the engraving by Charles Turner.

LUCY AUDUBON AT 44

A miniature on ivory by Frederick Cruikshank, painted in London in 1831, at the same time the British artist pictured her husband.

fact—that nature indifferently copied is far superior to the best idealities."

On a Sunday morning, when the snow was so deep that the Scots were wading through it as they made their way to church, Audubon dined with a minister, the Reverend Newbold, and afterwards was "toted to church" in a sedan chair. "I had never been in one before," he wrote his wife that night, "and I like to try, as well as see, all things that are going on on the face of this strange world of ours; but so long as I have two legs and feet below them, never will I again enter one of these machines, with their quick, short, up-and-down, swinging motion, resembling the sensations felt during that great earthquake in Kentucky."

In the land of Calvinism the man who had been reared a Papist but who eschewed all religion sat in a stiff-backed pew and heard the famed and popular Sidney Smith, then in his fifty-sixth year, preach the Church of England doctrine. "Oh! what a soul there must be in the body of that great man," Audubon added to the letter he sent his wife describing the events of that snowy Edinburgh Sunday. "What sweet yet energetic thoughts, what goodness he must possess.

"It was a sermon *to me!* He made me smile, and he made me think deeply. He pleased me at times by painting my foibles with due care, and again I felt the color come to my cheeks as he portrayed my sins. I left the church full of veneration not only towards God, but towards the wonderful man who so beautifully illustrates his noblest handiwork."

Waving away the sedan chair, Audubon and his friend Hay, the antiquarian, after services "walked, tumbled and pitched" through the deep snow to the outskirts of the city where he saw "Sky-Larks, poor things, caught in snares as easily—as men are caught!"

Early in February Audubon was due to read another paper before the Wernerian Society on the habits of the rattlesnake. He had not found time to complete the writing and was disturbed when he arrived. "When I entered the rooms they were as full as an egg," and Professor Graham arose as the long-haired naturalist entered and called the president's attention to Audubon's presence. "I was sorry I was not prepared to read to those assembled that a Rattlesnake rattled his tail, not to give knowledge to man of his presence, but because he never strikes without rattling—and destitute of that appendage *he cannot strike at all!*"

When he informed the presiding officer that he was not prepared to read his paper, but would do so at a later date, his engravings of birds were called for and upon being exhibited they "were highly praised."

In spite of flattering attentions showered upon him by the scientists, educators, and others of the Scottish capital interested in natural history; in spite of the attention and belief given his many startling statements concerning the habits of birds in distant and alluring America, all was not smooth going on Audubon's scampering ride to fame. In spots it was as bumpy as his ride in the sedan chair—for there were those in the Old World who refused to swallow at one gulp *everything* this eccentric woodsman told his hearers at Wernerian Society meetings.

Foremost among the non-believers was Charles Waterton, a recognized English naturalist, who read with a jaundiced eye Audubon's account of rattlesnakes with recurved fangs, and his experiments on the lack of nose-smelling powers of the carrion vultures. He had even written Audubon a letter protesting the accuracy of some of his observations and conclusions. Audubon, who termed the letter "scrubby," refused to answer it and dismissed the Englishman from further consideration, whereupon Waterton, constituting himself chief heckler of the Franco-American story-teller, published his stinging criticisms. These printed barbs found Audubon's skin rather thin and, at regular meetings of the Wernerian Society, he would sandwich between his accounts of bird habits some rather caustic appraisals of Mr. Waterton's abilities as a naturalist.

Attending the Edinburgh University in 1827 was a youth of eighteen who delighted to accompany Doctor Grant to the Wernerian gatherings. The fresh-faced young Englishman was greatly interested in everything pertaining to natural history—so much so that thirty years later he startled the scientific world with his theory of evolution and the origin of species. Charles Darwin, commenting in later years on one of these meetings, wrote: "I heard Audubon deliver some interesting discussions on N. American birds, sneering somewhat unjustly at Waterton."

It was in March, after the first number of his plates had been completed and Lizars was busy on his second number of five plates, that Audubon issued his *Prospectus* for his proposed work on *The Birds of America.* Many of his new-found friends in the British Isles endeavored to dissuade him from his intention of finishing his work on such a gigantic scale, avowing that the whole scheme was foredoomed to failure, but he brushed aside these gloomy predictions and began a diligent search throughout Britain for subscribers.

The work was to appear in parts of five plates each, at two guineas a part. In order to distribute the expense to purchasers, only five parts a year, or twenty-five plates, were to be engraved, colored, and delivered to subscribers. The paintings were to be reproduced from engraved copper plates, double-elephant size, printed on the finest paper procurable, and all of the birds and flowers reproduced in life-size, and colored by hand precisely like the originals. Subscribers were invited to take part or all of the completed work.

No sooner was Audubon embarked on his colossal undertaking and preparing to go to London in pursuit of subscribers, than his friends in Edinburgh suggested he give due attention to the matter of his personal appearance.

Robert W. Hay, the antiquarian, called with his son and found Audubon at work picturing two catbirds on sprays of blackberry briars, a painting he proposed presenting to the Countess of Morton. Hay, after voicing his admiration for the picture, bluntly came to the real reason for his early morning call.

"Don't you think it would be good policy for you to cut your hair and have a fashionable coat made before you reach London?" he demanded.

Says Audubon, in recording the conversation, "I laughed and he laughed, and my hair is yet as God made it."

The flowing locks that left a shining coating of bear's

grease on the velvet collar of Audubon's unfashionable coat—locks that offended the sight and, it might as well be confessed, the smell of Audubon's Edinburgh friends—remained an object of attack. Two days after Hay's unsuccessful effort to have them sheared, Mrs. Dickie handed her lodger two notes. One was from Captain Basil Hall, the other from his brother, Sir James Hall.

"They were filled with entreaties, couched in strong terms, that I should *alter my hair* before I went to London," writes Audubon.

. "Good God! if Thy works are hated by man it must be with Thy permission. I sent for a barber and my hair was mowed off in a trice. I knew I was acting weakly, but rather than render my good friends miserable about it, I suffered the loss patiently."

When the barber had finished his shearing and the desecration was complete, Audubon seized his diary and, after adorning the page with a heavy black border an inch wide, penned a single entry:

Edinburgh
March 19th 1827

This day My Hairs were sacrificed
and the will of God usurped by the
wishes of Man — as the Barber
clipped them rapidly it remainded
me of the horrible times of the French
Revolution when the same operation was performed
upon all the Victims murdered at the
Guillotine————My Heart sank Low.

John J. Audubon

At the time Captain Hall and his brother succeeded in persuading Audubon to cut his cherished locks, the bird artist was in a torment of indecision and evident retrospect. The "puzzling background" of his life had again surged to the fore and was once more taking possession of his innermost thoughts.

One Friday afternoon, four days before the barber was called in, Audubon and his George street lodgings were honored by a visit from Lady Selkirk and her daughter. Her Ladyship was the widow of Lord Selkirk, the late Governor General of Canada, the same who had fostered

Edinburgh

March 19th 1827.

This day My Hairs were sacrificed, and ~~the~~ will of God usurped by the wishes of Man — as the Barber clipped them rapidly it reminded me of the horrible times of the French Revolution when the same operation was performed upon all the Victims murdered at the Guillotine — My Heart sank low.

John J. Audubon

an ambitious emigration scheme in that part of North America and founded "Selkirk's Settlement" on Prince Edward's Island. Lord Selkirk's sister was the mother of Captain Basil Hall, the young British naval officer, traveler, and author, who had taken such a deep and mysterious interest in Audubon since the naturalist's appearance in Edinburgh.

Lord Selkirk had been dead three years when his widow called on Audubon. She examined his drawings, questioned him minutely concerning his life and residence in America, and heard something of his many adventures and his ambitions. She was strangely concerned about him and his antecedents, thought Audubon, and after Lady Selkirk and her daughter departed he sat to his journal and described the visit:

"The carriage rolled away and I sat alone—thinking how truly strange that the wife of the Earl of Selkirk should call on thy husband at Edinburgh. Did she know, I wonder, who *I am positively* or does she think that it is John J. Audubon of Louisiana to whom she spoke?

"Curious event, this life of mine!"

This entry of March 15, 1827, and one written three days later, were withheld by members of the Audubon family when copying journal entries for publication. They were included with other suppressed entries from letters, diaries and journals which a granddaughter declared proved to her that Audubon was the Lost Dauphin.

The day before he allowed his hair to be shorn Audubon was shaving. After finishing his work with the razor, he went to his journal and set down:

"Edinburgh, March 18, 1827—To day as I was shaving I was struck by my resemblance to my father, not my adopted father, but my *own* father."

CHAPTER 22

London Town

ON the fifth of April, shorn and uncomfortable and wearing a fashionable coat, Audubon left Edinburgh in his new rôle of *edition de luxe* book-agent to search out subscribers to his great work. His destination was London, but on his provincial canvass he first visited in succession Belford, Newcastle-upon-Tyne, York, Leeds, Manchester, and Liverpool.

He was successful in his quest for subscribers in some of these old English towns and met disappointment in others. Life in these quaint places proved irksome to the out-of-doors man and he spent nights filling his journal with confessions of his homesick longings for the woods of America. He was in England, but his heart was elsewhere, and a final entry one night read: "Oh, that I were in Louisiana, strolling about the woods, looking in the gigantic poplars for new birds and new flowers!"

Even in his moments of depression, when he was tormented by his "blue devils," when he was assailed with grave doubts as to the final outcome of his ambitious project, he never failed to be observant of humorous happenings.

His stay in York was not pleasant. It rained, then snowed, and the wind blew cold all day. "I could never make up my mind to live and die in England whilst the sweet scented jessamine and the magnolias flourish so purely in my native land, and the air vibrates with the songs of sweet birds," he wrote his wife, and then added that he felt as dull as a martin surprised by the weather.

The next morning his spirits were raised when visitors came to inspect his drawings of the birds of far-away America. Among these visitors was Mr. Phillips, curator of the local museum, who advised Audubon to call upon the local nobility and other gentry in the neighborhood of York and to take his birds with him.

Audubon thanked the museum director, "but I told him that my standing in society did not admit of such conduct, and that although there were lords in England, we of American blood think ourselves their equals. He laughed, and said I was not as much of a Frenchman as I looked."

2

When Audubon reached Newcastle-upon-Tyne his spirits were revived, although he found the River Tyne "as dirty and muddy as an alligator hole." His buoyancy of feelings was directly attributable to the securing of three subscribers to his work, and the fact that here he met Thomas Bewick, the aged wood engraver, whose works on birds were then famous. Bewick expressed himself astounded by the boldness of Audubon's understanding and praised the younger man's birds without stint.

"He welcomed me with a hearty shake of the hand, and took off for a moment his half-clean cotton night-cap tinged with the smoke of the place," wrote Audubon. "He is tall, stout, has a very large head, and his eyes are further apart than those of any man I remember just now. A complete Englishman, full of life and energy though now seventy-four, very witty and clever, better acquainted with America than most of his countrymen, and an honor to England."

Bewick showed Audubon how he made his engravings on box wood. On a piece not more than two-by-three inches he had represented a dog frightened during the night by false resemblances of men formed by curious roots and branches of trees and rocks. Audubon was as much impressed with Bewick as he was with the craftsman's skill, and termed him a true son of Nature. "Nature alone has reared him under her peaceful care, and he in gratitude of heart has copied one department of her works that must stand unrivalled forever; I say 'forever' because imitators have only a share of real merit, compared with inventors, and Thomas Bewick is an inventor, and *the first wood-cutter in the world!* These words, 'first wood-cutter' would, I dare say, raise the ire of many of our hearty squatters, who, no doubt, would take the axe, and fell down an enormous tree whilst talking about it; but the moment I would explain to them that each of their chips would produce under his chisel a mass of beauties, the good fellows would respect him as much as I do."

Before he left Newcastle, Audubon's room at the *Rose and Crown* Inn was "filled all day with people to see my works and *Me*, whom some one said resembled in physiognomy Napoleon of France. *Strange simile this!* but I care not whom I resemble, if it be only in looks, if my heart preserves the love of truth."

The following day, however, he confesses he had grown tired of holding up bird drawings for the curious and the *ton* of Newcastle, and although he was rewarded by the addition of five subscribers to his growing list, he was glad to leave for York atop a coach so he could better view the English countryside on the ride.

Although now established in his new rôle of book-agent, Audubon did not cease to study the habits of the birds of England that came under his observation. Tiring of showing his wares and asking for subscriptions, he seized upon every opportunity offered to walk out of the environs of the town and allow his feet, aching from battering the pavements, to ease their burnings on grassy meadows or flower-spangled river banks. Sauntering along the wend of the Ouse, his attraction was given to a large flock of starlings. It was April, a time of the year when he thought all birds should be paired and busy with nesting duties. He watched their motions, manner of walking over the short grass, and came to the conclusion "that the bird commonly called the Meadow Lark with us is more nearly related to the Starling of this country than to any other bird. I was particularly surprised that a low note, resembling the noise made by a wheel not well greased, was precisely alike, and that in *short* flights the movements of the wings had the same tremulous action before they alighted."

He had not secured a single subscriber in York, and the following evening, after he had returned from a long walk, he recalled how many times at the sunset hour he had walked with his wife through "the fragrant woods of Louisiana; how often have we stopped short to admire the works of the Creator; how often have we been delighted at hearing the musical notes of the timid Wood Thrush that appeared to give his farewell melody to the disappearing day! We have looked at the glittering fire-fly, heard the Chuck-will's-widow, and seen the vigilant Owl preparing to search field and forest! Here the scene is not quite so pleasing, though the charms brought youth and happiness to my recollection."

In spite of diligent canvassing he was only able to obtain three subscribers in York. Greatly disappointed he took an early morning saunter along the banks of the Ouse before packing up to continue his journey to Leeds. "During my walk I saw a large butterfly, quite new to me, and attempted to procure it with a stroke of my cane; but as I whirled it round, off went the scabbard into the river, more than half across, and I stood with a naked small sword as if waiting for a duel. I would have swam out for it, but that there were other pedestrians; so a man in a boat brought it to me for sixpence."

With his ever-present "American Stick" intact again he returned to his lodgings, but in a black mood. He was in the the dumps, deep in them—doubts were assailing him again. In spite of his ill humor, in spite of the fact that a bevy of "blue-devils" was hammering on the top of his cropped head, he penned a characteristic word picture of his landlady, Mrs. Pulleyn, and her emaciated meek spouse. "Her weight, in ratio with that of her husband, is as one pound avoirdupois to one ounce apothecary! She looks like a round of beef, he like a farthing candle. When he enters the room I think of Scroggins' ghost!"

One year after he had left Feliciana bound for his European adventures, Audubon found himself in Leeds. Armed with letters to many of the celebrities there, he entered the town confident he would meet with greater success than that which he had obtained in either Newcastle or York. Among those of importance whom he met was John Backhouse, "a good ornithologist—not a *closet naturalist* [this was a fling at Waterton], but a real true blue who goes out at night and watches Owls and Night-Jars and Waterfowl to some purpose, and who knows more about these things than any other man I have met in Europe."

On the May Day, realizing he had been away from his wife exactly a twelvemonth, he gave up his hunt for fame a few hours while he penned a lengthy communication to the woman who had made his quest possible. "It was this day, my Lucy, that I parted with thee at the corner of Mr. Bourgeat's Road, already twelve months and these might well have been with me as not but as it seems it was not ordered to be so. May God preserve thee."

He then apologized for allowing a whole month to slip by without sending her a letter, and detailed the many activities he had shouldered pending his leaving Edinburgh. He recalled she had written him asking advice on the prevailing mode in England as to the arrangement of hair by British ladies of fashion, and had asked him to purchase and send her a fashionable headdress. For, while the husband had been wondrously endowed with a hirsute adornment, Lucy had lost her hair, and it was necessary for her to wear a wig. Late in life she became quite bald.

"Do, my Lucy, arrange thy Hair according to thy own Taste," he advised, "and although to forward all that I have without one thing reaching thee is not encouraging to send more, I will most undoubtedly send thee a Head dress *à L'Anglaise* from Liverpool and a most fashionable one."

In the same letter he devoted attention to Mrs. Audubon's change of residence. In a letter he received just before leaving Edinburgh, Lucy had advised her husband she had left the Percy plantation in February, and had taken up duties as a teacher at *Beech Grove*, the plantation home of William Garrett Johnson, a well-to-do cotton planter in Feliciana, a few miles distant from *Beech Woods*. Audubon declared he was "particularly glad" she had left Mrs. Percy's, but complained that Lucy had failed to inform him of the reasons for the change.

That night he fell into retrospective mood and in his journal philosophized on what he had accomplished and what he hoped to do.

This is the day on which last year I left my Lucy and my boys with intention to sail for Europe. How uncertain my hopes at that time were as to the final results of my voyage,—about to leave a country where most of my life had been spent devoted to the study of Nature, to enter one wholly unknown to me, without a friend, nay, not an acquaintance in it. Until I reached Edinburgh I dispaired of success; the publication of a work of enormous expense, and the length of time it must necessarily take; to accomplish the whole has been sufficient to keep my spirits low, I assure thee. Now I feel like beginning a New Year. My work is about to be known, I have made a number of valuable and kind friends, I have been received by men of science on friendly terms, and now I have a hope of success if I continue to be honest, industrious, and consistent. My pecuniary means are slender, but I hope to keep afloat, for my tastes are simple; if only I can succeed in rendering thee and our sons happy, not a moment of sorrow or discomfort shall I regret.

The following day, after receiving a stream of visitors at his Leeds' lodgings at 39 Albion street, Audubon walked three miles out of town to visit Kirkstall Abbey, made a sketch of the scene for his wife on one of his visiting cards, and that night he wrote her:

"From that spot I heard a Cuckoo cry, for I do not, like the English, call it singing. I attempted to approach the bird, but in vain; I believe I might be more successful in holding a large Alligator by the tail. Many people speak in raptures of the sweet voice of the Cuckoo, and the same people tell me in cold blood that we have no birds that can sing in America. I wish they had a chance to judge the powers of the Mock-bird, the Red Thrush, the Cat-bird, the Oriole, the Indigo bunting, even the Whip-poor-will. What would they say of a half a million Robins about to take their departure for the North, making our woods fairly tremble with melodious harmony? But these pleasures are not to be enjoyed in manufacturing towns like Leeds and Manchester; neither can one praise a bird who sings by tuition, like a pupil of Mozart, as a few Linnets and Starlings do, and that no doubt are here taken as the foundation stone of the powers alloted to European birds generally. Well, is not this a long digression for thee? I dare say thou art fatigued enough at it, and so am I."

At Leeds his spirits were raised when the secretary of the Literary and Philosophical Society called at his lodgings and, after inspecting the bird drawings, subscribed for the forthcoming published work. Others called, singly and in gay parties, and the artist was forced to hold up for inspection his bird treasures. Many of his visitors were titled and Audubon confided to his journal that he was "sorry to say" he found it generally more difficult to please that class of persons than others, and that he felt in consequence more reserved in their presence, "I can scarcely say why."

That night he again wrote his "beloved Lucy" and recounted details of the day. He told of the many visitors, their comments and his reactions to what they said and did.

"I think I must tell thee how everyone stares when they read on the first engraving that I present for their inspection this name: 'The Bonaparte Fly-catcher,' — the very bird I was anxious to name 'The Rathbone Fly-catcher,' in honor of my excellent friend 'Lady' Rathbone, but who refused to accept this little mark of my gratitude. I afterwards meant *to call it after thee*, but did not, because the world is so strangely composed just now that I feared it would be thought childish; so I concluded to call it after my friend Charles Bonaparte. Every one is struck by the name, so explanations take place, and the good people of England will know him as a great naturalist, and my friend. I intend to name, one after another, everyone of my new birds, either for some naturalist deserving of this honor, or through a wish to return thanks for kindness rendered me."

Following this resolve Audubon named: "Children's Warbler," "Stanley's Hawk," "Cuvier's Regulus," "Selby's Flycatcher," "Henslow's Bunting," "Traill's Flycatcher," "Roscoe's Yellowthroat," "Harlan's Hawk," "Harris's Sparrow," "MacGillivray's Seaside Sparrow," "Swainson's Warbler," "Bewick's Wren," "Lincoln's Sparrow," and "Bonaparte's Flycatching Warbler." True, many of these baptisms have disappeared from our ornithological literature because some of the birds he claimed as new species when examined by ornithologists proved to be immature specimens of birds already named.

How nearly Bonaparte's Warbler came to be known, on Audubon's famous plate at least, as "Lucy's Warbler."

But no, her husband had to compliment the great—he must not be thought "childish," beloved Lucy!

3

Audubon was delighted to again meet Robert Bentley when Manchester was reached on the sixth of May. The next day he had his paintings and the first set of engravings on exhibition at the Royal Institution. He scoured Manchester for subscribers and in a week's time, aided by Publisher Bentley, had added eighteen names to his growing list, in all forty-nine in forty days of canvassing.

Then he went to Liverpool where he busied himself with preparations for his long contemplated visit to London, packed his drawings so they could be shipped there by caravan, as the covered wagon transport of that day was termed, and visited the Rathbones, the Roscoes, and even found time to call upon Alexander Gordon and his sister-in-law Anne.

In spite of the time entailed the round of calling, Audubon found opportunity to write his wife in quite some detail, his plans and hopes:

Mr. Lizars my engraver who wrote me in great Spirits and has begun the second number which will appear before the public in about 2 months — I conceive it is now time to give thee a regular detail of the manner in which this Great Work of mine has been undertaken and the means that are intended to carry it throughout in all its parts. In the first place I have been carefull not to have more copies struck than could possibly be help to try with the least cost the result of the *1st* number. this consisted of 50 copies only. Mr Lizars assured me that the filling of that quanity would save and balance the expense of producing them and I felt willing to make the trial at my own expense and risk.

The result has been a fortunate one, not only the first 50 copies engraved, printed & coloured have been subscribed for and delivered but more than 50 more have been *struck* or *printed since* and I am glad to say that I have subscribers enough to take the whole. in this way we follow the demand by printing more & more copies as they are required by the improvement of my list of Subscribers and take good care to have only a very small stock of copies over the demand — Thus now with one hundred subscribers (who all pay on delivery) hundred Copies of each number that consists of 5 plates averaging in quality and appearance those I have sent thee, leaving a benefit of 42 pounds 9 shillings and 4 pence Sterling, and that repeated 5 times during one Year gives — £212.6.8 sterling. When 200 Subscribers will be had the first amount will be more than double *because* the plates are paid for by the first 100 copies sold and of course the printing coloring and paper is the only additional expense

Therefore 200 Subscribers gives a profit on each number of £174.18.8 sterling and five times that amount £879.7.4 sterling which makes in Dollars about 3902 per annum — enough to maintain us even in this Country in a style of elegance and comfort that I hope to see thee enjoy. Should I be so fortunate to reach the number of 500 Subscribers and my health does not impair in consequence of my great exertions the sum per annum clear of expenses will be £2821 sterling, making in Dollars about ten thousand seven hundred and forty-nine!

Audubon added, near the close of this lengthy letter, that if she believed "the fair accounts given thee as Fairy tales," he would copy the actual words of Lizars and send them on. "If I fail, America is still my Country, and thou, I will still find my friend; I will return to both and forget forever the troubles and expenses I will have been at; when walking together arms in arms we can see our Sons before us, and Lisson to the mellow sounding notes of the Thrush so plenty in our woods of Magnolias."

In a postscript he apologized for not sending her the headdress *à l'Anglais*, claiming he had "little time to breathe," but as soon as he arrived in London he would send one or two. This reminded him of his own thatch. "My hair was long and curled beautifully on my shoulders until 2 months ago when I cut it off and am now *rather more* of an Englishman, but in good Circles and all societies Appearance has very little to do.

"Do write *why* thou left *Mrs. P.* I thought thou wert so attached to her that nothing would make you part," he ended the letter, which indicates that Lucy was keeping secret her reason for leaving Mrs. Percy's plantation.

It was a Sunday morning, the twentieth of May, when Audubon left Liverpool for London Town. To his "great joy," Robert Bentley elected to make the journey with him and the coach they selected dashed through Chester, Wrexham, Eastham, and Shrewsbury. In the latter town they were faced with a delay of five hours and they put in the time wandering along the banks of the river Severn. Even though they were wrapped in coats and cloaks, the two found the air chilly when the London coach left Shrewsbury after nightfall. Breakfast was secured at Birmingham at five in the morning, "where the worst stuff bearing the name of coffee that I ever tasted, was brought to us," writes Audubon. "I say *tasted*, for I could do no more."

The coach rolled through Stratford-on-Avon, Woodstock, and Oxford, and at ten in the morning passed through the turnpike gate, followed Oxford street its full length, and drew up at the *Bull and Mouth* tavern. The man from America surveyed the great city of London and that night seized journal and crow quill to set down his first impressions.

"I should begin this page perhaps with a great exclamation mark, and express much pleasure, but I have not the wish to do either; to me London is just like the mouth of an immense monster, guarded by millions of sharp-edged teeth, from which if I escape unhurt it must be called a miracle. I have many times longed to see London, and now I am here I feel a desire beyond words to be in my beloved woods."

The following day Audubon forsook the *Bull and Mouth* and took lodgings at the home of Mrs. Middlemist, 55 Great Russell Street. She was a sister-in-law of Mrs. Robert Percy of *Beech Woods*. After settling his effects there, Audubon set out to view the town and at the same time deliver letters of introduction he carried to many important personages in the British capital.

Guided by a map, he threaded the crowded streets of London Town, and endeavored to find his own way through the vast labyrinth of thoroughfares as he would through a dense magnolia forest of the Felicianas. He scurried about, he tells us, "like a post boy taking letters everywhere," until his feet were sore from battering the pavements.

"From one great man's door to another I went," he records, "but judge my surprise when, after wandering the greater part of three successive days, early and late, and at all hours, I found not a single individual at home!" One night he returned to his rooms at the Middlemist house completely worn out, declaring he must have walked "forty miles on hard pavements, from Idol Lane to Grosvenor Square, and across in many directions, all equally far apart."

AUDUBON AT 48
The oil portrait by Henry Inman, painted in Philadelphia in 1833.

THE HALL ENGRAVING
An engraving of the Inman portrait by H. B. Hall and frequently reproduced.

AUDUBON AT 53

An oil portrait by George P. A. Healy, an American artist, made in 1838. The portrait was painted at night by gaslight. Now owned by the Boston Museum of Natural History.

Each great man was out. Wearied and disappointed, he came to the conclusion that his only chance of having his letters delivered was to consign them to the post. He placed all of them there save one that was addressed to John George Children, an English physicist and naturalist, who was secretary of the Royal Society of London. Calling at the British Museum he was fortunate in finding Children in his office and received a warm welcome. During the course of their conversation Audubon related the difficulties he encountered delivering his letters and how he had solved the problem. Children at once pointed out the error the bird painter had committed in placing them in the post office and suggested that Audubon continue his calls, and in this way rectify the mistake. Children's words threw Audubon into a blue funk but, in the course of a week, when a few of the Londoners who had received his letters called at his lodgings and left their cards, his feelings underwent a marked change and his spirits climbed out of the mire of despond as he was wont to clamber out of a miry alligator hole in the Tunica swamps of Feliciana.

Invited by Children to dine with him and heeding the lessons of deportment drilled into him by Captain Basil Hall at Edinburgh, Audubon donned a suit of fashionable black, and "thus adorned like a mournful Raven," kept the appointment. Later he and Children attended a meeting of the Linnæan Society where Audubon exhibited the first five plates struck off by Lizars. "All those present pronounced my work unrivaled and wished me success," he penned in high glee to his wife that night before turning into bed.

In the next few days Children saw to it that the bird artist attended the meetings of other societies, where he met Londoners who stood high in the world of science and all of them were more than merely interested in his plans to publish *The Birds of America.* At the outset his introduction to the English metropolis bade fair to rival his speedy conquest of stolid Edinburgh and it appeared that the stir he created in Fair Edina would be equalled, if not outdone, in London Town.

Audubon had not been in London many days before he received dire tidings from Lizars. The Edinburgh engraver wrote that his colorists had struck, and all work on *The Birds of America* was at a standstill! Lizars suggested that until the matter could be mended that Audubon find someone in London who could and would color the black and white prints that had already been pulled from the copper plates.

The evil news threw Audubon into a panic. Where, where would he find a colorist? A London shop man directed him to call on a young man named Havell, said to be a finished colorist as well as an experienced engraver. Audubon hurried to the address but, even after five calls, failed to find the young man in. Anxiously he paced the streets. Gloomy thoughts and dire suspicions raced through his mind like hurricanes in the Gulf of Mexico during the autumn months. Lizars had written in such discouraging words that Audubon became convinced the Scot was planning to abandon the contract.

He was distracted! His cherished work was about to die a-borning! He was without funds, and money now was imperative. Someone must be found to take up the work where Lizars laid it down. Audubon was relieved on his sixth visit to the shop to meet the man he was seeking—Robert Havell, Jun., then a little-known artist, thirty-four years of age. Audubon explained his situation, showed the young man his bird drawings, exhibited the plates that Lizars had completed, displayed his list of subscribers, and made the Londoner a proposal. The upshot of the meeting was that Havell agreed to finish Audubon's great work, and through its publication and fame became recognized as one of the foremost engravers of history.

In a few days the publication office of *The Birds of America* was removed from Edinburgh to 79 Newman street, London, and the work begun anew under the auspices of Robert Havell & Son, for the senior Havell was also an engraver of note. No sooner had father and son started their part of the contract than Audubon realized his birds would be reproduced more perfectly and at less cost than in Scotland.

Audubon in writing his wife full particulars of the arrangement expressed himself as "truly glad" of the change:

London affords all sorts of facilities imaginable, or necessary for the Publication of such an immense work and hereafter my *Principal* business will be carried on here — I have made arrangement with a Mr. Havell an excellent Engraver who has a good establishment containing Printers — Colorers and Engravers So that I can have all under my eye when I am in London and no longer will be stopp[d] by the want of Paper, or Coppers that Mr Lizars was obliged to order from here; sometimes with risks and at all events with a considerable expense *extra*. Indeed the difference of cost from the number which Mr Havell is engraving (the *3d*) and those done by Mr Lizars I save about 25 pounds Sterling which is nearly one-fourth of what Mr. L. charges and yet the work is quite equal, and the sets colored by him are far surpassing in beauty those of Mr L — My business is now I think in such a train as will enable me to keep it going this year as the work is now able to pay for itself by good managem[t] and Industry and to try and give thee a true Idea of it I will explain more at length —

The price I pay Mr Havell for Engraving one Number or a set

		Sgs	Pce.
consisting of 5 Plates with the lettering and Coppers Included is	£42.	0.	0
the price of coloring 100 sets @ 8/6	42.	10.	0
Paper for Do. 1 Ream	14.	1.	0
Printing the 100 sets	11.	5.	0
100 tin cases to forward the sets to each person	5.	0	0
	£114.	16	0

These 100 sets thus delivered bring 210 pounds as I charge 2 Guineas per number so that my having been able to pay for the 1*st* number and also the 2*d* will enable me to keep going and if between this and January 1828 I procure 100 more Subscribers than I have at present, I will consider myself quite able to have thy sweet self and Johny here, because every subscriber after even now is all clear profit. the plates are of course my property and 1500 copies may be struck off before they will need any repair — to collect my money I take a round to the different Cities where my subscribers are and it is my Intention to go that round twice or three time a year so that I have really great Hopes of Success and the Prospect of having thee and our Sons once more Independent.

Audubon's task, now that the *Birds* were once more in flight, was to keep Havell's workmen supplied with cash. So he resorted to his painting as a means of raising the necessary funds. His lodgings at Mrs. Middlemist's became his studio, he painted morning, noon, and night; hawked his pictures of birds and mammals about London Town, selling to shops, to patrons—to anyone who would buy. He tells us:

> At that time I painted all day, and sold my work during the dusky hours of evening. As I walked through the Strand and other streets where Jews reigned; popping in and out of Jew-shops or any other, and never refusing the offers made me for the pictures I carried fresh from the easel. Startling as this may seem, it is nevertheless true, and one of the curious events of my extraordinary life.

"I do anything for money now a days," he wrote his wife. "I positively last week made 22 Pounds 10 Shillings by drawing trifles in a Scotch Lady's Album. That enabled me to purchase 6 Gilt frames to forward 6 Pictures to the Liverpool exhibition where I hope I may sell the whole of them—I painted them since I came to London in oil — one of Ducks — one of Rabbits — one of Common Fowls, one of Pigeons, one of Partridges, one of an Otter, all measuring 42. Inches by 28. — My prices for them are from 20 to 30 Guineas each according to difference of value judged by myself and some friends of mine — if I sell them it will put me quite afloat and at my ease — I will begin as soon as time will permit 2 very large Pictures of Peacocks, and Turkeys for the Spring London exhibition so as to have my name Cracked up here as well as in Edinburgh."

Finding his painting room and parlor too small, Audubon left the Middlemist home during the latter part of August, moving his effects to 95 Great Russell street, Bedford Square, to a house kept by a Mrs. Woodly, described by her new lodger as "an intelligent widow, with eleven children, and but little cash."

Shortly after this move Audubon made seven copies of his "Otter Caught in a Trap," which he had first painted at Henderson in 1812. He also made a number of copies of favorite bird portraits, especially of the mammoth wild turkey cock of the Sleepy Hollow woods of Feliciana.

"Without the sale of these pictures I was a bankrupt before my work was scarcely begun," he writes, "and in two days more I should have seen all my hopes of publication blasted; for Mr. Havell had already called to say that on Saturday I must pay him sixty pounds. I was then not worth a penny, but had actually borrowed five pounds a few days before to purchase materials for my pictures. But these pictures enabled me to pay my borrowed money, and to appear full handed when Mr. Havell called. Thus I passed the Rubicon!"

Audubon admits that he sold seven canvases of the entrapped otter. "In other pictures, also, I sold from seven to ten copies, merely by changing the course of my rambles; and strange to say, that when in after years at better times I called on the different owners to whom I had sold the copies, I never found a one of them on their hands. And I recollect that once, through inadvertence, when I called at a shop where I had sold a copy of a picture, the dealer bought the duplicate at the same price he had given the first! What has become of all those pictures?"

While Audubon scurried about London Town, selling his hastily painted canvases of wild life, the Havells, father and son, were busy with their reproductions of the American Woodsman's bird portraits. The younger Havell was a superior engraver to Lizars; the coloring done by Havell senior, too, was a vast improvement on the rather careless daubing of the colorists in the Scot's establishment.

An interesting story is told of Audubon and the younger Havell by the engraver's daughter, to the effect that when Havell had finished the first engraving and tendered the hand-colored proof of it for Audubon's inspection, the naturalist gave the sheet one fleeting look, snatched it out of the young man's hand, danced about the room, crying "Ze jig ees up, ze jig ees up!" Meaning just the reverse, of course.

Havell and his father at first thought that the woodsman artist was displeased, but when Audubon threw his arms about the younger, embraced him with genuine Gallic enthusiasm, implanting a kiss on each cheek and in excited words assured him he had found the right engraver for his precious birds, Havell realized he was being praised.

Although Havell's daughter stated that the plate which so pleased Audubon was that of the Prothonotary Warbler (which had already been engraved by Lizars), Audubon's correspondence at that period indicates that it was the reproduction of his painting of Baltimore Orioles and their hangnest which proved the Englishman's superiority over the Scottish engraver. This beautiful plate of the orioles and their pendant nest is today recognized as one of the finest examples of engraving and aquatint that Robert Havell, Jr., completed, and it did much to establish the Havells' fame.

Sir Thomas Lawrence was of assistance to the struggling naturalist during these first days in London. He called on Audubon at his lodgings, examined his drawing of quadrupeds and birds, both finished and unfinished, but said nothing of their merit. He merely asked what prices the woodsman placed on them. Disappointed at the titled portrait painter's seeming lack of appreciation, Audubon gruffly mentioned the prices of several. Sir Thomas, without another word, left. He was back in two hours with two gentlemen. He did not introduce them to the bird artist, but one of them purchased a copy of the otter caught in a trap for twenty pounds sterling while the other paid over to the astounded Audubon fifteen sovereigns for a group of common rabbits. "I took the pictures to the carriage which stood at the door," recalls Audubon, "and they departed, leaving me more amazed than I had been by their coming."

A few days later, Sir Thomas Lawrence again called at the Great Russell street studio. The portrait painter told Audubon he had been advised by the curator of the British Museum that Audubon was then making a painting to be presented to his majesty King George IV. Audubon admitted such was his intention and placed the large canvas on an easel for Sir Thomas' inspection.

It was the same work he had started and half-finished while in Edinburgh. He had at first depicted a group of frenzied pheasants startled from their covert by a fox, but dissatisfied with his rendition of reynard, painted out the animal and inserted a spaniel in its stead—for he had learned that the king was fond of this breed of dog. He had also renamed the effort, "English Pheasants Surprised by a Spanish Dog," and called it, in French, "*Sauve qui peut,*" (Let him save himself who can).

"Sir Thomas pushed off my roller Heasal, bade me hold up

the picture," records Audubon, "walked from one side of the room to the other examining it, and then coming to me tapped me on the shoulder and said, 'Mr. Audubon, that picture is too good to be given away; his majesty would accept it, but you never would be benefited by the gift more than receiving a letter from his private secretary, saying it had been placed in his collection. That picture is worth three hundred guineas; sell it, and do not give it away!"

Audubon followed Sir Thomas Lawrence's advice, placed the canvas on exhibition in Havell's shop, refused three hundred guineas for it, but later sold the painting for one-third that price to "my generous friend John Heppinstall of Sheffield, England, and invested the amount in spoons and forks for my good wife."

"English Pheasants Surprised by a Spanish Dog" is owned by C. H. Thordarson, Chicago, and a copy is in the Audubon collection exhibited by the American Museum of Natural History in New York City.

Audubon at times turned from the oil copies he was making of his drawings to revise many of his earlier water color paintings before turning them over to Havell to be engraved. One of these was his large drawing of the White-headed Eagle, the same he had painted in 1820 when making his way down the Mississippi river on Aumack's flatboat.

He had originally pictured the big bird of freedom feasting on a Canada goose. "Now I shall make it breakfast on a Catfish, the drawing of which is also with me, with the marks of the talons of another Eagle, which I disturbed on the banks of that same river, driving him from his prey. I worked from seven this morning until dark," he sets down in his journal. Two days later he records he is "still hard at it, and this evening the objects on my paper look more like a bird and a fish than like a windmill, as they have done. Three days more and the drawing will be finished, if I have no interruptions." Two months later Havell showed him the engraved reproduction. "A splendid plate, indeed," the artist commented.

Leaving the Havells, father and son, busy reproducing his birds, Audubon combed the English countryside for subscribers. While at Oxford he was the guest of Doctor and

Mrs. Edward Burton, the husband a professor of divinity at one of the colleges. Mrs. Burton, an enthusiastic collector of letters, autographs, and portraits, after dinner asked her guest to write his name, his date of birth and the present date. "The former I could not do," Audubon wrote that night in his journal, "except approximately, and Mrs. Burton was greatly amused that I should not know; what I *do* know is that I am no longer a young man."

Audubon returned to London disappointed with his visit to the famous university town. He noted while at Oxford that there were twenty-two colleges, all intended to promote science in its various branches, yet not one had subscribed for his work. He was clearly out of sorts when he dropped into Havell's establishment for, when he found one of the colorists "doing miserable daubing," he excitedly demanded that Havell dismiss the offender. Whereupon the other colorists threw down their brushes and went on strike.

Once more Audubon was faced with an abandonment of his cherished work, but the strike was of short duration, for others equally proficient with the water colors were secured and the coloring went on with unabated energy.

4

For many weeks Audubon neglected his journal, finally he set down: "It is three long months since I tarnished one of thy cheeks, my dear book. I am quite ashamed of it, for I have several incidents well deserving to be related even in my poor humble style—a style much resembling my *paintings in oil.*"

In the interim the king of England had looked over the preliminary plates of the projected work and had become a subscriber on the usual terms, "not as kings usually do, but as a gentleman." George the Fourth permitted the woodsman to publish the ambitious work under his particular patronage, approbation, and protection. His majesty took his volumes, but failed to pay for them.

This much accomplished, Audubon began another drive on rural England and the smaller towns, seeking new subscribers. "How often have I thought during these visits of poor Alexander Willson," he writes, "when travelling as I do now, to procure subscribers. He as well as myself was received with rude coldness, and sometimes with that arrogance which belongs to *parvenus.*"

While on this tour Audubon received several letters from friends in Liverpool, all protesting against his paintings in oils. "It proves to me the real taste of good William Rathbone; and *now I do declare to thee* that I will not spoil any more canvas," he penned in his ubiquitous journal, "but will draw in my usual old, untaught way, which is what God meant me to do."

His mind was full of this resolution when he once more visited Edinburgh. He was better groomed than he was the day he first entered the portals of "Fair Edina," but was otherwise unchanged. High on his shoulder was a huge portfolio. In the right hand his ever present "American stick" with its concealed blade. Under his hat flowed his abundant locks in their old-time luxuriance—the desecration of March nineteenth had been mended by the simple expedient of allowing no other barber's shears to touch his curls. Audubon was himself again!

Several subscribers, he found, had withdrawn their promise to support the work but Audubon, becoming accustomed to such disappointments, shrugged his shoulders and set to work to fill their places on his list. At Lizars' shop he met with a hearty welcome. Jubilantly he showed the Scot how Havell had turned out the plates for the third number. These included the Bird of Washington, the beautiful drawing of the Baltimore orioles and their hangnest, the snow bird on a branch of swamp ash, the blue yellow-backed warblers perched on a rare Louisiana iris, and the cruel great-footed duck hawks tearing at the breasts of captured teal and gadwall.

Lizars admired his rival's engraving with unstinted generosity and called his workmen to see how completely the Londoners had beaten them at their own game. Audubon paid his score with Lizars and the partnership that began so auspiciously was ended. "I think he regrets now that he decided to give my work up," Audubon gloated in his journal that night, "for I was glad to hear him say that should I think well to intrust him with a portion of it, it should be done as well as Havell's, and the plates delivered in London at the same price. If he can fall £27 in the engraving of each number, and do them in a superior style to his previous work, how enormous must his profits have been?"

The quest for subscribers carried the naturalist to Glasgow and there, so he wrote his wife, he "found on *Experiment* that the Scotch in Scotland are the same as they are in all parts of the world where they go—tight dealers, and men who with great concern untie their purses."

His return route was through Leeds, York, Manchester, and then Liverpool again, where he spent a number of days with the hospitable Rathbones at their *Green Banks* estate. One day, when Mrs. Rathbone asked Audubon to teach her to handle oils, he told her he could not for the want of talent. "My birds in *water-colors* have plumage and soft colors, but in oils—alas!"

Returning to Liverpool from *Green Banks*, Audubon walked alongside Mr. Rathbone, who was mounted on his horse. "I do not rely much on my activity as I did twenty years ago," he wrote in his journal that night, "but I still think I could kill any horse in England in twenty days, taking the travel over rough and level grounds. This might be looked upon as a boast by many, but, I am quite satisfied, not by those who have seen me travel at the rate of five miles an hour all day. Once, indeed, I recollect going from Louisville to Shippingport in fourteen minutes, with as much ease as if I had been on skates." That two-mile jaunt of his Louisville days, at the rate of a mile in seven minutes, seems to prove that many of Audubon's other tales of prodigious feats of pedestrianism, such as walking from Philadelphia to New York in three days, over snow- and ice-covered roads, were not figments of his expansive imagination.

Audubon's plans for the future of his work at this time were rather expansive. He advised his wife of his intention of sending a set of five numbers of the bird plates to the newly-elected president of the United States, Andrew Jackson, and ask his public patronage, such as had been given him by King George of Great Britain. "I will do the same with the King of France & the Emperor of Russia and I will not be much surprised if I find them *not Englishmen*," ran his letter.

"Now, thou must not think me flighty, and abandoning my dear America, rough as it is yet; and, swelled in thought in favor of all & everything in England.

"No, indeed, my Lucy, not even the metaphoric name of 'Sir John,' as Sir Wm Jardine was pleased to call me at Twizel, could make me relinquish the idea of knowing that in *my universe* of America, the deer runs free, and the Hunter as free forever.—No—America will always be my land. I never close my eyes without traveling thousands of miles along our noble streams; traversing our noble forests. The voice of the thrush and the rumbling noise of the Alligator are still equally agreable to my sense of recollection."

Christmas Eve in Liverpool found the man homesick for the country he loved. The population of the cotton mill town appeared to him to be engaged in "purchasing eatables for to-morrow. I saw some people carrying large nosegays of holly ornamented with flowers in imitation of white roses, carnations, and others, cut out of turnips and carrots; but I heard not a single gun fire, no fireworks going on anywhere,—a very different time to what we have in Louisiana," he scribbled in the journal, and then went to bed to dream of a happy Christmas morning with Lucy and the boys in far-off Feliciana. Only to be awakened at midnight by Doctor Monroe, who came into Audubon's room with a bottle of "that smoky Scotch whiskey which I can never like," and insisted on the bird artist taking a glass with him in honor of the day.

New Year's Day, 1828, found Audubon in Manchester. His first duty, he tells us, was to go to his journal and wish Lucy, his sons, and his friends a year of comfort, of peace, and enjoyment. "Now, my Lucy, when I wished thee a Happy New Year this morning I emptied my snuff box, locked up the box in my trunk and will take *no more*. The habit within a few weeks has grown upon me, so farewell to it; it is a useless and not very clean habit, besides being an expensive one. Snuff! farewell to thee. Thou knowest, Lucy, well that when I will . . . *I will!*"

Five days later he admits he so missed his snuff that whenever his hands went to his pockets in search of his box, he discovered "the strength of habit, thus acting without thought, I blessed myself that my mind was stronger than my body."

He had not been back in London many days, however, when the box was resurrected from the trunk and he was once more carrying pinches of the powdered tobacco to his aquiline Bourbon nose.

He was quite in the mode too, and affiliated with the learned and the stylish, for instead of clamping through the streets of London with his portfolio of drawings balanced on his shoulder and his long hair streaming in the breeze, The American Woodsman rode grandly from one address to another. "This afternoon I took a cab and with my portfolio went to Mr. Children's. I cannot, he tells me, take my portfolio on my shoulder in London as I would in New York, or even tenacious Philadelphia."

He further confided to his journal that he was feeling dull and wondered how long he would be confined in "this immense jail," as he termed the English metropolis. However, he continued to fling himself into his self-imposed task of painting pictures for sale to the shops, and superintended in person the coloring that Robert Havell, the younger, was doing on the set Audubon had decided to present to the congress of the United States. His wife was sending him not only letters of encouragement but money, and the husband penned for her eyes an entry in the journal in appreciation of her substantial assistance. "My Lucy, thou art so good to me, and thy advices are so substantial, that, rest assured, I will follow them closely."

On the first day of February, 1828, he exhausted the blank pages in the journal he had started on New Year's day the previous year, and on the first page of the new diary penned:

> Another Journal! It has now twenty-six brothers; some are of French manufacture, some from Gilpin's "Mills on the Brandywine," some from other parts of America, but *you* are positively a Londoner. I bought you yesterday for fourteen shillings; and what I write is for my wife, Lucy Bakewell, a matchless woman, and for my two Kentucky lads, whom I do fervently long to press to my heart again.

Audubon was at this time repeating his Edinburgh triumphs among the scientifically-minded of London. Early in February the Linnæan Society made him a member, and a number of publishers urged that he write for their publications accounts of his zoological quests in the New World, some of the unusual facts about the strange birds, beasts, and reptiles he knew so intimately. One seeking such contributions was John C. Loudon, editor of the *Magazine of Natural History*, but the man from America quickly and decisively declined to touch pen to paper. He was still smarting under the lash of criticism that had aroused a controversy on both sides of the Atlantic in the wake of his rattlesnake story. In refusing Loudon's request, Audubon vowed, "I will never write anything to call down on me a second volley of abuse. I can only write *facts* and when I write those, the Philadelphians call me a liar!"

This decision he kept. Letters from America, especially those mailed in Philadelphia, had much to recount of the cruelly barbed tittle-tattle being bandied about by word of mouth and even being put to paper regarding the "tall yarns" he had been telling the believing Scots and credulous Londoners. J. G. Children, when his advice was sought, advised against any more writings for the scientific periodicals. If he must write, Children told Audubon, he should confine himself to bird biographies in view of future publication to accompany his bird pictures.

Audubon reluctantly agreed to follow this sound advice; he even decided not to write his American friends regarding these withering attacks on his veracity. "It takes too much time," he penned his wife, "to write to this one and that one, to assure them that what I have written is *fact*. When Nature as it is found in my beloved America is better understood, these things will be accepted everywhere; till then they may wait."

A letter from Thomas Sully told him in a frank and generous manner that he had "been severely handled" in one of the Philadelphia newsprints. "The editor calls all I said in my papers read before the different societies in Edinburgh 'a pack of lies!'" fumed Audubon to his wife. "It is, however, hard that a poor man like me, who has been so devotedly intent on bringing forth the facts of *curious force*, should be brought before the world as a liar by a man who doubtless knows little of the inhabitants of the Schuylkill, much less of those elsewhere. It is both unjust and ungenerous, but I forgive him. I shall keep up a good heart, trust to my God attend to my work with industry and care, and in time outlive these trifles."

He soon received balm soothe his hurt. On the first of April he rushed to his journal to set down: "I have the honor to be a Fellow of the Linnæan Society of London, quite fresh from the mint, for the news reached me when the election was not much more than over." He was in high feather, and for the first time wrote after his name, in flourishing capitals—"F. L. S. L."

In spite of the honor that had been conferred on him he was waxing impatient over the manner in which his plates were being engraved and colored, and he was almost constantly at Havell's new establishment at 77 Oxford street. "How slowly my immense work progresses," he bewailed to his journal one night: "yet it goes on apace, and may God grant me life to see it accomplished and finished. Then, indeed, will I have left a landmark of my existence."

He grew apprehensive that the damp climate of London was affecting the original drawings. "This quite frightened me. What a misfortune it would be if they should be spoiled, for few men would attempt the severe task I have run through, I think." Then he sighs, considers his age, although he was only forty-three, and sets down: "And as to me, alas! I am growing old, and although my spirits are as active as ever, my body declines, and perhaps I never could renew them all. Indeed, should I find it necessary, I will remove them to Edinburgh or Paris, where the atmosphere is less dangerous."

London irked him and he wrote his wife: "Whenever I am in this London all is alike indifferent to me, and I in turn indifferent. Ah! my love, on a day like this in America I could stroll in magnificent woods, I could listen to sounds fresh and pure, I could look at a *blue* sky."

It was in May that all was bright and joyful in London, in spite of the lack of a blue sky and magnolia woods, for Loudon's *Magazine of Natural History* had appeared with a most laudatory review of Audubon's *Birds*. The critique was written by William Swainson, an English naturalist, and marked the beginning of an intimacy between the two, a friendly intercourse destined, however, to be rudely severed within two years. Audubon confided to his journal how Swainson "has Praised my talents. Would that I could do as well as he says I do; then indeed would my pencil be eager to portray the delicate and elegant contours of the feathered tribe, the softness of their plumage, and their gay movements. Alas, now I must remain in London overlooking engravers, colorers, and agents. Yet when I close my eyes I hear the birds warbling, nay, every sound; the shriek of the Falcon, the coy Doves cooing; the whistling note of the Grackle seems to fill my ear, again I am in the cornfield amidst millions of these birds, and then, transported afar, I must tread lightly and with care, to avoid the venomous Rattler."

Early in August an American portrait painter named C. R. Parker, whom Audubon had first met in Natchez, called on the naturalist and asked permission to paint his portrait in a woodsman's garb and, although protesting that it would prove very tiresome, agreed to the request. Fifteen days later the portrait, which was not painted in his hunting costume, but in the more sombre habiliments of civilization, was nearly finished, and Audubon writes that "Parker considers it a good one, and *so do I.*" This striking likeness of John James Audubon, which for a time was said to have disappeared, is now believed to be the one mistakenly attributed to "W. H. Holmes." In it Audubon is shown in a green coat, with a crimson fur-trimmed cloak thrown over his shoulder, while one hand is shown holding his portfolio of bird drawings.

For some weeks Audubon had in contemplation going to Paris in quest of subscribers for his work and to exhibit his bird drawings to the leading naturalists of France in hope of securing their approbation—and subscriptions. He urged the artist Parker to accompany him. William Swainson, who wanted to study new ornithological specimens at the museum of the *Jardin des Plantes*, also decided on the trip and arranged to take Mrs. Swainson with him.

When the party of four bound for France reached Dover it was with a prophecy, little then imagined this first day of September, that Audubon wrote:

"Now, my dear book, prepare yourself for a good scratching with my pen, for I have entered on a journey that I hope will be interesting."

This journey to the land of his boyhood, proved not only interesting, as Audubon predicted, but highly dramatic, for the "enigma" of his birth was brought once more to the fore, as will be shown by heretofore withheld entries in his well-scribbled journal.

The Feliciana Wild Turkey cock. A woodcut by John Woodhouse Audubon of his father's famous plate.

CHAPTER 23

PARIS

AS Audubon wrote his wife, the strange things that he saw and did in Paris would have made a mountain of volumes "if closely related." From the medley of fact and fancy which he penned one finds it expedient to record certain outstanding happenings.

Foremost among such was his meeting with the Baron George Chrétien Léopold Frédéric Dagobert Cuvier, who subsequently lauded Audubon's birds as "the greatest monument erected by art to nature." The woodsman also heard François Gérard, a noted French portrait painter, say, "M. Audubon, you are the *king of ornithological painters!*"

Viewing the Seine, Audubon wrote his wife, "it is not so large as the Bayou Sarah, where I have often watched the alligators while bathing." Wandering about old Paris with his companions, he chuckles to himself "the *gens d'arms* watches us as though we were thieves." He attempted to enter the *Louvre* with Mrs. Swainson to view the art treasures there and was stopped by a guard who laid down the edict that no one who wore a *fur cap* could enter. Whereupon Audubon arrogantly tried another gate, where the cap he wore atop his chestnut curls did not prove a bar.

He called on a Paris banker, bearing a letter of introduction from the friendly Rathbones, but the man of money, while most polite, informed his caller that all he knew about ornithology was that the large feathers of a bird were called *quills* and were useful in posting ledgers. Whereupon Audubon decided that his time would best be spent with the scientists who, if not overburdened with francs, had a wealth of understanding of the subject nearest his heart.

He visited the king's library where he learned from the librarian, "a perfect gentleman," that the court "had inspected my work, and were delighted with it; and he then told me that kings were not generally expected to pay for works; and I gave him to understand that I was able to keep my work if the king did not purchase."

Later, however, came word that Charles X, brother of the martyred Louis XVI and uncle of the Lost Dauphin, had subscribed to *The Birds of America.* Audubon wrote his wife: "Now, Lucy, I have certainly run the gantlet of England and Paris, and may feel proud of two things—that I am considered the first ornithological painter, and the first practical naturalist of America; may God grant me life to accomplish my serious and gigantic work."

As he walked through the streets of Paris, following an evening spent at the opera, Audubon commented that the "pure atmosphere of Paris, the clear sky, the temperature, almost like that of America, makes me light-hearted indeed, yet would that I were in the far-distant retreats of my happiest days. Europe may whistle for me! I, like a free bird, would sing, 'Never,—no, never, will I leave America!' "

One morning Audubon and Parker called at the residence of the Baron Cuvier, for the American artist had secured permission to paint a portrait of the distinguished French savant. While Parker sketched in the outlines of the baron's features on his canvas, Audubon chatted with Cuvier's daughter, discussing painters, painting, and nature.

"Great men as well as great women have their share of vanity," Audubon set down in his journal that night, "and I soon discovered that the Baron thinks himself a fine looking man. His daughter seemed to know this, and remarked more than once that her father's under lip swelled more than usual, and she added that the line of his nose was extremely fine.

"I passed my finger over mine, and, lo! I thought just the same."

2

A strange thing about this strange man's visit to the land of his boyhood is revealed and yet obscured by his own utterances. Extracts from his journal seem to prove that at this time he believed his foster mother and his half-sister still alive and that he had every intention of visiting them and his old home at Couëron while in France. That the tie which bound him to his foster mother was a strong one is evidenced by the outburst of a sentiment which we find in his journals.

"My mother," he wrote, "the only one I can truly remember; and no son ever had a better; nor more loving one. Let no one speak of her as my 'stepmother.' I was ever to her as a son of her own flesh and blood, and she to me a true mother."

That he should visit her seemed inevitable.

That he had every intention of doing so is attested by numerous entries, such as that made shortly after his arrival in Liverpool, when he wrote his wife that he proposed to visit "Manchester, Birmingham, London for three weeks, and then to France, Paris, Nantes, to see my venerable step-mother." Again, six weeks later, after telling his wife that he would visit her native place and then go on to London, he adds: "From there to France, but, except to see my venerable mother, I shall not like France, I am sure, as I *now* do England . . . Yet I love France most truly, and long to enter my old garden on the Loire and with rapid steps reach my mother—"

Two years later (he had not made his proposed visit to the land of his boyhood as we have seen) he again wrote Lucy on the subject of his contemplated journey to Paris to secure subscribers, adding, "I have it in contemplation to visit Paris in May and will go to see my sister, &c, &c." There was no mention this time, it will be observed, of Madame Audubon.

Lieutenant Jean Audubon's widow had been dead seven years when Audubon wrote this. She had been dead five years when he first set foot in Liverpool.

How was it that Audubon was ignorant of this fact?

Lines of communication were not as certain in those days as they are now, yet on the occasion of Jean Audubon's death news had reached Kentucky in a reasonable length of time.

This discrepancy in the biography of Laforest Audubon has never been explained. One incident which might shed light upon the fact that after writing with the enthusiasm quoted he made no effort to visit Nantes, is his meeting with Charles d'Orbigny, son of his old time companion of the happy Couëron days when the physician had given him his first lessons in natural history. The meeting came through Audubon's visit to René Primevère Lesson, the noted French naturalist and author. Audubon's journal reads:

"While with M. Lesson today, he spoke of a Monsieur d'Orbigny of La Rochelle; and on my making some inquiries I discovered he was the friend of my early days, my intimate companion during my last voyage from France to America; that he was still fond of natural history, and had the management of the *Musée* at *La Rochelle.* His son, Charles, now twenty-one, I had held in my arms many times, and as M. Lesson said he was in Paris. I went at once to find him; he was out, but shortly after I had a note from him saying he would call to-morrow morning."

The next day the young man was at Audubon's lodgings. "My god-son Charles d'Orbigny. Oh! what past times were brought to my mind. He told me he had often heard of me from his father, and appeared delighted to meet me. He, too, like the rest of his family, is a naturalist, and I showed him my work with unusual pleasure. His father was the most intimate friend I have ever had, except thee, my Lucy, and my father."

Is it possible that Audubon learned from young d'Orbigny that his foster-mother had died?—that this information prevented him from going to Nantes and Couëron?

The foregoing quotation from his journal under date of October 8, was printed by a granddaughter. It was, however, only a portion of the entry written by Audubon that night. That entry, and entries made on succeeding days, were withheld by Miss Audubon when she edited her grandfather's journals for publication. These entries had to do with, so she believed, not only the "enigma" of his birth and the oath of silence he had made at the request of Jean Audubon, but pointed to the fact, so Miss Audubon claimed, that her grandfather was none less than the Lost Dauphin of France.

Upon the question of his birth, entries in Audubon's journal of those days in Paris seem to shed some light. His words, penned in moments of great mental stress, confound the skeptical, illumine and intensify the hitherto vague insinuations and inferences contained in letters and diaries previously made public by his descendants.

In view of such expressions as the "enigma of his birth," his "extraordinary secret," he "who should command *all*" in Paris, that "he must flee France" before a dagger thrust would end his life, the belief of descendants that Audubon was the Lost Dauphin, Louis XVII, the Shadow King of France, now assumes startling proportions.

The heretofore withheld entries in his journal read:

"*October* 8, 1828. *Paris*—Oh, how much I wish that I could go to Nantes but alas! I cannot. thou only, my Lucy, knowest the reasons. The cloud that still hangs over my birth required silence—I must change the subject, my heart is ready to burst—

"A singular incident took place today while with M. Lesson; he told me he had a small work written by my grandfather (as he thought), & that he thought he still knew à la Rochelle a man of my name. Lucy, my blood was congealed in my veins—but what am I about? Oh, my Book, I dare not relate."

The following day he was still laboring in a maelstrom of emotion, for he penned:

"*October* 9, 1828—The name of that Audubon of La Rochelle haunted my body, and so disturbed my mind, that I felt as if to remain in France and to be known as I now must shortly be known to be in France was dreadful and made me tremble—

"As I was going to the minister I thought of my birth, of my curious life, and of the strange incidents that have brought me to what I am now known to be. I felt more than once as if now was the moment to dispel the cloud & again I reflected on the consequence, wiped the stream of water that ran cold over my forehead, & concluded to carry my extraordinary secret to the grave.

"Oh, my Lucy, oh, my father, oh, how cruelly situated I am—& yet perhaps it is best that it should be so. I sighed & walked faster and faster. How often I thought that I might once more see Audubon of la Rochelle without being known by him and try to discover if my father was still in his recollection, if he had entirely forgotten Selkirk's Settlement[1] and if—if I say more words I must put an end to my

[1]Note by Maria R. Audubon on margin: "Selkirk Settlement was a settlement of French émigrés in Scotland."

existence, having forfeited my word of honor and my oath.

"Lesson was in Rochefort at the time my father commanded the post, but too young, he said, to remember him.

"Had I told him that my father was———Stop! here I am again about to fly the track———peace, peace Audubon ———Good night, my Lucy, for myself I shall not close my eyes.

"*Paris, Friday, Oct*er 10th 1828.—Oh, my Lucy, what a night I have had. Oh, that I could see my father's mortal shape & obtain from his goodness the removing of the oath extracted from me in my youthful days. I turned over & over in my sweated bed until wearied (not by remorse but by sorrow). I was glad to see glimpses of daylight to change the scene. How much of my father's life I passed over would fill my book, and the strange scenes attached to my early life so stared me in the face that I saw naught but Spectres before me, St Domingo, France & my *beloved* country all had their turn—how dreadful—I have heard of men's hair & beard turning white on unexpected extraordinary incidents, but I was truly shocked at seeing myself in the glass while shaving and yet I am perfectly innocent, and so was my dear father.

"Oh, cursed———and my father's brother, too! Lucy, I am quite wild———When young I was easily taught to keep silence & thought nothing of it; but now that I have children myself, children that one word of mine would rise to eminence & would be———

"Stop thy pen, or forever be damned, Audubon!

"I see my father before me with his proud eagle's eye, frowning as if I had leaned over the abyss—but no—no, never———

"Oh, My Lucy, how I regret this journey; it has opened all my wounds afresh. La Rochelle is before me, my father bleeds & and I must flee France or the dagger may put an end to———

"I must bury the dreadful past in oblivion. Peaceful woods to you I must return, and under your dark shades consecrate my days to the only blessing left me on this earth, that of admiring the works of the Creator who alone knows who I am, and will repay me for my torments here below; what might this day have been if known here.

"Patient—silent—bashful & yet powerful of physique and of mind, dressed as a *common man* I walk the streets. I bow, I ask permission to do this or that or other things, I follow the publication of a work on Natural History that has apparently absorbed all my knowing life . . . *I, who should command all!*

"I understand now why my father demanded of me a most solem oath that I would never permit myself to be forced into becoming a priest; I would have had no legitimate heir, and yet—that other promise—demanded later prevents my sons from ever being known. Cruel, cruel, but who may forsee the future?"

3

Ten days after writing these cryptical entries, Audubon attended a grand review of the French troops as they marched by the king. He made for a high wall, which he scaled at the risk of breaking his neck, "and there, like an Eagle on a rock, I surveyed all about me." He was mainly interested in the appearance of King Charles for, after commenting briefly upon the nicely executed maneuvers of the Swiss troops, he writes he kept his eyes fastened on the monarch as he mounted his horse and rode about the parade grounds.

"Three times I was within twenty-five yards of the King and his staff, and, as a Kentuckian would say, 'could have closed his eye with a rifle bullet.' He is a man of small stature, pale, not at all handsome, and rode so bent over his horse that his appearance was neither kingly nor prepossessing . . . I saw a lady in a carriage point at me on the wall; she doubtlessly took me for a large black Crow."

During the Paris visit, Audubon visited Versailles, the palace and the gardens where Louis Charles Capet, son of Louis XVI and Marie Antoinette, was born and where the Dauphin played as a child. That Sunday night Audubon wrote his wife:

"Versailles, where we spent our day, is truly a magnificent place; how long since I have been there, and how many changes in my life since those days! . . . thus, my Lucy, once more have I been at Versailles, and much have I enjoyed it."

4

These messages Audubon addressed to his wife appear to indicate that she shared her husband's intimate thoughts. To the day of her death, according to intimate family history, she believed implicitly in his high birth. When her second son, John Woodhouse Audubon, passed away in 1862, the mother reached his bedside too late to see him alive. During her paroxysm of grief Mrs. Audubon exclaimed: "Oh, my son, my son! You died and never knew!"

Those gathered in the room did not ask the sorrowing mother the meaning of her words, because, according to Maria R. Audubon, "the members of the family had been taught that a secret might be imparted but never questioned."

Another granddaughter, Harriet B. Audubon, also a daughter of John Woodhouse, recalled an incident which lends color to the belief held by the family of Audubon's high birth. She and her grandmother were living with the family of a New York clergyman, the Reverend Charles C. Adams, soon after the Civil War. "He had expressed a wish to write a life of my grandfather if she would give him permission; she not only gave him permission but lent him his journals, which she then had with her," says Miss Audubon in a sworn statement. "One day, when he had been reading the journals, he came into our parlor, with a volume of the journals in his hand, exclaiming: 'Why, he was the Lost Dauphin!' My grandmother made him an evasive answer, neither denying nor admitting the statement. I think she said: 'I do not see why you should come to such a conclusion,' or something like that, and the subject was dropped."

Miss Harriet Audubon also told how she had read in her grandfather's journal one significant sentence. "He made a reference to 'my father,' meaning Jean Audubon—and in the next sentence says, 'my *own* father whom I saw shot.' He says 'shot' because he was only eight years old, and the verb 'to guillotine' was not then invented."

CHAPTER 24

Back in America

AUDUBON did not "flee France." It was twenty-four days after setting down in his journal that a dagger might put an end to his existence, before he left his companions, the Swainsons and the artist Parker, in Paris, and on the fourth day of November took the road to Boulogne for Calais where he was to recross the Channel.

He traveled in the *rotunda* of a coach with two nuns "that might as well be struck off the calendar of animated things," he tells us. "They stirred not, they spoke not; they replied neither by word or gesture to the few remarks I made. In the woods of America I have never been in such silence; for in the most retired places I have heard the gentle murmuring streamlet, or the sound of the Woodpecker tapping, or the sweet melodious strains of that lovely recluse, my greatest favorite, the Wood Thrush."

The passage from Calais to Dover was short and uneventful—for once Audubon escaped his usual seasickness. On the boat he recapitulated the results of his journey to France. In Paris he had spent two months and forty pounds sterling; he had been acclaimed by the scientists a foremost ornithologist, and he had appointed an agent to augment the list of thirteen subscribers he had signed up before he had said his *adieux* to the new friends he had made in the land of his boyhood.

He did not visit Nantes, nor had he gone to Couëron where his half-sister was living. Nor did he dash through the gardens of *La Gerbetière*, that enchanted spot on the banks of the Loire where he had played as a boy. Why?

Aside from the wild outbursts penned in his journal, letters and other papers now in the hands of his descendants contribute no further information on this clouded and puzzling period. Four years later, in 1833, Audubon wrote his son Victor, then in London, that his sister's husband had been in communication with him, evidently in regard to Jean Audubon's estate, "Puigaudeau's letter says that he wishes to settle with me, but gives no particulars and I know no more about the matter than the man in the moon—his address is George Loyen du Puygaudeau, Couëron Near Nantes, Dept of Loire Inferieur."

Two years later Victor visited Couëron, met his Aunt Rosa and her husband and son, Gabriel 2nd., who were under the impression he had come to settle financial affairs. Victor Audubon assured them, as his father had taken as his share Jean Audubon's *Mill Grove* plantation, that he had secured all that was due him and did not care to share any of the property Madame Audubon had bequeathed him. This appears to have been the last contact father or sons had with Rosa and her descendants.

2

Back in London Audubon sat at his easel from earliest morn to late at night turning out copies of his bird pictures to be sold in shops so that Havell and his crew in the engraving establishment could be paid regular wages each Saturday.

"I am painting as much as the short days will allow," he set down in his journal, "but it is very hard for me to do so, as my Southern constitution suffers so keenly from the cold that I am freezing on the side farthest from the fire at this very instant." He sadly neglected his journal during these dreary wintry days in London, when wayfarers carried torches through the streets to light their way home at noon time, and the entries are few and far between dates.

His second Christmas day spent away from America was not a joyous affair—he ate the Yule-tide dinner at a Mr. Goddard's home and the company was composed for the most part of Yankee sea captains. Although homesick and heavy of heart he stuck to his paintings and one large canvas finished was that of the Eagle and the Lamb, and the artist flushed with pride when Sir Thomas Lawrence designated it "a fine picture."

Soon after he had supplied Havell with the bird pictures that would make up the eleventh number of his work, he turned to the long neglected journal and on the last day of March, 1829, penned:

It is so long since I have written in my life book that I feel quite ashamed on opening it to see that the last date was Christmas of last year. Fie, Audubon! Well, I have made up my mind to go to America, and with some labour and some trouble perfected all arrangements. I have given the agency of my work to my excellent friend Children, of the British Museum, who kindly offered to see to it during my absence.

While perfecting his plans to return to America Audubon arrived at a strange decision. He would go incognito. He wrote his son Victor on this subject "with strongest injunctions to keep it a perfect secret." In a letter to his wife he said he would go to America "under the name of John James —and will travel through the U. S. by that simple name only . . . Only 3 or 4 friends in England will know *positively* when I have gone, my Subscribers and the *World* will think me on the European Continent after more Patronage—this is absolutely necessary for the safe keeping of my present subscribers, most all of which would become alarmed and would expect the work to fall through."

Ten days later he is writing his wife that he had abandoned the scheme of going back to the land he loved under an assumed name. "When I wrote last I thought of going *incog* but on mentioning it to my friend Mr Children he persuaded me not, but to go openly and I will now for many valuable reasons . . . When I reach the shore I will have my arrival published in the News Papers there."

The sale of paintings to the shops and the payment of subscriptions filled Audubon's purse and enabled him to make the return journey in style—he would be able to carry on his work of securing new American birds and to picture them without the harassment of scrambling after dollars.

Passage was engaged on the packet-ship *Columbus*, which he admits was chosen on account of its name, and on April Fool's Day the packet put out of the smoky harbor of Portsmouth.

A single entry in the journal tells us that "we have hoisted the anchor, am at sea, and *sea-sick!*"

3

A month and five days were passed on the heaving reaches of the Atlantic—with Audubon in the throes of his customary *mal de mer* daily, much to the amusement of his state-room companion, Sir Isaac Coffin, Bart., a gouty old American-born English admiral. Sir Isaac was a member of a celebrated Nantucket whaling family and was on his way to that island to supervise the building there of a school which he had founded and endowed for the education of descendants of his noted ancestor, Tristam Coffin, one of the original purchasers of Nantucket.

Consequently it was not until he felt the land under his feet did The American Woodsman reopen his journal and we read under date of May 5, 1829:

> I have brought thee, my English book, all the way across the Atlantic, too sea-sick to hold any converse with thee—sea-sick all the way, until the morning I saw my dear native land. The cry of 'land, land, land!' thrice repeated, roused me from my torpor, and acted like champagne to refresh my spirits. I rushed on deck, and saw in the distance a deep grey line, like a wall along the horizon. My heart swelled with joy, and all seemed like a pleasant dream at first; but as soon as the reality was fairly impressed on my mind, tears of joy rolled down my cheeks. I clasped my hands and fell on my knees, and raising my eyes to heaven — that happy land above — I offered my thanks to our God, that he had preserved and prospered me in my long absence, and once more permitted me to approach these shores so dear to me, and which holds my heart's best earthly treasures.

Safely landed, for Audubon always carried the presentiment that he would perish at sea, he did not at once hurry off to Louisiana and his wife, although it had been three years since he had seen her. He had other plans. Before leaving London he had written Lucy directing her to relinquish her position with the Johnsons, close her Feliciana school, and join him either in New York or Philadelphia, or, if that was not to her liking, meet him in Louisville. Mrs. Audubon had refused to do this, claiming it was his duty to join her in Louisiana, and in her spirited letter she accused her husband of losing his affection for her in the glory of his new prominence. This was the letter that greeted him upon his arrival in New York.

Seizing pen and paper, Audubon denied with vehemence the charge that he had lost his affection for his beloved Lucy, and in the course of a long letter claimed he had returned to America to remain as long as would be consistent with the safety of his publication venture. At great length and in numbered paragraphs he explained that he wished to employ and devote every moment of his sojourn to drawing such birds and plants as he believed were necessary to give his *Birds of America* the perfection he desired and which he believed his subscribers expected of him.

He called upon Lucy to make a decision. He made it very plain if she refused to come to him, as he commanded, they would in all probability part forever!

This letter, under date of May 11, 1829, and addressed to "My Dearest Friend," reads in part:

I wish to receive as *true* and *frank* an answer *as I know my Lucy will give me*, saying whether or no, the facts and the prospects, will entice her to join her husband and go to Europe with him; to enliven his spirits and assist him with her kind advices — the "no" or the "yes" will stamp my future years——if a "no" comes *I will never put the question again* and *we probably* never will meet again ——If a "yes" and a kindly "yes" comes bounding from thy heart my heart will bound also, and it seems to me that It will give me nerve for further exertions! We have been married a good time, circumstances have caused our voyage to be very mottled with Incidents of very different nature but our *happy days* are the only days *I now remember.* The tears that now almost blind me are the vouchers for my heart's emotions at the recollections of those happy days! *I have no wish to entice thee to come by persuasions;* I wish thee to consult thy ownself and that only, and to write to me accordingly to thy determination — the amount of thy own pecuniary means — and how soon I might expect thee *in Philadelphia* from after the time this reaches thee. *I cannot go to Louisiana* without running risks incalculable of not receiving *regular news* from London . . . Thy determination must be prompt either "yes" or "no."

I should like exceedingly to spend a week or two at Mr Johnson's with thee but it cannot be and probably for ever my eyes will not rest on the Magnolia Woods or see the mocking thrush gaily gamboling full of melody amongst the big trees of the South. A vessel arrived yesterday in 12 days from New Orleans the news of which shook my frame as if electrified; to know that in so short a time I might again see my Lucy and press her to my heart is a blessing beyond anything I have felt since three years.

His ultimatum dispatched in the mails, Audubon arranged

for an exhibition of his paintings and finished plates at the New York Lyceum of Natural History. This over he hurried off to Philadelphia where he resumed acquaintance with Doctor Harlan and some of the other few friendly Philadelphians, and then settled at Camden, where for three weeks he studied the habits of the migratory warblers and other birds at that time arriving in large numbers from the south for the annual breeding season. He wanted subjects for certain plates he had planned on issuing the following year, and his original drawings of the wood pewee flycatcher and the black poll warbler were made while there.

Another three weeks were spent at Great Egg Harbor, New Jersey, where he lived at the seashore in a fisherman's hut. The harbor was noted for the numbers and variety of its land and water birds, so Audubon worked every day painting or hunting specimens. Among the originals that carry penciled notations proving they were drawn at this resort are the bay-winged bunting, seaside sparrow, yellow-breasted chat, warbling flycatcher, golden-crowned thrush, small green-crested flycatcher and rough-legged falcon.

On his return to Philadelphia he found a letter from his wife. Lucy not only refused to join him, but accused him of a want of affection, a coolness in his style of writing, and declared that the fact he was not returning to Louisiana was sufficient proof of all her doubts and fears. She explained she was not able to go to him for want of funds and that she would not be able to collect the monies due her for teaching until late in the fall or at the end of the year. Her "no" was emphatic.

Audubon immediately penned a long letter to his son Victor, taking the boy to task for not writing him and asking "are you, as your Mother seems to be, *quite* unwilling *to believe* that I am doing all I can for the best of all of us; and in such a case have you abandoned the Idea of answering my letters? . . . Have you thought, as your Mother, that *although* I wrote that I could not go Westerly or Southerly that I would undoubtedly do so?—if you have? undeceive yourself and believe me I cannot go either to Kentucky or to Louisiana."

He launched into a lengthy explanation of his reasons for

not believing it wise to make the journey and reviewed all he had accomplished under difficulties and how he had planned his future course. He complained of the position his Lucy had assumed in urging that he drop all he was doing and return to her. He told Victor:

> *I cannot go to her* because was I to lose my Summer by so doing I would miss the birds that I want and that are not at all to be found *west of the Mountains.* She does not seem to understand this; she complains of my want of affection; of the coolness of my style of writing &c — and thinks that my not going to Louisiana for her is quite sufficient proof for all these her doubts and fears.— ever since I left her I never have had from her a letter containing the *facts of her situation,* never have known how much or how little she made or received; but on the contrary have always hoped that she was well and Happy.
>
> Now, as a man of business, I wish you to write to her taking in consideration what I have said . . . . .

In spite of all that Audubon urged and threatened, his "Beloved Lucy" remained firm in her determination not to leave the Feliciana country and go to him. He must come to her!

While awaiting a reply from his wife and son, Audubon outfitted himself for a trip of several weeks into the depths of a great pine forest in Northampton county, Pennsylvania. He went to Mauch Chunk and then plunged into the very heart of the pine-clad hills, carrying with him a wooden box containing a small stock of linens, drawing papers, his journal, colors,, and pencils, together with twenty pounds of shot, a due quantum of cash, his new double-barreled shotgun he had purchased abroad, and "a heart true to nature as ever." He remained in the pine forest until early in October putting up at the cabin of a settler named Jedediah Irish. Here he made his originals of bird pictures that afterwards were reproduced in his plates. The warblers he collected and drew were the Canada, pine swamp, black and yellow, hemlock, autumnal and Connecticut, as well as the barn and mottled owls. His pine swamp warbler, which he supposed was a new species, proved to be the young of the black-throated blue warbler.

The man, free of the artificiality of Europe, had thrown himself into his old-time field work with vigor and enthusiasm, as his own chronicle shows:

I am at work and have done much, but I wish I had eight pairs of hands and another body to shoot the specimens; still I am delighted at what I have accomplished in drawing this season; Forty-two drawings in four months, eleven large, eleven middle-size, and twenty-two small, comprising ninty-five birds, from Eagles downwards, with plants, nests, flowers, and sixty different kinds of eggs. I live alone, see scarcely anyone, besides those belonging to the house where I lodge. I rise long before day and work until nightfall, when I take a walk, and then to bed.

I returned yesterday from Mauch Chunk; after all, there is nothing perfect but *primitiveness*, and my efforts at copying nature, like all other things attempted by us mortals, fall far short of the originals. Few better than myself can appreciate this with more despondency than I do.

4

October was almost half done when Audubon returned to Philadelphia and met George Lehman, the Swiss artist he first encountered at Pittsburgh in 1824 when on his way back from Niagara. He engaged the Swiss to assist him in drawing flowers and plants on his new bird portraits, while he went about Philadelphia with his intimate, the sprightly Doctor Harlan.

His answer had come from Lucy. She had laid down a counter ultimatum. He must come to Louisiana or stay away forever. In consequence, he put in the next few days packing his effects, planning a trip to the magnolia woods of his cherished Feliciana. Lucy had won!

Audubon set out in a mail coach for Pittsburgh. There he took passage on a river boat for Louisville, embarking as a cabin passenger—in marked contrast to the same journey made five years before, when he slept in a bed of shavings on the open deck of a boat floating down the beautiful Ohio. He was now a success and was receiving the recognition that achievement and notoriety always earn.

It had been three years and six months since he had last seen his wife, five months and more had elapsed since he had returned to the land of his adoption before he set his wandering foot in the direction of the Feliciana woods and his heart was happy. At Louisville he found his two boys. Victor was still working for Nicholas Berthoud, while John Woodhouse, who had left his mother the year before, was employed in the office of his uncle Thomas W. Bakewell. The father took the boys in his arms in his usual demonstrative fashion, pressed them to his hungry heart, and remained with them a day or two while he poured into their eager ears tales of his adventures across the Atlantic. He also took keen delight in regaling—and in the pronounced Gallic accent that his stay in England had not erased nor dimmed—his various Louisville in-laws with his many triumphs in England, Scotland, and France; how he had dined with Sir This-and-That, or what Lord So-and-So had said of his "great work;" how Baron, and Prince, and even King had vied with scientific societies in doing him honor. Our Woodsman was most expansive, and the Bakewells and the Berthouds were impressed and, for the first time in many years, Laforest Audubon was welcomed to their homes and importuned to stay and visit awhile.

The Feliciana woods of Louisiana were now calling, so he took passage on an Ohio river steamboat, which made its way down the winding course of that river and the length of the twisting Mississippi, the same rivers on which he had floated southwards nine years before, tattered, penniless, downcast, and unknown.

It was night when the distinguished Mr. Audubon landed at Bayou Sarah. At daybreak the next morning he secured a horse from friend Nübling to carry him nine miles inland where his wife, unaware of his coming, was living.

He was once more in the magnolia forests of the state he loved. As he rode through them on his way to *Beech Grove* he exulted in the familiar sights that met his eyes on every side; as he galloped his mount along the Woodville road, he heard the post-nuptial song of his adored Mock Bird. At Wakefield he swerved to the right and a quarter of an hour later dashed into a plantation yard, turned the blowing horse over to a negro slave, and—

"I went at once to my wife's apartment. Her door was ajar, already she was dressed and sitting by her piano, on which a young lady was playing. I pronounced her name gently, she saw me, and the next moment I held her in my arms. Her emotion was so great that I feared I had acted rashly, but tears relieved our hearts—once more we were together."

5

The next day, in a letter written to his sprightly Philadelphia friend Doctor Harlan, Audubon recounted the many difficulties of travel he had encountered on his trip to the South," as you spoke of travelling westwardly I give you here an a/c of the Fare.—to Pittsburgh all included 21$.—to Louisville 12$.—and 25$ more to Bayou Sarah where I landed. 30$ is the price from Louisville to N. Orleans.—our Steam Boats are commodious and go well."

After sending his regards to a few mutual male friends in the Quaker City, he added:

"May I also beg to be remembered in humble words to a fine pair of Eyes; divided, not by the Allegany Mountains; but by a nose evidently from far *East*, to a placid forehead, to a mouth speaking happiness to——— ———your——— ———————————————"

A dash line, nearly the full width of the page, ended the message.

Black Vultures attacking the head of a deer
Redrawn from Audubon's plate.

CHAPTER 25

Final Days in Feliciana

LUCY AUDUBON had successfully taught the pupils of her school at Mrs. Percy's *Beech Woods* plantation for four years, from New Year's Day 1823, to February of 1827, when she suddenly closed the school and removed from the Percy home. A few weeks later she opened a new class of instruction at *Beech Grove*, the plantation home of William Garrett Johnson, situated only a few miles away from her first school.

A disagreement, the nature of which remains unrevealed to this day, had arisen between Mrs. Percy and Mrs. Audubon —Lucy even kept the reasons for the change from her husband when writing him of the break. In the reopened school she gave the daughters of the planter and others who attended the usual rudiments of education, as well as lessons in music and dancing. In a short time she won at *Beech Grove* the same high reputation she had enjoyed at *Beech Woods*, plantations named so near alike that they caused confusion in the chronicles of previous biographers. The financial arrangements she made with the Johnson family were much more satisfactory, as the planter agreed to pay her the annual stipend of one thousand dollars and to collect the tuition of the young ladies attending from their parents without leaving this task to Lucy Audubon.

Among the many young ladies she taught at *Beech Grove* were Susan Johnson, who married Pleasant Harbour; Malvina D. Johnson, who became the wife of Dr. Warren Stone; Jane Montgomery, who married a Mr. Smiley; Jane Harbour, later the wife of James Hill; Mary Harbour, who married Dr. McGhoon, and Mary Rucker, who became Mrs. James Leake. Margaret Butler of *The Cottage* was another member of the *Beech Grove* school, as were the three Carpenter girls, Mary, Anne and Louisa, sisters of Dr. William

Marbury Carpenter, later a noted Louisiana physician and botanist; while little Ellen Johnson, who became Mrs. William Broadner Walker, was the tiny mascot. Another girl, Isabel Kendrick, who married David Fluker, Jr., crossed Thompson's creek to attend the school, and it was her daughter, Mrs. Mary Fluker Bradford, who wrote a brief biography of Audubon, and was one of the leaders of a movement that in 1910 erected a heroic bronze monument to the artist-naturalist in a park in New Orleans that now bears his name.

The first day after his return to his favorite section of the United States Audubon was out with his gun after new specimens, for, as he had written the lively Doctor Harlan, "a friend of mine here *says* that he has discovered 2 or 3 New Birds!!!—new Birds are new birds in our days, and I shall endeavor to shew you the Facts Simile when I shall have the pleasure of shaking your hand."

As he was crossing a field he noted a dark-colored bird of prey winging its way across the opening between two groves of oaks. The hawk finally perched on the tip-top of a tree in an erect and commanding attitude. Audubon at once stalked the bird, for it was a "non-discript."

"When I saw it on its perch it looked so like the Black Hawk (*Falco niger*) of Wilson, that I apprehended what I had heard of it might prove incorrect," he writes. "I approached it, however, when, as if it suspected my evil intentions, it flew off, but after first sailing as if with a view of escaping me, passed over my head, when I shot it, and brought it winged to the ground. No sooner had I inspected its eye, its bill, and particularly its naked legs, than I felt it was, as had been spoken to me of its exploits, a new species. I drew it whilst alive."

So elated was the artist with his new bird of prey that he reopened his letter to Doctor Harlan to write:

> I have Just *now* killed a Large *New Falcon yes positively a Species of Hawk almost Black about* 25 Inches Long and 4 feet broad tail square Eye yellowish White, Legs and Feet bare short & strong — I will skin it!!!
>
> What I have said about the Hawk to You must be *Lawful* to *Academicians* and you will please announce *Falco Harlanii* by
>
> John J. Audubon
>
> *F.L.S.L.*

In such fashion was Harlan's hawk, or the "Black Warrior," taken and named. It is a bird that has created confusion among technical ornithologists ever since. In late years it has been accorded a position as a southern subspecies of the red-tailed hawk and designated *Buteo borealis harlani.* There is still contention among some of the closet naturalists as to its standing, many claiming this hawk is only a color phase and should have no standing even as a sub-species.

A few weeks after he had named his Harlan's hawk, Audubon saw a male bird of the same general blackish coloration perched on the very tree where he had first seen the female. Anxious to verify his first impression that he had discovered a new species of hawk, he endeavored to collect it, but as long as he flourished a gun the "Black Warrior" kept out of range, calling shrilly its characteristic *Pee-ank, Pee-ank, Pee-ank* as it flew to the safety of the thick woods. He pursued the bird day after day, determined to bring it down. On one occasion he took his wife with him to see the new bird, but only while they remained on horseback and unarmed could they approach the tree on which it perched without startling it into flight. He had hunted it in vain for a fortnight when Dr. John B. Hereford, of the neighboring plantation of *Wakefield*, knowing the artist's consuming desire to obtain the bird, brought the specimen down with a rifle ball and sent it alive, but with a broken wing, to Audubon at *Beech Grove.*

The male bird proved to be a handsome specimen, full of fight and energy and far wilder than the female. It erected its head feathers, opened its hooked bill menacingly and made ready to strike with its talons when Audubon essayed to place it in position for drawing. He added its portrait to that of the mate, and the two birds form the subjects of his plate of "Harlan's Buzzard."

This was not the only new species he described after his triumphs of Edinburgh and London. One of his Feliciana neighbors, returning from a trip from Natchez, saw one of the indolent or heavy-flying hawks, correctly called buzzards, circling a copse of thick woods not far from *Beech Grove,* shot it and delivered the female bird to Audubon. He at once placed it on his position board, and the "Black-winged hawk," as he originally called it, was made to live again in his drawing of the red-shouldered bird with the conspicuous white rump feathers. Later he named the new species in honor of Edward Harris, "who, independently of the aid which he has on many occasions afforded me, in prosecuting my examination of our birds, merits this compliment as an enthusiastic Ornithologist." Audubon's *Buteo Harrisii*, however, has been changed by present-day authorities to the more resounding and jaw-cracking *Parabuteo unicinctus harrisi* now found in our ornithological literature.

Audubon was happy to be back among his old friends of the Felicianas. Among the many bits of news with which Lucy regaled her husband was the information that Eliza Pirrie had forsaken widowhood on Christmas Eve the year before. She had married a young clergyman, William Robert Bowman, who came to St. Francisville from Brownsville, Pennsylvania, to erect the second Protestant church in Louisiana, Grace Episcopal, which still nestles in a forest of moss-draped oaks at St. Francisville.

For six years Eliza Pirrie Barrow Bowman labored with her clergyman husband in his church work, and two children, Isabelle and James Pirrie Bowman, joined little Robert H. Barrow in the nursery. In 1837 she again became a widow, but a few years later married Henry P. Lyons of Philadelphia. Audubon's pupil, his "beautiful Miss Pirrie of *Oakley*," passed away three months after The American Woodsman's demise.

Audubon was spending all his spare time in the woods and fields with the new gun he had brought back from London. It was a handsome, expensive weapon, with mountings of gold and silver. The fowling-piece was double-barreled, of 18-gauge bore, and was fired by means of a percussion cap, a remarkable advance over the old flint lock. The length was extraordinary, measuring 63 inches, and it weighed twelve pounds. Deeply engraved between the barrels was the inscription, "John James Audubon, Citizen of the United States, F. L. S. L.," the initials an evidence of his fellowship in the Linnæan Society of London. The gun carried a concealed trap door in the butt-plate, greatly exciting the curiosity of Doctor Pope and Augustin Bourgeat when they fondled and fired the beautiful weapon.

These two erstwhile companions of Audubon's days in the woods were delighted with their friend's success and proudly proclaimed his achievements abroad to the other folk of the Feliciana countryside, declaring they had always known that their long-haired French friend was destined for fame, even when others doubted.

Doctor Pope and his wife had left the village of St. Francisville when Audubon returned from his triumphs of Edinburgh, London, and Paris, and he found them installed in a log cabin in the country. "Audubon visited us for the purpose of procuring and studying the habits of the Swallow-tailed hawks, which were plentiful in the woods near us," Mrs. Pope recalls in her delightful memoirs of the Audubons. "One day Doctor Pope and Audubon went fishing in a lake, Garnharts, I believe, and on their return brought home the largest turtle I have ever seen. The head was eight inches across, and the shell was large enough for an infant's cradle. It snapped a large cane in two with a single bite.

"Audubon had lately returned from Europe, where he had gone to have his drawings engraved. He was obliged to visit England, Scotland, and France to have the work done. Each of his birds required a separate plate, a very tedious and expensive undertaking.

"Our dwelling was a log house, weather-boarded on the outside, but the logs inside were exposed. Between them I placed many odds and ends—eggs, bunches of feathers, garden seed, brooches of yarn; in fact, whenever anything was wanted, all I had to do was to turn to the log wall and I could generally find what I was looking for. Audubon often laughed at my 'museum,' as he called it. One day, he had been gathering forest leaves as souvenirs for friends in England, he came into the cabin and looked around at my museum and laughingly said: 'Madame, eef Hi could put theese 'ouse as eet stand in London, eet would make a fortune—for eet would be one of ze gr-r-r-reatest *curiosité* zat Hi could take zere!' "

While her husband was busy collecting, not only birds for drawings but other objects of natural history, Mrs. Audubon was making ready to relinquish her years of toil as a teacher and the bread-winner of the family. She resigned her position as a teacher-governess to the pleasant and hospitable Johnsons and prepared to accompany Audubon to Europe. A charming pen picture of *Beech Grove* has been left us by Colonel Thomas B. Thorpe, who wrote for an old number of *Godey's Lady Book*:

> In the hospitable mansion of W.G.J———, in the parish of West Feliciana, if one will look into the parlor, they will see over the piano a cabinet-sized portrait, remarkable for a bright and intellectual look. The style of it is free, and there is an individuality about the whole that gives assurance of a strong likeness. Opposite hangs a proof impression of the Bird of Washington, a tribute of a grateful heart to an old friend. The first is a portrait of Audubon painted by himself."

The portrait of Audubon was an oil painting on a thin canvas, bordered by a rough hand-made frame. The artist wears a dark green coat and an old-fashioned neckcloth and collar encircle the neck. The portrait, according to Mrs. William Broadner Walker (the little Ellen Johnson and mascot of Mrs. Audubon's *Beech Grove* school), was made by Audubon while looking into a mirror, and was given to the Johnsons as a token of his regard. He also left with these kind folk an unfinished oil portrait of his wife and sons made during his early days of trying his hands at oil painting. Audubon's self-portrait was treasured in after years by Mrs. Walker, who in turn bequeathed it to her daughter, wife of Lieutenant Mitchell Ford Jamar of the 13th United States Infantry. It was afterwards owned by Dr. David Gambel Murrell of Paducah, Kentucky. This painting, which is the earliest known likeness of The American Woodsman, is reproduced as the frontispiece of this biography.

Audubon, during the month and a half he stayed in West Feliciana, specialized in birds of prey, for a number of the portraits of hawks that grace his mammoth work were made at this time. He also turned his attention to the various species of squirrels so plentiful in the Feliciana woods, and here too drew the little chipmunk that appeared in *The Viviparous Quadrupeds of North America.* Heads of deer and a few other mammals, many of which remained unfinished drawings, were put to paper.

Recalling his account of the habits of the vultures, which he had written for the *Edinburgh New Philosophical Journal*, and the fact that his earlier drawing of the black vulture was not up to what he considered his standard, Audubon collected a pair of these carrion-eating birds and set them at work picking at the head of a deer when he made his new drawing. An amusing mistake, made first by Buchanan and perpetuated by all later writers of Audubon's life, is the statement that he drew at this time "Black Vultures Attacking the Herd of Deer." As a matter of fact, the birds are preparing to make a meal off the dismembered *head* of one deer.

2

As the year 1829 came to a close Audubon began his plan to return to England to take over once more active supervision of the issuance of *The Birds of America*. Although he had left his business affairs in the hands of John G. Children, and it was believed all was progressing favorably, Robert Havell became alarmed over the loss of a number of subscribers who had canceled subscriptions, and the failure of M. Pitois, the agent in charge of subscriptions in France, to make returns. So orders were given to pack belongings and make ready to leave the Louisiana bird paradise.

New Year's Day, 1830, when he was nearly forty-five, Audubon bade farewell to the magnolia woods of Feliciana never to return to them. Mrs. Audubon collected the monies due her and the husband and wife started for New Orleans, taking with them the three slaves "yet belonging to us, namely, Cecelia, and her two sons, Ruben and Lewis." At New Orleans they stopped for a few days at the home of William Brand, where the slaves were disposed of, and on the seventh of January Audubon and his beloved Lucy left for Louisville on the steamboat *Philadelphia*, a splendid new boat just put into the Mississippi river passenger service. They paid a fare of sixty dollars for the stylish journey.

Again John James Audubon traveled the Mississippi river, the same stream that had seen him floating down its surface nine years before, in rags and tatters, unknown and low in spirit. Now he was making the trip famous, admired, and with gold coins jingling in his pockets. The same long hair hung over his ears and curled on his shoulders, his eyes were as blue and as bright and as piercing, his nose as patricianly patterned, and his Gallic accent as pronounced. He was dreaming, this cold day of January, 1830, as he had done in January, 1821, when the keelboat in which he was drifting was approaching New Orleans. A portfolio of bird drawings was his prized piece of luggage then as now. Audubon the dreamer had arrived at the portal of his dreams.

At Louisville the two Audubons were enthusiastically welcomed by Victor and John; the *White House*, Nicholas Berthoud's home, was thrown open to the artist, and for two months he amused himself "stuffing birds" at the Falls of the Ohio. Possibly he did ride through old Louisville's streets in a coach and six, as he had sworn to do. Early in March he and his wife took a steamboat to Cincinnati, thence, via Wheeling, to the nation's capital by mail coach.

In Washington the congress was in session and through the help of Edward Everett, then a leader of the lower house, Audubon was introduced to President Andrew Jackson. Later he exhibited his drawings and engraved plates to the members of congress and received its subscription. At Philadelphia the naturalist and his wife were given a warm welcome by Doctor Harlan, Thomas Sully, and others. A week later Audubon was in New York arranging for passage to England, and the packet-ship *Pacific* landed The American Woodsman and his wife in Liverpool in twenty-five days.

The Common Gallinule. Redrawn from Audubon's plate.

Book Eight

Audubon The Publisher

"The reason why my works pleased was because they are all exact copies of the works of God, who is the Great Architect and Perfect Artist—nature indifferently copied is far superior to the best idealities."

JOHN JAMES AUDUBON, in his journal,
March 1, 1828.

CHAPTER 26

The Bird Biographies

IN London Audubon found his list of subscribers had not increased during his trip to America, but in spite of this and the further news that he had lost several patrons, he declared himself satisfied with all that had taken place during his absence. Undoubtedly the fact he had been elected a member of the Royal Society of London had much to do with this serenity. After paying his entrance fee of fifty pounds and taking his place in that august scientific body, he confided to his journal that he accepted the membership "although I felt my self that I had not the qualifications to entitle me to such an honor."

The hand-colored engravings were being turned out at Havell's establishment regularly and money was needed to pay the salaries and expenses of the engravers and colorists. Again Audubon resorted to his paints and brushes to provide the funds. Again the birds and mammals he put to canvas found, as before, ready sale in the London shops. As new subscribers were also needed Audubon decided upon another canvassing tour through England to Scotland. Accompanied by his wife he visited Birmingham, Manchester, Leeds, York, Hull, Scarbrough, Whitby, and Newcastle before his "fair Edina" was reached.

Again lodgings were taken at Mrs. Dickie's George street house and here The American Woodsman entered upon the second part of his ambitious project of delineating the birds of America. This time he was to wield the pen. He had been advised by friends who had his best interests at heart that however remarkable and valuable his pictures of the birds of America might be, it was absolutely necessary that a letter-press of some kind should accompany his life-sized pictures of the feathered inhabitants of the New World. It was with this in mind that he had gone to Edinburgh. He knew the habits of the birds. He knew their songs. He knew how to picture them with pencil and brush, but when it came to picturing them with words—he also knew his deficiencies.

"I know that I am a poor writer," he admitted, "that I can scarcely manage to scribble a tolerable English letter, and not a much better one in French, though that is easier to me. I know that I am not a scholar, but meantime I am aware that no man living knows better than I do the habits of our birds; no man living has studied them as I have done, and with the assistance of my old journals and memorandum-books, which were written on the spot, I can at least put down plain truths; which may be useful and perhaps interesting, so I shall set to at once. I cannot, however, give *scientific* descriptions, and here must have assistance."

This was no new realization. Nor had he just decided upon publishing books on the birds he had pictured. He had previously corresponded with William Swainson on the subject, and that English naturalist had agreed to undertake the work of revising and whipping Audubon's words into readable shape. It appears that Swainson was insistent that *his* name should appear on the work and equally with Audubon's. As this was not to Audubon's liking, negotiations were broken off, as was a friendship of several years' standing. This situation brought The American Woodsman to the Scottish capital seeking another ghost writer.

William Swainson never forgave Audubon for not including him in the fabrication of the *Ornithological Biography*, and later, in 1840, when the English naturalist published a volume of his own, one devoted to biographies of naturalists, he gave Alexander Wilson eight pages and accorded Audubon only a single page. On it Swainson said of Audubon, the man from whom he had borrowed money when in financial straits: "He can shoot a bird and make it live again, as it were, on canvas; but he cannot describe it in scientific, and therefore in perfectly intelligible terms. Hence he found it necessary, in this part of his work, to call in the aid of others; but being jealous that any other name should appear on the title page but his own, he was content with the assistance of someone who, very good naturedly, would fall in with his humour."

The "someone" who fell in with Audubon's humor proved to be William MacGillivray, a young Scottish naturalist, thirty-four years old, who afterwards won fame for himself with his *History of British Birds*, in five volumes; *The Rapacious Birds of Great Britain*, the *Natural History of Deeside and Braemar*, and other works. (Swainson ignored MacGillivray in his biographies of naturalists.)

Audubon tells of the compact with the Scot in his journal: "I applied to Mr. James Wilson to ask if he knew of any person who could undertake to correct my ungrammatical manuscripts, and to assist me in arranging the more scientific part of the *Biography of Birds*. He gave me the card with the address of Mr. W. MacGillivray, spoke well of him and his talents, and away to Mr. MacGillivray I went. He had long known of me as a naturalist. I made known my business, and the bargain was soon struck. He agreed to assist me and correct my manuscripts for two guineas per sheet of sixteen pages, and that day I began to write the first volume."

In estimating the influence of so remarkable an accomplishment as Audubon's *Birds of America* and his letterpress, the *Ornithological Biography*, Dr. Elliot Coues did not give Audubon the entire glory for what he termed the Audubon epoch, saying:

> Vivid and ardent was his genius; matchless he was with pen and pencil in giving life and spirit to the beautiful objects he delineated with passoniate love; but there was a strong and patient worker at his side — William MacGillivray, the countryman of Wilson, destined to lend the Scotch fibre to an Audubonian epoch. The brilliant French-American naturalist was little of a "scientist." Of his work, the magical beauties of form and color and movement are all his; his page is redolent of Nature's fragrance; but MacGillivray's are the bone and sinew, the hidden anatomical parts beneath the lovely face, the nomenclature, the classification,— in a word, the technicalities of the science. Not that MacGillivray was only a closet-naturalist; he was a naturalist in the best sense — in every sense — of the word, and the "vital spark" is gleaming through his works on British Birds, showing his intense and loyal love of Nature in all her moods. But his place in the Audubonian epoch in American ornithology is as has been said. The anatomical structure of American birds was first disclosed in any systematic manner, and to any considerable extent, by him.

The three most concerned with the publication of the famed

Ornithological Biography immediately set to work. Audubon, the one who knew the birds and their habits; MacGillivray, the "ghost author," who not only knew birds but how to write, and the ever helpful Lucy Audubon, who only knew how to answer any call her husband made for assistance.

"Writing now became the order of the day," Audubon penned for his sons' reading. "I sat at it as I awoke in the morning, and continued the whole long day, and so full was my mind of birds and their habits that in my sleep I continually dreamed of birds. I found Mr. MacGillivray equally industrious, but although he did not rise so early in the morning as I did, he wrote much later at night (this I am told is a characteristic of all great writers) and so the manuscripts went on increasing in bulk, like the rising of a stream after abundant rains, and before three months were passed the first volume was finished. Meanwhile your mother copied it all to be sent to America to secure the copyright there."

When this oddly-assorted trio began to write about the birds of America, a perfect epidemic of American bird books broke out in Europe. Audubon learned, and with some consternation at first, that no less than three editions of Wilson's *Ornithology* were to be published. Professor Jameson was having one put into print; Sir William Jardine, with Swainson as editor, was having another set in type, and Captain James Brown was getting out a third, a pirated edition.

"Most persons would probably have been discouraged by this information, but it only had a good effect on me," Audubon declared, "because since I have been in England I have studied the character of the Englishman as carefully as I have studied the birds in America. And I know full well that in England novelty is always in demand, and that if a thing is well known it will receive much support. 'Willson has had his day,' thought I to myself, 'and now it is my time.' I will write, and I hope to be read; and not only so, but I will push my publication with such unremitting vigour that my book will come before the public before Willson's can be got out."

Scratch, scratch, scratch went the iron pens over the snowy whiteness of the sheets of paper. The careful MacGillivray took the extra "l" out of Audubon's "Willson," made his

AUDUBON AT 41

An oil portrait by C. R. Parker, an American artist, painted in London in 1828. Considered one of the best likenesses of The American Woodsman. Owned by Mr. Morris Tyler, New Haven, Connecticut.

AUDUBON AT 59
Plaster cast of a cameo made in Boston in 1844 by John C. King, a Scottish artist and sculptor.

LUCY AUDUBON AND HER GRANDDAUGHTERS
Seated on either side are the two eldest daughters of John Woodhouse Audubon and Maria Rebecca Bachman. Lucy, later Mrs. De Lancy Barclay Williams, and, right, Harriet Bachman Audubon who never married. From a photograph made about 1855.

"watter" water, struck out the superfluous capital letters, and generally toned and polished the free-born thoughts into the orderly flow of words that characterizes the descriptions of birds in Audubon's *Ornithological Biography*.

When copy for the first volume was finished the work carried a perfect sequence of bird biographies to match the issuance of the double-elephant plates. The first life history was that of the wild turkey, for it was the giant Feliciana gobbler that led off the procession of pictured birds. Next came the account of the yellow-billed cuckoo, then the prothonotary warbler, purple finch, Bonaparte's flycatcher, and on through to the plate numbered one hundred, which pictured the blue-green tree swallow, the bird he had studied so intently at New Orleans.

The life histories written, Audubon looked about for a publisher for the work. None was to be found. None would venture to print the bird biographies. Here was a pretty pass! Was Audubon to be put to publishing his own work at his own expense?

"I offered this famous book to two booksellers, neither of whom would give a shilling for it," he complained, "and it was fortunate they did not, and most happy is the man who can, as I did, keep himself independent of that class of men called 'gentlemen of the trade.' Poor Willson, how happy he would have been if he had it in his power to bear the expenses of his beautiful work."

Consequently, The American Woodsman was forced to make an arrangement with Patrick Neill, the same printer who had guided him about on his first visit to Edinburgh, to print the work. The first volume bears the imprint of "Adam Black, 55 North Bridge, Edinburgh," as ghost publisher. The four subsequent volumes carry the colophon of Adam and Charles Black, but all the books attest that Neill & Co., Printers, Old Fish Market, did the necessary presswork.

Meanwhile the finished manuscripts were being set by Neill's typesetters and Audubon was in a fever of excitement. By the middle of March, 1831, the first finished book was turned over to the author and sheet copies were sent to Philadelphia so that Doctor Harlan and friend McMurtie could start simultaneous publication in America. One hundred pounds sterling had to be scraped together to secure copyright and pay the printing bill on the west side of the Atlantic. Then Audubon awaited the verdict of the critics.

The initial volume of the *Biography* proved an instant success. It was praised without reservation in all quarters; scientific journals were flattering in their reviews, magazines with a more popular appeal gave it unstinted commendation. Letters received from America were of a cheering nature, which Audubon admitted raised his dull spirits. For, in spite of the success that had come to him, he says he felt "dull, rough in temper, and long for nothing so much as my dear woods."

With the letterpress to his first hundred bird plates out of the way, Audubon began to balance his accounts. He made arrangements with Joseph B. Kidd to copy in oils some of his more notable plates so that he might sell them at good prices to defray the heavy publication costs he was now staggering under. In April he and his wife left Edinburgh.

Arrived in London, he had his portrait done in miniature on ivory by Frederick Cruikshank, and so well pleased was he over his own likeness that he had the artist make one of his beloved Lucy. He found it urgent that he visit Paris to collect subscription monies due him from M. Pitois, the agent he had appointed at Baron Cuvier's suggestion. He was delighted to exhibit Paris to his wife, and it was the last of May before he was back in the English metropolis.

Here he found flattering reviews of his book in the foremost magazines, men of science and letters were urgent in their invitations, he was fêted here and elected to august bodies there, but he was not satisfied. There were regions in America he had not explored. There were birds in those regions he had never glimpsed. Birds that had not been described by naturalists. His wandering foot was itching.

2

Therefore, the first of August found him at sea again, bound for "America—my country!" on the *Columbia*, the same trans-Atlantic packet that had carried him back to the land of his adoption the previous trip. With him and Mrs. Audubon was a young Englishman, a taxidermist named

Henry Ward, whom Audubon had engaged to accompany him on his proposed expeditions so that birds skins could be preserved, and cash raised on specimens that were wanted by various Old World museums.

"I have balanced my accounts with the Birds of America, and the whole business is really wonderful," he wrote on the eve of his departure from London. "*Forty thousand dollars!* have passed through my hands for the completion of the first volume. Who would believe that a lonely individual, who landed in England without a friend in the whole country, and with only sufficient pecuniary means to travel through it as a visitor, could have accomplished such a task as this publication?

"Who would believe that once in London Audubon had only one sovereign left in his pocket, and did not know a single individual to whom he could apply to borrow another, when he was on the verge of failure in the very beginning of his undertaking; and above all, who could believe that he had extricated himself from all his difficulties, not by borrowing money, but by rising at four in the morning, working hard all day, and disposing of his works at a price which the common laborer would have thought little more than sufficient remuneration for his work?

"To give you an idea of my actual difficulties during the publication of my first volume, it will be sufficient to say that, in the four years to bring that volume before the world, no less than fifty of my subscribers, representing the sum of fifty-six thousand dollars, abandoned me! And whenever a few withdrew I was forced to leave London and go to the provinces to obtain others to supply their places, in order to enable me to raise the money to meet the expenses of engraving, coloring, paper, printing, etc.; and what with all my constant exertions, fatigues, and vexations, I find myself now having but one hundred and thirty standing names on my list.

"England is most wealthy, and among her swarms of inhabitants there are many whom I personally know, and to whom, if I were to open my heart, there would be a readiness to help me for the sake of science; but my heart revolts from asking such a favor, and I will continue to trust in that Providence which has helped me thus far."

CHAPTER 27

In Florida Wilds

THE *Columbia* took thirty-three days to make the passage to New York. The weather was pleasant and Audubon did not suffer as much from *mal de mer* as was usually the case when he was on the high seas. He was frequently on deck, blazing away with his gun at gulls and other birds that circled the packet. He records that he was only able to secure sixteen that he reached with his charges of shot, the *Columbia* was going too fast, the captain said, to stop and pick up fifty other birds the naturalist killed from the vessel.

He was impatient to be off to the wilds. His plan, formed in England, was to go to Florida, then cross the country west of the Mississippi and even penetrate to California. He had long wanted to cross the Rocky Mountains and follow the Columbia river to its very mouth on the shores of the smiling Pacific. But his plans proved too ambitious for either his purse or his abilities. In consequence, these pretentious projects were boiled down to a single expedition, one Audubon had long in mind, to the heart of the Floridian peninsula.

Sending Lucy on to Louisville to visit her sister, Eliza Berthoud, and her brother, William G. Bakewell, Audubon journeyed farther south. At Philadelphia he again met George Lehman, the Swiss landscape painter, and persuaded him to join the expedition to the land of the everglades. The plan called for a land journey to Charleston, South Carolina, and thence by packet to St. Augustine.

October was half done when Audubon and his two assistants reached Charleston and delivered a letter of introduction to the Reverend Mr. Gilman. "There I found a man of learning, of sound heart and willing to bear the 'American Woodsman' a hand—he walked with me and had already contrived to procure us cheaper Lodgings," writes Audubon, "when he presented me in the street to the Revd Mr. Bachman!"

In such a fashion did Audubon and John Bachman meet. The latter was a Lutheran divine, also an amateur naturalist intensely interested in mammals. The Swiss-American minister of the gospel and the Franco-American bird painter found much in common; both delighted in the chase, both handled the gun well, and both had a fondness for objects of natural history. The friendship was instant and Bachman insisted that Audubon and his two assistants spend the time they were to be in Charleston, awaiting the steamer *Agnes*, under his roof.

"Mr. Bachman!! why, my Lucy, Mr. Bachman would have us *all* stay to his house—he would have us make free there as if we were at our own encampment at the head of Some unknown Rivers—he would not suffer us to proceed farther South for 3 weeks—he talked—he looked as if his heart had been purposely made of the most benevolent materials granted man by the Creator to render all about him most happy—Could I refuse his kind invitation? No!—It would have pained him as much as if grossly insulted. We removed to his house in a crack—found a room already arranged for Henry to skin our Birds—another for me & Lehman to Draw and a third for thy Husband to rest his bones in on an excellent bed! . . . This my Dearest Friend is the situation of thy husband at Charleston South Carolina."

Although the weather during the latter part of October was "shockingly hot" the whole party went into the fields after birds, and more than three hundred specimens fell before the guns. These feathered prizes were either prepared by Ward as museum specimens or pickled in "pale-faced rum" and sent to Doctor Harlan at Philadelphia for safe keeping. "Here I am the very pet of every body and had I the time or Inclination to visit the great folk I might be in dinner parties from now until Jany next—however I have other Fish to fry—I am positively busy—I have drawn 9 Birds since here which make 5 Drawings when finished," Audubon informed his wife, and after expressing his happiness at learning of her safe arrival at Louisville with Victor, who had journeyed to Philadelphia to escort his mother to the Kentucky town, the artist added: "I will not forget the Friend of 25 Years standing I think—neither will I forget her precept for I am also aware that the World has an eye upon me and was the World blind I feel that it is more suitable to become wise if possible than to become a poor & useless being."

The first week in November was passed and Audubon records he had drawn fifteen birds, making five completed drawings, all of which were finished by Lehman with views of the South Carolina country as backgrounds, and the birds were shown perched on typical plants of the locality. Henry Ward skinned and preserved two hundred and twenty specimens, representing sixty species, while the head of the expedition varied his hunting and drawing of birds with quests for subscribers to his work. It was the fifteenth of the month before the *Agnes* arrived, effects were placed on board, and the vessel set sail for Florida. The winds were contrary, "and so was the Capn, as poor a 'shoat' as I have ever seen." It was the twentieth of November before Audubon put up at a tavern in the ancient Florida town of St. Augustine.

Audubon regretted leaving the hospitable home of John Bachman, for his stay at Charleston witnessed the beginning of the enduring friendship of the two men whose names will ever be remembered through their joint work, *The Viviparous Quadrupeds of North America*, a friendship afterwards cemented by the marriage of John Woodhouse Audubon to Maria Rebecca Bachman, and Victor's marriage to her younger sister Eliza.

2

During the first ten days of the stay at St. Augustine the three hunters were busy shooting and drawing birds. One new specimen was secured, the one known to our bird books as "Audubon's Caracara." In a letter to his wife he tells of securing it: "Have drawn 13 different Species amongst which is a *new one* which proves to be a *new Genera* for the United States—a kind of Exotic Bird probably very common in South America but quite unknown to me or anyone else in this place—it is a mixture of Buzzard and Hawk and I have decided to call it *Catharses Floridaniis*—I have written to Doc[r] Harlan about it and its description will be published in the transactions of the A. S. S. of Phil[a]."

Audubon carried among the many letters given him to Florida plantation owners, one to General Hernandez, a wealthy orange grower, but as this gentleman "received me *rather* cooly," the naturalist decided not to trouble the general with his company, and visited another planter named McCraigh at Smyrna some forty-six miles further south.

"St. Augustine is the poorest hole in Creation," Audubon wrote his wife. "The living is very poor and very high—was it not for the fishes in the bay and a few thousand of oranges that grow around the Village, the people must undoubtedly abandon it or starve, for they are all too leazy to work, or if they do work at such price as puts it out of the question to employ them. The country around nothing but bare sand Hills—hot one day cold another &c &c."

In another letter, after his usual "God Bless Thee Dearest Friend Good night," he added "——by the way, *Know ye* all men that Rattlesnake *do clime Trees!!!*"

In January the bird hunter and his assistants penetrated to the interior of the state and were put up at the plantation home of John J. Bulow. From this headquarters they made a number of forays into the surrounding country, many of the adventures being detailed in Audubon's Florida *Episodes*. The first month of 1832 was half gone when the party returned to St. Augustine in consequence of receiving letters from Washington, which informed Audubon that the secretary of the treasury, Louis McLane, had advised commanders of revenue cutters in Florida waters to convey the naturalist to different points in that state within cruising limits of the vessels.

The United States Schooner of War *Spark*, as Audubon described it, was then in port, and although Lieutenant William P. Piercy, its commander, so Audubon was told, had expressed himself to others "very roughly" about transporting the naturalists on a projected trip up the St. Johns river, the officer changed his tone when the artist presented his letters. It was agreed the schooner should sail to Jacksonville and proceed south on the St. Johns as far as navigation and the vessel's draft would permit, a voyage of four or five weeks.

"These are my present Plans," wrote Audubon on the eve of departure, "and, if the Commandant and I agree, I will stick to the Schooner *Spark* until I have drawn many a fine Bird—Should he prove unkind or Two rough I will leave him."

The *Spark* left St. Augustine for the mouth of the St. Johns river in the teeth of a gale. The wind was so boisterous that Audubon, as usual when on rough water, became quite seasick and Lieutenant Piercy put back to St. Augustine and the haven of its harbor. In consequence the *Spark* did not reach the mouth of the noted Florida river and Jacksonville until the ninth of February. The southward trip began on that date.

The voyage up "this Dingy looking river," which Audubon claimed did not equal in beauty the Ohio, began under auspicious circumstances. He records that the commander of the war vessel was "jolly," that the shores of the river were low and swampy places "to the great delight of numberless herons that moved along in gracefulness, and the grim alligators that swam in sluggish sullenness." Audubon was at peace with the world. A few days before he had foresworn snuff. As he wrote his wife, "Thou wilt be surprised to read that I have *abandoned Snuff for ever!* and so has Lehman—I came to that determination on the 1st of this Month—I am So tanned and burnt that thou might easily take me for an Indian—My beard has grown unshorn these 5 weeks."

A week later, when the *Spark* was only one hundred miles up the river, Audubon began to complain of the trip. He wrote, "The Stink of the River Water I fear has caused one half of our Crew to be sick." The paucity of bird life fretted him, for since the beginning of the voyage he had succeeded in drawing only two species, and he complained bitterly to his wife: "I have been deceived most shamefully about the Floridas—Scarcely a Bird to be seen and these of the most common sort—I look to the leaving of it as an Happy event—I am now truly speaking in a *Wild* and *dreary* and desolate part of the World—No one in the Eastern States has any *true* Idea of this Peninsula—*My account* of what I have or shall see of the Floridas will be far, very far from corroborating the *flowery sayings* of Mr. Barton the Botanist."

So the naturalist and the members of the crew contented themselves to blazing away at alligators from the deck of the schooner. One morning when the *Spark* was anchored at Buenavista Lieutenant Piercy went ashore and, fearing to encounter rattlesnakes, sent a member of the crew back to the boat to secure his shotgun. In handing the weapon into the small boat it was accidentally discharged, the load passing through the seaman's hand. The commander decided the man needed medical attention and conveyed him down the river a few miles, thence by land, over a cutoff, directly east to St. Augustine. This caused enforced delay and idleness.

It had been planned to proceed up the river to Lake George, but when Lieutenant Piercy returned he pulled up the river in a small boat to within five or six miles of the lake, and then decided that it would be a useless expense of time and labor to move the *Spark* up the narrow and intricate passage.

Audubon was out of sorts and on the refusal of Piercy to proceed farther there was a clash of temperaments. The naval man probably proved "unkind" or "very rough," for Audubon quitted the *Spark* in a huff, and taking his assistants with him, journeyed some forty miles down stream in a hired skiff rowed by two natives, until they arrived at the Indian trail or short cut overland to St. Augustine. With every mile that divided him from the war vessel Audubon was breathing blistering imprecations on "the *Spark* blackguards!"

The naturalist had expected to procure a wagon at the cutoff for his trunks, kegs, and other effects, but was disappointed. So the bulky paraphernalia was piled on shore and Ward left to guard it, while Audubon, with Lehman and his big black and white Newfoundland dog *Plato*, set out on foot for St. Augustine at four in the afternoon. He describes this journey vividly in the *Episode* entitled *St. John's River in Florida*, but in it does not even hint at the unpleasant parting with Lieutenant Piercy.

The two men and the dog tore their way through tangled thickets of low trees, crossed streams running bank full with rain water, for they were overtaken by a furious night tempest. They trudged across open pine barrens on their eighteen-mile journey in the blackness, half lost and groping their way on an unknown course for hours. Suddenly the storm passed, the sky became spangled with the twinkle of sub-tropic stars and the pungent air off the salt marshes saluted their nostrils. "Like pointers advancing on a covy of partridges—we at last, to our great joy, descried the light of the beacon near St. Augustine," says Audubon. They crossed the causeway at the back of the town and made their way to the hotel, "drenched with rain, steaming with perspiration, and covered to the knees with mud."

The next morning Major Gates, commanding the fort, sent a wagon and soldiers for Ward and by afternoon the naturalists and their effects were again tied up at St. Augustine awaiting the arrival of the packet *Agnes* so they could return to Charleston. "I have been forced to perform a counter march," Audubon wrote his wife, "but it has proved, like some performed by Greater Generals than myself, a most Honourable and profitable retreat."

3

It was not until the fifth of March that the *Agnes* took the party and the bird skin collection out of "the miserable spot St. Augustine," and as the packet headed north it passed the *Spark* just as that schooner sailed out of the mouth of the St. Johns. The packet was hailed, Lieutenant Piercy had his gig manned, and was rowed over to Audubon's vessel.

"The Commandant came aboard us," he writes, "presented me with a most Superb pair of Swans and said *he hoped* I would not say to anyone the reasons why I had left his Vessel—The man may have a good heart, but if his head, like an empty box, contains no brains to enable him to be a *worthy Gentleman*—the man and the head may go a'drift for me."

One of the birds that Lieutenant Piercy gave Audubon as a peace offering served as his model for his plate of the American Swan, as he then termed the waterfowl we now call the whistling swan. When the plate was published in 1838, there were included in the composition three yellow waterlilies, which Audubon designated as *Nymphæa lutea*. The lilies have a history.

Writing on "Audubon's Lily Rediscovered," in the *Popular Science Monthly*, in 1877, Professor Samuel Lockwood, said:

> Beholding it with his own eyes, the great painter put it in one of his own glorious bird-pictures and, having given the portrait of his floral beauty, he named it *Nymphæa lutea*, or in plain English, the yellow water lily. But this pretty flower had never been seen by the botanists, and so, forsooth, the thing was absolutely ignored —treated as a pretty fable, a bit of art extravagance. Art, like history, may have its anachronisms, but the real artist, though he may err, cannot lie.
>
> So thoroughly was *Nymphæa lutea* snubbed, that it would have been as much as a poor mortal's reputation was worth to have mentioned credence in the thing in the hearing of sober science . . . the luckless lily of Audubon is scientifically tabooed.
>
> Last summer, in Florida, Mrs. Mary Treat rediscovered the long-lost flower of Audubon. Professor Asa Gray duly acknowledged it as the long-ignored *Nymphæa lutea* . . . Were it scientifically orthodox to rechristen the rediscovered flower we would have its history crystalized in a new scientific name — *Nymphæa Audubonii*. Which, after so long incredulity, would be doing the bonny thing; and thus the yellow water lily would dot, with golden memories of the gentle enthusiast, the waters of the rivers of time.

Audubon's "Lost Lily" has quite a different history. The lilies do not appear on the original drawing of the whistling swan, but were evidently added when the engraving was made by Havell in London in 1838, from a separate drawing by Audubon, or possibly Lehman. Nor did Audubon "discover" the strange yellow lily. Witness his own words to Victor:

> A Young German a good Botanist with whom I am well acquainted has lately returned to Charleston from the Floridas — he traveled the "Ever Glades" spent a summer there and discovered a bout 50 New Birds, a great Number of Plants &c. The New Birds John Bachman will secure for me — I will derive some knowledge from "*Lightner*"

In a letter to Doctor Bachman, under date of London, April 14, 1838, Audubon asked the Charleston divine:

> Has Leitner published the New Plants he discovered in the Floridas? I ask this latter question because on the 83 number of my work, Plate 411, I have represented a New Nymphea, which unpublished by him, I should like in my letter press to name after Doc^{r} Leitner's name, "*Nymphea Leitneria!*"

Doctor Edward F. Leitner was an enlightened, highly educated, and skillful German physician. At Charleston he was lecturer on botany at the Natural History Society, and accompanied a number of naval and army expeditions sent to Florida to keep the Seminole Indians in check in 1836 and 1838. Owing to the fact that he had pursued his natural history explorations in many out-of-the-way portions of the region he was able to guide the soldiers to Seminole villages. A report made by Lieutenant L. M. Powell of the United States Navy shows that on January 15, 1838, Doctor Leitner guided a detachment up Jupiter creek to an Indian camp commanded by Chief Tuskogee. The Indians ambushed Lieutenant Powell's command, and in addition to the four seamen and soldiers killed, Leitner was shot down, the savages took his scalp, and his body was not recovered.

The German scientist had already described the yellow water-lily, which he found in the St. Johns and Miami rivers, in Curtis' *Botanical Magazine of London* under the name of *Nymphæa flava*, or "Florida lily."[1] Doctor Bachman informed Audubon of Leitner's death, and why The American Woodsman called it *lutea* and not *Leitneria* is not known.

4

On its way to Charleston the *Agnes* ran into a storm and was forced to put into Savannah harbor so Audubon went ashore in a gig and "put up at the City Hotel with a beard and a pair of Mustachios and a dress which at once attracted all attention." He called on several of the residents of the city, displayed his drawings and finished plates, and before taking the mail coach for Charleston, secured two new subscribers and placed an additional six hundred dollars in his pockets.

At Charleston Audubon remained with the hospitable John Bachman, drawing birds, scouring the countryside for subscribers, and hunting birds. He taught the clergyman the delights of snuff, for in spite of his many resolutions to forswear the weed, Audubon was wedded to its use. The two would take long rides over the country roads, and as Audubon was

[1]Castalia flava of present works on botany.

continually grumbling about the jostling he received in the cumbersome vehicles of that period, Bachman gave him the nickname of "Jostle," and continued to use the nickname for many years in letters to the naturalist.

Audubon had written to friends having influence at Washington to secure the services of a government vessel which would cruise the eastern coast of Florida and he determined to remain at Charleston until his request was granted. During this wait he devoted much time to canvassing and was success-

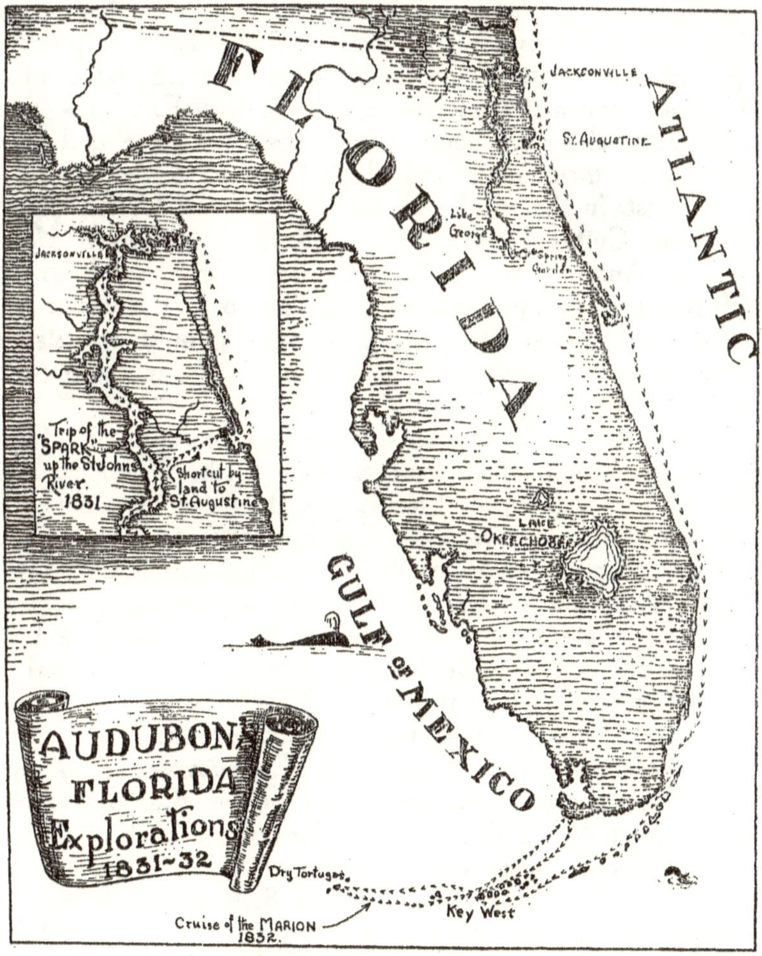

ful in placing his large work with the Charleston Society of Natural History, the legislature of South Carolina, and a number of well-to-do citizens of Charleston and Savannah. Although elated over the way subscriptions poured in, he was impatient to be off on a coastal tour of the Florida peninsula.

"What will my Philadelphia friends say or think when they read that Audubon is on board a U. S. Schooner of War going around the Floridas after *Birds?*" he exulted in a letter to his beloved Lucy. "I assure thee my Sweet Girl I begin to be proud of myself when I see that my Industry, perseverance and honesty has thus brought me So high from So Low as I was in 1820 when I could not even procure through my Relations and former Partners the Situation of a Clerk on Board an Ohio Steamer—now they Prize me—nay wish me well—very good, I wish them the same and may God grant them peace and plenty."

At last, in the middle of April, 1832, the United States Revenue Cutter *Marion*, "*The Lady with the Green Mantle*," so Audubon frequently called her in his episodes on the Florida trip, dropped anchor in the harbor. Its commander, Lieutenant Robert Day, called on the naturalist and stated his boat and crew were at his service. So began the historic cruise to the Florida Keys.

For six weeks the *Marion* visited all the coastal islands from St. Augustine to Key West, as well as the Tortugas, and there at the very tip of Florida Audubon met his old friend of New Orleans days, Napoleon L. Costé, who was taken aboard as pilot while the cutter was navigating the Keys. Here Audubon added another bird to our ornithological science, the great white heron, which he made the subject of one of his plates, while Lehman drew as a background a distant view of the island town of Key West.

Many of the more interesting events of this Florida trip were recounted in a number of the *Episodes* which first appeared in the original edition of the *Ornithological Biography*, but were omitted in the smaller editions of the *Birds of America.* Although many new drawings were made on his two expeditions to Florida wilds, over a thousand specimens secured, and two new discoveries made, Audubon declared his trips to Florida were "rather unprofitable expeditions."

5

The naturalist returned to the hospitable Bachman residence bearded and in torn clothes. In after years the Charleston clergyman wrote Audubon his remembrance of the naturalist's appearance: "As I saw you . . . when you came from Florida . . . your beard, two months old, was as gray as a Badger's. I think a grizzly-bear, forty-seven years old, would have claimed you as *par nobile fratum*." If Audubon was forty-seven in 1832, as he undoubtedly must have informed Bachman, this would have placed his birth-year as 1785.

Audubon remained in Charleston a few days, secured a few new subscribers for his monumental work, and then returned to Philadelphia where he was joined by Lucy and his two boys. Early in August he left with his family for a trip to the New England states, having decided to remain in America until he completed his collection of birds, but to insure the work being done by Havell having proper supervision, Audubon sent his eldest son Victor to London to attend to this very necessary superintendence.

While drumming up subscribers in the New England states, where he secured eighteen subscribers for the big work, he met and was successful in adding John Neal of Portland, Maine, a newspaper and magazine writer, to his list of patrons. Several months later when Neal defaulted in his payments, Audubon characterized him as a "scamp" and ordered his Boston agent to repossess the numbers already delivered. In 1835, when Neal was editor of *The New England Galaxy*, a Boston newspaper, he retaliated with a series of three viciously-worded editorials in which he attacked Audubon's stories of his birth, claimed he was a native of San Domingo, "if born anywhere!" and devoted a great deal of space to Audubon's relations with and treatment of Joseph Mason.

These remarkable articles were never answered by Audubon nor any of his friends, and appear to have escaped the attention of all previous biographers, in spite of their importance and the sidelights thrown on Audubon's character.

At this period of his career Audubon's growing irascibleness was given full sway. During the Florida trips he would frequently vent his temper on those about him and the language he used was usually the envy of the gruff seamen who manned the boats. At the close of the Florida explorations he "fired Lehman instanter" for some fancied grievance, and so harassed Henry Ward that the young English taxidermist tried to drown his woes, unsuccessfully of course, in rum. When Audubon informed Ward that he too was out of a job, he did it with a wealth of expletives that shocked Doctor Bachman.

Soon after Audubon left Charleston for New York the clergyman in a letter took "Old Mr. Jostle" to task regarding his habit of taking the Lord's name in vain and his free use of other oaths: "I want to see you once more to ascertain whether you have stuck to your good resolutions, viz: never to swear (which is a vulgar practice for one who is conversant with the most beautiful of God's works—the feathered race), and never to work on Sundays."

Audubon replied in a long letter assuring Bachman that he had made another resolution to that effect, and launched into intricate descriptions of some fellow-naturalists of Philadelphia. Nor were the word pictures flattering to the subjects. Bachman spent some time deciphering the communication and then wrote:

"Your last letter required a Philadelphia lawyer to decipher it, all pot-hooks; you must have taken lessons from some new-fangled writing-master in Yankee-town, who taught you to place the letters, as Henry Ward sometimes does his birds in a basket—heads to tails and crosswise."

Audubon had commented of the clergyman's reference to his, Audubon's, obstinacy, and assumed it was flattering.

"When I spoke of your *obstinacy*, I meant it as a compliment and I am glad that you understood me," explained Bachman, "and yet you are not as obstinate as your predecessor, Wilson, who was ready to quarrel with a man because he differed from him in opinion. I liked Wilson because he studied nature; I like you because you give theory to the dogs; because you give to the opinions of others just as much as they are worth; because you will examine and judge for yourself, and because you study where every naturalist ought, in the wide fields of nature.

"How different is *her* teaching to that expressed by men

EDWARD HARRIES
A daguerreotype of Audubon's friend and patron made in New Orleans in 1843.

ANNE BAKEWELL GORDON
A painting of Lucy Bakewell's sister by John Woodhouse Audubon.

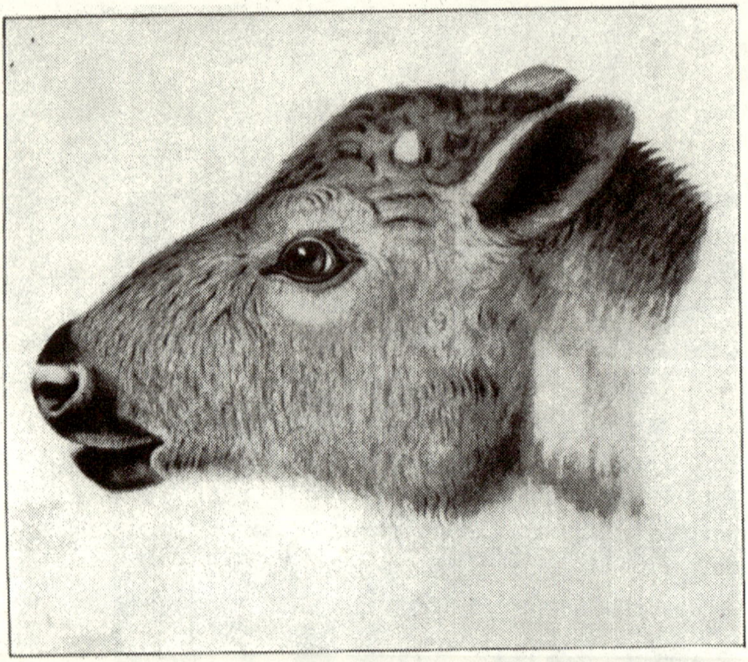

HEAD OF A BUFFALO CALF

From a painting by John James Audubon made on the Missouri River Expedition in 1843, who wrote his wife: "We procured yesterday morning a Buffaloe calf 2 months old, and the head of another." From the original owned by Mrs. Alicia Bakewell Shaffer Cincinnati, O.

HEAD OF A BLACK-TAILED DOE

Drawn on the Missouri River Expedition by Audubon who wrote on the original: "head of doe shot at Mt. Vernon by Edward Harris & Drawn by ME John J. Audubon. June 30 & July 1, 1843."

in general. I have read the speculations of men, I have listened to the tales of the ignorant traveler, and it seemed as if there were defects in all the works of God. Then I have turned to the fields and woods; to the air, the earth, and the sea; and I have perceived that all was order, harmony, and beauty, and I have acknowledged that all the defects were in the shortsightedness of man."

Audubon was mollified.

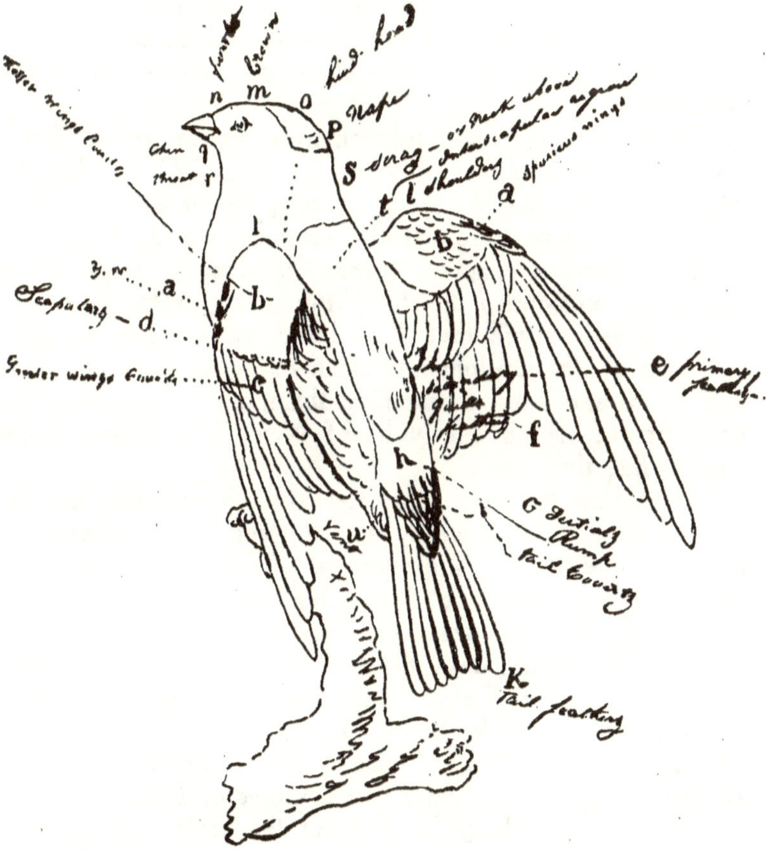

Audubon's own pen-and-ink sketch on a page of his journal which he used in naming the bird's various parts and feathers.

CHAPTER 28

Down to the Labrador

DURING the early summer of 1833 Audubon realized a dream of years, an expedition to the shores of Labrador. He selected Eastport, Maine, as the port of embarkation, and in June the schooner *Ripley* carrying a party of expectant naturalists surged through the rough waters of the Bay of Fundy, along the coast of Nova Scotia, and then to the bleak *terra incognitus* of the northland.

Those accompanying Audubon were his son John Woodhouse, Joseph Coolidge, Thomas Lincoln, William Ingalls, and George Cheyne Shattuck, all young men most enthusiastic over the great adventure that lay before them in this trip down to the Labrador. Captain Henry W. Emery, a friend of Lincoln's, commanded the stout little sailing craft. Audubon was surprised to find that the colored man he had engaged as a sort of "major-domo, to clean our guns, hunt for nests and birds, and assist in skinning them, etc.," had been the body-servant of Vincent Nolte of New Orleans and spoke French fluently.

It was June the sixth, and after a number of irritating delays which included a wordy war between Audubon and the man who outfitted the ship over cost of chartering it, that the *Ripley* set sail and two days later was dancing over the waters and Audubon was "shockingly sea-sick, crossing that worst of all dreadful bays, the Bay of Fundy." They passed through the Gut of Canso, landed at the Magdalen Island, saw the wonders of the famous Bird Rock, passed Anticosti Island, and on the 18th. of June landed at American Harbor. At last, Audubon had reached the shores of Labrador. For ten days all were busy hunting out the birds, seeking new species among the feathered multitudes, and drawing pictures of many taken.

Leaving American Harbor, at the mouth of the Natashquan river, the *Ripley* carried the party to many small islands where puffins, razor-billed auks, guillemots, and gulls were nesting and July 14 the schooner dropped anchor at Macatine and the whole party went ashore to seek out birds. In his journal Audubon described the taking of a mother spruce partridge which became the model for one of his Labrador plates. The mother grouse was moving along a tree-lined trail followed by a file of tiny little ones, not long out of their shells. "On seeing us she ruffed her feathers like a barnyard hen," so runs the entry, "and rounded within a few feet of us to defend her brood; her very looks claimed our forebearance and clemency, but the enthusiastic desire to study nature prompted me to destroy her, and she was shot."

When setting this adventure on paper for his *Ornithological Biography* the details were toned down: "The affrighted mother, on seeing us, ruffled up all her feathers like a common hen, and advanced close to us as if determined to defend her offspring. Her distressed condition claimed our forbearance, and we allowed her to remain in safety. The moment we retired, she smoothed down her plumage, and uttered a

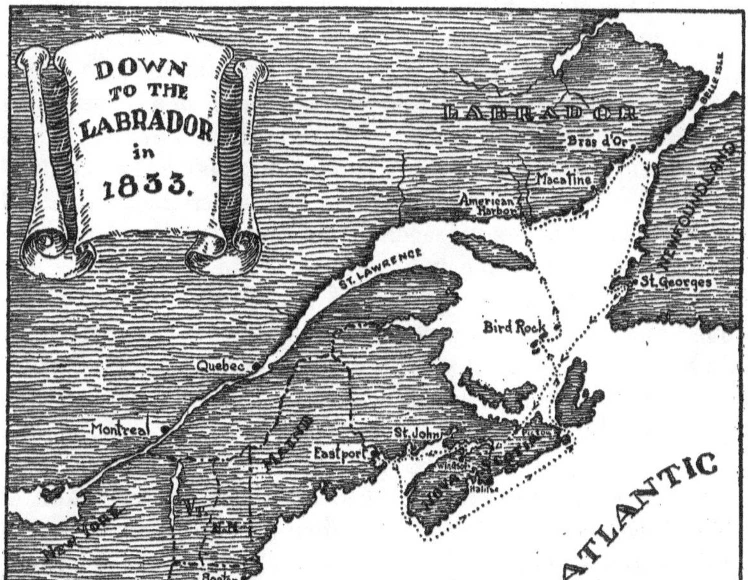

tender maternal chuck, when the little ones took to their wings, although they were, I can venture to assert, not more than *one week old*, with so much ease and delight, that I felt highly pleased at having allowed them to escape."

A number of birds were secured at Little Macatine during the stay and Audubon, working like one possessed, set many of the birds to paper. The next stop was at Bras d'Or Bay, where the party found the now extinct Labrador duck, which Audubon then termed the Pied Duck, bred there. By the middle of August Audubon decided that he had enough of Labrador and ordered the *Ripley* to head in the direction of Maine. The Labrador expedition proved to be another disappointment. Although the hard trip, which was a succession of cold and mosquitoes, and was not as successful as anticipated, Audubon was taking back with him a collection of nearly two hundred bird skins and a number of objects of natural history, such as marine plants, shells, and a few specimens of the smaller mammals, and twenty-three large drawings of the birds of Labrador.

Only a few new species were added to his growing list of American birds not described by others, and the only one that stands is the sparrow which was named for Tom Lincoln, the young man who secured the finch. Upon his departure from Eastport, The American Woodsman had expected to spend the two months in a land that would furnish him a wealth of new and undescribed forms. As he did with regard to his Florida explorations, Audubon has left us in his colorful *Episodes* a number of interesting and entertaining tales of what he saw and experienced in the bleak northern territory he explored from June until August. The night before the *Ripley* sailed into the harbor of St. George's Bay, Newfoundland, Audubon penned in his journal: "Seldom in my life have I left a country with as little regret as I do Labrador; the next nearest to this was East Florida, after my excursion up the St. John's River."

The party of naturalists did not remain on the *Ripley* until that stout little craft reached Eastport, but debarked at Pictou, went overland to Truro, then on to Halifax where a short stay was made. A coach took the party to Windsor, where Audubon recorded he saw the tide waters of the Bay of Fundy rise sixty-five feet, before a steamboat "The Maid of the Mist" carried the party to Eastport. So ended Audubon's long-desired trip down to the Labrador.

2

Upon his return to New York in September, Audubon decided to embrace an offer from John Bachman to remain with him in Charleston while awaiting another start to Florida, for in spite of the disappointments encountered in the two previous excursions, the naturalist felt that the west side of that peninsula and the shores of the Gulf of Mexico should be thoroughly combed for birds.

He started for South Carolina by the way of Philadelphia. His reception in the Quaker City was not to his liking, for he was arrested for one of his old partnership debts of the Henderson period. "In Philadelphia I, of course, received no subscriptions," he writes, "nay, I was arrested there for debt, and was on the point of being taken to prison, had I not met with William Norris, Esq., who kindly offered to be my bail. This event brings to my mind many disagreeable thoughts connected with my former business transactions, in which I was *always* the *single* loser, that I will only add I made all necessary arrangements to have it paid."

Dreading the perils of a new railway, which had just been put into commission, the naturalist and his wife left Richmond for Charleston in a horse-drawn carriage. There, at the Bachman's spacious home the Audubons spent the winter, the husband busy at his manuscripts. "I write a Bird or so every evening," he wrote Victor in London, who was attending to the publication of the plates at Havell's establishment, and added that in spite of subscribers dying they would have to "depend upon our Industry, our truth, and the regular manner in which we publish our Work—this will always prove to the *World* & to our Subscribers, that nothing more can be done than what we do, nay that I doubt if any other *Family* with our pecuniary means ever will raise for themselves such a *Monument* as 'the Birds of America' is, over their tomb!"

In the spring Audubon was definitely informed that no government cutters nor other boats could be put at his disposal for the Florida and gulf territory he wished to explore, so in March of 1834 the artist, his wife, and son John prepared to quit the Bachmans, but before going on to New York the question of the nose-smelling ability of the buzzards came up for a round of discussion—critics were still hammering Audubon in the papers for his claims that the vultures could only see their carrion food and not smell it.

Therefore, it was proposed that Doctor Bachman and a number of his ornithologically inclined friends and neighbors should make their own experiments and see whether the South Carolina buzzards differed from those of Louisiana. The series of experiments with the "nose-smelling of Turkey Buzzards proved *perfectly* satisfactory to my good friend and myself . . . that they come to their food by their sense of sight, and not by that of smell, and lastly they cannot discover by any sense of smell the most putrid matter, even when this putrid stuff is within a few feet of them, out of sight of their eyes." Audubon wrote his son Victor, adding that the experiments had been carried on for the purpose of refuting "the blackguardism of G. Ord and others."

Doctor Bachman wrote a paper on the subject which bore out the main parts of Audubon's contention. This printed article was hailed by Audubon as "a condemnation of My Dear Enemies, Messrs. Waterton & Ord," characterizing the clergyman's findings as a "plain paper, no nonsense, no fudge; but so simple & full of truth that I greatly fear that the *Armour* of Waterton will fall to the Earth, and leave the man, a poor worthless Carcase fit (if fresh) for the very Buzzards which he has so deeply abused."

Just as the Audubons were taking leave of Charleston the naturalist faced another embarrassing situation—he was sued in the Charleston courts for an old debt, dating back to the failure of the "infernal mill' at Henderson, Kentucky. He was forced to arrange matters for his future appearance in court by calling on new-found friends to come to his assistance by posting a bond.

When Audubon reached New York he had with him a goodly lot of material for the second volume of the *Ornithological Biography*, for during the winter days spent at Charleston he had put to good use every spare moment on the rough drafts he intended handing over to MacGillivray. While not sufficiently gifted to write his own descriptions in the manner they should be finished for presentation on the printed pages of such an ambitious scientific work, the structure that lay behind the published biographies of the birds he knew and loved so well was entirely his own. All that his talented ghost writer was called upon to do was to whip into proper English and spelling that which Audubon wrote.

By the middle of April, Audubon, his wife, and John, with a great sheath of written descriptions and pictures of the new bird drawings, were on board the fast packet *North America*, and nineteen days later were back on British soil. A little drumming up of subscribers was done in the provinces and then he and Lucy set their faces northwards to Edinburgh where they rented a house and remained in the Scottish capital for a year and a half. There was much to be done there.

3

The immediate task was the issuance of the second volume of bird biographies while Havell in London kept to his engravings. As was the case with the initial volume, Audubon's accomplished ghost writer, William MacGillivray, rewrote his descriptions to match the issuance of the second hundred plates in *The Birds of America*, and by the first of December the new matter was in the hands of Patrick Neill's typesetters and shortly thereafter the sheets were put to the presses in Old Fishmarket.

The talented Scotsman agreed to "revise and correct" the third and fourth volumes of the biographies at "two pounds two shillings per sheet" as well as to revise, for a sum subsequently to be determined, any other work which Audubon might intend publishing.

Just what a task MacGillivray had can best be estimated by a comparison of the original manuscript written by Audubon of the ruby-throated hummingbird, the first page of this manuscript being reproduced on another page, and the printed biography as it appeared in the work after MacGillivray had revised it.

The Ruby Throated Humming Bird

Audubon

Where is the person who on seeing, this lovely feathered miniature, moving humming, passing through, or suspended as if by magic in the air, with motions as easy, graceful as they are light & airy flitting from one flower to another & from blossom to blossom; eagerly pursuing its course over & across our extensive continent, affording new pleasures to mankind when ever it is seen, where is that person I ask of you Kind Reader who on observing this richly clad diminutive Sample of the feathery tribes, will not pause, not admire & not instantaniously feel the reverence we owe to the Almighty Creator whose bounties we at every step constantly discover and at every movement of our own superior organization feel how sublime & manifest *his* own wonderful system of arrangement throughout the whole of creation exists?—Such a one does not live—so kindly were we all blessed with that unate & noble feeling—admiration!

No sooner has the vivifying orb began to warn of spring once more the season, and caused millions of plants to spread the beauties of its benifiting rays, than the little humming bird is seen advancing on fairy wings, visiting carefully every opening calix & like an anxious florist, remove from each of them the injurious Insects that otherwise would ere long cause their beautious petals to droop & decay. — the little bird poised in the air is observed peeping cautiously and with a brilliant eye into their innermost recesses

MacGillivray

Where is the person, who on seeing this lovely little creature moving on humming winglets through the air, suspended as if by magic in it, flitting from one flower to another, with motions as graceful as they are light and airy, pursuing its course over our extensive continent, and yielding new delights wherever it is seen;—where is the person, I ask of you kind reader, who, on observing this glittering fragment of the rainbow, would not pause, admire, and instantly turn his mind with reverence toward the Almighty, the wonders of whose hand we at every step discover in his admirable system of creation?—There breathes not such a person; so kindly have we all been blessed with that intuitive and noble feeling — admiration!

No sooner has the returning sun again introduced the vernal season, and caused millions of plants to expand their leaves and blossoms to his genial beams, than the little Humming-bird is seen advancing on fairy wings, carefully visiting every opening flower-cup, and, like a curious florist, removing from each the injurious insects that otherwise would ere long cause their beauteous petals to droop and decay. Poised in the air, it is observed peeping cautiously, and with sparkling eye, into their innermost recesses, whilst

Plate 47. Ruby throated Humming Bird —

Where is the person who on seeing this lovely feathered miniature, moving humming, passing through, or suspended as if by magic in the air with motions as easy, as graceful as they are light and airy, flitting from one flower to another & from blossom to blossom; eagerly pursuing its course over the vast extensive continent, affording new pleasure to mankind wherever it is seen, where is that person I ask of you kind Reader who on observing the richly clad diminutive of the feathery tribe will not pause, not admire, & not instantly feel the reverence due to the Almighty Creator whose [illegible] boundless are at every step [illegible] of our own superior organization and at every movement of our own wonderful system manifested, our [illegible] feel how [illegible] through our [illegible] the whole creation exists! [illegible] of arrangement [illegible] with [illegible] & noble lives — so kindly may we all [illegible] blessed with the warmest of spirit and feeling — admiration! —

No sooner has the vivifying sun begun to warm of spring and to spread the healthy [illegible] more the season, and caused millions of plants to [illegible] the budding [illegible] is seen advancing to its benefiting rays, than the little humming bird is seen advancing on spring flower calix [illegible] on wings of [illegible] visiting cautiously each of them the injurious insects [illegible] & like an anxious florist, remove from them the injurious [illegible] that are otherwise would ere long cause their lovely [illegible] decay. — the little bird poised in the air is observed peeping cautiously and with a brilliant eye into their innermost recesses whilst the ethereal motions of its pinions are so rapid & light without doing any detriment to the flower, appear to fan and cool the flower, producing merely a delightful murmuring sound well adapted to lull the insects to repose — then is the moment for the humming bird to secure them, its long delicate bill enters the calix and the protruding double tubed tongue, imbued with its delicate saliva touches one after another each insect, and draws them from their hiding places into its mouth to be immediately destroyed. — the whole of this is accomplished in one instant and the bird as it leaves the flower sips a slight portion of its liquid honey, that probably considered with grateful [illegible] the theft is [illegible] relieved from the attacks of her [illegible] destroyers. —

The Prairies, the fields, the orchards & gardens, nay the deepest shades of the forests are all visited in their turn and every where the little bird meets with pleasure & with food — its gorgeous throat defies all competition in beauty & brilliancy, now it glows with a fiery hue & again it is changed to the deepest velvety black soft — [illegible] the upper parts of its delicate body are resplendent changing green, and it throws itself through the air with a swiftness & vivacity beyond all powers to describe — it moves from one flower to another like a gleam of light, either upwards, downwards, to the right or to the left & again downwards — and in this manner reaches the furthermost northern portions of our country following with extreme precaution the advancement of the season, & retreating with equal care at the approach of Autumn at the approach of Autumn.

I wish it was within my power at this instant to impart to you kind Reader the pleasures I have felt whilst watching the movements — the feelings excited by a single pair of these most favourite little creatures when engaged at [illegible] participating the emotions of their love to each other.

whilst the etheral motions of its pinions so rapid & so light appears to fan & cool the flower without any detriment to its once fragile texture, producing merely a delightful murmuring sound well adapted to lull the Insects to repose — then is the moment come for the humming bird to secure them, its long delicate bill enters the Calix and the protruding Inititive double tubed tongue, imbued with its glutinous Saliva touches one after another each insect, and draws them from their lurking places into its mouth to be immediately destroyed. — the whole of this is accomplished in one Instant and the bird as it leaves the flower, sips such a slight portion of its liquid honey that the theft is probably considered with grateful Initation by the flower thus kindly relieved from the attacks of her destroyers.

The Prairies, the fields, the orchard & Gardens, nay the deepest Shades of the forests are all visited in their turn and every were the little bird meets with pleasure and food — the gorgeous throat defies all competion in beauty & Brilliancy, now it glows with a fiery hue & again it is changed to the deepest velvety Jett — the upper parts of its delicate body are resplendent changing green, and it throws itself through the air with a swiftness & vivacity beyond all power to describe — it moves from one flower to another like a gleam of light, either upwards, to the right or to the left again downwards — and in this manner reaches the furthermost northern portions of our Country following with extreme precaution the advancement of the

the ethereal motions of its pinions, so rapid and so light, appear to fan and cool the flower, without injuring its fragile texture, and produce a delightful murmuring sound, well adapted for lulling the insects to repose. Then is the moment for the Humming-bird to secure them. Its long delicate bill enters the cup of the flower, and the protruded double-tubed tongue, delicately sensible, and imbued with a glutinous saliva, touches each insect in succession, and draws it from its lurking place, to be instantly swallowed. All this is done in a moment, and the bird, as it leaves the flower, sips so small a portion of its liquid honey, that the theft, we may suppose, is looked upon with a grateful feeling by the flower, which is thus kindly relieved from the attacks of her destroyers.

The prairies, the fields, the orchards and gardens, nay, the deepest shades of the forests, are all visited in their turn, and everywhere the little bird meets with pleasure and with food. Its gorgeous throat in beauty and brilliancy baffles all competition. Now it glows with a fiery hue, and again it is changed to the deepest velvety black. The upper parts of its delicate body are of resplendent green; and it throws itself through the air with a swiftness and vivacity hardly conceivable. It moves from one flower to another like a gleam of light, upwards, downwards, to the right, and to the left. In this manner, it searches the extreme northern portions of our country, following with great precaution the advances of the season, and retreats with season, retrograding at the appearance of autumn with equal care.

I wish it was within my power at this Instant to impart to you Kind Reader the pleasures I have felt whilst watching the movements; — the feelings exhibited by a single pair of these most favourite little creatures when engaged at participating the emotions of their love to each other.

equal care at the approach of autumn.

I wish it were in my power at this moment to impart to you, kind reader, the pleasures which I have felt whilst watching the movements, and viewing the manifestation of feeling displayed by a single pair of these most favorite little creatures, when engaged in the demonstration of their love to each other:

That a love of nature permeated Audubon's whole being is proved again and again in his unedited writings. In his journals, diaries, and letters a host of whimsical similies and metaphors are to be found, in every instance flavored by his association with creatures of the wild.

For example, he writes of finding the Earl of Morton "weaker than a newly hatched partridge." Another time, when cooped in his room in England by rain, he describes himself "as dull as a Martin surprised by the weather." Once when he rushed to an Englishman's home for dinner *en famille* only to find he was a day earlier than expected, he confessed to his diary he was "as ashamed of his blunder as a fox who had lost his tail in a trap." A sudden arising in the morning is described as "leaping from my bed as a hare from its form." In London, when he had been forced to purchase and wear a new and stylish black suit, he speaks of walking to J. G. Children's house "attired like a mournful Raven," and when his affairs were at a standstill in England's metropolis he declared he was "as dull as a beetle." He noted that the Earl of Kinnoul had a "face like the caricature of an owl." At Oxford, he and Doctor Kidd "ran after each other like Red-headed Woodpeckers in the spring," and he declared he was "panting like a winged pheasant" while showing his drawings to visitors in Liverpool. The students at Cambridge when he dined with them left the tables "as vultures leave a carcase."

On another occasion, when he was invited to a fashionable party, he says he was so ill at ease that he "stood motionless as a heron." In the home of a titled Englishman, the servants "moved as quietly as Killdeers." He recalled that the daughter of Baron Couvier, who was not attired to receive company, flew off at the entrance of a companion and himself "like a dove before falcons." He described fellow passengers on a cart in New York "perched about us as I have seen chimney swallows perched on a roof before their morning flight." When he visited Doctor Brewster in Edinburgh he recorded that the boy who answered the door stood "looking at my hair like an ass at a fine thistle." Many times he wrote that he had been "busy as a bee" writing letters. Once when he went to a meeting of the Wernerian Society he found the room was "as full as an egg."

4

The second volume of the *Ornithological Biography* met the same enthusiastic welcome the first had received, and one periodical in reviewing it stated that Audubon "has told what he has seen and undergone, not perhaps in the smooth nicely balanced periods of a drawing-room writer . . . but with the unstudied freedom, rising at times to eloquence, nor has been ashamed to utter the thousand affectionate and benevolent feelings which a close and enthusiastic communion with nature must nourish. The work is full of the man."

From the first of the year 1835 until springtime Audubon was busy with his material for the third volume and went to London to supervise the work Havell was doing on the new plates. He busied himself at his self-appointed tasks with unremitting vigor.

"Immediately on my arrival in London I set to writing, and finished in one month, one 4th. of the Biographies of my 3d. vol," he wrote to John Bachman. "This rendering me puffy, I could scarce breathe—my appetite was gone—my digestion bad—in other words I was attacked by Dyspepsia as bad as ever. Then I thought of a change of work—for in a change of labour the body and the mind undergo sure and certain relief. I took to Drawing! and what do you think—I have positively finished 33 drawings of American birds in England. This has enabled me to swell my 3d. vol. of Illustrations with 57 species not given by Willson and therefore forestalling my friend Charles Bonaparte."

At this time Charles Waterton was still hurling printed jibes at Audubon, and soon after Audubon's return to Edinburgh to again plunge into the task of writing bird biographies, he writes the Charleston clergyman regarding the attacks of the English naturalist. "As to the rage of Mr. Waterton, or the lucubrations of Mr. Neal, who by the bye is a subscriber to the Birds of America (bona fide), I really care not a fig —all such stuffs will soon evaporate, being mere smoke from a Dung Hill."

This reference to "Yankee Neal" appears to be the only attention Audubon ever paid to the Boston editor's bitter attack in *The New England Galaxy*.

5

Hard and unceasing labor enabled Audubon, with MacGillivray's assistance, to produce his third volume of letterpress, and by the end of 1836 Havell had engraved 350 plates, this left only a half a hundred of the projected 400 to be cut and bitten into the copper. To secure models for drawings of birds so necessary to fittingly conclude the ambitious undertaking, Audubon decided he must again return to America and make his long-contemplated expedition to the Gulf of Mexico, to the Rocky Mountains, to the Far West —to go, if necessary, to the Pacific Coast.

Taking his son John with him, leaving his wife and Victor in London to oversee the production of the remaining plates, Audubon again set forth across the Atlantic.

CHAPTER 29

To Louisiana for the Last Time

AUDUBON and his son proceeded immediately to Philadelphia, where they were welcomed by Doctor Harlan and several other old-time friends. The important news in ornithological circles at that time was that regarding the results of an expedition made to the Rocky Mountains and the far West by Dr. Thomas Nuttall and Dr. John Kirk Townsend. They brought back a rare collection of bird skins that had been deposited in the Philadelphia museum.

Audubon was tremendously excited. He said the lot of skins contained "about forty new species of birds, and its value cannot be described." He admitted he had "a great treat looking over and handling the rare collection," and at once wrote Edward Harris urging him to join in inspecting it at the Academy of Natural Sciences. Harris came at once and immediately offered to give Audubon five hundred dollars toward purchasing the collection. "Is not this a noble generosity to show for the love of science?" Audubon demanded of his journal.

The negotiations were not immediately brought to a head and the rare Western birds remained in the museum while Audubon went to Boston to round-up subscribers. He visited a number of naturalists, including Thomas Brewer, then a young man just developing his ornithological tastes. He met Thomas Nuttall and heard from that botanist, who never carried a gun when on an expedition, a first-hand recital of his adventures and travels to the far West with Townsend. Nuttall promised the artist duplicates of all the new birds brought back, and agreed to urge Townsend and the Philadelphia academy to allow Audubon to portray all the new species in his forthcoming plates.

This much accomplished, Audubon went to Salem to secure

subscribers, for he was at this time going about in his rôle of salesman for his own work. When he arrived at the ancient Massachusetts town he called on many of the "blue-bloods," as he termed the elite, and his account of one visit is interesting:

> I called alone on a Miss Sitsby, a beautiful "blue," seven or eight seasons beyond her teens, and very wealthy. *Blues* do not knit socks, or put on buttons when needed; they may do for the parlour, but not for the kitchen. Although she had the eyes of a gazelle, and capital teeth, I soon discovered she would be of no help to me; when I mentioned subscriptions, it seemed to fall on her ears, not with the cadence of the Wood Thrush or Mocking Bird does on mine, but as a shower-bath in cold January. Ornithology seemed to be a thing for which she had no taste; she said, however, "I will suggest your wish to my father, sir, and give you an answer tomorrow morning." . . . At last I bowed, she curtsied, and so the interview ended.

Returning to Boston, Audubon met Daniel Webster who, so Audubon recounts, "subscribed to my great work" (the God-like Daniel later fell behind in his payments); obtained a few more subscribers, and delivered finished plates to a number of patrons. When he returned to New York he called on Washington Irving, discussed birds with William Cooper and visited Henry Inman, who had painted Audubon's portrait in 1833 and found the portrait painter putting finishing touches to one of Mrs. Audubon. That night Audubon wrote Lucy, "Saw the sketch intended for thee, but found it not at all like thy dear self."

While in New York Audubon received a letter from John Bachman advising him to give up any plans he had formulated for visiting the Floridian peninsula because of the outbreak of the Seminole War. "Your Indian friends, the cut-throats, have scalped almost every woman and child south of St. Augustine, save those on Key West," wrote the clergyman, who added that, while the Indians' ardor would be subdued by the troops during the winter, nothing could be done there by naturalists for at least two years, and that many small predatory bands would remain "that will make no bones of scalping an Ornithologist *secundum artem*." Doctor Bachman suggested a trip along the gulf coast to Texas as an alternative.

Whereupon Audubon completed arrangements with Edward Harris to accompany him and John the following spring on a trip to New Orleans, where a revenue cutter would take the three along the Louisiana gulf coast to the new Republic of Texas, so that certain needed birds could be collected, their habits studied, the northward migration from South America watched, and portraits drawn as a magnificent finale to the great work.

Bachman insisted that Audubon and his son spend the winter at Charleston, an invitation that was instantly accepted, but before they set off to the South Edward Harris generously purchased a number of the duplicate skins taken by the Townsend-Nuttall expedition. Elated at this stroke of good fortune, Audubon dashed off an enthusiastic note to John Bachman:

"Now Good Friend open your eyes! aye open them tight!! Nay place specks on your probosis if you chuse! Read aloud!! quite aloud!!!—I have purchased *Ninety Three Bird Skins!* Yes 93 Bird Skins!—Well what are they? Why nought less than 93 Bird Skins sent from the Rocky Mountains and the Columbia River by Nuttall & Townsend! Cheap as Dirst too—only one hundred and Eighty Four Dollars for the whole of these, and hang me if you do not echo my sayings *when you see them!!*—Such beauties such rarities! Such Novelties! Ah my Worthy Friend how we will laugh and talk over them!"

But this was not all the delighted Audubon penned his clergical crony. "Have counted the points of exclamation? no, very well.—good then.—Titian Peale has given me a New Rallus and six young ones to draw, caught about 30 miles below this, last summer, and plenty more! *Wam* Cooper of New York has positively given me some very rare Bird Skins.—Friend Harris, a great number of *Do Do*—So you see or do you not see how lucky the 'Old Man' is *yet!* and why all this Luck?—Simply because I have laboured like a cart Horse for the thirty years on a Single Work, have been successful almost to a miracle in its publication thus far, and now am thought a—a—a—(I dislike to write it, but no matter here goes) *a Great Naturalist!!!*—That's all! oh! what a strange World we do live in, and how grateful to our God must we be, when after years of trouble, anxiety &

AUDUBON AT 56

From the engraving by Alonzo Chappel who founded his likeness upon the oil portrait John Woodhouse Audubon painted of his father in 1841.

AUDUBON AT 58

A portrait in oils by John Woodhouse Audubon who pictured his father as he appeared upon his return from the expedition in 1843 to The Mountains of the Winds.

sorrow, we find ourselves Happy because true to him! him without whose assistance, and ever parental care, we poor things never could be called Worthy the notice of even our own Race!"

Remaining ten days longer so that a few drawings Havell needed in London might be finished, Audubon and John hurried on to Charleston, after traveling for six days on what the naturalist described as "the most extraordinary railroad in the world." The father and the son were both impatient on this trip southward—the father eager to begin drawing pictures of the specimens just secured from Doctors Nuttall and Townsend, the son eager to hold in his arms his beautiful betrothed, Maria Rebecca Bachman, eldest of the clergyman's nine children.

Both found their loves. Audubon *père* put in the winter months drawing the birds, and was assisted by Miss Maria Martin, Doctor Bachman's sister-in-law, who afterwards became the clergyman's second wife. Miss Martin was an accomplished botanist and most of the floral decorations on Audubon's drawings of this period were from her brush. Her assistance in this respect was considerable, but not as extensive as was Joseph Mason's contribution, nor that of George Lehman.

2

The winter passed, and early in 1837 Audubon was joined by Edward Harris and plans were laid for the overland journey to New Orleans and the exploration of the long and deeply indented Louisiana coast line to the infant Republic of Texas. A few days were spent in shooting, Harris being given his first deer hunt and the opportunity to make his first kill—after which the customary honors were shown him. His face was well daubed with the blood of the buck and its tail stuck in his cap. It was the seventeenth of February when Audubon, Harris, and John bade farewell to the hospitable Charleston folk.

Although the Seminole War in Florida was said to have ended, it was found impossible to secure a government vessel to take the party by water along the east coast and thence into the Gulf of Mexico, so the overland journey was decided upon. Their way led through Georgia and Alabama and the roads, Audubon's letters recount, were bad and he was severely "jostled," he wrote back to Bachman. It rained almost incessantly. At Montgomery the mail coaches were abandoned for a steamboat which carried them down the Alabama river to Mobile.

A hasty visit was made to Pensacola in an endeavor to secure a government cutter, but the best Audubon could do was to obtain some snuff from the commandant. "Copenhagen *Snuff*," he wrote John Bachman, for if the truth must be known the naturalist had seduced the clergyman into its use, "that would make your nostrils expand with pleasure, and draw tears from your eyes—the stuff is so potent!"

Audubon returned to Mobile, leaving Harris at Pensacola to continue a hunt for a bird called by the natives a *Gris*, which Audubon suspected was the brownish ibis he had shot but could not retrieve in a Florida morass several years before. The two Audubons went to New Orleans on a steam vessel which made the journey from Mobile via the Sound, Lake Borgne, and Bayou St. John.

3

When John James Audubon reached New Orleans—the same city he had entered a down-hearted stranger sixteen years previously; where he had nearly starved while formulating the plans for picturing the birds that afterwards gained for him imperishable fame; where he had received rebuffs and snubs from high and low; where he had plumbed the depths of misery—he was received with extravagant acclaim.

He had arrived! He was now Mr. Audubon, the distinguished *savant*, naturalist, and scientist. Men now bowed to him when they passed this prosperous-looking individual on the narrow *banquettes* of old New Orleans. No one called him a *greenhorn* or snickered at the long locks that still curled on his broad shoulders.

Audubon was delighted to find some of his old-time friends, although, as he wrote his wife, "we have lost by death the greater portion of our numerous former acquaintances here."

Especially glad was he to hold in his arms Charles Alexandre LeSueur, his "good LeSueur," the same Frenchman who had been kind to him in Philadelphia twelve years before, when Audubon needed friends in that cold city of Brotherly Love. Delight was heaped on delight when he learned from the chief revenue officer that Napoleon L. Costé, the able pilot of the *Marion*, was now a lieutenant in command of the cutter *Campbell*, which was to be placed at his disposal for the cruise along the Louisiana gulf coast.

From his lodgings with James Grimshaw, who had married Mary Julia, a daughter of Nicholas Berthoud, he sallied forth to meet the notables of the town. He dined at the Royal street home of André Bienvenu Roman, former governor of the state who, while chief executive, had subscribed for *The Birds of America* for the State of Louisiana. Governor Roman saw to it that the local papers were properly informed of the distinguished naturalist's arrival. Said the *Courier*, on the English page of its issue of Saturday, March 11th:

AUDUBON THE ORNITHOLOGIST — It is with much pleasure we announce the arrival of this gentleman among us. He leaves here shortly in one of the cutters which our government has generously placed at his disposal, to examine all the coast and inlets of our state as far as the Sabine, to procure new specimens of birds &c, to add to those which he has already procured in the United States.

We regret that Mr. A's short stay precludes our citizens the pleasure of offering him a testimonial of their regard at the present time, while it gives us much pleasure to state that it is his intention to return amongst us in about two months, when our citizens will be afforded an opportunity to tendering that tribute of esteem which his talents and exertions in science eminently entitle him to.

This newspaper notice greatly pleased Audubon. We find him writing John Bachman the details of his arrival in New Orleans, his reception by different citizens, and something of his plans for the collecting trip along the coast:

"I am glad, and proud Too; that I have at last been Acknowledged by the public prints as a Native Citizen of Louisiana—and had it been supposed when we first arrived here that our stay would have been half as long as it has been —I really think that my Country men would have honoured us with a Public *Dinner!* Try and find out the Paragraphs in the New Orleans Courier (French & English) of the beginning of this month."

In writing his wife a few days later he tells of dining with Governor Roman, where a large company met him, and adds, "He is a fine man, and has written a few kind things in the Papers here—My '*Natal City!*' "

Which again brings us to the puzzling enigma of John James Audubon's birth.

His statement to Bachman was that the public prints acknowledged him a "Native Citizen of Louisiana." But what did he mean by underscoring and adding the exclamation point to "My Natal City!" when writing his wife?

A careful perusal of the age-worn *Courier* of that day shows that the abbreviated reading notice of his arrival on the page printed in English was duplicated on the page given over to the same news in the French language, save there was added to this latter item an extract from Baron Cuvier's review of Audubon's plates of *Birds*. This addition was headed:

EXTRAIT D'UN RAPPORT FAIT A L'ACADEMIE ROYALE
DE SCIENCES DE PARIS, PAR LE BARON CUVIER

and the second paragraph of this report merely repeated what Cuvier had stated in Paris regarding the author of the "most magnificent monument that art has ever erected to science":

L'auteur, né à la Louisiane, et qui s'est adonné dès sa jeunesse à le peinteur, est venu, il y vingt cinq ans, se perfectionner dans son art l'ecole de David.[1]

A rather extraordinary "acknowledgement" that the artist was a native of the state of Louisiana! These newspaper notices, and the extracts from Audubon's letters add just a little more mystery to the vexing enigma of his birth. Why the cryptic "My *Natal City!*" in his letter to his wife? It would appear she knew what he meant—even if we do not.

4

On the twenty-fourth of March, the *Campbell* dropped

[1] "The author, born in Louisiana, and devoted from his youth to painting, was twenty-five years ago a pupil in the school of David."

down the river, but it had not proceeded far before it was anchored on the western side of the Mississippi. The boat, in spite of the fact the crew numbered sixteen, was short-handed so Commander Costé and his first officer returned to New Orleans to find five more sailors to complete the crew. During this enforced wait John went into the nearby cypress swamp to outline cypress trees with the *camera lucida*. Edward Harris was taken on an alligator hunt down a bayou, where twenty of the saurians were slaughtered and observations made on a few birds. Harris was standing the trip admirably, wrote Audubon to Bachman. "He is in facto one of the finest Men of Gods Creation—I wish he were my Brother."

The alligator hunt was most successful. "We killed about 20 of these beautiful creatures, and brought only 7 on board. —Harris Killed several. he had never seen any before.—he likes their flesh, too, but not so Johnny, excepting the latter our *Mess* made a grand Dinner of the 'Tail end' of one, and after all, alligators flesh is far from being bad." In addition to this news Audubon informed Bachman as to conditions on the boat. "There is no Grog on board the Campbell!! What do you say to that?—Snuff is yet partially afloat—but will be dropped astern very soon!"

The want of sailors was at last filled. Costé, by raising the wages to forty dollars, procured some stout fellows for the journey and on March twenty-ninth the *Campbell* was sailing down the Mississippi bound for the mouths leading out into the gulf. The head of the passes was reached on the first of April, and the three naturalists were soon out in the marshlands with their guns and the collecting trip was in full blast.

The chattering red-winged blackbirds were seen in countless thousands, and from every bending cattail the epauletted males were singing their gleeful springtime *kong-gar-ree*, for the nesting season was on. Noisy glossy boat-tailed grackles fluttered about the extensive stretches of the three-cornered grasses. Sprightly, pugnacious kingbirds, lately arrived from the South after a journey over the wide stretch of the Mexic gulf, were busy building nests in the black mangroves. In spite of the lateness of the season, all the ducks had not returned to the North in answer to the call to reproduce their kind, for from the deck of the *Campbell* were to be seen the scurrying forms of gadwalls, blue- and green-winged teals, canvasbacks, and the Louisiana summer mallard, which Audubon believed to be the so-called black duck of the New England states and eastern Canada.

A showy spoonbill duck came within range of the guns—down it went *plop* into the water of a shallow lagoon. Edward Harris recorded a Harlequin duck, never observed in Louisiana since. Tiny busy sanderlings hurried up and down the sandy beaches of the gulf. The *pill-will-willet* of the frantic nesting willets rang shrilly in their ears. The little spotted sandpiper, tipping its tail and bowing politely as it trotted in front of them, thus indicated how it had gained its local name of *Chevalier de batture.* Audubon and his companions also found the "Tell-tale Tattler," as they then knew the greater yellowlegs, most abundant. Flocks of red-breasted snipe or knots were arriving on the hospitable Louisiana shores from their night flight over the gulf, and one of these travelers stopped a load of shot.

Clapper rails filled the marshlands with their weird cachinnation until the grasses seemed to vibrate with the laughter. A great squadron of white pelicans was soaring high in the blue sky above the passes where the mighty Mississippi empties into the green-blue of the gulf salt waters. A marsh hawk was seen to suddenly dive at a nest, seize a long-billed marsh wren in its talons and fly off with its catch—and the nest, too! the first act of this kind that Audubon had ever seen a hawk of this species perform.

Ah, here was a bird paradise indeed. For two days the low-lying territory was explored. Sea birds were also in abundance. Laughing gulls, black skimmers, brown pelicans and terns of many species. The marsh terns, as Audubon designated the gull-billed terns, were particularly beautiful. They were feeding on insects and evidently paired. Three were brought down and one selected as a model for his drawing showing a tern pursuing an insect in the air which was reproduced in his collection.

It was the third of April before the revenue cutter *Crusader*, commanded by W. B. G. Taylor, joined the *Campbell.* It proved to be a light draft boat provided with seines, cast-nets, fishing tackle, and other paraphernalia. The following day the two vessels sailed through Grand Pass and into Barataria Bay, anchoring off the island of Grande Terre. A variety of birds, mostly water birds, were seen including flocks of white pelicans, and pursuit was immediately given by Audubon for he was anxious to procure specimens for the purpose of studying their anatomical structure.

While the cutters remained in Barataria Bay the members of the expedition were the guests of M. Andry, a sugar planter, who was raising cane on the long sandy island, once the rendezvous of the famous pirate Jean Laffite. For six days the naturalists combed the region for birds, collecting various species of ducks, plovers, sanderlings, turnstones, herons, and egrets of many species, curlews, including the Esquimau curlew. Willets, snipe, sandpipers, and rails were very abundant, and the hunters saw great flocks of gulls, terns, and skimmers, as well as thousands of brown pelicans. The spring migration was on, and from the south, over the wide reach of the gulf, hosts of land birds were on their way from the wintering homes below the equator to their breeding grounds in the North. Consequently there was good hunting for the questing naturalists and their guns were kept hot.

When he went ashore on "Cayou" island Audubon found an Arkansas flycatcher lying in the doorway of a deserted hut, and apparently having just died after an exhausting flight over the gulf waters. He was delighted with the find, for it was the first time he had laid hands on one and it enabled him to take measurements of a species he had not previously described. The low sandy island was alive with feathered visitors, most of them shorebirds and land bird migrants, and

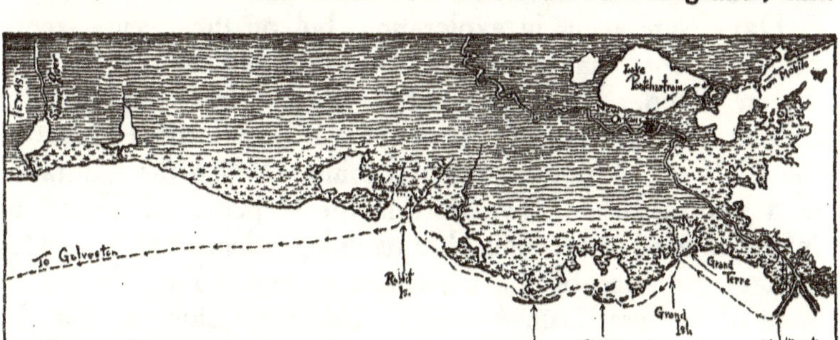

ROUTE OF AUDUBON'S FINAL TRIP TO LOUISIANA, ALONG THE GULF OF MEXICO, 1837.

Edward Harris' tabulation shows that one hundred and four different species of birds were collected during the three days given over to shooting.

At *Isle Dernier*, the celebrated "Last Isle" of Lafcadio Hearn's famous story of *Chita*, the bird collectors were again busy with their weapons and one hundred and twenty-five different species were found among the tremendous numbers of birds brought down. Napoleon Costé shot three American avocets out of a flock he discovered on the shore, and as a wisp of fifteen oyster-catchers swept compactly by uttering their *weep weep*, Audubon fired into the flock, bringing down two.

Birds were still plentiful when the expedition reached Atchafalaya Bay. The boats circled Rabbit Island, which the party visited, and Audubon naively concluded it was so named "because there were no rabbits on it!" The *Campbell* was anchored in deep water and the lighter-draft *Crusader* sailed into the shallow water of Vermilion Bay and approached the white cliffs of Côte Blanche. South of the cutter was a great marshy island which in later years became famous as the wild life sanctuary established by Mrs. Russell Sage for the migratory wild waterfowl of the United States and Canada, and now known to conservationists the world over as Marsh Island.

The *Crusader* made for the mouth of Bayou Salé and Audubon went ashore and visited Major Michael Gordy, who was raising sugar cane on the highlands. They spent several days in profitable shooting, Edward Harris recording that ninety-seven different kinds of birds were secured.

Days were spent in exploration, but on the twenty-second of April Costé hauled in his mud hook and set sail for Galveston island. When the cutters passed the mouth of the Sabine river the westerly limits of the then United States on the Gulf of Mexico were left behind. When the naturalists next stepped ashore they were in the Republic of Texas, an infant nation just recognized in its independence by the United States and three of the European nations. The Texans, in spite of General Sam Houston's brilliant victory at San Jacinto, were still being warred upon by the Mexicans and the trip to the new nation was considered in the light of a hazardous undertaking. As they were aboard a government vessel there was little apprehension as to what might happen should a Mexican gunboat descend on the bird hunters. As Audubon wrote Bachman, "We Intend Visiting the whole of Galveston Bay, and Islets thereabouts, in spite of the Mexican's *Flotilla* which after all 'I think is all 'My Eye!' "

Galveston island was combed for birds; many were secured and skinned, many others were pickled in rum, and even a deer hunt was enjoyed by the party. Officials of the infant nation were guests aboard the two vessels, and much new information on natural history was gained. In the middle of May, Audubon and Harris visited Houston, then the capital of Texas, and paid their respects to President Sam Houston. The naturalist has left a most interesting pen picture of *The Raven* in his journal, which was reproduced in Buchanan's biography and reprinted in various other life histories of Audubon.

It was the eighteenth of May when the *Campbell* headed back for the mouths of the Mississippi, and nine days later the cutter was tied up at New Orleans. The next night the bird men were dined by Governor Roman and his family and pressed to detail their adventures along the Louisiana coast. The proposed public dinner was not tendered the distinguished naturalist as the banks were closing one after another, and things financially were standing on end. After packing his collections and leaving the dog *Dash*, that had proved invaluable in retrieving birds on the trip, with William Bakewell Berthoud, Nicholas Berthoud's son, John James Audubon left Louisiana forever.

His son accompanied him when on the last day of May Audubon took the lake steamer *Swan* for Mobile to retrace the route he had journeyed in the spring. Edward Harris remained in New Orleans a few days arranging for the forwarding of the ornithological prizes to his New Jersey home.

Audubon was delighted with the results of what proved to be his last adventure in the state he loved the best, to judge by what he wrote Thomas M., Brewer of Boston:

"The weather during the principal portion of our absence was unusually cold, even for this season, and this gave us, perhaps, the very best opportunities ever afforded any student of nature to observe the *inward* migration of myriads of birds that visit us from the south and west when the imperative laws of nature force them from their winter retreats towards other countries to multiply. We found not one new species, but the mass of observations that we have gathered connected with the ornithology of our country, has, I think, never been surpassed."

5

When the last of June was marked off the calendar, John Woodhouse Audubon and Maria Rebecca Bachman bound the two families by closer ties by being united in matrimony. After the ceremony the couple went to Niagara Falls for the honeymoon, while Audubon spent a few days at Edward Harris' Moorestown farm.

Back in New York, Audubon had a business understanding with Nicholas Berthoud. Time had not proved kind to the brother-in-law who had rather lorded it over the impecunious fellow who spent all his time running after birds. The wheel of fortune had turned the wrong way, as far as Berthoud was concerned, and he was forced to desert Louisville. He applied to the "green horn" for assistance, suggesting that he could handle the affairs of publication in America while Audubon busied himself abroad. The upshot of the meeting was that Audubon, not mentioning the past, employed Berthoud as his American agent and prepared for a return to England satisfied that his affairs would be in capable hands.

"I have settled my accounts with my Brother in Law Berthoud in full to the present day; and we will go on as usual as he is willing to be my agent here," Audubon wrote Bachman. "N. Berthoud calls me one of the Happiest of Men —Free of debts, and having *available funds* and *Talents!*"

On the seventeenth of July Audubon with his son and daughter-in-law sailed on the packet *England* for Liverpool, and early in August the Audubons were reunited—the family augmented by the acquisition of a daughter to whom they became devotedly attached.

CHAPTER 30

The Great Work Completed

BACK in London Audubon at once plunged into the work of preparing material for the remaining volumes of the *Ornithological Biography*, turning over the sheets he had written to the diligent MacGillivray for needed revision. These out of the way, the bird biographer gave attention to touching up a number of his bird drawings so that Havell would be kept well supplied with material for the engravings.

When he was not drawing, writing life histories of his birds, or scouring England and Scotland for new subscribers, he was writing colorful letters to Edward Harris or John Bachman, begging these two staunch friends to pickle in rum all the birds they could shoot, and ship them on to London. In his letters to Bachman, written with all the pot-hooks and flourishes he was capable of making, Audubon gave many interesting sidelights on scientific personages in the British metropolis.

His one favorite topic of correspondence was none other than Prince Bonaparte. In a letter to the Charleston clergyman, Audubon said of the titled ornithologist:

> Charles Bonaparte came to London about 2 Weeks ago, and has spent 2 hours with us . . . he says that he will go on with the continuation of Willson's Work ? ? he is now publishing the Birds of Mexico. — he opened his eyes when he saw all *our* new species and complimented me highly on my *Industry* and *perseverance;* Where he will procure specimens, and *Matter* to go on with his Work on the birds of our country, you will easily guess! He is a most aimiable good Man, and I know you would enjoy his society much — He kissed me as if a Brother, and I really believe he is My Friend.

A few days later another letter to Doctor Bachman had a very different characterization of Prince Bonaparte. A portion of this communication reads:

Charles Bonaparte returned to London a few days ago, and came to see me after I had gone to bed; but there he came, sat by my side and talked of birds upwards of one hour, the consequences of which were that I scarcely closed my eyes afterwards that night. The next morning he called again, when Victor and I went off with him in search of private lodgings as he does not wish to be known that he is in London except by Naturalists, and because he dislikes the Humbug of the Nobles that are ever and anon at his Father in law, Joseph Bonaparte. He therefore is now in humble street. he came the third time to us for the purpose of shaving dressing &c and lastly that day whilst we were all at Dinner . . . The next morning I went with him to hire a Cabriolet and horse — he is almost constantly with Gould, at the Zoological Museum and Indeed every where, where there are bird Skins. Me thinks he is over anxious to *pump me*, but I am now no longer a green horn, and will not Write such accounts for him as I did when I sent him all the Habits of the Wild Turkey from Bayou Sarah to New York, for which *he* received all credit, and I scarcely any. I cannot well Imagine why he should continue Wilson's Ornithology after my Work is finished, unless it is Merely to arrange our Fauna in Squares, Circles, or Triangles, in the manner of Swainson and all other crazed naturalists of the closet — but we shall see.

Two months later Audubon is again writing his Charleston crony on their favorite topic. It appears although Bonaparte had promised to let Audubon print something regarding four or five new species the prince had secured from the Mackenzie River region (or "Russian America," as Audubon noted), the bird artist was not satisfied with the actions of the titled fellow-naturalist, and complained to Bachman:

I feel disposed to give you now my real view of the character of Charley! When he first came to London, he began by going the rounds, trying to pump each, and every one, of those men from whom he thought he might acquire Knowledge, and of Course as far as the Birds of North America are concerned, I was the very first on his list. Days after Days he has visited us, pumped me as far as I was willing to be, Made list of all our new species, examined each bird in the Skin, coresponded with his systematical arrangements, after asking me thousands of questions, and after all is still desirous that I should give him my Ideas or in fact Knowledge of their Habitats, Migrations &c! quite trifles you see; but in this, I will stop his carreer, and will tell him bluntly and honestly; when we come to the Scratch, and that as to acquiring the all of this from me (before being printed and before the World) he is mistaken as if he "had torn his shirt"! The beauty of his manouvers is that whilst doing all this for his own fame and benefit, he pretends that he is acting for my sake! Capital is it not? When I am as confident that he *positively speaking* Knows very little indeed of our Birds! Otherwise he is a mild, pleasant speaking personage, not at all of the Prince about him while with us at least, but so very fond of praise, that I doubt his sincerety, (I am sorry to say this) as it has become rather too clear to me, that he never possessed one half of the creadit which I have been wont heretofore to grant to him, blinded as I have been by the apparent friendly manners which he never ceases to assume . . .I now greatly regret my not having paid more attention to the strong language of Harlan respecting Charley, for if I had been more prudently guarded, he would at this moment Know still less than he does.

Just before the close of the year Audubon wrote Bachman that, much to his relief, Bonaparte had left London. But by the middle of April he was crying down all sorts of maledictions on the titled ornithologist's head, and writing Doctor Bachman that Prince Bonaparte "has treated me most shockingly—he has published the whole of our Secrets, which I foolishly communicated to him after his giving me his word of honour that he would not do so, and now I have *cut him*, and he will never have from me the remaining unpublished Number of My Work—(which by the bye he calls a poor thing) and the latter simply because I at last refused to give him my Knowledge of the Migratory or Geographical distribution of our Birds—So much for a Prince!"

Some months later Audubon congratulated Bachman by letter for "rising the bile of Mons. Bonap. What a dirty mean fellow he proved himself to be at Last!" Thus he dismisses the subject of Charles Lucien Jules Laurent Bonaparte, prince of Canino and Musigano.

2

In the summer of 1838 it became evident to the inmates of No. 4 Wimpole Street, Cavendish Square, that there was to be a new member in the Audubon family. All were delighted, none more than The American Woodsman. When he wrote the gladsome tidings to John Bachman that he too was soon to be a grandfather, he added to the missive which carried the information that Maria was shortly to enter on the sacred duties of motherhood: "Indeed My Dear Bachman, it may be possible that ere this reaches you, both of us will be Grand Fathers! Nay, Dr. Phillips thinks that the *chance* may be double, and if so how blessed I will feel to have a pair of them borned Audubons."

In the same letter, which is under the date of April 14, 1838, Audubon informs Bachman that he has just received a letter from Doctor Wilson, a mutual Charleston friend, which was "full of fun and just what was wanted to raise the spirits of a Hypocondrical of 53 Years of Age, and Thank God yet able to put his fore finger and thumb up to his nose holding withal a pinch of the 'American Gentleman.' (Snuff! Snuff!!)."

Why then all the mystery in the Audubon family, and from The American Woodsman himself, about his age, the date of his birth? If in April of 1838 he knew he was fifty-three years old, he likewise knew he was born in the year 1785, as can easily be demonstrated by simple subtraction. It will be remembered, too, that Jean Rabin, *créole de Saint-Domingue*, was born at Aux Cayes, April 26, 1785. Nor should the fact that Louis Charles, the Dauphin of France, was born at Versailles March 27, 1785, be ignored.

3

The fall of 1838 found Audubon in Edinburgh supervising the printing of the fourth volume of his letterpress and madly scratching away with a spluttering iron pen on the material for the fifth and concluding volume, which he planned to complete by the following March. So he and his ever valuable Scot kept at the pages which were soon whipped into shape for the typesetters. Mrs. Audubon, in spite of her poor health at the time, was, as always, an able assistant, although Audubon complained that his "good old Girl buys paper sadly too small in every way—it forces me to cramp my naturally beautifull hand Write, and more, force me to conclude a letter ere it is half finished."

So the great work which had been in process of production for twelve years was at last being completed. It proved "a triumph of human endeavor and of the spirit and will of man," as Professor Herrick has so properly evaluated *The Birds of America* and the *Ornithological Biography*.

May and June of 1839 found Audubon, MacGillivray, and Havell busy winding up their labors. Audubon finished his part of the writing for the fifth and concluding volume of the bird biographies and spent the better part of a month in outlining what he named *A Synopsis of the Birds of America*, which was a methodical presentation of the birds he had already described in the *Biography* and pictured in the mammoth plates. The *Synopsis* was a highly technical work in which, as was properly acknowledged, MacGillivray was the technician. The birds were presented in a scientific order, and not in the helter-skelter way Audubon had issued his plates. Its pages carried special references to the species pictured in the double-elephant plates and the five volumes of bird biographies, and in proper grouping the birds were collected in their orders, families, and genera, recognizing 491 species of birds inhabiting the artist's beloved America.

Audubon had actually accomplished his long-cherished "impossible" dream.

4

There was no tearing at heartstrings when the Audubon family pulled up stakes in Cavendish Square and set sail for America. From the deck of the packet, surrounded by his beloved Lucy, his two sons, a daughter-in-law, and a tiny Lucy Audubon, The American Woodsman waved his last farewell to England, the land of his success and triumphs.

The naturalist was followed across the Atlantic by Robert Havell and his family, for the engraver who had also won imperishable fame by his masterly reproductions of Audubon's original bird drawings had decided to abandon the land of his birth for a future in the New World. He had been lured to America by Audubon's glowing descriptions of American scenery, of the rush and grandeur of the mighty Niagara, of the magnolia woods of the South, and the great mountain ranges of the West.

Havell eventually settled on an estate on the Hudson river near Ossining where he found the Hudson as great an inspiration as the Thames or the Wye, and made many splendid pictures of the stream that flowed past his new home. Twenty-seven years after Audubon passed on, Robert Havell died at the age of eighty-five, and like the artist whose bird paintings he preserved for posterity on copper he was buried beside the same beautiful, quiet flowing Hudson.

5

Settled in New York town, there was no idleness for Audubon nor his two sons. Quarters were rented at 86 White street, where a second grandchild, Harriet Bachman Audubon, was born. In the midst of rejoicing over this event plans were laid for an American publication of the *Birds* but in a smaller format. With an energy quite resembling that of twelve years before, Audubon set to work on this reissuance of his original publication. It was to be a complete revision, he had decided, with the birds grouped and presented in scientific order instead of a haphazard parade. There would be seven volumes printed, carrying the general title of *Birds of America*, and this decision called for much preliminary work. John Woodhouse and Victor threw themselves into the task with an enthusiasm that matched their father's vigor and by the end of 1839 the plans were definitely laid.

As his fame had become fixed in the land of his adoption, Audubon decided upon a public exhibition of the original drawings that had given him this public notice, but the fickle public did not patronize the bird display and money, instead of being made, was lost and the show closed. In November the naturalist journeyed to Philadelphia to see his crony, Doctor Harlan, and Samuel Breck in his "Recollections," has left us a pen portrait of The American Woodsman. Wrote Mr. Breck in his notebook under date of November 16, 1839:

At the Academy of Natural Sciences today Dr. Morton introduced me to the justly celebrated Audubon, so well-known by his great work on ornithology. He is a man of fifty, with the countenance of a bird, having a projecting forehead, a sunken black eye, a parrot nose, and long protruding chin, combined with an expression bold and eagle-like. I asked him to bring to Philadelphia for public exhibition his original drawings. He observed that, having failed of success in showing them in New York, where he lost

AUDUBON AT 63
A daguerrotype by Mathew B. Brady made in 1849.

AUDUBON AT 65
His last portrait. A daguerreotype taken in 1850.

AMERICA'S TRIBUTE
A bronze bust in the Hall of Fame
by A. Stirling Calder.

NEW ORLEANS' TRIBUTE
Bronze statue by Edward V. Valentine
in Audubon Park.

fifty-five dollars, he had not the courage to encounter the expense of another display before the public.

"If I had," he continued, "an extra ordinary fat hog to show, and should place him in a large room on an elevated pedestal, with a comfortable bed of straw, I could draw thousands from far and near; but painting, however beautiful or well done, will not attract enough people to cover the expense. In London I should be sure of constant visitors to my gallery, but not here."

He spoke like a disappointed man, and did not seem to think that the great success of the panorama here, which I brought to his notice, was suited to change his plans.

Audubon returned to New York to supervise the revision of the *Ornithological Biography* for the purposes of the projected smaller illustrated edition of his beloved birds. In December Victor took time out to attend to a very important personal matter—he journeyed to Charleston where he and the Reverend Bachman's second daughter, May Eliza, were married, thus binding the Audubons and the Bachmans by double ties.

In the *petite edition*, as Audubon termed the American reissue of the bird books, the illustrations were reproduced by a lithographic process, the birds of the elephant folio being reduced by aid of *camera lucida* to fit the demands of the royal octavo format, this work being done by John Woodhouse Audubon, and the colored lithograph sheets inserted in the text. In the original edition made in London the copper-engraved and hand-colored plates measured thirty-by-forty inches and were separate from the five bound volumes of reading matter. In the new American work the illustrations measured seven-by-ten inches.

The *Episodes*, or "Delineations of American Scenery and Manners," which were innovations and gave a rather unique touch to a bird book, were deleted in the small work. The text of the bird biographies were in a very few instances revised, but many errors of identification were corrected. The nomenclature was made to conform to that of the *Synopsis*, and the work was issued in one hundred parts. Each part contained five of the bird plates and text, and the systematic listing of the birds began with the vulturine. The first volume, containing the first twenty parts, was completed in 1840; the seventh and concluding volume containing the pelicans, gulls and other seabirds, and grebes and loons, left the hands of the printers in 1844.

Victor and John devoted themselves to the work of publication while the father once more assumed his rôle of book agent, seeking subscribers for the new American edition, as well as ferreting out those who would purchase the remainder of the big English work. On this quest he traveled incessantly through the eastern part of the United States.

At this time Audubon, while only fifty-five, was already feeling age creeping upon him. When writing John Bachman on the subject of their projected joint work, *The Viviparous Quadrupeds of North America*, he said:

"My Hair are grey, and I am growing old, but what of this? My spirits are as enthusiastical as ever, my legs fully able to carry my body for some Ten years to come . . ." He declared that while the task he had set for himself, to draw a complete series of mammals of America, presented "difficulties innumerable, but *I trust* not insurmountable, provided We Join our Names together, and you push your able and broad shoulders to the Wheel, I promise you that I will give the very best figures of all our quadrupeds that ever have been thought of or expected, and that you and I can relate the greatest amount of *Truths* that to this time has appeared connected with their dark and hitherto misunderstood Histories!"

Disliking life in the bustling city, Audubon searched about to secure a country estate within reach of New York, and in the spring of 1842 settled on a spot overlooking the Hudson in what was then called Carmensville, but in later years better known as Washington Heights (presently 155th to 158th streets). Here, on this thirty-acre tract, Audubon erected his home at the foot of the river bluff. It was April when the family moved into the new house, and at that time Audubon christened the estate "Minnie's Land," in honor of his wife because Victor and Johnny since their residence in Edinburgh had fallen into the practice of calling her "Minnie", the Scottish term for mother.

At *Minnie's Land* was begun the task of making drawings for the *Quadrupeds* on which The American Woodsman worked with unremitting vigor, taking time off only for forays about the eastern country to secure subscribers for the small edition of the *Birds*. One of these trips took Audubon to Boston and other sections of the New England States and into Canada to Quebec and Montreal, where a number of patrons were obtained, and on his return to New York made a side trip to the island of Nantucket.

While the Audubons were basking in fame's brilliant rays they were not flush with funds. In consequence the naturalist went to Washington, where he was received by President Tyler who promised to assist him in his quest for subscribers to all three of his works, the double-elephant folio of *The Birds of America*, the *Birds* in miniature, and the *Quadrupeds*. Audubon also called on Daniel Webster and told that statesman, who had subscribed to his work some years before, something of his financial status. That night he wrote back to the family:

"Mr. W. would give me a fat place was I willing to have one; but I love indepenn and piece more than humbug and money!"

"Minnie's Land" Audubon's home on the Hudson River.

CHAPTER 31

To the Mountains of the Winds

FROM the time of Audubon's earliest quests for the secrets of nature, the Far West had always been a goal. Many resolutions—resolutions born of his traveling thigh, resolutions never kept—were to ease the itch of his wandering foot by journeying to the "Mountains of the Winds," as he so frequently designated the Rockies. Years passed over his head before he realized this ambition. He had progressed from obscurity to fame ere he saw with his own eyes the thundering herds of bison or listened to the sweet-voiced Western birds on their breeding grounds.

He was nearing sixty, in the year 1843, when he decided on making his final expedition to the wilds of his adopted country. It was his intention to gather material and models for the *Quadrupeds*, principally pictures for this work, as John Bachman was doing most of the writing, but he also had it in the back of his head that he might find something new on birds.

This last collecting trip, the Missouri River Expedition, carried the naturalist to the Yellowstone country and almost to the headwaters of the Missouri river. In the party was his constant friend and patron, Edward Harris, who was manager and treasurer of this foray after creatures of the wild; John G. Bell, taxidermist; Isaac Sprague, artist and botanist, and Lewis Squires, who served as general assistant and secretary.

Arrangements had been made the winter before to take passage on the first of the boats ascending the Missouri after the ice cleared, and the St. Louis fur company headed by the Choteaus had agreed to assist the naturalists in their quest.

The land journey to distant St. Louis was made via Wheeling, Cincinnati, and Louisville in coaches. At the Kentucky town, the scene of his mercantile failure in 1810, and where he had been a guest of the town's jail in 1819, the now famous naturalist was greeted by many old-time friends, including Captain John D'Hart, the skipper of the river boat *Columbus*, "who looked just the same as he did 21 years ago." An evening was spent at the home of Ormsby Hite, a brother-in-law to Lucy's brother William Bakewell. Audubon wrote his wife that at the Hite home "we had quite an assembly and *I did* dance until half past 12 of the night."

It was Thursday March 23, 1843, when the party set out down the Ohio river for St. Louis on the *Gallant*. "Harris and I have one *State room*, he sleeps on 3 boards and I on 4, our meals are none of the best, all is greasy and nasty," Audubon wrote Lucy. "A first rate initiation for the trip to Yellow Stone," he concluded philosophically.

It was five days later when the party debarked at St. Louis. Audubon was greeted by Nicholas Berthoud, who, after a number of business vicissitudes, including that of acting as Audubon's book agent, had finally settled in the Missouri town with his family. He it was who broke the news to the expectant naturalists that there would be an enforced delay owing to the fact that the winding course of the Missouri was almost a solid mass of ice. When Audubon met Captain Sire, commander of the *Omega*, the river boat that was to make the trip to Fort Union, the skipper confirmed the bad news and set April 20 as the date for departure.

Audubon had also expected to meet at St. Louis a titled Englishman, Sir William Drummond Stewart, Bart. The Britisher was a sportsman contemplating a hunting trip to the mountains after buffalo and other big game. There was a remote chance, it appeared, that the naturalists might accompany the sportsmen who were then bound up the Mississippi river from New Orleans.

"Sir W. D. Stewart is expected every day and there is a roumour that he will charter a steamer and follow us to the Yellow Stone," Audubon wrote his wife. "*Entre nous et vous tous!* Major Sandford and Miss C. Chouteau are desperately in love with each other, but being Brother & Sister in Law, *the Pope* Will not allow their marriage, although a large amount of Money has been offered the Long Cap for his consent—What fools there are in this Wicked World!"

It was the first day of April before Lord Stewart and his party reached St. Louis. The Britisher and his friends had started from New Orleans on the *J. M. White*, then the finest and fastest boat on the Mississippi river, but when only a dozen miles below St. Louis the *White* struck a ledge of rocks, called the Grand Chain, and in a few moments was sunk in deep water. Although the boat was a total loss all the passengers and most of the baggage were saved.

Sir William thereupon changed his mind about penetrating the wilds via a steamboat, and decided to organize a land expedition. He and Audubon held conference, "Sir Wm is so desirous that we should accompany him & party, that he offered me 5 Mules and a Waggon for ourselves; but we will not Change my plans!" Audubon informed his wife by one of the frequent letters that were mailed back to *Minnie's Land*. A week later he reported, "Sir William Stewart and his gang cannot however go off until about the 10th or 11th of May.—No one *here* can understand that Man, and I must say that in my opinion he is a very curious Character. I am told he would give a great deal that we Should Join him. If So why does he not proffer some $10,000; who Knows but that in such a Case I might Venture to leap on a Mule's back and trot some 7 or 8 thousand Miles."

In consequence the expedition to the Mountains of the Winds dallied in St. Louis awaiting the breaking up of the river ice. Edward Harris, with Sprague, Bell, and Squires, filled in the time making side jaunts, shooting prairie chickens, and collecting small birds. A young man who claimed that as a boy he knew Audubon in New Orleans, turned out to be the son of Doctor Louis Heermann, and that night Audubon wrote his wife, "Young Heermann, to Whose Mother I gave formerly Drawing lessons for about 6 months, brought me several letters of introduction, thinking I was going to join Sir Wam's Expedition. He is sadly disappointed at my not going *that Way*."

Several other meetings were held between Audubon and Stewart, but in spite of the Britisher's offers Audubon clung to his original intention of going to the Yellowstone country by the river route, and a few days later wrote his wife:

"Sir Wam Stewart goes off in about a week to Indepence with his 70 followers of all Sorts.—They start from thence when the grass is sufficient to feed their beasts, and take with them 16 days provisions only; then comes the tug of War.—Buffalo meat, when it can be got, and dried when not fresh.—Water very scarce at times &c. How many of the *Young Gents* will return before they have a sight of the Mountain is more than I can say?—He has done all he could to persuade me to Join his party, but it was no go. he promises *now* to let me have all the Animals I do not procure, since I have procured a German Youth, to preserve Bird & Beasts for *him!* This is the way with this World."

A word picture of Audubon has been left us by an unknown writer who met the party of naturalists at Saint Louis while they were waiting for the ice to clear in the Missouri. The writer, who sent his description to the Buffalo *Courier*, where it was published without a signature in the issue of August 22, 1843, stated:

> Mr. Audubon is a man about the middle statute; his hair is white with age and somewhat thin; he combs it back from an ample forehead, his face being sharp at the chin; has gray whiskers, an aquiline nose, and a hazel eye, small, keen and indicative of great tranquility, and sweetness of temper, cheerfulness and genius.
>
> He is a man of robust constitution though not of stout frame. He told me he had not taken a particle of medicine for twenty years. He is capable of any fatigue; can walk thirty-five miles a day with ease, for months; can sleep anywhere in the open air; endure all climates; his principal food being soaked sea biscuits and molasses on account of having lost all his teeth, from which he suffers and is obliged to boil his meat to rags.
>
> He says he can live a hundred years with temperate habits, regularity, and attention to diet.
>
> Starting up the Missouri he said he was entirely done with ornithology, his object now being to classify American quadrupeds. He was severe on Buffon, whose book he regarded as no authority; said Bouffon was a man of wealth, resided in Paris, and wrote his descriptions from dried skins.

The loss of his teeth did prove a handicap to Audubon on this foray into the wilds, and he made sure that a goodly store of sea biscuits and New Orleans molasses was made part of the cargo of the river boat. He also saw to it that there was some whiskey stowed away in a secret hiding place on the *Omega*, for it was against Federal regulations to transport firewater into the Indian country.

Finally Joseph A. Sire had the *Omega* in readiness, reports from upstream were to the effect that the Missouri was clear of ice, consequently on Tuesday, April 25, the *Omega* cast off its wharf ropes and the paddles started their steady churning of the muddy waters of the river. Edward Harris leaves us this pen picture of the start:

"At last we are off on our long talked of expedition. The captain had great difficulty in getting the trappers on board, they were nearly all drunk and it was about noon before we got underway, amid the shouts and yelling and firing of guns from our drunken trappers . . . Our boat makes a very poor attempt at stemming the current of this great river, now more filled with water than it has been for many years. We look for a tedious passage."

When the *Omega* reached Fort Pierre on the first of June Audubon mailed back to his family a lengthy and lively letter he had been writing during the slow up-river trip. He pictured in vivid words the appearance of the members of the party and added, "Neither Harris, Squires or Myself have Shaved since we left St. Louis, and I have not once pulled off my breeches when I have tumbled down at night to Sleep."

Their destination, Fort Union, was situated on the banks of the Missouri just where that river crosses the present boundary line of North Dakota and Montana, and it was the twelfth of June before the wood-burning *Omega* reached that headquarters of the Western fur trapping company, making the trip in seventeen hours less than seven weeks, the best time that had been made on an upriver trip from St. Louis since the boats had been put in operation.

Eight weeks were spent in the upper Missouri river country. From old Fort Union frequent forays were made into the surrounding country. Many interesting observations on mammals were made, Edward Harris, Bell, Squires, and Sprague enjoying the excitement and hazard of killing the bison from horseback. Audubon did not attempt such strenuous hunting, confining his buffalo collecting to watching the others engage in the chase.

Many new things about birds were noted and, best of all, many birds new to science were collected. Audubon, with the assistance of Bell and Sprague, added a number of names to the ornithology of North America—among them a vireo for Bell, a titlark for Sprague, and a sparrow for Harris. Although the scientific designation of the last was afterwards changed to the name that Nuttall had given the same bird previously collected by Townsend, it still carries the name "Harris's sparrow" in our bird books of today. The sweet-voiced western meadowlark was among the other new species obtained and described for the first time.

On the expedition Edward Harris secured and named a new species of titmouse, which he called the "Long-tailed Chickadee," but no mention of this discovery was made by Audubon in the later editions of his American work, although he did not fail to record and print his own bird discoveries on the Missouri River trip. A year after the return from the West Victor informed his father by letter that Harris had written asking permission to publish his description of the little chickadee with the long tail. Audubon replied, "Write to Friend Harris *at once* that he is welcome to publish the Titmouse found at the 3 Mamelles, and tell him that if *he* will show me a titmouse without *blue legs and feet*, I will be grateful to him." However, the little bird did prove to be a valid sub-species and is so designated in present day bird books, the sole contribution of Edward Harris to the ornithology of North America.

Audubon has left us a vivid and pulsating account of this hazardous expedition to the Indian country of the far West in his journal, which was transcribed and published by his granddaughter. His day-by-day recital proves to be far more romantic, more interesting than Edward Harris' record of the same adventure, for Audubon knew how to dramatize and his diary gives us a most colorful series of pictures of that part of our country in the hectic days of 1843.

The exposures and hardships of the trip to the Mountains of the Winds exacted their toll of Audubon's vitality. On the homeward trip he wrote in his diary, under date of September 29, "I am getting an old man, for this evening I missed my footing on getting into the boat, and bruised my knee and my elbow, but at seventy and over I cannot have the spring of seventeen."

The American Woodsman was only fifty-eight in this year and, if his journal entry was exactly copied, one wonders why he misstated his age.

However, he did return to New York in October, bearded and a trifle bent in frame. Back in *Minnie's Land* he endeavored to throw himself into the task of painting mammals with the old-time vim and vigor he had put into his bird drawings, but he was not at his best. He was not as talented in depicting mammals as he had been in picturing his beloved citizens of the air.

The strenuous life he had led was telling on him and it was necessary for John Woodhouse to do practically half of the work necessary to properly illustrate the *Quadrupeds*, and at times so tardy was Audubon in forwarding to John Bachman data on certain species of animals, and in returning corrected proofs of the text matter, that there was a near-rupture in the long friendship.

The work on the drawings for the *Quadrupeds* progressed slowly and finally The American Woodsman was forced to lay down his brushes.

The zenith had been passed and the sun of Audubon's life was slowly setting in the west of his existence—the twilight hours were at hand.

Audubon on his return from the Missouri River Expedition. From an old woodcut.

Epilogue

THE FINAL JOURNEY

"I can never recollect the name of an enemy . . .
it is only my friends whom I can remember."

JOHN JAMES AUDUBON, in his
journal January 1, 1827.

THE FINAL JOURNEY

THREE years after his return from the Missouri River Expedition Audubon's eyes failed him, although he never became actually blind. When he could no longer handle his pencil, black chalks, and brushes, his heart seemed to wither with his body.

Then Audubon's mind began to fail and for five years he wandered in a shadowland which must have been like a sweet restful gloaming to the strenuous, adventurous, mysterious life he had led. The pressure of a blood clot on the brain deprived him of the power of speech and he became entirely mute. He recognized no one but his devoted Lucy. She he always knew and showed it by grieving and fretting should she leave the room after sitting with him.

When John Bachman visited his old friend in May of 1848, the clergyman was shocked at the change he found and pictured the scene he had witnessed at *Minnie's Land* in a letter to a daughter:

"Audubon has heard his little song sung in French, and has gone to bed. Alas, my poor friend Audubon! the outlines of his countenance and his form are there, but his noble mind is all in ruins.

"I have often, in sadness, contemplated in ruins a home that, in former years, I have seen in order and beauty, but the ruins of a mind once bright and full of imagination, how much more inexpressibly melancholy and gloomy."

Audubon spoke but once thereafter. William G. Bakewell visited his sister in the fall of 1850 and when he entered the room where the naturalist sat in his easy chair, hailed him in his bluff Kentucky manner.

"Ha! Squire! How are you now?"

Audubon looked up with a sudden animation flooding his eyes. "Yes, yes, Billy!" he cried. "You go down that side of Long Pond and we'll get the ducks!" and then lapsed into his customary brooding silence.

His reference to the Long Pond of Henderson days, where he and little Billy Bakewell hunted the wild waterfowl, were the last words he ever uttered.

Audubon's hair now fell in great waving locks of snowy whiteness on his drooping shoulders. The pressure on his brain happily did not cause paralysis and he loved to wander in the tiny copse of woods surrounding *Minnie's Land*. For hours he would sit in silent retrospect at the base of a giant poplar growing in front of the house. Barred from seeing distinctly the beauties around him, doubtless in his weakening mind's eye he beheld the bejeweled Hum-bird robbing nectar from the red trumpet flowers, or heard, in the deep recesses of his fading recollections, the pleasing *tea-kettle tea-kettle* note of the Carolina wren; the more melodious utterance of the wood thrush, the far-away crepuscular call of the chuck-will's-widow, the tinkling vocalization of the Louisiana wood-wagtail, and the polyglot of song from his favorite Mock Bird of the distant magnolia forests of his beloved Feliciana happyland.

As he wandered along the bank of the river on his slow uncertain tread, led by a servant, his dimmed eyes strained to take in the majestic flow of the beautiful Hudson and the rugged palisades of the opposite shore.

His wife, the devoted, helpful Lucy to the last, read to him in the evenings, sang his favorite little French song, and played soft music on her piano—for the soul of the portrayer of the birds was about to take wing.

On January twenty-seventh, 1851, The American Woodsman left the borderland in which he had been wandering these few blank years and entered upon his final adventure in the domain of the unknown.

That adventure, however, is a sealed book.

Appendices

"When all is said and done, I am somewhat cosmopolitan—I belong to every country."

John James Audubon to Vincent Nolte

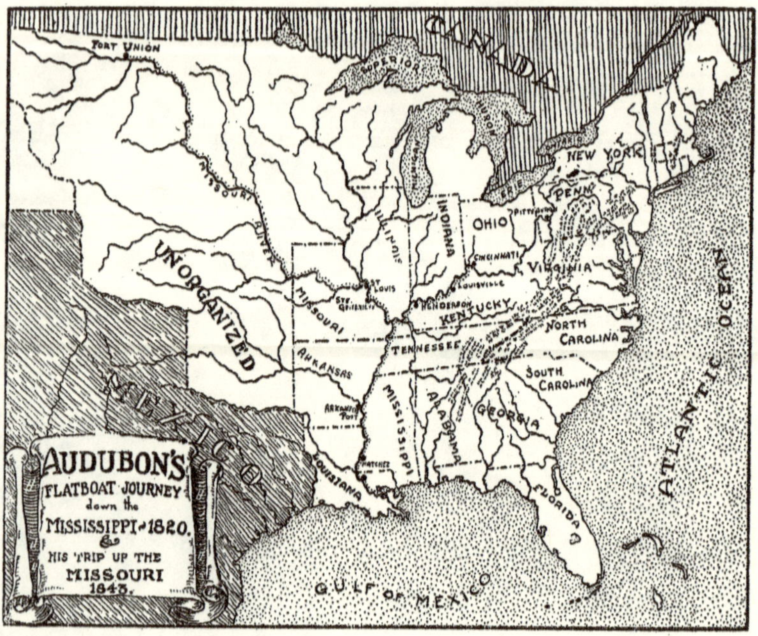
AUDUBON'S
FLATBOAT JOURNEY
down the
MISSISSIPPI—1820.
&
HIS TRIP UP THE
MISSOURI
1843.
FORT UNION
MISSOURI
RIVER
UNORGANIZED
MEXICO
CANADA
SUPERIOR
HURON
ERIE
NEW YORK
PENN
OHIO
INDIANA
ILLINOIS
CINCINNATI
VIRGINIA
LOUISVILLE
ST LOUIS
HENDERSON
KENTUCKY
MISSOURI
NORTH
CAROLINA
TENNESSEE
ARKANSAS
SOUTH
CAROLINA
MISSISSIPPI
ALABAMA
GEORGIA
NATCHEZ
LOUISIANA
FLORIDA
GULF OF MEXICO
ATLANTIC OCEAN

A

THE ENIGMA AND THE LOST DAUPHIN

Who was John James Audubon?

A granddaughter who had access to all her grandfather's original manuscripts copied from a number of them certain references which she excluded from her printed versions of *Audubon and His Journals*, and his autobiography *Myself*. These withheld extracts, however, she set down in small memorandum books for the eyes of immediate members of the Audubon family.

At the foot of these suppressed extracts she wrote:

> "I have never known *who* John J. La Forest Audubon *was*, and these extracts from his letters and journals seem to me to point to the fact that he was 'The Dauphin' who so mysteriously disappeared during the French Revolution.
>
> Maria R. Audubon."

Miss Audubon also transcribed from her grandfather's papers:

"In Nantes in 1812 Jean Audubon & Anne Moynette gave over some property to 'Jean Rabin, Créole de St. Domingue,' which he refused to accept, saying, 'My own name I have never been permitted even to speak; accord me that of Audubon, which I revere as I have cause to do.' "

These extracts have been withheld from the public through the years. In view of the conclusions adduced by Professor Herrick's biography, which were to the effect that Audubon was the love child of Captain Jean Audubon and a "Mlle. Rabin, *Créole de Saint-Domingue*," and the belief held by descendants of the great bird artist that he was of noble birth, as proved by his Bourbon features and certain cryptic writings in his journals, these heretofore suppressed extracts were sent to me by the late Miss Harriet Audubon without reservation as to their use for the purposes of this intimate study of The American Woodsman. They have been inserted in their proper sequence in my unfolding of the bird artist's life story.

2

Audubon's published autobiographical sketch begins with these words: "The precise period of my birth is yet an enigma to me, and I can only say what I have often heard my father repeat to me on the subject. It seems that my father had large properties in Santo Domingo, and was in the habit of visiting frequently that portion of our Southern States called, and known by the name of, Louisiana . . . . During one of these excursions he married a lady of Spanish extraction, whom I have been led to understand was as beautiful as she was wealthy, and otherwise attractive, who bore my father three sons and a daughter.—I being the youngest of the sons and the only one who survived extreme youth. My mother, soon after my birth, accompanied my father to the estate of Aux Cayes, on the island of Santo Domingo, and she was one of the victims during the ever-to-be-lamented period of negro insurrection of that island." He tells how Captain Audubon, after escaping, "took me to France, where, having married the only mother I have ever known," entered the French Navy.

Biographers writing of Audubon's early days have been forced to rely on printed versions of this sketch, the original manuscript mysteriously disappearing until it was found "in an old book which had been in a barn on Staten Island for years." It was said Audubon wrote it in 1835, but the date of its recovery was never given. Nor has the original document ever been exhibited and it is supposed that it was burned by the granddaughter who transcribed it for publication.

In his own printed works, the *Ornithological Biography*, Audubon began the first pages of his famous letterpress with an *Introductory Address* leveled, as was the custom at that time, at "Kind Reader." In it he presented "some account of my life, and of the motives which have influenced me in thus bringing you into contact with an American Woodsman."

Regarding his birth he merely stated he was born in "the New World," not specifying the exact spot nor the date, and made no references to parentage—his exact words, "I received light and life in the New World."

Mrs. Audubon, when she prepared her husband's papers for publication, wrote that while Jean Audubon, "the father of the naturalist," was residing in the West Indies he frequently visited North America and on one of these visits "met and married in Louisiana a lady of Spanish extraction, named Anne Moynette,[1] whose beauty and wealth may have made her equally attractive." In the matter of date and place of birth, Mrs. Audubon set down, "The naturalist was born on his father's plantation, near New Orleans, Louisiana, May 4, 1780." This assertion, however, was made for "the purpose of concealing his noble birth," according to Miss Harriet Audubon in a letter to the present author.

Audubon's journal of 1820-21, containing his uncensored although defaced statement on his parentage and birth (reproduced in this biography just as he wrote it, pages 115 to 122) remains the sole example of his testimony on this clouded phase of his existence unedited. In it he does *not* claim Louisiana as his birthplace. He does make certain references to his age . . . that he was fourteen when at Rochefort on January 1, 1800, and seventeen when he went to America in 1803, both of which would fix his birth year as 1785. One entry has to do with a reference to other children, that he and his half-sister Rosa were

[1]Miss Maria Audubon wrote that her name was Rabin.

two of a family of five children. His written statement that he had three "younger" brothers was changed by a different hand, by different ink, and evidently at a much later date, to read "three *older* brothers killed in the wars." Why was this so changed? His first two lines in reference to his mother have been so defaced that they are not decipherable. His statement that his father "having married in France," was changed to read "*re*married."

Audubon's granddaughter, in the introduction to her *Audubon and His Journals*, stated that her grandfather was born at Mandeville, Louisiana, in the plantation home of the Marquis de Mandeville de Marigny, called *Fontainebleau;* that very little of Audubon's mother was known, save that recently acquired papers "prove her *name to have been Rabin*," and that "he may have been born anywhere between 1772 and 1783."

When she penned these statements, Miss Maria Audubon was in possession of the very passages in her grandfather's journals and letters which prompted her to believe that he was the Lost Dauphin of France, a belief she successfully kept from the public.

Audubon's curious statements in his journal and letters to his wife are puzzling. We have already read those declarations: that he was of "high birth," that he was "an aristocrat!", his references to his "noble nose!", his resemblance to his father "not my adopted father, but my *own* father;" of the oath of silence exacted by Captain Audubon, and his desire that the boy he reared should have "children, legitimate children." How he walks the streets of Paris "dressed as a common man," how he must bow and ask permission to this or that —"*I, who should command all!*" Then he mysteriously writes his wife he "must flee France or the dagger may but an end to ————." The dash line, almost half across the page, meaning, it is supposed, himself.

His curious journal entry, "Versailles, is truly a magnificent place; how long since I have been there, and how many changes in my life since those days!" only adds to the mantle of mystery that enshrouds the prospect of his early life and identity.

3

The conclusion long held by Miss Maria Audubon, and believed in too by her half-sister, the late Miss Harriet B. Audubon, that Audubon was none other than the Lost Dauphin presents many curious coincidences in the lives of two little boys of history.

According to Professor Herrick's documentary proof—a series of sworn, signed, and sealed legal papers—Jean Jacques Fougère, originally called "Jean Rabin, *créole de Saint-Domingue*," was born April 26, 1785, at Aux Cayes, in what is now Haiti, to Captain Jean Audubon and a woman set down in the attending physician's bill for services as "Mlle. Rabin."

Almost exactly one month earlier, March 27, 1785, the second son of Louis XVI was born at Versailles, France, the child who afterwards became the Dauphin and the central figure in the most amazing riddle the world has been called upon to solve. This son of the king of France and Marie Antoinette of Austria was baptized Louis Charles Capet, and was born the Prince Royale. His brother, Louis Joseph, four years his senior, was the Dauphin, but died in 1789, hence Louis Charles, at the age of four, automatically became the Dauphin—the heir-apparent to the Bourbon throne.

A brief recital of his life's story lends added interest to that of Audubon, in view of the claims and beliefs of Audubon's descendants.

In August of 1792, when the Dauphin was seven, the mobs of the French Revolution swept the royal family from power in the palace of the Tuileries to imprisonment in the towers of a feudal fortress, originally the abode of an ancient order of Knights Templar and called "The Temple."

Here the king, his queen, the dauphin, the king's daughter, Marie Thérèse Charlotte, called the Princess Royale; the king's sister, Princess Elizabeth; Madame Pauline de Tourzel, governess to the heir-apparent; the Marquis and Marquise de Saint-Brice, and several other royalists who remained true to the court of Saint Louis, together with several loyal servants, were incarcerated.

Louis XVI was torn from the members of his family by the fanatics who had overthrown royalty and made a solitary prisoner in one of the towers of the Temple; his queen, son, daughter, and sister, confined in other sections of the prison, were forced to endure privations, insults, taunts, reproaches, and vile indignities from their guards, who were hilarious and cruel over the success of their *coup d'etat.* The most bigoted of the revolutionists, the *san-culottes,* saw to the degradation of the king and jeered when on January 21, 1793, the guillotine sliced the monarch's head from his shoulders.

The *Commune* thundered forth its abhorrence of royalty and, not sated with the blood of *Louis Seize,* heaped further indignities on his widow and children, and then was written the vilest tyranny and cruelty with which the pages of French history are blemished. Several months after the king's execution, because of increasing rumors that Royalists were plotting a rescue of the Dauphin from the Temple, the little child-king was separated from his mother, placed in the tower room formerly occupied by his father, and on the order of Robespierre was given over to the custody of a shoemaker revolutionist named Antoine Simon and Marie Jeanne, his wife. For the Dauphin's amusement the guard Simon procured a dog, which the kinglet named *Castor,* and later, as a diversion for his charge, the cobbler built an aviary because "the Dauphin had a great desire to keep birds." In such a manner did the little prisoner spend his time, playing with his birds and having cages built for the feathered songsters that shared his incarceration. Under the teachings of Simon and his wife the boy learned not only low language but many obscenities and, after being made to drink wine to excess, the Dauphin was prompted to denounce his mother for certain private actions he claimed to have witnessed, and to recite atrocious practices she had done him while in prison. The child's testimony was taken down in writing by members of a special committee and on the following day the boy was made to face his sister and repeat the accusations against his mother. Among the members of the Committee on General Safety listening to what was being said, was Jacques Louis David, the celebrated artist of the revolution, the same David who was so fond of sketching the stiff attitudes of the victims of the guillotine; the same David who, a few days after listening to the drunken mouthings of a boy of eight, leaned from a window in the *rue de Honoré* so he could make a pencil sketch of Marie Antoinette as she was carted through the cobbled streets of Paris to meet Madame Guillotine; the same David who, nine years later, was teaching drawing to a boy from Nantes, a boy named Jean Jacques Fougère Laforest Audubon.

In January of 1794, the cobbler Simon, on the plea that his wife was in ill health, resigned his position as guardian for the Dauphin and, after insisting upon a receipt for his royal prisoner, took up his residence in a building whose windows overlooked the stables and courtyard of the Temple. From that time on the story of the Dauphin becomes shrouded in mystery; from that time on the child-king became a solitary prisoner. According to some accounts, which are today doubted, the boy was *walled up*, whereupon the robust fiery youngster was transformed in a few days to a "whelp, dirty and consumed with vermin, disputing with the rats the bread" his captors threw him; and, according to reports that are believed genuine, he was a boy both *deaf* and *dumb!*

In May of 1794 the Dauphin's sister was the only other royal prisoner in the Temple, for Madame Elizabeth, the king's sister, had gone the way of Marie Antoinette and her brother. In spite of the fact that the brother and sister were the only prisoners, they were not allowed to see one another and, therefore, it was impossible for Marie Thérèse to know whether the boy in the tower was her brother—or someone else.

On the twenty-seventh of July Robespierre fell from power, so did his head the next day from his own blood-smeared guillotine, and with his end came the end of the dread Paris Commune. Followed thick and fast rumors that the young Dauphin had escaped and members of the Committee on Convention ordered General Paul F. N. Barras, who had downed Robespierre, to visit the Temple and personally see that the young king was still a prisoner. He reported that he had indeed seen the boy Capet, and the next day he placed a new guardian in the Temple, a young patriot named Jean Jacques Christophe Laurent, a *créole de la Martinique*, noted for his turbulent zeal. The selection of Laurant was at the behest of another *créole*, Joséphine de Beauharnais, the beautiful mistress of General Barras . . . she who afterwards became the first wife of Napoleon Bonaparte and Empress of the French.

The former guard Simon had gone to the guillotine with Robespierre, but his wife lived and years afterwards, when an inmate of the *Hospicé des Incurables*, the old *chouanne* confided a secret to the nuns of Saint Vincent de Paul. She claimed that on the day she and Simon moved from the Temple, January 19, 1794, they brought to the Temple, for the removal of the shoemaker's effects, a pushcart which contained a wicker-work hamper with a double bottom, a pasteboard rocking-horse, and several other toys intended for the child-king. In the interior of the pasteboard horse they had concealed a child whom they substituted for the Dauphin and, after the exchange had been made, little Louis Charles Capet was wrapped in a bundle of soiled clothes and placed in the hamper which was loaded on the pushcart. The child was afterwards removed from their house by unrecognized Royalists, so Mère Simon said. She did not know what eventually became of him, but she was convinced at the time she told her story, in 1814, that the child was alive and would someday wear the crown of France.

Whether it was the son of Louis XVI or a substitute boy who occupied the tower room from July 28, 1794, until June 8, 1795, will always remain a riddle. For almost a year a boy was kept in solitary confinement in a tower room of a feudal fortress in the heart of Paris. During that time the character of the royal prisoner underwent a marked change. From a lively lover of birds, a boy who was turbulent, vivacious, wilful, from one who was always jumping about and singing the day long, the prisoner became a stupid child with an air of imbecility, who sat at a table day and night building little houses with playing cards.

In May of 1795 the child was reported ill and in need of medical attention and a commissioner was instructed to visit the prisoner and report his condition (the créole Laurent had retired at his own request from his position the previous March). The commissioner reported that the face of the sequestered boy was covered with ulcers and pimples, and had scabs, resulting from an itch on the back of his head. He could not talk and did not appear to be able to understand or hear what was said to him. On June eighth the boy in the Temple died. Two days later his passing was publicly announced, and at nine that night the body was buried in a small grave in *Le Cimetiere de la Madeline* with elaborate secrecy as armed soldiers kept away the curious citizens of Paris. Officially, and with what appears to be too many attesting documents, the boy so secretly buried was declared to be the child Capet, once known as the Dauphin of France.

The son of Louis XVI was a child with blue eyes, acquiline nose, slender waist, and ten years old when he was supposed to have died. In 1846, fifty years after the interment, the Abbé Haumet, curé of Sainte-Marguerite, had the body of the boy buried as the Dauphin secretly exhumed and allowed physicians to make an examination. In the opinion of the doctors, "It is absolutely impossible that this skeleton could have been that of a child of ten years and a few months; it can only have belonged to a boy of fifteen to sixteen."

This tale of the incarceration of the Dauphin proves only the prologue to the strangely mystifying story of the Little Lost Prince, the celebrated Sovereign Without Subjects. Immediately upon the announcement of the Dauphin's death arose a rumor in Paris. Royalists went about whispering to one another "*Quelle est moitiée de trente-quatre?*" ("What is the half of thirty-four?".) Fellow royalists answered, in the same guarded tone: "The half of thirty-four is seventeen—the seventeenth Louis of France."

For it was general street talk that the "Little Fellow" had escaped from the Temple and would return to rule over his royalist subjects, because the "Boy of the Temple" who had died was a substitute. Even his sister, after her release and banishment to Austria, wore no mourning until she arrived in Vienna, and only then when she was told it was expected of her.

It was not strange, in the circumstances, that many pseudo-Dauphins, each with an aquiline nose, blue eyes, and long chestnut hair falling on the shoulders, sprang up everywhere. All with their plausible tales and claims from time to time threw France into ferments of excitement, for royalists were praying for a return of their phantom king as there was no doubt in their minds that The Boy had escaped his captors. Thus the door was thrown wide open to imposters.

All through the dread days of the Revolution the anxious interest of all France, as well as other parts of the civilized world, was centered upon the fair head of the Dauphin—the little boy who had committed no fault, merited no reproach, whom no law condemned, yet who was paying the penalty for no crime save that of being the son of a king.

When the Dauphin died, or was supposed to have died, the concern in him was acute. One hundred and forty-three years have passed, yet the interest in him holds the anxious attention of France and the world. There have been many explanations as to how he escaped the Temple and his ultimate fate, some plausible and many not. One that has been put forward in late years, and which appears to bear out the contentions of the Audubon family believing in the Dauphin story,[1] is that Joseph Fouché, Napoleon's infamous spy and police terror, had something to do with such a plot. That he decided The Boy must be secretly taken from France and hidden in some colonial possession. San Domingo was selected as the best retreat, and the Creole Laurent, the child's former jailer, was selected by Fouché as the one best fitted to accomplish this act. A man named Leblanc was appointed *commissionaire Isles-sous-le-vent*, was directed to sail without delay to his post San Domingo, and that Laurent, in charge of the Dauphin, should accompany him to this retreat.

Laurent and the young king went *en chaise de poste* to Nantes and at that city on the Loire the two remained in seclusion for some weeks, awaiting the frigate that would take them to the island with the new *commissionaire*. The Dauphin at that time, 1796, would have been just eleven.

Nantes was then in a state of great agitation and turmoil. The *Nantais* had enthusiastically embraced the revolutionary cause and their

[1]Le Roi Perdu. Memories le comte de Vaisons, Octave Aubry.

city had been the scene of a number of battles between contending royalist and revolutionary forces. The Vendean leader Charette was executed in March, and years afterwards John James Audubon wrote in his journal that he had seen Charette shot down in Nantes' *place de Viarme.*

Lieutenant Jean Audubon was, on the surface at least, an enthusiastic revolutionist. He served on various republican committees, was appointed a civil commissioner, helped organize the national guard, and enlisted in the republican navy with the rank of ensign. At the time Laurent and his charge were said to have arrived in the city on the banks of the Loire, Jean Audubon was on port duty at La Rochelle, but his rank permitted him to make frequent trips to visit his family then living in the *rue de Crébillon* in the heart of Nantes. The boy he had brought back from Aux Cayes, Saint-Domingue, the alleged son of Mlle. Rabin, was just eleven.

Where Laurent and his charge lived while in Nantes, whom he met while in that city, who saw the youngster he was guarding and spiriting out of France, or who possibly recognized his royal prisoner, is not stated in comte de Vaisons' alleged memoirs. The count is made to say that when the frigate sailed, Laurent and Leblanc had on board "a boy" who was represented by them as the nephew of the *commissionaire,* and that Laurent reported to Fouché by letter under date of June 17, 1796, of their safe arrival at San Domingo.

Could there have been another substitution at Nantes? ask those interested in Audubon's claim of "noble birth."

Once safe at San Domingo (we are still following Octave Aubry's *Memoires du comte de Vaisons*) the boy carried from France was placed in charge of an elderly well-educated woman named Madame de Rolland de la Toste, who became his *marraine,* or godmother. The youngster was called a *Nantais* by his playmates, "because he came from Nantes," so Laurent is said to have reported to Fouché. While France writhed in the toils of the revolution the boy spirited away to San Domingo was growing fair and strong. In 1803, when he was eighteen, the blacks revolted, overrunning the French part of the island with fiendish ferocity. During an attack upon the home where he lived with his *marraine,* the young man bravely battled the revolting negro slaves and was killed. In such fashion, according to the alleged memoirs of the count de Vaisons, so ended the riddle as to the ultimate fate of the Lost Dauphin.

4

The foregoing accounts are only a few of the many tales that have engaged public attention from time to time during the past century regarding the possible fate of "the half of thirty-four," the long-mourned Louis XVII, the little Shadow King of France, the pathetic little Prisoner of the Temple.

In a retrospective analysis it seems quite probable that in the year 1810 the ultimate fate of the Dauphin was as much a subject of discussion and conjecture as it is today, if not more so. Can there be any doubt that this son of Marie Antoinette and his probable escape were the subject of interlocution among the many noble émigrés who made Louisville their New World rendezvous? Can there be any doubt that the *ci-devant* Marquis de Saint-Pierre and his wife, she who had been *dame d'honneur*, so she said, to the Dauphin's mother, and who knew the golden-haired boy of seven who played in the garden at Versailles, discussed the horrors of the revolution many times with the young merchant Audubon who was just then starting a business career in the frontier Kentucky town named in honor of a King Louis of France? Can there be any doubt that the marquis and his wife told of their exciting escape from the clutches of the Terror, when every mile of the journey from Paris to the seaport was filled with dread that their son Nicholas, who was then eight years old, would be taken for the escaping Dauphin and beheaded?

It is quite possible, also, that the beheaded monarch, *Louis Seize*, father of the Dauphin, was discussed. This particular King Louis, history bears witness, was more a huntsman than he was a ruler, one who was passionately fond of bird shooting. Days on which he had not killed a bagful of game were blank days for him. Louis the Sixteenth had an obsession for setting down all he did in a diary, and in these journals the king wrote many intimate things. An entry for July 14, 1789, a day on which he had been out bird shooting and had failed to fill his bag, contains a laconic, but illuminating, "Nothing!"

If the Dauphin did escape, and most authorities today agree that in all probability the true Dauphin was smuggled out of the Temple, and they acknowledge the story of the substitution of another boy well substantiated, what became of the child-king is still unsolved beyond any doubt.

The supposition held by a number of his descendants that John James Audubon might have been the Lost Dauphin is based on a series of coincidental factors and a collection of peculiarly worded paragraphs in communications meant only for his wife's eyes. In not one of the extracts withheld from the public by descendants does their grandfather make the direct assertion that his "noble birth" meant he was actually the lost child of the martyred Louis and Marie Antoinette.

One explanation that has been advanced by a student of this phase of Audubon's life is that after his marriage and the birth of his children he was forced to render some sort of explanation to his wife regarding his position in life and the charge of illegitimacy brought to light by a court action in France, when distant relatives of Lieutenant Jean Audubon endeavored to obtain what little was left of his estate by bringing before the court the French law that a "natural child" could not inherit such property.

To explain this effectively, did Audubon conceal the truth under a cloak of mystery and an enigmatic gloss of high birth? Did he feel that public knowledge of his true parentage would defeat his lofty aspirations? Did he realize that he could not emblazon his arms with the bend sinister? Is that why he whispered to his devoted and believing Lucy that he was indeed "the half of thirty-four" but was bound by the oath exacted of him in his youth never to reveal it? Was that the root of his superstition about odd numbers? Did he deliberately create confusion as to his birth? about Selkirk's Settlement? the uncle of la Rochelle whom he cursed? his secret? his age? and his real name?

If he did, that is why those who have studied Audubon's eccentric character and glowing personality in later years have found themselves groping in a confusion he so deliberately constructed.

That John James Audubon actually could have been the Lost Dauphin seems most unlikely, in spite of the amazing chain of circumstances which appear to bind him to the little prisoner of the Temple. His own written autobiographical sketch, the authenticity of which cannot be doubted, which he wrote on that winter day he was floating down the Mississippi river on a flatboat, appears to be the repository of truth—he was sick in mind and body, he was in a mood that dreary, rainy December day to write only facts—and apparently he did so, not even withholding that part of his life's history which revealed to his sons that his mother was not the wife of his father, if the two defaced lines can be so interpreted.

The long-held belief of descendants that their distinguished ancestor was in truth Louis the Seventeenth of France is an enthralling, if highly improbable, answer to the enigma of this strange man's birth, but one which a biographer cannot ignore. To study this a little more intelligently we should examine once more into what is known and what is surmised as to his actual parentage.

B

CRÉOLE DE SAINT-DOMINGUE

There is no question as to the place and time of Audubon's death—in New York "just as sunset was flooding the pure snow-covered landscape with golden light, at five o'clock Monday, January 27, 1851, the pard-like spirit, beautiful and swift . . . outsoared the shadow of our night."

But where was Audubon born, and when?

Practically all published biographies have stated that the naturalist was a native of Louisiana—that he was born "somewhere in Louisiana." A granddaughter, claiming she based her statement on information furnished by the Reverend A. Gordon Bakewell, a son of Thomas Woodhouse Bakewell, published that the plantation *Fountainebleau* located on the shores of Lake Pontchartrain near Mandeville, Louisiana, was the birthplace.

According to the story he told the Reverend Bakewell, Bernard de Mandeville de Marigny remembered the event vividly—he was there in person, for he had extended the hospitality of his home to Admiral Audubon and his Spanish-Créole wife, described by Marigny as "*une dame d'une beaute, incomparable et avec beaucoup de fierte.*" If Audubon was born "anywhere between 1772 and 1783," or even May 5, 1780, the date set down by Lucy Audubon, the evidence adduced by Bernard Marigny must be discarded on two important counts . . . Marigny himself first saw the light of day October 28, 1785, and could not very well have been an eyewitness to an event that took place five years before he was born! As a matter of strict fact Marigny did not purchase *Fountainebleau* until 1820, and did not erect buildings there until some years later—sufficient proof that Audubon could not have been born in a house built thirty-five years after his birth!

For years it was generally accepted that the naturalist was born in Louisiana, and this impression persisted until 1917 when, persumably, the enigma was an enigma no longer. A distinguished ornithologist, educator, and man of letters, Francis Hobart Herrick, professor of biology of the Western Reserve University at Cleveland, discovered documents in France which seemed to prove conclusively that Audubon was not a Louisianian by birth. The curtain of mystery which had so long concealed this period of his life was lifted, and Doctor Herrick made known to the world who Audubon apparently was, and where, and in what circumstances The American Woodsman was born.

2

Jean Audubon, the man John James Laforest Audubon called father, was an adventurer and a rover. He was possessed of a "wandering foot." Jean Audubon's birthplace was Les Sables D'Olonne, France, and his ancestors were fisherfolk. He was one of twenty-one children. The exciting life Jean Audubon led began when he was thirteen and shipped as cabin-boy aboard his father's fishing boat. By the time he was fourteen he had participated in a sea battle between the French and English off the Gulf of St. Lawrence and was wounded in the leg. As his ship was captured by the British tars, Jean spent the next five years of his life a prisoner of war in England. The most he gleaned from this adventure was an admiration for the English people and a knowledge of their language. It will be noted that Jean Audubon has been termed a lieutenant, his rank in the French navy; a captain, as he was the commander of merchant vessels, and even "Admiral Audubon" by descendants—a rank he never held. For the purposes of this biography he has been called Captain Audubon.

When set at liberty, Jean Audubon, just emerging from his teens, returned to the sea. For nearly a score of years he made many voyages, saw the West Indies, the fishing banks off Newfoundland, enlisted in the French navy as a common sailor and served for almost a year before he reentered the *service au commerce*, or French merchant marine. Late in 1770 he made a number of voyages to the island of San Domingo, then a French possession, his ship carrying cargoes of coffee and sugar back to Nantes, a French port that came to know Jean Audubon well in later years.

While he was commanding the ship *La Dauphine*, and nearing the age of twenty-eight—this was in the year 1772—Jean Audubon married a childless widow named Anne Moynet Ricordel, nine years his senior. The Widow Ricordel was then living at Paimbœuf, where she owned several pieces of property. She also had a dwelling in her native city of Nantes, and it was in this pleasant little town on the banks of the River Loire, that she lived while her young sailor husband was either on the ocean or having adventures in far-off lands.

Two years after his marriage Jean Audubon became captain of his own ships and in them made several profitable voyages for a firm of Nantes colonial agents, Messrs Coirond Brothers. In the spring of 1779, when leaving San Domingo for France with a cargo of sugar, Jean Audubon's ship, *Le Comte d'Artois*, was attacked by four British corsairs and two galleys. In spite of a desperate defense, Audubon was defeated, his ship taken as a prize, for a second time he became a prisoner of the British, was sent to New York, then in possession of Lord Howe, and for thirteen months lanquished in a prison-ship. Upon his release he became an enthusiastic supporter of the American colonists' cause, joined them in their battle for freedom, and in 1781 he was with the forces of Comte de Grasse before Yorktown and witnessed the surrender of Lord Cornwallis. Before final peace came Jean

Audubon, as an officer of the United States navy, sank a British privateer off the coast of France. The war ended, the sailor-man returned to Nantes and his wife, and settled down to a life of quietude.

But not for long. San Domingo lured him. He decided to try for fortune there. Leaving his wife in France he sailed for the West Indies to locate in the most important colonial possession owned by France. He made his headquarters at Aux Cayes, in the western part of the island, where as merchant, planter, and dealer in slaves from Africa he amassed what is said to have been a considerable fortune.

This port, originally and properly named *Les Cayes*, a Spanish name meaning "The Keys," is in that section of the island now dominated by the Republic of Haiti, but designated on most maps as *Aux Cayes*.

The corruption was caused by early French settlers who, when dating a letter or receipting a bill, dropped the article from *Les Cayes* and wrote "aux Cayes" (pronounced *o'ka*) and meaning "at the Cayes." All merchandise bundled at this seaport carried the designation *aux cayes* stenciled on the wrappings. In the early days, when cargoes from all over the world were landed at New York, all bundles were opened and minutely examined as they came off the ships to ascertain if the contents agreed with the manifests or labels. Items, quantities, and the nature of goods "from the Cayes" in almost every instance were found to be correct and the shippers gained a reputation for honesty, consequently, when the freight handlers picked up a bundle marked *aux Cayes* it was not inspected but heaved on a waiting truck with an expression "o'kay" voiced by the English-speaking longshoreman. In such fashion we came by our present colloquial designation of "O. K.", and not from Andy Jackson's humorous abbreviation of "oll kerrect," as usually stated.

Jean Audubon was soon recognized as an influential *négociant*. He was successful in his dealings in slaves, as the head of a group of productive plantations devoted to the cultivation of sugar cane, as owner of refineries and many inland trading posts. He lived in a style befitting his position. His wife never visited him at his island home—she remained in Nantes.

3

He did not face a lonely existence for living with Captain Jean Audubon at Aux Cayes was a young woman then styled a créole of San Domingo, whose name, as it appeared on a physician's bill and other documents, was "Mlle. Rabin." To this pair, on April 26, 1785, was born a boy who in later documents is named "Jean Rabin, *créole de Saint-Domingue.*" Later, when he was nearly eight and living with Captain Audubon in France, apparently this same boy was adopted by the sea captain and still later baptized Jean Jacques Fougère, which in English would be John James Fern.

A receipted bill of the attending physician, a Doctor Sanson, approved and paid by Jean Audubon, was found in France through Professor Herrick's diligent researches, and this, with other documents still possessed by descendants of Audubon's half-sister, appeared to remove all doubt as to where and when, and in what circumstances John James Audubon was born and why there was an enigma in his life.

Mlle. Rabin, in feeble health to judge from other entries on the physician's bill, probably did not live long after the birth of her son, for further documentary evidence indicates that her place in Jean Audubon's ménage was filled by another *créole de Saint-Domingue.* The other was Catherine Bouffard who, on April 29, 1787, became the mother of a baby girl who was at first named Muguet (May-lily or Lily of the Valley). Mlle. Bouffard had another daughter, named Louise, also born at Aux Cayes, but whether she too was a daughter of Captain Audubon is not known. Catherine Bouffard subsequently went to France, but in all probability never entered Jean Audubon's life again.

Captain Jean Audubon left San Domingo in the fall of 1789. With him, in charge of slaves, were two of his children acquired so unconventionally in the New World. He returned to France by the way of Philadelphia and not via New Orleans, as has been stated, and purchased a plantation named *Mill Grove* just outside the Quaker City. The boy, Jean Rabin, was then four and a half years old and his half-sister two years younger.

Back in Nantes Jean Audubon presented his wife with the little boy and the little girl acquired without benefit of clergy at Aux Cayes. Madame Audubon, childless herself, opened wide her arms and received the little ones tenderly, and became to them the kind and over-indulgent foster mother John James Audubon affectionately mentioned in recitals of his early life in France.

Three years later, March 7, 1793, Madame Audubon and her husband legally adopted the boy and girl by an act passed before a notary and in the presence of necessary witnesses. The boy was then eight and the girl six. When these papers were signed, Jean Audubon, then commanding a *corvette* named *Le Cerbèré,* and his wife declared they adopted and recognized from that moment as their lawful children, viz, "A male child named Fougère, born since their marriage . . . to him Jean Audubon, and a woman living in America, who has been dead about eight years, and a female child, named Muguet, born also since the marriage aforesaid, to him and another woman living in America, named Catherine Bouffard, of whose fate he is ignorant."

When the boy was nearing sixteen, in October of 1800, he was baptized Jean Jacques Fougère Audubon by a Catholic priest in the church of Saint-Similien at Nantes. The girl's name was changed from Muguet to that of another flower, Rosa, persumably after Captain Audubon's sister Marie Rosa. This sister, the only daughter in a family of twenty-one children, had married a Nantes lawyer named Pierre de Vaugeon, and she, according to records in the possession of Maria R. Audubon, had been "killed by the *Chouans* about 1796."

4

The reason for the change of the boy's name from *Rabin* to *Fougère* has proved obscure. In his later life he never made use of the name Rabin, and evidently cared very little for that of Fougère. He did adopt the name of La Forêt, for it appears as part of his signature on a number of early drawings made in France. Some of his work in depicting birds he found near Nantes and Couëron carry the initials "J. L. F. A." and "J. J. L. Audubon." His writings tell us that his father usually addressed him as "Laforest," and his signatures on many letters addressed to his wife are frequently signed "Laforest."

The change of names in the articles of adoption could tend to indicate that the mother's name was not Rabin, but Fougère, a name that has several meanings, such as "fern," a "brake of trees," or even a "drinking glass." It is a peculiar fact that while the name of the mother of the little girl was set down in the adoption papers, the name of the mother of the boy Jean was not mentioned.

Miss Maria Audubon writes in a confidential memorandum, "In Nantes in 1812 Jean Audubon and Anne Moynette gave over some property to 'Jean Rabin, Créole de St. Domingue,' which he refused to accept, saying, 'My own name I have never been permitted even to speak; accord me then that of Audubon, which I revere as I have cause to do.' "

However, one use of the name Rabin by the naturalist himself is noteworthy. In 1817, after his marriage to Lucy Bakewell and the birth of his two sons, and while he was living at Henderson, Kentucky, Audubon executed a power of attorney in favor of G. Loyen du Puigaudeau, husband of his half-sister Rosa. This unique document was drawn up a year after Captain Jean Audubon had written his last will, about eight months before his death, and was evidently designed to faciliate a division of property between the two children. In this power of attorney the naturalist named himself "Jean Rabin, husband of Lucy Bakewell," and signed the paper, "John J. Audubon," swearing to his signature before Ambrose Barbour, clerk of the court at Henderson, then acting in his capacity of notary public.

In 1827, when in England, the woodsman writes Mrs. William Rathbone of Liverpool, "My name is John James Laforest Audubon. The name Laforest I never sign except when writing to my wife, and she is the only being, since my father's death, who calls me by it."

We have also seen that the naturalist had his name engraved as "Laforest Audubon" on the Souvenir Gun given him by the fascinating Madame André, after he had drawn her figure in the nude.

5

The mystery concerning the exact identity of Jean Rabin's mother is yet to be solved. The use of the term *Créole* in describing her has caused some to assume this indicated a touch of color in her blood. Which, of course, is unfortunate because it is untrue. In the West

Indies, Spanish America, and Louisiana the term *créole* denotes children of those countries born of or descended from European ancestors and has nothing to do with color. *Créoles* there are of the purest French and Castilian blood and it is a designation proudly borne by many splendid families today.

The fact that San Domingo is now ruled by the blacks is no indication of such a strain. The downfall of white supremacy in French San Domingo, that part of the island now designated at Haiti, and the establishment of the so-called "Black Republic," resulted from causes far less simple than is generally realized.

That horrible and bloody revolution brought about by the black slaves of the resident French was caused by the color line being tightly drawn. In Captain Audubon's time at Aux Cayes the different elements constituting the population included, first and foremost, the "whites," those born in the colony and known as *Créoles de Saint-Domingue;* French-born bureaucrats, plantation owners, merchants, and poor whites. Second, there were the "mulattoes," both freedmen and slaves. Third, the "blacks," the negro slaves who outnumbered the combined white and partially colored population almost ten to one.

In the exceedingly complex society of San Domingo of that period it is found that the white society was divided by educational or financial qualifications, and that the "Europeans," as the resident French were called, had little in common with the "Créole" whites. The only policy in which all classes of whites were united, was the irrevocable determination to draw the color line, to keep clearly and definitely to the established principle that the mulattoes were in fact negroes, and that no consideration of shade or wealth could alter or minimize this fundamental fact. The white men who occasionally married women who were not *all* white, or consorted with them, were not only ostracised by their white associates, but were deprived of civil rights and prohibited from holding any office.

These being facts, it is most unlikely that a man of Jean Audubon's standing would have adopted a child of his from any but a white woman.

Records from the island show that Captain Audubon enlisted with the National Guard at Aux Cayes, July 14, 1789. He must have left the island shortly thereafter, because it is proved he visited Virginia, then went to Philadelphia and purchased the *Mill Grove* estate on the Perkioming before the close of that year.

While it has been generally written that Audubon's mother was killed in an uprising of the blacks, and that this revolution caused his father to flee the island, a review of the occurences of that period do not bear out such statements. In 1789 there was an uprising of the mulattoes in the valley of the Artibonite which, while quickly suppressed, was followed by others in various parts of the island. Although active rebellion was averted, all classes were greatly excited and only a spark was needed to set the whole island ablaze.

The first massacres of the white planters of the Plaine-du-Nord by the blacks occurred late in August of 1791. It was followed by equally brutal reprisals on the part of the whites. Accounts of this period vie with one another in the recitation of almost incredible ferocities. In fiendish cruelty there seems to have been little to choose between the whites and the blacks. The French burned captured negroes alive, broke them on the wheel, or buried them to their necks in sand and poured melted hot wax in their ears. These awful atrocities were paralleled by equally revolting exhibitions of black savagery.

But during this massacre Jean Audubon and the little boy and baby girl he had taken from Aux Cayes were in Nantes, France, and had been for two years, far from these horrible scenes, and from documentary evidence it is most certain that Mlle. Rabin died in 1785 from a fever shortly after the birth of that boy called Jean Rabin. The first negro uprising came six years later.

France was still in the throes of the Revolution. There was dissention among the French Royalists and French Republicans in San Domingo. Finally, in 1793, the great mass of blacks held in bondage, realizing their strength, rose against their masters. They ravaged the western part of the island with fire and sword, drove out the whites they did not kill, and eventually Dessalines, nicknamed the "Black Tiger," standing on the seashore, tore the *tricolor* of Republican France into three pieces. Dramatically hurling the white portion into the ocean, the negro leader united the red and blue of the desecrated banner and created the ensign of independent Haiti, the famous Black Republic.

6

Those who have studied the ability of Audubon to delineate birds have concluded, and with some reason, that young Audubon could not have inherited his artistic talents from Captain Jean Audubon's family, fisher folk all of them; but undoubtedly this gifted faculty came to him from his mother's line, and that, ordinarily, grandparents handed down such talents. Therefore, it appeared in the face of Professor Herrick's almost complete and valuable discoveries in France, that there was much more to be learned of "Mlle. Rabin" in Aux Cayes.

Was the name Rabin assumed? Had it been spelled correctly in the bill Doctor Sanson rendered Captain Audubon? Was it a first or given name, and was the mother's last name Fougère? Why did her son adopt the fanciful name of Laforest?

The Blacker Library McGill University, of Montreal, Canada, acquired in Paris, in 1928, a series of watercolor paintings depicting the flora and fauna of Haiti, many being of birds found there. According to the inscription on the volumes they were a *Collection des oiseaux de St. Domingue peints d'apres nature par M*[r]. *de Rabié maréchal de camp, ingénieur en chef de la partie du nord de St. Domingue, mort à Paris, en* 1785.

From the signatures and dates on the various drawings it appears that M. Rabié began depicting objects of nature on his sketch pads in 1771 and continued such work up to August of 1784, at which time he evidently left San Domingo for Paris, dying there a year later. He was well-known during his residence on the island and is described in Moreau de Saint-Méry's work, *De la Partie Francaise de l'Isle Saint-Domingue*, as the engineer who designed and constructed an elaborate fountain, a doorway to a church, and a number of other structures on the island.

M. Rabié's drawings of birds, all in full color, in life size and life-like attitudes against a landscape background, and apparently made from living birds, are very much like those John James Audubon made years later and which so astonished the ornithologists and scientists of the Old World. Curiously enough, Engineer Rabié—and we have this on the authority of Dr. Alexander Wetmore of the Smithsonian Institute—depicted birds that were not scientifically recognized until 1929. His drawings of the Hispaniolan goatsucker and the black-capped petrel were so exact that Doctor Wetmore had no difficulty in noting the sub-specific differences.

What *work* of Audubon's grandfather did Lesson show Audubon in Paris in 1828?

7

The most recent contribution to a possible solution of the enigma comes from Stéphane A. Fougère, for many years mayor of *Les Cayes*, later préfect of that same district and a lawyer and commercial agent of that Haitian city. According to his records and written testimony, another of Captain Audubon's sons, a brother to Jean "Rabin," was named Belony Fougère. This son remained on the island and married Francine d'Opsant Dumont, a native of Jérémie, a town located not far from Aux Cayes. Mlle. Dumont was a descendant of a family named Laforest whose plantations and holdings were in the neighborhood of Jérémie. From the union of Belony Fougère and Francine Dumont issued several daughters and a son named Oxilus. One son of Oxilus was Antoine Fougère, father of S. A. Fougère who has supplied these statements.

In the *Dictionnaire Geographique et Administration Universal d'Haiti* it is shown there are two communities called Fougère in Haiti. One is the military station of Petit-Anse in the commune of Cape Haiti; the other located in the rural section of Roucou, in the commune of Limonade. In the commune of Les Cayes is found the county of Bouffard. A review of the list of land-masters of the ancient French colony reveals the name of Raffin, a white colonel in the colonial army; and a white plantation owner was named Rabouin, but the name *Rabin* is not encountered.

The code of Louis XIV forbade natural sons the right to use their father's name, and young women in San Domingo bearing children when they were not married were termed *Mademoiselle*, and, according to S. A. Fougère's conclusions, "*Mlle.* Rabin, who was probably Rabin by her mother and Fougère by her father, was not in harmony with her relatives, especially her father, because of her relations with Captain Audubon. Therefore, she was not willing that her child should bear her paternal name. Her father, in all likelihood, possessed considerable wealth and was an important planter of those early days, and was not willing to see his daughter, a *créole de Saint-Domingue*, a mother-girl in a Frenchman's home. The *créoles de Saint-Domingue* were the children of European white men and white women—all held high reputations that went with well-to-do people."

The other sons of Mlle. Rabin (again according to S. A. Fougère), those who remained in San Domingo, including his direct ancestor Belony Fougère, retained the name of their mother's father instead of that of Rabin or Audubon. These "other sons" being a reference to Audubon's own statement that he had "three younger brothers killed in the wars." Or was the correction to "older" brothers correct?

"It is evident that John James Audubon's dislike for the name Fougère was because his mother was not willing to bear it," writes S. A. Fougère, "therefore he would not. For that reason he adopted her other family name of Laforest, and this is a possible solution of the enigma of names. It is also my opinion that while in Aux Cayes, Captain Audubon could not use the name of Fougère for his son and was compelled to wait until his return to France to have it written into his son's birth register. As Mlle. Fougère had died she could not enter a legal objection, but, on the contrary, Mlle. Catherine Bouffard, who had succeeded her in the Audubon home, was still alive and when her daughter Rosa was adopted, Captain Audubon was forced to record her name because, as she was then in France, she could have entered a legal objection."

8

All the foregoing evidence merely adds to the mystery of the actual identity of John James Laforest Audubon. One fact remains clear and permanent . . . . he was not a native of Louisiana as has been so long supposed.

Was he the boy that was born to Jean Audubon and "Mlle. Rabin" in Aux Cayes April 26, 1785?

A preponderance of evidence appears to prove that he was that little boy.

To counter this mass of testimony, the descendants of The American Woodsman today reveal the evidence upon which they base their belief that their distinguished ancestor was of noble, of royal birth—that he was that mysterious figure of history, the elusive Lost Dauphin.

Miss Harriet B. Audubon, in a statement made before a notary public September 3, 1931, details as "a rather striking evidence of the truth of what we believe," the remark made by a French lady who saw for the first time a portrait of Audubon, and not knowing who he was, "exclaimed as she laid a hand on her heart, 'A Bourbon! Where did you get it? Look at those eyes, that mouth, that chin!'

"Another evidence of his royal birth is given by the education he received," continues Miss Harriet Audubon, "aided, no doubt, by some of the aristocrats; he was taught, in addition to his school education, music, drawing, and painting (from one of the greatest French artists, 'David'), dancing and *fencing*. That is not the education a sailor gives to his son."

Miss Harriet Audubon recited her recollection of an incident of many years ago when the Reverend Charles C. Adams assisted Mrs. Audubon in writing a life of Audubon, and was loaned a number of the naturalist's original journals. He "came into our parlor, with a volume of the journals in his hands, exclaiming, 'Why, he was the lost Dauphin!' " Miss Audubon says her grandmother made the clergyman an evasive answer, "neither denying nor admitting the statement. I think she said, 'I do not see why you should come to such a solution," or something like that, and the subject was dropped."

In the heretofore unrevealed extracts of Audubon's journal, written when he was in Paris, which have been printed in full in this biography on pages 373-375, the naturalist makes mention "of that Audubon of La Rochelle," the brother of Jean Audubon, and heaps curses on his memory. This Audubon, whose first name is believed to have been Claude, receives attention in documents that have also been withheld by descendants. An entry reads:

"Audubon, the elder brother of Jean Audubon, was an active politician in Nantes, La Rochelle and Paris from 1771 to 1796, when he disappeared for two years—next heard of in La Rochelle living in great affluence and *piety*. At his death his wealth went to the Roman church and various charities—he and the Admiral were not on speaking terms for many years."

Another entry is to the effect that "the brother of Admiral Audubon" left three daughters at Bayonne, Anne Audubon, Dominica and Catherine Françoise; the last married Louis Lissablé, a pilot, "but no descendants could be traced."

For the rest, the strange outbursts penned in his journal, a Bourbon resemblance and his declarations "not my adopted father but my *own* father," his friendship with the Marquise de Saint-Pierre—she who claimed to have been *dame d'honneur* to Marie Antoinette—constitute the evidence offered by descendants that Audubon was in fact that elusive character of history . . . The Lost Dauphin.

C

THE WORKS OF JOHN JAMES AUDUBON

A BIBLIOGRAPHY OF HIS ORNITHOLOGICAL AND OTHER IMPORTANT WRITINGS

I *The Birds of America*, 435 folio plates (double-elephant 30 x 40 inches) of bird portraits, 1,065 life-sized figures, printed from engraved copper plates, colored by hand, reproducing in this medium Audubon's original paintings. Numbers one to ten were first engraved and printed in Edinburgh, Scotland, and the remainder in London, England. This is known as the first, original, or, more usually, the "Elephant Edition" or "Elephant Folio," and plates from this issue are the ones prized by collectors.

II *Ornithological Biography, or An Account of the Habits of the Birds of the United States*, which contained the life histories of the birds depicted in his plates, the continuity matching the order in which the bird pictures were issued. This "letter-press" consisted of five volumes of text, *without* pictures, save for anatomical woodcuts which appeared in Vol. V only. Printed in Edinburgh, Scotland, with American reprints of volumes I and II only.

III *A Synopsis of the Birds of North America*, a systematic summary of the birds described in the *Ornithological Biography* and pictured in his large copper-engraved plates. A single volume without illustrations. Printed in Edinburgh, Scotland.

IV Several magazine articles on birds, alligators, rattlesnakes, methods of drawing, episodes, etc., printed in scientific journals in New York, Edinburgh, London, and Philadelphia.

V *The Birds of America*, (the "Birds in miniature"), in which the colored pictures are combined with the text. Issued in seven octavo volumes. All editions published and printed in the United States. The small bird portraits (approximately 5 x 7 inches on 6 x 9 pages) were reproduced by lithography and should not be confused with the original large copper-engraved and hand-colored plates produced in Great Britain. It appears that nine different editions of the octavo-sized *Birds* were offered to the public. One re-issue of *The Birds of*

America in double-elephant size, but by a chromo-lithographic process, and in one volume of 106 plates, was undertaken in the United States in 1859-60.

VI *The Viviparous Quadrupeds of North America*, a joint work of John James Audubon and the Reverend John Bachman. The original issue of plates picturing the mammals was in large size, Imperial folio, followed by octavo volumes to match the small *Birds*. The mammals pictured in both sizes were reproduced by a colored lithographic process. The original drawings were by the elder Audubon and his son John Woodhouse Audubon, the father painting 76 subjects and his son 74 of the 150 plates that made up the original work. The octavo volumes carried a shorter title, *The Quadrupeds of North America*, the difficultly pronounced "*Viviparous*" being dropped. Six editions were issued, all published and printed in the United States.

DATA ON THE VARIOUS WORKS

I

THE BIRDS OF AMERICA

(Usually called "the original Audubon Prints")

The Birds of America, reproductions of original drawings by John James Audubon. Copper plate engravings printed on double-elephant (untrimmed 29½ x 39½ inches) Whatman's hand-made drawing paper and colored by hand. Each sheet has the watermark of the manufacturer, the name of the mill, and a date. An example: "J. WHATMAN TURKEY MILL 1828." Issued to make four volumes of pictures only, no text. Total of complete sets variously stated—187 to 190, the number of sets never reached 200 sets of 435 individual plates picturing 1,065 figures of birds, all reproduced life size.

The first ten plates were engraved in Edinburgh, Scotland, in the winter of 1826-27 by William Home Lizars. Only 50 of the first five plates were printed and colored by Lizars; he did not color any of the plates vi to x. The remainder of the plates, xi to ccccxxxv (11 to 435) were engraved in London, England, by Robert Havell, Junr., who also retouched and reengraved several of the Lizars' plates. The coloring on plates vi to x, engraved and printed by Lizars, was done by Robert Havell, Senr.

Audubon's original plates were issued in "parts" of five plates or "numbers" to each part, or 110 plates to each volume, 105 in the fourth, in this manner:

VOL. I, parts 1 to 22	pl. i to cx	eng. 1826 to 1830
VOL. II, parts 23 to 44	pl. cxi to ccxx	eng. 1831 to 1834
VOL. III, parts 45 to 66	pl. ccxxi to cccxxx	eng. 1834 to 1835
VOL. IV, parts 67 to 87	pl. cccxxxi to ccccxxxv	eng. 1835 to 1838

These hand-colored engravings were issued to subscribers *without* text depicting 1,065 life-sized figures of birds, including, so Audubon then claimed, 489 distinct species. These plates were sold for two guineas for each part of five plates (a guinea equaled a pound or 21 shillings). The complete work selling in England for £182, 14 shillings, and in the United States for $1,000.00.

Publication data: 1 to 27, published in 1826-27; 28 to 50, in 1828; 51 to 75, in 1829; 76 to 100, in 1830; 101 to 125, in 1831; 126 to 155, in 1832; 156 to 185, in 1833; 186 to 235, in 1834; 236 to 285, in 1835; 286 to 350, in 1836; 351 to 400, in 1837, and 401 to 435, in 1838.

The first plate in each *part* of five has a large bird picture practically filling the whole paper. The second plate in a part is usually given over to large-sized birds in a composition arrangement, while the remaining three plates are of smaller birds, each with a distinct "plate mark." This arrangement is strikingly illustrated in Part One. The huge Wild Turkey Cock led off the procession of birds and is "Part 1. No. 1." The Yellow-billed Cuckoos, shown in good size among pawpaw blossoms, are "Part 1. No. 2." The third plate shows the Prothonotary Warbler; the fourth is the Purple Finch, and the fifth is his Bonaparte's Fly-catcher.

On the Lizars' plate of the celebrated Wild Turkey gobbler the inscription reads: "Great American Cock Male. Vulgo (Wild Turkey) *Meleagris Gallopavo*, Linn." When Havell reprinted this plate the engraved wording was changed to: "Wild Turkey, *Meleagris Gallopavo*, Linn. Male." In the lower right-hand corner: "Engraved by W. H. Lizars, Edin^r^." and "Retouched by R. Havell, Junr."

Other changes made to the first Lizars' plates are: Plate 2. Lizars' plate—"Black-billed Cuckoo, *Coccyzus erythrophthalmus.*" Havell's retouched plate—"Yellow-billed Cuckoo, *Coccyzus americanus.*" Plate 3, Lizars' plate—"Protonotary Warbler, *Dacnis protonotarius.*" Havell changed the generic scientific name to "*Sylvia protonotarius.*" Plate 6: Lizars' plate "Great American Hen & Young. Vulgo, Female Wild Turkey, *Meleagris gallopavo.*" Havell changed this to "Wild Turkey Hen & Young." Plate 7: after the words "Purple Grackle" on the Lizars' plate, Havell added "or Common Crow Blackbird." Plate 10: Lizars' inscription "Brown Lark, *Anthus aquaticus,*" was changed by Havell to "Brown Titlark, *Anthus spinoletta*, Bonap."

Collectors of Audubon plates will note that on each plate the engraved number of the *part* has Arabic numerals while the plate numbers are frequently Roman. In some plates, however, both part and number are in Arabic figures. Examples: The Prairie Warbler has on its upper left "Plate 14.", on the upper right "No. 3." While on the plate of the Yellow-throated Vireo is "No. 24." and "Plate CXIX." The lower right-hand corner carries the engraver's name as: "Engraved, Printed, & Coloured by R. Havell, Junr., London, 1830." Most of the plates do *not* carry the year they were engraved.

II

ORNITHOLOGICAL BIOGRAPHY

Audubon's letterpress, or his first published volumes of life histories of the birds, was published in Edinburgh, Scotland, in five volumes from 1831 to 1839. This work is titled *Ornithological Biography, or an Account of the Habits of the Birds of North America*, and is not as well known as his smaller works in which bird pictures and text were combined. These biographies furnished word pictures of the birds he had depicted in his mammoth engraved plates, interspersed with "Delineations of American Scenery & Manners," sometimes designated as "Episodes."

The *Ornithological Biography* was issued in five volumes, Royal octavo (Roy. 8vo.), page measurement 10 x 6¼ inches, as follows:

VOL. I Adam Black, 55 North Bridge (with names of agents); Neill & Co., Printers, Old Fishmarket, Edinburgh, MDCCCXXXI. Preface dated "March 1831."

VOL. II Adam and Charles Black, Edinburgh, MDCCCXXXIV. Preface dated "1st. December 1834."

VOL. III Adam and Charles Black, Edinburgh, MDCCCXXXV. Preface dated "1st. December 1834."

VOL. IV Adam and Charles Black, Edinburgh, MDCCCXXXVIII. Preface dated "1st. November 1838."

VOL. V Adam and Charles Black, Edinburgh, MDCCCXXXIX. Preface dated "1st. May 1839."

Volumes I and II of the *Ornithological Biography* had American reprints. Vol. I was reprinted in Philadelphia by Dr. Richard Harlan for Audubon, and Vol. I and II were issued by different publishers. Data on these American reprints are:

1st. American reprint has same pagination of original Edinburgh issue. Title page carries the imprint: Judah Dobson, Agent, 108 Chestnut St., Philadelphia, MDCCCXXXI. Copyright by R. Harlan, M.D., 1831. Printed by James Kay, Jun. & Co., Printers to the American Philosophical Society, No. 4, Minor St.

2nd. American reprint of Vol. I follows closely the original edition but carries the names of E. L. Carey and A. Hart, Chestnut St., Philadelphia, MDCCCXXXV.

3rd. American reprint Vol. II follows the original European volume and has the imprint of Hilliard, Gray, and Company, Boston, MDCCCXXXV.

There were no American reprints of Volumes III, IV, and V of the *Ornithological Biography*, and neither the Edinburgh issues nor the American reprints had colored illustrations of the birds although Vol. V of the original edition contained 98 woodcuts of the anatomical structure of the birds. It is believed that these drawings were the work of William MacGillivray who rewrote Audubon's text for publication.

The *Ornithological Biography* was intended as a letterpress to the engraved plates. There was no endeavor to follow a biological system but followed the order in which the bird pictures were given to the public. The first three volumes contained an even hundred life histories, Vol. IV had 88 descriptions, Vol. V had 47 bird biographies.

Vol. I described birds on plates 1 to 100 (i to c); Vol. II, 101 to 200 (ci to cc); Vol. III, 201 to 300 (cci to ccc); Vol. IV, 301 to 388 (ccci to ccclxxxviii); Vol. V, 389 to 435 (ccclxxxix to ccccxxxv).

III

A SYNOPSIS OF THE BIRDS OF NORTH AMERICA

A Synopsis of the Birds of North America was published in Edinburgh in 1839. It is a one-volume octavo edition which proves to be a methodical and systematic index to the birds of America carrying references to Audubon's engraved plates and notes on the distribution and nomenclature found in the *Ornithological Biography*, and was not illustrated. The title page imprint is:

Edinburgh / Adam and Charles Black, Edinburgh; / Longman, Rees, Brown, Green, and Longman, / London. / MDCCCXXXIX.

Overleaf: Printed by Neill and Co., Old Fishmarket, Edinburgh.

This rather scarce book, i-xii + 359 pages, was to a great extent the work of William MacGillivray, as Audubon acknowledged in his prefatory address.

IV

MAGAZINE ARTICLES ON NATURAL HISTORY

On the Hirundo fulva of Vieillot, Annals of the Lyceum of Natural History of New York, Vol I, pp. 163-166. New York, 1824.

Facts and Observations connected with the permanent residence of swallows in the United States, Annals of the Lyceum of Natural History of New York, Vol. I, pp. 166-168. New York, 1824. These two articles being Audubon's first published works.

Account of the Habits of the Turkey Buzzard (Vultur aura) *particularly with the view of exploding the opinion generally entertained of its extraordinary power of Smelling.* Edinburgh New Philosophical Journal, Vol. II (Oct.-Apr.). pp. 172-184. Edinburgh, 1826-27.

Observations on the Natural History of the Alligator. Edinburgh New Philosophical Journal, Vol. II, (Oct.-Apr.), pp. 270-280. Edinburgh, 1826-27.

Account of the Carrion Crow or Vultur atratus, Edinburgh Journal of Science, Vol. VI, (Nov.-Apr.), pp. 156-161. Edinburgh, 1826-27.

Notes on the Habits of the Wild Pigeon of America, Columba migratoria. Edinburgh Journal of Science, Vol. VI, (Nov.-Apr.), pp. 256-265. Edinburgh, 1826-27.

Notes on the Rattlesnake (*Crotalus horridus*), *in a letter addressed to Thomas Stuart Traill, M.D.*, &c., Edinburgh New Philosophical Journal Vol. III (Apr.-Oct.), pp. 21-30. Edinburgh, 1827. Reproduced in Journal of the Franklin Institute and American Mechanics' Magazine, vol. ii, n. s., pp. 32-37, Philadelphia, 1828.

Account of the Method of Drawing Birds employed by J. J. Audubon, Esq., F. R. S. E., Edinburgh Journal of Science, vol. viii, pp. 48-54. Edinburgh, 1828.

Notes on the Bird of Washington—(*Falco Washingtonia*) *or Great American Sea Eagle*, Loudon's Magazine of Natural History, vol. i, pp. 115-120. London, 1828-29.

An Account of the Habits of the American Goshawk (*Falco palumbarius, Wils.*), Edinburgh Journal of Natural and Geographical Science, vol. 3 (March), pp. 145-147. Edinburgh, 1831.

V

THE BIRDS OF AMERICA

(The *Birds* in miniature.)

The first American issue of *The Birds of America*, in which the pictures and text were combined, sometimes called "the *Birds* in miniature" so they will not be confused with the large copper plate originals, was published in 1840-44 by J. J. Audubon and J. B. Chevalier in New York and Philadelphia. This work consisted of seven volumes differing from the order of the biographies in the *Ornithological Biography* in that the bird histories are systematically grouped in orders, families, and species, a number of changes made in names and in the body of the text, and the *Episodes* deleted.

The work was illustrated with Audubon's bird drawings but they were reproduced by a lithographic process. These small bird portraits, about 5 x 7 inches on 6 x 9 paper, were drawn on stone with the aid of the *camera lucida*, printed black and white, then colored by hand.

Issued, unbound, in blue paper covers when accompanied by the colored illustrations, or in drab wrappers when without pictures. The complete work consisted of 100 parts, each part having five lithographic plates. The cost was $1.00 a part, and $100.00 for the complete set. Binding was usually done by the subscriber after he received all the parts. This reduced format was usually Royal 8vo.

Data on the first edition and its reprints are:

1st. Edition

The first of *The Birds of America* in this format was issued in seven volumes. Volumes I to V published by J. J. Audubon, New York, and J. B. Chevalier, Philadelphia; Vols. VI and VII were published by J. J. Audubon, 77 Williams St., New York, and 34 North First St., Philadelphia, 1840-1844. The 500 illustrations, from colored lithographic plates, printed on paper 6½ x 10 inches, bear the legends "Drawn from Nature by J. J. Audubon, F. R. S., F. L. S." and "Lith^{d}., Printed & Col^{d}. by J. T. Bowen, Phil^{a}." These prints do not have the lithographic tinted backgrounds found on the same plates in subsequent editions. The title pages read: The / Birds of America, / from / Drawings Made in the United States / and their Territories. / by John James Audubon, F. R. SS. L. & E. / (follows 11 lines giving his membership in societies) / Vol. I. / New York: / Published by J. J. Audubon. / Philadelphia: / J. B. Chevalier. / 1840. The over-leaf copyright date is 1839, and the printer's imprint is: E. G. Dorsey, Printers, / Library Street. (See cut page 506.)

This is the more valuable of the smaller editions of Audubon's *Birds*. Unbound sets, in the original 100 parts in blue paper wrappers, are rare and command good prices. Each of the volumes concludes with a "List of Subscribers," the original list and the six supplementary lists. Frequently book binders failed to include these lists. Sets with the names of subscribers are more valuable than those without them.

2nd. Edition

The second edition of *The Birds of America*, in which the text and lithographed plates are combined, was published by "V. G. Audubon, New York, 1856." Seven volumes, Roy. 8vo, as in the one mentioned above, but Vol. I has a steel engraving of John James Audubon by H. B. Hall after Henry Inman's portrait, the same that appeared as a frontispiece in Lucy Audubon's biography of her husband.

3rd. Edition

The third edition, Imperial 8vo., in seven volumes, was issued: "New York, V. G. Audubon, 1859." This edition contains the same text and 500 lithographic illustrations, and can be identified by the imprint on the reverse of the title page, "Entered, etc., 1839," and "R. Craighead, Printer, Stereotyper, & Electrotyper, Caxton Building, 81, 83, & 85 Center street." The title pages read: The / Birds of America, / from / Drawings made in the United States / and their Territories. / by / John James Audubon, F. R. S., &c., &c. / Vol. I / New York: / V. G. Audubon. / Roe Lockwood & Son, 411 Broadway. / 1859.

4th. Edition

The fourth octavo edition of *The Birds of America* was also issued by V. G. Audubon from the house of Roe Lockwood & Son, New York, 1860, and contained the 500 lithographic illustrations.

5th. Edition

Only one attempt was made to reissue the double-elephant folio plates in their original size. This work, published by John Woodhouse Audubon, was an American edition from lithographic plates. It consisted of 106 plates, representing 151 of the original 435 copper engravings. Roe Lockwood & Son, New York, 1860, undertook this work for young Audubon, but the outbreak of the Civil War put a stop to the ambitious plan to reproduce all of the birds, on the original large scale, by color lithography. This attempt to reissue *The Birds* proved a financial failure, John Woodhouse Audubon standing the brunt of the losses.

These large chromo-lithographs were much inferior to the hand-colored engraved plates turned out by Lizars and Havell. In many of the plates the backgrounds were changed, many of the bird figures grouped, and, all in all, the birds and floral decorations poorly done. In consequence they are not as much in demand by collectors as the original plates. This issue can readily be identified by the legend on the lower right-hand corner: "Chromo-lithography by J. Bien, 180 Broadway, New York." These plates are frequently offered for sale by some dealers as "original" Audubon plates.

John Woodhouse Audubon also issued an edition of *The Birds of America*, but *without* illustrations combined with the text, as a letterpress to the above chromo-lithographs, in seven volumes Roy. 8vo., bearing the imprint: "Roe Lockwood & Son, New York, 1861."

6th. Edition

The Birds of America, seven volumes, Roy. 8vo., with 500 lithographic plates 7 x 10 inches, Roe Lockwood & Son, New York, 1861, a reissue by John Woodhouse Audubon, following his issuance of the fifth edition.

7th. Edition

The seventh edition, according to Dr. Elliot Coues, carries the designation: "*The Birds of America; a Popular and Scientific Description of the Birds of the United States and Their Territories. New Edition, New York,* 1863." Seven volumes, Imperial 8vo.

8th. Edition

The Birds of America in eight volumes, Imperial 8vo. and Royal 8vo., instead of the usual seven volumes, illustrated with 500 lithographic plates, was issued by J. W. Audubon, "New York, 1865."

9th. Edition

The ninth and apparently final edition of the *Birds* in miniature, with text and 500 lithographic plates combined. Probably a reissue of the eighth edition of 1865 and, while not dated on the title page, is said to have been published in 1871. It is the second eight-volume edition, Imperial 8vo., published by "George R. Lockwood, late Roe Lockwood & Son, 812 Broadway, New York." Vol. I contains a memoir of J. J. Audubon, signed "G. R. L., 1870."

VI

THE VIVIPAROUS QUADRUPEDS OF NORTH AMERICA

Data on the first and following editions are:

1st. Edition

Originally issued in hand colored lithographic plates only, 1845-1848, and sold to subscribers in 30 parts of five plates each, at $10.00 a part, or $300.00 complete. Size of plates 22 x 28 inches. Legends: "Drawn from Nature by J. J. Audubon, F. R. S., F. L. S." and "Lith. Printed & Cold. by J. T. Bowen, Phila.," followed by year. This issue was without text, except titles, tables of contents, and names of the mammals. When bound, issued in three volumes.

Publication data: Imperial folio. Published by J. J. Audubon, New York, 1845-1848. Vol. I, parts 1 to 10, plates 1 to 50, 1845; Vol. II, parts 11 to 20, plates 51 to 100, 1846; Vol. III, parts 21 to 30, plates 101 to 150, 1848.

John James Audubon drew 76 of the originals, the remaining 74 being reproductions of painting made by his son John Woodhouse, legends on plates identifying the work of each. There were no copper plates, colored by hand, as in the original *Birds*, done for this work.

2nd. Edition

A text-only edition, Royal 8vo., of *The Viviparous Quadrupeds of North America*, issued as a letterpress to the lithographic plates, was printed in three volumes. Published by J. J. Audubon and V. G. Audubon, New York, 1846-1854. Data: Vol. I, text only, J. J. Audubon, New York, 1846. (Vol. I, had an European edition, same as American, but carrying the imprint of Wiley & Putnam. London, 1847.); Vol. II, text only, published by V. G. Audubon, 1851; Vol. III, text with 6 colored plates, V. G. Audubon, 1854.

3rd. Edition

This is the first octavo edition of this work in which text and lithographic plates were combined. Published so as to be uniform with the small *Birds*.

The Quadrupeds of North America (note the absence of "*Viviparous*") issued in three volumes, Royal 8vo., with 155 colored lithographic illustrations, 7 x 10½ inches. Title page:

The / Quadrupeds / of / North America / by / John James Audubon, F. R. S. &c., &c. / and / The Rev. John Bachman, D.D. LL.D., &c., &c. / Vol. I / New-York: / Published by V. G. Audubon / 1851.

Overleaf: Entered, according . . . etc., 1849 by V. G. Audubon, and U. Ludwig & Co., Printers, 70 Vesesy-street, N. Y. The copyright notice in Vol. II is dated 1851, in Vol. III, 1854.

All plates in Vol. I, and 28 in Vol. II, total 78, are after drawings by John James Audubon. The remaining 22 in Vol. II, and all in Vol. III, total 77, are after drawings by his son John Woodhouse Audubon. These illustrations were "Lith. Printed & Col[d]. by J. T. Bowen, Phil[a].," with the exception of 17 plates in Vol. I which were "Printed by Nagel & Weingæartner, N. Y." Practically all carry the name of the artist who reproduced the animals on stone. Those produced by the Bowen firm carry the line: "Drawn on Stone by W. E. Hitchcock." Those printed by Nagel & Weingæartner were "Drawn on Stone by R. Trembly." Plate xxxiii, *The Mink*, reproduced on stone by Trembly, was printed by Bowen in Philadelphia.

4th. Edition

This, the second octavo edition of the *Quadrupeds*, with text and plates combined, was issued in 1854 by Victor Audubon. It is practically identical with the one just described, the title pages are the same except dates at bottom: Vol. I, 1852; Vol. II, M DCCC LIV; Vol. III, 1854. Overleaf carries same copyright data as above. On lower left corner is: "R. Craighead, Printer and Stereotyper, 53 Vesey Street, New York." in Vols. I and III, missing in Vol. II. Usually seen in Roy. 8vo. size.

5th. Edition

A third issue of this octavo edition is said to have been run off the presses in 1856. No example examined by present author.

6th. Edition

A fourth issue of the octavo, bearing the printer's date of 1860 has also been recorded.

Finely bound, Imperial folio volumes of the first edition of *The Viviparous Quadrupeds of North America*, plates only, 22 x 28 inches, in the three volumes are sometimes in demand. It must be remembered the *Quadrupeds* are never such valuable collectors' items as are the *Birds*.

Individual plates from broken up volumes are frequently offered for sale. Care should be taken to note whether such mammals pictured are the work of the father or son.

D

AUTHENTIC LIKENESSES OF JOHN JAMES AUDUBON

1. *Audubon by himself*—1822

The earliest known, and unquestionably the best likeness of The American Woodsman, is a portrait by himself made in 1822 at the Percys' *Beech Woods* plantation, West Feliciana parish, Louisiana, soon after learning the use of oils from John Steen, and painted while looking into a mirror. Audubon was then 37 years old and his own portrait undoubtedly represents him as he actually appeared when at the zenith of his powers. He presented it, in 1830, to Mrs. William Garrett Johnson of *Beech Grove* plantation, who bequeathed it to her youngest daughter, Ellen (Mrs. William Broadner Walker); in turn the portrait went to Mrs. Walker's daughter, Mrs. Mitchell Ford Jamar; to David G. Murrel, of Paducah, Kentucky, and then bequeathed by Mrs. Murrel to the late Miss Sadie Randolph, of New Orleans. Audubon painted his portrait on thin, 8½ x 12 inches, canvas and attached it to what is evidently a hand-made frame. His coat is dark green and the background is of a rose tint shading to light blue above. His hair is brown and the large eyes are blue. Reproduced as a frontispiece to this biography from a photograph by the author.

2. *Audubon by himself*—1826

A black chalk sketch by himself made while at *Green Banks*, the home of William Rathbone just outside Liverpool, England, and given to Mrs. Rathbone. He wrote upon it: "Audubon at Green Bank *Almost*, Happy!!—Sepr 1826." Audubon was then 41 years old. First reproduced as a woodcut on the title page of Buchanan's biography. Later from the original sketch in Maria R. Audubon's *Audubon and His Journals*. The Buchanan woodcut is reproduced on page 322 this work.

3. *Audubon by Syme*—1826

An oil portrait made by John Syme at Edinburgh, Scotland, for W. H. Lizars who intended to use it to further the publication of *The Birds of America*. Audubon was 41 years old on November 27, 1826, when: "At twelve I went to *stand up* for my picture, and sick enough I was of it by two; at the request of Mr. Lizars I wear my wolf-skin coat, and if the head is not a strong likeness, perhaps the coat may be—but this is discourteous of me, even to my journal." On the last day of the month the portrait was finished and Audubon gazed upon, "a strange-looking figure, with gun, strap, and buckles, and eyes that to me are more of an enraged Eagle than mine." As the Lizars-Audubon partnership was dissolved soon after, the engraver did not publish the portrait. In 1833 Charles Wands made an engraving from Syme's oil which appeared as a frontispiece to one of the volumes of *The Miscellany of Natural History*, by Sir Thomas Dick Lauder and Captain Thomas Brown. Thus it became the first published likeness of The American Woodsman. He did not like it and wrote John Bachman: "I have seen my portrait engraved—the Devil himself could not wish better fun than to catch me in such a trim as this fellow has represented me in—Like Me? God bless you not a bit of it." Later copies of the Wands engraving appeared in Baron Cuvier's English edition of *The Animal World*, in 1834, from an engraving on steel by J. Brown; it was also copied as a woodcut in *Audubon Naturaliste Américain Etude Biographique* by P. A. Cap, 1851, and in *Gleason's Pictorial* in 1852. The whereabouts of Syme's oil portrait is not known but Wands' engraving is reproduced facing page 336 of this work.

4. *Audubon by Parker*—1828

An oil portrait by C. R. Parker, an American artist who accompanied Audubon to Paris. On August 25, 1828, Audubon set down in his journal: "Mr. Parker has nearly finished my portrait, which he considers a good one, and *so do I*." This portrait, which pictures Audubon at 43, is the one mistakenly attributed to "W. H. Holmes," and shows the bird artist holding a portfolio, garbed in a green coat, with a fur-edged crimson cloak thrown over his shoulder. Long in the possession of the Bentley family of Manchester, England, the Parker portrait, which Audubon descendants consider an excellent likeness, is presently owned by Mr. Morris Tyler, of New Haven, Connecticut, a great grandson of Victor Audubon. It is reproduced facing page 400 of this work.

5. *Audubon by Cruikshank*—1831

A miniature painted on ivory by Frederick Cruikshank in London, May 1831, who at the same time did a miniature of Lucy. The bird man was then 46 years old. In 1834 he wrote John Bachman that "Cruikshank has Improved my Miniature very considerably—he has worked over the Hair &c—This picture goes to *Turner* to be engraved in Mezzotints." Charles Turner, A. R. A., did engrave the Cruikshank miniature and it was published by Havell, January 12, 1835. A favorite portrait of Audubon and his admirers, it becomes the likeness so well known through it many reproductions. The original miniature was destroyed in a fire at Shelbyville, Kentucky, along with many other valuable family relics in 1874 soon after Mrs. Audubon's death. The two Cruikshank miniatures are reproduced on the same page facing 337 of this work.

6. *Audubon by Inman*—1833

A portrait in oils by Henry Inman, Philadelphia, April 1833, showing The American Woodsman when 48 years old. Audubon wrote his son Victor: "and *I say* it is a truer portrait of me than even the Miniature." The Inman portrait has become well known through its engraving by H. B. Hall, which first appeared in the second octavo, 1856, publication of the *Birds* in miniature, and later as the frontispiece of Mrs. Audubon's *Life* of her husband. The Hall engraving is the likeness fixed upon the public mind through its numerous reproduction. Both the original Inman painting and Hall's engraving of it are reproduced on the same page, facing 352 of this work, for the purposes of comparison. The original Inman oil portrait is now owned by Mr. Morris Tyler, New Haven, Connecticut, who inherited it from his cousin, the late Miss Harriet Bachman Audubon.

7. *Audubon by Healy*—1838

Oil portrait by George P. A. Healy, an American artist, while in London in 1838 when Audubon was 53 years old. Healy induced Audubon to pose for him but, as The American Woodsman would not pose during the day, the portrait was made at night by gas light. "I painted him in a costume he wore when he went in search of his birds—a sort of Backwoodsman's dress. The portrait was a curiously bright one, as though it had been painted in sunlight." The Healy likeness now hangs in the lecture room of the Boston Museum of Natural History, and is reproduced facing page 353 of this work from a photograph from the late Ruthven Deane.

8. *Audubon by Havell*—1839

Life mask made in London by Robert Havell, Jr., when Audubon was 54. Long in the possession of the Havell family the mask was acquired by Colonel John E. Thayer who presented it to Harvard University where it now is in the Museum of Comparative Zoology. An earlier life mask made by a man named O'Neill in Edinburgh, Scotland, in 1827, and presented to the Antiquarian Society, has apparently disappeared.

9. *Audubon by King*—1840

John C. King, a Scottish artist and sculptor, made an intaglio cameo in a shell during one of Audubon's visits to Boston. The original of the King cameo has disappeared but a cast in plaster, which was presented to Mr. Martin Parry Kennard by King, was bequeathed to his son, Mr. Frederic H. Kennard, of Newton Centre, Massachusets. A reproduction of the cast faces page 401 of this work.

10. *Audubon by his son*—1841

A portrait in oils by John Woodhouse Audubon made at *Minnie's*

Land, New York, who represented his father, when 56 years old, seated with a gun in his arms and a dog lying on the ground near him. In a letter written Victor Audubon, February 11, 1841, the father wrote: "John has painted one of Trudeau in an Indian dress, as well as his 'old Dad' Sitting in the Wilds of America admiring Nature around him, with a *Dog Companion*, lying at 'his' feet." This painting, now owned by Mr. Victor Morris Tyler, New Haven, Connecticut, has been reproduced many times—by Mrs. Horace St. John, in her *Audubon;* by Miss Maria R. Audubon, in her *Audubon and His Journals*, and was used by Alonzo Chappel for his painting which was later engraved for Duyckinck's *National Portrait Gallery of Eminent Americans.* The Chappel engraving of John Woodhouse Audubon's painting is reproduced facing page 432 of this work.

11. *Audubon by his son*—1841

Another full length oil painting by John Woodhouse Audubon done about the same time as the above. In it the son again pictured his father seated, with his gun, in hunting costume, the same dog crouches at his feet, and to Audubon's right is a horse. The original now hangs in the American Museum of Natural History, New York City. A reproduction will be found on page 244, Vol. II, of Herrick's *Audubon the Naturalist.*

12. *Audubon by Sprague*—1842

A pencil sketch by Isaac Sprague made before he accompanied Audubon on the Missouri River Expedition in 1843, when The American Woodsman was 58 years old. Sprague's drawing is reproduced in Maria R. Audubon's *Audubon and His Journals.* The original sketch is owned by the Sprague family, Wessley Hills, Massachussets.

13. *Audubon by his son*—1843

A portrait in oils by John Woodhouse Audubon picturing his father as he appeared at 59 upon his return from the Missouri River Expedition. The original painting is presently owned by a granddaughter, Miss Florence Audubon, Salem, New York. Reproduced facing page 433 of this work.

14. *Audubon by Brady*—1849

A daguerreotype, said to have been made by Mathew B. Brady in New York in 1849, is familiar to Audubon admirers from its frequent reproduction. The halftone, facing page 448, is from a photograph of the original sun portrait once owned by the late Miss Meta Grimshaw, of New Orleans, a granddaughter of Nicholas Berthoud and Eliza Bakewell, but now owned by Mrs. Alicia Bakewell Shaffer, of Cincinnati, Ohio. A duplicate daguerreotype is also owned by Mr. Victor Morris Tyler, of New Haven, Connecticut. This, the first known camera likeness of Audubon, shows him at 64 nearing the twilight of his adventurous, colorful career.

15. *Audubon by an unknown artist*—1851

A woodcut of Audubon, supposedly representing him as he appeared on his return from his Missouri River Expedition. It was printed in 1851 in *The Hunter-Naturalist. Romance of Sporting or Wild Scenes and Wild Hunters by* Charles Wilkins Webber. The Brady daguerreotype was used as a basis for the drawing by the artist. A reproduction is on page 458 of this work.

16. *Audubon's Last Portrait*—1850

A daguerreotype, the last ever made of Audubon, which shows the portrayer of the birds as he appeared a short time before his death. The original portrait is owned by Mr. Victor Morris Tyler, New Haven, Connecticut, and a reproduction faces page 448 of this work.

17. *Audubon in Death*—1851

A pencil sketch of his father after death by John Woodhouse Audubon reproduced in Maria R. Audubon's *Audubon and His Journals.*

18. *Audubon's Death Mask*—1851

A profile from the original death mask is to be found in Scribner's Magazine, March 1898, when Maria R. Audubon first published her grandfather's *Myself*. The original death mask was destroyed in the Shelbyville, Kentucky, fire of 1874.

Various Likenesses Done in Later Years

An oil painting, erroneously attributed to Victor and John Woodhouse Audubon, proves to be a portrait by Thomas W. Wood who based his likeness upon former portraits by Inman and Audubon's younger son. It was painted in 1905 by Wood upon order from Morris K. Jessup who gave it to the American Museum of Natural History in New York City, where it now hangs.

A marble bust by William Couper, made in 1906, is on exhibition in the American Museum of Natural History, New York City. Couper based his likeness upon the several portraits by Healy, Inman, Cruikshank, and John Woodhouse Audubon.

The full length bronze statue in Audubon Park, New Orleans, by Edward Virginious Valentine, was unveiled November 26, 1910, when the name of Exposition Park was changed to that of Audubon, thus honoring the artist who drew many of his famed bird portraits in the Crescent City.

A bronze bust of The American Woodsman now occupies a conspicious niche in the American Hall of Fame, New York University. It is the work of A. Stirling Calder and was unveiled in 1927. These two bronzes are reproduced facing page 449 of this work.

E

LIST OF PLATES

Comprising the Original Issue of Audubon's
"*The Birds of America*"

With notes showing where and when the original drawings were made.

Quoted references are from the writings found on the original drawings. Example: No. 119 "James Pirrie's Plantation, Louisiana, July 11, 1821." Other data are from his journals, letters, or printed works.

1. Great American Cock. Wild Turkey. Sleepy Hollow Woods, West Feliciana Parish, Louisiana, 1825.
2. Yellow-billed Cuckoo. **Beech Woods,** West Feliciana parish, La., 1825.
3. Prothonotary Warbler. **Oakley,** West Feliciana parish, La., 1821.
5. Bonaparte's Fly Catcher. "Bayou Sarah, Oct. 5, 1821." La.
4. Purple Finch. West Feliciana parish, La., "November 1825."
6. Great American Hen. Wild Turkey. West Feliciana, La., 1825.
7. Purple Grackle. **Beech Woods,** West Feliciana, La., 1825.
8. White-throated Sparrow. "Louisiana, March 25."
9. Selby's Flycatcher. **Oakley,** West Feliciana, La., July 1, 1821.
10. Brown Titlark. New Orleans, La., February 21, 1821.
11. Bird of Washington, New Orleans, La., January 1821.
12. Baltimore Oriole, Concordia parish, La., 1822.
13. Snowbird. Louisiana.
14. Prairie Warbler. **Oakley,** "Bayou Sarah, Sept. 5, 1821."
15. Blue Yellow-back Warbler. New Orleans, La., "March 27, 1821, plant by Jos. Mason."
16. Great-footed Hawk. On Mississippi river, La., "Dec. 26, 1820."
17. Carolina Dove. **Beech Woods,** West Feliciana, La., 1825.
18. Bewick's Long-tailed Wren. **Oakley,** Feliciana, La., "Oct. 2, 1821."
19. Louisiana Water Thrush. **Oakley,** Feliciana, La., "Sept. 27, 1821."
20. Blue-winged Yellow Warbler. "Louisiana."
21. Mockingbird. Feliciana, La. **Oakley,** 1821, and **Beech Woods,** 1825.
22. Purple Martin, **Beech Woods** West Feliciana, La., 1825.
23. Maryland Yellowthroat. "Louisiana, April."
24. Roscoe's Yellowthroat. "Bayou Sarah, Louisiana. Sept. 29, 1821."
25. Song Sparrow. "Montgomery county, Penn. 1812."
26. Carolina Parrot. **Oakley,** West Feliciana, and New Orleans, 1821-22.
27. Red-headed Woodpecker, **Oakley,** West Feliciana, La., 1821.
28. Solitary Flycatcher. "Mouth of Bayou La Fourches" on Mississippi river, January 1, 1821.
29. Towhee. "near Natchez, Miss., April 13, 1822."
30. Vigor's Wren. "Penna. April 21, 1812."
31. White-headed Eagle. On Mississippi at Little Prairie, Nov. 24, 1820.
32. Black-billed Cuckoo. "Louisiana."
33. Yellow Bird or Goldfinch. Louisiana 1825.
34. Worm-eating Warbler. Concordia parish, La., April 1822.
35. Children's Warbler. **Oakley,** West Feliciana, La., August 4, 1821.
36. Stanley Hawk. **Beech Woods,** West Feliciana, La., lower figure on stump redrawn from painting made at Louisville, Ky., Dec. 5. 1805.
37. Golden-winged Woodpecker. Louisiana 1825.
38. Kentucky Warbler. **Beech Woods,** West Feliciana, La., 1825.
39. Crested Titmouse. "Penn."
40. American Redstart. **Oakley,** West Feliciana, La., August 27, 1821.
41. Ruffed Grouse.
42. Orchard Oriole. "Louisiana, April 12, 1822."
43. Cedar Bird. Cincinnati, O., April 11, 1820.
44. Summer Red Bird. "Bayou Sarah, Louisiana, August 27, 1821."
45. Traill's Flycatcher. "Fort of Arkansas, April 17, 1822."
46. Barred Owl. **Beech Woods,** West Feliciana, La., 1825.
47. Ruby-throated Hummingbird. **Beech Woods,** West Feliciana, La., 1825.
48. Cerulean Warbler. **Oakley,** West Feliciana, La., 1821.
49. Blue-green Warbler. **Oakley,** West Feliciana, La., August 12, 1821.
50. Swainson's Warbler. New Orleans, La., October 29, 1821.
51. Red-tailed Hawk. West Feliciana, La., 1825.
52. Chuck-Will's-Widow. Natchez, Miss. May 7, 1822.

53. Painted Bunting. "City of New Orleans, April 9, 1821."
54. Rice Bird. New Orleans, La., "March 11, 1822."
55. Couvier's Wren. "**Fatland Ford,** Pennsyla., June 8, 1812."
56. Red-shouldered Hawk. Louisiana 1825.
57. Loggerhead Shrike. **Beech Grove,** West Feliciana, La., 1829.
58. Hermit Thrush. New Orleans, La., February 2, 1822.
59. Chestnut-sided Warbler. "May 17, 1812, Penna."
60. Carbonated Warbler. "Henderson, Ky., May, 1811."
61. Great Horned Owl. "Henderson, Ky., Sept. 21, 1814."
62. Passenger Pigeon. "Pittsburgh, Pa." No date, probably 1824.
63. White-eyed Flycatcher. "New Orleans, April 11, 1821."
64. Swamp Sparrow. The legend in pencil on this drawing is: "SWAMP SPARROW, male, **Spiza palustris**, plant vulgo May Apple, **Podaphyllum pellatum.** Drawn from nature by Lucy Audubon. Mr. Havell will please have Lucy Audubon name on this plate instead of mine." It is one of the Bayou Sarah drawings with the floral decoration drawn by Joseph Mason.
65. Rathbone's Warbler. "Drawn from nature, Falls of Ohio July 1, 1808."
66. Ivory-billed Woodpecker. "Drawn from nature by John J. Audubon, Louisiana." Probably 1825 in Feliciana parish.
67. Red-winged Starling. "Feliciana, Louisiana."
68. Republican Cliff Swallow. "Cinn. May 20, 1820."
69. Bay-breasted Warbler. "Drawn May 12, 1812, Penna."
70. Henslow's Bunting. "Cinna. April 12, 1820.
71. Winter Hawk. New Orleans.
72. Swallow-tailed Hawk. "1821." **Oakley,** West Feliciana, La. Copious lead pencil notes on original drawing have been erased.
73. Wood Thrush. "Weight 8½ ounces. April 21, 1822." Natchez, Miss.
74. Indigo Bird. "Louisiana, July. J. J. A."
75. Le Petit Caporal. "April 23, 1812." Taken at **Fatland Ford,** Penn. while in pursuit of a dove.
76. Virginia Partridges Attacked by Hawk. **Beech Woods,** West Feliciana, La., 1825.
77. Belted Kingfisher. Background scene Little Bayou Sarah, Feliciana, La.
78. Carolina Wren. Feliciana, La.
79. Tyrant Flycatcher. "April 10, 1822." Natchez, Miss.
80. Prairie Titlark.
81. Fish Hawk. New Orleans, 1822.
82. Whip-poor-will.
83. House Wren. **Fatland Ford,** Pennsylvania.
84. Blue-gray Flycatcher. New Orleans, 1821.
85. Yellow-throat Warbler. **Oakley,** West Feliciana, La. "August 1821."
86. Black Warrior. West Feliciana, La. **Beech Grove.** "Nov. 18, 1829."
87. Florida Jay. Drawing made from captive birds, New Orleans, 1821.
88. Autumnal Warbler. "Great Pine Swamp, August 20." 1829.
89. Nashville Warbler. Kentucky.
90. Black-and-white Creeper. West Feliciana, La.
91. Broad-winged Hawk. Combination drawing: Female from drawing made at **Fatland Ford,** Penn., May 27, 1812; Male, West Feliciana, La., 1825.
92. Pigeon Hawk.
93. Seaside Finch. "Great Egg Harbour, June 14." 1829.
94. Bay-winged Bunting. "Great Egg Harbour, June 26." 1829.
95. Blue-eyed Yellow Warbler. "Near Natchez, Miss." 1822.
96. Columbia Jay.
97. Mottled Owl. "New Jersey Dec." 1824.
98. Marsh Wren. "New Jersey, June 22." 1824.
99. Cow Bunting. Feliciana, Louisiana.
100. Green-blue or White-Bellied Swallow. "Philadelphia, May 17, 1824."
101. Raven.
102. Blue Jay. **Beech Woods,** Feliciana, La., 1825.
103. Canada Warbler. "Great Pine Swamp, August 1." 1829.
104. Chipping Sparrow. Louisiana, 1821.
105. Red-breasted Nuthatch.
106. Black Vulture. **Beech Grove,** West Feliciana, La., 1829.
107. Canada Jay.
108. Fox-coloured Sparrow. Charleston, S. C., January, 1834.
109. Savannah Finch. "Male, New Orleans February 6, 1821."
110. Hooded Fly-Catcher. **Oakley,** Feliciana, "La., August 11, 1821."
111. Pilated Woodpecker. West Feliciana, La., 1825.
112. Downy Woodpecker. **Oakley,** Feliciana, La., 1821.
113. Bluebird. **Beech Woods,** Feliciana, La., 1825.
114. White-crowned Sparrow. "Henderson, Ky., 1814, Oct. 14th."
115. Wood Pewee Flycatcher. "New Jersey, May . ." 1824.
116. Ferruginous Thrush. West Feliciana, La., 1825.
117. Mississippi Kite. Male, upper figure, only. "Drawn from nature by John J. Audubon, Louisiana, parish of Feliciana, James Pirrie's Esq. Plantation, June 28, 1821."
118. Warbling Flycatcher. "N. J. May 23d." Camden, 1824.
119. Yellow-throated Vireo. "James Pirrie's Plantation Louisiana July 11 1821."

120. Pewit Flycatcher. Feliciana, La.
121. Snowy Owl.
122. Blue Grosbeak. "April 15, 1821, New Orleans."
123. Black and Yellow Warbler. "Great Pine Swamp, Aug. 12," 1829.
124. Green Black-capt Flycatcher. "Great Pine Swamp, Aug. 12," 1829.
125. Brown-headed Nuthatch. Louisiana.
126. White-headed Eagle. Young. New Orleans, 1821.
127. Rose-breasted Grosbeak. New York State, 1824.
128. Catbird. New Orleans, 1821.
129. Great Crested Flycatcher. "April 17,1821." Natchez, Miss.
130. Yellow-winged Sparrow. "May 12, 1812, Pensla."
131. American Robin.
132. Three-toed Woodpecker.
133. Black-poll Warbler. "New Jersey, May."
134. Hemlock Warbler. "Great Pine Swamp, Aug. 12." 1829.
135. Blackburnian Warbler. "12th May, 1812, Pennsa."
136. Meadowlark. New Jersey, May.
137. Yellow-breasted Chat. "June 7, Jersey."
138. Connecticut Warbler. "Delaware River, New Jersey, Sept 22d."
139. Field Sparrow. "Great Egg Harbour, July 11th."
140. Pine-creeping Warbler. "James Pirrie's Plantation, Louisiana, June 10, 1821. Plant by J. R. Mason."
141. Goshawk and Stanley Hawk. Adult, Henderson, Ky.; young, Great Pine Forest, Penn.; Stanley Hawk, Feliciana, La., 1825.
142. American Sparrow Hawk. Audubon's pet "Nero." **Beech Woods**, Feliciana, La., 1825.
143. Golden-crowned Thrush. "New Jersey, May."
144. Small Green-crested Flycatcher. "New Jersey, May."
145. Yellow Red-poll Warbler. "Bayou La Fourche, January. 1, 1821."
146. Fish Crow. New Orleans, "Mississippi River, January, 14th. 1821."
147. Night Hawk.
148. Pine Swamp Warbler. "Great Pine Swamp, Penna. August 11th." 1829.
149. Sharp-tailed Finch. Charleston, S. C., 1832.
150. Red-eyed Vireo. New Orleans.
151. Turkey Buzzard. West Feliciana, La., 1825.
152. White-breasted Black-capped Nuthatch. Feliciana, La.
153. Yellow-crowned Warbler. "Penna. April 22, 1812."
154. Tennessee Warbler. **Oakley**, Feliciana, La., Oct. 17, 1821.
155. Black-throated Blue Warbler.
156. American Crow. West Feliciana, La.
157. Rusty Grackle. "Louisiana."
158. American Swift. "July 18th." Saint Francisville, La.
159. Cardinal. **Oakley**, Feliciana, La., July 1821.
160. Black-capped Titmouse. "My drawing of the Carolina titmouse was made not far from New Orleans late in 1820. I have named it so partly because it occurs in Carolina, and partly because I was desirous of manifesting my gratitude."
161. Brazilian Caracara Eagle. St. Augustin, Fla., Nov. 27, 1831.
162. Zenaida Dove. Florida Keys, April 30, 1832.
163. Palm Warbler. Florida.
164. Tawny Thrush. "State of Maine." Dennisville, 1832.
165. Bachman's Finch. Charleston, S. C., June 1832.
166. Rough-legged Falcon. New Jersey, July, 1832.
167. Key West Pigeon. Key West, Fla., May 6, 1832.
168. Forked-tailed Flycatcher. Camden, N. J., June, 1832.
169. Mangrove Cuckoo. "Key West, May 1832."
170. Gray Tyrant, Florida Keys.
171. Barn Owl. "New Jersey, July, 1832."
172. Blue-headed Pigeon. Florida Keys, May, 1832.
173. Barn Swallow. New Jersey.
174. Olive-sided Flycatcher, Boston, August 8, 1832.
175. Nuttall's lesser-marsh Wren.
176. Spotted or Canada Grouse, Dennisville, Me., Aug. 1832.
177. White-crowned Pigeon.
178. Orange-crowned Warbler. Feliciana, La., 1825.
179. Wood Wren. Dennisville, Me., 1832.
180. Pine Finch. Charleston, S. C., Oct., 1833.
181. Golden Eagle. Boston, 1833.
182. Ground Dove. St. Augustine, Fla., 1832.
183. Golden-crested Wren. Charleston, S. C.
184. Mangrove Hummingbird. From specimen, Charleston, S. C.
185. Bachman's Warbler. Charleston, S. C. "Plant by Miss Martin."
186. Pinnated Grouse.
187. Boat-tailed Grackle. "Bonnet Carre's Church, January 4, 1821." La.
188. Tree Swallow. Boston. "drawn by John Woodhouse Audubon."
189. Snow Bunting. "Louisiana."
190. Yellow-bellied Woodpecker. Feliciana, La.
191. Willow Grouse or Large Ptarmigan. Labrador, July 6, 1833.
192. Great American Shrike or Butcher Bird. "Banks of Mississippi River in Louisiana."

193. Lincoln Finch. Labrador, American Harbour, June 28, 1833.
194. Canadian Titmouse. "Labrador, July 20, 1833, opposite Island of Macatine."
195. Ruby-crowned Wren. Labrador, June 30, 1833.
196. Labrador Falcon. "near Bras d'Or, Labrador, August 6, 1833."
197. American Crossbill.
198. Brown-headed Worm-eating Warbler. From specimen taken by Doctor Bachman, Charleston, S. C., butterfly and azalia by Miss Martin.
199. Little Owl.
200. Shore Lark. Labrador, Bras d'Or, July, 1833.
201. Canada Goose. Henderson, Ky.
202. Red-throated Diver. Labrador, July 6, 1833.
203. Fresh-Water Marsh Hen. New Orleans, 1821.
204. Salt Water Marsh Hen.
205. Virginian Rail, New Orleans, 1821.
206. Wood Duck. Beech Woods, West Feliciana, La., 1825.
207. Brown Booby. Key West, May 14, 1832.
208. Esquimaux Curley. August 4, 1833, Bras d'Or, Labrador.
209. Wilson's Plover.
210. Least Bittern. Young bird on left of plate, Cincinnati Museum, 1820.
211. Great Blue Heron. New Orleans, 1821.
212. Common Gull. New Orleans, January 31, 1821.
213. Puffin. Labrador, July 1, 1833.
214. Razor-billed Auk. Labrador.
215. Hyperborean Phalarope. Boston.
216. Wood Ibis. Tunica Swamps, West Feliciana, La.
217. Louisiana Heron. Florida Keys, April 29, 1832, 1825.
218. Foolish Guillemot. Labrador, June 30, 1833.
219. Black Guillemot. Magdeline Islands, Gulph of St. Lawrence, 1833.
220. Piping Plover.
221. Mallard Duck. New Orleans, 1822.
222. White Ibis. Tunica Swamps, Feliciana, La., 1825.
223. American Oyster-catcher.
224. Kittiwake Gull.
225. Killdeer Plover. Bayou Sarah, La., 1825.
226. Whooping Crane. New Orleans, 1822.
227. Pintailed Duck. New Orleans, 1822.
228. American Green-winged Teal. "New Orleans, February, 1822."
229. Scaup Duck. "New Orleans, February, 1822."
230. Sanderling or Ruddy Plover.
231. Long-billed Curlew. Charleston, S. C.
232. Hooded Merganser. New Orleans.
233. Sora Rail. New Orleans, February 5, 1821.
234. Ring-necked or Tufted Duck. New Orleans, 1822.
235. Sooty Tern. Tortugas, Florida, May 9, 1832.
236. Night Heron or Qua Bird. Thompson's Creek, Feliciana, La.
237. Great Esquimaux Curlew.
238. Great Marbled Godwit. Keys of Florida, May 31, 1832.
239. American Coot. General Hernandez's Plantation, East Florida.
240. Roseate Tern. St. John, New Brunswick, 1833.
241. Black-backed Gull. Labrador.
242. Snowy Heron. South Carolina.
243. American Snipe. New Orleans, February 8, 1821.
245. Large-billed Guillemot.
246. Elder Duck. Labrador.
247. Velvet Duck. Labrador.
248. American Pied-billed Dabchick. New Orleans, 1822.
249. Tufted Puffin. Kennebec River, Me., 1832.
250. Arctic Tern. American Harbour, Labrador, June 25, 1833.
251. Brown Pelican. Florida.
252. Florida Cormorant. Florida Keys, 1833.
253. Pomarine Jager. Bras d'Or, Labrador, August 1, 1833.
254. Wilson's Phalarope. New York, 1824.
255. Red Phalarope. Louisville, Ky., 1808.
256. Reddish Egret. Florida Keys, 1832.
257. Double-crested Cormorant. Labrador, 1833.
258. Hudsonian Godwit. Female by John Woodhouse Audubon, Boston. 1832; male by J. J. Audubon, London, 1835.
259. Horned Grebe.
260. Forked-tailed Petrel. On board transatlantic packet Columbia, 1831.
261. Hooping Crane (Sandhill) Florida.
262. Tropic Bird. Tortugas Keys, Florida, 1832.
263. Curlew Sandpiper. Long Island, N. Y., 1829.
264. Fulmar Petrel.
265. Buff-breasted Sandpiper.
266. Common Cormorant. Labrador, July 3, 1833.
267. Arctic Jager.
268. American Woodcock. New Orleans.
269. Greenshank. St. Augustine, Fla.
270. Wilson's Petrel. On board ship Delos on way to England, 1826.

271. Frigate Pelican. Key West, Fla., May, 1832.
272. Richardson's Jager.
273. Cayenne Tern. St. Augustine, Fla.
274. Semipalmated Snipe or Willet. Florida.
275. Noddy Tern. Florida Keys, May 11, 1832.
276. King Duck.
277. Hutchin's Barnacle Goose. London, from specimen.
278. Schinz's Sandpiper. St. Augustine, Fla., Dec. 2, 1831.
279. Sandwich Tern. May 26, 1832, Florida Keys.
280. Black Tern.
281. Great White Heron. Florida, May 26, 1832.
282. White-winged Silvery Gull.
283. Wandering Shearwater. Labrador.
284. Fork-tailed Gull.
286. White-fronted Goose. New Orleans, Nov. 13, 1821.
287. Ivory Gull.
288. Yellowshank. Charleston, S. C.
289. Solitary Sandpiper, Bayou Sarah, Feliciana, La.
290. Red-backed Sandpiper. Florida.
291. Herring Gull. St. Augustine, Fla.
292. Crested Grebe.
293. Large-billed Puffin. From Specimen in London from John Gould.
294. Pectoral Sandpiper. Dennisville, Me., Aug., 1832.
295. Manks Shearwater. St. Georges, Newfoundland.
296. Barnacle Goose.
297. Harlequin Duck.
298. Red-necked Grebe. Boston.
299. Dusky Petrel. On ship Delos off Florida on way to England, 1826.
300. Golden Plover. New Orleans, March 16, 1821.
301. Canvasback Duck. Baltimore, Md.
302. Dusky Duck. New Orleans, February, 1822.
303. Bertram's Sandpiper. Bayou Sarah, La., 1825.
304. Turn-stone. Philadelphia, Pa., May, 1824.
305. Purple Gallinule. New Orleans, April 23, 1821.
306. Great Northern Diver or Loon. Labrador, July 9, 1833.
307. Blue Heron. New Orleans, March 20, 1821.
308. Tell-tale Godwit or Snipe. Florida.
309. Great Tern.
310. Spotted Sandpiper. Bayou Sarah, Feliciana, La.
311. American White Pelican.
312. Long-tailed Duck, Bras d'Or, Labrador, July 28, 1833.
313. Blue-winged Teal. "New Orleans, February 7, 1822."
314. Black-headed Gull. "shot in New Jersey."
315. Red-breasted Sandpiper.
316. Black-bellied Darter. "New Orleans, 1822."
317. Black or Surf Duck. Labrador.
318. American Avocet. New Orleans, Nov. 7, 1821.
319. Lesser Tern.
320. Little Sandpiper. Bayou Sarah, Feliciana, La.
321. Roseate Spoonbill. Tunica Swamps, Feliciana, La., 1825.
322. Red-headed Duck. Boston. From pair given by Daniel Webster.
323. Black Skimmer. St. Johns River, Florida, 1831.
324. Bonapartian Gull.
325. Buffleheaded Duck.
326. Gannet. Gannet Rock, Gulph of St. Lawrence, June 22, 1833.
327. Shoveller Duck. New Orleans, La., February 1822.
328. Long-legged Avoset. New Orleans, La., May 2, 1821.
329. Yellow-breasted Rail. "New Orleans, December 21, 1821."
330. Ring Plover. "Philadelphia, May 11, 1824."
331. Gossander. Cohoes Falls, N. Y.
332. Pied Duck. Boston, 1833. From pair sent him by Daniel Webster.
333. Green Heron.
334. Black-bellied Plover.
335. Red-breasted Snipe.
336. Yellow-crowned Heron. "Louisiana Oct. 2."
337. American Bittern. Drawn by John Woodhouse Audubon.
338. Bemaculated Duck. "New Orleans, February 1822."
339. Little Auk.
340. Least Stormy-Petrel.
341. Great Auk.
342. Golden-eyed Duck.
343. Ruddy Duck. New Orleans.
344. Long-legged Sandpiper.
345. American Widgeon. "New Orleans, 1820."
346. Black-throated Diver.
347. Smew or White Nun. "New Orleans, November 14, 1821."
348. Gadwall Duck. New Orleans, November 10, 1821.
349. Least Water Hen. Philadelphia.
350. Rocky Mountain Plover.
351. Great Cinereous Owl. London.

352. Black-winged Hawk. Charleston, S. C., Feb. 8, 1834.
353. Titmice.
354. Tanagers: Louisiana & Scarlet. Feliciana, April 1823.
355. MacGillivray's Finch.
356. Marsh Hawk. Mississippi River, 1820.
357. American Magpie.
358. Pine Grosbeck.
359. Flycatchers: Arkansas, Swallowtailed & Say's.
360. Wrens: Winter & Rock.
361. Long-tailed or Dusky Grouse.
362. Yellow-billed Magpie, Steller's Jay, Clark's Crow.
363. Bohemian Chatterer. Pictou, N. S.
364. White-winged Crossbill. Labrador, June 30, 1833.
365. Iceland or Jer Falcon. Bras d'Or, Labrador, Aug. 12, 1833.
367. Band-tailed Pigeon.
368. Rock Grouse.
369. Mountain Mockingbird & Varied Thrush.
370. American Water Ouzel.
371. Cock of the Plains.
372. Common Buzzard.
373. Grosbeaks: Evening & Spotted.
374. Sharp-shinned Hawk. Bird on left "Red Banks, Oct. 10, 1812;" right "Cincinnati, O., March 28, 1820."
375. Lesser Red-Poll. Labrador, July 27, 1833.
376. Trumpeter Swan, young. New Orleans, Dec. 16, 1821.
377. Scolopaceous Courlan.
378. Hawk Owl.
379. Ruff-necked Hummingbird.
380. Tengmalm's Owl. Bangor, Me., September 1832.
381. Snow Goose. New Orleans, February 1822.
382. Sharp-tailed Grouse.
383. Long-eared Owl.
384. Black-throated Bunting. "near Natchez, April 20," 1822.
385. Swallows: Bank & Violet-green. Banks of Schuylkill river 1824.
386. White Heron. "New Orleans, March 29, 1821."
387. Glossy Ibis. Florida.
388. Nuttall's Starling, Yellow-headed Troopial & Bullock's Oriole.
389. Red-cockaded Woodpecker. "Oakley, West Feliciana, La., July 20, 1821."
390. Lark & Prairie Finch, Brown Song Sparrow.
391. Brant Goose.
392. Louisiana Hawk. West Feliciana, La., "J. J. A. 1837."
393. Townsend's Warbler, Arctic & Western Bluebird.
394. Chestnut-coloured Finch, Black-headed Siskin, Black-crowned Bunting, Arctic Ground Finch.
395. Warbler: Audubon's, Hermit & Black-throated Gray.
396. Bourgomaster Gull.
397. Scarlet Ibis. Drawn from specimens.
398. Finches: Lazule, Clay-coloured & Oregon Gray.
399. Warblers: Black-throated, Blackburnian & Mourning.
400. Arkansas Siskin, Mealy Red-poll, Louisiana Tanager, Townsend's etc.
401. Red-breasted Merganser. Charleston, S. C.
402. Black-throated Guillemot, Nobbed-billed Auk, Curled-crested Auk, etc.
403. Golden-eyed Duck.
404. Eared Grebe.
405. Semipalmated Sandpiper.
406. Trumpeter Swan.
407. Dusky Albatross.
408. American Scoter Duck. Labrador.
409. Terns: Havell's & Trudeau's. Havell's—Mississippi river near New Orleans, January 6, 1821. Trudeau's from specimen.
410. Marsh Tern. Mouths of Mississippi river, April 1837.
411. Common American Swan. Florida, 1831.
412. Cormorants: Violet-green & Townsend's.
413. California Partridge.
414. Warblers: Golden-winged (Feliciana) & Cape May (specimen from Edward Harris).
415. Brown Creeper & California Nuthatch. London, specimens.
416. Woodpeckers: Hairy & Red-bellied (Feliciana); Red-shafted, Lewis' & Red-breasted from specimens.
417. Woodpeckers: Maria's, Three-toed, Phillip's, Canadian, Harris' & Audubon's. specimens.
418. American Ptarmigan & White-tailed Grouse.
419. Little Tawny Thrush, Ptilogony's Townsendi & Canada Jay.
420. Prairie Starling.
421. Brown Pelican, young. New Orleans 1821.
422. Rough-legged Falcon.
423. Thick-legged Partridge & Plumed Partridge. London from specimens.
424. Lazuli Finch, Crimson-necked Bullfinch, Gray-crowned Linnet, etc.
425. Columbian Hummingbird.
426. California Vulture.

427. Oyster-catchers: White-legged & Slender-billed.
428. Townsend's Sandpiper.
429. Western Duck. By John Woodhouse Audubon, in London, specimen.
430. Slender-billed Guillemot.
431. American Flamingo. Florida, 1832.
432. Owls: Burrowing. Large-headed Burrowing, Little Night, & Columbia.
433. Bullock's & Baltimore Orioles, Mexican Gold Finch, Varied Thrush.
434. Flycatchers: Little Tyrant, Small-headed (Louisville, 1808, Audubon said it was copied by Wilson).
435. Ouzels: Columbian & Arctic water ouzels.

The foregoing compilation indicates that, at least, 167 of Audubon's original bird drawings were drawn in Louisiana; that 56 were drawn in New Orleans; 40 were made at Percy's **Beech Woods** plantation, and 26 while Audubon was with the Pirrie family at **Oakley** plantation in West Feliciana parish. These figures are quite likely under-estimates and many more bird pictures which can not be accurately credited were probably made in Louisiana and his Feliciana Happyland.

Where no note follows the number and name of the plate, it must be understood that no positive data could be secured as to the time or place of the original drawing.

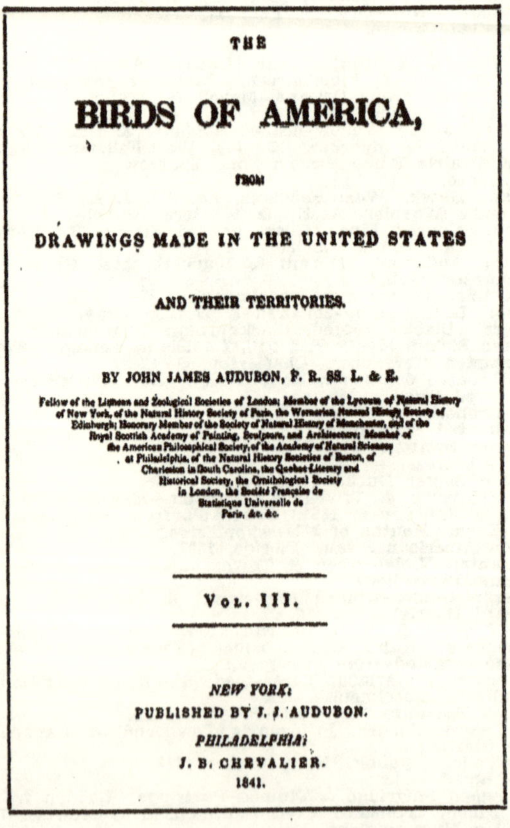

THE

BIRDS OF AMERICA,

FROM

DRAWINGS MADE IN THE UNITED STATES

AND THEIR TERRITORIES.

BY JOHN JAMES AUDUBON, F. R. SS. L. & E.

Fellow of the Linnean and Zoological Societies of London; Member of the Lyceum of Natural History of New York, of the Natural History Society of Paris, the Wernerian Natural History Society of Edinburgh; Honorary Member of the Society of Natural History of Manchester, and of the Royal Scottish Academy of Painting, Sculpture, and Architecture; Member of the American Philosophical Society, of the Academy of Natural Sciences at Philadelphia, of the Natural History Societies of Boston, of Charleston in South Carolina, the Quebec Literary and Historical Society, the Ornithological Society in London, the Société Française de Statistique Universelle de Paris, &c. &c.

VOL. III.

NEW YORK:
PUBLISHED BY J. J. AUDUBON.
PHILADELPHIA:
J. B. CHEVALIER.
1841.

Title page of first American or octavo edition of "The Birds in Miniature."

F

AUTHORITIES

The principal printed works consulted in the compilation of the life of *The American Woodsman*

JOHN JAMES AUDUBON: *The Birds of America,* 1827-1838; *Ornithological Biography,* 1831-1839; *A Synopsis of the Birds of North America,* 1839; *The Birds of America,* 1840-1844; *On the Hirundo fulva of Vieillot,* Annals Lyceum Nat. Hist. of N. Y., vol. i, pp. 163-166, 1824; *Facts and Observations Connected with the Permanent Residence of Swallows in the United States,* Annals Lyceum Nat. Hist. of N. Y., vol. i, pp. 166-168; *Account of the Turkey Buzzard,* Edinburgh New Philosophical Journal, vol. xi, pp. 172-174, 1826; *Observations on the Natural History of the Alligator,* Edinburgh New Philosophical Journal, vol. ii, pp. 270-280, 1827; *Notes on the Rattlesnake,* Edinburgh New Philosophical Journal, vol. iii, pp. 21-30, 1827; *Account of the Method of Drawing Birds employed by J. J. Audubon, Esq., F. R. S. E.* Edinburgh Journal of Science, vol. viii, pp. 48-54, 1828.

JOHN JAMES AUDUBON and JOHN BACHMAN: *The Viviparous Quadrupeds of North America,* 3 vols. 1846-1854.

JOHN NEAL: *Audubon—the Ornithologist,* New England Galaxy, Boston, January 3, February 7, April 18, 1835.

VINCENT NOLTE: *Fifty Years in Both Hemispheres, or Reminiscences of a Merchant's Life,* London, 1854.

MRS. HORACE ROSCOE STEBBINGS ST. JOHN: *Life of Audubon, the Naturalist in the New World, His Adventures and Discoveries,* London, 1856.

PAUL ANTOINE GRATACAP (called "Cap"): *Audubon, Naturaliste Americain Etude Biographique,* Paris, 1862.

BRADFORD KINNEY PEIRCE: *Life in the Woods; or, the Adventures of Audubon,* New York, 1863.

ROBERT BUCHANAN: *The Life and Adventures of John James Audubon, the Naturalist,* London, 1868.

LUCY AUDUBON: *The Life of John James Audubon, the Naturalist*, New York, 1869.

SAMUEL BRECK: *Recollections of Samuel Breck with passages from his note-books* (1771-1862), London, 1877.

JOHN GILMER SPEED: *John Bachman, D.D., LL.D.*, Charlestown, 1888.

GEORGE PETER ALEXANDER HEALY: *Reminiscenses of a Portrait Painter*, Chicago, 1894.

MARIA REBECCA AUDUBON: *Audubon's Story of His Youth*, containing her grandfather's autobiography *Myself, J. J. Audubon*, Scribner's Magazine, vol. xiii, pp. 267-289, March 1893; *Reminiscences of Audubon by a Granddaughter*, Scribner's Monthly, vol. xii, pp. 333-336, 1876; *Audubon and His Journals*, 2 vols., New York, 1898.

MARY FLUKER BRADFORD: *Audubon*, New Orleans, 1897.

HEZEKIAH BUTTERWORTH: *In the Days of Audubon, A Tale of the "Protector of Birds."* New York, 1901.

JOHN BURROUGHS: *John James Audubon*, Boston, 1902.

WITMER STONE: *A Bibliography and Nomenclature of the Ornithological Works of John James Audubon*, The Auk, vol. xxiii, pp. 298-312, Philadelphia, 1906.

ALEXANDER GORDON BAKEWELL: *Reminiscences of John James Audubon*, Pub. La. Hist. Soc., vol. v, pp. 31-41, *New Orleans*, 1911.

FRANCIS HOBART HERRICK: *Audubon the Naturalist, A History of His Life and Times*, 2 vols. New York, 1917. (The best and first accurate life of Audubon.)

LOUIS LEAR THÉODORE GOLSELIN (G. Lenôtre): *The Dauphin (Louis XVII), The Riddle of the Temple*, New York, 1921.

LOUISE BUTLER: *West Feliciana, A Glimpse of Its History*, Pub. La. Hist. Soc., vol. 7, No. 1, 90-120, New Orleans, 1924.

OCTAVE AUBRY: *Le Roi Perdu. Memoires le comte de Vaisons*, Paris, 1924.

SUSAN STARLING TOWLES: *John James Audubon in Henderson, Kentucky*, Henderson, Ky., 1925.

HOWARD CORNING: *Journals of John James Audubon* 1820-1821 *and* 1840-1843, 2 vols. Club of Odd Volumes, Boston, 1929; *Letters of John James Audubon* 1826-1840, 2 vols. Club of Odd Volumes, Boston, 1930.

IRVING T. RICHARDS: *Audubon, Joseph R. Mason, and John Neal*, American Literature, vol. 6, No. 2, May, 1934.

ACKNOWLEDGMENTS

MY INTIMATE study of the life of John James Audubon is the result of more than twenty years of investigation and research of the literary, pictorial, and familiar works of The American Woodsman, and of personal exploration of his happy hunting grounds in Louisiana, Florida, Pennsylvania, Mississippi, Kentucky, and Labrador. Reference has, of course, been made to former biographies, historical works, and various published correspondence of contemporaries.

Principally I have relied upon letters, journals, and heretofore withheld extracts of correspondence in the possession of the Audubon and Bakewell families for drawing the new portrait found in the foregoing pages. These were placed at my disposal unconditionally and without reservation as to their use.

Although impossible to record every instance of cooperation and courtesy extended during the lengthy preparation of the present work, I explicitly desire to express acknowledgments to certain friends and correspondents for assistance rendered.

To members of the Audubon family I am deeply obligated, in particular to Mr. Victor Morris Tyler, of New Haven, Connecticut, grandson of Victor Audubon, who permitted examination of family documents and who furnished portraits; to the late Miss Harriet Bachman Audubon, of Louisville, Kentucky, daughter of John Woodhouse Audubon, for a number of manuscripts pertaining to her distinguished grandfather's early life in relation to his enigmatic parentage; to Mrs. Alicia Bakewell Shaffer (Mrs. Frank H. Shaffer), of Cincinnati, Ohio, and her daughters, the Misses Lucy and Susan Shaffer, for many generous contributions of Bakewell family letters, manuscripts, family data, and portraits; to the late Miss Meta Grimshaw, of New Orleans, Louisiana, granddaughter of Nicholas Berthoud and Eliza Bakewell, for much data and information pertaining to the Marquis and Marquise de Saint-Pierre, and to Mr. Nicholas Berthoud Ringeling, of Philipsburg, Montana, for assistance in matters concerning the Berthoud family as well as for portraits.

I am indebted to my friend Professor Francis Hobart Herrick, of Cleveland, Ohio, author of *Audubon the Naturalist*, whose two-volume biography is today the standard work, for his helpful guidance and contributions of certain facts he did not use in his own work on Audubon. I am also in the debt of the late Mr. Ruthven Deane, of Chicago, Illinois, long the foremost authority on *Audubonia*, for much data, pictures, and sound advice. To Mr. Howard Corning, of the Essex Institute, Salem, Massachusetts, formerly of the Baker Library, Harvard University, who placed at my disposal many notes, letters, and other helpful documents. To my friend the late Mr. Frederic H. Kennard, of Newton Centre, Massachusetts, for many courtesies and a copy of the King Cameo of Audubon. To Mr. Irving T. Richards, of Cambridge, Massachusetts, who directed my attention to the John Neal articles in the *New England Galaxy*.

Mr. W. U. Harris, of Jackson, Alabama, was generous in placing at my disposal the original letters, journals, ornithological memoranda, and data gathered by his grandfather, Edward Harris, on his expeditions with Audubon. My investigations in the Feliciana country of Louisiana were materially aided by my friend and companion of numerous bird jaunts, Mr. Edward Butler, of *The Cottage*, West Feliciana parish, Louisiana, who located for me many of Audubon's old haunts in his bird heaven.

Others to whom I am indebted include Miss Lucy Matthews, of *Oakley Plantation*, granddaughter of Eliza Pirrie; the late Miss Sarah Turnbull Stirling, of Wakefield, Louisiana; Mr. J. Hereford Percy, of Baton Rouge, Louisiana; Mr. George M. Lester, of *Waverley Plantation*, West Feliciana parish; Miss Claribel Drake, of *Mount Ararat Plantation*, Church Point, Mississippi; Mrs. Charles Brandon, and the late Mrs. John A. Walworth, of Natchez, Mississippi.

I am under very special obligations to Mr. Robert J. Usher, librarian of the Howard Memorial Library, New Orleans, Louisiana, for advice, constructive criticism, and use of many archives. Also to Miss Josie Cerf, formerly of the Louisiana State Museum, and Miss Carrie Freret, librarian of the Louisiana Historical Society. Mr. Alexander J. Wall permitted an extended examination of the valuable collection of Audubon's original drawings owned by the New York Historical Society. I am indebted to Mr. Alfred C. Potter, librarian of the Widener Library, Harvard University, and to Dr. Thomas Barbour, of the Museum of Comparative Zoology, Harvard University, for permission to examine and make transcriptions from Audubon's journal of 1820-21 and other original documents. Miss Annie Nunns, of the Wisconsin Historical Society Library, at Madison, kindly traced certain data in the century-old files of the Cincinnati *Western Spy*. Miss Susan Starling Towles generously furnished much information regarding Henderson, Kentucky.

To learn the identity of the Marquis de Saint-Pierre, who in America preferred to be called "James Berthoud," the name of his faithful Swiss coachman, it was necessary to contact authorities in France's old Normandy by correspondence. I am indebted to Albert Le Cannellier, *avocat, Batonnier du Barreau de Valognes*, also president of the *Société Archeologique* of that French town, who traced the geneology of the titled émigré who proved such a staunch friend to Audubon in Louisville.

Research of the Santo Domingo region was limited to correspondence, and for help in this direction I am indebted to Mr. Donald R. Heath, American consul at Port au Prince, Haiti, and to Captain Roy C. Swink, U. S. M. C., of the *Guarde d'Haiti*, for placing me in contact with Mr. Stéphane A. Fougère, former mayor of Les Cayes, who furnished data on the Fougère, Laforest, and Audubon families.

Dr. Witmer Stone, editor of *The Auk*, assisted with sound advice and many matters relative to the bibliography of Audubon's works. Mr. William Schively, of New Richmond, Ohio, furnished information regarding his uncle, Joseph R. Mason, thus clearing up much which was heretofore obscure appertaining to Audubon's young assistant and his subsequent career. Dr. Alexander Wetmore, assistant secretary of the United States Museum, Washington, D. C., allowed the reproduction of heretofore unpublished early drawings of Audubon's birds now a part of the museum's collection of the artist's originals. Professor Charles S. Sydnor, of Duke University, was good enough to call my attention to certain matters pertaining to Audubon's dancing school in Woodville, Mississippi. Mr. Linden E. Bentley read the manuscript and Miss Joyce Comeaux read the final proofs.

To all these friends, acquaintances, and interested strangers who have given so freely of their time I tender my sincere appreciation, as they have had a definite part in making this new portrait of The American Woodsman.

STANLEY CLISBY ARTHUR

New Orleans, April 26, 1937.

INDEX

www.ingramcontent.com/pod-product-compliance
Lightning Source LLC
Chambersburg PA
CBHW030329240426
43661CB00052B/1571